RANDOM
HOUSE
LARGE
PRINT

BEING NIXON

BEING NIXON

A Man Divided

EVAN THOMAS

RANDOM  HOUSE
LARGE PRINT

Published in the United States of America by
Random House Large Print in association with Random
House, an imprint and division of Penguin Random
House LLC, New York.

Cover design by Fort

Front cover photograph by Katherine Young/Getty Images

The Library of Congress has established a
Cataloging-in-Publication record for this title.

ISBN: 978-0-8041-9496-9

www.randomhouse.com/largeprint

FIRST LARGE PRINT EDITION

Printed in the United States of America

10 9 8 7 6 5 4 3 2 1

This Large Print edition published in accord
with the standards of the N.A.V.H.

To my daughters
Louisa and Mary

Contents

Introduction

THE FATALISTIC OPTIMIST

Richard Nixon loved the movies. His favorite, contrary to myth, was not **Patton**, the 1970 biopic of the bellicose, war-loving American general George S. Patton. It was **Around the World in 80 Days,** the whimsical, lighthearted 1956 film, based on a Jules Verne novel, about a nineteenth-century British gentleman and his valet who circumnavigate the world on a bet.[1] "Watch! Here comes the elephant!" Nixon would exclaim, bouncing in his chair at his favorite scene. He sat for over five hundred movies at Camp David and in the White House theater during his five and a half years as president, and the eager moviegoer depicted by his daughter Julie bore no resemblance to the brooding Rex more commonly imagined. "No matter how terrible the first reel is, he always thinks it will get better," Julie told William Safire when he was working as a presidential speechwriter. " 'Give it a chance,' he'll say. Oh, we sat through some real lemons. Bebe [Rebozo] would fall asleep, Mother and Tricia would tiptoe

The candidate.
**Courtesy of the Richard Nixon Presidential
Library and Museum**

out, but Daddy would stick with it. 'Wait,' he'd say. 'Wait—it'll get better.' "[2]

Nixon wanted to be upbeat, to be an optimist. He often tried to, as he put it, "buck up" his followers and his family. Late at night, sitting alone in his Executive Office Building hideaway, or the Lincoln Sitting Room in the White House, or his lodge at Camp David, he would take out his yellow legal pad and begin making notes about the leader and person he wished to be. He imagined, in the spirit of his mother's Quaker faith, "peace at the center"; he would use words like **joyful, serenity,** and **inspirational**.[3]

Those descriptive words fit him only occasionally. In his daily life, he was more often fretful. He wished to be seen as cool and calm in crisis, and he could be, but he was subject to episodes of venting and lashing out. He was socially anxious and could be hopelessly, helplessly awkward. At his White House dinner for the artist Andrew Wyeth, he welcomed Wyeth's daughter-in-law Phyllis, who was in a wheelchair, and exclaimed, "Just last week I met with the Easter Seal children!"[4] Nixon was famously clumsy. The president dropped so many medals at awards ceremonies (or inadvertently stabbed the recipient), that Brent Scowcroft, at the time a White House military aide, had the medals affixed with clip-on devices instead of pins.[5] Nixon's almost painful self-consciousness made him seem uncomfortable while doing the simplest human task. Gregg Petersmeyer, a young White House aide, recalled watching the president at a cabinet meeting. When a new person entered the room, Nixon could not bear to turn his head to face him. Instead, his eyes darted sideways to get a peek.[6] He was being bashful, but he looked sneaky. Tenderhearted and devoted to his wife and daughters, he could seem callous to them in public.

Hope and fear waged a constant battle in Nixon. At the end of his presidency, fear won out. Nixon was often driven by fear—he was, he believed, surrounded by enemies. At the same time, he understood the hopes and fears of others, the insecurities of the people he memorably named "the Silent Majority." He was an introvert in an extrovert's business; incredibly, he was also one of the most successful politicians in American history. Weak at human relations but cunning at power, he made politics into a science and also an art; "for him it had a cadence, precision, and beauty," wrote his daughter Julie.[7] He ran on five national tickets and won four times, the last (1972) in one of the greatest presidential landslides ever. Only Franklin Roosevelt exceeded his electoral record. Though Ronald Reagan usually gets the credit, it was Nixon who created the modern Republican Party, by breaking the New Deal coalition and siphoning off disaffected Democrats who sensed that the native Californian, born to the lower middle class, was more sensitive to their wants and needs than the liberal elitists Nixon so enthusiastically scorned.

His accomplishments at home and abroad were great: opening up China, achieving arms control with the Soviet Union, ending (if too slowly) the

Vietnam War, desegregating the Southern schools, increasing benefits for the elderly and the disabled, creating the Environmental Protection Agency. Indeed, some historians call him a liberal.[8] He was not, but he was a crafty activist who loved to outflank and confound his foes.

Did he achieve all this in spite of—or perhaps because of—his anxieties? Nixon's inclination toward the dark side has long been a cliché. Less understood (possibly even by Nixon himself) is his heroic, if ill-fated, struggle to be a robust, decent, good-hearted person. In the battle against his darker impulses, he fought with a kind of desperate courage. At some level, I believe, he was aware of this struggle, though he gave every indication of a man with little or no self-knowledge.

Nixon believed deeply in his country, and he largely realized his ambition to be a statesman. Nonetheless, anyone listening to the tapes of his White House conversations will cringe—not, perhaps, at the profanity (common among men of his World War II generation under stress) but at the sheer hubris. Nixon and his lieutenants rarely, if ever, stopped to wonder if they possibly were wrong and their opponents were right. Such arrogance was and is probably characteristic of the conversations of most presidents—the Oval Office is a cockpit of sycophancy—but Nixon's brittle pridefulness was so disturbing and at moments ugly that it makes you want to cry out. (Did he really rail against Jews in government? Yes, he did.)[9] Ultimately, Nixon's obsession with smiting his enemies—combined with an utter inability to confront his friends—was fatal to his presidency.

Even so, his constant attempts to be a better man, generous and big-spirited—and to control his fate, knowing, perhaps, that he was destined to fail—are poignant. Improbably, this anxious boy from a pinched background believed that he was meant to do great things. Shy and bookish, he wanted to wake up every morning and ask, "What will we accomplish today?"

This is not a book intended to weigh the success and failure of Nixon as a policy maker, and, although the Watergate scandal figures inevitably and prominently, I do not attempt to solve its many mysteries. Rather, I have made an effort to understand what it was like to actually be Nixon. Drawn from the memories of three dozen or so men and women who worked for him as well as from the growing flow of new and rich archival material, this book is a chronicle of a fantastically contradictory and intriguing figure who set out to change the world and, for better and for worse, did just that. The story is best told from the beginning.

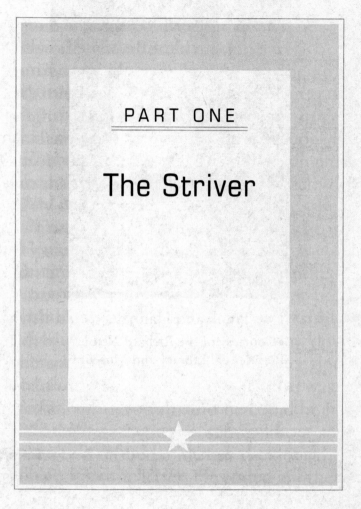

PART ONE

The Striver

Frank and Hannah.
**Courtesy of the Richard Nixon
Presidential Library and Museum**

Yorba Linda.
**Courtesy of the Richard Nixon Presidential
Library and Museum**

CHAPTER 1

Lives of Great Men Remind Us

In May of 1929, the Latin Club of Whittier High School celebrated Virgil's two thousandth birthday with a banquet and a production of the story of Aeneas and Dido from the **Aeneid**. The students wore togas and ate with their hands; the dry California hills passed for ancient Rome. Richard Nixon, the top student in the club, played Aeneas, Trojan hero and founder of Rome, and a girl named Ola Florence Welch played Dido, queen of Carthage.

Virgil's **Aeneid** imagines the ill-fated romance of Aeneas and Dido. Dido is under the sway of Juno, who stands for domesticity and marital fidelity. Aeneas is ruled by Venus, goddess of passionate, sexual love. Dido beds Aeneas and regards herself as married. Aeneas, rather coldly, abandons Dido to fulfill his greater destiny. ("To Italy I must go. There is the fatherland I must love.") Bereft, Dido throws herself on a funeral pyre, the gods' reckoning for her hapless devotion.[1]

It is doubtful that Nixon, age sixteen, was pondering the complexity of human nature and the vagaries of passion and commitment as he took the stage in the Whittier High gym. He had other worries. His feet hurt. It had taken both Latin teachers several minutes to tug the size-9 silver boots over Nixon's size-11 feet. "The hour on stage in them was agony beyond belief and almost beyond endurance," Nixon recalled.

Worse, Nixon was supposed to take Dido in his arms, on stage, in public. He had never kissed a girl before, or even close—Whittier was an upright Quaker town and Nixon was bashful. When Aeneas in his toga and too-small boots awkwardly reached out to embrace Dido, the student audience, heretofore bored, erupted in catcalls, hoots, and derisive laughter. Cheeks burning, the leading couple had to stop until the clamor died down.

Nixon later described the performance as "an unbelievably horrendous experience."[2] As the curtain fell to polite applause, the desperate-to-please high school junior volunteered to play the piano to entertain the disgruntled audience. "I'll do anything to make the party a success," he told one of the Latin teachers.[3] He was humiliated, however, and he lost his temper when one of the teachers criticized his clumsy performance.

Such a painful experience might have ended the thespian ambitions of any high school student (and Nixon did take away a lifelong aversion to wearing boots). But Nixon went on to act in several plays in college, with growing assurance and emotional range. Indeed, in 1952, when Nixon publicly wept after clearing his name from calumny with the so-called Checkers Speech, his old acting coach, Albert Upton, exclaimed, "That's my boy! That's my actor!"[4]

Nixon's dramatic debut was a crisis, but for Richard Nixon, crisis was already normal—to be expected; endured; even, as time went on, welcomed. Defeat was what one overcame; rejection was to be reversed, if not avenged.

Two months before the Latin play, Nixon had been the choice of the Whittier High School faculty to become student body president. Nixon was responsible, dutiful, and attentive to his elders. But at the last moment, another boy, a popular athlete named Robert Logue, had entered as a surprise candidate and won the students' votes. Nixon, who had been nicknamed "Gloomy Gus" by a few of the girls, had to settle for the position of "administrator," appointed by the faculty. In photos in the Whittier High yearbook, the **Cardinal and White,** Logue looks like a tanned Adonis, with a confident smile, cleft chin, and swept-back blond hair. In his photo, the dark-haired Nixon looks young and anxious.[5]

One of the girls who had voted for Bob Logue was Ola Florence Welch—Queen Dido. At the time of the election, she had written in her diary, "Oh how I hate Richard Nixon." She had been mortified by her stage embrace with Nixon. "We never practiced it. When we came to do it, it was very awkward and the kids went to pieces. I just about died," she recalled.

But when it was over, after briefly lashing out at

his carping teacher, Nixon calmed down and grew purposeful. "He never said a word about the play but he insisted that I must come over and meet his folks immediately," Ola Florence later recounted. Nixon wrote her a letter, apologizing for his "caddish behavior" (getting mad at the teacher) and explaining why, as he put it, he was "so cracked up about you. . . . You are not a boy chaser. You use your brains to good purposes. You never show your anger to anyone. . . ." He did not say anything about her looks, which, judging from photos, were striking, almost sultry.

Ola Florence reconsidered her opinion of Nixon. She decided that the dark-haired, brooding boy was "really quite handsome" and that he was interesting, articulate, and unusual. They began going steady and remained a couple all through college. Indeed, while the romance was rocky, they would come close to marrying.[6]

Aides to President Nixon like to reminisce and joke about Nixon's oft-expressed dislike for Ivy Leaguers, particularly graduates of Harvard. In his memoir, H. R. Haldeman, Nixon's chief of staff, describes the president exclaiming, "None of them in the Cabinet, do you understand? None of those Harvard bastards!"[7] Alexander Butterfield, a presidential assistant, recalled being summoned to the Oval Office after Nixon had somehow heard that the president of Harvard, Derek Bok, was on the White House premises. "What is that son of a bitch doing here?" Nixon demanded. Butterfield explained that Bok was a member of the Committee for the Preservation of the White House, and that Harvard had donated some paintings. "Never again!" cried Nixon. "How did he get in here in the first place?" John Ehrlichman, another top Nixon aide, recalled that "Nixon used to talk about the Eastern Establishment, but a lot of good people came from Harvard and similar places. He took them on, muttering and chirping all the time, about how deplorable it was, but he took them on and confided in them."[8] Indeed, Theodore White noted that Nixon hired far more Harvard men than all the Harvard men who had been president (the two Adamses, the two Roosevelts, and Kennedy).[9] Nixon chose as his foreign policy adviser a Harvard grad and Harvard professor, Henry Kissinger, and an equally intimidating Harvard professor, Daniel Patrick Moynihan, as his first domestic policy adviser. This was ironic but actually not surprising. Nixon was smarter, more intellectual, more open to ideas than almost any president who had come before him, including the ones who had gone to Harvard.

At graduation from Whittier High in June 1930, Nixon won the Harvard Club of California's award for outstanding all-around student, "which will probably irritate many of my friends who did go to Harvard," Nixon recalled a half-century later.[10] The award entitled Nixon to apply for a tuition scholarship from Harvard (he received a similar offer from Yale). But Nixon had to stay home. It was the Depression, and there was no money for travel or living expenses.

Nixon was not poor, exactly, but his family was cash-strapped. Frank, his blustery, bullying father, was a rolling stone who had worked a number of low-paying jobs, including as a trolley car conductor, factory hand, and oil roustabout. His mother Hannah, born to more genteel circumstances, endured lean times with a kind of tense grace. Frank would loudly denounce his bad luck and all who caused it; Hannah would smile sweetly, if a bit grimly, and keep her resentments bottled up.

Frank had planted some failing lemon groves in the thin soil of Yorba Linda in 1913, the year Nixon was born. The tiny town to the east of Los Angeles smelled sweetly of orange blossoms in the spring, but in the fall, when the Santa Ana—the fierce wind the Indians called "Devil's Breath"—blew in off the desert, young Nixon could hear rocks bouncing off the side of the little bungalow his father had built. The dust seeped in everywhere. On many nights, Hannah had to serve a dinner of fried mush.

Frank Nixon gave up the citrus groves and started up a gas station and grocery store on the road at the edge of Whittier, a nearby college town nestled amid eucalyptus and palm trees on a steep hillside. In the boom-and-bust of California's Southland of the 1920s, the gas station prospered. There had been enough money to send Richard's older brother, Harold, back east to Mount Hermon, a Christian boarding school in Massachusetts.

Harold Nixon was tall, blond, and handsome. The girls "swooned over him," Richard recalled. Harold was fun-loving and mischievous, outgoing and popular. He was a hellraiser and a cut-up. Richard, as a little boy, was the opposite. He was solemn and fastidious and preferred his own company. His cousin Jessamyn West observed that "he didn't seem to want to be hugged." He dressed in starched white shirts, and he carried his shoes in a bag when he went barefoot. He complained to his mother that other boys on the school bus smelled.[11] "He was very fussy, always neat," his mother Hannah recalled. "He seemed to carry quite a little weight for a boy of his age."[12]

If there is a lasting impression of Richard Nixon as a boy, it is one of solitariness. Friends and relatives remember him lying by himself in the grass, staring up at the sky, or wandering past the clusters of playing boys, lost in his own thoughts.[13] He was a stickler for order. His uncle recalled that when the Nixon cousins were playing with a football, young Richard, age eight or so, took away the ball and sat by himself on the porch, insisting that he would give it back only when the others played by the rules.[14] The sad-faced boy with the unruly shock of black hair seemed to yearn for order and certainty.

Young Richard was a dreamer. He recalled listening to train whistles in the night, and when, on his thirteenth birthday, his grandmother Almira Milhous gave him a portrait of Lincoln, he hung it over his bed, along with a copy of Longfellow's **Psalm of Life,** written out in his grandmother's hand:

> Lives of great men oft remind us
> We can make our lives sublime
> And departing leave behind us
> Footprints in the sands of time.

It was a heavy burden for an impressionable boy. And yet Nixon had a slight subversive streak. As a boy as well as a man, Nixon could be painfully ill at ease, and his jokes sometimes fell flat. He would never be mistaken for a wit. But he did possess a mordant, dry hint of humor, even as a thirteen-year-old. In history class a few weeks after Grandmother Milhous set up Lincoln as a role model with Longfellow's poem, Nixon penned a parody—not a knee-slapper, but a looser, more puckish try than might be expected from such a solemn, eager-to-please boy:

> Now the lives of great men all remind us
> We can make our lives that sort
> And departing, leave behind us
> Footprints on the tennis court.[15]

Hardship, familiar to the Nixon household, became tragedy in 1925, the year Richard turned twelve. Arthur, the fourth son, died of a mysterious illness. In his memoirs, Nixon wrote that he cried every day for weeks. Nixon's mother, Hannah, recalled him just sitting and staring into space, silent and dry-eyed.[16] A couple of years later, Harold, too, became sick. Nixon knew something was wrong as soon as the family picked up the oldest boy at the train station after his first year in Massachusetts. Harold was coughing and feverish. He had tuberculosis, a dangerous, frequently fatal disease.[17]

Frank Nixon refused to take handouts, so he passed up the county hospital where "lungers," as TB victims were sometimes called, could get free care, opting instead to pay for an expensive private sanatorium.[18] When the money ran out, Hannah Nixon took her sick eldest son into the dry mountains of Prescott, Arizona, and set up a boarding house for Harold and a couple of other TB patients. Richard and his younger brother Donald were left at home in Whittier to fend with their father. It was a life of constant work, some of it drudgery. From the time he was fifteen or so, Richard arose every morning at four o'clock to drive into the vegetable markets in Los Angeles to buy fresh produce for the family grocery store before heading off to school. In the summer, Nixon joined his mother in Arizona, where he did odd jobs (including as a carnival barker) while his mother changed bedpans and cleaned basins of bloody sputum.[19]

Nixon referred to his mother as a "saint." She spoke in a gentle voice but refrained from hugging or using expressions of endearment. True to her Quaker faith, she looked to an "inner light" and disliked showy religion. She said her evening prayers in a closet. Nixon feared his father's temper, but he was more frightened of his mother's "look." Hannah had an "iron hand inside her velvet glove," recalled Nixon's girlfriend, Ola Florence Welch. Hannah could punish just by her silence.[20]

Nixon followed his mother's example of trying not to antagonize Frank Nixon.[21] When his father grew belligerent, Richard would hide with a book.[22] Near the Nixon bungalow was an irrigation ditch that was quite dangerous to small children. Hannah's sister, Elizabeth Milhous Harrison, recalled watching in horror as Frank grabbed his boys out of the irrigation ditch where they had been playing and then threw them back in again, yelling, "If you want water, I'll give you enough." Their aunt cried out, "Frank, you'll kill them, you'll kill them!"[23]

Hannah's family disapproved of Frank, who had never graduated from elementary school and was semi-literate. Her sisters warned her not to stoop. The day Hannah and Frank were married, her little sister carved on a cherry tree, "Hannah is a bad girl."[24] The Milhous family was haughty, recalled Jessamyn West, and held itself above everyone but the other proper Quaker families who lived in Victorian houses on and around Whittier Hill. Nixon may have first felt the sting of snobbery within his own family.[25]

Nixon was caught between his two parents, trying to please both. He sought love from one, then the other; one wonders if he ever really found it from either. "Can you imagine," asked Henry Kissinger, "what this man would have been like if somebody had loved him?"[26] Kissinger was exaggerating for effect, but Nixon's insecurities seem so profound that he must, as a child, have lacked for some essential assurance. Self-protection, more than nurturing, seems to have been the order of the day in the Nixon household. Young Richard learned to avoid his father's temper and his hand. (As small boys, Richard and his brothers were not spanked but "thumped," rapped on the head.)[27] Richard watched as his mother intercepted customers in the store before Frank could bombard them with his vehemently held political views. If she didn't get there in time, she sometimes followed the browbeaten customers out the door, trying to soothe them.[28] In his memoirs, Nixon was still abashed by the shouting matches between his father and his brothers that could be heard "all across the neighborhood." In a rare instance of self-reflection, Nixon wrote, "Perhaps my own aversion to personal confrontations dates back to these early recollections."[29]

For a small shy boy, uncertain but eager to please, the space between Frank and Hannah may have felt at times like no man's land. "They were both explosive persons, one outwardly, one inwardly," recalled Richard's niece (brother Don's daughter), Lawrene Nixon Anfinson. "My grandmother exploded inwardly, kept it all in, but was very quiet and gave everybody the silent treatment, which just killed them, because she was so sweet. If she became angry you better watch out. . . . She kept at it for days, maybe, and nobody could talk to her."[30] Nixon may have learned by watching his mother deal with his father. "She would say, 'That's right Frank, that's right Frank,'" recalled Nixon's cousin, Sheldon Beeson. "But at the same time, you knew she was sort of scheming as to how she could kind of smooth things over and do it some other way."[31]

Years later, as a husband and father, Nixon would not abide conflict in his own home. He always wanted to hear up-beat music, symphonies and show tunes, even through dinner and wanted to hear only cheerful conversation. Acutely sensitive to moods, he would abruptly and insistently end any family conflict by saying, "Oh, there's no problem." He never raised his voice and left all discipline to his wife, Pat. "My father doesn't like arguments," recalled his daughter Julie in 1972. "He wants to be an optimist."[32] It is perhaps unsurprising that, as a high school student, Nixon brought home Dale Carnegie's relentlessly positivist **How to Win Friends and Influence People** and suggested to his family that they "all read it together."[33]

Nixon learned how to fight back against his father's bullying in a sort of abstracted, lawyer-like way. Animated and boisterous, Frank was often on his soapbox, in his store, at Sunday School, in his parlor. A precocious newspaper reader, socially but not intellectually reticent, young Richard began discussing politics with his father when he was still in grade school. His opinions began to overcome his shyness. As a second grader in 1920, Richard would sometimes lecture bewildered young children on the candidates in the upcoming national election. Over time, he found he could outsmart his father by scoring debating points.[34]

Frank Nixon was a Republican with a deep populist streak. He identified with the "little man" and was drawn by the hurt or angry crowd. California in the 1920s was a paradise of sunshine and fragrance, but it was filling up with dispossessed Okies from the Dust Bowl. The influx disturbed a middle class grown fearful of Reds and labor agitators. Revivalism was in the air. After Arthur's death, Frank took his grieving sons (but not Hannah, who shunned public religiosity) to come-to-Jesus meetings in Los Angeles. The Nixon boys were swept along with the five thousand congregants at "Sister" Aimee Semple McPherson's Angelus Temple—L.A.'s first megachurch—to accept Salvation. It was young Richard's first, unforgettable exposure to a mass audience moved by the power of righteous fulmination.

Inside the massive temple, which still stands in L.A.'s Echo Park, there was a room where miraculously healed congregants could leave their crutches and canes. At the turn of the century, millions of lower-middle-class whites from the all over the country migrated to California seeking good health and personal salvation. The culture they created stressed looking to the future and not to the past, pasting on a sunny smile whatever one's mood, and earnestly accenting the positive. Still, the dark side sometimes peeked out. In 1926, shortly after Nixon saw the flaming red-haired evangelist in person and began listening to her nightly radio broadcasts, Sister Aimee was caught up in a scandal—accused of staging her own kidnapping. The charges were never proved, but for months the press shrilly sensationalized the story. For the thirteen-year-old Nixon, avid consumer of newspapers, it was an early lesson in the murkiness and malleability of truth.[35]

Whittier College in 1930 did not, in its Quaker rectitude, allow fraternities (or drinking or dancing on campus), but it did permit "literary societies." The most select society was known as the Franklins (after the most famous Quaker of them all, Ben Franklin). "We were the socialites," recalled Hubert Perry, a member of one of Whittier's ruling families. Perry recounted that Nixon was rejected by the Franklins. Nixon insisted that he had turned down the Franklins.[36] The different versions are not insignificant in trying to understand Nixon. There is the insecure Nixon who never got over the social slights of his youth; then there is the resilient Nixon who rose above the snobs and shaped his own persona. Both are the real Nixon: He used anxiety to create strength, but a brittle strength.

Either by choice or necessity, Nixon created a rival power base to the Franklins. He became the first president of a new society called the Orthogonians (Greek, roughly speaking, for "Square Shooters"). "The Orthogonians were the Franklins' castoffs," sniffed Perry. Maybe so, but while the Franklins might have a star quarterback, the Orthogonians had most of the linemen. They may not have been the elite, but "Nixon understood there were more of them," said Perry. Nixon, who immediately began running for student office, was building a political organization. In the yearbook, the Franklins were photographed wearing tuxedos, while the Orthogonians purposely wore open-neck white shirts.[37] Nixon (who owned a tuxedo all four years at Whittier and bought a new one his senior year) knew that there was considerable resentment of the Franklins on campus. "They were the Haves and we were the Have Nots," Nixon recalled.[38] The Depression was settling in, and the poorer students sometimes slipped into the avocado orchards at night to forage for food.[39] Nixon wrote a kind of blue-collar manifesto for the Orthogonians. "We were officially dedicated," Nixon recalled, "to what we called the Four B's: Beans, Brawn, Brain, and Bowels."[40]

By "bowels" Nixon meant guts, which he had when he went out for football. At five-eleven, 145 pounds, he was undersized for a tackle, but he was too uncoordinated and slow-footed to play in the backfield. Mostly he was used as cannon fodder for the first team at practice and sat on the bench during games. He took enormous punishment in practice—"we used him as a punching bag," said his coach—but won the admiration of his teammates by coming back for more. "Anyone who could take the beating he had to take, the physical beating, was brave," said Perry.[41]

The coach of the Whittier Poets was a part–Native American named Wallace Newman, known, inevitably, as "Chief." A former University of Southern California star who probably should have been coaching in big-time football, Newman made no effort to hide his grudges. He hated losing, disdained quitters, and was loud about it: "Show me a good loser and I'll show you a loser!" he bellowed to his charges. Nixon worshipped him, understood the large chip on his shoulder, and would, throughout his life, invoke the Chief's life lessons in grit.[42]

Nixon was a grind in the library, but more "analytical" than "philosophical," according to his history and political science teacher, Paul Smith.[43] He read Shakespeare's **Julius Caesar** and wrote papers with titles like "The Causes of the Fall of Rome" and "The Greatness of Julius Caesar." But the essays are turgid and plodding.[44] He did not remark upon, perhaps missed altogether, Shakespeare's lessons about hubris and betrayal.[45]

On March 7, 1933, Richard, then a twenty-year-old junior, was in the library studying, when he got a note to go home immediately. He found a hearse outside. The undertaker was carrying away Harold's body. For the first time, Richard saw his father weep. The fair-haired first son had been "the flower of the family," recalled cousin Jessamyn West. "Why is it," Frank Nixon asked West, "that the best and the finest of the flock has to be taken?"[46] Richard had taken second place to his doomed brother. Harold had been a Boy

Scout, but by the time Richard's turn came, there was no money to buy a uniform.[47] Richard would have to find a different way to measure up. Harold's death had a "deep effect" on Richard, as his mother recalled: "He sank into a deep impenetrable silence. From that time on, it seemed Richard was trying to be three sons in one, striving even harder than before to make up to me and his father for our loss."[48]

Within a few weeks of Harold's death, Nixon plunged into a fierce campaign for student body president. He had been running for the position all along. By his second-to-last year at Whittier, he was the student body vice president, and, thanks partly to his assiduous maneuverings, the outgoing president was an Orthogonian. Just as in high school, the way was clear, or so it seemed.

Nixon was not a natural "buddy." "I don't think he had anybody that you would call a close friend," said Hubert Perry.[49] Some regarded him as prickly and cold—"cocksure," according to one coed who could not see through his defensive veneer.[50] He could be edgy and subject to nervous fits and explosions before he went on stage for a play or debate (which he did frequently, notwithstanding his studies and the 4 A.M. wholesale market run). But he worked at being an enthusiast, cheering himself hoarse from the football bench, constantly organizing rallies and feeds, even handing out sticks of chewing gum.[51] He became familiar with the peculiar lonesomeness of a politician—friend of all, intimate of none. Through hard work and ubiquity, he made himself seem inevitable as student body president. By a bit of political sleight of hand—the trading of some student offices—he thought that he had arranged to run unopposed in May of 1933.

Then, at the last moment, the Franklins entered their own candidate, a charismatic cheerleader named Dick Thompson. The student newspaper turned on Nixon. "It is a likely fact that the students' choice for next year will be Dick Thompson for student body president," wrote "Scoop," the political columnist of the **Quaker Campus**. It was as if the ghost of Bob Logue, his handsome high school nemesis, had appeared to torment "Gloomy Gus."

Nixon, not for the first or last time, was cast into a defeatist despond. He told a confidante, the mother of his English teacher and drama coach, that he was dropping out of the student body race. He said that he had too many other responsibilities, which was true, if not the whole truth. He did not mention Thompson.

But, as he would throughout his life, Nixon rallied. After a few days, he mustered his courage and his wiles and came up with an opportunistic plan. For some time, students had been agitating to hold dances on campus. The administration, beholden to the board of trustees dominated by the straitlaced Society of Friends, had balked. In his opening campaign speech, Thompson, the suave Franklin, suggested that an old building could be converted into a student center, which, he hinted, might eventually be used for dances. Nixon saw the chance to outflank his opponent. He came right out and proposed campus dances. To appease the administration, Nixon cleverly argued that it would be more wholesome for the school to allow dances on or near campus than to just say no—which would only encourage students to go off to smoke-filled dives in Los Angeles.

Nixon was playing to a larger audience, the "non-orgs," the students who belonged to no organization. The organization kids, the societies and clubs and teams, already had dances, usually not in honky-tonks but at nearby country clubs or Los Angeles hotels. Dances on campus for all students were sure to be crowd-pleasers, and so they were. In May 1933, at the end of his junior year, Nixon was elected student body president. He did not hide his pleasure at having outsmarted the Franklins. His smile, which could be surprisingly wide and warm, beamed as he greeted students and handed out sticks of chewing gum in thanks for their support. In August, the Board of Trustees grudgingly lifted its ban on dances, which they decorously described instead as "large social affairs," and rented out the local Ladies Club, still technically off campus.[52]

Nixon himself did not know how to dance. Under pressure from Ola Florence, he took some lessons, but he had two left feet. Ola Florence's friends asked her how she could abide such a "stuffy" boyfriend. But Ola Florence was taken by Nixon. "I thought Dick was wonderful . . . so strong, so clever, so articulate," she told a Nixon biographer, Jonathan Aitken. "He wrote me notes which I just couldn't believe, they had such beautiful words and thoughts."

The two were secretly engaged for a time, though there was "no hanky panky," recalled Welch.[53] But then the romance seemed to cool. There were fights; Nixon began dating other girls, apparently to arouse Ola's jealousy. She once had to call her parents to pick her up at a dance while Nixon went off with another girl. Welch wondered if her steady had become arrogant, "now that he's president." He seemed lonely, solemn, preoccupied.

Ola Florence was sad about her boyfriend. "I'm a very emotional person, outgoing. I like being silly, I love dancing," she said. Ola's mother "just couldn't stand Dick," according to Ola Florence's younger sister, Dorothy; she thought he was a "two timer." But Ola Florence couldn't bring herself to break with Nixon. "We had a stormy relationship, more stormy than most. . . . sometimes he'd be harsh and I'd cry. Then we'd make up," she said. Angered at his son's behavior, Frank Nixon took Ola Florence's side. "He'll hang himself if he's not careful!" Ola Florence remembered Frank shouting.

Then, one night in May 1934, a few weeks before graduation—he would sweep all the prizes—Nixon learned that he had won a full scholarship to Duke Law School, which was just then trying to establish itself in the first rank by attracting top scholars. "The night he found out, oh we had fun that night," Ola Florence recalled. "He was not only fun, he was joyous, abandoned—the only time I remember him that way. He said it was the best thing that ever happened to him. We rode around in his car and just celebrated."[54] He shared his dreams with her—possibly to become, he dared hope, chief justice at the United States Supreme Court. "I always thought he would achieve something extraordinary in life," she said, although "never in my wildest dreams did I ever picture him as president of the United States." Dido also recalled about her Aeneas, "I think I never really knew him."[55]

How well did Nixon, at age twenty-one, know himself? He knew that he could be temperamental, even "caddish," as he put it in his letter to Ola Florence. He knew that crisis was normal and that the temptation to give up had to be resisted, suppressed, conquered. He learned that a will toward optimism could efface, if not eliminate, pessimism. He learned, perhaps without quite realizing it, that power and control over others were antidotes to feelings of helplessness and isolation. He sensed that he was a clever politician and was relieved that, on stage, his shyness fled. He knew that he had an unrelenting work ethic. He saw himself as morally principled and, aside from occasional expedience, he was. Whittier had very few black students, but Nixon made sure that one of them, a halfback named William Brock, was welcomed into the Orthogonians, at a time that almost all fraternities around the country were racially segregated.

During his senior year, Nixon was required, for a course on Christian philosophy, to write a series of twelve essays on the theme of "What Can I Believe?"

Some of the essays were earnest attempts to turn the mystery of faith into social science. In one, Nixon designed an elaborate, largely incomprehensible chart filled with arrows pointing back and forth between categories like "neural energy" and "sensory experiences intelligent adaptation." He decided that he had moved beyond the literal Biblical interpretations of his parents, "fundamental Quakers," but he had trouble articulating what, beyond vague Christian bromides, he did believe.[56]

Curiously, he seems to have missed the best lesson, taught by Grandmother Milhous, a Quaker who used "plain speech," addressing her family as "thee" and "thou." Nixon's youngest brother, Edward, recalled how their grandmother told her grandchildren not to hate their enemies. "She said, 'Let them sound off. Let it go in one ear and out the other and settle some place else. Listen and say nothing, that's the best thing to do," according to Edward. She compared anger and the desire for revenge to a spring flower that would die out. "Never say, 'I hate,'" said Grandmother Milhous. "Don't call anyone a liar. You're not sure and if you are sure why advertise it? Let the lie die. Use silence."[57]

Nixon was more heedful of a verse from a Longfellow poem she sent him:

The heights of great men reached and kept
Were not attained by sudden flight
But they while their companions slept
Were toiling upward in the night.[58]

CHAPTER 2

Pat and Dick

At Princeton and Yale in the early twentieth century, wealthy donors self-consciously celebrated Anglo-Saxon superiority by building collegiate gothic campuses after the model of Oxford and Cambridge.[1] Eager to catch up, Duke University in Durham, North Carolina, used a family tobacco fortune to build a turreted dreamland, a stage set for future champions of the race. Finished a few years before Richard Nixon arrived for law school in 1934, the instant-ancient campus was belied only by its sapling trees.

Nixon was dazzled. "For someone accustomed to California architecture and a small college like Whittier, Duke was like a medieval cathedral town. There were spires and towers and stained glass everywhere. Dozens of buildings were set in clusters amid acres of woods and gardens," he remembered. His awe turned to anxiety when he began counting the Phi Beta Kappa keys on the watch chains of his classmates. Duke had recruited top scholars from Ivy League schools; thirty-two of Nixon's forty-five

Richard and Ola Florence.

classmates were members of the academic honor society. Whittier did not even have a Phi Beta Kappa
chapter.

Nixon knew that he would lose his full scholarship if he did not get top grades. He worked alone,
avoiding study groups. "I'm a reader, not a buller,"
he later explained (he may have used a stronger term
than "buller"). In letters home to Ola Florence, he
contemplated quitting. One night he poured out his
fears to an upperclassman, who had remarked on
the long hours the lonely first-year student seemed
to be spending in the library. The upperclassman
was consoling. "You don't have to worry," he told
Nixon. "You have what it takes to learn the law—an
iron butt." At the end of the year, Nixon was third
in his class.[2]

Nixon lived in a tool shed without heat or plumb-
ing. Breakfast was often a Milky Way candy bar. He
wrote longing letters to Ola Florence, which she answered, coolly. Upon returning home for the summer, he called his college flame to announce that he
was coming over. She could not see him; there was a
boy in her living room. Nixon became agitated. "If I
never see you again, it will be too soon," he swore
and slammed down the phone. He was at her house
the next day, pretending that nothing had happened.
He bragged to her about facing down his intimidating professor, Douglas Maggs, who was renowned
for badgering students in his personal injury law
class, known as "Torts." Ola Florence quipped,
"Torts, that's something you cook." Nixon became

pompous and proprietary. "You're going to have to learn something about law terms now," he intoned. She dumped him and by Christmas was engaged to the boy in the living room, Gail Jobe. Nixon wrote a few more beseeching letters before giving up. It does not appear that he ever talked to anyone about his rejection.[3]

By his third year, Nixon's living situation at Duke had improved, marginally. He lived in an unheated house in the woods with three other men; they shared two brass beds. But the residents of "Whip-poorwill Manor," as they dubbed the one-room shack, seemed to have had some fun. Nixon was teasingly nicknamed "Gloomy Gus" (again), but he loosened up. He yelled, jumped, and waved with such abandon at Duke football games that he became something of a stadium character; students would want to sit near him just to see the show. The former college thespian found the occasional outlet for his acting skills—uncharacteristically, as a stand-up comic. At the "Senior Beer Bust," he stood on a picnic table and gave a deadpan speech about social security—"social insecurity"—in which he intentionally mangled the facts and mimicked confused bureaucrats. (Nixon was already an anti–New Deal, anti-FDR Republican.) He was so entertaining that for days afterward, in the cafeteria, students would gather around and cajole him to give a funny speech. He shyly begged off; he had no more jokes.[4]

At Duke, Nixon also showed his tender side. One of his classmates, Fred Cady, had been disabled with polio. As students rushed up the stone steps, Nixon stopped to help Cady with his books and his crutches. It became a routine; every day Cady would wait for his friend to help carry him up the steps. Another student, Charles Rhyne, was hospitalized for months with a poisoned arm. Nixon showed up by his bed every night to read his lecture notes. (Many years later, Rhyne would represent Nixon's faithful secretary, Rose Mary Woods, when she testified before a federal grand jury about the infamous eighteen-and-a-half-minute gap in the White House tapes.)

On Sundays, Nixon attended church in Duke's vast gothic chapel. He was bothered that neither of the regular ministers, a Methodist and a Quaker, ever discussed race relations. Nixon observed that the blacks in Durham lived in a separate and unequal world, waiting on tables and working in the factories, speaking only when spoken to. Other students from outside the South were bothered by the strict segregation, but only Nixon spoke out about it, recalled several of his classmates, one of whom noted, "He looked upon the issue as a moral issue and condemned it as such."[5]

Over the Christmas holiday during his final year, Nixon, along with two of the other top law students, drove to New York to look for jobs as Wall Street lawyers. Nixon recalled anxiously waiting in the lobby of one of the venerable firms, Sullivan and Cromwell, noticing the thickness of the oriental rugs and the glow from the wood-paneled walls. Years later, Nixon could vividly summon the feelings of rejection. "I knew that these firms were virtually closed shops, which hired only from the establishment elite of the Ivy League law schools, but I thought it would be worth a try," he recalled. "I must have looked pretty scruffy sitting in those plush polished mahogany and leather reception rooms in my one good suit."[6]*

The summer of 1937 found Nixon back home in Whittier, living over his parents' garage. He was morose, his family recalled. He applied to become an FBI agent and never heard back, possibly because of a bureaucratic snafu.[8] Finally, his mother got him a job working at a local law firm, Wingert and Bewley.[9] Nixon wrote up wills for the prosperous families living on the hill. He occasionally and uncomfortably handled their divorces. "This good-looking girl, beautiful really, began talking to me about her intimate marriage problems," Nixon later recalled to journalist Stewart Alsop. "Were you embarrassed?" asked Alsop. "Embarrassed! I turned fifteen colors of the rainbow," Nixon replied.[10]

Nixon struggled. He became entangled in a nasty malpractice action after he made a mistake filing a

---

*Nixon was rejected by Sullivan and Cromwell and other posh "white shoe" Wall Street firms. At the Wall Street litigation firm of Donovan, Leisure, General William "Wild Bill" Donovan, the firm's founder, did offer Nixon a job. Donovan, who had been a poor Irish Catholic boy from Buffalo, had been known to hire up-and-comers like Nixon, but for whatever reason, Nixon declined the offer.[7]

deed; the firm had to settle the case for twice Nixon's salary. He started a small business freezing orange juice, and it failed, costing Nixon his first year's savings. He still felt the condescension of the Franklins. The senior partner's wife, Judith Wingert, recalled that the Nixons were "lower middle class," their grocery someplace where "you stopped on your way back from the golf course."[11]

Whittier was very conservative—despite the Depression, the town refused to take New Deal money from Washington to create jobs because, the town council decreed, public relief was "Bolshevik."[12] Drinking, dancing, and card playing were proscribed by the Quakers. Some of the Whittier men were hardly Quakerish in their intolerance; when a saloon had opened in town in the late 1880s, some locals burned it down and beat the proprietors with ax handles.[13]

Strict moralism notwithstanding, southern Californians had a soft spot for show business and theater, even in straitlaced Whittier. The film industry was well-rooted in Hollywood by the 1930s, and the Spanish Catholic heritage of pageantry had seeped into religious revivalism.[14] At the Angelus Temple (from the Roman Catholic devotion commemorating the Incarnation), Sister Aimee staged "theatrical sermons." In Whittier, there was an amateur theater company, and in 1937, Nixon decided to try out for a part in a drama called **The Dark Tower**. At the audition, Nixon read for the role of Barry Jones, who according to the play was a "faintly collegiate, eager,

blushing youth of twenty-four." The lead role of
Daphne would be "a tall, dark, sullen beauty of
twenty, wearing a dress of great chic and an air
of permanent resentment." The girl trying out for
the part of Daphne was named Pat Ryan. Nixon had
never seen her before, and he thought he knew everyone in town. She had a mass of red-gold hair, high
cheekbones, and (weighing about twenty pounds
more than she would as First Lady) a curvy figure. "I
could not take my eyes away from her," Nixon recalled. "For me it was a case of love at first sight."

Pat Ryan was well known by the boys she taught
at Whittier High. "She was so sexy you can't imagine," recalled one of them, Robert Blake (later an
ambassador in the Nixon administration). "She
wore tight sweaters, unlike the old bags around
town. When she walked down the hall, we'd go
around the corner and whistle."[15] Interviewed in
1950, her English professor at the University of
Southern California recalled:

She was a quiet girl and pretty. And it always used
to disturb me how tired her face was in repose.
There seemed to have been plenty of reason for it.
As I recall it, if you went into the cafeteria, there
was Pat Nixon at the serving counter. An hour
later if you went to the library there was Pat Nixon
checking out books. And if you came back to the
campus that evening there was Pat Nixon working
on some student research program. Yet with it all,
she was a good student, alert and interested. She

stood out from the empty-headed, overdressed little sorority girls of that era like a good piece of literature on a shelf of paperbacks.[16]

Nixon wrangled a ride home with the girl and a friend that night, and the next, and the next. On the third night, Nixon asked, "When are you going to give me that date?" Pat Ryan laughed. "Don't laugh," said Nixon, pointing a finger at her. "Some day I'm going to marry you." She was taken aback; the two had barely spoken. When she got home, she told a friend, "I met this guy tonight, who says he is going to marry me."[17]

Nixon noticed something deep and kindred about Pat. In one of his first love letters to her, he wrote, "you with the strangely sad but lovely smile." He pursued; she resisted. She turned him down for dates; he appeared, unannounced, at her door. She more than once locked him outside. She was a little unnerved by his devotion, and he could be impetuous. "Please forgive me for acting like a sorehead when you gently ushered me out the door the other night," he began one letter. He ended another: "Yes, I know I'm crazy, and that this is old stuff and that I don't take hints, but you see, Miss Pat, I like you!"

Warily, she agreed to let him drive her into Los Angeles on weekends—often, so she could go on dates with other suitors. Nixon would patiently sit in hotel lobbies, reading a book. She liked to ice skate, so he took her ice skating, and fell down so many times that he was bloody by the end of the evening.

Slowly—very slowly, over the course of two years—Pat allowed herself to know Nixon. She discovered that she had much in common with this clumsy, eager, dreamy, moody young man on her doorstep. Pat Ryan (born Thelma, but she changed her name because she disliked it) came from an even more hardscrabble background; her father made Frank Nixon seem relatively tame. Will Ryan drank and would pick fights with his wife until the children cried out, "Don't, Daddy, don't!" He could be cruel. With his drinking buddies, he pretended to auction off little Thelma as a slave. Sitting very straight, trying not to cry, Thelma feared that her father truly would sell her. Years later, Julie Nixon Eisenhower recalled in her memoir, **Pat Nixon: The Untold Story:**

> My mother resolutely buried the unpleasant memories of her childhood. Only once did she admit to me her father's temper and confrontations with Kate [Pat's mother]. Then, firmly, so I would know she was speaking her final words on the subject, she said, "I detest temper. I detest scenes. I just can't be that way. I saw it with my father." She paused for a moment and added: "And so to avoid scenes or unhappiness, I supposed I accommodated to others."

Both Pat and Dick were sensitive to the jeers and put-downs of their social "betters." Pat bitterly recalled a carload of rich college boys hooting at her as

she swept trash out of a building while she was working briefly as a house cleaner. Both fantasized about
escape. Pat told Nixon that she did not want to be
tied down, that she wanted to travel to exotic, far-
off places. Nixon, who used to lie in his boyhood
bed listening for the train whistle, who had spent
hours lying in the grass watching the clouds go by,
began calling her "my Irish gypsy" and "Miss Vaga-
bond." Pat began to soften. "He was handsome in a
strong way," she later told Julie. Nixon had a mellifluous baritone voice, fine for public speaking and
stage, and it reached Pat. "He had a wonderful quality in his voice that I have never heard in another
man," she told Julie. She also saw and felt his drive
and was not put off by his ambition for power and
office. Indeed, she shared it. Her roommates wondered why she put up with this persistent and slightly
bumptious suitor. She answered: "He's going to be
President some day."

All his life, Nixon was drawn to the sunshine. He
was fair-skinned and burned easily, but he liked to
walk the beach for hours at a time or to stare out at
the sunset. In March of 1940, Richard drove Pat to
Dana Point, a rocky promontory on the Pacific coast
south of Los Angeles. Parked in his Oldsmobile,
looking out over the long white beach sweeping
down the coastline, he proposed marriage. She said
yes, though as she later told her daughter Julie, "even
as she consented, she was not sure she wanted to
marry."[18]

Throughout their marriage, at intimate moments like anniversaries, Nixon could be oddly distant from Pat. On the day Nixon was to give Pat their engagement ring, he was a no-show at their luncheon date. Back at her desk grading papers in the afternoon, a disappointed, perplexed Pat received a basket from a messenger. Inside was tucked the ring. Impulsively, she shoved the ring away. Finally a teacher next door came in and declared, "Look, you are going to put on that ring right now." The teacher had to slip the ring onto Pat's finger.

In later years, Pat would be seen as long-suffering. To her admirers, she was a saintly figure, like Nixon's mother Hannah, sad but stoical. To her husband's legion of critics, she was a doormat, if not a neglected wife. Because Pat was so private, it is hard to know her true feelings. As a public figure, Nixon could seem insensitive and preoccupied. But there can be no doubt that when young Richard Nixon, the ardent suitor, spoke expansively and dreamily of his hopes and dreams of attaining greatness as a lawyer or as a politician, Patricia Ryan felt her own hopes rise. She had grown up in a home with a dirt floor. She wanted a finer, better, more respectable life, and her husband-to-be promised to give her one. Fiercely, she would hold him to that promise. Though she could appear frozen in the public glare, she was tender and warm in private, and loving to Nixon. She must have also sensed his vulnerability and experienced his well-concealed sweetness. The notion that there could be any kind of physical attraction between them has been blotted out by too many photographs of Nixon glowering and Pat pretending to smile and looking stricken. Nixon's small circle of intimates knew better. People who thought of Nixon as rather grim and hunched over were sometimes surprised by the warmth of his smile. When he was happy—especially with his family—his posture was confident.

Pat and Dick were married on June 21, 1940, in a small, private ceremony at the Mission Inn in the town of Riverside, south of Whittier. The Mission Inn is a southern California folly, a fanciful jumble of architectural styles, an effusion of balconies, minarets, and spires. The ceremony was held in the Presidential Suite, where Theodore Roosevelt had stayed; it was chosen not for its history but because it was the smallest and cheapest room to rent. "Both my parents remember how happy the reception was," recalled their daughter Julie.

On their honeymoon, they drove down to Mexico. Short of money, they had stocked up on canned food to avoid the expense of restaurants, but, as a wedding prank, their ushers had removed the labels on the cans. "Several times we ended up having pork and beans for breakfast and grapefruit slices for dinner," recalled Nixon.

The young lawyer and schoolteacher watched their pennies. Still, they were able to get away for a cut-rate Caribbean cruise in the summer of 1941. Nixon was seasick most of the time, and their cheap berth in the bowels of the ship stank of diesel fuel. "My sharpest recollection of the trip is of the evening of June 22, 1941, when our elderly black steward told us that word had just come over the radio that Hitler had invaded Russia. We both hoped this would lead to a Russian victory and Hitler's downfall."[19]

The world war was coming closer. As a Quaker, Nixon was, nominally at least, a pacifist who wanted America to stay out of the conflict. But he wanted, in some way, to serve and to be closer to the action, a wish hardened into resolve by Pearl Harbor. When he was recruited through Duke Law connections to take a job in the federal government, he and Pat moved to Washington in January 1942. He was bored and frustrated as a lawyer in the Office of Price Administration's tire rationing division. That summer, he joined the navy.

His letters to Pat from Officer Training School in Quonset, Rhode Island, were ardent and touching. "I may not say much when I'm with you—**but all of me loves you all of the time.**" After a two-day leave in New York City, he wrote:

This weekend was wonderful. Coming back I looked at myself in the window and thought how very lucky I was to have you. I certainly am not the Romeo type and you are so beautiful. I was proud of you every minute I was with you. . . . [20]

Winning his ensign's bars, Nixon "expected to be assigned to a battle fleet in the South Pacific or the

North Atlantic. I could hardly believe my eyes when I opened my orders and found that I was being sent to the Naval Air Station in Ottumwa, Iowa." The unfinished runway, he discovered, "stopped abruptly in the middle of a cornfield."[21]

He continued to badger the navy for duty in the war zone, and finally, in the summer of 1943, found himself on a troop ship to the South Pacific. But not to sea duty—probably fortunate, given his susceptibility to motion sickness—or to the front lines. Rather, he became an air transport officer on hot, fetid bases in the rear areas of the American island-hopping campaign. The airfields were bombed a few times, but the greatest threat, he wrote Pat, was from poisonous insects.

Yet he was a good officer. He took an interest in his men, helping them write letters home and to transfer to better postings, bucking up morale, taking off his shirt and pitching in to load airplanes on the way to the battle zone. He was an expert scrounger and found ways to treat exhausted aircrews at "Nick's" hamburger stand. In later years, more than one officer compared him to the sympathetic, thoroughly decent character played by Henry Fonda in the play and movie, **Mr. Roberts**.[22]

He also learned to swear and to play poker. He may have seen a bit of the seamier side of life when he worked as a carnival barker while his brother wheezed in the Arizona desert, but Nixon's true education in profanity came as a green young officer commanding rough Seabees and Marines in the

South Pacific. His swearing sounded a little posed, even on the White House tape transcripts that got him in such trouble for the frequent appearance of "expletive deleted" during the Watergate scandal. Hannah Nixon's son was not naturally crude. But he was hardly effete, and he was not easy to fool or take advantage of. He was a very good card player, keeping a poker face, playing it safe, but then bluffing boldly. He sent home about $6,000 (roughly $80,000 in 2014 dollars) in poker winnings, far more than his lieutenant's pay.[23]

Always, he wrote aching letters to Pat. "I think of you when I see beautiful things," he wrote. He called her "Dear One"; she called him "Dear Plum." Dick began imagining his return home. "I'm going to walk right up to you and kiss you—but good. Will you mind such a public demonstration?"[24] When he arrived home in San Diego in the summer of 1944 after fourteen months overseas, Pat later recounted, she "ran to the airport gate and threw her arms around him in all-encompassing embrace."[25]

In an early letter home from the war, Nixon wrote his bride, "I'm anti-social, I guess, but except for you—I'd rather be by myself as a steady diet rather than with most people I know. I like to do what I want, when I want. Only where you are concerned do I feel otherwise—Dear One."[26] One wonders how someone who preferred to be alone, who often seemed so ill at ease in company,

chose as his life's calling a profession that requires
constant attention to others—in the stereotype of
the classic pol, endless glad-handing, schmoozing,
shoulder-squeezing, and baby-kissing. Even Nixon
would later acknowledge the incongruity of an introvert in an extrovert's business.[27]

Yet Nixon had a great capacity to accept discomfort and endure blows. It was normal to him, even
necessary. And politics, he knew, was something at
which he could succeed. He may have lacked the
natural gifts of the smooth sophisticates, the Bob
Logues and the Franklins, but by dint of shrewdness
and hard work, he could work around, compensate,
overcome. Ever alert to slights himself, he could read
people and situations; he knew what made people
fearful and hopeful and how to sense what they
wanted, even if they didn't quite know it themselves.
He could identify and empathize with the lonely
and left behind. As if to defy his own shyness, he
liked to be on stage; he had a prodigious memory;
he didn't mind pressing the flesh. Indeed, he seemed
to welcome plunging into crowds. As a student
leader, he had developed a taste for power, the getting and using of it. Quite possibly, in the validation
of elected office, he found a replacement for the ad-
oration he missed as a child, which even Pat could
not replace. Heeding his grandmother Milhous, he
wanted to make his mark by doing good in the
world, to leave "footprints in the sands of time." In
his eighth-grade autobiography, he had seen the way,
more or less:

My plans for the future if I could carry them out are to finish Whittier High School, and College and then take post-graduate work at Columbia University, New York. I would also like to visit Europe. I would like to study law and enter politics for an occupation so that I might be of some good to the people.[28]

In September 1945, a month after V-J Day, Nixon received an airmail letter from a bank manager and Whittier College trustee named Herman Perry, asking him if he would like to be "a candidate for Congress on the Republican ticket in 1946." An ardent foe of the New Deal active in local Republican politics, Perry had been watching Nixon since his days as a high school debater. He liked Nixon's aggressiveness and hoped that marriage had softened the boy's natural glower. Perry's short note said that Republican and Democratic registrations in the local congressional district were split "about 50-50" and that "the Republicans are gaining." The letter ended, "Please airmail me your reply if you are interested. P.S., Are you a registered voter in California?"

Nixon was, though he was living outside of Baltimore, serving out his time terminating navy contracts. He and Pat had saved about $10,000, including his poker money, to buy a house, and Pat was pregnant. Nixon took less than forty-eight hours to say yes.[29]

Victory in World War II brought global power to America but not contentment to its people. America's former ally, the Soviet Union, loomed as the menacing foe, and the atom bomb threatened to make the next war the last. Housewives shopping for groceries and clothes for their families complained of high prices and shortages left over from rationing. Strikes and labor unrest plagued industries trying to convert back to peacetime production. Government bureaucracy created by the New Deal was held to blame. "HAD ENOUGH?" asked the Republicans in 1946.[30]

The Republicans were looking for fresh political faces, preferably young veterans. In November 1945, Nixon auditioned before a citizens committee looking for a GOP candidate to take on Democratic Jerry Voorhis, a five-term incumbent. Nixon wore his naval lieutenant commander's dress blue uniform because Pat had given away his one good suit while he was overseas. Crisp and hard-charging in his presentation, he got the job. As Roy Day, the Republican committee chairman, told his fellow Republicans, a mix of wealthy Pasadena gentry and small businessmen scattered around the 12th Congressional District, "He's saleable merchandise."[31]

Day was not just being flip. In California politics, candidates were becoming commodities. Under Governor Hiram Johnson, California had reformed city machine politics through statewide referenda and open primaries, substituting the will of the people for the backroom politics of party hacks. Inevitably, however, a new class of operators rose up to manipulate popular opinion. Their goal, as Theodore White put it, was to "twitch an uninformed electorate by its nerve ends," to use emotion and visceral appeal by hyping a few simple issues.[32] The pioneer "political consultants," a term that would later become ubiquitous but was virtually unknown outside of California in the 1940s, were a husband-and-wife team, Clem Whitaker and Leone Baxter. Using advertising and a pliable press (later, "free media"), they were magicians at image making and what decades later would become known as "spin." "For a million dollars," boasted Whitaker, "I could make tuberculosis popular."[33]

One of their early disciples was a short, pudgy lawyer and PR man named Murray Chotiner. A sallow-faced Runyonesque figure who smoked cigars and found his law clients from the bail bondsmen, Chotiner would become known as a Svengali figure, Richard Nixon's supposed tutor in the art of the political smear. "California has a cult of the smear," recalled Lou Cannon, biographer of California's other master politician of the era, Ronald Reagan. "Chotiner did not invent it, but he refined it."[34] Chotiner always insisted, "It is not a smear, if you please, if you point out the record of your opponent."[35] Nonetheless, he was straightforward about his approach to campaigning. Standing like a professor at a blackboard at a political breakfast in Pasadena, he pointed to Rule One: "Destroy your opponent."[36]

In 1946, Chotiner was acting as campaign manager for the GOP's senate candidate, William Knowland, for whom he had dreamed up the slogan "WE WILL NOT SURRENDER" (suggesting, not subtly, that Knowland's opponent would). The Republicans hired Chotiner to write some press releases and advise their young and green candidate for California's 12th Congressional District. Legend, spread largely by Chotiner, held that he played a key role in the making of Richard Nixon, attack dog. Actually, he was only marginally involved in that first campaign, but the advice he gave was useful. He told Nixon to debate his opponent and sent him to see Kyle Palmer, chief political reporter of the **Los Angeles Times**.[37]

In California politics, Palmer, a dapper, cheerfully cynical man with an ingratiating manner, was known as "Mister Republican" and "the Little Governor." An endorsement from the **Los Angeles Times** was worth hundreds of thousands of votes. Palmer was the one who told the Chandler family, owners of the paper, whom to endorse. He wrote speeches for politicians and instructed them on whom to hire and what bills to support. In a state that had supposedly rid itself of old-fashioned machine-style political bosses, historian David Halberstam has written, Palmer **was** the political boss.

Granting an audience to Nixon, Palmer found the young man "gawky" and earnest—but just the ticket to unseat Congressmen Voorhis, a liberal New Dealer whose ability to hang on to his seat for the past decade had been a reproach to Palmer's domain. In his column, "The Watchman," Palmer began playing up Nixon—the clean-cut young war veteran, the Quaker not afraid to fight. "Voorhis," on the other hand, wrote Palmer, "was once a registered Socialist and that streak will not rub out." The phrase Palmer and others used was "creeping Socialism"; the choice facing the voters, as Nixon quickly picked up the refrain, was "slave or free."[38] Nixon would later regard the press as his undying enemy. But in 1946, he had Palmer's **Los Angeles Times** and the backing of almost every other paper in the Southland.

Nixon's closest adviser, at least at first, was his wife, Pat. She was stoical and dogged. After they had their first child, Tricia, in February 1946, the Nixons moved into a rented, one-bedroom Spanish-style bungalow. The crib went in the living room. No one got much sleep. A mink farm next door kept them awake with round-the-clock screeching as well as an unmistakable stench. Within three weeks of Tricia's difficult breech birth, Pat was out campaigning day and night. She quietly bore the snobbery of a Pasadena matron who, at a Republican ladies' lunch, questioned whether she knew the right nail polish to wear.[39] She quit smoking in public and swallowed her reserve to go out and meet and greet.

Pat could be blunt, even caustic with her husband. "God, she made it rough for him," recalled Adela Rogers St. Johns, a Hearst reporter and later novelist and screenwriter who traveled with the Nixons. "She would say, 'That was a disaster' or 'Well, I've heard you make lousy speeches, but that was the worst.'"[40] At the same time, she knew when to back off. She did not much like Murray Chotiner, but she stopped criticizing him. "When she voiced her disapproval, my father decided that Chotiner's hardline, street-smart political advice was more important to him than his wife's objections," Julie Nixon recalled. "So the subject of Murray became a nonsubject."[41]

In later years, campaign aides and reporters would observe that Pat Nixon rarely spoke to her husband on campaign planes or buses. The pattern was established early. That summer of 1946, Tom Dixon, a radio announcer paid by the campaign to introduce Nixon at rallies, watched as Nixon prepared to record some speeches at a local radio station. When Pat entered the studio, according to Dixon, "Nixon flared at her like a prima donna and said, 'You know I don't ever want to be interrupted when I'm working.'" Dixon's wife, Georgia, was in the studio and observed that, "just before air time, [Nixon] looked up and he looked at Pat and pointed at her and pointed at the door, like he would telling a dog to go outside." Mrs. Dixon followed Pat outside. Pat explained, "You know, Richard doesn't like to have me in there. I don't know why but I make him nervous." The candidate's wife did not appear to have been too upset. She added, "He's such a great man."[42]

She believed it. She was willing to put up with a great deal because she saw her husband as he saw himself—as a man of destiny. If anything, she was more sure, more committed. When he wavered, she would brace him, sometimes harshly. More often, she put on a stoical mask. She understood a volatile temper; she had seen her father abuse her mother. Sharing her husband with a rough-edged operator like Murray Chotiner was a small price to pay to achieve the success both of them dreamed of and spoke of late into the night. She learned to deal with her husband's moods. Under stress, Nixon was prone to outbursts. Pat simply learned to avoid them.

Preparation was an obsession with Nixon. He wanted to know everything about his opponent, especially anything that could be used against him. Nixon had been given a brief tutorial in the art of negative campaigning by Chotiner. Rule number one was dig up some dirt. Although Chotiner's wiles and energy that summer of 1946 were devoted largely to William Knowland's Senate campaign, he was able to feed Nixon some useful political intelligence from time to time. Someone leaked to Chotiner that Congressman Voorhis had been endorsed by an organization called the National Citizens Political Action Committee, or NC-PAC. It was a liberal group, but not nearly as leftist as the similarly named and better-known CIO-PAC, a pro-union group that was regarded as socialist. Voorhis had **not** been endorsed by the far-left CIO-PAC. In his campaign, Nixon artfully blurred distinctions between the two, handing out twenty-five thousand red thimbles while urging voters, "Nixon for

Congress—Put the Needle in the PAC" (without saying which one).[43]

Frustrated by Nixon's clever, if slightly dodgy, tactics and the unwillingness of the pro-Nixon press to probe into them, Voorhis made a classic mistake for an incumbent. He agreed to debate the underdog. Characteristically and carefully, Nixon prepared, slipping quietly into the back of auditoriums to watch his foe give speeches.

What he saw was a ponderous, stuffy professor type. Voorhis was a patrician reformer, a graduate of Hotchkiss and Yale, an East Coast establishment liberal transplanted to the West. After five terms, he seemed to have a safe seat; he had been lazy and slow to react. Nixon was happy to be underestimated, especially by a snob.[44]

It had been a brutally hot summer in the Los Angeles basin, with temperatures rising above 100 degrees day after day. Friday, September 13, 1946, started hot and smoggy, but the evening turned warm and lovely by the time nearly a thousand people jammed into the auditorium at San Marino Junior High. Voorhis went first, rambling and droning on in his slightly weary way.

Nixon arrived in the middle of Voorhis's speech. He had learned, early in his political career, to make an entrance. When he walked alone, he often seemed slumped and lost in thought. But for speeches and debates, he would square his shoulders and stride confidently in the room. Nixon's own speech was pithy—he denounced Washington bureaucracy and labor agitators—and drew loud applause.

Both candidates had planted questioners in the audience. A Democrat asked Nixon why he had made the "false charge" that Voorhis had been endorsed by the CIO-PAC. Nixon was ready. He reached into his pocket and pulled out a bulletin from NC-PAC endorsing Voorhis. Then he got up from his chair and walked across the stage to hand the document to Voorhis, so he could see for himself. Flustered, Voorhis got up to take the pamphlet, realized that he was being led into a trap, and blurted out that NC-PAC was not CIO-PAC. While he fumbled for words to explain, Nixon calmly read lists of directors from both organizations, pointing out that many of the names were the same. The audience lustily cheered Nixon and booed Voorhis.

Staggering off the stage, Voorhis asked a campaign follower, Chester Holifield, how he had done. "Jerry, he murdered you," said Holifield. "He used every trick in the book."[45]

Nixon "scored a hit," crowed the **Los Angeles Times**. For the next six weeks, Nixon tirelessly banged away at Voorhis for being the tool of the Washington establishment. Skillful at stealing opposition thunder, Nixon became the avatar of the "forgotten man," the financially strapped shopkeepers and out-of-work laborers to whom FDR had appealed with the New Deal. Nixon deftly turned the New Deal on the bureaucrats and their flunky, Jerry Voorhis.

On election day, Nixon won easily, with 57 percent of the vote. Palmer invited Nixon and his whole family to celebrate in the private suite of the paper's owners, Dorothy ("Buff") and Norman Chandler, in the Los Angeles Times Building. Asked what he wanted to drink, Nixon answered, "Milk." But then he followed Mrs. Chandler into the kitchen and asked, "Could you get me a straight bourbon? I don't want my mother to see me drinking it."[46] The evening went on until dawn. Nixon recalled in his memoirs, "Pat and I were happier on November 6, 1946, than we ever were to be again in my political career."[47]

The investigator.
**Courtesy of the Richard Nixon Presidential
Library and Museum**

CHAPTER 3

The Greenest Congressman

*T*he Washington Post called him "the greenest congressman in town."[1] His cramped office was tucked away on the fifth floor—called the "attic"—of the Old (now Cannon) House Office Building. Despite the jolt of World War II, the nation's capital in 1946 was still a small, somewhat Southern town, inbred and hierarchical.[2] Lacking seniority, Nixon was denied a coveted seat on the Judiciary Committee. Knowing no one, unsure of his place, not a member of any "in" group, Nixon, as ever, made do. He didn't need the Franklins; he would once more start his own club. It took some time to bond with other congressional newcomers, but within a couple of years, he had become a charter member of the jauntily named Chowder and Marching Club. The fifteen freshmen and junior Republicans who got together once a month or so for food and drink were hale and hearty, just like the Orthogonians. One of them was a former football lineman from the University of Michigan named Gerald Ford. Ford later remembered an evening out with the fellows. Nixon was spirited, even a bit of a showman—he could play popular tunes on the piano and lead sing-alongs. But afterward, as Nixon waited outside on the curb for a car, Ford noticed that his fellow bon vivant seemed to be "mumbling to himself. He seemed sad and detached," Ford recalled.[3]

On the Education and Labor Committee, Nixon took his seat at the very end of the Republican side of the table. At the opposite end sat another newly elected navy veteran, Congressman John F. Kennedy of Massachusetts, last man on the Democrats' lineup. "We were like a pair of unmatched bookends," Nixon recalled. Kennedy was all languid grace and lofty manners, a prince of the city, or so he seemed to the anxious young striver whose father had not been able to give him Harvard.

On April 21, 1947, "we had the first Kennedy-Nixon debate," Nixon recalled. As part of a House Education Committee road show, the two freshmen argued over labor policy in the steel town of McKeesport, Pennsylvania. On the **Capital Limited** train back to Washington that night, Nixon and Kennedy drew straws for the lower berth ("this time I won," recalled Nixon). They "sat up late," talking about domestic issues and especially foreign policy, the subject they both most cared about. Years later, Nixon would come to regard Kennedy in the way that Macbeth saw Banquo's ghost. But that night he felt kinship. He was able to see that Kennedy, despite his apparent ease of manner, was not unlike him, after all. Both men had lost golden older brothers; both felt the heavy burdens of parental expectation. "We shared one quality which distinguished us from most of our fellow congressmen," Nixon recalled. "Neither of us was a backslapper, and we were uncomfortable with boisterous displays of superficial camaraderie. He was shy, and that sometimes made him appear aloof. But it was a shyness born of an instinct that guarded privacy and concealed emotions. I understood these qualities because I shared them."[4]

During the January social season of his first winter in Washington, the Nixons were invited to a dinner party at the home of Christian Herter, a former State Department diplomat and future secretary of state, at the time a ranking member of the House Foreign Affairs Committee. Very tall, stooped by the arthritis that would eventually disable him, Herter was an elegant man. "He's the cream of the bottle," declared New York governor Tom Dewey, the Republican candidate for president in the upcoming election. **Time** magazine described Herter as "aristocratic, somewhat aloof." He was "the example of the good clean man in politics," a diplomatic historian later wrote of the Harvard-educated reformer who once described Washington as "a dirty kitchen where cockroaches abound." Married into a Standard Oil fortune, Herter lived in tastefully refined grandeur.[5]

The Nixons were excited but nervous to be invited to such a glamorous soiree. The invitation from the Herters said "informal," so Pat Nixon "bought a beautiful teal-blue cocktail dress for the occasion and my father wore his dark blue suit," wrote Julie Nixon Eisenhower. "When they walked into the Herters' home that night they were stunned to see that they were the only two guests not dressed in black tie and long, formal gowns." In Washington society at that time, "informal" meant a tuxedo; "formal" meant white tie and tails.[6]

One can only imagine the tense smiles on the faces of the carefully, nicely, but inappropriately dressed "greenest congressman" and his wife. It was one of those embarrassing, awkward moments that rubbed raw Nixon's feelings of alienation, just under the skin. And yet Congressman Herter, who had himself been shy in college (and liked to say that his "watchword" was a Chinese proverb that exalted "gentleness, frugality, humility"), was probably not offended by Nixon's modest blue suit. Herter must have been impressed by what his well-prepared guest had to say at dinner. Nixon's sartorial faux pas did him no lasting harm; a couple of months later, the junior member of the California delegation learned that he had been chosen to serve on an important committee chaired by Herter. The nineteen members—Nixon was the youngest and the only Westerner—were to go to Europe and report on the prospects for a massive foreign aid plan announced by Secretary of State George C. Marshall at Harvard Commencement in June. "I was probably the most surprised man in Washington when I opened the morning newspaper and read that I had been chosen" for the committee, Nixon recalled. He had never spoken to anyone about the committee because, as he explained, "I had not thought there was any chance of being appointed to it."

Nixon was thrilled. Here was a break, a chance to see statesmen in action, perhaps, in some minor way, to become one. Nixon may have been "the greenest congressman," but he was also a most ambitious one. Like many young men of his generation, he had been given, by service in a world war, a first-hand education in the importance of America's global role. Unlike most returning servicemen, he was not content to find a job and raise a family or even, as a politician, to be satisfied by tending to the needs and wishes of the voters back home. Determined to prove himself on the biggest stage he could find, he understood that as America entered a new Cold War, the main event for a national politician was international relations. The Herter Committee was Nixon's chance to begin to fulfill a lifelong ambition. "I would now have the opportunity to work with some of the most senior and influential men in the House," he wrote, "and a chance to show what I could do in the field of foreign affairs."[7]

At the end of August, the Herter Committee sailed from New York on the **Queen Mary**. It was to be all business: Herter instructed the committee members to leave behind "their wives and their tuxedos."[8] Apparently wishing to make sure work would be balanced with play, Nixon's new friend, Jack Kennedy, gave Nixon the names and addresses of three

young ladies in Paris. "I don't think Mr. Nixon even
took the numbers away with him," recalled his secretary, Dorothy Cox. "He was far too embarrassed."⁹

Less than a year after he had debated Jerry Voorhis in the San Marino Junior High gym, Nixon was
discussing foreign affairs over tea with the British
prime minister, Clement Attlee, at 10 Downing
Street. The scenes of postwar devastation on the
continent left a lasting impression on Nixon. In
Berlin, the congressman found people living like
rats in caves. "As we stood in the vast ruined hall of
what had been Hitler's Chancellery, small, thin-
faced German boys tried to sell us their fathers'
medals as souvenirs," he recalled. On an island in
Greece, the mayor introduced the visiting congressmen to a woman whose left breast had been cut off
by the Communists because she had refused to betray her brother, a leader of the loyalists fighting the
Communist guerrillas. Nixon was shaken and impressed by the fierceness and ubiquity of the Communist insurgents. In Trieste, he witnessed an
organized mob carrying red flags and singing "The
Internationale" as the men, fists clenched, paraded
by his hotel. "Suddenly, there was an explosion at
the end of the block. The crowd cleared and I saw
the body of a young man whose head had been
blown off by a grenade," he wrote. "I was sure what
was happening in Trieste would soon be re-enacted
throughout Western Europe unless America helped
to restore stability and prosperity." Nixon's anti-
communism was not just a politically useful stance.

After the Herter Committee trip, it deepened into conviction.[10]

Before Nixon left for Europe, he had been warned by Herman Perry, the Whittier banker who had recruited him to run for Congress, not to be swayed by State Department "propaganda" into wasting taxpayer money.[11] Perry accurately reflected opinion back home in the 12th Congressional District. Nixon's own poll found that three out of four of his constituents were resolutely opposed to any foreign aid. Nixon followed his conscience instead.

Nixon was not unmindful of his constituents. Few politicians have been more attuned to the wants and needs of the folks back home. But Nixon possessed a long-range vision that most of his congressional peers lacked. He understood that the Republican Party was doomed to irrelevance if it regressed to pre–World War II isolationism.

The man who as a boy had listened for train whistles in the night could hear a distant call. America was at that moment on the verge of becoming the world's great superpower, and Nixon understood that his political future lay as an internationalist, not as an isolationist. This was a time to lead, not to follow; in time, public opinion would come along. In December, he voted for the Marshall Plan to rebuild Europe. Then he flew to California to make his case that American intervention would save Europe from starvation—-and help safeguard the West from Communism, a more persuasive argument back home.[12]

Nixon also had some repair work to do in his own home, the modest apartment he had rented with Pat just outside Washington in the Virginia suburbs. Pat was feeling neglected and overwhelmed by the burden of caring for a two-year-old and Nixon's aging and ailing parents, who had moved to a farm in Pennsylvania, partly to be closer to their rising-star son. "Mother always had scorned complainers," Julie recorded in her memoir of her mother. But, about eighteen months into their Washington life, Pat finally unburdened herself to her distracted and often absent husband. "My father was stunned when she finally told him how deep her discontent was," Julie wrote. Shy about expressing himself face-to-face, Nixon wrote his wife a long letter, declaring his "abiding love" and promising to spend more time at home.

It was a promise he could not possibly keep. More than likely, his wife was not fooled. Her discontent may have been deep, but her capacity for suffering was deeper. She stoically accepted his good intentions and swallowed her doubts. Nixon wrote the letter shortly before Pat went into labor with their second daughter on a scorching Fourth of July night (Congressman Nixon was at least able to get Pat a corner room with cross ventilation at the un-air-conditioned hospital.)[13] A month after Julie's birth, Nixon met Alger Hiss.

The first Washington institution to tap into America's massive postwar disillusionment was the House Un-American Activities Committee. Many people saw Communism as an incubus, like an evil possession or a disease; it was foreign and unclean; **un-American,** in a popular usage of the era. The threat was not imaginary. During the 1930s, the Soviet Union had actively recruited agents and planted spies; decades later, declassified cables from FBI wiretaps would show that Moscow had aggressively penetrated the federal government, though the spy rings were mostly rolled up after the war.[14]

HUAC, as the congressional committee was known, was a poor scourge of the Red Menace. Its members tended to be blowhards or worse. The ranking Democrat, John Rankin of Mississippi, a flagrant anti-Semite and racist, was known to paw through a dubious volume entitled **Who's Who in American Jewry** to see if witnesses were hiding their ethnicity.[15] The committee had a reputation for trampling on constitutional rights and for engaging in general foolishness. A parade of left-leaning movie stars and screenwriters trooped before HUAC to deny that they were taking orders from the Kremlin; Gary Cooper was guarded but testified that communism was not "on the level."[16] An embarrassed House GOP leadership had put Nixon on the committee in the hope, correct as it turned out, that with his legal training he would act as a force of moderation and steer the committee toward some real Soviet spies.[17]

In August 1948, President Harry Truman, largely as a stunt to revive his flagging reelection campaign, called the "Do-Nothing" Congress back to Washington from its summer recess. On the morning of Tuesday, August 3, HUAC returned to its Red hunting, calling as a witness a dumpy, vacant-looking man named Whittaker Chambers. "Chambers was one of the most disheveled-looking persons I had ever seen," recalled Nixon. "Everything about him seemed wrinkled and un-pressed." Speaking in a bored monotone, forced to repeat himself (the microphone was broken), Chambers told the story of how, as a disaffected intellectual, he had first joined the Communist Party in the 1920s, then broken with it during the Stalinist show trials of the late 1930s. He named other communist agents in America. One of them, he said, was Alger Hiss.

"A ripple of surprise went through the room," recalled Nixon. Hiss was a pillar of the Eastern Establishment. A graduate of Harvard Law School, he had clerked for Justice Oliver Wendell Holmes Jr. and risen through a series of State Department jobs, winning the backing and patronage of such worthies as Secretary of State Dean Acheson and his presumed successor John Foster Dulles. He had held important postings at the Yalta Conference in 1945 and at the San Francisco conference creating the United Nations later the same year. He had seemed assured of a glorious diplomatic career.

The next morning Hiss telegraphed the committee demanding the right to formally and publicly deny Chambers's charge. He appeared before a packed hearing room on August 5. Hiss was tall and handsome, elegantly dressed, "coldly courteous, and at times, condescending," Nixon recalled. He denied ever having heard the name Whittaker Chambers. Shown a picture of Chambers, he paused, looking up at Congressman Karl Mundt, the acting chairman of the committee. "He looks like a lot of people. I might even mistake him for the Chairman of this Committee." Mundt, who was pudgy like Chambers, looked taken aback. "I hope you are wrong about that," he said.

The spectators tittered. When the hearing was over, a crowd clustered around Hiss to congratulate him. "It was a virtuoso performance," Nixon recalled. "Without actually saying it, he left the clear impression that he was the innocent victim of a terrible case of mistaken identity."[18] The liberal press agreed. A **Washington Post** editorial compared Hiss to "an innocent pedestrian, splattered with mud by a passing vehicle." The **Post**'s cartoonist, Herbert Block—"Herblock"—who would later become one of Nixon's great tormentors, drew a picture of an innocent man cornered by a tiger; the tiger was labeled "Smear Statements."[19] At a press conference, President Truman was asked about HUAC's latest foray into the underworld of communist espionage rings. "A red herring," said the president, dismissively and perhaps a little too cleverly.

Most of the committee members folded like the schoolyard bullies they were. "We've been had. We're ruined," moaned one. "Let's wash our hands of the whole mess," said another. Only Nixon wanted to keep going.[20]

At lunch, he said to his secretary, Dorothy Cox, that there was something a little too suave, a little too sure about the man in the Ivy League suit. Hiss seemed to be overplaying his hand. Nixon decided to press forward with his own investigation.

In his 1962 memoir, **Six Crises,** Nixon asserts that he had known nothing of Hiss until Chambers named him to the committee. Various historians have insisted that Nixon was tipped off by a "Red hunter" named Father John Cronin who had good FBI ties. Toward the end of his life, Nixon insisted to biographer Jonathan Aitken that he didn't discuss Hiss with Cronin until after he had broken the case. Cronin largely backed up Nixon's version, according to Aitken: "Nixon may have read something about Hiss in my reports . . . but we didn't discuss the case until after Hiss made his public denial."

Nixon scholar Irwin Gellman has pored over Nixon's diaries and papers and found no trace that Cronin tipped off Nixon beforehand. It is possible that Nixon read Cronin's 1945 document, "The Problem of American Communism," which mentions Hiss four times in 146 pages. But, using the colloquial smear of the day, Cronin lumped Hiss in with "fellow travelers" like Eleanor Roosevelt and FDR's Secretary of the Interior Harold Ickes, who were hardly reporting to the Kremlin.[21] Cronin regarded Hiss as a communist sympathizer, but he had no inkling that the diplomat was a Soviet spy.

Nixon could not know, either. But even as an obscure congressman, he had an instinct for what he liked to call "the big play." Nixon may not have known that Hiss had served the Soviet intelligence service, but he could tell a phony when he saw one, especially one who affected an upper-class accent.

On August 17, Hiss appeared before Nixon and a committee investigator at a suite in the Commodore Hotel in New York City. Hiss noted that he was supposed to meet his wife at the Harvard Club that night; he hoped someone would let her know if he had to be late.[22] The patrician Hiss, who came from a genteel, if threadbare, Wasp family, had an almost incurable need to remind Nixon that he was dealing with a social better. At a later session, as Nixon and Hiss were sparring over some point of law, Hiss huffily declared, "I am familiar with the law. I attended Harvard Law School. I believe yours was Whittier?" Robert Stripling, the committee's chief investigator, observed that "Nixon turned red and blue and red again. You could see the hackles on his back practically pushing his coat up." Stripling later said that "Nixon set his hat for Hiss. It was a personal thing."[23]

Nixon's pursuit of Hiss has been portrayed by some as a class vendetta, by others as a noble crusade. Stripling was too cynical; Nixon was a true anticommunist. Still, ideology was not his sole, or even his primary, motivation. Personal ambition, patriotism, and an almost eerily prescient sense of timing moved Nixon more than fixed political principle. Nixon always emphasized the loneliness of his quest, and he must have **felt** alone as he defied conventional wisdom in Washington, including, at first, the opinions of his own colleagues on the committee. But Nixon was not one to swing wildly. Quietly, before he went public with his attack on Hiss, Nixon checked in with some paragons of the ruling order. The first was Christian Herter. Nixon was "particularly disturbed," he recalled, by his conversation with Herter. "I don't want to prejudge the case," Herter told Nixon, but he warned against getting "taken in by Chambers."

Nixon admired Herter, but he also knew that Herter was a member of Hiss's tribe and was perhaps blinded by class loyalty. So Nixon pressed on. He went to see John Foster Dulles, the senior partner at Sullivan and Cromwell, the same Wall Street firm where Nixon, as a needy Duke Law student, had sat forlornly in the lobby worrying about the shabbiness of his one good suit. Dulles was Governor Dewey's chief foreign policy adviser in the presidential campaign of 1948, but he took the time to see young Congressman Nixon, possibly because he was shrewd enough to see some risk of his own exposure in the Hiss case. Dulles had recommended Hiss for his current job as head of the Carnegie Endowment for International Peace. Nixon showed Dulles the testimony of Hiss and Chambers. A careful lawyer, Dulles read the document closely, noting that Chambers was able to identify personal details about Hiss's life. "There's no question about it," he finally said. "It's almost impossible to believe, but Chambers knows Hiss." Should Nixon proceed with the investigation? Dulles told Nixon, "In view of the facts Chambers has testified to, you'd be derelict in your duty if you did not see the case through to a conclusion." Dulles displayed a curious mixture of high righteousness and expedient cunning; he had already begun writing memos to files distancing himself from Hiss.[24]

Nixon got a little help from the FBI, but not much. The Bureau's J. Edgar Hoover regarded himself as the nation's chief bulwark against communism, but he was ultimately interested in preserving his own vast power above all. He deftly played politicians against each other, dispensing or threatening to expose secrets, national and personal, as it suited his purposes and ambition. With Nixon he entered a dance that, as it turned out, would go on for another twenty-five years. An FBI agent shared evidence on Hiss with Nixon, partly to help goad the Truman administration, but he did it selectively and warily. In late September, Hoover's trusted assistant, Clyde Tolson, wrote a memo to Hoover asserting that Nixon was a headline seeker who "plays both ends against the middle." Hoover wrote in the margin: "I agree."[25]

Certainly, Nixon worked hard to play reporters. He would invite groups of them to his office in the evening, making sure, with characteristic studiousness, to memorize their names and favorite cocktails. Bert Andrews was the Washington Bureau chief of the **New York Herald Tribune**, an organ of moderate Republican reason, widely regarded as

second only to **The New York Times** in clout. Andrews had won a Pulitzer Prize a year earlier for articles critical of HUAC's heavy-handedness. Nixon
offered Andrews what newsmen prize: exclusive access. He invited Andrews to come with him to visit
Chambers on his farm in Maryland.[26]

Thanks partly to Nixon's leaks, press interest in
the Chambers-Hiss investigation began to mush-
room during the hot Indian summer of 1948. Nixon
had to sneak out a window of the Old House Office
Building to slip past the press pack and drive to
Chambers's farm, where he spent days quizzing the
moody ex-Red. Chambers had a shadowy past—he
had been arrested for homosexuality and had told a
great many lies during his underground existence as
the member of a communist cell. Chambers was
gloomy and martyrish, shy and tortured, and Nixon,
for his part, may have related to him; certainly, he
understood him. The two became family friends.
Nixon took Chambers to meet his mother, while
Chambers later wrote that his children worshipped
"Nixie, the kind and good, about whom they will
hear no nonsense."[27]

During several days of testimony in late August
and September, at the first-ever televised congressional hearings, Nixon, Chambers, and Hiss parried
over the facts that might—or might not—expose
Hiss as a Soviet agent who had worked in cahoots
with Chambers in the 1930s. The details were petty
and arcane—Chambers was able to show that he
knew that Hiss's Quaker wife, Priscilla, used the

"thee" and "thou" of "plain speech" and that Hiss was an avid bird watcher. Slowly, under hot lights in a crowded hearing room, Hiss's veneer of aloofness and haughty innocence peeled away.[28]

Nixon drove himself harder. He "immersed himself in the case with an intensity that was almost frightening," recorded his daughter Julie.[29] Nixon later wrote that he felt enormous tension, that he was caught in a constant state of crisis—but that he regarded his feelings as normal and healthy in a way, or at least necessary for any warrior girding for the fight. In **Six Crises,** he was quite frank about the emotional and physical toll: "I began to notice . . . the inevitable symptoms of tension. I was 'mean' to live with at home and with my friends. I was quick-tempered with members of my staff. I lost interest in eating and skipped meals without even being aware of it. Getting to sleep became more and more difficult."

He continued, a little self-consciously:

I suppose some might say that I was "nervous," but I knew these were simply the evidences of preparing for battle. There is, of course, a fine line to be observed. One must always be keyed up for battle but he must not be jittery. He is jittery only when he worries about the natural symptoms of stress. He is keyed up when he recognizes those symptoms for what they are—the physical evidences that the mind, emotions, and body are ready for action.

If these passages are to be believed, Nixon did not look inward in any truly self-scrutinizing way. There was no attempt at self-analysis, as there might have been by a member of a later generation; surely, he did not see what some future biographers would discern—a frightened boy cowering before his father's hand or an over-eager youngster desperately seeking to win his withholding mother's conditional love.[30] Rather, he saw a fighter, a battler. Sleeplessness and short temper were not signs of neurosis or even "jitteryness." They were, for Nixon, the predictable manifestations of the "mind, emotions, and body" bracing for noble combat. What Nixon really felt, deep down, is unknowable, but no one ever worked harder at maintaining a facade of upbeat stoicism, not just to the outside world, one suspects, but in his own mind as well. He was determined not to worry about being worried.

He was not insensitive. He was not a blunt instrument, a "planing machine gouging a deep self-beneficial groove through life," as William James had described Justice Oliver Wendell Holmes Jr. Indeed, despite his later jealousy, he had been able to see past JFK's show of effortless grace to a kindred shyness. Nixon felt that he had overcome his disadvantages not by giving in but by fighting back—by audacity and grit, not equivocation and self-doubt. He rarely lowered his guard or stood down.

Still, it was exhausting always to be on alert, like a ship in harm's way. Nixon could not sustain such a high state of readiness indefinitely. On the eve of a big hearing on August 25, Bert Andrews stopped by Nixon's office and said, "You look like hell. You need some sleep." That night Nixon took his first sleeping pill.[31]

The Nixons had not taken a vacation in three years. The Herter Committee ruined a planned holiday in 1947, and the Alger Hiss affair put off a trip to the beach in August of 1948. Finally, in December, Nixon took Pat on a Caribbean cruise. On the first night at sea, they were dining at the captain's table when the purser brought over a radio telegram. It was from Stripling, the committee investigator. Chambers had produced some documentary evidence proving that Hiss was a Soviet spy. Stripling's "cablese" was breathless indeed: "Case clinched. Information amazing. Heat is on from the press and other places. Immediate action appears necessary. Can you possibly get back?"

Nixon read the telegram aloud at the table. Pat threw up her hands and said, "Here we go again."

A telegram followed from Bert Andrews, the **New York Herald Tribune** man who was working so closely with Nixon that he was practically on staff: "Documents incredibly hot. Stop. Link to Hiss seems certain. Stop. . . . Love to Pat. Stop. (Signed) Vacation-Wrecker Andrews."

Stripling arranged to have a Coast Guard seaplane pick up Nixon at a mid-ocean rendezvous. (Pat was to make her way home, alone, from the ship's next port of call.) The press, duly tipped off, was waiting in Miami when Nixon emerged from the co-pilot's seat, hero to the rescue. Reporters yelled for Nixon's comments on the "Pumpkin Papers." Nixon, befuddled, asked, "What is this, a joke?" The reporters explained that Chambers, leading investigators out into the fields on his farm, had taken the top off a pumpkin and produced five rolls of microfilm containing photographs of secret State Department documents—and, most damningly, summaries in Hiss's own handwriting.[32]

The revelation of the microfilm sparked an intense media circus. Nixon was photographed peering through a magnifying glass at the evidence, like a modern-day Sherlock Holmes (never mind that the film could be read only on a microfilm projector).[33] The film of the Pumpkin Papers, announced Nixon, was "conclusive proof of the greatest treason conspiracy in this nation's history"—true enough, because America, since Benedict Arnold, had experienced relatively little treason.

But then, with a sickening lurch, the balloon plummeted: An expert from Eastman Kodak, the film's manufacturer, reported that the film had been manufactured in 1945—seven years **after** Chambers had allegedly photographed the incriminating documents as an insurance policy against assassination, as he had explained with his typical penchant for drama.

"The news jolted us into almost complete shock," Nixon later wrote. "We sat looking at each other without saying a word. This meant that Chambers was, after all, a liar." Nixon called Chambers and told him what the committee had just learned from Eastman Kodak. "What is your answer to that?" Nixon demanded. There was a long silence over the phone. Nixon wondered if Chambers had hung up. Finally, Nixon recalled, Chambers answered in a "voice full of despair and resignation: 'I can't understand it. God must be against me.'" Nixon exploded "with all the fury and frustration that had built up within me, 'You'd better have a better answer than that!'"

Gloomily, Nixon braced himself for "the biggest crow-eating performance in the history of Capitol Hill." But five minutes before the scheduled mea culpa press conference, the man from Eastman Kodak called back to say there had been a mistake, the film had been manufactured in 1938 after all. Chambers was vindicated. Stripling, a Southerner, let out a rebel yell, grabbed Nixon's arms, and began to dance him around the room. Extricating himself, Nixon tried to call Chambers but couldn't reach him. It later turned out that the despairing Chambers had tried to poison himself. Fortunately, he failed.[34]

The Hiss case dragged through the courts for months before Hiss was finally convicted of perjury—for lying that he was not a spy—and sent to jail (the statute of limitations for treason had run out). Years later, documents declassified from American and Soviet archives seemed to prove that Hiss had been feeding State Department secrets to the

Soviets. Right up to his death in 1996, Hiss stead-
fastly maintained his innocence. He told author
Herbert Parmet that although Nixon was not a
"yahoo" he was "crude" and "crass." Hiss allowed,
"From time to time I was guilty of a certain snob-
bishness toward him. He may have sensed some of
that, and it may have annoyed him."[35]

For the nation, as well as Nixon, the Hiss case was
a turning point and a catalyst. If someone as reputable as Alger Hiss could be a Soviet spy, who was to
say where the subversion ended? America entered a
fearful age. In 1949, the Soviet Union successfully
exploded an atomic bomb; it was soon learned that
spies had given the Soviets some of America's nuclear
secrets. In 1950, the junior senator from Wisconsin,
Joe McCarthy, sallied forth on a reckless witch-hunt
that exposed no real Reds but fomented widespread
suspicion, even panic, for the next four years until
McCarthy collapsed under the weight of his own
scurrility.

It can be argued that the decades-long culture war
that divided the "Silent Majority" from the Establishment, Middle America from the East Coast elite,
commenced with the case of **Richard Nixon v. Alger
Hiss**. For Nixon, the Hiss case became an almost
sacred touchstone. He would, in almost any situation and seemingly for almost any reason, urge his
followers to read the Hiss chapter in **Six Crises**. At
the same time, he always considered his victory to
be a Pyrrhic one. He claimed that the East Coast
elite and its minions in the press never recovered

from the embarrassment of backing the gentlemanly but Kremlin-serving Hiss against the lowly but righteous Nixon.[36]

After the Pumpkin Papers came out, Nixon was invited to a dinner party at the home of Virginia Bacon, an in-crowd Washington hostess whose father-in-law had been a contemporary of Theodore Roosevelt. After dinner, Paul Porter, a leader in the Washington legal establishment, was getting needled for his support of Hiss. Didn't he think that HUAC had done a good job exposing Hiss? "No!" declared Porter. The hearings should be stopped because they were reflecting badly on FDR's foreign policy, he insisted. Years later, Nixon contemptuously recalled Porter's stubborn refusal to concede:

Well, there you had it. That was perhaps typical, typical of people in the foreign service, typical of people closely associated with Harvard and other great universities. They couldn't bear to find one of their own like Hiss being involved in this kind of thing. They considered the Hiss case as being an attack on the whole elite establishment, an attack on the foreign service, an attack on those who were there for the UN, and even an attack on Roosevelt's foreign policy. Those attitudes were all crap, but that was what I had to fight against.[37]

In **Six Crises,** Nixon claimed that after the Hiss case, he was "subjected to an utterly unprincipled and vicious smear campaign. Bigamy, forgery, drunkenness, insanity, thievery, anti-Semitism, perjury, the whole gamut of misconduct in public life, ranging from the unethical to downright criminal activities—all these were among the charges hurled at me, some publicly and others through whispering campaigns which were even more difficult to counteract."[38] Nixon was exaggerating; with the possible exception of the far-left press or some way-out Drew Pearson columns, the public record does not support this litany of slander (the whispering is unverifiable, of course). Indeed, Nixon's press was mostly positive. At the start of 1950, **Newsweek** called Nixon "the most outstanding member of the present Congress," and the **Saturday Evening Post**, another mass-circulation mainstay, featured him as an up-and-comer to watch. But Nixon, ever alert to put-downs, sensed that liberal columnists and opinion-makers and their social friends in Georgetown and on Capitol Hill were beginning to privately sneer at him as a charlatan and demagogue. There is no doubt that Nixon regarded himself as an object of scorn and calumny. So did Pat. When Julie was asking her mother about the Hiss case in 1979, her answers were "brief and strained." When Julie changed the subject, Pat interrupted her "with an edge of vehemence in her voice." She said that after Hiss, her husband became a "target."[39]

Frank Gannon, who worked closely with the Nixons on **RN**, Nixon's massive 1978 memoir, believed that the Nixons had enjoyed Washington in the early years—Pat even got Dick out on the dance floor at the Shoreham Hotel—but that "Hiss queered it all. Doors closed on them. Invitations were withdrawn. She discovered that politicians were weasels."[40] At the time, even as he became a national figure for "getting Hiss," Nixon was so downcast that he was considering giving up his congressional seat to go back to practicing law, recalled Herb Klein, a young newsman who had covered Nixon on the Herter Committee trip (he astutely observed that Nixon avidly plunged into street crowds partly to avoid going to embassy cocktail parties).[41]

But Nixon did not quit Congress. He doubled down and ran for the U.S. Senate.

Ike and Dick.
**Courtesy of the Richard Nixon Presidential
Library and Museum**

CHAPTER 4

Rock 'Em, Sock 'Em

For all his feeling that reporters were out to get him, Nixon still had more friends than enemies in the press, particularly back home on the West Coast. His most powerful ally was Kyle Palmer, the political editor of the **Los Angeles Times**. In the fall of 1949, Palmer called Nixon and asked, "Dick, have you thought of running for the Senate?" Nixon answered that he had not, which, as David Halberstam wrote, "was not exactly true." Ever since the Democrats had taken back the House on the coattails of Truman's surprise victory in 1948, Nixon had realized that in the House of Representatives he was, as he put it in his memoirs, "a comer with no place to go."

Palmer pressed Nixon on a run for the U.S. Senate: "Well, I wish you'd give it some thought because we'll all support you if you do."[1] The backing of the **Los Angeles Times** was a major boon: It meant no primary challenger and instant access to deep pocket contributors. On November 3, Nixon announced his candidacy for the Senate. Picking up his cudgel as champion for the "forgotten man," he warned of an immense "slush fund" controlled by a "clique of labor lobbyists" and vowed, with words that would later be used against him, "We must put on a fighting, rocking, socking campaign." At the time, it worked: "'Fighting, rocking, socking campaign.' The phase has caught on," Murray Chotiner wrote Nixon. "It is one of our greatest assets. It would be a colossal blunder to revert to the conventional campaign. Scores of people have written and asked if YOU REALLY MEAN IT? . . . NOW YOU HAVE TO SHOW THEM." Nixon wrote "yes" in the margin.[2]

In the early going, Nixon and Pat drove around small towns in a beat-up station wagon with a loudspeaker on top. His opponent, Congresswoman Helen Gahagan Douglas, bought up radio and TV ads across the state. (Ultimately, Nixon would raise and spend much more money than Douglas.) A rarity as a woman in politics, Douglas, wife of the famous actor Melvyn Douglas, was a high-cheekbone dish, a former actress and light opera star who attracted the wandering eye of Congressman Lyndon Johnson of Texas, among others. She was a bleeding heart liberal, an early model of radical chic (she once stood in a pulpit of a black church and simpered, "I just love the Negro people").[3] She was also, fortunately for Nixon, a poor politician.

Nixon would later be pilloried by his media critics for smearing Douglas as "the Pink Lady." Actually, he didn't have to. Her opponents in the Democratic primary had called her that, as well as "a pinko" and "the red queen," while spreading anti-Semitic taunts against her husband. In the edgy, wide-open, media-driven world of California politics, the incentives to sling mud were great, and Douglas slung back, eagerly and indiscriminately.

Amazingly, she attacked Nixon as soft on communism. She distributed a leaflet shouting "THE BIG LIE! (Hitler invented it. Stalin perfected it. Nixon uses it . . .)" and claimed that Nixon—not she—was the congressman "the Kremlin loves."

For Chotiner, now Nixon's campaign manager, this was too good to be true. He countered with a flyer comparing Mrs. Douglas's voting record with that of Congressman Vito Marcantonio, a notorious communist sympathizer from New York. The pamphlet described the "Douglas-Marcantonio Axis." Douglas's flyer had been printed on yellow paper. Chotiner had an inspiration, and printed the attack on Douglas on pink paper.

The "pink sheet" became notorious in campaign lore. Chotiner had to increase the press run from 50,000 to 500,000 copies. Douglas spluttered that the leaflet was misleading (it did, in fact, exaggerate her ties to the left) and bought a series of newspaper ads declaring, THOU SHALT NOT BEAR FALSE WITNESS, in which she foolishly, and baselessly, reiterated her charge that Nixon was a fellow traveler in the Marxist cause. She also called Nixon a "pipsqueak," "Pee Wee," and, most lastingly, "Tricky Dick."[4]

Nixon was later said to have remarked that Douglas was "pink right down to her underwear." The line, which Nixon never uttered publicly and perhaps not even privately, has entered the Nixon lore, along with the Tricky Dick label.[5] In the Eastern press, especially, Nixon was constantly described as a schemer and a bully. In his memoirs, Nixon complained about the unfairness of it all, pointing out that the Douglas campaign repeatedly recruited hecklers to shout him down.[6]

Nixon may have acted and looked peevish from time to time, but he was, for the most part, having a good time. People generally like to do what they are good at, and Nixon was very good at electoral politics. Hecklers were just an opportunity to stand up for free speech. Besides, he liked being the center of attention. Driving their dented, yellow, woodpaneled Mercury station wagon, Nixon and Pat traveled ten thousand miles around the state of California, stopping wherever they could attract a crowd. Pat handed out sewing thimbles printed with the words SAFEGUARD THE AMERICAN FAMILY. Nixon speechified, scowled, smiled, and shook hands. He was hardly a natural at pressing the flesh, but he had an attribute far more important than a hearty handshake: an amazing memory for names. He worked at it, compiling thousands of note cards with the identities of supporters and small personal details about each person. He routinely astounded small-town politicians, businessmen, and shopkeepers by calling them by name and asking after their children, also by name. In time, these note cards, which he studied at night and filled with notations about favors earned and expended, became a "cash register of political memory," noted Irwin Gellman.

Nixon micromanaged his own campaigns, to the frustration of Murray Chotiner, but he enjoyed Chotiner's darkly mischievous turn of mind. The two men talked about ways to set traps for the clumsy Mrs. Douglas, who talked too much and could be bombastic. Feeling increasingly excluded, Pat disapproved of Chotiner's tactics and manner. On the other hand, she was not shy about wanting to hit back at Douglas's personal attacks. "How can you let them do that?" she would demand of her husband.[7]

Nixon was outraged, or perhaps pretended to be, when Douglas hinted strongly that he was a fascist, surrounded by men in "dark shirts." He kept his temper. He told his advisers that he must not appear "ungallant" to a woman, and he demurred when Chotiner wanted to print a flyer on even brighter red paper. Better to let voters think that **she** was the smear artist.[8]

Nixon tended to turn pessimistic just when things were looking up, and Election Day, November 7, 1950, gave him a chance to sulk—at least at first. Nixon went to the beach with Pat and the girls, but the day turned gloomy and overcast. He was shivering and morose, sure that voter turnout would be low and that he would lose. With his family, he retreated to a nearly empty movie theater to brood some more. Meanwhile, at the polls, he was clobbering Mrs. Douglas. His nearly twenty-point margin of victory was the biggest in the country for any senatorial candidate. Nixon was only thirty-seven years old, and he was already a senator from one of the largest and most powerful states in the union. That night, he moved from one victory party to another, playing "Happy Days Are Here Again," the Democratic theme song—which he appropriated—on the piano. Nothing pleased him more than outfoxing his enemies.

Among the smart set back East, "Tricky Dick" became a favorite object of derision. The lead satirist was Herbert Block, whose "Herblock" cartoon appeared daily on the editorial page of **The Washington Post**. More than anyone else, it was Herblock who created the physical caricature of Nixon—the dark jowls, the ski-jump nose, the beady eyes. Liberal journals—**The New Republic, The Progressive, The Nation**—seemed to delight in poking fun at Nixon as a morality-free parvenu. "If he did wrestle with his conscience," William Costello wrote mockingly in **The New Republic,** "the match was fixed." The magazines were small but influential among intellectuals and academics, particularly Ivy Leaguers.[9]

"Eggheads," they were called; an egghead was a pretentious highbrow, out of touch with the common man. In later years, the term would be used effectively by Nixon himself against Adlai Stevenson (who was bald), but it first showed up in the widely read column of Joseph and Stewart Alsop.[10] The Alsops were pure-blooded scions of the establishment, products of Groton and Harvard and Yale, related by marriage to Theodore Roosevelt. Joe Alsop, the older brother, was regarded as effete by the standards of the time—he collected art and was a closeted homosexual—but there was nothing soft about his politics. On foreign policy, he was a hard-liner who preached toughness and interventionism. In 1949, when the Red Chinese triumphed in their civil war, Alsop led the cry, absurd but maddening to the Truman administration, of "Who lost China?"

Alsop was a powerful Washington figure during the early Cold War, a high age of punditry, and he cultivated leaders whom he could lecture in return for scoops. Right from the beginning he spotted Nixon as a Republican internationalist—and a potential source—writing him letters and offering to share with Nixon his interviews with ambassadors from Iron Curtain countries.[11] A few weeks after Nixon won his senate seat in November 1950, Alsop invited the Nixons to dinner at one of his famous "Sunday Night Suppers."

The Sunday Night Supper, which became a Georgetown institution, was informal. "We'd get bored with our children on Sundays and abandon them and have dinner with each other," recalled Tish Alsop, Stewart's wife. But this supposedly casual maid's-night-out potluck supper became a prized invitation in the insular world of postwar Washington.[12] Senators and statesmen were flattered to join the Alsops' in-crowd circle for boisterous, alcohol-fueled debate and conviviality.

When they arrived at 2720 Dumbarton Street on a Sunday night in early December 1950, the Nixons may have been a little puzzled by Alsop's quirky abode amid the gracious Federalist and Greek Revival houses in Georgetown. It was severely modern—"garage Palladian," Alsop joked.[13] But within, beneath ancestral portraits, the atmosphere was old-school and genteel. Tish Alsop observed that Nixon was ill at ease from the moment he walked in. He did not mingle but "sank quickly into a big wing chair," she recalled. His discomfort became acute embarrassment at dinner. At the table across from Nixon sat Ambassador Averell Harriman, also Groton and Yale, but not exactly a gracious gentleman on this night. "The Crocodile," as he was known for his habit of snapping at people, looked straight at Nixon and announced in a loud voice (he was slightly deaf), "I will not break bread with this man!" Harriman had been a supporter of Helen Gahagan Douglas and regarded Nixon as an inferior being. He turned off his hearing aid, refused to eat anything, and shortly left the dinner.

The Nixons left no record of the evening, but it is not hard to imagine how they felt. It probably did not help that Alsop, confused, called his guest "Russell Nixon." Tish Alsop, the Nixons' hostess at a dance party on another occasion, was almost as judgmental as Harriman. She found both Nixons "wooden and stiff" and "terribly difficult to talk to," she told historian Fawn Brodie. "Nixon danced only one dance, with me. He's a terrible dancer. Pat didn't dance at all. They stayed only half an hour. It was as if the high school monitor had suddenly appeared. I couldn't wait for him to go."[14]

The Georgetown set was influential and would become more so as Washington emerged as a super-power capital. Joe Alsop's closest female friends were Polly Wisner, wife of the chief of operations at the CIA, and Katharine Graham, daughter of the owner of **The Washington Post**. They were bonded by ties of school and club, class and ritual. There was the "nine o'clock network," as Phil Graham, Kay's hus-band, called the three-way phone conversation and gossip exchange that took place every morning among Mrs. Graham, Mrs. Wisner, and Evangeline Bruce, wife of America's most worldly diplomat, David Bruce. At the Cooking Class, the same three women joined the wives of several top CIA and State Department officials to learn how to cook French cuisine with a Foreign Service wife named Julia Child. "Dancing Class" was what the set called the triannual formal balls at the posh Sulgrave Club (politicians were generally excluded).[15] Social Georgetown was not the Nixons' world; indeed, in Nixon's mind and in truth, it was to become the enemy camp.

The Nixons were hardly social outcasts, but get-ting on with the swells was never easy. That same December of 1950, they were invited to a dance at the Sulgrave Club hosted by Luvie Pearson, the wife of Drew Pearson, the muckraking columnist who was socially well connected. During the Senate campaign, Pearson had written that Pat had to wear costly dresses because she was too bony to wear regular sizes. "I thought that was the height of viciousness," Pat wrote a friend. About the Pearsons' party at the Sulgrave, she wrote, "They had the nerve to invite us."[16]

The Sulgrave party turned into a near-brawl. Pearson, who liked to stir the pot with his "Washington Merry-Go-Round" column, also invited Senator Joe McCarthy, the Red baiter whom Pearson had attacked in his columns. At the end of the evening, Nixon came into the coatroom to find McCarthy with his hands around Pearson's throat. Seeing Nixon enter, McCarthy gave Pearson a hard slap for good measure. "That one was for you, Dick," said McCarthy. "Let a good Quaker stop this fight," said Nixon (according to his memoirs) and pulled the two apart. He later said that he thought McCarthy was going to kill Pearson.[17]

In February 1951, the Nixons settled in Spring Valley, a new development several miles north of Georgetown. For the first time, Pat could afford a decorator. A reporter from the **Christian Science Monitor** described the living room of the Nixons' Spring Valley house as having "a bright California look with its cheerful aqua walls."[18] Pat Nixon often went to her husband's office on Capitol Hill to help with the mail, and while there she became close to Nixon's secretary, Rose Mary Woods. In time, Woods, smart, tough, tight-lipped and utterly loyal, would become almost a member of the family, "Aunt

Rose" to Julie and Tricia. His staff regarded Nixon as a considerate, kind boss, although given to occasional fits of temper. "He was very thoughtful and private," recalled Marjorie Acker, an assistant to Woods.[19] Rose Woods was a true believer. At the beginning of one political campaign (1956), she would write Nixon's mother: "The next few months will be hard to take when we read things about the Boss that are entirely untrue and, in many cases, vicious lies. I know it is particularly hard on you and Mr. Nixon, but just remember that most of the people who are against him, whether they are aware of it or not, are being led around by propaganda which was originally started by the decidedly left-wing element of the country."[20]

Nixon worked incessantly. On weekends, Pat and the girls would take picnics to the office in order to see him. During the first six months of 1951, he crisscrossed the country, visiting twenty-five states to tell the tale of how he had exposed Alger Hiss. In September, Pat wrote a friend that "Dick is more tired than I have ever seen him."[21]

For some months, Nixon had been suffering from neck and back pains. During one speech, he had felt like passing out, and he began to feel twinges near his heart and a twitch in his eye. Seeking relief, he had heard about a New York doctor named Arnold Hutschnecker, and in January of 1952, he traveled to New York City to visit Hutschnecker's Park Avenue office. In later years, Hutschnecker would be known, erroneously, as "Nixon's psychiatrist." At the time, he was an internist with an interest in psychosomatic illness.[22] During Nixon's four appointments with Hutschnecker in 1952, doctor and patient talked about healthy living habits and discussed politics and the search for world peace. "I was so, so careful not give him the feeling that he was being analyzed," Hutschnecker told Jonathan Aitken some forty years later. "And it was true. I never analyzed him. But naturally, I did form my own private theories about him. In a nutshell, these were that he felt he owed everything to his mother—his superior intellect, his success, and his ideals. The driving force in his life was that he wanted to prove to his mother that he was a good boy. He could not be a loser because this would mean letting his mother down."[23]

Hutschnecker, finding nothing physically wrong with his patient, prescribed strong barbiturate-based sedatives, a common treatment for anxiety at the time. Nixon tried to relax by following the sun. In December 1951, he was invited to Miami by the junior Democratic senator from Florida, George Smathers, who was worried that Nixon was having a "nervous breakdown." An affable, hard-partying playboy, Smathers was known as "the Collector" because he collected friends—among them, John F. Kennedy and Lyndon Johnson—whom he would take on bacchanals to Miami.

It was Smathers who introduced Nixon to the man who would become his best, lifelong friend, Charles Gregory "Bebe" Rebozo. A Cuban immigrant's son who had attended Miami High School with Smathers and once worked as a steward on Pan American Airways, Rebozo had made a fortune on leveraged real estate. He and Smathers tried to help Nixon unwind with speedboat trips around Miami. Smathers recalled that Rebozo was, at first, put off by Nixon. "Don't ever send another dull fellow like that down here again," Rebozo wrote him, according to Smathers. "He doesn't drink whiskey; he doesn't chase women; he doesn't even play golf." Rebozo's recollection of their first meeting was kinder: "He had a depth and genuineness about him which didn't come through because of his shyness, but I saw it." Nixon and Rebozo were both, at heart, lonely men who had to work at being part of the crowd. They found comfort and companionship in each other's silence.[24]

Back in Washington, Nixon gamely joined in the tomfoolery and boozy camaraderie of his old pals in the Chowder and Marching Society, but his recreation wasn't limited to boys' nights out. In April 1952, the Nixons stole away for a second honeymoon in Hawaii. They went dancing every evening at the Royal Hawaiian Hotel, wrote Julie Nixon Eisenhower, "even taking one hula lesson at the Queen Surf Hotel." They took a midnight swim and "thought nothing of going through the staid, formal lobby swathed in towels. Looking back, my mother recalls, 'It was the last carefree vacation I ever had.' "[25]

Richard Nixon admired Dwight Eisenhower, and he would come to feel warmly toward him. But

Nixon was never entirely comfortable around the five-star general and former Supreme Allied Commander. Ike had a sunny, winning smile, but he could be aloof, even to those closest to him.

As a junior officer doing navy contract termination work in New York City after V-E Day in May of 1945, Nixon had looked down from his twentieth-floor window to witness General Eisenhower welcomed home by a tremendous ticker-tape confetti parade. Nearly four million people had turned out that warm spring day to see the returning hero. In his memoirs, Nixon recalled that he could see that "Eisenhower's arms were raised high over his head in the gesture that soon would become his trademark." Nixon would make that gesture—arms outstretched, fingers forming the V-for-victory sign—his own.[26]

Nixon met Eisenhower, for a moment or two, in 1948 when Ike briefed Nixon and the other members of the Herter Committee on the military situation in Europe. Then, in July of 1950, Nixon was invited to Bohemian Grove, the summer encampment of a men's club in a redwood forest north of San Francisco. At the time, Nixon was in the midst of his fierce election campaign against Helen Gahagan Douglas, but ambitious men did not often decline invitations to Bohemian Grove.

The two-week all-men's party at "the Grove"—with its "Low Jinks" opening party, "Hi Jinks" closing ceremony, and an elaborate ritual conducted by hooded, torch-bearing figures to "cremate Care"—

was a chance for high-powered businessmen and political figures to unwind in a private, sylvan setting. Bohemian Grove has a rule, "weaving spiders come not here," a line from Shakespeare warning visitors against making deals and promoting oneself—but the real sin was to be too obvious about it.[27]

Nixon was invited by former president Herbert Hoover, who presided over one of the Grove's camps, each with its own rustic bar and dining room. Hoover's camp was known as "Cave Man," and President Hoover, also known as "Chief," was "Number One Cave Man." Every day, Hoover invited important men to lunch in a scene that was as informal, intimate, and thoroughly intimidating as the Alsops' Sunday Night Supper. Hoover sat at the head of the table. "As the Republican nominee in an uphill Senate battle, I was about two places from the bottom," Nixon recalled. The guest of honor, seated at Hoover's right, was Dwight Eisenhower.

Nixon watched Eisenhower closely. He noted that the general was deferential but not obsequious with the former president and that he responded to Hoover's toast with a gracious one of his own. At his "Lakeside Talk" to the encampment later that afternoon, Eisenhower spoke without notes. Later, around the campfire, the men of Cave Man weren't quite sure that Ike was ready to be president. "But it struck me forcibly that Eisenhower's personality and personal mystique had deeply impressed the skeptical and critical Cave Man audience," Nixon wrote.[28]

Nixon again met Eisenhower in May 1951 on a

congressional junket to Europe, where the general was reprising his Supreme Commander role. Nixon observed that Eisenhower was "erect and vital and impeccably tailored." He "carefully steered away from American politics, but it was clear he had done his homework." Ike had read about the Hiss case. "The thing that most impressed me was that you not only got Hiss, but you got him fairly," he told Nixon, whose heart swelled and whose political support swung into the Eisenhower column.[29]

By the spring of 1952, Nixon was hearing rumors that he might be Ike's running mate if Eisenhower secured the Republican nomination. "I considered my chances almost impossibly remote," he recalled. But he got a strong hint that he was a contender on May 8, 1952. Nixon had been invited by Governor Thomas Dewey, the Republican nominee for president in 1948, to address a hundred-dollar-a-plate GOP fundraiser at the Waldorf-Astoria in Manhattan. Nixon—speaking without notes—finished his tough-on-communism national radio broadcast speech in twenty-nine minutes, leaving time for thunderous applause. When he sat down, Dewey snuffed his ever-present cigarette and grasped Nixon's hand. "That was a terrific speech," he said. "Make me a promise: don't get fat, don't lose your zeal, and you can be president some day."[30]

Dewey was one of several close advisers to Eisenhower who quietly plotted and planned his entry into the race, while their duty-honor-country hero pretended, for as long as possible, to remain above politics. After the dinner, Dewey said to Herbert Brownell, a New York lawyer who was in Eisenhower's inner circle, "We've found our man for vice president."

Nixon was young, not yet forty and still only six years past his first congressional campaign. But he was, in fact, a logical running mate for Ike. Eisenhower was tied to the East Coast foreign policy establishment. Nixon was an internationalist, too, but he was close to the grass roots. He could bash communists and political opponents with equal fervor—letting Ike float above the fray. And he could deliver California.

Nixon needed some private advice. Though Washington cocktail parties put him off, there was one in-crowd hostess he admired and liked and who very much liked him. Alice Roosevelt Longworth, the daughter of Theodore Roosevelt—"Princess Alice" to the press—had sat through every day of the Alger Hiss hearings, rooting Nixon on from the front row. Mrs. Longworth was a pureblood but also a provocateur. She liked troublemakers, and she liked making trouble. Her cousin Franklin Roosevelt finally banned her from the White House in 1940 after she publicly, for outrageous effect, likened FDR to Hitler. "Stalin is my pin-up boy," she'd say to get a rise out of a dinner guest. She admired Joe McCarthy—"You're wonderful," she once told him. She asked him to tea—until he became a drunk and she tired of him.[31]

Despite the social gulf between them, Mrs. Longworth had an affinity for Nixon. "Princess Alice" had been a lonely girl. For all her pedigree, she had felt alienated from the Roosevelt family; after the death of Alice's mother, her father had remarried and had had five more children.[32] She was teasing and blunt with Nixon, who could almost relax with her. In the late spring of 1952, Dick and Pat went to dinner at her ghostly mansion near Dupont Circle, and he asked what he should do if Eisenhower offered him a place on the ticket.

"Father used to tell me that being vice president was the most boring job in the world," she said. But, she added, Nixon was the best man Ike could pick. Nixon protested that the whole prospect was so unlikely that he couldn't take it seriously. She looked at him skeptically and said, "You and Pat should talk about it so that just in case it does happen you aren't caught with your drawers down!"[33]

At midnight on the night of July 10, 1952, in an un-air-conditioned hotel room near the Chicago Stockyards, Dick and Pat began a conversation that would take all night. Dick had just returned from the Republican National Convention at the nearby International Amphitheatre. There had been rumors in the newspapers that Ike would pick Nixon when the party chose its nominees the next evening, but Nixon professed to be doubtful. He wanted to save the newspapers, he told Pat, as a souvenir "for the grand children."[34]

For the next four hours, Pat and Dick talked. If

the call came, what would he say? Pat was uneasy, still bruised by the Hiss case and the donnybrook with Helen Gahagan Douglas. Finally, shortly before dawn, Nixon summoned Murray Chotiner to his room. "As a political professional, he might have a different perspective about the whole question," is the way Nixon explained the call to Chotiner in his memoirs. It's doubtful that Pat was eager to countenance Chotiner and his cigar-smoke cynicism.

Nixon recalled that he "filled him [Chotiner] in on our discussion and asked for his opinion. He answered in his usual blunt way, 'There comes a point when you go up or go out.'" If Nixon lost, he'd still have his Senate seat; if he won and didn't like it, he could quit after a term and still be a young man. After Chotiner left, Nixon and his wife continued to talk. Any arguments were likely quiet ones. "Tricia and I rarely heard voices raised at home because both parents had memories of angry verbal clashes and they cherished harmony," wrote Julie Nixon Eisenhower.[35]

Pat was resigned—or pretended to be. "I guess I can make it through one more campaign," she finally said. Her true feelings were probably ambivalent. She must have known that at least two more campaigns lay ahead. If Eisenhower won and ran again in 1956, Nixon would then be positioned to run for president in 1960. She understood and shared her husband's ambition to keep on going. After all, before they were even engaged, she had told her friends, "He's going to be president some day."

With little or no sleep, Nixon stumbled off to the
GOP convention that morning and staggered back
to take a nap until the evening session, when the
balloting would commence. The temperature outside was 98 degrees, and inside the hotel room it was
about the same. Nixon stripped down to his underwear and lay on the bed, "trying to think cool
thoughts." Chotiner burst through the door—
Nixon was on Eisenhower's short list! "It's still wishful thinking," replied Nixon. He had just started to
drift off to sleep when the phone rang. It was Herbert Brownell Jr. "We picked you," said the New
York lawyer and future attorney general.

Nixon jumped up and put on his wrinkled gray
suit for an audience with the general. "I felt hot,
sleepy, and grubby," he recalled. There was no time
to shower and shave. A few minutes later, Nixon
emerged from the motorcycle-escorted limousine
and ascended to Eisenhower's suite at the Blackstone
Hotel. Nixon greeted his new running mate with a
boisterous, "Hi, chief!" He immediately regretted
his attempt at bonhomie.[36] Ike's wide smile faded.
General Eisenhower, Nixon was discovering, harbored a certain reserve and did not appreciate infor-
mality from those down the chain of command.
Nixon would later say that he "always felt like the
junior officer coming in to see the commanding
general."[37]

Pat Nixon was in the Stockyards Inn coffee shop,
biting into a sandwich, when she heard the news of
her husband's selection. "That bite of sandwich

popped right out of my mouth," she recalled. She went upstairs and put on her prettiest black-and-white print dress and a white hat and headed for the Amphitheatre. She kissed her husband once, then again for the photographers.[38] An enormous roar went up from the ten thousand revelers jamming the hot, loud convention hall. Nixon, wide-eyed, thrilled, gripped General Eisenhower's wrist and held up his arm. He sensed that Eisenhower "resisted it just a little."[39]

On a brief holiday in the mountains, the running mates attempted to bond. Eisenhower tried to teach Nixon how to fly cast. "I caught his shirt on the fourth try," Nixon recalled. "The lesson ended abruptly. I could see he was disappointed."[40] (The next year, Ike would try to instruct Nixon at golf. The lessons went no better. "Look here," Ike told Nixon, "you're young, you're strong and you can do a lot better than that.")[41]

Nixon's role in the campaign, traditional for a running mate, was to go on the attack so that Eisenhower would not have to. Nixon duly compared Eisenhower's opponent, Adlai Stevenson, to a "waltzing mouse" and, before a Texas audience, went further, accusing the Truman administration of "coddling communists." Nixon was performing a part, but he seemed to relish it. "Rock 'em, sock 'em" politics kept him in the news.[42]

In mid-September, the **Nixon Special**, the vice-presidential candidate's whistle-stop tour, was chugging up central California, when Nixon's press secretary, Jim Bassett, told the candidate that the **New York Post** had published a story under the headline "SECRET NIXON FUND!" The subheading read: "Secret Rich Man's Trust Fund Keeps Nixon in Style Far Beyond His Salary." The greatest crisis of Nixon's young life had arrived.

CHAPTER 5

Checkers

"The **Post** story did not worry me," Nixon recalled in **Six Crises.** "It was to be expected." At the time a liberal paper, the **New York Post** was given to tabloid salaciousness. "Six Sex Arrests" was a larger headline on the **Post**'s front page that day than "Secret Nixon Fund."[1] The story, written by a Hollywood reporter who doubled as the **Post**'s West Coast political writer, wasn't even a scoop. Other news organizations had reported the existence of the roughly $18,000 fund (almost $160,000 in 2015 dollars) in less lurid terms. The money had been raised from private donors to allow Senator Nixon to run what Murray Chotiner called a "permanent campaign"— largely, to meet travel expenses. It was not a secret, and Nixon did not use it to maintain a lavish lifestyle.[2]

At whistle stops that day aboard the **Nixon Special,** Nixon was mostly concerned with protecting his sore throat as he yelled out to the crowds, "Who can clean up the mess in Washington?" ("Ike can!") But by the end of Friday, September 19, Nixon and

The vice president and Mrs. Nixon.
Courtesy of the Richard Nixon Presidential Library
and Museum

his increasingly anxious staff began to note that more newsmen were coming on the train, and they were persistently asking Nixon about "the secret fund."

At ten o'clock that night, as the train pulled off on a siding in southern Oregon, a reporter asked Nixon if he had any comment on the **New York Herald Tribune** editorial. Nixon asked, reasonably enough, "What editorial?" The newsman reported that the next morning's paper would have an editorial calling for Nixon to step down from the ticket.

"This one really hit me," Nixon recalled. He felt as if the train had suddenly jolted. The **New York Herald Tribune** was his ally. Its Washington bureau chief, Bert Andrews, had been his friend and partner in chasing Hiss. The newspaper was known as the voice of the Republican establishment. But that was the problem. The true loyalty of Andrews and the editors at the **Herald Tribune** was to a culture and a set of customs that were far removed from the failed citrus orchards of Yorba Linda or the smash-mouth politics of Murray Chotiner. The editorial, Nixon realized with a growing dread, could reflect the thinking of General Eisenhower and, just as certainly, the bankers, lawyers, and retired generals in Brooks Brothers suits who surrounded him.

He had not heard directly from the Eisenhower campaign for two days. Three time zones separated the **Nixon Special** from the Eisenhower campaign train, the **Look Ahead, Neighbor! Special**, and communications in that pre–cell phone age were primitive. Still, the silence was ominous.

Nixon called in Chotiner and Pat. The candidate suddenly felt exhausted and depressed. He told his wife about the **Herald Tribune** editorial—Chotiner already knew about it—and she was "shocked," Nixon recalled. "Much of the fight had gone out of me by this time, and I was beginning to wonder how much more of this beating I was going to be able to take." Maybe, he suggested to his wife, he should resign.

Pat reacted "with fire in her eyes," he recalled. He later reprised her words:

> You can't think of resigning. If you do, Eisenhower will lose. He can put you off the ticket if he wants to, but if you, in the face of attack, do not fight back but simply crawl away, you will destroy yourself. Your life will be marred forever and the same will be true of your family, and particularly, your daughters.

How well she knew her husband! "I was never to receive any better advice," he reminisced, "and at a time when I needed it most."[3]

By the time the train pulled into Portland on Sunday, the crowds were turning ugly. Hecklers carrying signs that read "NICKLES FOR POOR NIXON" were throwing coins at Pat and Dick until they had to duck. At the hotel, Nixon received a massage for his agonizingly tense neck and back. He was handed a telegram from his mother—"Girls are okay. We are thinking of you."—which Nixon understood as her Quaker way of saying that she was praying for him. He had to step into a vacant room to hide his tears.

In the living room of his suite, Nixon huddled with his campaign advisers. Bill Rogers, a Washington lawyer who would later become Nixon's secretary of state, said that Nixon would have to resign. Chotiner said no—the PR man was savvy enough to know that if Nixon were dumped from the ticket, it would be a confession of Republican corruption and Eisenhower would lose the election. Nixon got up from the table and said, as though to himself, "I will not crawl."[4]

Finally, at 10:05 P.M., came the long-awaited telephone call from the Eisenhower campaign. Nixon was slouched in an armchair with his feet propped up on a coffee table. His arms were hanging listlessly by his sides.[5] Rose Woods stuck her head into the room and said, "General Eisenhower is on the phone."

Nixon braced himself. "Hello Dick," came the flat Kansas twang over the line, "warm and friendly," Nixon would recall. "You've been taking a lot of heat the last couple of days. I imagine it's been pretty rough," said Eisenhower. Nixon did not disagree.

"You know," the general continued, "this is an awfully hard thing for me to decide. I have come to the conclusion that you are the one who has to decide what to do."

Nixon let the line hang silent. Eisenhower suggested that Nixon go on national TV to make his case to the American people. Nixon had already been considering such a step, but he wanted to know if Ike would back him up—or at least put him out of his misery. "General," he asked, "do you think after the television program that an announcement could be made one way or another?"

The man who gave the order on D-Day hesitated. "I am hoping that no announcement would be necessary at all," he replied, "but maybe after the program we could tell you what ought to be done."

This was too much for Nixon. He could no longer "yessir" his commander. "There comes a time in matters like this," Nixon blurted, "when you've either got to shit or get off the pot."

Nixon could see that his language startled the others in the hotel room. He assumed that it shook Eisenhower, "who was certainly not used to being talked to in that manner." But Eisenhower, who was hardly unfamiliar with barracks language or intemperate subordinates, would not be stirred. "We will have to wait three or four days after the television show to see what the effect of the program is," he said.

There was nothing more to discuss. Eisenhower never asked whether the fund story was true. "Keep your chin up," said Ike and hung up.[6]

Nixon went to find Pat. She was resting in bed nursing a painfully stiff neck. Her friends, Jack and Helene Drown, had been trying to comfort her. Over and over, she had said to them, "It can't be happening. How can they do this? It is so unfair.

They know the accusations are untrue." Helene later told Julie Nixon Eisenhower, "It almost killed me to look at her. She was like a bruised little kitten."[7]

But with her husband Pat was firm: "We all know what you have to do, Dick," she told him. "You have to fight it all the way to the end, no matter what happens." Nixon returned to his own room—he did not share a bed with Pat, who found it impossible to sleep with her husband when he was constantly getting up in the middle of the night to write notes to himself.[8] Nixon sat up most of the night, thinking, girding himself, alternately swallowing or channeling his self-pity, forging the power of his resentment.

On the plane to Los Angeles in the morning, Nixon tried to doze but couldn't. He began jotting notes on some postcards he had found in the seatback. He recalled a quote from Lincoln that "God must have loved the common people because he made so many of them." He remembered that during the 1944 election, FDR had ridiculed his critics for attacking his dog Fala. Here was a chance to turn the tables on the Democrats. He made a note: "They will be charging that I have taken gifts. I must report that I did receive one gift after the nomination—a cocker spaniel dog, Checkers, and whatever they say, we are going to keep her." He recalled a Truman scandal involving a $9,000 mink coat to a White House secretary. He made a note that Pat had no mink coat—just a "good Republican cloth coat."

He turned to Pat in the seat beside him and told her that Eisenhower had said that they would have to disclose all their personal finances. She burst out, "Why do we have to tell people how little we have and how much we owe? Aren't we entitled to at least some privacy?" Nixon answered, "People in political life have to live in a fishbowl," but he knew, as he later recalled, that "it was a weak explanation for the humiliation I was asking her to endure."[9]

Chotiner dropped by Nixon's seat. He noted that all the Democrats except the presidential candidate, Governor Adlai Stevenson, were attacking Nixon. "I smell a rat," said Chotiner. "I'll bet he has something to hide." Chotiner's typically base and shrewd instinct was confirmed when they arrived in Los Angeles, where Nixon was to go on national television the next day. Stevenson confirmed that he had his own private fund for campaign expenses, just like Nixon. But he refused to take reporters' questions, and—gallingly to Nixon—the press "treated him with kid gloves."*

All through the night and into the next day, Nixon holed up in the Ambassador Hotel, working on his speech, "scarcely bothering to touch the hamburgers that were ordered from room service."[11] He was troubled, also thrilled. Here was crisis in the extreme, politics in its purest, most trying and exalted form. He was alone, with the whole world watch-

---

*Decades later, as he was writing his memoirs, Nixon was still outraged at "the blatant double standard." Not unreasonably: In 1976, Stevenson's official biography disclosed that Stevenson's private fund was more than four times larger than Nixon's and went to private expenses like paying for the orchestra at a dance for Stevenson's son.[10]

ing. In **Six Crises,** Nixon would lay out an elaborate rationale for his relentless work ethic in stressful times. "It has been my experience that, more often than not, 'taking a break' is actually an escape from the tough, grinding discipline that is absolutely necessary for superior performance. . . . Sleepless nights, to the extent the body can take them, can stimulate creative mental activity." He added, revealingly, "For me, it is often harder to be away from the job than to be working at it."[12]

Republican Party officials had paid $75,000 to buy a half-hour of airtime on the NBC network at 6:30 P.M. (9:30 P.M. Eastern time). At 4:30 P.M., while Nixon was grinding away at the third draft of his speech, he received a phone call from a "Mr. Chapman" in New York. That was the code name for Governor Dewey. Nixon instantly sensed trouble in Dewey's pinched voice.

"There has been a meeting of all of Eisenhower's top advisers," Dewey began. "They have asked me to tell you that it is their opinion that at the conclusion of the broadcast tonight you should submit your resignation to Eisenhower. As you know," Dewey continued, in the time-honored tradition of political cowardice, "I have not shared this point of view, but it is my responsibility to pass this recommendation on to you."

Nixon was struck dumb. Dewey jiggled the receiver. "Hello, can you hear me?"

Nixon asked, "What does Eisenhower want me to do?" Dewey hedged and equivocated.

"It's kind of late for them to pass on this kind of recommendation to me now," Nixon said. His anger was rising. He looked at his watch. He had a half-hour to get cleaned up and read over his notes.

"What should I tell them you are going to do?" asked Dewey.

Nixon exploded: "Just tell them I haven't the slightest idea as to what I am going to do and if they want to find out they'd better listen to the broadcast. And tell them I know something about politics too!" He slammed down the receiver.[13]

The 750-seat El Capitan Theater in Hollywood was empty. Nixon wanted no reporters. They watched over a monitor in a separate room. NBC had constructed a flimsy, fake-home set with a desk, a chair, and a bookcase set into the wall. A makeup man applied beard-stick to Nixon's five o'clock shadow, even though he had shaved a half hour before.

Nixon was "suddenly overwhelmed with despair," he later recalled. His voice trembled. "I just don't think I can go through with this one," he told Pat. "Of course you can," she answered, and took his hand. They walked on stage.

The director gave the signal. "My fellow Americans," Nixon began, "I come before you tonight as a candidate for the vice-presidency and as a man whose honesty and integrity has been questioned. . . ."[14]

Nixon had warned Pat that he would lay bare their personal finances, and he did. To show the nation that he was not a sleazy politician on the take, he earnestly, painfully recited their modest income and considerable debts, including a $3,500 loan from his parents and a $500 loan to buy life insurance and the $80-a-month rent he and Pat first paid on their little apartment in northern Virginia. "Well that's about it. That's what we have," said Nixon, "and that's what we owe. It isn't very much. But Pat and I have the satisfaction that every dime we've got is honestly ours. I should say this, that Pat doesn't have a mink coat. But she does have a respectable Republican cloth coat, and I always tell her she'd look good in anything."

The camera cut to Pat Nixon, sitting beside her man on the set. She looked noble, exposed, tragic, and stricken.

"One other thing I should probably tell you," Nixon went on, "because if I don't they'll probably be saying this about me, too. We did get something, a gift, after the election. A man down in Texas heard Pat on the radio mention the fact that our two youngsters would like to have a dog. And believe it or not, the day before we left on this campaign trip we got a message from Union Station down in Baltimore, saying they had a package for us. We went down to get it. You know what it was? It was a little cocker spaniel in a crate that he'd sent all the way from Texas, black and white, spotted. And our little girl, Tricia, the six-year-old, named it Checkers."[15]

As he wound up his speech, Nixon referred to his pursuit of Alger Hiss and said that he was "not a quitter." Watching at home, his mother Hannah, normally so restrained, shouted at her television set, "No, and you never have been!"[16] But, Nixon went on, "the decision, my friends, is not mine." The candidate urged his audience to telegraph or write the Republican National Committee whether he should stay on the ticket or get off it.

Watching TV in his living room in Washington, Walter Lippmann, the most respected newspaper columnist in America, turned to his guest, John Miller of **The Times** of London, and said, "That must be the most demeaning experience my country has ever had to bear."[17] In the years to come, the ridicule would rain down from sophisticates like Lippmann and his fellow pundits. The "Checkers speech" was mawkish and maudlin ("And you know, the kids just love that dog and I want to say this right now," said Nixon, his voice oozing humble sincerity, "that regardless of what they say about it, we're going to keep it"). The chattering class verdict was unanimous: Nixon was guilty of emotional fraudulence. His delivery had been hammy, hokey, and holier-than-thou ("Now what I'm going to do—and incidentally this is unprecedented in the history of American politics," said Nixon, all noble sacrifice, "I am going to give to this television and radio audience a complete financial history"). After the Checkers Speech, self-righteous self-pity became indelibly associated with the Nixon speaking style. Critics even pointed out that Nixon had gotten the Lincoln quote wrong. The Great Emancipator did not say,

"The Lord must have loved the common people because he made so many of them." Rather, Lincoln was talking about his own plain looks: "Common-looking people are the best in the world; that is the reason the Lord makes so many of them."[18]

Yet Nixon's misquotation reveals that he was making a far more profound political pitch than Honest Abe's self-effacing quip. Nixon's speech was brilliant political theater. The man who had fashioned the Orthogonians' mission statement knew his audience—knew that the Franklins might make fun of his speech but that the vastly more numerous common people would be moved. Liberal Democrats who fancied themselves as tribunes of the working man suddenly saw Nixon outfox and supplant them. It is no wonder that hating Nixon became a mantra of the liberal elite. In the Checkers Speech were seeded the roots of Nixon's later appeals to the Silent Majority—which would again leave the chattering classes spluttering.[19]

Dwight Eisenhower watched his running mate's speech with an inner circle of wise men, New York lawyers like Governor Dewey and military pals like General Lucius Clay. "Sophomoric!" "Sugary sweet!" they exclaimed.[20] For a more meaningful reaction, Eisenhower had only to look to his wife, Mamie. She was crying. Eisenhower turned to Arthur Summerfield, the head of the Republican National Committee, which had paid for Nixon's TV time. "Well," said Ike, with cold understatement, "you certainly got your money's worth."[21]

· · ·

Dazed, drenched with sweat, Nixon stumbled off the stage. He had run out of time before he could tell viewers the address of the Republican National Committee. He feared that he had blown his only chance. He mournfully told Pat, "I was a flop." Chotiner, who had been watching on a TV monitor, knew better. So did the cameramen, some of whom were crying. Nixon was told that the NBC switchboard was lighting up "like a Christmas tree."[22]

In the car back to the hotel, Nixon saw a barking Irish setter and mordantly quipped, "Well, I won the dog vote tonight." Only once he was at the hotel did he begin to appreciate the torrent he had unleashed. The telegrams were arriving by the basket. The Checkers speech had reached scores of millions by TV and radio, perhaps half the country; in those early days of mass media, Nixon's audience was the largest ever for a TV broadcast.

Eisenhower sent a glowing telegram, but it got lost among the thousands pouring in. All Nixon learned was that Ike still appeared to be publicly equivocating. Nixon was crestfallen. "What more can he possibly want?" he asked Chotiner. Desolate, Nixon began dictating a telegram resigning from the ticket. Rose Woods dutifully typed up the message but wisely gave it to Chotiner. The campaign manager tore it up.

Eisenhower summoned Nixon to meet him on board the **Look Ahead, Neighbor! Special** in Wheeling, West Virginia. When the plane landed, Eisenhower himself bounded up the steps into the cabin. Nixon was taken aback. "General," he said, "You didn't need to come out to the airport." Eisenhower flashed the famous smile. "Why not?" he said. "You're my boy!"

That night, the Republican running mates, together again, spoke at a football stadium. The ovation was overpowering. "I want you to know," Nixon told the crowd, "this is the greatest moment of my life." Afterward, newspaper cameras caught him weeping on the shoulder of California senator Bill Knowland.[23]

In the freezing night air—it was still late September, but winter was coming to the West Virginia mountains—Mamie let Pat share her white fur coat. There was silence between them. Plaintively, Mamie began, "I don't know why all this happened when we were all getting along so well." Pat could not contain herself. "But you just don't realize what **we've** been through," she said. That ended the conversation.

In later years, Nixon would regard the fund crisis as a personal victory, the ultimate vindication of his fight-back philosophy. His daughter Julie remembered him saying during her teen years, "Did you know today is the anniversary of the fund speech?" But Pat did not wish to know. Many years later, in 1978, while writing a memoir of her mother, Julie asked Pat about those weeks in September 1952. Mrs. Nixon turned her head to the wall and said, "Do we really have to talk about this? It kills me."

When she turned back to face Julie, there was so much pain in her eyes that Julie had to look away.[24]

During the fund crisis, Nixon had seemed to waver, while Pat remained resolute. But Nixon had been perhaps seeking his wife's sympathy and support, knowing that she would respond with loving firmness. After the fund crisis, Pat's political ambition waned. She never stopped loving and supporting her husband, but she no longer quite shared his dreams.

Nixon was exhausted. "The fund crisis made me feel old and tired," he recalled. He was shocked to learn that "my combative father had been reduced to bouts of weeping as each new smear surfaced." But Nixon himself responded by becoming more aggressive on the campaign trail, attacking Stevenson—"Adlai the Appeaser"—as "a weakling and a waster." Burned by Andrews of the fickle **Herald Tribune,** he no longer tried to cultivate reporters. When some newsmen were late to the campaign bus, he was overheard to say, "Fuck 'em, we don't need them."

The Eisenhower-Nixon ticket won easily. Anxious on Election Day, Nixon joined a pick-up touch football game with some Marines on the beach near Camp Pendleton. When he dropped a pass, a Marine remarked, "You'll make a better Vice-President than a football player." Then the Marine caught himself: "Sir."

On inauguration night, his mother handed him a note in her small, crabbed handwriting:

To Richard

You have gone far and we are proud of you always—I know that you will keep your relationship with your maker as it should be for after all that, as you must know, is the most important thing in this life. With love, Mother.

Nixon put the note in his wallet and kept it there for the rest of his life.[25]

In 1953, after his first few months in the White House, President Eisenhower wrote out a list for PROJECT X, a secret recollection of his presidency to be deposited in a time capsule at his Gettysburg farm. The first item was Nixon. Eisenhower wrote, "Energetic-physically strong-politically astute-ambitious-good personality. Only weakness that I can detect (or think I can) is that he is very fond of the nightlife in Washington. Sometimes has a bedraggled morning appearance."[26]

In fact, Nixon actively disliked Washington nightlife, but he may have appeared a little bleary-eyed in the mornings. He had trouble sleeping, and sometimes took a drink or a pill—or both—to make himself drowsy. Nixon was not a big imbiber, but he had a notoriously low capacity for alcohol, and on occasion he let drink get the better of him. Congressman Pat Hillings, who had taken over Nixon's California district, recalled Nixon getting tipsy at a dinner with the Eisenhowers early in the 1952 campaign. He got through the dinner all right, but in the elevator he startled his entourage by giving the wall a smack and loudly exclaiming, "I really like that Mamie. She doesn't give a shit about anybody—not a shit!"[27]

In **Six Crises,** Nixon described Eisenhower as "a far more complex and devious man than most people realized," adding, "and in the best sense of those words." Eisenhower was a military man who delegated to his subordinates. He had been put off by the confusion that reigned when a green, unprepared Harry Truman took over from FDR, and he was determined that Nixon would not fulfill the old stereotype of a vice president as a useless appendage.[28] Eisenhower ran a "hidden hand presidency": He let Nixon and others take public roles and, when necessary, do the dirty jobs.[29]

In the fall of 1953, Eisenhower sent Nixon to Asia for two months. This was not a pointless vice-presidential junket. Nixon had to deliver difficult messages to Syngman Rhee of South Korea and Chiang Kai-shek of Taiwan, both of whom were threatening attacks on their communist neighbors that risked dragging America into World War III. Nixon skillfully handled both men and at the same time managed to like them, or at least honor their orneriness.

Nixon did not like personal confrontation. But delivering a message from the president of the United States, however unwelcome, was different. Nixon loved politics as the exercise of power, of finding a way to get things done. While sensitive to the pride of these heads of state, Nixon saw them as pieces on a chessboard, objects that had to be moved—gently, carefully—in the greater cause of world peace. Nixon was thrilled to be acting on such an exalted stage, not as a messenger boy for the great president-general but as a superpower diplomat who could show his worldliness and finesse.

Genuinely curious and open-minded, doggedly well-prepared, the future statesman in Nixon emerged, to the surprise of some hosts. From Malaya, the British High Commissioner, Field Marshal Sir Gerald Templer, wired Foreign Secretary Sir Anthony Eden that Nixon was

> an extremely nice man in every way. He was very anxious to learn and to help. He has got charming manners and in fact was the very reverse of everything that one had expected after reading press reports of the American election. He is easy in his conversations and got on extremely well with the many Asians he met. . . . He seemed to me potentially to be a much bigger man than Adlai Stevenson, who, as you know, stayed with us a few months ago.[30]

The Nixons satisfied their childhood wanderlust. Nixon wrote disapprovingly, and also a little dreamily, about Sukarno's gleaming white palace in Indonesia, "filled with some of the most exquisite women I have ever seen," adding that "my briefings had stressed this side of his character." Pat was a nonstop goodwill ambassador, gamely leaving the lavish dinners—served on gold plates in Sukarno's palace, lit by a thousand torches—to tour hospitals and orphanages. (On a later trip in 1955, U.S. foreign service officers protested when she went to a leper colony.)[31] Nixon was proud to face down anti-American demonstrators in Burma. He greeted a protester carrying a sign reading "Go Back Warmonger" by saying, "I am Mr. Nixon and I'm glad to know you. What's your name?" The man scuttled away.

When he returned, the vice president got a glowing two-page handwritten letter from Eisenhower—gratifying indeed, Nixon noted in his memoirs, coming "from one who meted out praise in very small and careful doses." The 1953 trip "had a tremendously important effect on my thinking and on my career," Nixon wrote. It established him as a globetrotting foreign policy expert and put him on a familiar footing with world leaders such as India's Jawaharlal Nehru and the Shah of Iran. More important, it assured him that he had the skills and confidence to thrive in the political game that most engaged him: structuring a system of alliances and opposing interests in the cause of building a lasting foundation for peace.[32]

Dealing with Senator Joe McCarthy back home was more vexing. Eisenhower wanted to avoid tangling with the demagogue, whose communist witch-hunt had spun out of control. "Never get into a pissing match with a skunk," the president told his brother, Milton.[33] So he sent Nixon to be his go-between and informant. Nixon was deft with McCarthy, restraining him on occasion, then cleverly working with Ike to undermine him. Nixon persuaded McCarthy not to chase William Bundy, a CIA official and son-in-law of Truman's secretary of state Dean Acheson, who had contributed to Alger Hiss's defense fund. (" 'Joe,' I said, 'you have to understand how those people up in Cambridge think. Bundy graduated from the Harvard Law School, and Hiss was one of its most famous graduates. I think he probably just got on the bandwagon without giving any thought to where the bandwagon was heading.' ") When the time came to attack McCarthy openly, Eisenhower tapped Nixon to give a speech on national TV—and told him to make sure he smiled. Nixon spent four days in a hotel room trying to figure out how to ding McCarthy without alienating the anticommunist right. In his televised speech on March 13, 1954, Nixon reached for a metaphor:

> Now, I can imagine some of you will say, "Why all this hullabaloo about being fair when you're dealing with a gang of traitors?" As a matter of fact, I have heard people say, "After all, we are dealing with a bunch of rats. What we ought to do is go out and shoot them."
>
> Well, I agree they are a bunch of rats. But just remember this. When you go out and shoot rats, you have to shoot straight, because when you

shoot wildly, it not only means the rats will get away more easily—but you make it easier on the rats. Also you might hit someone who is trying to shoot rats, too.[34]

The press and public took notice: Here was one famous "Red hunter" turning on another—only Nixon was representing the president of the United States. McCarthy began muttering about "the constant yak-yakking from that prick Nixon."[35] In the spring of 1954, McCarthy finally brought himself down, a drunken bully exposed in nationally televised hearings. "McCarthyism," chortled Ike, "is now McCarthywasm."[36]

But some of McCarthy's mud splattered on Nixon. Adlai Stevenson accused Nixon of "McCarthyism in a white collar," implying that he was less reckless but still odious to the American sense of fair play. "The president smiles while the vice president smears," said Stevenson, who was still smarting because Nixon had dubbed him "Side-saddle Adlai" in the 1952 election.[37]

In the fall of 1954, Eisenhower spent the first month of the mid-term congressional campaign at the Denver White House (his in-laws' home). "After a few hours of work in the morning he would golf in the afternoon," Nixon recorded in his memoirs with a trace of bitterness. Nixon, meanwhile, traveled twenty-six thousand miles in six weeks, visiting ninety-five cities in thirty states and speaking on behalf of 186 GOP candidates. For the last three weeks he slept no more than five hours a night.

His heart was not in it. "I still resented being portrayed as a demagogue or a liar or as the sewer dwelling denizen of Herblock cartoons in the **Washington Post**," he later wrote. "As the attacks became more personal, I sometimes wondered where party loyalty left off and masochism began. The girls [who turned eight and six in 1954] were reaching an impressionable age, and neither Pat nor I wanted their father to become the perennial bad guy of American politics."[38]

Nixon canceled his home delivery subscription to **The Washington Post** so that the girls would not have to see their father climbing out of the sewer in a Herblock cartoon, but they could not altogether avoid the press.[39] The night their father had been nominated for the vice presidency, cameramen and reporters burst into the Nixon house in Spring Valley; their popping flashbulbs frightened the girls. (Lurking outside a few days later was a **Washington Times Herald** reporter named Jacqueline Bouvier, soon to be Kennedy. When the girls emerged she asked them if they ever played with Democrats. "What's a Democrat?" asked four-year-old Julie.) In 1954, a reporter chatted up Tricia, age seven, by telling her that her father was "famous." She responded, "If he's famous why can't he stay at home? Why is he gone all the time?"[40]

Georgetown society dined out on Nixon. In the

drawing room of Averell Harriman's mansion on N Street, his wife Marie and her bridge group snickered that Marie's pet dog, a terrier, had thrown up watching the Checkers Speech.* Closer to home, Spring Valley was not always so welcoming, either. Connie Casey, the daughter of a Democratic congressman, recalled that when a rumor spread that Nixon was starting a petition to get rid of neighborhood housing covenants against Jews and blacks, her mother refused to sign. Normally, Mrs. Casey was a good liberal, opposed to racial and ethnic discrimination, but she declared, "If **he** is for it, I'm against it."[41]

The barbs and cold looks caused Nixon to question his calling. This seems hard to believe, in retrospect—after all, never was there a more committed politician than Richard Nixon. But Nixon's large capacity for self-pity was aroused by the constant attacks, real and perceived, and he was bothered by the change in Pat's attitude. She had always shared his ambition, but after the ordeal of the Checkers Speech, she seemed truly sick of politics. As early as February 1954, Nixon had scribbled some notes on a yellow pad weighing whether to quit politics. At the top of the page he had written, "Reasons to get out"; under "personal" he wrote

---

*Joe Alsop would occasionally backslide and write a positive column about Nixon in the **Post**, but his friends would try to yank him back in line. "He does—must!—feel a sense of shame in his Nixonite mood; and it must be the business of all of us to keep activating it," Arthur Schlesinger Jr. wrote Georgetown society matron Evangeline Bruce after one such lapse.[42]

"Wife—(columns, personal, staff hurts)."[43] He was stung in April when the Duke faculty voted not to give him an honorary degree and was wounded again in June when Whittier students formed two lines at commencement—one for those wishing to shake his hand, the other for those wishing **not** to shake his hand.[44] At the Capitol, presiding over the Senate, he seemed to be going through the motions. "He had to sit up front in the Senate, but when he was off duty you would see that hunched figure trying to skulk off down the back ways," recalled Hugh Sidey of **Time** magazine.[45]

On Election Day, November 2, as he flew back to Washington, he took out a folder of notes he had made for an election-eve broadcast. Nixon handed them to Murray Chotiner in the seat beside him. "Here's my last campaign speech, Murray," he said, wallowing a bit. "You might like to keep it as a souvenir. It's the last one, because after this I'm through with politics."[46]

The Republicans lost control of the House and Senate. Nixon was despondent, and Pat was too. A few weeks after the election, their daughter Julie recalled, they talked about their future. Pat worried that if things turned out well, Eisenhower would get the credit. If they did not, Nixon would get the blame. They were not in control, and their relationship with Ike was, as Julie described it, "so delicate and tenuous."[47] Pat made Dick write down a promise that after the vice presidency he would quit politics and go back to California to practice law.[48]

The fan.
**Courtesy of the Richard Nixon Presidential
Library and Museum**

CHAPTER 6

"El Gringo Tiene Cojones"

On a warm Saturday afternoon, September 24, 1955, Nixon was lazily reading batting averages in the **Washington Evening Star** when he got a call from Jim Hagerty, Eisenhower's press secretary. Hagerty told Nixon that the president had suffered a heart attack. Nixon's silence lasted so long that Hagerty wondered if he was still on the line.[1]

For ten minutes, Nixon would later recall, he sat in his living room, his mind whirling. Then he called Bill Rogers, his close friend who had offered support during the Checkers crisis. Nixon's voice was "hoarse and charged with emotion," recalled Rogers. " 'It's terrible! It's terrible!' he said over and over again." Nixon asked Rogers if he could give him sanctuary from newsmen. Then, remembering that he had forgotten to tell Pat the news, he rushed upstairs to tell her.

Rogers's wife, Adele, parked a block away as reporters and photographers descended on Nixon's house in Spring Valley. As Rogers later told the story, it was decided to use the two Nixon girls, aged seven and nine, "as decoys" to engage the reporters in "small talk" while Nixon slipped out the back. Nixon spent the night at Rogers's house in Bethesda, Maryland, wide awake as he endured Rogers's fifteen-year-old-son playing with his ham radio on the floor above all night.[2]

At the White House, Nixon was careful not to sit in Eisenhower's chair when he presided over an emergency meeting of the president's advisers. He knew, as he recalled, that he was "walking on egg shells."[3] In the Cabinet Room, Nixon was not necessarily first among equals. Even before the heart attack, Eisenhower's powerful chief of staff, Sherman Adams, was rumored to be the White House regent, at least for domestic affairs. John Foster Dulles, the secretary of state, was widely regarded in the press as the true architect of American foreign policy, puppetmaster to the syntactically challenged, golf-loving Ike.

This was a misperception fostered by the wily Eisenhower, who liked to work behind the scenes—mainly so that he could use others to play the heavy or take the blame. With Ike gone, Dulles appeared to be the senior partner. Dulles was a public moralizer and aspirant Great Man. In his public appearances, he displayed more gravitas than the "rock 'em, sock 'em" Nixon of the campaign trail. Nonetheless, Nixon had quietly grown close to the pious and outwardly pompous secretary of state. The two were alike: socially awkward, intense, off-putting to some but possessed of a well-disguised gentleness and profoundly absorbed by the task of advancing America's world role. Nixon would stop by Dulles's house on some evenings for a drink and a chat. Dulles would teach Nixon about the world, and Nixon would teach Dulles about politics; the overlap was considerable and mutually beneficial.[4] Now, as President Eisenhower was slowly recovering in a hospital bed in Denver, Nixon and Dulles kept the nation on course with a minimum of disruption. The Cold War was in a temporary lull, allowing Nixon time to advance his little-noticed education in statecraft. White House speechwriter Emmett Hughes was impressed with Nixon's poise and restraint during the fall of 1955, when the world wondered if the American president would be able to resume his duties. It was, Hughes later wrote, Nixon's "finest official hour."[5]

Fully engaged in leading while trying not to look like it, Nixon was no longer thinking of quitting politics, his promise to Pat notwithstanding. Later, when reporter and early Nixon biographer Earl Mazo asked him why he changed his mind, Nixon answered, "Once you get into this great stream of history you can't get out."[6]

On the day after Christmas in 1955, President Eisenhower, now back in the Oval Office, invited his vice president over to the White House for a chat. Nixon's sensitive nerves began twitching almost right away. After some desultory chatter, Ike began the real conversation by noting that Nixon's poll ratings were lower than Adlai Stevenson's in

head-to-head surveys. Sensing a put-up job by Eisenhower's advisers in the East Coast establishment,
Nixon tried to protest that his poll ratings were im-
proving. In his avuncular style, Ike went on: Maybe
Nixon should consider taking a cabinet position in
a second Eisenhower term. The jobs of attorney
general and secretary of state were filled, but the Defense Department might come open, said Ike.

Nixon's spirits sank. He knew what the headline
would read: NIXON DUMPED.[7] Six or seven times over
the winter of 1956, Ike blandly suggested that Nixon
take a cabinet post—Commerce, perhaps? Health,
Education, and Welfare?—rather than run for re-
election as vice president. He said the choice was up
to Nixon. Stubbornly and grimly, Nixon replied that
the choice was Eisenhower's, that Nixon would do
whatever the president deemed best for the country.
This "no, after-you" routine might have been comic,
but to Nixon it was deeply demoralizing.[8]

Eisenhower looked at Nixon the way a general
does at an up-and-coming colonel. He believed that
the young politician needed seasoning, maturity,
and training in management and leadership.[9] Secretary of defense would do nicely. Nixon could think
only of the political ignominy of demotion. He took
it personally. In mid-winter, Republican National
Committee chair Leonard Hall was dispatched by
the president to give Nixon a gentle shove. Nixon's
eyes "turned dark, dark, dark," Hall recalled. He
turned to Hall and said of the president, "He's never

wanted me. He's never liked me. He's always been against me."[10]

That was not entirely true, but Nixon could not be blamed for failing to read Eisenhower's inscrutable demeanor. The emotional toll of the situation became physical. Nixon checked into Walter Reed Medical Center that winter suffering from exhaustion and various ailments, both real and imagined. He saw at least ten different doctors, and Dr. Hutschnecker prescribed Equanil, a habit-forming, barbiturate-based tranquilizer that would be discontinued a few years later; Dexamyl, an amphetamine-based upper; and Doriden, a sleeping pill later deemed to be hypnotic. These drugs, widely prescribed in the 1950s, made a potent drug cocktail, especially when mixed with actual cocktails. On a desperately needed Florida vacation in March of 1956, Nixon reported to Hutschnecker that two or three drinks in the evening made him "feel good."[11]*

All through the winter of 1956, Eisenhower blandly fended off press inquiries about Nixon's future. At a news conference on March 7, asked if he intended to drop Nixon from the ticket, Eisenhower

*It should be noted that Nixon's political peers took drugs or intoxicants of equal or greater potency. Eisenhower was on a number of medications, including barbiturate-based sleeping pills; LBJ was at times a heavy drinker; JFK was on cortisone for Addison's disease and during his presidency consumed a combination of uppers and downers prescribed by Dr. Max Jacobson, who came to be known as "Dr. Feelgood."[12]

answered that his vice president would have to "chart his own course." That was the last straw. On the morning of March 9, desolate and bitter, the vice president drafted a press statement to the effect that he would not run for reelection in 1956 and intended to call a press conference later that day.

Once again, Pat Nixon stood defiant. Wishfully, if not naïvely, she had been holding on to her husband's written promise, secured just a year earlier, to quit politics and become a private lawyer. But she was shocked by the toll political rejection had taken on her husband. He seemed to be literally wasting away. She would later tell her daughter Julie that she had never seen him so depressed. Realizing that private life could be a kind of death to Nixon, she tore up his "contract." Eisenhower was being unfair, she argued to her husband. To her friend Helene Drown she wrote, "No one is going to push us off this ticket."[13]

A few days later, still feeling wobbly despite Pat's newfound resolve, the Nixons went to dinner at the home of their one defender in social Washington, Alice Roosevelt Longworth. As they entered her turn-of-the-century mansion just off Dupont Circle, she called out from the top of the stairs, "Have you been listening to the radio? There's a write-in vote for you in New Hampshire." Eisenhower was the only name officially on the ballot in the New Hampshire primary, but a surprisingly large number of voters had gone to the trouble to write in Nixon's name as well. (New Hampshire senator Styles

Bridges, an archconservative and ally of Nixon's, had been quietly beating the local bushes.) A devoted lover of politics, Mrs. Roosevelt rushed through dinner, Nixon recalled, so that they could retire to the drawing room and listen to the radio. Beneath the pelts of wild animals shot by her father, "Mrs. L.," as Nixon called her, and her guests sipped coffee and discussed the redemptive returns. The ordinary people, the have-nots, the "Silent Majority," as Nixon would later call them, had spoken, and Nixon got to celebrate the news with the doughty daughter of Teddy Roosevelt, Nixon's beau ideal of the "man in the arena."

Eisenhower got the message from the voters. "Anyone who attempts to drive a wedge of any kind between Dick Nixon and me has just as much chance as if he tried to drive it between my brother and me," he told reporters. Nixon arranged an audience with the president and said that he would be honored to continue as vice president. With Jesuitical innocence, Eisenhower asked why he had taken so long to say so.[14]

In later years, Nixon's closest aides—men like Henry Kissinger and H. R. Haldeman—would laugh at the popular image of Nixon the Imperial President, barking orders at cowed subordinates.[15] Nixon's desire to avoid awkward scenes was so great that he rarely, if ever, directly braced an underling. His outbursts were not infrequent, but they were very rarely aimed directly at the subject of his ire.

He would loudly complain about an aide or adviser, but not face-to-face. More admirably, he went to great lengths to avoid hurting people's feelings. Chuck Colson said that Nixon could be "brutally cold, calculating, a manipulator of power"—but also marveled that he "could never bring himself to point out to a secretary her misspellings. I once saw him re-dictate a letter to eliminate a troublesome word, rather than embarrass the secretary."[16]

He disliked personal confrontation of any kind. Yet he seemed to welcome **public** confrontation. He was a tireless hand-shaker and baby-kisser and was fearless about taking on hostile crowds. On a trip to Africa in 1957, a reporter from an African-American newspaper wrote with some wonder, "Oft times . . . [I] had heard that Mr. Nixon lacked warmth, soul, sincerity . . . that everything he did was motivated by cold, calculating logic. The Nixon I observed did not fit this stereotype. I can't forget the sight of Dick Nixon kissing the upturned faces of little black babies."[17]

Some of his willingness to risk exposure was just political necessity, a burden shouldered, grudgingly but dutifully, by a private man living a public life. To his speechwriter William Safire, Nixon quoted Walter Judd, a right-wing congressman who had been a mentor of sorts. "Walter Judd used to say, 'You have to make love to the people.' It's always been a very difficult thing for me to do, but you must plunge into the crowds. You have to show you care, and of course," Nixon added, "you must care."[18]

As ever, Nixon's motivations were cloaked in apparent contradiction. While Nixon could be, or pretend to be, cynical about voters, he more often identified with them. Still, the way in which Nixon waded into crowds—doggedly, bravely, even a little recklessly—suggests some deeper, more personal driving force than political expediency or democratic sympathy. Fear of heights made Nixon a cliff diver.

Elected to a second term in a landslide in November 1956, Eisenhower continued to use his vice president as a kind of forward observer, sending him abroad to scout out trouble spots and report back.[19] With its tiny landed oligarchy and vast dispossessed poor, South America was an obvious target for leftist agitators, and by the late 1950s the universities and labor movements in parts of Latin America were seething with unrest.

In the spring of 1958, Nixon was invited to attend the swearing-in ceremony for the first democratically elected president of Argentina since the fall of strongman Juan Perón. Nixon did not want to go. He was busy organizing Republicans for the 1958 elections, eager to establish himself as the head of the party and the presumptive heir to the GOP presidential nomination in 1960. But Eisenhower leaned on his vice president and laid on a trip that would take the Nixons to every South American country but Brazil and Chile.[20]

Pat was also not eager to travel. She was in bed suffering from a bad back, a recurring ailment usually exacerbated by stress, in this case brought on by lifting her daughter to look at a bird's nest.[21] Shopping for a wardrobe for the South America trip, she had called Mollie Parnis, a dress designer for First Lady Mamie and other powerful Washington women. When Miss Parnis mentioned this to Mamie, the First Lady breezily responded, "No, no dear, don't do that. Let the poor thing go to Garfinckel's and buy something off the rack."[22]

The Nixons' capacity to endure small indignities was further tested in Buenos Aires at the presidential inauguration. The Nixons arrived too late at the white-tie event to see the swearing in; the embassy had miscalculated the traffic. At first, the South American crowds were peaceful, even friendly. But ever since a CIA-backed coup had overthrown the leftist government in Guatemala in 1954, the last vestiges of FDR's Good Neighbor Policy in Latin America had given way to suspicions of American meddling. Among students and workers, resentment of **los norteamericanos** was on the rise. In Peru, as his motorcade entered Lima, Nixon heard for the first time an oddly shrill, derisive whistle that signaled mocking disrespect. Nixon was scheduled the next day to visit the city's ancient University of San Marcos. Leaflets encouraged workers and students to bar the American dignitary—GATHER TO SHOUT WITH ALL YOUR FACES—DEATH TO YANKEE IMPERIALISM—AGENT OF GREAT NORTH AMERICAN MONOPOLIES AND PARTISAN OF ATOMIC WAR—and the local police warned Nixon against going, suggesting instead a visit to the tamer Catholic University.[23] Lying in bed that night in the grand old Hotel Bolivar, Nixon recalled how Ike had once told him that he had suffered from sleeplessness in the lead-up to D-Day, but that once he had decided, he had slept well. Nixon could not sleep. He could hear chants of "Fuera Nixon"—Nixon Go Home—and, occasionally, "Muera Nixon"—Death to Nixon.

Nixon decided to go to San Marcos only after he was in his car the next morning. At the gates of the university, he faced about two thousand people, chanting and emitting that high, jeering whistle. Along with his translator, Colonel Vernon Walters, and a Secret Service agent, Jack Sherwood, Nixon walked up to the crowd. He told Walters to translate: "I want to talk to you. Why are you afraid of the truth?" (Walter later recalled he heard a student say, "El Gringo tiene cojones"—the Yankee has balls, high praise in Latin America.)[24] Suddenly, a rock glanced off Nixon's shoulder and hit Sherwood in the face, chipping a tooth. As more rocks began to fly, Nixon ordered retreat—but slowly, still facing his attackers. In the open limousine, Nixon instructed Sherwood to brace his legs as he stood to shout, with Walters translating in rapid-fire Spanish, "You are cowards, you are afraid of the truth! You are the worst kind of cowards!"

Back at the hotel, Nixon was within fifty feet of the door when the crowd closed in again. A demonstrator spat in his face. Sherwood spun the man away, but not before Nixon had kicked him in the shins. "Nothing I did all day made me feel better," Nixon recalled.[25]

Nixon's brave stand drew international attention. Ike sent him a cable—"Dear Dick, Your courage, patience, and calmness in the demonstration directed against you by radical agitators have brought you new respect and admiration in the country." Clare Boothe Luce, wife of Time-Life founder Henry Luce, sent Nixon a one-word cable that pleased Nixon, the Teddy Roosevelt worshipper. It read: "Bully."

A still more severe test awaited. The CIA had picked up rumors in Venezuela of a plot to assassinate the visiting American vice president. Venezuelan authorities reported back that everything was under control.

From the window of his airplane at the Caracas airport on the morning of May 13, Nixon could see and hear demonstrators whistling and chanting. On the red carpet leading into the terminal, the Nixons paused while a band played the national anthems of both countries. "For a second," Nixon recalled, "it seemed as if it had begun to rain." Nixon looked up at the observation deck. The crowd was spitting. Pat Nixon recalled that the gobs of spit looked like giant snowflakes.[26] Nixon turned to look at his wife. Her bright red dress was splotched with brown stains (the mob was chewing tobacco).

Inside the terminal, Pat tried to reach out and touch the shoulder of a girl who was screaming at her. The girl turned and burst into tears. Inside the limousine, the Venezuelan foreign minister tried to use his handkerchief to wipe the spit off Nixon's suit. "Don't bother," Nixon said. "I am going to burn these clothes as soon as I can get out of them."

Exiting the highway near the National Pantheon, the motorcade ran into a roadblock. Nixon's Secret Service man, Jack Sherwood, looked out the window and said, "Here they come!" Hundreds of people came boiling up out of the alleys and side streets. They were yelling and armed with crowbars and stones. The first rock hit the supposedly unbreakable window and lodged in the glass, spraying the car with tiny glass slivers. One struck the foreign minister in the eye. Bleeding, he began to moan, "This is terrible, this is terrible."

A man began smashing at the window with an iron pipe. Glass fragments cut the mouth of Nixon's interpreter, Colonel Walters. Nixon began to feel the car rocking back and forth. He had read about mobs overturning cars and setting them on fire. For the first time, he later said, he wondered if he was about to die.[27]

Sherwood pulled his gun from his holster. "Let's kill some of these sons of bitches," he said. In a cool, even voice, Nixon told him to hold his fire. As Walters later recalled Nixon's words, the vice president said, "Put away that gun. If they open one of those doors and pull me into the street—and only if I tell you—do you use it."[28]

The press truck ahead managed to pull out of the mob and lumber over the traffic island. Nixon's limousine followed, plowing through the crowd. The Venezuelan police reasserted some measure of control, and the motorcade roared away and headed for the embassy. Nixon had been trapped for twelve minutes. A later investigation found a cache of Molotov cocktails waiting at the Pantheon.[29]

Nixon flew home from the Caracas airport, which was empty this time, cleared by troops and tear gas. Eisenhower, the cabinet, leading members of Congress, the diplomatic corps, and about fifteen thousand people were waiting for him at the airport in Washington. Crying, Tricia and Julie hugged their parents. For several weeks thereafter, Nixon wrote, "neither Pat nor I could appear anywhere in public without people standing up to applaud. For the first time I pulled even with Kennedy in the Gallup presidential trial heat polls."[30] Jack Kennedy had been a war hero, celebrated (after some skillful family promotion) for his bravery as a PT boat captain in World War II. Now Nixon, too, was seen as a heroic figure—a **popular** hero.

Every summer vacation that Nixon had planned since he came to Washington in 1947 had been cut short, and 1958 was no exception. Nixon had just arrived with his family at the Greenbrier Hotel in West Virginia on August 25 when the White House called. The president was on the line. "I wonder if you could talk to Sherm. . . ." he began.[31]

Sherman Adams, Ike's chief of staff, had gotten caught up in an influence-peddling scandal. Adams had taken a Vicuna coat and other favors from a New England textile manufacturer named Bernard Goldfine. Adams, an acerbic New Englander who usually hung up without saying good-bye, had few friends left in Washington. The president needed to cut Adams loose, and he wanted Nixon to do it for him. At the Greenbrier, Nixon abandoned his family and drove back to Washington to see Adams. The encounter with the president's top aide was painful. The vice president, who hated personal confrontations, hemmed and hawed with the phlegmatic Adams, who stared stonily back at him. More unsuccessful meetings and failed delegations followed. Grumbling about his feckless subordinates, Eisenhower himself finally had to fire his chief of staff.

"My mother would remember always that particular episode," Julie Nixon Eisenhower recalled, "not only because the vacation plan was ruined, but also because she foresaw that for her husband it was a no-win proposition: Adams would resist, and the President would be disappointed."[32] Nixon recounted the incident more obliquely, but tellingly. In his memoirs, he remembered a conversation from about that time with Walter Bedell Smith, Ike's World War II chief of staff. In his cups, the hard-bitten Smith began to tear up. "I was just Ike's prat boy," he told Nixon. "Ike always had to have a prat boy, someone who would do the dirty work for him. He always had to have someone else who could do the firing, or the reprimanding, or give orders which he knew people would find unpleasant to carry out.

Ike always had to be the nice guy. That's the way it is in the White House, and the way it will always be in any organization that Ike runs."[33] In a later interview, Frank Gannon asked Nixon if the experience with Sherman Adams and Bedell Smith affected him during Watergate by making him reluctant to fire his top aides until it was too late. Nixon answered, guardedly but with uncharacteristic self-awareness, "It probably had some effect."[34]

Nixon resumed his globetrotting. He continued to surprise foreign observers who had formed a sour impression by reading the American press. America's relations with its most valuable ally—Great Britain— were shaken after the 1956 Suez Crisis, in which Eisenhower had peremptorily stopped a British-French-Israeli invasion of Egypt. On a trip to London in November 1958, Nixon was able to reassure the British government that the Atlantic Alliance remained necessary and strong. After meeting privately with Nixon at Whitehall, the British foreign secretary, Selwyn Lloyd, wrote a memo-to-file:

> After Dulles's ponderous evasions, Nixon's incisive frankness was a great relief. He has a first class mind backed up by a masterly understanding of the world scene. . . . The president's deputy does not appear to be, as was sometimes feared, a kind of political ogre without principle or integrity, but rather a tough politician who possesses common sense as well as formidable energy, charm, and a

lively intelligence . . . if he succeeds Eisenhower, the world will have nothing to worry about. He may well be a considerable improvement![35]

At the Grosvenor Square residency of the U.S. ambassador, Jock Whitney, Nixon hosted a Thanksgiving Day dinner for the Queen of England. Nixon had packed his white tie and tails, only to learn at the last moment, in a reversal of his embarrassment at Christian Herter's, that the Queen expected less formal attire—black tie, not white tie. "Frantic," Nixon's military aide Don Hughes recalled, Nixon's aides stripped an American PR man of **his** tuxedo and put it on Nixon.* The comic opera wardrobe changes might have worked, but Nixon couldn't resist blurting out to the puzzled young Queen, "I'm afraid this isn't my suit!"[36]

Nixon described himself to an admiring early biographer, Bela Kornitzer, as a man who rose above political invective, who did not take the bait. Kornitzer tried to get a rise out of his subject: "I believe you are the most maligned figure in political history," he said to Nixon in an interview on March 25, 1959. "I acquired from my mother a great tolerance, an understanding of human failings," Nixon responded, a bit piously, invoking the Quaker tolerance of his parents. "I'm not as tolerant as they are,"

---

*The PR man was Jim Bassett, a newspaperman hired to handle press for the Nixons. Nixon "looked at me in sort of a wolfish way and said, 'What size are you?' "[37]

he said. "But I have a considerable degree myself. I do not hold on to grudges. I inherited from my father a hot temper but I inherit from my mother an ability to control it."[38]

Nixon's remark about "not holding grudges" seems preposterous, given the events that were to come, but there is little reason to doubt that he saw himself that way. In any case, he was given a chance to demonstrate his self-control with one of history's brashest provocateurs, Kremlin leader Nikita Khrushchev, on a trip to Moscow in late July 1959. In the Cold War America of the late 1950s, still shaken by Sputnik and the doomsday specter of Soviet rockets raining down nuclear weapons, Khrushchev was a figure of fascination and not a little fear. Bragging and bombastic, the Kremlin leader had threatened, "We will bury you!" at a meeting with Western ambassadors in 1956. He had meant that communism would ultimately triumph over capitalism, but Americans took his threat more literally. Eisenhower wanted to meet with Khrushchev, to talk him down, but first he sent Nixon to Moscow on a scouting trip.

Even by his law school "iron butt" standards, Nixon's preparation for his first trip to the Soviet Union was epic: For nearly six months he studied CIA and State Department briefings and interviewed all manner of experts. His wariness of Harvard notwithstanding, he used as his tutor Harvard professor William Yandell Elliott, who in turn put Nixon in touch with a prodigy of international secu-

rity named Henry Kissinger.[39] Arriving in Moscow
on July 22 on a brand-new Boeing 707—the age of
jet travel had just arrived—Nixon, typically, could
not sleep. His first encounter with Khrushchev at
the Kremlin the next morning was not elevating.
The Kremlin boss swore that a congressional bill
calling on the Soviet Union to release its "captive nations" in Eastern Europe "stinks like fresh horse shit,
and nothing smells worse than that." Not to be one-
upped in the barnyard, Nixon countered that "there
is something that smells worse than horse shit—and
that is pig shit."[40]

Nixon tried to be statesmanlike when the two
drove together to a trade fair, where they stopped at
a TV studio built by RCA to show off to the Russian
people the novelty of color television. But he fretted
that he came across as meek next to the browbeating
Khrushchev. When the vice president left the studio
he was "sweating profusely," recalled William Safire,
then a twenty-nine-year-old PR man working for a
homebuilder who was exhibiting "the typical American house." Nixon wasn't being paranoid; Khrushchev had "clobbered him," Safire recorded in his
memoirs.[41]

But when the debate moved to a different set—an
ultramodern American kitchen—Nixon rallied and
hit back in measured fashion.

"We are strong. We can beat you," blustered
Khrushchev, heaving his bulk around.

Nixon responded sternly but calmly: "No one
should ever use his strength to put another in a posi-

tion where he has in effect an ultimatum. For us to argue who is the stronger misses the point. If war comes we both lose."

There was more posturing and finger-pointing and some raised voices, but Khrushchev seemed to sense that Nixon was not an adversary he could easily bully. At a banquet afterward, Nixon followed Khrushchev's lead and threw his vodka glass into the fireplace.

Nixon was given the unprecedented opportunity of addressing the Russian people on TV, a speech he sweated over but delivered calmly. Afterward, Nixon may have become a little tipsy, because Milton Eisenhower, the president's brother who had joined them on the trip, later told historian Michael Beschloss that Nixon consumed "six or seven" martinis and became sloppy. That many martinis would have put Nixon under the table; Nixon more likely drank two or three. With his limited capacity, one or two would have made him wobble, especially when he was exhausted and excited, as he surely was that night.[42]

Nixon's euphoria, no matter how gin-induced, was understandable. Khrushchev was an enormous figure in the Cold War world, menacing with his rockets, meaning to frighten and succeeding. By standing up to him in the kitchen debate, Nixon had shown his mettle to a global audience. That Nixon could keep his cool while Khrushchev blustered was a tremendous confidence builder. Nixon had begun the 1950s showing that he was ready for a California-wide political campaign. He ended the decade demonstrating that he was ready for global statesmanship. He had "won" by remaining cool; for an excitable, decidedly uncool kid in high school, the face-off with Khrushchev was immensely redeeming and self-affirming. Nixon had found, through politics, a confident identity.

The so-called Kitchen Debate, widely reported back home, proved a turning point for Nixon. He emerged to many Americans as a stand-up statesman who could handle the Russians. **Time** magazine, the flagship of the Luce Empire, put Nixon on the cover, with the Kremlin towers in the background. Widely distributed photos showed Nixon poking Khrushchev in the chest. Nixon even received grudgingly respectful notices from James Reston, the **New York Times** columnist who functioned as a kind of Voice of the Establishment and who had been scratchy, if not caustic, in his earlier commentary on Nixon.[43] The 1960 election was coming.

Dick and Jack.

**Courtesy of the Richard Nixon Presidential
Library and Museum**

CHAPTER 7

Jack

From their first debate, as freshmen congressmen attending a field hearing of the House Education and Labor Committee in McKeesport, Pennsylvania, in 1947, Nixon and Kennedy seemed bound together in a drama of personal and national destiny. They recognized in each other shyness and profound ambition, a kinship of generational politics, a fascination with America's global role. They might have remained friendly, if not quite friends, had not fate—and its human instruments, jealousy and pride—pitted them against each other.

One afternoon in the winter of 1950, when Nixon was working in his congressional office on Capitol Hill, preparing for his race for the Senate against Helen Gahagan Douglas, his secretary let him know that that he had a visitor. It was the congressman down the hall, Jack Kennedy. Young Kennedy pulled an envelope out of his breast pocket and handed it to Nixon. "Dick, I know you're in for a pretty rough campaign," said Kennedy, "and my father wanted to help out." Inside the envelope was a check for $1,000 (almost $10,000 in 2015 dollars). Nixon might have seen this offering from the multi-millionaire patriarch as mildly condescending, but he needed the cash, and he was grateful.[1]

The two saw each other fairly often during their years on the Hill. As senators, their offices were across the hall from each other. In 1953, Kennedy invited Nixon (along with hundreds of political figures) to his wedding to Jacqueline Bouvier; Nixon had to decline in order to play golf with his boss, President Eisenhower.[2] In 1954, when Kennedy was gravely ill after near-fatal back surgery at Bethesda Naval Hospital, Nixon went to see him and emerged in tears, according to his Secret Service escort Rex Scouten. "Oh God, don't let him die," Nixon choked. Nixon's tearful prayer may seem extreme—the two men were not that close—but Kennedy seems to have touched some chord of fellow-feeling in Nixon.[3]

In 1960, a month before the Democratic Convention, Nixon ran into Joseph Kennedy, the patriarch of the clan, outside the Colony Restaurant in New York City. After a warm handshake, Kennedy said to Nixon, "I just want you to know how much I admire you for what you've done in the Hiss case and in all the Communist activity of yours. If Jack doesn't get it," said father Joe, "I'll be for you." A few days later, Nixon had another chance encounter with Joe Senior, this time in the first-class cabin of a United Airlines flight from New York to Los Angeles. Accompanying the ambassador was a "real raving beauty" less than half his age, recalled Nixon. Kennedy introduced his companion as his "niece" and gave the nonplussed Nixon a wink.[4]

Decades later, recounting these stories in his 1983 interviews with Frank Gannon, Nixon seemed as much admiring as disapproving. He could scorn the Kennedy philandering and mock the Kennedy privilege, but he envied the Kennedy macho and charisma, and he admired the cold efficiency of the family political machine. "The Kennedys were effective. They got it done," said Nixon. With mild disdain, Nixon described the Kennedy style: "suave, smooth, debonair, and that appealed, of course, to many in the media, who are more frankly suckers for style than the average people." On the other hand, Nixon allowed, "People aren't going to vote for the man next door. They want their leader to be somebody who is different, bigger than life, different from themselves. Not one that is like them." Nixon knew that to many voters, he seemed "like them." Jack Kennedy did not.[5]

The 1960 election has been portrayed as the ultimate battle of the Franklins against the Orthogonians, the cool guy against the striver.[6] But that image, while illuminating, does not fully capture the clash of societal forces, nor the outsize characters of their champions. JFK was not just any Franklin. He was certainly not smug or complacent. He may have been a spoiled rich boy, languid in his charms, but he was also a new-money scion whose father had felt

so shunned by the Yankee aristocracy that he literally left town, moving his family from Brahmin Boston to the less class-ridden New York. "When will
the nice people of Boston accept Catholics?" his
beautiful Irish Catholic mother Rose had bitterly,
beseechingly asked one of Jack's posh Harvard
friends.[7] To many, the Kennedys represented an
American dream of immigrant arrival, the wide-
open, G.I. Bill promise of postwar social and economic advancement. In less heart-warming fashion,
the family also knew how to do whatever it took.

Richard Nixon, for all his Orthogonian cheer-
leading, was hardly a regular guy himself. What Average Joe, in the name of democratic debate, takes
on a South American mob? Or models himself—as
Nixon would later—after Charles de Gaulle? At
times Nixon belonged on Olympus, at other times
in Hades; either way, he was no mere mortal in the
reach of his ambition or the tragedy of his flaws.

A half-century later the issues of the 1960 election seem obscure or hyped. The candidates argued
over Cold War hotspots long forgotten, like Que-
moy and Matsu (disputed islands on the Red Chinese coast, occupied by the Nationalist Chinese),
and vaguely spoke of "getting the country moving
again" (Kennedy's mantra). But the real issues were
never really addressed or even recognized by the candidates, the press, or the voters. America in 1960
stood on the verge of a decade of profound
change—on matters of sex, gender, and race, on
America's role in the world—and not in a calm or

measured way. Half the country wanted to go forward and half wanted to go back, but the path forward—or back—was never clearly defined. Kennedy,
very roughly speaking, seemed to represent the future, while Nixon, as Ike's heir, seemed to represent
the status quo, though neither man came close to
articulating what that meant, if they even knew. The
country was evenly split between the two candidates
in the beginning and evenly divided—almost dead
even—at the end. But there was nothing static about
the campaign. Between spring and fall, the race
twisted and turned in ways that exposed Nixon at
his noblest and his most ignoble.

On July 16, 1960, sitting in his Washington office,
Nixon closely watched Kennedy's acceptance speech
after the senator from Massachusetts won the Democratic nomination. Nixon was encouraged. Kennedy seemed effete, elitist, and also gaunt and tired.
Too much Harvard accent, and a tinge of weakness,
even illness, Nixon thought. He could be beaten in
a debate—on television.[8]

Nixon underestimated Kennedy's public character, but not his family's dark side. During the primary season, Nixon had seen that the Kennedy
operation—well-greased by Ambassador Kennedy's
fortune—could be just as ruthless and underhanded
as the roughest Irish pols of Boston. In the Wisconsin primary in April, Senator Hubert Humphrey of
neighboring Minnesota seemed to have a clear
home-grown edge. But a few days before the vote,

anti-Catholic literature, postmarked from Minnesota, began to pour into the Catholic areas around Milwaukee. There was an enormous backlash, and Humphrey was blamed for trying to incite anti-Catholic prejudice against Kennedy. Shortly after Humphrey lost, Nixon learned who had done the mailings: operatives working for JFK's brother and campaign manager, Robert Kennedy. Nixon put the information in his mental "never forget" file.[9]

Richard Nixon loved classical music. He had taken piano lessons as a child and could bang out Broadway tunes and popular songs on the piano, but he was most moved by the great, romantic symphonies of the classical masters. In private, at home or in a hotel suite, he liked to listen to Beethoven and Brahms and Tchaikovsky on a record player, to allow his emotions to be stirred and lifted.

At the Republican National Convention in Chicago in July 1960, Len Hall, the former head of the Republican Party who was advising Nixon, heard loud music late one night coming from the suite reserved for the Republican nominee. He wandered into the suite's living room and found Nixon in a trance, conducting the trumpets and thundering drums of the **1812 Overture**.[10]

Nixon usually hid his emotions—but not always well. In the 1960 campaign, he functioned as his own campaign manager, a major mistake. (Murray Chotiner had been sidelined by an influence-peddling scandal.) He was determined to outwork (the soft, spoiled) JFK, which led Nixon to make another mistake. Ignoring the cautions of his advisers, he decided to campaign in all fifty states. He fell behind right away when he banged his knee on a car door and had to spend two weeks in the hospital with a serious staph infection that almost cost him his leg. Emerging from the hospital on September 9, he took off on a twenty-five-state, fifteen-thousand-mile tour. Within three days, he was running a fever over 103 degrees.[11] He couldn't sleep. He kept a Dictaphone by his bed so that he could dictate memos, and he would be up at all hours spitting out orders on campaign minutiae.[12]

In Iowa in mid-September, a new advance man, John Ehrlichman, had scheduled a full day's drive through the farm state's small towns. The hours between stops were long, and Nixon became increasingly frustrated by the wasted time. Nixon may have willed himself to dive into crowds, but the effort cost him. Harrison Salisbury of **The New York Times** observed Nixon's stiff-legged gait and clenched fists as he approached the rope line—his smile was fixed, but there was nothing easy or natural about his manner.[13] In the Indian summer warmth, as Nixon's open convertible headed down the empty Iowa roads, the candidate "seethed with anger," recalled the chief advance man, H. R. "Bob" Haldeman. One of Nixon's aides, Air Force Major Don Hughes, was riding in the seat in front of Nixon's. "Suddenly—incredibly—Nixon began to kick the back of Hughes's seat with both feet," recalled Haldeman. "And he wouldn't stop!"

Thump! Thump! Thump! The seat and the hapless Hughes jolted forward jaggedly as Nixon vented his rage. When the car stopped at a small town in the middle of nowhere, Hughes, white faced, silently got out of the car and started walking straight ahead, down the road and out of town. He wanted to get as far away as he could from the Vice-President. I believe he would have walked clear across the state if I hadn't set out after him and apologized for Nixon and finally talked him into rejoining us.[14]

Both Haldeman and Hughes later played down the incident. Nixon had reason to be angry—the endless drive between small farm hamlets to speak to sparse crowds was an immense waste of time, a blunder of scheduling and advance work. Nixon could be petulant, it was true, but he was far more often considerate of his aides, seeing it as his duty to cheer them up when they became worn down and discouraged. Nixon worked at being upbeat. Generally, he succeeded, but—in the course of a grueling campaign—not always.

When, just before midnight on September 25, Nixon arrived in Chicago for the first nationally televised debate, he was exhausted and still sick. He had lost ten pounds, and his shirt hung limply around his neck. He wore himself out some more by giving a speech to a hostile labor audience in the morning and then spent five hours trying to cram facts into his head. On the way to the studio, he once again cracked his knee on the car door. His face turned ashen as he pretended to ignore the pain.[15]

His rival had spent the day sunning, napping, and listening to Peggy Lee records. When Kennedy sauntered into the studio, tan, crisp, and fashionably late, he ignored his opponent. Nixon couldn't take his eyes off Kennedy. A producer asked Kennedy if he wanted makeup. "No," said Kennedy, offhand and cool. Did Nixon want makeup? Nixon declined, too. He told his press secretary, Herb Klein, that he didn't want to look like a "sissy."[16] But the five o'clock shadow was a problem. Someone was sent down to Michigan Avenue to buy some Lazy Shave, a kind of cosmetic "shavestick," at a drugstore. Nixon smeared the white ointment over his beard, adding a ghastly sheen to his pallid complexion (back in his dressing room, Kennedy used Max Factor Creme Puff to keep the shine down).[17] In the control booth, a Nixon aide uneasily asked Bobby Kennedy how he thought the vice president looked. "T'rific," replied Kennedy. "T'rific."[18]

Kennedy and Nixon came into the debate, the first of four, essentially tied in the polls. About 80 million people, the biggest political audience since the Checkers Speech, were watching. A few minutes before the camera light went on, Nixon took a phone call from his vice-presidential ticket mate, Henry Cabot Lodge Jr. A Boston Brahmin who had lost his Senate seat to Kennedy in 1952, Lodge turned out to be a poor choice as a running mate. He was an unenthusiastic campaigner who liked to take the weekend off and had no common touch. (Kennedy, whose own family knew something about Wasp snobbery, had been bemused when Nixon chose the aristocratic Lodge. "If Nixon ever tries to visit Lodge at Beverly," JFK said, referring to Lodge's estate on Boston's swank North Shore, "they won't let him in the door.")[19]

In his pre-debate pep talk, Lodge urged Nixon to "erase the assassin image," the Herblock cartoon of the scowling scourge of Hiss, and to be "the nice guy" instead. As the debate began, Nixon made an obvious, almost pained effort to show restraint. The panel of newsmen tried to provoke him. Sander Vanocur of NBC pointedly asked Nixon about President Eisenhower's apparent, if unintentional, putdown of his vice president. In late August, as he was ending a press conference, Eisenhower had been asked to cite an example of Nixon's contributions to U.S. foreign policy. "If you give me a week, I might think of something," Eisenhower had testily responded. Nixon struggled to explain away Eisenhower's words as "facetious" (what Ike had meant to say, Nixon later argued, was, "I'll talk about that at next week's press conference").[20] But the damage done by Ike's careless remark was severe. Vanocur's question particularly rankled Pat Nixon, who (rightly, as events would show) suspected newsmen of doing the Kennedys' bidding.[21]

Few who saw that debate or read about it later would forget the contrasting images: Kennedy, calm and confident, presidential; Nixon, eyes furtively watching his opponent, sweat streaking the smear of Lazy Shave, shoulders hunched. A British diplomat reported to the Foreign Office: "He seems in the last few weeks to have aged and shriveled, and the way in which his tongue kept darting in and out of his lips was positively reptilian."[22] Columnist Joe Alsop wrote that Nixon "looked like a suspect who was being questioned . . . in connection with a statutory rape case."[23] Mayor Richard Daley of Chicago tastelessly joked that Nixon had already been embalmed.

In the aftermath, Nixon was in a mild daze, unsure what to think. A supporter tried to console him: "That's all right. You'll do better next time." She spoke loudly so that the microphones could pick up her words. She was in fact not a supporter but a woman hired by Dick Tuck, a campaign prankster. The wily Tuck had first crossed Nixon's path as a Democratic operative in the 1950 campaign against Helen Gahagan Douglas. Posing as a Republican advance man, he had embarrassed Nixon by hiring an empty hall. By the time of the 1960 election, Tuck was on the Kennedy payroll.[24]

Back at his hotel, Nixon's secretary, Rose Woods, tried to be gentle with "the Boss," but she did have to report that Nixon's own mother had called to ask, "Is Richard ill?" Watching from his hotel room in Texas, Nixon's running mate Lodge was harsh. "That son of a bitch just lost the election," he said to his aides.

In political lore, Lodge's verdict has become conventional wisdom, but in fact Nixon—fattened up by two milkshakes a day and kept cool by frigid air conditioning in the studios—won or held his own in the next three debates. The evidence from polling data suggests that the debates were probably a wash. Even so, there is no question that the first debate established Kennedy, heretofore regarded in many quarters as a playboy and a dilettante, as a mature leader, while raising questions about Nixon's stamina and steadiness.[25]

What really spelled Nixon's defeat happened off-stage.

Nixon's Quaker mother raised him to be free of racial prejudice. Ever eager to please and honor her, Nixon went out of his way to show consideration to black people. In college and law school, he stood up against the unthinking racism of the day. In an underappreciated role, Nixon was Eisenhower's point man on civil rights. Although Lyndon Johnson has been credited with passing the 1957 Civil Rights Act, it was the Eisenhower administration that pushed the bill. Earlier, Nixon had taken the lead by steering government contracts to black businesses. His evident sincerity impressed Ethel Payne, the leading black newspaperwoman, especially when, late in the winter of 1958, the vice president showed up at a party at her D.C. apartment with Pat and a bottle of bourbon. (At the time, Payne wrote off Jack Kennedy, by contrast, as "glassy-eyed" with ambition for 1960 and too pliant to segregationist Southern Democrats.) Nixon became friendly with Martin

Luther King Jr. after a trip to Africa in 1957 and was close to Jackie Robinson, the baseball player who broke the color line for the Brooklyn Dodgers.[26] On the campaign trail, Nixon practiced what he preached. In Springfield, Missouri, when a hotel refused to rent rooms to some black reporters covering the campaign, Nixon moved his whole entourage out.[27]

On October 19, 1960, three weeks before election day, Martin Luther King Jr. was arrested during a sit-in at a "whites only" restaurant in Atlanta. The civil rights leader was sent in chains to the state pen on an old charge of driving on an expired license. His wife, Coretta, understandably feared that he would be killed there. At the urging of his advisers, JFK called Coretta to express his concern—and to let the press know. Meanwhile, his brother Robert maneuvered to get the judge to release King. Nixon's press secretary, Herb Klein, was asked to respond. "No comment," said Klein.[28]

Nixon had explained to his spokesman, Herb Klein, that calling Mrs. King would look like "pandering." He was huffy about Bobby Kennedy calling the judge ("improper!").[29] He may have also worried about alienating white voters, particularly Southern Protestants whom he hoped to peel away from the Democratic "Solid South." Nixon was already a little suspect in the South for his friendly remarks about the NAACP, and he didn't want to arouse a backlash. Privately, Nixon did think that King's constitutional rights had been infringed, and he spoke to his friend Bill Rogers—who had become attorney general in the Eisenhower administration—about announcing a Justice Department investigation. But the White House refused to sign off on the idea.

Nixon's apparent inaction was galling to blacks. Martin Luther King's father—"Daddy" King, a prominent Baptist minister in Atlanta—had been a Nixon supporter. But the elder King switched sides. He told his congregation that he never thought he could support a Catholic, but "Kennedy can be my president, Catholic or whatever he is. . . . I've got all the votes and I've got a suitcase, and I'm going up there and dump them in [Kennedy's] lap." The Kennedy machine revved up, though not out in the open: In black churches and bars all over the country, thousands of handbills were distributed. On one side the flyer read, "Jack Kennedy called Mrs. King." The other side read, "Richard Nixon did not." In the large black populations of Detroit, Philadelphia, and New York and in the black press, Kennedy operatives reached out, sometimes with cash.* High black turnout on Election Day may have made the

---

*"Walking around money" may have been a bigger factor than the flyers, which were not distributed in time to affect the vote. The Kennedy operation made large payments to black preachers and local politicians to make sure that they got out the vote.[31] The Nixon campaign passed up chances to reach out to black leaders. Jim Bassett recalled that Haldeman at the last minute canceled a brunch for Nixon with "leading blacks of Chicago, clergymen, businessmen, etc." Nixon later claimed he had never heard of "walking around money" until the 1960 election—and that when his GOP operatives did try to use cash to win black preachers, they were outbid by Joe Kennedy.[32]

difference for Kennedy, who carried a half-dozen states in the industrial Midwest and Northeast by narrow margins.[30]

Nixon's black supporters could not understand what had happened to their candidate. William Safire, who was doing some PR for the campaign, ran into Jackie Robinson as he was leaving Nixon's hotel room, where Robinson had gone to plead the case for helping King. Robinson was in tears. "He thinks calling Martin would be grandstanding," Robinson reported and burst out, "Nixon doesn't deserve to win."[33]

Nixon learned how he had miscalculated only after it was too late. Two days after the election, his black chauffeur, John Wardlow, told him ("with an emotion I had never before seen him show," Nixon recalled), "Mr. Vice President, I can't tell you how sick I am about the way my people voted in the election. You know I had been talking to all my friends. They were all for you. But when Mr. Robert Kennedy called the judge to get Dr. King out of jail— well, they just all turned to him."[34]

Nixon's surprise and rue at losing a constituency he had consistently courted and supported was genuine. Nixon was not completely free of prejudice, but more than most white politicians—including John F. Kennedy—he identified with the plight of blacks who needed jobs and education to enter the American middle class. Characteristically, Nixon turned his disappointment into anger at the Kennedys for stealing black votes with underhanded tricks.

· · ·

During the campaign, the mainstream press missed the story of how Kennedy was winning—and Nixon was losing—the black vote. In Nixon's view, the press hacks were too busy fawning over Kennedy to pay attention to the Democrats' more devious maneuvers: the walking-around money and the dirty tricks like hiring hecklers, sending out salacious or prejudiced campaign literature under Nixon's name, and changing street signs on the way to rallies. (Kennedy's operatives did not advertise their cultivation of the black press because they did not want white voters to notice.) Once again, Nixon was not being paranoid. Though most publishers, who tended to be Republican, endorsed Nixon on their editorial pages, reporters from the big papers widely favored Kennedy. They regarded Nixon as slippery and insincere, a reputation Nixon exacerbated with his off-putting manner.

Nobody played the press better than John F. Kennedy. He was earthy, clever, confiding; he admitted chosen reporters to his very select club. The most prominent was Theodore H. White, whose **Making of the President, 1960** became the ur-campaign book, at once an exaltation and embarrassment of access journalism. ("Cher Pierre," White began a letter to Pierre Salinger, JFK's press secretary, a month before the election, "my chips are so heavily committed to Jack.")[35] In **Breach of Faith: The Fall of Richard Nixon**, written partly to revise the too-credulous record left by the last of his campaign books, **Making of the President, 1972,** White wrote, with inadvertent hauteur, "When Nixon talks unguardedly on the stump, he talks the hard language of the underprivileged; he can get down to bedrock communication so directly and coarsely as to mystify not only his advisers but his friends." White described how, when he visited President Kennedy in the Oval Office shortly after the 1960 election, he found the new commander-in-chief "indulging himself by reading verbatim transcripts of Nixon's stump speeches in the campaign." Kennedy was "puzzled," wrote White. "He said, 'You know Nixon is really smart—how can he talk such shit?' "[36]

Kennedy was cozy with reporters like White ("another Harvard grad," Nixon would mutter) because he literally lived among them. Jackie and Jack Kennedy had moved into a red brick row house at 3307 N Street in Georgetown, a block away from Joe Alsop's street, Dumbarton, and just a few doors down from Ben Bradlee, the **Newsweek** reporter who became JFK's personal friend and, later, Nixon's nemesis as editor of **The Washington Post.** Joe Alsop was particularly smitten with Kennedy's combination of machismo and style—"Stevenson with balls," Alsop called him. Stewart Alsop, Joe's brother and writing partner, was more balanced—indeed, in 1958, he had written a sympathetic and insightful profile called "The Mystery of Richard Nixon" in the mass-circulation **Saturday Evening Post.** But Joe Alsop was at the center of an elite that embraced JFK and just as firmly rejected Nixon.

On October 11, 1960, Katharine Graham of **The Washington Post** threw a fiftieth birthday party for Joe at her parents' home; among the hundred guests were the peers of the Georgetown set, including all the top officials of the CIA and all the leading pundits, most notably Walter Lippmann and James Reston of the **Times**. Surveying the crowd, Kennedy adviser Arthur Schlesinger Jr. told former secretary of state Dean Acheson: "They cannot stand the thought of a Nixon victory." From the campaign trail, the Kennedys sent champagne and a note from Jackie to Joe: "I cannot express—& become tearful when I try—in this supercharged emotional time—how we appreciate your friendship." On inauguration night, when all the balls were over, JFK would repair to Alsop's house for more champagne.[37]

On the campaign plane, reporters joined the Kennedy staff in sing-alongs about the New Frontier.[38] Bouncing along on the campaign plane, separated from the traveling reporters by a red curtain (and, in some cases, by a gaping cultural divide), Nixon could not possibly compete with the glamorous Jack. Reporters could be savage to Nixon. They called him "the cardboard man" because he seemed to be hiding behind a cardboard image, even when he tried to have drinks with reporters and chat with them. Bryce Harlow, who counseled Nixon, recalled watching reporters try to trap and provoke Nixon at a press conference in Marvin, Illinois, interrupting him, even insulting him. "I was aghast at the viciousness of it, the malice, the open hatred," Harlow recalled. That night, on the plane back to Washington, Nixon wearily said to Harlow, "I've tried everything anyone can do. . . . I've given interviews one on one, lots of them. I've had small, intimate interviews. I've had parties at my home. I've made myself accessible to them. I've given them news and information. I've played their game. It has never changed a thing. I don't know what can be done about it."[39]

Hounded by reporters, Nixon had to stop holding press conferences on the campaign trail. His last, desperately clumsy attempt to be "one of the boys" backfired. In Billings, Montana, in mid-October, Nixon's spokesman, Herb Klein, arranged a party for the traveling press corps and the American Airlines crew of Nixon's campaign plane. Nixon, who came in "a little late," tried to mingle. The reporters tried to turn the party into "an informal press conference, violating the rules," recalled Klein. When Klein stepped in, Nixon awkwardly tried to make a joke by referring to the two American Airlines stewardesses—both favorites with the crew, staff, and press—as "bar girls," that is, prostitutes. The "girls" gamely laughed, but many of the reporters grumbled about Nixon's tastelessness. "I could not help but think that the same type of remark made by Kennedy would have brought laughter," wrote Klein.[40]

As Election Day approached, the race appeared to be too close to call. "The hard language of the underprivileged" may have offended Theodore White and the Georgetown set, but Nixon's "rock 'em, sock 'em" stump speeches played well in many parts of the country, particularly in the Midwest and in rural areas. Nixon needed one last push to take the lead. The obvious man to give it was President Eisenhower, who was still enormously popular.

On October 31, eight days before the polls opened, Len Hall, the former head of the Republican Party, organized a White House lunch with Nixon and Eisenhower. Hall had gotten the president to agree to a series of campaign events in Illinois, New York, and Michigan. Unaccountably, however, Nixon seemed petulant, as if he did not wish to be there. Anxiously, Hall waited for Nixon to ask for the president's help. He was astonished when Nixon said, "Mr. President, you've done enough." Ike turned an angry shade of red familiar to his subordinates. After the meeting, the former D-Day commander summoned Hall to his office. "Did you see Nixon?" Ike demanded. "Did you see him?" Ike launched into an imitation of Nixon hunched over, shoulders bent, head down. "When I had a front line officer like that in World War II, I wanted to relieve him," Eisenhower growled. He paused and said, "He doesn't look like a winner to me."[41]

Years later, in his memoirs, Nixon explained his reticence with Eisenhower. The night before the White House lunch, he recounted, Mamie Eisenhower had called Pat and begged her to stop the president from campaigning. The strain on his heart might kill him, the First Lady had said. According to Nixon's account, she had also implored, "Ike must never know I called you."[42] So Nixon had behaved nobly by refusing, without explanation, Ike's help on the campaign trail. The diary of Dr. Howard Snyder, Ike's physician, supports the claim—it records Snyder himself asking Nixon to "either talk him out of it or just don't let him do it—for the sake of his health."[43] Susan Eisenhower, Ike's granddaughter, later said that Mamie denied to her that she had called Pat asking her to intervene; Susan's brother, David, speculated to the author that his future father-in-law just didn't want to rely on Ike, that he wanted to win the presidency on his own—a sin of pride forgivable in such a self-made man.[44] The misunderstanding between Eisenhower and Nixon was just the last in a long series. Though he was put off by Nixon from time to time, Eisenhower knew that, together, the two men had reinvented the modern vice-presidency; that Nixon had been an active and respected participant on the National Security Council; and that he had acted exceptionally well as Ike's envoy and executor. Even Mamie, though she had been catty about Pat's off-the-rack wardrobe, had defended Nixon against the criticisms of Ike's brother Milton and his son John.[45] For his part, Nixon showed remarkable loyalty to a man who on occasion treated him shabbily. Nixon could behave like an angry child when he was exhausted and stymied, but he also showed remarkable forbearance and acceptance of the things he could not change.

· · ·

Between the Republican Convention in July and Election Day on November 8, Nixon traveled sixty-five thousand miles and gave 180 formal speeches. By the end he was drained and, at moments, near delirium. In Stockton, California, he fell so profoundly asleep that his aide Don Hughes was not able to shake him awake. Finally, Nixon opened his eyes and announced, "I think God is with us."[46] After an endless day of jumping from airport to airport, rope line to rope line, Nixon turned to Haldeman as he staggered to his limousine and said with exhausted seriousness, "Bob, from now on, there will be no more landings at airports."[47] A few days before the vote, in Detroit, the candidate became upset when an advertising consultant named Everett Hart refused to run an errand; Nixon punched him in the chest.[48]

After a grueling trip to Alaska to fulfill his pledge to visit all fifty states, Nixon slept for two hours—his first time in a bed in seventy-two hours—before arising on Election Day to cast his vote and to visit his mother in Whittier. Nixon wanted to get away, anywhere. He sent Pat and the girls to get their hair done and told Herb Klein, "No reporters." With Hughes and Jack Sherwood, the Secret Service man who had pulled his gun in Caracas, he motored south ("no radio"), eventually reaching Tijuana, just over the Mexican border, where he drank margaritas at a German restaurant. On the way back, he summoned Hughes ("You're my fa-

vorite Catholic") and sat in the back pew of the old
Mission at San Juan Capistrano, lost in thought or
prayer.[49]

His election night headquarters was the gaudy
Royal Suite at the Ambassador Hotel, a riot of pur-
ples, pinks, reds, violet silk, and velour. While Pat
retreated to her room upstairs, Nixon watched the
early returns. All the anchormen in New York were
predicting a Kennedy victory, perhaps a landslide.
Nixon was skeptical; he knew it was going to be
close. By midnight on the East Coast, the anchormen were looking less smug: Nixon was doing well
in the Midwest and his native West. But by 2:30
A.M. (11:30 P.M. in Los Angeles), Nixon's extraordi-
narily accurate internal vote counter—supplemented
by columns of figures on his ubiquitous yellow
pads—told him that victory was probably impossible. He would have to carry Illinois as well as his
home state, California, and at least one other.

Nixon summoned Pat and told her that they
needed to go down to the ballroom, face the TV
cameras, and concede that Kennedy was likely to be
elected president "if the present trend continues."
She refused. She had been hearing the rumors of
voting shenanigans in Illinois and considered Kennedy a fraud and scoundrel. Two weeks before the
election, she had asked adviser Bryce Harlow, "How
can we let the American people know in time what
kind of a man Kennedy is?"[50] Now, she angrily told
her husband, "I simply cannot bring myself to stand
there with you while you concede the election to

Kennedy."[51] She turned and went back upstairs to her room.

Her friend Helene Drown followed her. "You've got to go with him," she said. Pat knew she was right.[52] She had come this far with a mixture of fortitude, fatalism, and a certain dry humor (she was thinking of titling her memoirs **I Also Ran**.)[53]

Pat went to Nixon, who was alone scribbling notes, and said, "I think we should go down together." But it was hard. She would always feel pained to remember the television image of her face, almost skeletal (she had lost ten pounds from her thin frame) and desolate as she choked back tears standing beside her man. "No, no, no!" came cries from the audience. "You're still going to win!"

After his almost-concession, Nixon watched the returns—still agonizingly close, but not close enough, and went to bed around 4 A.M. Barely two hours later, he recalled in **Six Crises,** "I felt someone shaking my arm insistently and urgently. I opened my eyes and saw it was Julie." The Secret Service had showed her to his room. The twelve-year-old girl asked, "Daddy, how did the election finally come out?"

Trying to be as gentle as possible, Nixon answered, "Julie, I'm afraid we have lost."

"She started to cry," Nixon recalled, "and the questions tumbled through her tears: 'What are we going to do? Where are we going to live? What kind of job are you going to be able to get? Where are we going to school?' "[54]

. . .

On the grimly silent plane back to Washington, Nixon summoned his campaign aides, one by one, to the front of the plane to thank them. Peter Flanigan, a twenty-seven-year old New York investment banker, was brooding over the Catholic vote. It had been split 50-50 in 1956, but in 1960 it swung 75 percent to Kennedy. JFK had made a campaign issue out of religious bigotry, going on national TV to say that nobody had asked his religious beliefs when he was serving in World War II. Meanwhile, behind the scenes, Kennedy's brother Robert had been using every surrogate he could find to get out the Catholic vote. "Bobby played it like a yo-yo," Flanigan recalled. Young Flanigan, who had been a contemporary of Robert's at Portsmouth Priory, a small Catholic boarding school (from which RFK had been dismissed for cheating), had wanted to "stem the tide" of Catholic defection from the GOP with "independent" advertisements aimed at Catholic markets. Nixon had chewed him out. "Don't play the religious card under any circumstances whatever," he told Flanigan. Nixon undoubtedly picked up anti-Catholic votes from Protestants, but he had been smart—and principled—enough to leave the issue alone.

Now, as he made his way up the aisle of the plane to see the boss, Flanigan prepared himself to apologize for not trying harder to win Catholics. "I thought it was my job to tell him we had let him down," Flanigan recalled. "But his purpose was to ease our disappointment. He said, 'Peter, we've laid to rest the dragon of religion in politics.' "[55]

Flanigan and others in the campaign, including those who had endured the candidate's occasional tantrums, would always remember Nixon's decency in defeat—and his unwillingness to match the Kennedys' slickness and dirty tricks. Nixon had a different takeaway from the 1960 campaign. "Kennedy's organization approached campaign dirty tricks with a roguish relish and carried them off with such insouciance that captivated many politicians and overcame the critical faculties of many reporters. I should have anticipated what was coming. . . ."

He made up his mind not to make that mistake again: "I vowed that I would never again enter an election at a disadvantage by being vulnerable to them—or anyone—on the level of political tactics."[56] Or, as his daughter Julie put it more succinctly, Nixon "vowed never to be at the mercy of such political hardball himself."[57]

CHAPTER 8

Over the Wall We Go

On the night after the election, Nixon's plane "landed in one of those dreary, drizzling rains which plague the Washington area during the late fall," Nixon recalled. Within two days he was on a boat off Key Biscayne, having a drink and trying to let the sun soak out his nearly existential fatigue. Len Hall, the Republican Party leader (who had felt marginalized in the campaign), somewhat cruelly dredged up the recent past by asking, "Why did you debate?" Nixon looked up at the sky with his eyes closed. "He looked incredibly tense, that terrible tension was there," remembered Hall. "And there was no answer."[1]

Nixon was having dinner at the Jamaica Inn in Key Biscayne that night when the maître d' told him he had an important phone call. Herbert Hoover ("the Chief") had been enlisted by Joe Kennedy to set up a meeting between Nixon and President-elect Kennedy.[2] The Kennedy patriarch was worried that Nixon would contest the results. Kennedy had won the popular vote by an official count of 112,827

On vacation.

Courtesy of the Richard Nixon Presidential
Library and Museum

votes out of approximately 68.8 million cast, a
paper-thin margin. In Chicago, where a switch of
just 4,500 ballots would have given the critical state
to Nixon, there were rampant charges that Mayor
Daley had turned out the graveyard vote. In the wee
hours of the morning of November 9, Daley had
called Kennedy and said, "Mr. President, with a little bit of luck and the help of a few close friends,
you're going to carry Illinois."[3] (In one mostly black
precinct of Chicago, there were more votes cast for
Kennedy than people living there.)[4]

Nixon graciously offered to meet Kennedy at his
father's Palm Beach home, but Kennedy answered
that it would be easier to come to him ("I have a
helicopter at my disposal," said the commander-in-
chief-to-be). When the two men met at the Key Biscayne Hotel on November 14, Kennedy began,
"Well, it's hard to tell who won the election at this
point. . . ." The president-elect was fishing, trying
to gauge whether Nixon would go to court.[5]

The two men skirted around the issue, trading political shoptalk, but Kennedy needn't have worried.
To be sure, Nixon was under pressure from his daughters at home: "How can you possibly talk to that man
after what he said about you in the campaign?" Nixon
answered that it was the only proper thing to do.
Julie interjected, "He didn't win. Haven't you heard
about all the cheating in Illinois and Texas?"[6] Leading Republicans from President Eisenhower to Len
Hall to Senator Everett Dirksen urged Nixon to consider a legal challenge. Nixon permitted some "inde-

pendent" groups to test the legal waters.[7] But by mid-December he had confirmed his initial instinct that a challenge would be counterproductive, making him look like the sore loser and putting a cloud over the new president at a dangerous time in the Cold War. To Bryce Harlow, who was sure that Lyndon Johnson had stolen Texas for Kennedy and that the vice president had a "responsibility" to assure the country of an honest election, Nixon replied, "It'd tear the country to pieces. You can't do that."[8]

Nixon did the right and honorable thing, and he showed his grace again when he found himself in the awkward position, as vice president, of formally certifying his opponent's election in Congress. On January 6, presiding over a Joint Session in the House chamber, Vice President Nixon announced the electoral vote (Kennedy 303, Nixon 219) and made a short speech:

> This is the first time in 100 years that a candidate for the presidency announced the result of an election in which he was defeated and announced the victory of his opponent. . . . In our campaigns, no matter how hard fought they may be, no matter how close the election may turn out to be, those who lose accept the verdict and support those who win.

Republicans and Democrats alike stood and loudly applauded until the vice president took a second bow.

Two weeks later, on a cold clear day at the East Front of the Capitol, Nixon listened as President Eisenhower audibly ground his teeth through his successor's Inaugural Address. Vowing to "bear any burden" sounded like dangerous over-promising to Ike.[9] That night, Nixon, alone, was driven to the Capitol, past the couples struggling through the new snow in their ball gowns and tuxedos. Nixon opened a door off the empty Rotunda and looked out over the West Grounds, toward the Washington Monument, stark and clear against the sky, and the Lincoln Memorial shining in the distance. "As I turned to go inside, I suddenly stopped short," Nixon recalled in his memoirs, "struck by the thought that this was not the end—that someday I would be back here. I walked as fast as I could back to the car."[10]

The message was waiting by the telephone in the hall of Nixon's home in Wesley Heights. It was from Tricia. "JFK called," read the note from the precocious eighth grader. "I knew it! It wouldn't be long before he would get into trouble and have to call on you for help." Nixon was being summoned to the White House. It was April 20, 1961; the headlines were all about the new president's first bold stroke, a fiasco at the Bay of Pigs in Cuba. A CIA-backed rebel force had been driven into the sea by the army of communist strongman Fidel Castro.

Entering the Oval Office, Nixon was shocked by JFK's appearance. The vigor had vanished. He looked "beaten, very wan, tired, harassed," Nixon later recalled. Kennedy got up from his rocking chair and started to pace, "using a string of four-letter words that he didn't use at Harvard," Nixon recalled.[11] ("He said shit six times!" Nixon wrote at the top of his notes of the meeting.)[12]

Kennedy asked Nixon what he should do. Flattered to be consulted, the former vice president responded, "There's no question about what should be done. You've got to get Castro out of there."[13] By instinct as well as by dint of his long tutorials with John Foster Dulles, Nixon was an interventionist. He believed that the United States should use military force to drive back communism. In 1954, when the French had abandoned Vietnam, Nixon had been more inclined than Eisenhower to send in ground troops.[14] Pondering what to do about Cuba, President Kennedy was reluctant to send in the Marines. Nixon told him he would support him whatever he decided to do.

As Kennedy walked Nixon out to the Rose Garden, the president suggested that "every public man" should write a book—as a good way to "elevate himself in popular esteem" as "an intellectual." Then Kennedy remarked, "It really is true that foreign affairs is the only important issue for the president to handle, isn't it? I mean, who gives a shit if the minimum wage is $1.15 or $1.25, in comparison to something like this?"

Nixon's devotion to politics, dimmed by the painful loss, was renewed by his Oval Office visit. Nixon could not help but feel that he, not Kennedy, belonged there and that, in time, he would find his way back. In the meantime, partly inspired by Kennedy's offhand advice, he did produce a book. For a memoir by a politician, **Six Crises** is remarkably candid about the author's moods and temper, his visceral turmoil as he fought through the Hiss case, the Checkers Speech, the "Dump Nixon" campaign, and other struggles of his fourteen years in Washington. But the book is ultimately more tendentious than intentionally revealing. It is a carefully constructed argument designed to show how Nixon's emotionalism was a sign of strength, not weakness—that his sleeplessness, his testiness, his occasional explosions were all necessary steps, even welcome in their way, toward facing down his enemies. The book says everything about how he psyched himself up to deal with crisis. It says nothing about the risks of exaggerating his enemies or becoming oversensitive to slights.

Of course, it is just a book, a political memoir designed to buff the reputation of a recently vanquished candidate for president, not a confessional intended to bare his soul. Maybe the memoir is simply incomplete; we cannot know what he was thinking in the darkness before the dawn. At some deep level, Nixon may have grasped that he was caught in an elemental contest, wrestling atavistically with his fears. But Nixon never admitted to such a struggle. Nixon's essential nature remains elusive in part because he took steps to hide who he was—from the

public and his family, and, perhaps, at a conscious
level, even from himself. In an unusually frank interview with Stewart Alsop in 1958, Nixon said, "I
can't really let my hair down with anyone, anyone at
all."[15] It is not glib to suggest that Nixon could not
have honestly looked inward and still been Nixon.
Nixon had to overcome his extreme shyness, his essential aloneness, to meet the demands of vote-
getting and projecting a public persona in a
mass-media democracy. There is something undeni-
ably brave about his determination to convert his
insecurities from debilitating weakness to propulsive
power. If he had to put on blinkers to run on a
muddy track, so be it.

And yet, blinkers can blind. Again and again,
Nixon faced the question of how to reconcile his
introverted nature with his extrovert's calling. That
conundrum, of course, begs a larger question: How
many great men of history were truly self-aware?
Could they afford to be, and still see themselves as
great? In Greek tragedy and later in Shakespeare,
hubris is less a warning than an inevitability—**the**
fatal flaw, unavoidable even when recognized. It is
not an accident that two of history's greatest leaders,
Abraham Lincoln and Winston Churchill, showed
signs of manic depression, at times suffering from
what the clinicians call "delusions of grandeur." Yet
in their mania, if that's what it was, they were very
grand indeed. Nixon was not manic, but he could
be at once visionary and blind.

Nixon was a proud writer. Like all politicians, he

used ghost writers and speechwriters, but he labored over drafts, and his work—and the voice behind his published words—can be truly called his own. He recalled that writing a book was surprisingly hard and draining. He became run down and lost ten pounds.[16]

Nixon drafted **Six Crises** while living alone in an apartment, then a rented house in Los Angeles, eating TV dinners off trays. He had gone to work at a law firm run by one of his old political supporters, Earl Adams, to make some money. Pat was back in Washington while the girls finished the school year before moving to California. Nixon was, by his own account, lonely, short-tempered, and bored. He missed politics and the public stage.[17]

"The pressures to run for governor began almost from the day I arrived back in California," Nixon wrote in his memoir **RN**. As he was leaving the Oval Office in April, even President Kennedy wanted to know if he would run for governor. Nixon answered no, but over the next few months he changed his mind. A rematch against Kennedy in 1964 seemed like a prohibitive long shot, and the California governorship was a way to keep his hand in politics. At first, Nixon was ahead in the polls. Still, he had some reasons to hesitate. One was that he really wasn't interested in being governor. Another was Pat—he had promised that he would spend more time with her and the girls, who were just entering their teenage years.

Nixon was building a "dream house" for his family in Trousdale Estates above Sunset Boulevard, with white carpeting, seven bathrooms, and large picture windows as well as a full-time staff—Manolo and Fina Sanchez, Cuban refugees who were to become part of the Nixon family. "I had never seen Pat so happy. She was so glad to be out of politics," Nixon biographer Earl Mazo later told Julie.[18] On September 25, 1961, Nixon apprehensively gathered his family at the dinner table and told them that he was thinking of running for governor (he had already told an aide to schedule a press conference for September 27). Nixon expected Pat to balk, and she did. "If you run this time, I'm not going to be out campaigning with you as I have in the past," she said. The girls were more positive: Tricia wanted Nixon to run "just to show them."

Nixon repaired to his study to make some notes, as he recalled, "announcing that I had decided not to run for governor." After about half an hour, Pat came in. Nixon could not really see her face in the shadows outside the circle of light from his desk lamp. He could hear that her voice was struggling with emotion. "I have thought about it some more," she said. She was "more convinced than ever" that running would be a mistake. But if he did run, she said, "I'll be there campaigning with you just as I have always been."[19]

And so the play went on. Nixon seemed to need to test Pat, to win her support by saying that he was ready to give it all up—so that she would rescue him once more by pledging her devotion. The Nixons may not have been aware of the drama they were staging, but they certainly knew their parts.

On the campaign trail, Pat's driver, Jack Carley, a twenty-one-year old college grad, noted that Mrs. Nixon was savvy, good-humored, and deliberate. She was so fastidious that Carley once had to pull off into the emergency lane of a roaring freeway to fetch a fresh pair of white gloves from the trunk. Pacing herself, she would ask Carley to circle the block rather than get to an event before almost everyone else had shown up. But she was steadfast; she never complained. Late in the campaign, she cracked three ribs in a fall. Her doctor told her to go to bed, and instead she taped up her rib cage and kept campaigning.[20]

On the stump, her husband was oddly flat. He had to fend off a challenger from the right, ultraconservative Joe Shell, and the incumbent governor, Edmund G. "Pat" Brown, was not dazzling, but he was gregarious and available. By autumn, Nixon was running behind Brown in the polls and needed to debate to try to catch up. At the face-off in San Francisco on October 1, Tom Braden, publisher of the **Oceanside Blade-Tribune,** asked a loaded question: Was it moral or ethical for Nixon to permit his family to take a "secret loan from a major defense contractor"?*

Nixon had heard this one before. Hoping to cash

---

*Nixon had reason to be miffed at his inquisitor, Tom Braden. The newspaper publisher served on a Brown-appointed state board of education. Before moving to California, Braden had been one of the CIA Ivy Leaguers in the "Sunday Night Supper" crowd that gathered at the Alsops.[21]

in on his brother's celebrity, Donald Nixon had started a restaurant business selling "the Nixon Burger," but it had gone broke, and Don had been unable to repay a $205,000 loan from, as it turned out, an agent of Howard Hughes, the mysterious billionaire whose holdings included Hughes Aircraft. The story had first surfaced in the column of Washington muckraker Drew Pearson before the 1960 election. Now the scandal—seemingly minor but nonetheless nagging—was threatening to cost Nixon some votes. (At a stop in San Francisco's Chinatown, Nixon, oblivious, had posed with a banner that read "Welcome Nixon" in English and underneath, in Chinese characters, "How about the Hughes loan?" The trick was the handiwork of the ubiquitous Dick Tuck.)[22] At the debate with Brown on October 1, Nixon swatted away any charge of wrongdoing, challenging his opponent to publicly accuse him of misconduct.[23]

The Hughes loan faded as a campaign issue, though it lodged in Nixon's store of old grudges. Braden was hardly Nixon's only problem in the press corps. He had always been able to count on the unquestioning support, indeed the boosterism, of the **Los Angeles Times**. Repeatedly on the campaign trail, an **L.A. Times** reporter named Dick Bergholz got under Nixon's skin, asking pointed, hostile questions whenever Nixon tried suggesting that Brown was soft on communism.[24]

Nixon knew that he was going to lose on Election Night. The Cuban Missile Crisis in mid- to late October had distracted the press and reversed some Nixon progress in the polls. (From Washington, President Kennedy had sent an Air Force jet to pick up Governor Brown to "consult" on the crisis, an outrageous ploy to boost the Democratic candidate that Nixon added to his bag of Kennedy grudges.) The morning after the election, Nixon looked bleary-eyed, exhausted, unshaven. His press secretary, Herb Klein, told him that the reporters wanted to speak to him. "Screw them," said Nixon. But then, watching TV in his hotel suite, he saw reporters pelting Klein with cries of "Where's Nixon?" and decided to face the mob of newsmen.[25]

"Good morning, gentlemen," he began. "Now that all the members of the press are delighted that I have lost, I'd like to make a statement of my own." He could see reporters "exchanging glances," he recalled, and yet—or so—he plunged on. His voice was not abject, but his rambling sarcasm would become permanently enshrined by Nixon's foes in the annals of what reporters were by now calling "Nixonland."* He famously ended, "Just think of how much you're going to be missing. You won't have Nixon to kick around anymore, because, gentlemen, this is my last press conference."[26]

*Wincing from Nixon's assaults—and resorting to his own hyperbole—Adlai Stevenson had coined the pejorative term in 1956: "A land of slander and scare; the land of sly innuendo, the poison pen, the anonymous phone call and hustling, pushing, shoving; the land of smash and grab and anything to win. This is Nixonland."[27]

There was stunned silence. Klein looked aghast. Nixon wrote in his memoirs, "I have never regretted what I said at 'the last press conference,'" but his gloom became positively Stygian when he returned home. Watching on TV in the den, Pat had been rooting for him, shouting "Bravo!" But she and the girls standing in the front hall were in tears when he arrived. "She said brokenly, 'Oh, Dick,'" recalled Julie. "He was so overcome with emotion that he brushed past and went outside to the backyard." Pat disappeared into her room, darkened by shutters, and wept. "Bewildered," Julie recalled, the girls were swept off to stay with friends for a few days. Years later, talking to Julie, Tricia wondered aloud if her parents had made too much of losing. Julie asked what she meant, since neither parent had ever talked to them about the 1962 campaign. Tricia answered, "There was a sadness, and the sadness went on for years."[28]

The punditry wrote Nixon off for good. "Exit growling," scoffed Mary McGrory of **The Washington Star**. ABC News screened a half-hour special, "The Political Obituary of Richard Nixon"—with special guest Alger Hiss. Concluded **Time** magazine: "Barring a miracle, Richard Nixon can never hope to be elected to any political office again."[29]

Three months later, Nixon's tax returns were audited again (they had been audited in 1961 and 1962 as well). The Justice Department opened a criminal investigation into the Hughes loan. Neither probe amounted to anything, but Nixon blamed

Bobby Kennedy, who was attorney general under his brother Jack, for the aggravation and cost. "I thought that kind of harassment is hard to forgive or forget, particularly when it's aimed at your family ... but on the other hand the Kennedys play hardball," Nixon told Jonathan Aitken many years later. "They had me down. They knew I wasn't out, and they wanted to put a couple of nails in the coffin. They almost succeeded."

On November 22, 1963, Nixon was pulling up in a cab to his new home, an apartment building in New York, when the doorman rushed up and said, "Oh, Mr. Nixon, have you heard, sir? It's just terrible. They've killed President Kennedy." The next night, Nixon wrote a gracious letter to Kennedy's widow, who responded with an empathy Nixon did not normally associate with the Kennedy name. Jackie's handwritten, nearly stream-of-consciousness note read:

> I know how you must feel—so long on the path—so closely missing the greatest prize—and now for you, all the question comes up again— and you must commit all you and your family's hopes and efforts again—Just one thing I would say to you—if it does not work out as you have hoped for so long—please be consoled by what you already have—your life and your family—[30]

Earlier that year, Nixon had told his family that he was thinking of practicing law in New York. "Tricia's and my immediate reaction was anywhere but

California," Julie recalled (at school, Tricia had felt taunted by the daughters of their father's right-wing Republican political foes). "Mother was enthusiastic about a move to New York, since it would be a clean break with politics." Nixon would be abandoning his political base to go on the turf of a Republican rival, former New York governor Nelson Rockefeller, but in some ways that appealed to Nixon's subversive sensibility—and in any case, New York was, as he put it, "the fast track." As it happened, the Nixons bought a stately Fifth Avenue apartment overlooking Central Park in a building adjoining Nelson Rockefeller's.[31]

Nixon joined a Wall Street law firm, Mudge, Stern, Baldwin & Todd—staid, well-established, but a notch below the top tier "white shoe" establishments. The firm was renamed Nixon, Mudge, Rose, Guthrie & Alexander. One of Nixon's new partners, Leonard Garment, vividly recalled Nixon's enormous, leonine head "and a sunny smile that lit up his face, smoothed out his jowls, and transformed him, momentarily, into the antithesis of Herblock's scowling, stubble-faced caricature." Their first conversation was interrupted by phone calls, and Garment could see that Nixon was enjoying showing off a little: "The phone, I started to learn, was his favorite instrument of persuasion. It separated him from the disturbing emanations of another person's physical presence, enabling him to concentrate his words without having to compose his eyes and coordinate his hands to harmonize with them."

Nixon adjusted his conversational style to his audience and his objective, Garment observed. The adjustments could be radical—from pol to intellectual to lawyer to regular-guy sports nut, with minute variations in between. The conversation was not linear or necessarily logical. "The rambling start-and-stop and the hem-and-hawing spiked with profanity"—much later to horrify and titillate readers of the Watergate tape transcripts—"were always part of Nixon's conversational technique," Garment later wrote. "They were his improvisational method of feeling his way through an uncertain conversation, probing, testing, targeting, gauging what the other fellow really had in mind (or what Nixon himself had in mind)."[32]

Nixon and Garment were an odd couple. Garment was a Jewish liberal who had held a Senate campaign fundraiser for Bobby Kennedy in his Brooklyn apartment. He had played clarinet in a jazz band, and his brother was a psychiatrist. But Nixon and Garment were both curious and restless. They enjoyed each other.

While Nixon was preparing for an important case, he and Garment flew to Florida for a speaking engagement. They were supposed to spend the night in a high-end real estate development near Miami. "Nixon took one look at the place, and his always operational political instincts and suspicions told him that in the morning the developers would expect to get pictures of him in the house in order to use his name and picture for publicity purposes,"

Garment recalled. Nixon told Garment to get back in the car, and then told the driver to go to the estate of Elmer Bobst, a pharmaceutical manufacturer and a Nixon friend and donor. The estate was forty miles away, and when they arrived there, after midnight, the gates were locked. A high wall surrounded the estate. Garment wondered, **What now?** Nixon told the driver to come back for them at 7:30 A.M. Then he turned and said, "Come on, Garment. It's over the wall we go." So the two New York lawyers, briefcases and all, clambered over the wall in their wing-tipped shoes. They found an unlocked pool house with twin beds and settled in, turning out the lights "like summer camp," Garment later wrote.

Nixon couldn't sleep. He began to talk about his dreams and ambitions. He said that he felt driven by his mother's pacifist idealism and the profound importance of foreign affairs. Accumulating money and joining exclusive clubs to play golf did not interest him, he insisted. He had lived "in the arena," and that's where he wanted to be, even if it meant shortening his life. He would do anything, make any sacrifice, anything, he said, "except see a shrink."[33]

Nixon told Garment that he would not "whore around" by lobbying Congress, but he was a profitable door-opener for the firm, lining up clients like Pepsi-Cola from his old friend Don Kendall, who had seen the 1959 Nixon-Khrushchev kitchen debate while he was peddling Pepsi franchises in Moscow. Nixon wanted to practice some real law, so Garment brought him in to argue a case called **Time,**

Inc. v. Hill. The Hill family was suing Time, Inc., for invasion of privacy for sensationalizing in the pages of **Life** magazine a terrible home invasion they had suffered. Nixon was only too happy to take the case—Time, Inc.'s First Amendment defense was "pious bullshit," said the old press basher.[34]

Nixon was to argue the case in the United States Supreme Court. He began by "virtually committing the trial record to memory," by poring over First Amendment tomes and legal opinions, and by scribbling "endlessly" on drafts of briefs. "His preparation was almost obsessive," recalled Garment. "He left nothing to chance."

As Garment bustled into the High Court on April 27, 1966, Nixon laid a hand on him. "Never rush into a public place," he said. "We strode slowly to our assigned seats, as if to the strains of 'Hail to the Chief,'" Garment related. By all accounts, Nixon delivered an excellent oral argument. His client lost the case, by a 5 to 4 vote of the justices. When Garment called Nixon to tell him the result, he asked a couple of legal questions then said, "I always knew I wouldn't be permitted to win a big appeal against the press. Now, Len, get this absolutely clear: I never want to hear about the Hill case again." He wanted no reminders of defeat and the distasteful press. Always look forward, he believed, even as he dwelled on the wounds of the past.[35]

Nixon was already plotting his comeback. On January 9, 1965, after a small family dinner party to celebrate his fifty-second birthday, he had repaired to his study, put his feet up on his favorite brown ottoman, and pulled out his yellow pad. He had been thinking of Winston Churchill during his "wilderness years" in the 1930s, written off as a national political leader. Nixon wrote a list: "New Year's Resolutions for 1965." The first item was, "Set great goals." He wrote a long list of items, most of them unremarkable ("Daily rest," "Brief vacations," "Golf or some other daily exercise," "Begin writing book"). Some, like golf and the book, fell by the wayside. One item is intriguing: "Knowledge of all weaknesses."[36]

Did he mean personal weaknesses? The record is devoid of any personal search. Nixon was quite honest about his political liabilities. He knew, he wrote in his memoirs, that he had the image of a loser, and not just a loser but a **sore** loser. "He was unemotional as a politician," recalled Stuart Spencer, a California political consultant who traveled with him in the mid-1960s. "Coldly analytical, including about himself. He knew his shortcomings. But he was paranoid," said Spencer, using the term too loosely, "and as time went on, he thought he was bulletproof, that he knew better, and he stopped listening to people."[37]

Alone with his thoughts that January night in 1965, Nixon turned off the light and stared into the fire. "For the first time in seven years," he recalled in his memoir, "I started not only to think seriously about running for the presidency again but to think about where I should begin."

He decided that "the best way to prepare for 1968 was to do well in 1966." So once more he took to the road on behalf of Republican candidates. The party was reeling after Barry Goldwater's debacle in 1964. At the GOP convention, when Pat Nixon automatically began to rise from her seat with the other party faithful to applaud Goldwater's famous line, "Extremism in the defense of liberty is no vice," Nixon had put his hand on her arm to restrain her.[38]* He wanted to bring the party back to the center. He was hawkish on Vietnam—he wanted more bombing, more troops—but moderate on social policy, accepting Big Government, albeit slimmed down.

John Sears, a young lawyer in the Nixon, Mudge firm, often traveled with Nixon, taking the aisle seat on the plane so that Nixon could avoid strangers and work on his yellow pad. "He loved his privacy and took enormous pains to hide things," recalled Sears. "He didn't like people getting into his head."[39] Nonetheless, he left Sears with some memorable impressions. "Politics would be a hell of a good business if it weren't for the goddamned people," Nixon grumbled to an aide after a long day campaigning for congressional candidates. Nixon was cheerfully cynical with Sears. As he was going up the steps of the Mormon Tabernacle in Salt Lake City, he turned and said, "Whatever I say in here, don't you believe

*Or so Nixon later recalled to his daughter Julie. The video of the speech shows him talking to Barry Goldwater Jr. during the speech.

a word of it." As if in unself-conscious homage to his "Tricky Dick" reputation, Nixon on the stump adopted a somewhat convoluted view of the truth. "John," he said one day in a holding room, "you've got to understand one thing. I can say things that if someone else said them, they would be lies, but when I say them, no one believes them, anyway."[40]

Nixon may have been broadly joking with Sears; it was sometimes hard to know. Nixon liked to crack lame jokes: "I got stoned in Caracas. I'll tell you one thing, it's a lot different from getting stoned at a Jaycees convention."[41] His speeches could be a little stagy and, to his critics at least, a bit mawkish. But he was sensitive and thoughtful, too. When a congressional candidate who had begged Nixon to stump for him got cold feet and embarrassingly told the crowd that Nixon was on the platform of his own volition, Nixon just played along. Why? Sears asked. "I was afraid his mother was there," Nixon answered, not cynical at all. "Mothers don't understand all that happens in politics. I didn't want to criticize him in front of his mother."[42]

On election night, November 6, 1966, Nixon was joyous when the returns showed a huge Republican rally—a net of forty-seven House seats, three Senate seats, and eight governorships. Nixon had backed winners in the vast majority of the thirty-five states and nearly eighty congressional districts where he had campaigned. At his headquarters at the Drake Hotel in Manhattan, he lay on the bed, "a phone in one hand and a highball in the other," Garment recalled. By then "reasonably well-oiled (it didn't take much to do the trick)," Nixon said " 'You're never going to make it in politics, Len. You just don't know how to lie."[43] Nixon may have just been jabbing at Garment for being a boy scout; on the other hand, Nixon did believe that deviousness was an important attribute for a successful politician.

"This is too great a night to go home!" Nixon exclaimed as they went into the night to hail a cab. "We won! We won!" he shouted to an aide. "Let's go to El Morocco and have some spaghetti!"[44] (An odd choice for such a famous nightclub. "It was a whim," Nixon later explained. "I had never been there.")[45]

On the day before Thanksgiving, Nixon's money men—investment bankers Peter Flanigan and Maurice Stans—told him that the time had come to make a move if he intended to run in 1968. He needed to head off Rockefeller and an up-and-coming conservative and heir to the Goldwater vote named Ronald Reagan, who had just unseated Pat Brown in California.[46]

The advice of the money men was not welcome at home. At Christmas time, on a bleak day, Pat, Julie, and Tricia huddled together on the beach at Key West, their legs wrapped in towels. "My mother said flatly, almost tonelessly, that she could not face another presidential race. She spoke of the 'humiliation' of defeat.' "[47]

In the beginning of 1967, Nixon declared a "moratorium" on politics. He did not travel any more around the country, making speeches, raising money, wooing Republicans, picking up IOUs. Rather, he disappeared into his study to read political philosophy: Plato, Aristotle, St. Thomas Aquinas, Kant, Pascal, Hegel, Rousseau, Hobbes, Locke, Montesquieu. He read Toynbee, Gibbon, and the memoirs of statesmen (all of Churchill's), biography, and some fiction, Tolstoy and Dostoevsky (but not, unfortunately, the tragedies of Sophocles, Euripides, or Shakespeare).[48]

Nixon's "holiday from politics" was a shrewd maneuver. Nixon was justifiably proud of his sense of political timing, and 1967 was a good time to be off the political stage, if not out of the country. Race, sex, and war were colliding in ways so extreme that America seemed on the brink of revolution. "Hey, hey, LBJ, how many kids did you kill today?" chanted the college kids. Some were desperate to hang on to their draft deferments in order to avoid the fate of their fifteen thousand or so peers—mostly non-college—thus far killed in Vietnam. Some were ducking military service; many were moved by sincere antiwar sentiment. Meanwhile, polls showed that a quarter of the country wanted to use nuclear weapons to win the war.[49] Rioting by blacks in Detroit was so severe that LBJ had to send in paratroopers from the 82nd Airborne Division to suppress sniper fire and looting. In the Long Island, N.Y., suburb of North Amityville, a mob of blacks yelled "Kill those cops" and threw Molotov cocktails at meetings intended to improve police-community relations.[50] Crime was soaring, and with it, middle-class fear. Closer to home, Tricia Nixon was afraid to go across town to the Port Authority Bus Terminal in New York, near seedy Times Square, to meet her boyfriend traveling from Princeton.[51] The Harris polling organization devised an "alienation index" to measure public anger: It was off the charts. And politicians tried to ride the wave without getting rolled. In California, Governor Ronald Reagan, a former actor, found an audience by inveighing against the "morality and decency gap."[52]

While other Republicans—principally, Michigan governor George Romney and, to a lesser extent, New York governor Nelson Rockefeller—uneasily exposed themselves to the roiled public, Nixon was offstage. He was preparing himself. He heard that the Kennedy family was creating an Institute of Politics at Harvard, as a kind of think tank for out-of-office Democrats. After brooding for a while about East Coast wealth and privilege, he became inspired and created his own, highly personalized tutorial. He had his in-house academic, a Columbia Business School professor named Martin Anderson, and a new assistant named Patrick Buchanan bring in deep thinkers, particularly conservative economists like Milton Friedman and Alan Greenspan. Nixon never stopped ridiculing academics—he liked to point out that when Frederick the Great wanted to punish a German province, he appointed a professor as governor. But he listened to scholars and thinkers in his fashion (usually by spouting his own theories and then querying, "Or am I wrong?")[53] He did not like long-winded or didactic seminars, preferring to work the telephone, which he could use without looking anyone in the eye and which he could abruptly hang up. Annelise Anderson, Martin's wife, recalled that her husband wrote a libertarian argument for ending the draft and creating an all-volunteer armed force. "Marty heard nothing from Nixon," she recalled, but the Andersons gathered from others that he was calling around, testing the idea, which in 1967 was very radical, opposed by the military and the foreign policy establishment. Finally, Nixon simply announced to Robert Semple of **The New York Times** that, if elected president, he would end the draft. (And he did.)[54]

Nixon liked to bluster that he had no interest in domestic or "local" policy issues. On the day he lost the California governor's race in 1962, he gloomily told speechwriter Stephen Hess, "At least I'll never have to talk about crap like dope addiction again." His domestic policy platform for the 1968 election would be a collection of bland bromides designed mostly not to offend interest groups. Nixon was hardly an expert on the ins and outs of social policy. Indeed, walking out of their first meeting in November 1968, his chief domestic adviser Daniel Patrick Moynihan would say to a friend, "He's ignorant! He doesn't know anything!"[55] But, as Moynihan would soon learn to his delight, Nixon was ready to learn. The very fact that Nixon would hire a liberal intellectual Harvard professor as his

chief domestic policy adviser suggests Nixon's openness to new and transformative ideas. As he read
philosophy and the biographies of statesmen in the
winter of 1967, he was preparing intellectually for
the sort of bold strokes that would confound his
enemies as president.

Nixon's main interest remained foreign policy,
partly because presidents can have more impact in
an arena where they are less often checked and
second-guessed by the legislative branch. In mid-
1960s America, foreign policy was still the main
event for an aspiring chief executive. LBJ was flailing in anguish as the Vietnam War undermined his
Great Society. Nixon was already thinking beyond
Vietnam, scribbling into the night on his yellow
notepads, searching for a model that would preserve
American preeminence in a world of enemies and
rivals large and small.

That spring of 1967, he traveled abroad, opening
doors for law clients, but making sure to renew his
acquaintances from his journeys as vice president and
to meet new and upcoming world leaders. In Israel,
he was snubbed by the leadership in the socialist government, but the far-sighted chief of the Israeli Defense Forces, Yitzhak Rabin, took him on a helicopter
ride to show him Israel's strategic vulnerability—the
Golan Heights, the short distance of ten miles from
the West Bank to the sea.[56] Nixon could see with his
own eyes the challenge of peace-keeping in a world
where ancient enemies lived on top of each other.

In Paris, he met with the French president, Charles

de Gaulle. It was their second visit. In 1963, still tending the wounds of the "Last Press Conference," Nixon had been served a simple lunch by "Le Grand Charles" in the garden of the Élysée Palace. The towering de Gaulle had stood to offer a toast to Nixon: that he had suffered defeats—like de Gaulle, like France, like others born to greatness—but that he would be back to serve his nation in some "very high capacity."[57]

Nixon was fascinated by de Gaulle and his mystique of the leader. In Nixon's personal library, one of the most heavily underlined books was a 1932 volume of de Gaulle's lectures, **The Edge of the Sword**. The passages underscored by Nixon are specifications on a blueprint to the New Nixon, not the periodic political "New Nixon" who popped up at campaign time to try to get along with the press, but someone deeper, more mystical—Nixon the Statesman, striving for peace on earth:

Powerful personalities . . . capable of standing up to the tests of great events frequently lack that surface charm which wins popularity in ordinary life. Strong characters are, as a rule, rough, disagreeable, and aggressive.

Great men of action have always been of the meditative type. They have without exception possessed to a very high degree the faculty of withdrawing into themselves.

And also, some self-identification:

There is nothing harder for the human spirit to bear than being cold-shouldered.[58]

In de Gaulle, Nixon saw a model of **l'homme serieux,** to be admired and, if possible, emulated—reserved, aloof, dignified; grand and all-powerful. De Gaulle's impact on Nixon is hard to overemphasize. Nixon placed Teddy Roosevelt ("in the arena") and Woodrow Wilson (the thinker who acts) in his pantheon, but first among equals was de Gaulle.

In West Germany on his European swing in the summer of 1967, Nixon also met with Konrad Adenauer, the great Cold War statesman known as "Der Alte," "the Old One." "Der Alte" had some interesting geostrategic advice for Nixon: Tilt American policy toward Red China to counterbalance the growing Soviet threat. Four years earlier, de Gaulle had advised much the same course, urging Nixon to open China to the West.[59]

Nixon was listening. To establish his bona fides with the intellectual elite, he wrote an article for the journal **Foreign Affairs,** published by the Council on Foreign Relations, an East Coast Establishment bastion, called "Asia After Vietnam." ("You know, he really **is** interesting," the editor of **Foreign Affairs** told Nixon aide Ray Price).[60] The key sentence began, "In the long run, it means pulling China back into the world community. . . ."[61] But the import of that sentence was lost at the time, missed by reporters more focused on Nixon's immediate political ambitions.

Nixon's audition with "the Powers That Be" of the business and political worlds came at Bohemian Grove, the summer camp of the establishment, in July 1967. There is a telling photo hanging over the bar in one of the camps, Hillbillies, of Nixon with Dwight Eisenhower at lunch in the Grove. A group hovers fawningly around Ike, while Nixon sits alone, as usual, across the table.[62] But Nixon was no longer the outsider, the supplicant. He had been asked to give the Lakeside Speech. "If I were to choose the speech that gave me the most pleasure and satisfaction of my political career, it would be my Lakeside Speech at the Bohemian Grove in July 1967," Nixon recalled. The speech was off the record and so got no media attention. "But it was an unparalleled opportunity to reach some of the most important and significant men, not just from California but from across the country."[63]

Typically, Nixon skipped all the Hi Jinks and Low Jinks and his cabin at Cave Man and holed up for a week in a cheap motel outside the Grove, eating Kentucky Fried Chicken out of a paper bucket and laboring over his speech. Nixon began with a usual jape: "It's much more pleasant to get stoned in Bohemia than in Caracas." But he quickly launched into a sophisticated tour of the world that brought the tycoons and senators and governors roaring to their feet.[64]* Reading the speech many years later, it is difficult to understand what moved them so. Nixon's tour of the horizon is intelligent and carefully considered but hardly inspiring. But his **manner**—confident and effortlessly knowledgeable—was inspiring. Nixon offered a hard-headed, realistic view of the many challenges America faced around the world and called for patience, strength, and wisdom—suggesting, neither too baldly nor too subtly, that he was the one who embodied these qualities. His words, nonetheless, came as a soothing tonic to a gathering of power brokers who saw their power threatened by the convulsions of the 1960s. There, amid the cavorting bankers and lawyers, Nixon emerged as de Gaulle's **homme serieux**. The Orthogonian had won the Franklin endorsement.

*Nixon's "world tour" speech became his staple, a sure winner, his equivalent of Ronald Reagan's "A Time for Choosing" oration, which came to be known as "the Speech." Nixon would stand up and, speaking without notes, take the audience on a tour of the world—analyzing all the hot spots and trouble spots, dissecting world leaders, weighing threats and opportunities. Sometimes, Nixon would order the podium removed to accentuate how good he was on his feet. He got the idea of using a "naked mike" from the entertainer Art Linkletter right after his Bohemian Grove speech in 1967.[65]

Bowling alone.
**Courtesy of the Richard Nixon Presidential
Library and Museum**

CHAPTER 9

The New Nixon

At Chapin, an exclusive girls school on the Upper East Side of Manhattan, Nixon was regarded as a popular father, according to Ruth Proffitt, a long-time Chapin teacher.[1] Unlike some of the distracted Wall Street lawyer-fathers, Nixon was attentive and upbeat with his daughters' friends when they came over, playing the piano and asking them about their lives. "Aunt" Rose Woods would remember coming in with Nixon from work on her frequent visits and watching as Nixon immediately turned on all the lights in the living room and his study, lit a fire, and put a record on the stereo. "Within minutes the room would be warm and bright and filled with happy voices and the music from **Carousel** or **The King and I** or Strauss waltzes," Julie Nixon recounted in her memoir of her mother.

The Nixons were loving parents. "Mommy is pretty, sweet, unselfish, kind, understanding and her same self—if not better than ever—which is near perfect," Julie wrote in her diary after the Nixons moved to New York in 1963. "Daddy is nice and busy and seems happy. He tries hard to have a fun 'family life.' "[2] It is possible to detect a note of skepticism in her teenage observation—"he tries hard. . . ."—but there can be no doubt that Nixon adored his daughters and they loved him back, fiercely.

Less than two weeks after the Nixons had moved into their apartment at 810 Fifth Avenue in the summer of 1963, Pat looked across the dinner table and said to her husband, "I hope we never move again."[3] She probably knew that her hope was forlorn. In the summer of 1967, Julie observed, "Mother was unmistakably troubled as she faced the prospect of another political race."

On December 22, 1967, after the Nixons' annual Christmas party, Nixon repaired to his study, pulled out a yellow pad ("his closest friend," quipped Leonard Garment), and started writing down a list of all the reasons why he shouldn't run for president. "Losing again could be an emotional disaster for my family," he wrote. He weighed the burden of ambition and duty. "I startled myself," he later recalled, by writing at the bottom of the page: "I don't give a damn."[4] That Christmas, Julie wrote in her diary that her father had told Tricia and her "that he had decided—almost definitely—not to run. He was depressed. I have never known him to be depressed before—not even after 1962." At Christmas dinner, Pat said she couldn't bring herself to urge her husband to run, but that she was "resigned to helping out," as Nixon put it in his memoirs. Julie, however, was insistent: "You have to do it for the country."

And Tricia spoke the final truth: "If you don't run Daddy, you will have nothing to live for."

When Nixon scrawled, "I don't give a damn," he was lying to himself, as he certainly knew. Certainly he worried about his family's emotions, and with equal certainty he cared intensely about fulfilling his political destiny. Among his favorite readings was a book called **The Will to Live,** by Arnold Hutschnecker, the physician who had helped Nixon with his psychosomatic illnesses in the 1950s. Borrowing from Goethe, Hutschnecker wrote that when "men of destiny" left the public stage, they lost their will to live and soon died. Nixon feared that the same would happen to him. But he also worried that Pat's willingness to play the rescuer—to urge him to run, whatever his or her doubts—was waning.[5]

As he often did in trying times, he headed alone to Florida to stay with his friend Bebe Rebozo at Key Biscayne. Under the warming sun, Rebozo and Nixon sat in silence. ("I already knew what he thought," Nixon recalled.) As Nixon moodily walked on the beach, he was joined—providentially, if improbably—by the Reverend Billy Graham, who was in Florida recovering from a lung infection.

Graham, with his affinity for political power, was a familiar face. Nixon had taken his mother to Graham's revival meetings in Los Angeles and talked politics with him from time to time. When Nixon's beloved mother had died that September, Graham presided at the service. Nixon had been in a state of near-collapse. He was furious at the newsmen who filled the pews, forcing many of Hannah's friends from Whittier to stand outside the church. After the service, Nixon had laid his head on Graham's shoulder and sobbed.

Back at Rebozo's house, Graham read from St. Paul's Epistle to the Romans. Nixon needed to look to faith for strength, said Graham. The world was full of woe. It needed a true leader, and Nixon was being called. In Nixon's retelling of his decision to run, the walk and talk with Graham is presented as quasi-divine intercession. Family lore culminates with a dinner on January 15, 1968, when Fina, the housekeeper, emerges from the kitchen to tell her boss that he was destined to be president: "You are the man to lead the country! This was determined before you were born!"[6]

It all sounds a little romanticized. Nixon's aides never believed his periodic vows to get out of politics for the sake of the family. When Nixon had said he wasn't going to run again in 1956, Jim Bassett, his sometime press aide, bet ten dollars that he would and then upped the stake to thirty when Nixon repeated his promise.[7] At the very least, as he solemnly took counsel or comfort from his daughters and Bebe, Billy, and Fina around the New Year, he seems to have been trying to create a bandwagon effect to get Pat on board. Nixon had been running for president for years, if not decades. With Dr. Hutschnecker in mind, he privately told others that if he kept practicing law he would soon be dead— mentally dead even sooner.[8]

To cock an eyebrow over his call to the mountaintop is not to denigrate his motives, however. He really did want to fulfill his mother's (and grandmother
Milhous's) dream that he go forth and serve in some
good and great way and "leave footprints in the
sands of time." Nixon did regard himself as a man of
destiny, and so did his family, Pat's reluctance notwithstanding. He would not give in to the bitterness
of his "last press conference" blurt in 1962. Whatever else he was, he was not a quitter. His mother's
last instruction, as she had lain dying just a few
months earlier, were words more persuasive than
any sermon Billy Graham could summon: "Richard, don't **you** give up. Don't let anybody tell you
you are through."[9]

Despite his deep feelings, churning and thinly
disguised, Nixon seemed at times to deny that he
had an inner self. "He was never into self-analysis,"
recalled a longtime friend and adviser, Ken Khachigian. "[To him] it was weak and phony. To obsess
over your psyche, that never occurred to him."[10]
Emotion suggested vulnerability, and vulnerability
was a sign of weakness, and weakness, for Richard
Nixon, was intolerable. "There was nothing he
feared more than to be thought weak," wrote Henry
Kissinger in his memoirs.[11]

Nixon wanted to be around strong men, never
weak ones, and the composition of his political inner
circle reflected his idealizations and dislikes. "Eggheads" were suspect. Though a bookworm himself,

Nixon protested that he preferred the company of non-intellectuals. "God I hate spending time with intellectuals. There's something feminine about them. I'd rather talk to an athlete," he once said.[12]

It was sometimes hard to tell when Nixon was being disingenuous or exaggerating for effect—he enjoyed provoking and playing devil's advocate ("You agree, don't you?" he would demand, and if the answer was yes, then maybe his interlocutor was just a sap or a toady).[13] Even so, it is not hard to understand why, as he pondered running for the presidency in 1968, Nixon was drawn to the persona, if not necessarily the actual person, of one of his new law partners, John Mitchell.

Mitchell was a brilliant lawyer with workingclass roots (check that box!) who had turned down Harvard Law to go to Fordham (check, check!). He was an ice hockey star and, in World War II, a highly decorated commander of a PT boat squadron that was reputed to have included Jack Kennedy (check, check, check!). He was a bond lawyer, which doesn't sound very political, but in fact it was: He was extremely well connected to leaders in state and local governments around the country who needed to raise capital. His manner was offhand, taciturn, but tough-guy. He turned a limp from a sore hip into a swagger. He would fiddle with his pipe (disguising a hand tremor) while arguments raged around him, then gruffly deliver the last word.[14]

Nixon put Mitchell on a pedestal. "I've found my heavyweight!" he said to Bill Safire, who was doing political PR work for Nixon before he formally decided to run.[15] Nixon knew that he had erred by trying to run his own campaign in 1960. Now he approached Len Garment about sounding out Mitchell for the job. Following Mitchell into the men's room at the University Club after a bibulous partners' dinner at Christmastime 1967, Garment asked, "Say, John, how would you feel about managing a presidential campaign?" Pipe in mouth, Mitchell leaned back and said, "Are you out of your fucking mind, Garment?" which Garment understood was Mitchell's way of saying yes.[16]

But John Mitchell was not quite what he appeared to be. His biographer, James Rosen, was unable to find any records of naval decorations or that he had ever been wounded in action (supposedly the source of the limp) or that he had even met JFK, much less commanded him. Nor was Mitchell as modest as his pose; he joked, crudely, "Nixon couldn't piss straight in the shower if I wasn't there to hold him."[17] He had a troubled second marriage to the alcoholic, out-of-control Martha Mitchell, and the more troubled she became, the more he drank, too. His phlegmatic style, doused with alcohol, would become a mask over anguish.

Nixon liked to be surrounded by attractive, vigorous young men. His "body man," the traveling aide who looked after his immediate needs, fended off unwanted strangers, and charmed the people who needed to be charmed, was Dwight Chapin. A young University of Southern California grad, Chapin had

the social graces of an Ivy Leaguer without the attitude. Chapin was drawn to Nixon by his worldiness
and ambition, and he was willing, by and large, to
overlook Nixon's moods and quirks. Nixon, even
more than most, did not like to have his privacy in-
truded on or his routines disrupted. Scheduling snafus could make him angry enough to lash out. He
once pushed Chapin into a wall, bruising his arm.
(Nixon apologized. Such physical outbursts were
rare. "He was mostly calm, he'd just say, 'Chapin,
you don't understand,'" Chapin recalled years
later.)[18]

Chapin was a handsome, warm extension of the
handsome, chilly H. R. "Bob" Haldeman, the campaign's chief of staff. Haldeman was Nixon's self-
styled "S.O.B."—the zero-defects enforcer of order
and timeliness in the Nixon campaign, the man
who, as time went on, would spend more waking
hours with Nixon than anyone else. Smart, tough,
capable of humor and even gentleness, Haldeman
kept his sweet side under cover. He had a certain
scowl—tight lips, furrowed brow, steely eyes—that
staffers grew to fear. The campaign "was so warm
and friendly and cozy," recalled his rival for Nixon's
attentions, Rose Mary Woods, "until Bob Haldeman arrived."[19]

Haldeman, a Big Man on Campus at UCLA and
an advertising man by trade, had stood outside the
El Capitan Theater to volunteer to work for Nixon
on the night of the Checkers Speech in 1952. By
1956, he was a regular advance man for Nixon cam-

paigns. It was said that Haldeman was drawn to Nixon by his unmasking of Alger Hiss—Haldeman's family, prominent in Los Angeles business and social circles, was hard-line anticommunist—but Nixon's real appeal to Haldeman was more ineffable. "He was to me that rare species, the uncommon man," Haldeman told Jonathan Aitken. Haldeman had a knack for handling troublesome geniuses, or so he believed. As the manager of J. Walter Thompson's Los Angeles office, Haldeman had been in charge of "the terror clients" such as Walt Disney. "By comparison, Nixon wasn't that bad!" laughed Haldeman.[20]

Haldeman's best advance man was his friend, another UCLA grad named John Ehrlichman. Quick, mordantly funny, Ehrlichman liked to tell stories of campus politics tomfoolery at UCLA after the war. He had worked for Nixon as a mole in the Rockefeller campaign in 1960 (he got a job as driver), and he was a resourceful and clever infighter. He was also unusually direct with Nixon. A teetotaling Christian Scientist (just like Haldeman), Ehrlichman had seen the candidate "pie-eyed" in a hotel suite at the 1964 GOP convention, and he extracted a promise from Nixon that he would "lay off the booze." ("The Christian Scientists believed one drink made you 'pie-eyed,'" observed a Nixon aide.)[21] As the Nixon campaign geared up in the winter of 1968, Haldeman and Ehrlichman brought discipline and a touch of youthful arrogance to the operation. "The approved advance man's style around Nixon was supercool," Ehrlichman recalled.[22] The New Nixon—colder, but also cooler—was born.

Nixon launched his campaign for the presidency at the last possible moment, on February 2, 1968, in a sleet storm in New Hampshire, where the nation's first primary was a little over a month away. "Gentlemen, this is **not** my last press conference," he drolly began (his joke writing had improved with the addition of Paul Keyes, a former Jack Paar comedy writer and producer of the TV show **Laugh-In**).[23] The media's darling in the earlier going, Governor George Romney of Michigan, was fading out. He had gotten his words tangled up about Vietnam, saying truthfully, but disastrously, that he had been "brainwashed" by the U.S. military briefers in Saigon. Nixon, meanwhile, was trying on his de Gaulle robes. He instructed that he would not be kissing babies or slapping backs in this campaign; the "rock 'em, sock 'em" campaign style would be replaced by something more dignified.*

Nixon avoided saying much of anything about race riots or the sexual revolution, and he was studiously vague on Vietnam. As vice president, he had

---

*Murray Chotiner had stayed in the background. In 1956, he had been called before a U.S. Senate Committee and investigated for influence peddling. A member of the committee was John F. Kennedy; the chief investigator was Robert Kennedy. Nixon could not afford to use Chotiner as a main adviser, but he later found a way to bring him back as a behind-the-scenes counselor, in a reduced role.[24]

been hawkish, but his interventionist rhetoric became more generalized over time. Privately, he told aides that he thought the war could not be won, but he wanted to keep some leverage against the enemy.[25] With an eye on both the North Vietnamese and the divided American voters, he advocated a middle-of-the-road approach.[26] "End the war and win the peace in the Pacific" was his motto, and because no one was quite sure what that meant, word began to circulate that Nixon had a "secret plan."

With some trepidation, Tricia's boyfriend, Edward Cox, asked Nixon about the "secret plan" at the Nixons' apartment one night in February 1968. There was, in fact, no "secret plan" to end the war, but Nixon was already thinking of a bold approach to pressure the North Vietnamese to make a deal. He told Cox, "I'm going to Moscow and Peking." No American president had ever been to either place, and Peking, or Beijing as it is called today, had been closed to all Americans since the Communist revolution in 1949. At the time, Cox did not understand the significance of what Nixon was saying; he was just trying to make conversation. The press and the experts also missed the significance of Nixon's opaque wording ("win the peace **in the Pacific**"), just as they had missed his signal about Red China in his article in the October issue of **Foreign Affairs**. That was fine with Nixon. He was a believer in surprise—in "audacity."[27]

Still, the New Nixon was just as shy and awkward as the old Nixon. He invited Walter Cronkite, the

CBS anchorman, up to his room and offered him a drink while declining one himself. Realizing that refusing a drink seemed a little prissy, he said to Cronkite, "I tell you what, I'll have sherry." But that didn't quite sound like one of the boys either, so he blurted, "In fact, I'll have a **double** sherry."[28] Down in the hotel bar, reporters were making up a ditty about the "Newest Nixon."

But Nixon's **homme serieux** strategy was working. Theodore White, a barometer of the conventional wisdom, was coming around. "I myself in 1960 had found him banal, his common utterances too frequently a mixture of pathetic self-pity and petulant distemper," White would write in **Making of the President, 1968,** but "to my surprise, [I] found in myself a slow and ever-growing respect for him."[29] "Powerful political columnists such as Scotty Reston of **The New York Times** and Joe Kraft of **The Washington Post** hailed the 'new' Nixon who seemed so reasonable and calm, a welcome relief from the tumultuous LBJ," recalled Haldeman.[30] Even the Georgetown set, also sick of LBJ, let up for a brief time on their favorite object of ridicule. Stewart Alsop made the case for Nixon in the pages of **Newsweek**.[31]

Nixon won big in New Hampshire, with about 80 percent of the vote. But less than a week later, Robert F. Kennedy jumped into the race for the Democratic nomination, and two weeks after that, Johnson announced that he would not run again for president. Nixon was watching the TV in a hotel in

Portland, Oregon, when RFK, surrounded by members of the Kennedy clan, announced his candidacy. When it was over, John Ehrlichman recalled, Nixon sat and stared at the black TV set "for a long time, saying nothing." Finally, like some Greek oracle, he shook his head and spoke. "We've just seen some terrible forces unleashed. Something bad is going to come of this."[32]

Right away, the Kennedy presence was felt. Pat Buchanan, one of Nixon's speechwriters, recalled a gloom settling over the Nixon campaign. Dick Tuck, the Kennedy prankster, was already bribing the band at Nixon rallies to play "Mack the Knife," so that the smiling, waving Nixon would be greeted to the strains of, ". . . and the shark has pearly teeth." He also hired pregnant women to carry signs saying, "Nixon's the One." John Mitchell was outraged. "We'll get even, we'll get even," he muttered.[33] Haldeman wanted to know whether the Nixon campaign could hire someone as creative at "black advance" as Dick Tuck.[34]

The year 1968 veered toward madness. On April 4, four days after LBJ announced that he would not seek reelection, Martin Luther King Jr. was assassinated in Memphis. Rioting broke out in dozens of cities. Nixon was in a personal and political quandary. Alabama Governor George Wallace was entering the race as a magnet for angry poor whites. "Send 'em a message!" was his line. With an eye on Wallace coming up on the right, Nixon had to walk a fine line between appealing to the populist vote in the South and antagonizing northern moderates. He wanted to reach out to Mrs. King, but he didn't want to "grandstand," as he put it. (William Safire, a member of the more liberal wing of the Nixon camp, groaned when he recalled that Nixon's refusal to "grandstand" in 1960—by publicly sympathizing with Coretta King when her husband had been jailed—had cost him the black vote).[35]

Quietly, Nixon traveled to Atlanta to console Mrs. King. From Key Biscayne, where he had flown afterward, he asked his campaign staff, "How's it playing?" He was told that his visit to the King family wasn't playing at all—because it had been kept secret. "Damn it!" Nixon exclaimed, "I'm going to have to go down there to that funeral."

Back in Atlanta on April 9, Nixon jammed into the Ebenezer Baptist Church basement after King's service with other high-profile mourners. One of them was the pro basketball star Wilt Chamberlain. "Are you going to march with us?" Chamberlain asked. Nixon's personal assistant, Dwight Chapin, was watching the unlikely scene unfold. He recalled: "I see this look on Mr. Nixon's face like, 'March?'" But off they went, along with Bill Cosby, Jackie Robinson, Marlon Brando, and Bobby Kennedy, beginning the solemn three-and-a-half mile procession to King's resting place. Nixon made it a block or two and said to Chamberlain, "Got to go to the airport." Chamberlain asked, "Can I get a ride?" The 7′1″ basketball star and the 5′11″ presidential candidate piled into a car ordered by a scrambling advance man.[36]

Less than six years after he had been declared a political has-been, Nixon seemed on course to cruise to the GOP nomination for president. Romney had dropped out, and Nelson Rockefeller was dithering. But Ronald Reagan was gaining. The summer before, Nixon had defeated Reagan in the Bohemian Grove primary—the governor, who had also attended the Grove and warily met with Nixon, was dismissed by the well-heeled campers as a "lightweight." But Reagan's denunciations of hippies and black radicals played well in the South, and Nixon feared a Rockefeller-Reagan "Stop Nixon" pincer movement.

In the South, former Governor, now Senator Strom Thurmond of South Carolina was pulling together all of the Republican state party chairmen to cast their delegates' votes as a block at the GOP convention in early August. They summoned Nixon, along with Reagan and Rockefeller, to audition on May 31.

Returning to Atlanta just six weeks after King's funeral, Nixon was once more trying to navigate the treacherous politics of race. The Supreme Court had just struck down the attempts of Southern governors to get around the 1954 school desegregation ruling, **Brown v. Board of Education**, by instituting "freedom of choice" plans that would, in effect, keep blacks and whites separate. Nixon knew there was no going back on **Brown v. Board of Education**, and, faithful to his Quaker roots, he opposed segregation. Instead, he promised to put "strict constructionists" on the Supreme Court who would not **force** integration by, for instance, busing school children.

Nixon needed Thurmond's endorsement. He had been courting "States' Rights Strom" for years; when the family dog of Thurmond's closest adviser, Harry Dent, was killed by a car, Nixon sent the Dent family a new dog.[37] Now, as he rode in a limousine with Thurmond on the way to meet with all the GOP state chairmen, Nixon was sweating profusely, recalled Bob Ellsworth, a longtime Nixon adviser who was riding along in the jump seat. Nixon wanted to ask Thurmond for his formal blessing, but he was afraid that Thurmond would demand in return that Nixon pledge to support "freedom of choice"—in practice, segregation. "I can't do that," Nixon had said to Ellsworth. "I can't do that and win the presidency."

Nixon asked ("with a lot of nice circumlocutions") for Thurmond's endorsement. In his barely comprehensible low country drawl, Thurmond responded, "You'd be a great president, and I'd like to endorse you." He paused and grew silent. Nixon sweated some more. Finally, Nixon croaked, "What would you like me to do?" Thurmond leaned forward and said, "I want you to promise me you'll never let up on the communists." Like a man who had been offered a pardon instead of a hanging, Nixon instantly answered, "It's a deal." He looked "just drained," Ellsworth recalled. Thurmond was cagey, and he understood Nixon's predicament on civil rights. He thought he'd have a better chance to defeat the Democrats than Rockefeller (too privileged) or Reagan (still too green).[38]

The night of the California primary, June 4, Nixon went to bed in New York before the results were in from the West Coast. He was awakened by a voice calling his name over and over. "Mr. Nixon, excuse me, Mr. Nixon." Nixon opened his eyes and saw Julie's fiancé, David Eisenhower. "What is it?" he asked. "They shot Kennedy," Eisenhower said. A mad gunman had mortally wounded RFK after his victory speech at the Ambassador Hotel in Los Angeles, where Nixon had spent election night in 1960. Nixon attended the funeral at St. Patrick's Cathedral in New York, a communion of the shaken in a season of tumult.

Young Eisenhower and Julie had fallen in love in college—she was at Smith, he was at Amherst—bonded in part by their strange celebrity and out-of-fashion politics. In July, Nixon went to Walter Reed Hospital to ask for the campaign endorsement of David's grandfather, President Eisenhower, who was slowly dying of a heart condition. For once, Ike did not equivocate about Nixon. "Dick, I don't want there to be any more question about this," he said. "You're my choice, period."[39]

At the GOP convention in Miami in August, Nixon gave a sentimental but moving acceptance speech, recalling himself as a child who "hears a train go by at night and he dreams of a faraway place where he'd like to go. It seems like an impossible dream."[40]

At 1:30 A.M., Nixon summoned one of his speechwriters, Bill Safire, to his penthouse suite in the Hilton Plaza. The candidate, who had slept only two hours the night before, couldn't sleep and wanted to talk about the speech. Safire found him slouched in an easy chair, tinkling the ice in a light scotch. "Professionally," Nixon asked, "what did you think of the speech?"

The train whistle was nicely evocative, said Safire. But another line, "Let's win it for Ike," sounded too much like a line out of the old Ronald Reagan movie **Knute Rockne, All-American:** "Let's win one for the Gipper."

"Yeah, I know, you intellectuals don't go for that sort of thing. The press won't like it at all, they'll climb the wall. None of them could write a speech like that, one that reaches the folks, and they'll hate me for it. . . ." Holding his glass by the rim, he took slow sips.

"They call me 'intelligent, cool, with no sincerity'— and then it kills them when I show I know how people feel. I'd like to see a Rocky or Romney or [New York Mayor John] Lindsay do a moving thing like that 'impossible dream' part, where I change my voice." He frowned, thinking of somebody else who could. "Reagan's an actor, but I'd like to see him do that."[41]

He chatted on, dozed off, woke up, ordered some ham and cheese sandwiches from the Secret Service man, and kept peppering questions as Safire eased toward the door. Nixon punched his speechwriter in the arm. "They won't like my speech, will they, **The New York Times** and those boys. . . ." He shrugged, pretending not to care. "Fuck 'em."

Pat had long since retired. For most of the night, Pat and the girls had waited in a trailer outside the convention hall for their grand family entrance at the final balloon drop. Tricia grumpily asked, "Whose brilliant idea was it to sit out in a trailer all night?" Pat looked at her and replied evenly, "How about your father's?"[42]

Ed Cox, soon to be Tricia's fiancé, was doing his best to fit in with the Nixon family. He found his prospective father-in-law to be formal but sometimes surprisingly approachable. In the hotel suite, he watched TV with Nixon as Nixon's new running mate, Maryland Governor Spiro Agnew, fielded questions at a press conference. "What do you think?" Nixon asked his daughter's boyfriend. Taken aback, Cox stammered, "Well, he's got presence." A few minutes later, when Nixon met reporters, the Republican nominee said of Agnew, "He's got presence."[43]

The choice of Agnew—a first-term governor who was not well known—surprised many, including those close to Nixon. But Nixon was intrigued by Agnew, who had been a strong Rockefeller supporter. Nixon took particular delight in stealing away Rocky's talent—he was already eyeing Rockefeller's chief foreign policy adviser, Henry Kissinger. He saw Agnew, the son of a Greek immigrant, as an anti-elitist subversive and a populist. Presciently, he understood Agnew's potential appeal to the silent voters turned off by the noisy liberal media. From a border state, Agnew was regarded as a moderate on race, but he was not afraid to tell off black militants. Campaign manager John Mitchell knew the law and order issue would play well. "Mitchell particularly liked Agnew's Baltimore speech chewing out black leaders," Bob Ellsworth recalled.[44]

In 1967, Nixon read a memo written by an intellectually ambitious young congressional aide named Kevin Phillips with the title "Middle America and the Emerging Republican Majority." Dubbed "the Computer" by Len Garment, the pale and dour Phillips was hired by the campaign as the "ethnic specialist" to provide charts and demographic statistics, but his secret boiled down to, as he bluntly put it, "knowing who hates who."[45] The enmities were not hard to find in a year when John Wayne's **Green Berets** was showing across town from **Wild in the Streets** (a fantasy of a president, elected by newly enfranchised fourteen-year-olds, who forces everyone over thirty-five to take LSD). Nixon did not have to be taught: He had practiced the politics of resentment all the way back to his pursuit of Alger Hiss. But Nixon was not overtly playing to anger in 1968; rather, he was appealing to voters who were tired of all the yelling. He was appealing to what he called the "silent center, the millions of people in the middle of the political spectrum who do not demonstrate, who do not picket or protest loudly."[46]

The loud angry voice of the 1968 campaign belonged to Governor Wallace. He was running as an independent, attacking both the Democratic nominee, Vice President Hubert Humphrey, and Nixon as tools of the establishment: "There's not a dime's worth of difference between them!" With a gleeful snarl, Wallace played the defender of the ordinary folks, railing against the "**swaydo**-intellectual morons tellin' 'em how to live their lives."[47] Wallace was so brazen in his attacks on "them"—the government, the media, the universities, the blacks, the students—that he left ample space for Nixon to be the sober, responsible leader who only subtly, indirectly played to people's pervasive fear of disorder. Nixon could see that with all the fist-shaking and shouting (and bombing and burning) most voters wanted someone who was calm, grown-up, seasoned. He was all those things, more or less, but he needed a good packager who could smooth down the rough spots.

On January 9, 1968, Nixon was a guest on the **Mike Douglas Show**, an afternoon TV talk show that reached a large audience of housewives. The candidate was introduced to the show's producer, an unusually confident young man named Roger Ailes. "Mr. Nixon, you need a media adviser," said Ailes. "What's a media adviser?" asked Nixon. "I am," said Ailes.[48]

In **The Selling of the President,** as Joe McGinniss entitled his 1969 bestseller, Ailes is portrayed as a Svengali figure.[49] Mythmaking aside, Ailes was smart enough to see that Nixon—sweaty and earnest on the stump—was not a natural at TV, and Nixon was smart enough to hire Ailes, almost immediately, to fix the problem. Ailes developed a series of televised citizen forums called "Man in the Arena," after Nixon's hero Teddy Roosevelt. They were highly controlled, right down to the makeup (more white on Nixon's upper eyelid, to lessen the glower), and there was nothing spontaneous about the hand-picked audience (no psychiatrists, Nixon decreed). The press was kept in a separate room.[50]

The Nixon campaign staff loved the productions; Pat Nixon, less so. McGinniss described an encounter between the media adviser and the candidate's wife on the elevator:

"Hello, Mrs. Nixon," Roger Ailes said.
　　She nodded. She had known him for months.
　　"How did you like the show?" he asked.
　　She nodded very slowly; her mouth was drawn in a thin, straight line.[51]

CHAPTER 10

October Surprise

"Richard Nixon used to disappear in the middle of the night during campaign trips," Haldeman would later recall. "I would call for him at his hotel room in a small Midwestern city in the morning and find that he was missing. Some time in the early dawn he had gotten out of bed and slipped away, with a nervous Secret Service man tailing him. We'd search all over town until we found the candidate looking haggard and wan in a flea-bitten coffee shop." One wonders what the Republican candidate for president was thinking on these occasional pre-dawn walkabouts.[1]

Haldeman wanted to protect Nixon: from the stresses of campaigning, from his enemies, from his own family—or so it seemed to them—and from Nixon himself. Haldeman, who would later describe Nixon as the "strangest man I ever met," admired his lonely courage, his vision for the country, and his devotion to duty, but he knew that the candidate was vulnerable.[2] Nixon was tough and prized his toughness, but like anyone, perhaps more than most,

The campaigner, 1968.
**Courtesy of the Richard Nixon Presidential
Library and Museum**

he was susceptible to emotional outbursts. Dwight Chapin recalled a trip on a small jet from Wisconsin to Florida. Nixon was talking to his chief speech-writer, Ray Price, discussing his acceptance speech at the GOP convention. Reminiscing about his mother, father, and two dead brothers, Nixon consumed "one or two little bottles of scotch" and began to cry—perfectly understandable, but awkward for Nixon, who liked to say that he never cried.[3]

On September 18, as the campaign plane landed in Peoria, Illinois, Bill Safire asked Nixon if he was enjoying the campaign. "Never do," Nixon responded. He was looking out at the crowd lined up along the airport fence, the politicians waiting to shake his hand. "Campaigns are something to get over with." Nixon relished plunging into crowds, especially when he was showing defiance, but day after day of airport rallies wore him out. He wearied of the hangers-on and glad-handers and favor-seekers, even the ministers and priests who went on too long in God's name. After one windy prayer, he turned to Safire and said, "No more goddamned benedictions." On the same plane ride to Peoria, he vented at his favorite target, the press: "You see the way they hate to get up and look at the size of the crowds? Remember, the press is the enemy."[4]

The New Nixon had made some gains with the members of the Fourth Estate, but the old Nixon knew they were temporary. The anti-Nixon bias was too deeply rooted. While Nixon still enjoyed the support of the conservative press—the Hearst papers, the **Chicago Tribune,** many small and medium-sized city newspaper publishers—reporters on the political beat were becoming increasingly liberal. In 1960, reporters leaving the Nixon plane for the Kennedy plane felt they were "coming home," wrote Teddy White. Jack Kennedy had asked Ben Bradlee of **Newsweek** what the Nixon plane was like. "Different, joyless, strangely dull," was the answer.[5] Nixon's well-run, highly punctual campaign plane in 1968 fared better against Hubert Humphrey's chaotic, shambling operation. "In 1968, one left the Nixon tour to join the Humphrey tour as if leaving a well-ordered and comfortable mansion for a gypsy encampment," wrote White, the most prominent New Nixon convert.[6] Yet, with the press, as with so much else, Nixon could not escape Kennedy's shadow. Looking back, Tom Brokaw, an up-and-coming TV newsman in 1968, recalled, "Developing a style, I wanted to be JFK, not Richard Nixon." He recalled meeting Nixon outside a hotel in San Francisco, where Nixon had been talking with former California lieutenant governor Bob Finch in preparation for a meeting with Governor Reagan. "Did you discuss 1968?" Brokaw asked. "No, we're just old friends," Nixon answered, looking at Brokaw with "flat eyes, through the heavy pancake makeup," Brokaw recalled (Nixon had started wearing makeup when there were TV cameras around). "I thought to myself, he's lying through his teeth—but it seemed so unnecessary. Why didn't he just say, 'We're all interested in 1968?'"[7] (Actually, given

Nixon's indirect style, it's possible that they didn't discuss 1968.)

Only very rarely, and poignantly, could Nixon let down his guard around staff and newsmen. Jack Carley, the advance man who had driven Mrs. Nixon in 1962, recalled Nixon trying to be thoughtful and considerate in his way. As their plane bounced through a storm to the Westchester County Airport, he reached into a bag of gifts he had been given at the last stop in New Hampshire. He pulled out some golf tees. "Anyone want these?" he asked. He offered some to Bob Semple of **The New York Times**. Then some golf socks. "Want these, Jack?" he asked his advance man. Startled, Carley said, "What size?" "Fits any size!" Nixon exclaimed, pulling on the socks. "They're stretchable!"[8]

His stamina was extraordinary. Always grinding, speaking without notes or from a teleprompter, he could carry reams of minute information in his capacious political brain. His memory store compensated for his shyness. "He had connections everywhere," recalled a political adviser, Stuart Spencer. "He always knew the guy's button. Oil, water, whatever. He could talk about it." Spencer remembered Nixon standing in 110-degree heat in Arizona, dressed as usual in a dark suit, scribbling away on his yellow pad. "He was oblivious," Spencer recalled. "But then he'd drink a little scotch and a switch would click and he'd get paranoid."[9]

The Haldeman operation tried to keep Nixon healthy and rested, scheduling downtime, which

Nixon preferred to think of as "sacred thinking time." Chapin's travel bag carried a sunlamp to refresh Nixon's tan (just like JFK's) and a bottle of sleeping pills, carefully counted out by Rose Woods.[10] For stress, Nixon took an anti-seizure medicine called Dilantin. He had learned about the drug from Jack Dreyfus, a mutual fund operator to whom Nixon had confided that he could not sleep and that he was too "excitable." When Dreyfus told him he would need a prescription for Dilantin, Nixon said, "Screw the doctors." Through his medical research foundation, Dreyfus had a vast store of "the wonder drug," as he called it, and he gave Nixon a thousand pills. Whether Nixon took them is not a matter of record, but in October 1968, three weeks before the election, Nixon asked Dreyfus, "Is it all right if I take two pills every day?" Dreyfus told him yes.[11]

Dilantin, which suppresses nerve impulses, may or may not have relieved Nixon's stress, but its side effects include slurred speech, especially when combined with alcohol. There is debate about how much Nixon drank, but none about his tendency to sound inebriated after only a drink or two. Len Garment recalled that Nixon would call him late at night from the campaign trail and talk until he drifted off. Ehrlichman later told Garment that, at around midnight, he would hand the candidate a scotch and a sleeping pill (Seconal) as well as the telephone to call Garment. The cocktail would kick in after twenty minutes or so, sometimes in mid-sentence.[12] (Chapin has disputed this version, telling the author that, as

Nixon's body man, he would retire for the night with two beers, one for him, one for Nixon. "That was it. No more," he said.)[13]

In trying to monitor and shield Nixon, the campaign sometimes marginalized his wife. Haldeman and Ehrlichman took their cues partly from Nixon, who could be aloof from Pat, even though he was devoted to her.* In his book, Ehrlichman wrote that Nixon "seldom included [Mrs. Nixon] in his deliberations on strategy or scheduling. He treated her as a respected but limited partner." Haldeman did not need much encouraging from Nixon to believe that, on the campaign trail, women were to be seen but not heard. "It was clear that Haldeman gave little weight to her opinions," observed Ehrlichman. But Pat, an old campaign trooper, had decided opinions of her own, and her skin was not as thick as it appeared. She "was not slow to read others' feelings towards her," Ehrlichman recalled.[15] On the plane, she and Haldeman were cool and correct with each other, but behind her back, the chief of staff referred

---

*Nixon's apparent inattention to Pat could be misleading, as his aides came to understand. "Nixon really worried about her," recalled Dwight Chapin.[14] "He'd ask, 'Who is with Pat?' He wanted to make sure Rose was with her." She, in turn, was not shy about asserting her pride of place. Arriving at a lodge in Lake Geneva, Wisconsin, an advance man said to her, "Here is where Chapin will stay"—pointing to a bedroom right next door to Nixon's. "And Mrs. Nixon," he continued, "you'll go down the hall."

"Young man," Pat said, "Take Dwight down the hall."

to the candidate's wife as "Thelma," her real name, which she disliked and dropped as a girl. She, in turn, complained bitingly about Haldeman to her daughters and to Rose Mary Woods, who was also feeling the chief of staff's sangfroid. Shortly after Haldeman took over in the summer of 1968, Pat was offended that she was not introduced at one of her husband's speeches. Then it happened a second time. "My father noticed also and gave orders that it not happen again," daughter Julie wrote.[16]

Like many in their generation (including Jack and Jacqueline Kennedy), the Nixons were not physically demonstrative. Nixon's handlers would have to continue to remind the president to attend to his First Lady: "I think it is important for the President to show more concern for Mrs. Nixon as he walks through the crowd. At one point he walked off in a different direction. Mrs. Nixon wasn't looking and had to run to catch up. From time to time he should talk to her and smile at her. Women voters are particularly sensitive to how a man treats his wife in public. The more attention she gets, the happier they are," Roger Ailes wrote Haldeman in May 1970.[17]

Political spying is as old as politics. In America, certainly in the big time, nearly all campaigns spy on their opponents, some more effectively (or more brazenly) than others. Dirty tricks are also a hallowed, if disreputable tradition. In 1960, recalled Ehrlichman, the Nixon campaign staff had "always

felt a little outclassed; the Kennedy fellows were really much better at the dirty stuff than we were."
Indeed, it's not clear that the Nixon campaign did
any "dirty stuff" in 1960. By 1968, "Nixon demanded that his staff conduct his campaign as if we
were an all-out war," wrote Ehrlichman, and that
meant air war, ground war, and covert war. As tour
manager, Ehrlichman had "countless talks" with the
candidate about the orchestrated jeering and heck-
ling at Nixon's speeches, which grew worse as the
campaign wore on. Nixon appeared calm in public,
but in the privacy of the airplane cabin, "it was obvious that he was extremely upset by the opposition's
tactics." The Secret Service refused to quash "legitimate political dissent." Frustrated by bureaucratic
foot-dragging, Nixon looked for other ways to work
his will. He declared that he wanted, as Ehrlichman
put it, "some kind of flying goon squad of our own
to rough up hecklers." Mostly by borrowing or rent-
ing local cops, his campaign tried to weed out "the
weirdos and beardos," as Nixon called the hecklers.
Ehrlichman knew Nixon's history of defying crowds.
He worried that, fatigued and under assault, he
might do something "unpredictable and dangerous."[18] Jack Carley recalled, "We were asked to recruit some beefy types who would surround the
protesters, and, without touching them, outshout
them and try to intimidate them into silence. Sometimes it worked and sometimes it didn't."[19]
Partly rehabilitated from his influence-peddling
scandal by the passage of time, Murray Chotiner

was put in charge of minor skulduggery. He recruited a "mole" to look and act like a reporter on the Humphrey campaign. Daily reports would come in from "Chapman's Friend," as the spy was codenamed, detailing internal squabbles and snafus in the Humphrey campaign. There was some "tasty gossip," Ehrlichman recalled, but nothing earth-shattering.[20]

Intelligence could come from many sources. At the Fontainebleau Hotel in Miami during the Republican Convention, Nixon's national security adviser, Richard Allen, was spotted by reporters speaking to a short, roundish man with curly hair and black-framed glasses. The man was Henry Kissinger, the Harvard professor who was at the time a foreign policy adviser to Nelson Rockefeller. For the reporters, Allen staged an elaborate pantomime to pretend that Kissinger was a long-lost friend, lest the press suspect any collusion between the campaigns. They were, in fact, trying to work out a deal on the GOP foreign policy platform. (At other times, to avoid being overheard, they spoke in German.)[21]

After the convention and Rockefeller's defeat, Allen asked Kissinger to serve on Nixon's foreign policy advisory board. Kissinger demurred, saying, "I can help you more if I work behind the scenes." Kissinger was playing both sides: He was hoping to get a high-ranking job in the Humphrey administration if the Democrats won. Kissinger was already consulting with the Johnson administration on its secret attempts to negotiate peace with the North

Vietnamese. With his Harvard peers and quite a few others, Kissinger was scathing about Nixon.[22] "Six days a week I'm for Hubert," he told Daniel Davidson, a young lawyer on Averell Harriman's negotiating team in Paris, "but on the seventh day I think they're both awful."[23]

"Like millions of other Americans watching television that night," Nixon wrote in his memoirs, he had been amazed by the violent scenes at the Democratic National Convention in Chicago that August.[24] The riots in the streets, the protesters shouting "Dump the Hump" and "Sieg Heil," the images of police beating demonstrators with nightsticks on national television all seemed to fulfill the vision of a nation spinning out of control. The political impact was devastating to the Democrats. Days later, their candidate, Vice President Humphrey, trailed Nixon by twelve points in the polls. On September 4, with just the sort of jiu-jitsu he prized, Nixon stood in an open car in a motorcade making its way through the Loop of Chicago and over to Michigan Avenue, the same street that, only a few days before, had been the scene of pitched battle between cops and Yippies, as a crowd of four hundred thousand cheered. Nixon was greeted respectfully by Mayor Richard Daley—the same Mayor Daley, Nixon believed, who had stolen the 1960 election from him.[25] By mid-September, Nixon was ahead of Humphrey by fifteen points.

It was not like Nixon to take success for granted,

to count on any sure bet. In early October, Humphrey, inevitably, started to come back, as angry blue-collar voters who had favored the spoiler candidate, Wallace, began to "come home" to the Democratic Party. As the race tightened, Nixon fretted. Kissinger was not Nixon's only source reporting on Lyndon Johnson's foreign policy machinations. The campaign began to hear from a source inside the White House that Johnson was close to declaring a bombing halt to spur peace negotiations with the North Vietnamese. On October 22, Nixon adviser Bryce Harlow received information "from a source whose credibility was beyond question . . . from someone inside Johnson's innermost circle." The report read:

> The President is driving exceedingly hard for a deal with North Vietnam. Expectation is that he is becoming almost pathologically eager for an excuse to order a bombing halt and will accept almost any arrangement. . . .
>
> Careful plans are being made to help HHH [Hubert H. Humphrey] exploit whatever happens. . . .

Nixon read Harlow's memo several times, and with each reading, he recalled, he became "angrier and more frustrated."[26] Here it was: the ultimate dirty trick. The president was playing politics with national security to enable his vice president to overcome the lead of the Republican challenger. Nixon could hardly be blamed for feeling a surge of rage and vexation. He felt that it was happening again: In 1960, he had been the true winner, but his opponents had conspired to steal the election and deny him the presidency.

Nixon was not going to roll over. He had "done the right thing" in 1960 and, in the name of national unity, held back his supporters who had wanted to go to court to challenge the voting returns. This time would be different. The political equation was not hard to balance: Any rough stuff was more than justified by the rougher stuff of his enemies. Fighting back was the only way to go; that was his most basic life lesson. Pat was a believer; if anything, she and the girls wanted him to be more defiant toward his adversaries.

Nixon, it's true, did not tell his wife everything about his campaigns, particularly the harsher or seamier sides. (**Nut-cutting** was a term he sometimes used, though never with her; he did not even swear in front of her.) He knew that she disapproved of Murray Chotiner and did not care for Haldeman, and he more or less condoned their efforts to cut her out of the day-to-day campaign. Nonetheless, he was convinced that Pat, more than anyone except possibly Julie and Tricia and his "sainted" mother, wanted him to go all-out to win—no compromises, no equivocating, no turning back.

It was the women in Nixon's life who gave him the determination to go on and to do what it took to win. It is true that Nixon often professed to ad-

mire manly men. He was a fan of John Wayne, who
had supported him in his first campaign against
Jerry Voorhis, and he wished to emulate the strong
and silent type of the westerns he liked to watch.
Nixon liked to lower his voice when he was in tense
situations; he prided himself on never getting sick or
even having a headache, which he somehow saw as a
feminine malady.[27] But, from his mother to his wife
to his daughters, he was drawn to examples of feminine strength. His father may have fervently waved
his arms at revival meetings, but it was his mother
who truly kept the faith. Nixon's self-image was
hardly as a trickster who trimmed and hedged.
Rather, he saw himself as a grand and noble figure.
At the same time, he saw the need to dare greatly in
his ambition. He was not going to fritter away his
life's dream if he could act boldly and decisively.

By mid-October, Nixon could not afford to wait.
His lead in the Gallup poll had fallen to eight points.
Nixon knew that an "October surprise" could vault
Humphrey past him into the White House.

Nixon could see his redemption from 1960 and
'62, his vindication by the polls, slipping away. Still,
he was not powerless. He had made plans; he was, as
usual, prepared.

He knew that South Vietnam, America's ally and
client state, would have to agree to the peace talks.
Nixon had his own agent, his own way of reaching
out to the government of President Nguyen Van
Thieu in Saigon, in the form of stylish and flamboyant Anna Chennault, well known around Washing-

ton as the "Dragon Lady" (from the comic strip "Terry and the Pirates"). The widow of World War II General Clare Chennault of the "Flying Tigers" (he had been fifty-seven and she was twenty-two when they married), Chennault gave lavish parties at her Watergate apartment and used her charm and money-raising ability for the so-called China Lobby supporting Taiwan. Nixon had once instructed an aide, "Keep her away from me, she's bad news," but he began to see that she was useful after she raised $250,000 for his 1968 campaign.[28] Among the friends of the "Dragon Lady" was Bui Diem, the South Vietnamese ambassador to the United States.

Months before Nixon learned that a bombing halt was imminent, he had set up his own back channel to Saigon. On July 12, 1968, three weeks before the Republican Convention, Nixon had met with Mrs. Chennault, Ambassador Diem, and John Mitchell in New York. Nixon expressly asked for a secret meeting—no Secret Service (lest their "boss," Lyndon Johnson, find out). With the South Vietnamese ambassador, Nixon supposedly designated Mrs. Chennault as "the sole representative between the Vietnamese government and Nixon campaign headquarters."[29]

What happened next—what transpired over the four months between that first meeting and election day, November 5, 1968—has been a source of fascination and mystery to historians for decades. The Chennault Affair has loomed as one of the great litmus tests in the history of Richard Nixon—in understanding his character and his methods, in measuring just how far he would go to attain power. Did Nixon, through Chennault, secretly conspire to persuade the South Vietnamese to thwart LBJ's "October Surprise" that would halt the bombing and bring peace negotiations—and possibly hand the November election to Hubert Humphrey?[30]

Nixon had trained himself to expect the worst from his enemies, but he was caught slightly off guard by Johnson's perceived gambit. Nixon's relationship with LBJ was a complex mix of respect, empathy, and suspicion. LBJ "personally liked" Nixon, he wrote an aide in 1966, and earlier, in 1956, he told another aide that Nixon had "stuck his neck out" by praising the majority leader when he returned to the Senate from a heart attack. In September of 1968, Nixon summoned Billy Graham to send President Johnson a private promise that he would never "embarrass" Johnson. On October 14, speechwriter Bill Safire asked Nixon why he had excised a pointed reference to the Johnson-Humphrey administration and penciled in "the past eight years" of Democrats in the White House. "He fudged," wrote Safire. "Not fair to LBJ," Nixon said. Safire speculated in his diary, "I wouldn't call this a mariage de convenance, but I'd compare it to two fighting roosters, circling each other, the knives attached to their spurs. Nothing will happen unless one makes the first move. Each is waiting for the other to knock the chip off his shoulder. RN doesn't want to knock it off, because LBJ can be vindictive and who knows what he might pull off on an international scale."[31]

By the last week of October, rumors and reports were surfacing in the press that President Johnson had agreed to halt the bombing of North Vietnam and open peace talks. Knowing that such a diplomatic breakthrough would be a boon to the Humphrey campaign, Nixon on October 26 put out a statement that remains a classic of political doublespeak:

> In the last 36 hours I have been advised of a flurry of meetings in the White House and elsewhere on Vietnam. I am told that top officials in the administration have been driving very hard for an agreement on a bombing halt, accompanied by a cease fire, in the immediate future. I have since learned these reports are true.
>
> I am . . . told that this spurt of activity is a cynical, last-minute attempt by President Johnson to salvage the candidacy of Mr. Humphrey. This I do not believe.[32]

This I do not believe. Nixon, the injured but still-trusting innocent—determined to stay on the high road no matter how low his opponents stooped. In fact, Nixon absolutely believed that LBJ's motives were political and that the bomb halt was a desperate attempt to rob the front-running Republican nominee of the election.

Nixon's suspicion that Johnson was politically
motivated seems perfectly sound, given LBJ's own
reputation as a ruthless master of the game. But the
historical record shows that Johnson initially **opposed** the bombing halt and had to be persuaded to
go along by the military and his own hawkish advisers. Johnson was so resistant that he made his Vietnam commanders fly home and brief him in the
middle of the night to assure him that a bombing
halt would not cost American lives.[33] Ironically, it
was not LBJ but the Soviet Union that wanted to see
Humphrey win and Nixon lose. The Kremlin pushed
the North Vietnamese to accept U.S. terms for peace
talks because Humphrey was regarded as a less formidable Cold War foe than Nixon.[34]

By October 29, a deal appeared to be in the works:
The bombing would stop, and a few days later the
peace talks would begin. But then, at the last moment, South Vietnam backed away from the table
and refused to sign off on the peace talks in Paris.

Johnson smelled a double cross. Nixon had publicly and privately promised not to undermine any
chance for peace. In Johnstown, Pennsylvania, on
October 17, Nixon had told voters that only the
president could decide whether to stop the bombing
and start talking. "We will support him," Nixon
said, "because he wants peace and we do not want to
play politics with peace."[35] But now President Thieu,
who had seemed amenable to the peace talks, was
suddenly balking. Why?

Johnson had his own intelligence sources, and he

was getting reports that Nixon was trying to sabotage the peace process before it even began. A Wall
Street source had picked up from a banking friend
in Nixon's inner circle that Nixon was finagling with
the Thieu government. "It all adds up," grumbled
the conspiracy-minded LBJ. His suspicions were re-
inforced when he was shown an intercept by the National Security Agency, the government's top-secret
gatherer of "signals" intelligence, of a cable from
Ambassador Diem to President Thieu. "I am still in
contact with the Nixon entourage," Diem told
Thieu, "which continues to be the favorite despite
the uncertainty provoked by the news of an imminent bombing halt." The "entourage" included Mrs.
Chennault and John Mitchell.[36]

Johnson wanted hard proof that Nixon was directly trying to block the deal. The Logan Act, a
two-hundred-year-old law, made it a crime for private U.S. citizens to interfere in negotiations of the
U.S. government with foreign powers. The president ordered the FBI to wiretap and physically
monitor the South Vietnamese embassy in Washington and to tap Mrs. Chennault's phone in her
Watergate apartment. The FBI duly recorded Mrs.
Chennault visiting the South Vietnamese embassy
for thirty minutes, then going to an unmarked
Nixon campaign office on Pennsylvania Avenue (her
phone was apparently never tapped).[37]

To Johnson, who didn't need much convincing,
Chennault's mere presence at the South Vietnamese
embassy was proof enough of meddling by the

Nixon camp. He got Senate Republican Minority Leader Everett Dirksen on the phone and ranted. "It's despicable, and if it were made public I think it would rock the nation," LBJ stormed. "Now, I rather doubt Nixon has done any of this, but there's no question but what folks for him are doing it." LBJ vented to Dirksen about Nixon's sanctimonious "This I do not believe" line: "I thought Dick's statement was ugly the other day, that he had been told that I was a thief, and a son of bitch and so forth, but he knew my mother and she really wasn't a bitch. . . ." He went on fulminating, in his vulgar LBJ way, about Nixon "fartin' under the covers" and "getting his hand under somebody's dress."[38]

When he spoke by phone with Nixon and Humphrey later that evening, the president played it cool. He mentioned some "minor problems" from the "China Lobby" (code to Nixon, he knew, for Mrs. Chennault) and said, with the same unctuous insincerity Nixon had shown him, "I know that none of you candidates are aware of it or responsible for it."

Nixon craftily played the last-minute glitch in the peace initiative as a Johnson blunder, one more bulge in Johnson's "credibility gap." Nixon had his adviser, Robert Finch, speaking as a "Nixon confidant," tell the press, with feigned surprise, "We had the impression that all the diplomatic ducks were in a row." Johnson was furious when he called Nixon on this charade, referring to Finch as "Fink."[39]

Johnson became even more indignant when the FBI supplied him with the latest report from the wiretap on the South Vietnamese embassy. Mrs. Chennault was delivering a message from "her boss." The message was: "Hold on, we're gonna win." The report did not identify "her boss," but LBJ had no doubt: Nixon was telling the South Vietnamese to hold on, he was going to win the election. Johnson called Senator Dirksen and did not mince words: "This is treason."[40]

Dirksen frantically called Bryce Harlow, who awakened Nixon in his hotel room in Los Angeles to let him know the depth of the president's anger. Nixon had to scramble—and he did, brilliantly. The next morning, November 3, the final Sunday before Election Day, Nixon went on **Meet the Press** and offered to be the solution to the problem he had created. He offered, if elected, to go to Saigon to persuade Thieu to join the peace talks. Calling Johnson, he was all wounded innocence. "My God," he told LBJ, "I would **never** do anything to encourage Hanoi—I mean, Saigon not to come to the table. . . ."

The phone call ended, and "Nixon and his friends collapsed with laughter," reported the **Sunday Times** of London in a post-election reconstruction of the episode. "It was partly in relief that their victory had not been taken from them at the eleventh hour."[41] Humphrey's surge slowed over the final weekend. But that laughter was nervous; the polls generally saw the race as too close to call.

For decades after, historians argued. The colorful Mrs. Chennault bragged about playing the role of spy in her memoirs, but was she exaggerating?* The FBI wiretaps strongly suggest that the Nixon campaign was signaling Saigon to go slow, but they are not conclusive. The image of Nixon as a dark trickster, paranoid about Johnson stealing the election from him, skirting if not breaking the law to stop the plot, perhaps fits the familiar Nixon narrative a little too neatly. In 1991, asked about the "myth" of the Chennault Affair by his friendly biographer, Jonathan Aitken, Nixon did not deny a role for Mrs. Chennault, but he downplayed it. She would "bend John Mitchell's ear as to what was going on and what our position should be," Nixon wrote Aitken in 1991. "Mitchell would puff on his pipe, listen respectfully, and pass on any informa-

---

*Professor Luke Nichter of Texas A&M, the leading scholar on Nixon's White House tapes, notes that Mrs. Chennault's name only shows up once in taped conversations, when she came looking for a job. Nixon and Kissinger pumped "the Dragon Lady," as they privately called her, for gossip about Asian leaders but then put her off. Although Nixon instructed an aide to find a commission or two for Mrs. Chennault to sit on, it does not appear that Nixon considered himself to be much in her debt. Nichter also points out that U.S. intelligence sources at the time backed up Nixon's later assertion that Thieu did not need to be persuaded by Chennault or Nixon to hold out—he was under pressure at home not to make any deals. It's highly unlikely that North and South Vietnam would have struck a peace deal regardless of any meddling by Nixon—both sides were firmly dug in. But that does not absolve Nixon, who knew that the election was so close that the merest perception of progress toward peace might have swung the election to Humphrey.[42]

tion only when he thought it might involve important facts which I did not have from other sources." In other words, Mitchell's role was entirely passive. So was Nixon's. Furthermore, "Thieu didn't need to hear what Chennault claims she told him," Nixon said. "Thieu knew I was hardline. . . . Thieu didn't need to be told by Mrs. Chennault that his interests would be better served by having me in the White House than Humphrey."[43]

What is the truth? The most credible account may come from a Nixon loyalist. After the election, at Nixon's behest, Haldeman assigned a young aide, Tom Charles Huston, to investigate LBJ's role in the "October Surprise." On his own initiative, Huston decided to look into Nixon's role as well. He found "no smoking gun," he told Nixon Library chief archivist Tim Naftali in an oral history that was declassified in 2014. But, he added, "there was no doubt that the Nixon campaign was aggressively trying to keep President Thieu from agreeing. . . . In typical Nixonian fashion, he wasn't going to leave anything to chance." The phlegmatic Mitchell was not just smoking his pipe and listening. "Mitchell was directly involved," Huston found and concluded, "It's inconceivable to me that John Mitchell would be running around, you know, passing messages to the South Vietnamese government, et cetera, on his own initiative."[44] The whole truth will never be known, but the evidence suggests that Nixon, through layers of deniability, took measures to make sure that Thieu would not agree to the peace talks in time to swing the 1968 election to Humphrey. Johnson did declare a bombing halt, and the Paris negotiations did (fruitlessly) commence, so no permanent harm was done to the peace process, which was not likely to go anywhere. The effect on Nixon was more long-lasting. He continued to believe that LBJ had tried to steal the election from him.

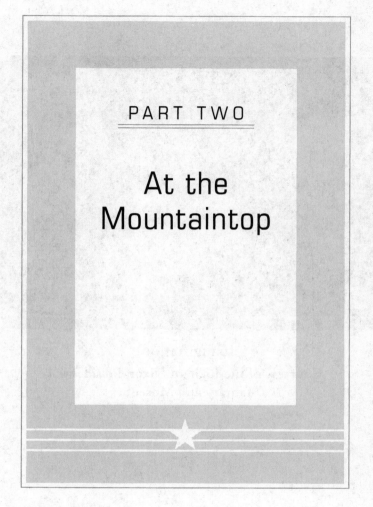

PART TWO

At the
Mountaintop

Inauguration.
**Courtesy of the Richard Nixon Presidential
Library and Museum**

CHAPTER 11

"He Loves Being P!"

Nixon wanted to be alone on election night. He put Pat, Tricia, and Julie in a separate suite on the thirty-fifth floor of the Waldorf Towers because, he wrote in his memoirs, "I did not want to make them feel that they had to keep up a cheerful front for my sake."[1] On the plane from Los Angeles to New York, he had brought his daughters up front to prepare them for not winning. "Actually," Dwight Chapin said to Bill Safire, "that's the way he prepares himself."[2] His family memories from the last two election nights were painful. He wanted to be alone, reflected Henry Cashen, an advance man, "because he couldn't bear to see the girls cry."[3]

There was no TV in his room. He thought network anchors and commentators were all blather and no substance. Bringing in totals from election officials around the country, Chapin found the candidate, wearing slacks, undershirt, and a bathrobe, propped up on pillows, working out of his briefcase. On yellow pads, he jotted columns of numbers, adding and subtracting electoral votes, looking for the path to victory.[4]

The race seesawed through the night. After midnight, it appeared—to the dismay of the Nixons—that the outcome might be decided, once again, in Illinois. Nixon had already organized Operation Eagle Eye, a team of lawyers to go to Chicago to watch the polls on election night.[5] Now he led in Illinois by a hundred thousand votes—but a number of Cook County precincts were still unreported. Nixon told Bryce Harlow to get Larry O'Brien, Humphrey's campaign manager and an old Kennedy hand, on the line: "Tell O'Brien to tell Hubert to quit playing games. We won Illinois, so let's get this thing over with." O'Brien was either out or refused to take the call.[6]

By 4 A.M., Nixon, smoking his fifth cigar of the night, was almost, but not quite, letting himself believe he had won.[7] His advisers kept telling him, "Don't worry . . . we're almost there," recalled Nixon. "**Almost**. I had been **almost** there in 1960." Haldeman and Mitchell told Nixon to take a nap, but he couldn't sleep.

At 6 A.M., the network commentators reported that Mayor Daley was holding back precincts in Cook County. In the suite where Pat, Julie, and Tricia sat watching the TV, Pat "got up from the couch without a word and went into the bathroom. We could hear that she was sick to her stomach," recalled Julie.[8] Mitchell, sitting in the half-darkened suite down the hall with the men, called CBS News reporter Mike Wallace and cajoled him into challenging Mayor Daley to release the votes: "You tell the Mayor for every ballot box they bring in, we will bring in one. This"—he meant the 1960 election—"isn't going to happen again."

As the sun rose in New York, the television networks one by one called the election for Richard Nixon. At 8:30 A.M., as ABC News rounded out the parade, Dwight Chapin burst into Nixon's room and shouted, "You won!"

Still in his bathrobe, Nixon joined the others in the living room. He put his hand on John Mitchell's shoulder. "Well, John," he said, "we'd better get down to Florida and get this thing planned out." (Chapin recalled Nixon saying, "We're going down to Florida to put together a government.") "Mr. President-elect, I think I'd better go up to be with Martha." Mitchell's wife was in a sanatorium in Connecticut, drying out. Nixon was moved, he recalled, by the Mitchells' struggles but also because this was the first time he had ever been addressed as "Mr. President." Chapin was watching Mitchell. He saw a teardrop trickle down the cheek of the man Nixon regarded as the Gary Cooper of Wall Street.[9]

Humphrey called Nixon to concede. The voice of Minnesota's "Happy Warrior," normally so ebullient, was full of fatigue and disappointment. Nixon was gracious and sympathetic. He made an effort to be kind with defeated politicians; he knew how they and their families felt.[10] Then he went home to his

apartment at 810 Fifth Avenue. He went to his study
and opened the windows wide. He put a recording
of Richard Rodgers's **Victory at Sea** on the stereo. "I
turned the volume up high," he recalled, "so everybody on Fifth Avenue, five floors below, could hear
it," Nixon recalled. He thought of a long struggle,
with many reversals, but, at last, "final victory."[11]

Nixon was president-elect, by a narrow plurality
of 43.4 percent to Humphrey's 42.7 percent (Wallace picked up 13.5 percent of the vote). He began,
right away, to build a government. But first he had
to clean up some loose ends. On Friday night, November 8, President Johnson called him, still steam-
ing about Mrs. Chennault. Johnson told Nixon
what his intelligence agencies had picked up on the
wiretap of South Vietnam Ambassador Diem: "He
has just talked to the Nixon people and they say
hold out, don't do anything, we're going to win and
we'll do better by you. Now, that's the story, Dick,
and it's a sordid story." Nixon did not argue. He
quickly agreed with LBJ to send word to the South
Vietnamese that he wanted the Saigon government
to join the peace talks.[12]

Johnson may have been, not too subtly, threatening to expose Nixon with this "sordid story." But in
this era of American politics, when campaigns stole
secrets but still believed in secrecy, there persisted a
kind of honor among thieves. Campaigns routinely
amassed files on the sexual habits, hidden illnesses,
and financial and moral peccadilloes of their

opponents—what, in a later era, would be called "opposition research" or simply "oppo." But campaigns very rarely aired their opponents' dirty laundry in public, and the press, more passive as well as more discreet in those days, chose not to pry into private lives. Rather, the files were used as deterrents. Roughly speaking, the unstated understanding was: If you leak my secrets, I'll leak yours. To borrow a nuclear-arms metaphor from the time, the campaigns were restrained by the threat of mutual assured destruction.

On the eve of the election, Johnson had briefly considered going public with the Chennault Affair, but he knew that Nixon could accuse him of politicizing national security by boosting Humphrey's chances with a bombing halt. (He also did not wish to reveal that the United States was wiretapping the South Vietnamese embassy in Washington and offices in Saigon.) From the LBJ ranch, the president consulted his old comrade and resident sage, Defense Secretary Clark Clifford. Speaking elliptically, in his trademark mellifluous voice, Clifford held forth in a way that was at once orotund and to the point: "I think some of the elements of the story are so shocking in their nature that I'm wondering whether it would be good for the country to disclose the story and then possibly have a certain individual elected. It could cast his whole administration under such doubt that I would think it would be inimical to our country's interests."[13] Johnson took the story to his grave—carefully avoiding any suggestion in his memoirs that Nixon was directly to blame in the Chennault Affair.[14]

Despite his menacing phone call on November 8, President Johnson was all grace and goodwill with the Nixons. He provided a plane, "Air Force Five," to fly them to Florida right after the election. It was a transport plane with a windowless fuselage, Julie recalled, but "even to step aboard one of the presidential aircraft was an exhilarating experience." Julie watched her parents exit the plane on the dark, cool night. "Once under the shelter of the plane, they turned to each other. Simultaneously, they embraced, and my father swung Mother around in a pirouette."[15] This intimacy was not unprecedented; Dwight Chapin recalled the Nixons holding hands when they thought no one was looking.[16]

There was one other high-ranking person who knew a great deal about the Chennault Affair, and Nixon took pains to deal with him quickly. On November 12, J. Edgar Hoover, the director of the Federal Bureau of Investigation, reported to a job interview of sorts at Nixon transition headquarters at the Pierre Hotel in New York.

Hoover and Nixon had been courting each other, at first warily, then more warmly, for nearly two decades. Over the years, they had exchanged a constant stream of gifts, gossip, political tips, and flattery. The Nixons had stayed at Hoover's summer cottage at Hotel Del Charro in La Jolla, near Hoover's favorite race track. During the 1960 election campaign, Hoover had called Nixon to tell him that JFK had fainted on a visit to the governor of New Jersey, so that Nixon's surrogates could leak it to the press. "Reference should be made to your perfect physical condition," Hoover instructed, in cloying bureau-cratese.[17] Hoover had worked hard to assure his re-appointment in a Nixon administration. Still, he wanted to guarantee his long-term employment.

To get through security and into Nixon's private suite at the Pierre, Hoover had to climb a flight of stairs and then step over a mass of telephone and TV cables. At seventy-two, Hoover looked "florid and rumpled," Haldeman recalled. "His appearance sur-prised me," recalled Ehrlichman. "He was florid and fat-faced, ears flat against his head, eyes protruding. He looked unwell to me."[18]

Hoover "quickly got down to business," Halde-man wrote. He told Nixon that, on Johnson's or-ders, the FBI had bugged Nixon's plane. The request had been based on "national security." "This angered Nixon, but he remained still as Hoover poured out more information," wrote Haldeman, who quoted the FBI director as warning Nixon: " 'When you get into the White House, don't make calls through the switchboard. Johnson has it rigged, and little men you don't know will be listening.' " In fact, said Hoover, LBJ had the whole White House bugged.

Hoover was exaggerating, though not carelessly. LBJ had wired the White House. But it was not true that the FBI had bugged Nixon's plane. Johnson had not made the request, and even if he had, the FBI never would have gotten past the Secret Service, according to Cartha "Deke" DeLoach, Hoover's number three and his official "bagman" to LBJ.[19]

Hoover was playing his great game of bureaucratic blackmail. He was making Nixon **think** that the all-powerful FBI knew his darkest secrets. Nixon would always believe that LBJ had bugged his plane, even after his own aides informed him to the contrary. Not coincidentally, by planting in Nixon's mind the fear that the FBI director was in a position to know a great deal—about, for instance, how Nixon communicated with his go-betweens to Mrs. Chennault—Hoover effectively created a valuable insurance policy for his own continued employment. Over the next three years, Nixon's aides would repeatedly try to get Nixon to fire Hoover, who was dangerous and disloyal in addition to being over the hill. The FBI director would die in office late in Nixon's first term.

Nixon's most complex and consequential presidential appointment showed up at the Pierre Hotel at 10 A.M. on Monday, November 25. Henry Kissinger was led to a large living room and told to wait for the president-elect. When Nixon at last swept in ("always keep them waiting and act like you own the room"), it seemed to Kissinger that Nixon was putting on a "show of jauntiness" to disguise "an extraordinary nervousness." Like another close Nixon observer, Leonard Garment, Kissinger noticed an odd gap between speech and hand movements, as if

Nixon was struggling to synchronize the two and not quite succeeding.

Nixon dispensed with the small talk and announced that he wanted to keep foreign policy under the tight control of the White House. He didn't trust the State Department or the "Ivy League liberals" at the CIA. Kissinger offered that a strong president would run his own foreign policy. At first Kissinger was struck by Nixon's "perceptiveness and knowledge," but then the conversation, as Kissinger put it, "grew less precise." Nixon rambled on about the goals of diplomacy and Kissinger's patron, Nelson Rockefeller. Kissinger would come to understand that Nixon was often elliptical in his speech. "I learned that to Nixon words were like billiard balls; what mattered was not the initial impact but the carom," he wrote. In time, Kissinger would be able to translate Nixon's circumlocutions. But at that first formal meeting, Kissinger was left slightly bewildered. What did Nixon want from him?

The next day he was summoned to John Mitchell's office. He found Mitchell puffing a pipe, "self-confident and taciturn." Mitchell came straight to the point. "What have you decided about the National Security job?"

"I did not know I had been offered it," Kissinger replied.

"Oh, Jesus Christ," said Mitchell, "he has screwed it up again."[20] A week later, after Kissinger had made a show of asking his friends if he should take the job,

Nixon announced that Kissinger was his new national security adviser.

In Nixon's version of his meeting with Kissinger, the president-elect was seized "by a strong intuition" and "decided on the spot that he should be my National Security Adviser." Nixon was less intuitive and more methodical than he let on in his memoirs. Among the many contradictions of Richard Nixon is this: The shy loner Nixon was "a great people person," recalled Donald Rumsfeld, who in 1968 was a young Illinois congressman whom Nixon persuaded to run the Office of Economic Opportunity (mostly to dismantle the less effective parts of LBJ's War on Poverty). By "people person," Rumsfeld meant that Nixon was "interested in horse flesh." He was a great talent scout for up-and-coming politicians and statesmen. "He spotted them, mentored them, urged them along," recalled Rumsfeld.[21] Nixon had identified Kissinger in the late 1950s, when the Harvard professor was a protégé of William Yandell Elliott, the Harvard don who acted as a kind of bridge between the Cambridge groves of academe and the Washington corridors of power. Overlooking his anti-Harvard animus, Nixon took Professor Elliott with him as an adviser on his 1959 Moscow trip. Kissinger sent Nixon his book on nuclear policy, and the two men began exchanging flattering letters. Kissinger only actually met Nixon for five minutes at a book party thrown by Clare Boothe Luce, but Nixon had been reading Kissinger quite closely for years.[22]

From his reading, Nixon knew that Kissinger looked at the world in the way he did. Like his nineteenth-century hero, Klemens von Metternich, Kissinger was a practitioner of realpolitik. He believed in searching for a balance of power. Nixon's greatest dream was to be the statesman who created a new world order that preserved American preeminence, if not dominance, by balancing the power of its friends and foes. Nixon understood instinctively that Kissinger could help him shape bold plans into reality. Together, they would leave a remarkable legacy of diplomatic achievement. But they did not always agree on who should get the credit—usually, Nixon was the idea man, Kissinger the executioner—and their relationship was Shakespearean in its jealousies, passions, and betrayals. Rarely have two men been at once so perfectly and awfully matched.

Nixon wrote that the "combination was unlikely—the grocer's son from Whittier and the refugee from Hitler's Germany, the politician and the academic."[23] But he must have sensed that in many important ways, they were alike. Kissinger may have gone to Harvard, but he had been an outsider there, lonely. As a professor, Kissinger may have been a star, but he was never entirely accepted by the Yankee hierarchy. Kissinger knew what it was like to be condescended to by McGeorge Bundy, the high Wasp Harvard dean and JFK's assistant for national security.[24]

Like Nixon, Kissinger loved to surprise and confound his enemies. Like Nixon, he preferred secrecy and harbored a devious streak. During the campaign, Nixon had been impressed by Kissinger's ability to work behind the scenes feeding information to the Nixon camp. But this knowledge raised an obvious question in Nixon's mind. If Kissinger had snuck around behind the backs of the Democrats, what was to stop him from doing the same to Nixon? According to Kissinger's biographer Walter Isaacson, Nixon told one of Kissinger's rivals at the outset of his administration, "I don't trust Henry, but I can use him."[25]

There were other differences. A gifted courtier, Kissinger was funny and charming. Unlike Nixon, he joked about himself in ways that disarmed others, particularly cynical journalists. By the time Nixon came along, Kissinger was no dumpy academic; he had bought a Mercedes and a sunlamp and had learned how to flirt. He also knew how to manipulate people, including Nixon, whose insecurities he could read at a glance. He sensed that Nixon was not nearly so black-and-white as he appeared to be and that his ambivalence could be exploited. "Nixon was afraid of Harvard, and he was attracted to it," Kissinger told the author. "He aspired to it."[26] Another nineteenth-century statesman whom Kissinger admired was Prince Otto von Bismarck. Bismarck's genius, Kissinger saw from close study, was the ability to deal with contending forces "by manipulating their antagonisms."[27] Like Nixon, Kissinger knew how to play off his enemies and rivals. But Kissinger also knew how to play off Nixon against Nixon.

· · ·

On November 28, Nixon flew back to Key Biscayne, this time on the Boeing 707 used as Air Force
One, generously loaned by President Johnson. Bill
Safire watched with amusement as Nixon swiveled
around in the president's easy chair, pushed a button
that elevated the coffee table into a desk, put up his
feet, and grinned: "It sure beats losing." Nixon was
in high spirits. With Safire, he discussed possible
cabinet choices. Nelson Rockefeller had been suggested for several different posts. "At Treasury," Safire
said, "what about David Rockefeller—no, you can't
have two Rockefellers in the Cabinet." Nixon answered, deadpan: "Is there a law that you have to
have one?"[28]

In Key Biscayne, Nixon had bought two houses,
dim within and barely furnished, next door to his
friend Bebe Rebozo. Lugging around briefing books,
Nixon pretended to work and mostly tried to catch
up on months of lost sleep. There were awkward
dinners with the new staff, at which Nixon announced that he wanted **Victory at Sea** played frequently at the Inaugural. The president-elect tried
to tease Haldeman's wife, Jo, asking her, "How's the
drinking problem?" The Haldemans were Christian
Scientists and teetotalers. Mrs. Haldeman smiled
gamely and played along, which got harder when
Nixon repeated the joke every time he saw her.[29] Pat
Nixon, normally very warm with her own family,
was a little reserved with Mrs. Haldeman. Julie observed that her mother was "putting her mind into

neutral" so that she could cope with the avalanche ahead.[30]

Nixon took a few minutes to pay a consolation visit to Hubert Humphrey. Dwight Chapin came into an upstairs waiting room at Opa Locka Air Force Base to find Nixon with his arm around Humphrey, who was dabbing his face with a handkerchief. On the plane home, Nixon said to Chapin, referring to Humphrey's close loss, "That's so hard, so tough. It's so tough," said Nixon. "But I never cried."[31]

On his Sunday mornings in New York City, Nixon had often attended Dr. Norman Vincent Peale's Marble Collegiate Church. Nixon liked Dr. Peale's sermons, which discouraged self-examination of one's flaws and weaknesses as a trap set by trendy psychiatrists. Instead, he preached "the power of positive thinking," the title of his 1952 mega-bestseller. On December 22, Nixon walked Julie down the aisle of Dr. Peale's church to give her away to David Eisenhower. Julie was effervescent and lovely but also tough-minded. She had endured a lot, including seeing her beloved father mocked in the Smith College student newspaper.[32] Earnest and thoughtful, out of step with his pot-smoking, anti-war classmates at Amherst, David had served as head of Youth for Nixon. (His grandfather, President Eisenhower, had offered him a hundred dollars to get his hair cut for the wedding. David got a light trim but never collected.) Julie and David would provide a refuge of positive thinking for Nixon in the years ahead, a source of love to a man who needed affection but sometimes had trouble showing it. Suffering from the flu on Julie's wedding day, Nixon wondered if maybe he should have spent more time with his daughter, but he also felt "tremendous joy and pride," he wrote, as he danced with the bride to "Edelweiss" from **The Sound of Music**.[33]

Julie, who had wanted to marry before her family entered the fishbowl of the White House, refused to allow press at the wedding. On Christmas Day, she and David slipped away from their Florida honeymoon cottage to surprise her parents at Key Biscayne. Nixon insisted on a post-dinner fire. The fireplace had never been used before, and smoke steadily began to fill the room, Julie recalled. "My father kept repeating, as if to reassure himself, 'Isn't this wonderful? Isn't this fun having a fire and being here together?' Eyes began to water; it became harder to breathe. 'My mother was the first to slip quietly out. . . . David lay down on the floor next to the dogs, who had stretched out very low in order to breathe more easily.'" Soon, even the dogs gave up, and Manolo and "several Secret Service agents" put out the fire.[34] "As 1968 came to a close," Nixon recorded in his memoirs, "I was a happy man."[35]

Inauguration Day, January 20, 1969, dawned gray and cold. The sun came out, but a raw wind blew on the thousands massed at the East Front of the Capitol. H. R. Haldeman began the diary he would keep for the rest of his time as Nixon's chief of staff:

> Most outstanding moment: fanfare, Nixon and Pat Nixon come to top of steps, stand at attention for musical salute. Expression on his face was unforgettable, this was the time! He had arrived, he was in full command, someone said he felt he saw rays coming from his eyes. Great ovation. Then slowly, dignified, down the steps to the front of the platform.[36]

Arthur Burns, a longtime Nixon economics adviser who had been given the title of "Counsellor" and cabinet rank, recalled watching Nixon "closely as he walked down the steps of the Capitol. I could not detect a touch of humility in his demeanor or in his facial expression. This bothered me very much."[37] Kissinger, seated nearby, observed that Nixon's "jaw jutted defiantly and yet he seemed uncertain, as if unsure that he was really there." The sharp-eyed Kissinger cattily recorded that Nixon's pants legs were, "as always, a trifle short."[38]

Nixon's address, written by him with help from Safire, Ray Price, and others, included a wise call to "lower our voices. . . . We cannot learn from one another until we stop shouting at one another." Nixon was not temperamentally suited to fulfill his mother's gentle Quakerisms, but he absolutely believed one simple declarative sentence, later carved on his gravestone, that he had written himself: "The greatest honor history can bestow is the title of peace-maker."[39]

As he rode in his limousine on the parade route up Pennsylvania Avenue, he noticed a cluster of signs. "Nixon's the One. . . . the Number One War Criminal" said one. "Ho, Ho, Ho Chi Minh, the NLF is going to win!" read another. Protesters were burning little American flags handed out by the Boy Scouts.[40] At Twelfth Street, the rocks and bottles, beer cans and pieces of garbage began to fly, and the riot cops moved in. Nixon was "angry that a group of protesters carrying a Vietcong flag had made us captives in our car," he recalled. So, as soon as the limo had swung up Fifteenth Street, where the crowds were cheering again, Nixon "ordered the driver to open the sun roof and let the other agents know that Pat and I were going to stand up so the people could see us."[41] Nixon emerged defiant, with his arms raised up in Ike's V-for-Victory sign— which had, more recently, been adopted as a peace symbol by the youth protest movement. Nixon relished recapturing the flag.

Nixon moved to rid the White House of ghosts. His first diary entry was: "H check EOB for bugs."[42] He wanted Haldeman to make sure that nobody, particularly LBJ, was bugging the old Executive Office Building, where Nixon decided to establish his "hideaway office."[43] The Oval Office was too ceremonial. Nixon would spend much of his time in a homey office in the Executive Office Building across a closed-off street from the West Wing, where he could take naps in the afternoon. The naps were kept secret, marked on the calendar as "staff time." Nixon was determined to be seen working at all times, and he did work, prodigiously. But, in his constant battle with sleeplessness, he needed afternoon respite.[44] In the evening, he sometimes read in the Lincoln Sitting Room, his feet up on his favorite brown ottoman, brought from New York by Pat.

Nixon looked under his bed on the first night and saw a mass of electronic gear for LBJ's taping system. Out it went.[45]* So did the three TV sets, which LBJ had liked to watch simultaneously, as well as the two wire service tickers. LBJ had installed on his phone sixty-four separate buttons to reach staffers, and he had ordered phones put in bathroom stalls so he could reach them anywhere.

Nixon slept only four hours his first night. He stepped into the shower and tried to figure out LBJ's complicated panel of knobs controlling the various jets and showerheads. The blast of water nearly knocked him down. While he was shaving, he remembered a hidden safe LBJ had showed him in November. He reached in and found one thin folder containing the casualty list in Vietnam on LBJ's last day. In Johnson's last year of office 14,835 men had

*On a tour of the White House during the transition, LBJ aide Joe Califano showed Nixon adviser Bob Finch a "hand-initiated" audio taping system LBJ had installed in the Oval Office and the Cabinet Room. When Finch told Nixon about the taping system, Nixon replied immediately: "Get rid of it. I don't want anything like that."[46]

been killed, 95,798 wounded. Those ghosts would not go away. Nixon closed the folder and put it back in the safe.[47]

After Nixon's first week in office, Haldeman wrote in his diary that the "P," as he referred to the president, "still loves every minute and shows it all the time." Nixon especially loved the pomp of office. After the first formal diplomatic reception, Haldeman described Nixon following the Color Guard as the Marine Band played "Hail to the Chief." "P was like a little kid or a wooden soldier, arms still, trying not to look as tickled as he obviously was. P really ate it up. . . . He loves being P!"[48]

Nixon counted on Haldeman to run his office. (He was borrowing, as he often did, from President Eisenhower: the model was Ike's coldly efficient chief of staff, Sherman Adams.) The forty-two-year-old, permanently tanned Californian with a buzz cut was the only staffer who had permission to awaken the president. He did everything from making sure the right cottage cheese was flown in weekly from Knudsen's Dairy in Los Angeles for Nixon's spartan lunch (cottage cheese, canned pineapple ring, rye crackers, skim milk) to trying, futilely, to make Nixon's new dog, an Irish setter named King Timahoe, like his master ("he's trying dog biscuits, no use," Haldeman recorded in his diary).[49] The perfectionist chief of staff set up a "tickler system" to make sure that Nixon's commands, issued via Haldeman, were being obeyed. More consequentially,

as time went on, Haldeman acted as a restraint on
Nixon's impulses. Increasingly, he understood when
not to carry out Nixon's orders. Nixon, in a rare moment of self-awareness, wanted it so.[50]

Nixon told Haldeman, "I must build a wall
around me."[51] He wanted to keep hangers-on and
favor-seekers away, as well as annoying or self-
aggrandizing cabinet officers and congressional leaders. "Basically, the Boss doesn't like to see people,"
Bill Safire wrote in his diary after ten weeks at the
White House. "That's what this machinery is set up
to avoid—and to give him time to think."[52]

Staffers began noticing that Nixon was referring
to himself in the third person, as "RN." He wanted
to emulate de Gaulle, majestic in his remoteness. As
Nixon's sympathetic biographer Conrad Black
pointed out, "De Gaulle, in referring to himself in
the third person, was imitating Julius Caesar. This
was a hazardous road for Nixon to take. . . ."[53] Gradually, over time, Nixon's campaign "body man,"
now his "special assistant," Dwight Chapin, observed that in the White House "Nixon's character
began to change. He became more formal and
aloof—worst of all, he wouldn't see congressmen
and senators. He made a lot of enemies that way."[54]

Dutifully, at times a little too enthusiastically,
Haldeman took on the role of no-excuses enforcer.
"Every president needs a son of a bitch," Haldeman
told one of his minions, Jeb Magruder, "and I'm
Nixon's. I'm his buffer and his bastard. I get done
what he wants done and I take the heat instead of

him."[55] Painfully, he had to cut off Rose Woods's direct access to her beloved boss. So informed, she stormed past Haldeman to tell the president-elect, with a word she seldom, if ever, used before or after, to "go fuck yourself." Later, when Nixon tried to make conversation with her on the elevator, she refused to talk to him.[56] They made up—Woods was no mere "secretary," in the dated use of the term. She was a member of the family, another strong-willed woman Nixon counted on. But Nixon was erecting walls that kept out people he loved as well as those whom he merely tolerated.

Haldeman, in the view of his friend Ehrlichman, was "joined at the hip"—linked in a "true marriage"—to Nixon. Haldeman had been a true believer in Nixon's destiny since the 1950s, Ehrlichman told writer Tom Wicker. Like a good wife, Haldeman believed that he could anticipate Nixon's weaknesses better than anyone, including Pat.[57] Still, Haldeman could be irreverent toward Nixon, at least when he was talking to Ehrlichman. (Together they were nicknamed by resentful reporters, as well as a few staffers, "the Berlin Wall" and "the Germans.")[58]* Haldeman "called Nixon Rufus, The Leader of the Free World, Milhous, and Thelma's Husband, depending on the occasion," wrote Ehrlichman, who could be even more acerbic. Haldeman quotes Ehrlichman refer-

*"The Germans" included Kissinger. After visiting his successor in the Oval Office, LBJ exclaimed to an aide that Nixon "had just one dinky phone" with three buttons. "That's all! Just three buttons! And they all go to Germans!"[59]

ring to Nixon as "the Mad Monk." There is a tone of gentle amusement, though not condescension, in Haldeman's contemporaneous diary. Ehrlichman's memoir, written after he went to prison, dragged down by Watergate, is almost derisive in places. Noting that reporters sometimes confused Haldeman and Ehrlichman, Ehrlichman wrote, "Richard Nixon had the same problem: he was forever calling me Bob. He'd start out to tell me to do something: 'Ah, Bob— ah—Bob—ah John—' Haldeman once wrote that Nixon could never remember how many children the Haldemans had or their names. In my case it was **my** name. Not only was I 'Bob' much of the time, but Nixon never mastered the spelling of my last name. Notes to me came addressed to 'E.' "[60]*

Neither man felt personally close to Nixon, notwithstanding the many hours spent in his company. "I'm not Nixon's friend," Haldeman explained to his personal aide, Larry Higby. "Nixon treats us like employees." Haldeman did not seem bitter; he understood Nixon's quirks. "I've met three or four geniuses," Haldeman told Higby. "All have uneven personalities."[62]

Alexander Butterfield would later become a footnote in history: the Nixon staffer who, at the 1973

---

*Long after Watergate, Nixon sent Ehrlichman one of his books—they never spoke otherwise—inscribed to him. Ehrlichman told Haldeman about it, noting that he had spelled his name without the first **h**. Haldeman responded, "Well, at least you know he wrote it himself."[61]

Watergate hearings, disclosed the existence of the president's secret taping system. In the winter of 1969, in the first days of the administration, Butterfield was an outsider, an Air Force colonel who had served as a staff assistant to LBJ. Impressed with his White House experience and military pilot's check-point precision, Haldeman made him responsible, Butterfield recalled, "for the smooth running of the president's day."

A forty-two-year-old veteran who had flown ninety-eight missions in Vietnam, Butterfield felt apart from the handsome young aides Nixon liked to hire, "the young guys who liked to say 'over and out' on their walkie-talkies," as Butterfield liked to describe them. On Butterfield's first day at work, January 25, Haldeman tried to explain his new boss. "This is a strange man," Haldeman told Butterfield. "He doesn't like people he doesn't know." In his diary, Haldeman described Butterfield's first encounter with the president: "Rather awkward. Will take time to develop. President awkward with stranger there but tried to cover it up. He's not very good at that."[63] In a later oral history, Butterfield described his wonder at watching Nixon's near-mortification as the president greeted his new assistant. Nixon made some indistinct guttural noises, spun his hands helplessly, and looked down at the carpet. "He never said a word," recalled Butterfield.

Butterfield came to see Nixon as a solitary but sympathetic figure. According to Butterfield, the president would dine alone "four out of five nights," usually going to the Residence only when his children were there.* Manolo would serve Nixon one Scotch; the president, who did not like to be seen looking too informal, would eat in his tie and jacket while Butterfield sat outside. Then, still wearing a necktie, he "might go down [to the White House bowling alley] and bowl a line." Sometimes he would engage Butterfield in conversation. The president would become engaged, genuinely curious. "What about these young people?" he would ask. "Why are they rioting? What is it that they're after?" In recalling those late-night conversations in Nixon's Executive Office Building hideaway, Butterfield mused, "I used to have trouble in there sometimes, but you know, the guy cared. He seemed to be struggling with that."

At formal White House dinners, Nixon would position himself to talk to "as few people as possible," with instructions that no conversation was to last more than five minutes. This was to be rigidly enforced; conversations were to be broken off in mid-sentence if necessary. Nixon urged Butterfield to try the same system for the First Lady. "Dick is crazy," Pat Nixon breezily told Butterfield. "I would never do that."[65]

Butterfield had been ordered by Haldeman to act as staff liaison to the First Lady (replacing Chapin, who had been caught up in the inevitable friction

---

*The president's daily diary suggests that Nixon dined with the First Lady more often, perhaps half the time.[64]

between Haldeman and Pat). Butterfield found Mrs. Nixon to be "sweet" and "smart" and "not Plastic Pat," the misnomer attached to her by journalists who mistook her sad-eyed, frozen candidate's wife's smile for emptiness.* Staffers who spent time around the Nixons knew that the First Lady was formidable and opinionated as well as loving and warm with her family and her daughters' friends. But they also saw her ignored or slighted by her husband, not intentionally or cruelly, perhaps, but nonetheless marginalized in the creation of "RN."

The first year in the White House was hard for the First Lady, Dwight Chapin recalled.[67] Ehrlichman described her receding to "near invisibility" at a fancy dinner for Henry and Christina Ford. Nixon, as he often did, rose to the occasion, spilling over with information about his guests' interests and philanthropies, gleaned from briefing memoranda.[68] Julie unhappily observed the diminished role for her mother, "especially since my father tried increasingly to separate his political and personal life," as she delicately put it.

There was no escaping. The president lives over the store. The First Lady tried to make the most of it, even if her husband was off reading de Gaulle and Churchill in the Lincoln Bedroom. The night she attended one of her first state dinners, Julie came

---

*The name "Plastic Pat" was popularized by Kandy Stroud of **Women's Wear Daily**. Nixon was bitterly resentful and, in his harshest language—referring to Stroud as "the kike girl"—ordered Stroud's White House press pass revoked.[66]

down later from her third-floor bedroom to get a snack from the family kitchen on the second floor. Dimly, down the darkened hallway, she spotted her mother, still dressed in her evening gown.

She was swaying to the faint sound of music coming from the Grand Foyer where some of the guests were still enjoying the dancing. On tiptoes, she moved gracefully across the gleaming parquet floor. I did not intrude but rather turned and went on to the kitchen.[69]

CHAPTER 12

Statesman and Madman

Nixon liked order and regimentation, uniforms and uniformity. He suggested that Kissinger dress his national security staffers in blue blazers emblazoned with emblems. (Kissinger put him off.)[1] And yet, Nixon welcomed **dis**order too. He wanted original thinkers, iconoclasts, visionaries unafraid of seeking to create **new** orders. He loved the word **moxie**, noted speechwriter William Safire, and he admired President Woodrow Wilson, Democratic activist, as a "man of ideas and action."[2]* Nixon's openness to new ideas and willingness to convert them into action constituted one of his great strengths—and also indicated much about his inner courage. At the same time, Nixon knew when to cut his losses or settle for less. His oscillations can seem

---

*Nixon proudly used "the Wilson Desk" in the Oval Office in tribute to the Democratic president who pushed progressive legislation and tried to make the world "safe for democracy." Safire had to inform Nixon that he had the wrong Wilson—the massive desk brought in by Nixon had actually been used by Henry Wilson, a vice president in the Grant administration.[3]

With Moynihan.
**Courtesy of the Richard Nixon Presidential
Library and Museum**

dizzying—the bold risk-taker one moment, the canny calibrator the next. But he was moved by one overriding concern—to be a doer, an achiever, and not just a talky ideologue or a wishful thinker.

Feeling isolated by the "Beaver Patrol," as the press referred to Nixon's young aides, Alex Butterfield was drawn instead to Nixon's most iconoclastic hire: Daniel Patrick Moynihan, maverick of the West Wing. The former Harvard professor occupied a tiny office in the basement, wore striped shirts when others wore only white ones, and was the only staffer who took up Nixon's invitation to use the White House pool. "Come on Alex, let's have a belt," Moynihan, his too-long hair still dripping, would say as he handed Butterfield a late afternoon cocktail.[4]

Haldeman put up with Moynihan's unbuttoned habits—like drinking Heinekens in the morning—because he knew that the president was taken with his new domestic affairs adviser.[5] "He's in love again," Nixon staffers would say, by now accustomed to Nixon's crushes on dynamic men who could shake up the status quo.[6] A Kennedy liberal, Moynihan was a prize defector. His own family and friends were shocked. "How could you even meet with him!" exclaimed his wife, Liz, when Moynihan told her he had just taken a job working for Nixon. She and the kids stayed in Cambridge. "We didn't trust them, we didn't know them. We didn't want to be hostages," she later recalled.[7]

Judged by later eras, when presidents tend to appoint faceless loyalists as domestic policy advisers, Moynihan was an astonishing choice—a freewheeling former Kennedy adviser welcomed into Nixon's inner council. Nixon was pleased to have not one but two Harvard professors as his top advisers. (The other one was less thrilled. "Moynihan will only go off and write a nasty book about you," Kissinger advised Nixon.)[8] Irish Catholic, son of a bar owner in Hell's Kitchen in Manhattan, Moynihan was, like Kissinger and Nixon, largely self-made.[9] As an assistant secretary of labor in the Kennedy and Johnson administrations, he had warned the limousine liberals against putting down poor whites and poked holes in liberal cant.[10] Moynihan's honest writings about the breakdown of the "Negro" family had made him an apostate, looking for a new home. "Pat was in a pretty bleak place in 1968," recalled a young aide, Chris DeMuth.[11]

Moynihan's ability to flatter rivaled Kissinger's. During the transition, at his first meeting with Moynihan arranged by house liberal Leonard Garment, Nixon said he was thinking of creating an Urban Affairs Council, as an equivalent to the National Security Council, to try to save America's rotting, racially torn inner cities. "Capital idea!" Moynihan exclaimed.[12] Nixon asked Moynihan if he would like to head it. Moynihan "said 'yes' on the spot. Very uncharacteristic," recalled his wife, Liz. Like Nixon, Moynihan matched his periodic gloom with determined optimism. On inauguration night, Nixon had ordered the lights turned on in every room in the White House to cheer up the place (and its new occupants).[13] Only five days before, Moynihan had sent a memo to the president-elect suggesting that he reverse a money-saving order by LBJ to douse the exterior lighting around the White House. While other public buildings were "brilliantly lit at night, the White House appears to be in permanent mourning," Moynihan had written. Nixon agreed; soon the White House glowed from within and without.[14]

Moynihan and Nixon bonded over the British statesman Benjamin Disraeli. Nixon had read and underlined a biography of the nineteenth-century iconoclast, an ethnic Jew who had stepped over and outmaneuvered the toffs to become prime minister.[15] Disraeli had been a great conservative reformer, able to achieve more than the liberals because of his drive and intelligence—in part because no one expected him to.

Nixon, who once pooh-poohed running the welfare state as "building outhouses in Peoria," would spend only about 20 percent of his time on domestic affairs. To presidential chronicler Teddy White, he had said, "I've always thought the country could run itself domestically without a president. You need a president for foreign policy."[16] But Nixon liked bold gambits, and Moynihan offered him a dramatic way to reform the welfare state and trump the liberal bureaucrats who ran it.* Drawing from free market economist Milton Friedman, Moynihan proposed cutting out the bureaucrats and social workers altogether and giving money directly to the poor in the form of a negative income tax. The welfare rolls would expand at first, but there would be more incentives to preserve families and find work. Nixon was sold. In a speech on welfare reform delivered in December 1969, Nixon declared that he wanted to free the poor from "the soul-stifling, patronizing attitude that follows the dole"—his own words, written in the pre-dawn hours when he rejected a speechwriter's draft. Nixon knew something about the struggles of the poor to preserve their dignity.[18]

Decades would pass before welfare reform would become law in 1996 (in altered form, with Moynihan, by then a senator, ironically voting in opposition). But Nixon began the march, and his administration was an active player in other traditionally liberal realms like health care, consumer and job safety, and the environment.[19] Nixon came to power in an era—following FDR's New Deal, World War II and the Cold War, and LBJ's Great Society—

---

*The tenor of Nixon's attitude to the liberal bureaucracy is captured in this memo to Moynihan, among others, the week before the inauguration, demanding a thorough investigation of Great Society welfare programs: "I do not want this swept under the rug or put aside on the grounds that we are want to have an 'era of good feeling' with the bureaucrats as we begin. This whole thing smells to high heaven and we should get charging on it immediately."[17]

when the public assumed that their representatives went to Washington to govern, not just posture for the next election and cash in on K Street. While Nixon is universally, and not wrongly, regarded as a cynic, his approach to governance was essentially positive. He believed that he could get things done— and that it was his **duty** to try. "He was an activist," recalled Bill Timmons, his congressional liaison. "He wanted to do a lot of things no one had ever tried."[20]

His faith—optimistic, unabashedly patriotic— seems almost quaint, if not naïve, judged by cable-TV era standards of negativism and passive-aggressiveness. It is striking, from the perspective of a later, less confident age, to see how incredibly **busy** the Nixon administration was. Nixon was often thwarted, and he lashed out in frustration or turned to connivance, and he was at times motivated more by political expedience than principle. But he embraced the mid-twentieth-century ethos that government existed to solve problems, and he kept at them until he was swallowed by Watergate. Although Nixon was in some ways a conservative who wanted to cut back on Big Government, he was an activist constantly looking for ways to have an impact. "Decentralization is not an excuse for inaction but a key to action," he scrawled on a memo from Moynihan.[21]

Nixon liked big bets, but he also liked to hedge. As a "counterweight" to the liberal Moynihan, Nixon created an amorphous but potentially powerful job as White House "Counsellor" for Arthur Burns, a conservative economist. Ponderous and long-winded, Burns wanted to slow down the quick-witted Moynihan by maneuvering him into writing up a formal position paper that could be picked apart by critics like Burns. At the first meeting of the President's Urban Affairs Council on January 23, Moynihan cheekily responded to this clever but unsubtle bureaucratic ploy. "I would be glad to undertake such a task," Moynihan said, "on the condition that—and I realize that one does not ordinarily impose conditions on the President of the United States—on the condition that no one take it seriously." The room roared with laughter. President Nixon "first blinked," reported the note taker, Ray Price, "and then joined in the laughter."[22]

Later debates by historians over whether Nixon was really a liberal or a conservative are largely beside the point. He was at heart a pragmatist in a deep American tradition. True to his puritanical heritage, he was a fatalist who knew that he faced harsh, unknown challenges in an untamed world and that outcomes could not be predicted confidently. He would make grand pronouncements from time to time, and he loved the idea of the "big play" that would surprise his enemies. But by and large, he favored modest steps, or at least slowly cementing his bold ones. "I wanted to be an activist president in domestic policy," he wrote in his memoirs, "but I wanted to be certain that the things we did had a chance of working."[23]

Like the eighteenth-century British statesman Edmund Burke whose writing he studied, Nixon viewed the world as it is, not as one might wish it to be. He was very open to new ideas and thought deeply about them, but he oddly discouraged open debate in his own councils. As vice president, he had been invited to join the vigorous back-and-forth President Eisenhower encouraged in his cabinet and National Security Council. Eisenhower eagerly jumped into the discussion, sometimes switching sides to provoke more debate. Nixon learned much from observing Ike, but this was an example he did not follow, perhaps because he was incapable of such confident face-to-face leadership. His essential shyness, shaped by his mother's Quaker reticence and his father's bullying, made Nixon avoid loud, open clashes of ideas. He relied on Kissinger—with the attendant subterfuge and gamesmanship—instead of formally engaging the National Security Council. Stimulated by Moynihan, he did chair most meetings of the Urban Affairs Council in his first year. But he came to regard cabinet meetings as troublesome and largely a waste of time; increasingly, he repaired to his hideaway to read and think.

On the night of February 6, his seventeenth day in office, Nixon took out a yellow pad and made a list. It's an expression of the way he saw himself, or wished to see himself, and how, in any case, he wanted to be seen by others:

Compassionate
Bold
New
Courageous
Strong—in charge President

The list went on: "Open Channels for Dissent" . . . "Trustworthy" . . . "Openminded" . . . "On the ball" . . . "Honest" . . . "Zest for job (not lonely—awesome)" . . . "Mrs. R.N.—glamour, dignity" . . . "Not concerned by Press, T.V., or personal style."[24] This last item was so far from reality that it almost calls into question what he really believed about all the others. On February 2, just four days earlier, Haldeman's diary had recorded Nixon badgering his press secretary, Ron Ziegler, to do a better job of persuading reporters that Nixon worked night and day, taking only five minutes for lunch.[25] Nixon made his list of resolutions while preparing for an interview the next day with Hugh Sidey of **Time** magazine, whose column, "The Presidency," was highly influential, particularly among middle Americans. Nixon could not stop worrying about his media image. He was at once determined to win over the press and sure that he would fail.

Nixon warily regarded Sidey as a pal of JFK and LBJ. In truth, the genial Sidey was prepared to like any president who gave him access, and he wrote a flattering column about Nixon.[26] Indeed, Nixon enjoyed a honeymoon with the press in his first few weeks in office. Even Herblock grudgingly agreed to give Nixon a shave and dispense with the dark jowls.[27] On February 17, James Keogh, a former **Time** editor who ran Nixon's speechwriting shop, wrote a memo, "Media treatment of the President is uniformly excellent. . . . The usual media character-izations are 'efficient,' 'cool,' 'confident,' 'orderly.'"[28]

Nixon had enjoyed success going over the heads of the press, via television, to the people. Not a few reporters resented his ability to circumvent them. He had moments of clarity about press relations, like the time he wrote Haldeman, "The greatest mistake we can make is to try to do what [President] Johnson did—to slobber over them with the hope that you can 'win' them. It can't be done."[29] But then he would fool himself into thinking that he could somehow manipulate reporters into doing his bid-ding. He was encouraged in this wishful thinking by Haldeman, who came from an advertising back-ground and believed, perhaps too well, in "media campaigns." It was Haldeman who invented the term **news cycle**.[30]

The press was highly skeptical of the White House spin machine. "We thought these PR techniques were bizarre in their lack of subtlety," recalled **Washington Post** editor Ben Bradlee (who, during the Kennedy administration, had dined privately with the president and their wives). "It was like they were running some sort of sleazy hotel in the Caribbean. 'Give 'em a free trip, and fill 'em up with booze if they're for us. Buy 'em off if they're neutral. Knee 'em in the groin if they step out of line."[31] Nixon would let himself get wound up by the "daily press summary," initiated by conservative speechwriter Pat Buchanan, who enjoyed pointing out the latest outrages of the liberal press. Goaded by the fiery Buchanan (who delegated much of the job to his assistant Mort Allin), Nixon would scribble commands in the margin, usually of the "off with their heads!" variety.[32] Nixon would routinely cut off all White House contact with reporters from papers like **The New York Times** and **The Washington Post**—"cut him," "freeze him," "dump him"—and then just as routinely forget about it.[33] Larry Higby, Haldeman's assistant, recalled his boss emerging from the Oval Office with long "to do" lists from the president. Haldeman would wisely draw a line through most of Nixon's impetuous orders—meaning, ignore them—but not always.[34]

Within six months, Nixon was on to his dilatory aides. "I have an uneasy feeling that many of the items that I send out for action are disregarded when any staff member just reaches the conclusion that it is unreasonable or unattainable," Nixon wrote his chief of staff on June 16. Notably, suggesting that he **wanted** to be protected from himself, the president added: "I respect this kind of judgment." But he insisted that he be informed when no action was taken. Often, he wasn't.[35]

Nixon reached out to his most recalcitrant foe, **The Washington Post**, through its colorful editor, who was not yet famous but was becoming quite a force, potentially a dangerous one to Nixon. On a Saturday morning, the president telephoned Bradlee at his office at the newspaper on Fifteenth Street, just to chat. Nixon was no doubt ill at ease—he knew that Bradlee had been not just cordial with JFK but a close personal friend. In his recollection of the call, Bradlee, who like Nixon had learned to swear in the navy, was characteristically profane and dismissive of the president:

> By God, one morning the operator said that the President was on the phone. I thought it was [humor columnist] Art Buchwald or somebody pulling my leg—and it was Nixon! It was most uncomfortable, awkward; there was no way to explain the call, except that somebody had said: "You know, you ought to try to get to know Bradlee." He talked about OPA [the World War II Office of Price Administration] and tire prices; I didn't give a shit. He tried it two more times and then realized it was a bad, bad idea.[36]

Nixon had the misfortune of coming to power at a time when the press was hardening in opposition to authority. The "credibility gap" created by President Johnson's lies about the Vietnam War and the rising ferment of the 1960s had produced a new generation of journalists who were hypercritical—sometimes, like Bradlee, swaggeringly so. **The Washington Post** was becoming a bastion of doubters. "You could certainly say that from the mid-60s onward we became a more anti-establishment paper than we had ever been," recalled Bradlee. "As far as the presidency was concerned there was an awe for the office under [Russ] Wiggins, my predecessor. I guess I changed all that. By the time Nixon got in we were already anti–White House, and we sure stayed that way."[37]

The Washington Post may have been "anti-establishment," but it was, at the same time, the Establishment, the hometown paper and favorite organ of the Georgetown set. Nixon tried, in ways that usually backfired, to make some inroads or at least send out peace feelers. In addition to telephoning Bradlee at his office, he used Henry Kissinger as a kind of ambassador to the court of Katharine Graham. The **Post**'s owner, who had taken over the paper five years earlier after her brilliant but unstable husband, Phil, had killed himself, had her own insecurities and was uncomfortable in the role of rival to the throne. But in Nixon's worldview, she would increasingly loom as a threatening usurper.

Mrs. Graham's closest friend, columnist Joe Alsop, was inclined to support Nixon's muscular foreign policy, and Nixon wanted Kissinger to stoke Alsop with flattery and leaks. On February 14, Kissinger, who taped some calls, recorded Nixon telling him, "Very subtly you can let Alsop know" that Nixon intended to be resolute on foreign policy. "He is already writing that. If you can convince Alsop—you know what I mean."[38] Two days earlier, Nixon had hosted his first formal dinner at the White House—a birthday party for Alice Longworth. The only other guests, besides the Nixons and Mrs. Longworth, were Kissinger, Joe Alsop, and his wife, Susan Mary Alsop. "Nixon would have Henry perform, and he would sit back and beam with pride, as if Henry were some sort of prized possession," Mrs. Alsop recalled. Nixon would lean toward his dinner partner and say, "Mrs. Longworth, I think you'll be interested in what Henry has to say about that."[39]

In March, Nixon called Mrs. Graham and suggested that she invite Kissinger to "an editorial lunch to brief us on administration thinking on Vietnam," she recalled in her memoirs. "It was clear that Henry was brilliant and at lunch that day he was both funny and articulate." The "lunch was the start of a long relationship with the paper and me," Graham wrote.[40] Before long, Kissinger was a regular at dinner at Mrs. Graham's and, even more frequently, at the Georgetown salon hosted by her best friend, Polly Wisner, the widow of the late CIA chief of covert operations, Frank Wisner. Cynthia Helms, the wife of CIA Director Richard Helms, was a frequent guest and joined in the fun as Kissinger made self-deprecating jokes and slyly mocked the president, usually for going overboard before Kissinger could restrain him. "Henry was the center of attention at Polly's. He made Nixon a cartoon. There was no empathy for the President in that room," Mrs. Helms said. At tables for eight crammed in amid Mrs. Wisner's French antiques, there was a thrilling sense of being in the know—indeed, socially, intellectually, even morally, a cut above. "Nixon called us the 'Georgetown Set,'" recalled Mrs. Helms. "I don't think we knew we were until he called us that."[41]

John Freeman, the new British Ambassador, took up his duties in February and was immediately folded into the capital elite. He was shocked by the animus against the president. "Nixon was treated abominably by Georgetown society," he told Jonathan Aitken. "It was not just a question of political disagreements. Really beastly attitudes were on display towards him, largely to do with social class."

Freeman recalled "one not uncharacteristic example of this at Mrs. Alice Longworth's house one evening. . . . Over drinks before dinner she asked me what I thought of the new President. I gave some sort of respectful reply. Alice then hushed up the whole company, saying in her wickedest voice, 'How extraordinary! Listen. The Ambassador thinks well of Mr. Nixon! Such a common little man!' and her guests all roared with laughter."[42]

How wounded Nixon would have been! To know that his singular upper-crust ally—"Mrs. L.," as he affectionately called her, his one faithful defender among the Washington cognoscenti—was taking such gleeful pleasure in sneering at him as a "common little man," even if, as was likely, she was indulging in broad irony. Mrs. Longworth liked to play the provocateur and was no doubt taking malicious pleasure in shocking her British guest. Still, her betrayal would have confirmed Nixon's suspicions, not just about Georgetown but more existentially about why he needed to keep his guard up. He would have stoically filed Mrs. L.'s slight away with other hurts in the place where he stored grudges and grievances—to be burned later as fuel. Nonetheless, Nixon was human, and he could not have helped but feel hurt when the whisperings of a supporter's perfidy came back to him as malevolent gossip. (Nixon heard about some of Kissinger's **lèse-majesté** from Haldeman, who had his own spies; other betrayals he probably intuited.) On some evenings, Nixon would joke with Haldeman about where Kissinger might be. "I guess Henry's out with his Georgetown friends," Nixon would say and brood for a moment. "He would joke about it," recalled John Connally, who later became one of Nixon's closest advisers. "But it bothered him badly."[43] The president tried to be philosophical. Career army officer Vernon Walters, Nixon's translator to the Caracas mob in 1958, later installed by Nixon to be deputy director (and Nixon watchdog) at the CIA, told Nixon that Kissinger was making snide comments about him at Washington parties. "I know this," Nixon replied. "Kissinger likes to be liked and I understand that."[44]

On February 17, Anatoly Dobrynin, the Soviet Ambassador to the United States, called on Nixon in the Oval Office. An experienced diplomat, Dobrynin was neither heavy-handed nor fearful of his Kremlin masters like many communist-bloc envoys, Kissinger wrote in **White House Years**. With Nixon, on this raw winter's day, the Soviet Ambassador hinted at the idea of a summit meeting between Nixon and his Kremlin opposite, Leonid Brezhnev. Nixon, "in the formal manner he adopted when he was keyed up," recalled Kissinger, replied cautiously, but he indicated he was interested. Determined to create a new balance of power, Nixon wanted to make Moscow a realpolitik partner in a new world order, not some scary Marxist aggressor waving nuclear missiles and spouting off about world revolution. The French word was **détente;** Nixon's savvy pursuit of it would push the nuclear superpowers away from the brink.[45]

At Kissinger's suggestion, the White House and Kremlin decided to open a back channel—direct, secret communications that cut out the bureaucracy. About once a month—as often as every day during tense periods—Dobrynin would slip into the White House through a little-used and little-noticed entrance in the East Wing and join Kissinger in the Map Room, where the two men would begin the long, tedious, and vital slog toward a nuclear arms control treaty. The State Department would be left on the sidelines and in the dark. Nixon had made his old friend Bill Rogers secretary of state; Rogers had been an adviser to Nixon during the Hiss case, the Checkers speech, and other Nixon crises. But Rogers, Eisenhower's last attorney general and a lawyer at heart, tired of Nixon's endless geostrategic conversations with Kissinger and forfeited his place at the foreign policy table.[46] Kissinger was only too happy to cut out Rogers, and Nixon, too, sought the sort of close control and secrecy provided by "The Channel," as the Dobrynin-Kissinger relationship was called. Kissinger, in his insouciant way, admitted to "vanity and quest for power" as "less elevated motives" for wishing to monopolize the relationship to America's greatest adversary and potential partner for peace. After that first meeting with Dobrynin, Kissinger wrote, "It was characteristic of Nixon's insecurity with personal encounters that he called me into his office four times that day for reassurance that he had done well."[47]

Nixon's insecurities were so evident that they made easy targets, but he could perform with surprising confidence and generosity of spirit. Eager to be seen as a statesman and wishing to repair alliances frayed by time and distress over the Vietnam War, he left for Europe on a ten-day trip after barely a month in the White House. In London, he ran straight into a flap caused by his overzealous aides. Britain's ambassador to the United States, John Freeman—the very one who noted Nixon's shabby treatment by Georgetown society—was supposed to accompany Nixon to a welcoming dinner at the home of the prime minister, 10 Downing Street. Freeman's appointment to Washington had been an awkward mistake—misreading U.S. politics, the Labor Government of Harold Wilson had picked Freeman, a leftist editor of the **New Statesman,** in anticipation of a Hubert Humphrey victory. In his

role of partisan journalist, Freeman had been harshly
critical of Nixon as an unprincipled right-wing hack.
So when Nixon's overprotective minders saw Freeman's name on the guest list, they rashly attempted
to strike it off.[48] The story leaked, as it was sure to.
Wisely, Nixon ordered his staff to stop fussing about
Freeman. Then, with the carefully rehearsed "im-
promptu" eloquence he often showed when called
on to speak at formal occasions, he rose after dinner
and began by saying that American journalists had
written far worse things about him than Freeman
had. "Some say there's a new Nixon and wonder if
there's a new Freeman," he went on. "I would like to
think that's all behind us. After all, he's the new diplomat and I'm the new statesman." The guests, in
British clubman style, thumped the table and called
out, "Hear! Hear!" On the back of his menu, Prime
Minister Wilson wrote Nixon a note: "That was one
of the kindest and most generous acts I have known
in a quarter of a century of politics. Just proves my
point. You can't guarantee being born a lord. It is
possible—you've shown it—to be born a gentleman."[49]

   Nixon did not pause long in Berlin—"a Kennedy
city," he said, recalling JFK's stirring "Ich bin ein
Berliner" speech—and from a speech he struck a
mention of "The Battle Hymn of the Republic"—
"That's a Kennedy song," he said, remembering that
Robert Kennedy had used it as an anthem in his
1968 campaign.[50] Peering out the window of Air
Force One on an icy morning in Paris, Nixon saw

that President de Gaulle, standing erect at the foot of the stairway, was not wearing an overcoat. Nixon took off his overcoat. De Gaulle spoke without notes. Nixon spoke without notes.[51] In his own mind, Kissinger had been giving Nixon only a "B plus" on the trip, and was weary from staying up late reassuring a happy but slurry Nixon in his suite at Claridge's. "Nixon desperately wanted to be told how well he had done," recalled Kissinger. "As he would do on so many other occasions, he asked me to recount his conspicuous role in the day's events over and over again."[52] But on the freezing tarmac at Orly Airport, as he watched his boss keep pace with "Le Grand Charles," Kissinger turned to William Safire and said, "God, to stand up there without notes and say the right thing, do you have any idea what that takes?"[53]

At the Élysée Palace, de Gaulle lectured Nixon about China. Better to recognize the Red Chinese when they need the United States as a counterweight to Russia, said de Gaulle, than to wait until China was a fully capable nuclear power and the United States would hold fewer chips. Nixon was listening closely. He had read that a Kremlin military official had compared Chairman Mao to Hitler and that Chinese and Russian troops were skirmishing on the border. Nixon knew the old adage, "the enemy of my enemy is my friend." The president's resourceful mind was already turning.[54]

On the most difficult question facing him, Nixon asked de Gaulle, "Mr. President, what would you do regarding Vietnam?"

De Gaulle paused for a long time before he spoke. "What is it you expect me to do, Mr. President?" he asked. "Do you want me to tell you what I would do if I were in your place? But I am not in your place!" Even de Gaulle did not have an answer to Vietnam.[55]

There was no good answer. Lyndon Johnson had been consumed by the war and was driven from office by it. During the election Nixon had talked about "peace with honor," a phrase borrowed from Disraeli, and hinted vaguely that he had a plan, but he did not.[56] He had gut responses, geopolitical theories, and innate political savvy, but these could be contradictory and lead to muddle and spasms.

Nixon hoped, unrealistically in retrospect, to end the war quickly. In November, at the Hotel Pierre, shortly after J. Edgar Hoover falsely told the president-elect that LBJ had bugged his campaign plane, Nixon seemed more forgiving to LBJ than angry, according to Haldeman. Nixon stared into his coffee cup for a while and said, "Well, I don't blame him. He's been under such pressure because of the damn war, he'll do anything." Nixon went on: "I'm not going to end up like LBJ, holed up in the White House, afraid to show my face on the street. I'm going to stop that war. Fast. I mean it."[57]

Walking on a foggy beach with Haldeman earlier that summer, Nixon had said, "I'm the one man that can do it, Bob." Nixon believed that the communists feared him above all other American politicians, and he wanted to manipulate this perceived fear to end the war. "They'll believe any threat of force that Nixon makes because it's Nixon," he said.

Nixon loved unpredictability and surprise, and he didn't mind being seen, under the right circumstances, as a little unhinged. "I call it the Madman Theory, Bob. I want the North Vietnamese to believe I've reached the point where I might do **anything** to stop the war. We'll just slip the word to them that, 'for God's sake, you know Nixon is obsessed with Communists. We can't restrain him when he's angry—and he has his hand on the nuclear button'—and Ho Chi Minh himself will be in Paris in two days begging for peace."[58]

Nixon was drawing inspiration from President Eisenhower, who was widely believed to have bluffed with nuclear weapons to end the Korean War. The real truth about the end of the Korean War was more complicated, and in other ways Eisenhower's model wasn't transferable. Eisenhower, the former Supreme Allied Commander and conqueror of Europe, possessed a credibility and an understated confidence that Nixon lacked. Nixon's "Madman Theory" would surface now and again in his frustrated attempts to bring the North Vietnamese to heel, but he would never show a willingness to go all the way—to flood North Vietnam by destroying its dikes or to actually use nuclear weapons.

Kissinger, too, believed that the war could be ended quickly—in a matter of months, he told various acquaintances and friends.[59] He had faith in diplomacy backed by the threat of force, in carrots and sticks, and in his own skill. In his many strategic musings with Nixon, he spoke of "linkage." Reduced to its essentials, "linkage" meant persuading the Russians that they were more likely to get arms control and trade agreements if they put pressure on their allies in Hanoi to end the war. The State Department was not keen on linkage, since it placed Kissinger as the spider at the center of the web.[60] Nor were the Russians, nor were the North Vietnamese. Moscow had some influence over Hanoi, which it was supplying with weapons. But Kissinger overestimated the degree to which the Soviets could control their ally.

The North Vietnamese were willful, stubborn, patient, and intransigent, not to mention wily and deceitful. In time, Kissinger would be reduced to ranting that they were "tawdry, filthy shits."[61] The apparatchiks in Hanoi could wait. They had been fighting the Japanese, then the French, then the Americans, for decades. They could see that the peace movement was gaining strength in the United States. Washington could ignore the noise from the campuses and, increasingly, the hinterlands, but not forever; possibly, not much longer.

Nixon's secretary of defense, Melvin Laird, was listening to the political signals. Foxy, crafty—a "rascal, but our rascal," according to Kissinger, who was half-amused, half-exasperated by him—Laird had been one of the most respected Republican members in the House of Representatives.[62] Nixon valued Laird's political judgment and skills, but he understood that Laird was a double-edged sword, a skilled infighter against his bureaucratic foes, a group Laird sometimes construed to include the president.

Asked about Vietnam, Laird once declared that Nixon "had no plan. I developed the plan." That was not entirely accurate, as historian Melvin Small has pointed out, but more than anyone else, it was Laird who tried to cover the president's political flanks while the war raged on.

Laird's plan was called "Vietnamization." It was not original—the Johnson administration had already begun work on "de-Americanizing" the war. But Laird was clever enough to see that American voters wanted to turn the fighting over to the South Vietnamese and bring the boys home—and that if they did, then America could reduce and ultimately end the draft, the source of so much student dissent.[63]

Nixon knew he had to do something. He inherited 530,000 American troops in Vietnam, dying at the rate of roughly two hundred a week. The Johnson strategy, such as it was, could be called middle-of-the-road. Johnson had stopped the bombing of North Vietnam right before Election Day, and all sides were talking in Paris. But the talks were going nowhere.

With Kissinger.
Courtesy of the Richard Nixon Presidential
Library and Museum

CHAPTER 13

"Need for Joy"

On February 22, 1969, the North Vietnamese launched an offensive into South Vietnam. Nixon took it personally. "It was a deliberate test, clearly designed to take the measure of me and my administration at the outset. My immediate instinct was to retaliate," Nixon wrote in his memoirs.[1] According to Henry Kissinger, Nixon was "seething" as he read the briefing books on Air Force One on the flight to Europe the next day. The president, who as a politician had often favored military intervention but was brand new to the role of commander-in-chief, "suddenly ordered the bombing of the Cambodian sanctuaries," Kissinger recorded.[2]

For years, the military had wanted to bomb the communist sanctuaries in Cambodia. The North Vietnamese moved supplies and men down the so-called Ho Chi Minh Trail, the ever-shifting web of jungle roads and paths just across the border from South Vietnam in neighboring Cambodia and Laos. From Cambodia, the North Vietnamese and their Vietcong allies could mount attacks on nearby Sai-

gon. In the first weeks of the administration—even
before Nixon's order—Kissinger instructed Air Force
Colonel Ray Sitton, whose Pentagon nickname was
"Mr. B-52," to plan for bombing attacks on what
the United States had heretofore regarded as neutral
territory. In the view of the new administration,
lines on the map in this region had not much meaning; the North Vietnamese controlled Cambodia's
bordering territory.

But then Nixon reversed course. Tugged and
pulled by advisers, he rescinded the order, then
changed his mind and reordered the bombing, then
rescinded the order again. His decision was extremely difficult. "Hot pursuit" into neutral territory is an old military doctrine. But bombing
Cambodia seemed sure to set off international protests and inflame the antiwar movement at home.
Nixon's immediate solution would become familiar:
to do it secretly. Impractically, the White House
even requested that the pilots of the B-52s not be
informed they were bombing a different country.

Nixon's desire to bomb was opposed by both Secretary of State William Rogers and Secretary of Defense Melvin Laird, though for different reasons.
Laird was for the bombing, but he wanted to be
open about it, figuring that the news would leak
anyway and just cause a bigger flap. Rogers followed
the State Department's line that the bombing was
morally and legally wrong. Rogers had been excluded from the original decision to bomb; Kissinger was already trying to get him fired.[3]

On Saturday, March 15, the North Vietnamese fired five rockets into Saigon. At 3:35 P.M., National Security Adviser Kissinger received a call from the president. He was ordering the B-52s to bomb the Cambodian sanctuaries. "State is to be notified only after the point of no return. . . . The order is not appealable," Nixon announced, speaking impersonally and emphatically. In his memoirs, Kissinger noted that "not appealable" was a favorite Nixon phrase that meant "considerable uncertainty" and, in the end, served to encourage appeals.[4] A student of Eisenhower, Nixon tried to play the commander-in-chief, but he did not exactly convey Ike's command presence. William Safire recalled a "stray order from the 'Boss'" to press secretary Ron Ziegler: "That's an order. No discussion, unless of course you disagree."[5]

On Sunday afternoon, March 16, Nixon assembled Kissinger, Rogers, Laird, and the chairman of the Joint Chiefs of Staff, General Earle Wheeler, in the Oval Office. It was the first time he would confront an international crisis, but it was a strange meeting, since he had apparently already decided on the outcome.

Kissinger had just brought in a new assistant, Colonel Alexander Haig, a much-decorated and phenomenally ambitious army officer at the Pentagon. One of Haig's duties was to pass messages from his boss to the president late at night. The colonel would find Nixon slid so low in his favorite easy chair that he was essentially lying on his spine, feet up on the ottoman, writing, crossing out, inserting words on his yellow legal tablet. Haig also sat against the wall at important national security meetings at the White House like the one on March 16. Haig recognized that Nixon was "the best informed, best prepared, most articulate, and least predictable person present. It was clear from the earliest moment that this was a man who did not respond to the system but dominated it." But Haig also observed that Nixon was painfully shy, "with an almost pathological distaste of confrontation." Haig was "puzzled" by this flaw, but as he wrote in his memoirs, he "could not yet see that it was fatal."[6]

Over Cambodia, sixty B-52s unleashed their thirty-ton payloads over a "box pattern" 1.5 by 2 miles long. In the jungle, a Vietcong official was jolted awake by "thunder . . . the concussive **whump-whump-whump** came closer and closer," he recalled. The North Vietnamese soldiers hugged the ground, some were "screaming quietly." But, "miraculously," the official recalled, "no one had been hurt." A U.S. Special Forces team was sent in to the area to mop up. The unit was wiped out. A second Special Forces unit was ordered to go but mutinied.

The B-52 operation was called "Breakfast." It would be followed by "Lunch," "Snack," "Dinner," and "Dessert." During the course of these "Menu" bombings, 3,825 B-52s dropped 103,921 tons of munitions. Historians still debate whether the bombing had any effect, other than to widen the war.[7]

· · ·

On the evening of March 16, within hours of his contentious non-meeting on the Cambodia air strike, the president hosted a surprise fifty-seventh birthday party for the First Lady. He had ordered the Army's Strolling Strings to play Pat's favorite Broadway show tunes and invited eighty guests. Nixon was excited about the party. White House social secretary Lucy Winchester recalled that he got so involved in the planning that he sang to her the entire "Happy Birthday" song.[8] But when the night came, he was understandably distracted. At dinner, he stood to raise his glass but said nothing about his wife, just that he wanted Mamie Eisenhower to give the toast. Pat's smile froze, and Mrs. Eisenhower appeared to be caught off-guard. "To a great friend and girl," said the former First Lady and sat down.[9] Cynthia Helms, who was at the dinner, remembered how hard it was to speak to Nixon and that Mrs. Nixon looked "numb." "It dawned on me that he had never mentioned her name," Mrs. Helms recalled.[10]

In later years, Nixon's aides would laugh about the boss's helplessness with anything mechanical and his almost comic clumsiness—the time, on a campaign swing to Maine, when he picked up a lobster and it clawed on to his suit lapel; the time he clunked heads with Anna Chennault at a state dinner; the time he dropped the ball throwing out the first pitch on Opening Day; the many times he dropped medals he was awarding soldiers. (They did not laugh when they recalled how Nixon would weep with the families of the dead ones.) Nixon had to have a specially made Dictaphone with as few buttons as possible, and he could not open pill containers or, according to his wife, hammer a nail.[11] Jeb Magruder, a PR man brought in by Haldeman, described a bill signing ceremony:

> A pen had been placed in front of the President on his desk with the top off. Nixon picked it up, put its top on, and tried to sign the bill with the top on the pen. Realizing his mistake, Nixon took the top off the pen, started to sign his name, but only managed to jab himself in his left hand. At that he dropped the top of the pen on the floor, and total chaos ensued, as half the Cabinet dropped to its knees trying to find the top of the pen.[12]

At 10 Downing Street on his European tour in February, Nixon spilled sauce on his tuxedo, then overturned an inkwell when he tried to write in the guest book. At his first state dinner, for Canadian Prime Minister Pierre Trudeau, on March 24, he spilled soup on his vest. The next morning, he told Haldeman, "We've got to speed up these dinners. They take forever. So why don't we just leave out the soup course." Haldeman hemmed, "Well. . . ." Nixon cut him off: "Men don't really like soup."*

---

*Nixon got excited by all the ways dinner could be speeded up—he hated the chitchat with his guest's wife—and got Haldeman to "put a stop watch on it." Haldeman was able to get a state dinner down to fifty-eight minutes.[13]

• • •

Nixon was meeting with Mel Laird in the Oval Office shortly after noon on March 28 when the president received word that Dwight Eisenhower had died. Nixon stared out the window and "started to cry, just standing there," Haldeman wrote in his diary. The crying became sobs. The president stepped into a small side office and returned, red-eyed, and sat on the edge of the desk, "half-crying."[14] Eisenhower had asked Nixon to deliver his eulogy, not surprising given Nixon's position, but still a deep honor after all of Nixon's years of longing to please and to live up to Ike, who had never quite reciprocated.

Feeling suddenly ill and feverish, Nixon headed to Camp David, the presidential retreat named for Ike's grandson, now Nixon's son-in-law. Sitting by the fire on a cold early spring evening, Nixon began to muse to his speechwriter, Ray Price, about one particular quality that set Eisenhower apart. "Everybody loved Ike," Nixon said, not a little enviously. "But the reverse of that was that Ike loved everybody." Nixon went on: "He never hated his critics, not even the press. He'd just say, 'I'm a little puzzled by those fellows.'"

Price could "picture Nixon's mind working, catching himself." Nixon knew that what he had said was not quite true. It was too much to believe that Ike never felt anger. The difference was that, after a blowup, the anger passed, while Nixon let it fester.[15] At some level, Nixon might have wished to emulate

Eisenhower.* But he couldn't. Possibly, he did not want to; resentment, though toxic, was vital to Nixon.

Nixon's desire to control—and to be seen to be in control—dominated his first nine months in office. He was not so naïve as to believe that he could truly control either events or perceptions, but his realism did not stop him from making heroic, sometimes overly theatrical, attempts to dominate the world stage and all who stood upon it. He was helped and hindered by Kissinger, whose acting skills matched his own.

Nixon, like all presidents, leaked, and, like all presidents, complained about leaks. On April 25, he brought J. Edgar Hoover up to Camp David to ask him what he could do to catch leakers, and Hoover, as expected, told him he could use the FBI to wiretap. Every president since FDR had done so, said Hoover, usually glad to be of service in such matters.[18] On May 9, **The New York Times** disclosed the secret bombing of Cambodia. Kissinger howled

---

*Nixon's eulogy—the first ever by a sitting president—perfectly captured the one great quality that Eisenhower had—but that the incumbent lacked: "His was the humility not of fear but of confidence."[16] Eisenhower welcomed naysayers, but Nixon was ambivalent. Nixon wanted debate, and he made sure to read conflicting views. But he increasingly avoided personal confrontation. "There are no 'no' men around the President. He's surrounded by sycophants," Price lamented to Bill Safire as he worked on the Eisenhower eulogy.[17]

loudest, stomping around the presidential bungalow in Key Biscayne shouting, "We must do something! We must crush these people!"

Kissinger called Defense Secretary Laird, getting him off the course at Burning Tree, the men's golf club just outside Washington. The national security adviser raged, "You son of bitch, I know you leaked that story, and you're going to have to explain it to the President." Laird hung up on Kissinger.[19] Kissinger was protesting too much. He was anxious about the leakiness of his own staff, which was heavy with Harvard liberals. The FBI was put to work.

Over the next twenty months, the FBI electronically eavesdropped on thirteen staffers and four newsmen, seventeen wiretaps in all. In 1973, Nixon would grumble that the taps "never helped us. Just gobs and gobs of material. Gossip and bullshitting." Nixon blamed Kissinger: "He asked that it be done."[20] Curiously, the **New York Times** story disclosing the secret bombing of Cambodia, which was highly classified information, caused no stir. The wiretaps, on the other hand, were evil seeds. They started the White House down a path that would lead to the White House Plumbers and the Watergate break-in.

The president ordered an eighteenth wiretap—not installed by the FBI, which was sending the transcripts to Kissinger—but by a former New York City cop named Jack Caulfield, who did odd jobs for Ehrlichman.[21] Caulfield tapped the phone of **Washington Post** columnist Joe Kraft. The **Post** columnist was regarded suspiciously as a Kissinger conduit. As Kissinger left the White House one night, Nixon, who liked to needle, called out, "There goes Henry, out to call the **Washington Post!**" The irony, noted Kissinger biographer Walter Isaacson, is that "when Nixon had some line he wanted to push, he would send a memo to Kissinger telling him to leak it to Kraft."[22]

Nixon was often restless.[23] Lyndon Johnson had been a prisoner in the White House, he believed, besieged by antiwar protesters. The protesters were still there, and their chants kept Nixon awake at night. So he escaped—on foreign trips and often to Camp David or Key Biscayne or, beginning in the summer of 1969, to a fourteen-room house overlooking the Pacific in San Clemente, California. The Spanish-style Casa Pacifica, adjacent to a compound of offices called the Western White House, was financed with the help of Bebe Rebozo and Robert Abplanalp, the Aerosol magnate ("Let us spray!" joked Nixon's staff). Nixon spent about half his first year away from the White House, and Pat accompanied him about half of that time.[24]

Camp David, the mountain retreat created by Franklin Roosevelt, who had called it Shangri-La, was rustic and a little seedy when the Nixons arrived. Nixon told Haldeman to fix it up, and the chief of staff spared no expense, installing a pool over the bomb shelter and a bowling alley.[25] Shabby genteel was not the Nixons' style. "FDR, born to wealth, appreciated rusticity; Nixon, born poor, appreciated a heated swimming pool right out front," observed William Safire. It suited Nixon's self-image as a Man of Mystery to be on mountaintops and remote beaches, noted Safire—a little out of reach, though never out of touch.[26]

Haldeman was almost always in attendance. On one dog day in summer, he sat in the humid sunshine with the president, who was in his bathing trunks. Haldeman was, as usual, wearing a tie out of respect. "I darn near melted," he wrote in his diary that night. "Was dripping and had a horrible time trying to take notes."[27] Nixon graciously invited Haldeman to bring his wife and children to Camp David, but Haldeman, ever conscious of the president's privacy, instructed his family to scatter whenever the president or his family drew near. More difficult, Haldeman tried to protect the president from Kissinger's insecurities. The latter railed against his rival at State, Secretary Rogers, calling him a "threat to world peace." "Kissinger is on Rogers kick again. . . . Comes in 2–3 times a day. Insists Rogers is trying to get him. . . . Just keep this stuff off his [Nixon's desk]," Haldeman noted at a meeting in San Clemente in August. "The President got into a snit and asked us to form a Henry-Handling Committee to deal with it."[28]

In July, Kissinger had persuaded Nixon to go on a round-the-world trip that was a classic of diplomacy, showmanship, and intrigue. The trip was code-named Operation Moonglow, in honor of the American astronauts who were the first men to walk on the moon. On the first leg of the trip, from the deck of an aircraft carrier in the middle of the Pacific Ocean, Nixon watched the splashdown of Apollo 11.[29] "P was exuberant, really cranked up, like a little kid. Watched everything, soaked it all up," wrote Haldeman in his diary. When the astronauts came on board, Nixon ordered the band to play "Columbia, Gem of the Ocean" (the spacecraft was named **Columbia**).

The press sniped that Nixon was a little too eager to bask in the reflected glory of a moon-launch program started by JFK, but the president was genuinely energized by the example of American can-do spirit. Borrowing from NASA jargon ("All systems go"), Nixon had the idea of using the word **go** as a theme for his presidency. "Means all systems ready, never to be indecisive, get going, take risks, be exciting," Haldeman recorded in his diary. "Must use the great power of the office to **do something**."[30]

Nixon paid a surprise visit to cheering troops in Vietnam and was moved by their resiliency. As Air Force One continued westward, Nixon instructed Haldeman "to never let the hippie-college types in to see him again."[31] In Saigon, President Thieu had greeted Nixon less enthusiastically. To him, "Vietnamization" and the withdrawal of American troops loomed like a potential death sentence. Earlier that summer, at a meeting on an American air base on the Pacific island of Midway, Thieu arrived to find only one big chair flanked by several smaller chairs.

Thieu went and found an equally big chair and placed it directly opposite the chair intended for President Nixon.[32]

In Pakistan, Nixon was impressed by the bluff military bearing of President General Yahya Khan.* Always thinking, Nixon began imagining a role for his new friend General Khan—as a secret go-between to the Red Chinese. In Romania, in a first-ever visit to a communist country by an American head of state, Nixon was overwhelmed by the roaring, freedom-hungry crowds, just as he had been a decade earlier on a vice-presidential trip to Poland. In Romanian strongman Nicolae Ceauşescu, "a strong, independent leader who had cultivated good relations with the Chinese," he found another potential ally in a plan that was taking more distinct form in his mind.[34]

In his vision, Nixon was way ahead of his closest foreign policy adviser. Aboard Air Force One, Haldeman came and took an empty seat beside Kissinger. "You know," said Haldeman, "he actually seriously intends to visit China before the end of the second term." In Haldeman's retelling, Kissinger took off his glasses and polished them. A small smile spread on his face. He turned to the president's chief of staff and said, "Fat chance."[35]

---

*On the ground in Lahore, where Nixon was to review the troops, advance man Henry Cashen radioed up to Air Force One as it circled the airport. Cashen asked for the reason behind the delay; the president's personal assistant, Dwight Chapin, called back and joked, "The Old Man is practicing his goose step."[33]

. . .

With a peculiar blend of affection, admiration, and pity, Kissinger regarded Nixon as a kind of Walter Mitty character, after the funny-sad James Thurber short story "The Secret Life of Walter Mitty," about a meek, mild man who fantasizes about becoming a hero—a combat pilot, an emergency room surgeon, a death-defying explorer—to escape his ordinary life. On August 29, at San Clemente, Nixon was having a drink with his pals Rebozo and Abplanalp when he received word that Palestinian terrorists had kidnapped a TWA flight and flown it to Damascus. "Bomb the airport," Nixon ordered. Kissinger was not sure what to do, but he decided the best option was, as he later put it, "to give the president the opportunity to have second thoughts." To strike Damascus, an aircraft carrier had to be moved closer to Syria in any event, buying time. (Defense Secretary Mel Laird recalled that he planned to cite "weather delays" to stall some more.) At the morning briefing, Kissinger reviewed the steps taken to get the carrier in launch position. Nixon asked, "Did anything else happen?" Kissinger replied, "No." "Good," said Nixon. "I never heard another word about bombing Damascus," said Kissinger. (The passengers, except for two Israeli hostages, were released.)[36]*

*It was not always easy to tell when Nixon was being serious. Nixon once told Secretary of State Bill Rogers, "Fire everybody in Laos." Rogers did not, but apologetically reported to Nixon, "I'm sorry I couldn't carry out your wishes on the Laotian staff

． ． ．

The day before the astronauts landed on the moon, Senator Edward Kennedy drove off a bridge in the middle of the night on Chappaquiddick, an island connected to Martha's Vineyard. The young girl who was with him, a former secretary to Robert Kennedy named Mary Jo Kopechne, did not survive. Nixon's interest in the case was constant as he flew to greet the returning astronauts and continued on around the world. "Wants to be sure he doesn't get away with it," Haldeman wrote in his diary. "Obviously (P feels) he was drunk, escaped from the car, let her drown, said nothing until the police got to him. Shows fatal flaw in his character, cheated at school, ran from accident."[38]

Nixon allowed himself to be hopeful, for a moment, that the press would uncover the true story. "It'll be hard to hush this one up; too many reporters want to win a Pulitzer Prize," he told William Safire. ("In the back seat!" he added, in an apparent sexual reference.)[39] But, before long, he suspected the fix was in. "Check out police chief—Mafia," Haldeman cryptically wrote in his notes while talking to Nixon the day of the accident.[40] Nixon ordered Ehrlichman to use his man, the ex–New York cop Jack Caulfield, to investigate.[41] (Caulfield sent his sidekick, Tony

---

situation, there's the problem of replacement." Rogers recalled that the president "looked at me funny, and asked, 'Was that what I wanted?'" Rogers said, "To fire everyone in Laos, remember?" Nixon responded, "Oh, hell, Bill, you know me better than that."[37]

Ulasewicz, who, posing as a reporter, was unable to dig up any new dirt.) Rattling off these orders, Nixon's mind seems to have darkened, as it sometimes did when he thought of the Kennedys. He still bristled over JFK's comment after the 1960 election—"No class"—when asked to describe Nixon, the same Nixon who had shown the grace not to challenge the shady election results.[42]

On July 21, two days after the accident, Haldeman wrote in his notes while meeting with the president,

> Reg meetings—dirty tricks dept.
> use of power of WH more ruthlessly
> in deadly battle—use all weapons[43]

Nixon was already using some dirty tricks on Kennedy. On March 26, after little more than two months in office, Nixon had ordered "a tail" put on Senator Kennedy, hoping to catch him "girling," as he put it.[44] Alex Butterfield later revealed that he had, to his ultimate regret, carried out a presidential order to use a Secret Service agent as a spy on Kennedy.[45]

And yet, the empathetic Nixon soon emerged. On August 4, meeting with congressional leaders after his global tour, Nixon took aside an obviously shattered Ted Kennedy and talked to him out of earshot of the others for about ten minutes. In his diary, Haldeman, who had asked Nixon what he told Kennedy, wrote:

Told him he understood how tough it was, etc.
Said he was surprised to see how hard the press
had been on him, especially because they like him,
but have to realize they are your enemy at heart
even if they do like you, because their prime motivation is the story.[46]

Safire watched the political rivals from across the
room. "Nixon, who had experienced premature political burial himself, was talking gently and reassur-
ingly, and Kennedy was listening," he recalled. Safire
could not hear what Nixon was saying, but he could
guess from a note Nixon had jotted down, scrawled
on a scrap of paper as he prepared to be asked about
Kennedy's troubles at a press conference. The note
read:

Defeat—doesn't
finish a man—
Quit—does—
A man is not finished
when he's defeated
He's finished
when he
quits.[47]

On September 7, as he flew back to Washington
from the Western White House, Nixon once again
pulled out a yellow pad and described the man and
the president he wanted to be:

Most powerful office
Each day a chance to do something memorable
for someone
Need to be good to do good
Need for joy, serenity, confidence, inspirational
Goals: Set example, inspire, instill pride

1. Personal image of Presidency—Strong, compassionate, competent, bold—Joy in job
2. Nation is better in spirit at end of term[48]

Twice, he used the word "joy" to express a feeling he only rarely showed, usually in moments of high pomp. But he needed to believe, to find sources of optimism and confidence. He was gearing himself up to face his biggest, most intractable problem: ending the war in Vietnam.

It was becoming "Nixon's War." In June, polls suggested that the country was evenly divided on Nixon's performance on Vietnam, but by September, 52 percent disapproved while only 35 percent approved.[49] Nixon was trying to bluff, covertly. On July 15, Nixon sent a secret letter to Ho Chi Minh, warning that if no peace breakthrough came by November 1, the president would be obliged to resort to "measures of great consequence and force." On August 25, the North Vietnamese leader, who was on his deathbed, coldly rebuffed Nixon's threat.[50]

On October 3, on a hot humid morning in Key Biscayne, Nixon, dressed in trunks and a sports shirt, summoned Haldeman and Ehrlichman. In his diary,

Haldeman, in his mildly sardonic way, described the scene: "Sort of one of those mystic sessions, which he had obviously thought about ahead of time." Nixon informed his top aides that he wanted to set aside large chunks of time to work on Vietnam. Then Nixon called in Kissinger, and according to Haldeman's diary, told them that "we have only two alternatives, bug out or accelerate, and that we must escalate or P is lost."[51]

Kissinger was already agitating to step up the war. He had pulled aside a "trusted group" of aides to work on war plans code-named "Duck Hook." (The origins of the code name are murky—according to one mock-serious account, it stood for "all the ducks of American power circling in for the kill"; in another, it was borrowed from golf slang for a wicked shot that curves violently off line.)[52] Kissinger told his staff, "I refuse to believe that a fourth-rate power like North Vietnam doesn't have a breaking point," and set no preconditions on finding it. The staff came up with plans for a four-day blitz in early November, after the expiration date of Nixon's six-month ultimatum to Ho Chi Minh: the bombing of cities and dikes, the mining of harbors, an invasion of North Vietnam, and, possibly, the use of a nuclear device to close the railroad pass to China.[53] If Hanoi didn't sue for peace after four days, America would repeat the punishment.

Kissinger was playing to the president's "madman" side. Although it's very unlikely he would have ever used nuclear weapons, Nixon wanted his foe to fear that he might.* While he had no "secret plan" to end the war, Nixon had been heavily influenced by Dwight Eisenhower's stratagem for ending the Korean War in 1953—to let it be known, through subtle signals—that the new Eisenhower administration was seriously contemplating the use of nuclear weapons. The Korean War was probably ended less by nuclear threats than war-weariness in communist capitals, but Nixon believed that Ike's bluff had paid off.

As vice president, Nixon had spent considerable time observing Eisenhower at national security meetings. Ike's practice was to encourage vigorous debate by asking provocative questions, including whether the time had come to end the "taboo" on the use of nuclear weapons.[55] But Eisenhower never shared with anyone whether he would actually use the weapons and indeed may not have known himself. Eisenhower came to the presidency with years of experience as a wartime commander after a long apprenticeship as a peacetime staffer. Nixon, who had served as a low-ranking supply officer and reached high office after a brief apprenticeship (elected vice president before he turned forty), was much less seasoned and prepared for the loneliness of command. Eisenhower

*In 2006, the National Security Archive disclosed documents suggesting that Nixon ordered a Strategic Air Command show of force in October 1969 that was tantamount to a nuclear alert. The purpose was to try to "jar" the North Vietnamese and their Soviet sponsors into making concessions. Hanoi apparently was not moved by Nixon's nuclear saber-rattling.[54]

had learned to keep an iron grip on his hot temper and always projected calm. Nixon was **usually** calm in crisis, almost preternaturally so at times. At other times, he allowed his emotions to take control and seemed to lurch unsteadily.

Nixon, at first, favored Kissinger's plan to strike the North with a heavy bombing campaign. But then he pulled back. He could not be absolutely sure that North Vietnam—fourth-rate power or no— would break under the onslaught. He worried that the Russians and Chinese would react violently (and that he would undermine his plan, still half-formed, to create an opening to China). His own secretaries of state and defense were opposed to Duck Hook. Kept in the dark by Kissinger, they found out about the plan only in early October, when Nixon floated the essence to some senators, who promptly leaked it to columnists Rowland Evans and Robert Novak.[56] Rogers and Laird worried that escalation would drive the antiwar movement into a frenzy. They favored further troop withdrawals as a way of defusing protest and calming the country.[57]

Nixon was a political pragmatist. He worried that Laird and Rogers would resign if he went ahead with Kissinger's plan, and he was getting tired of Kissinger's constant feuding with Rogers. "I sense a growing intolerance of K's attitude and habits. He overreacts and this bothers the P," Haldeman wrote in his diary on October 13.[58]

By then, Nixon had already decided to shelve Duck Hook. The roll-the-dice, go-for-broke gambler in Nixon was at odds with the careful poker player who measured the odds and knew when to fold. More often than not, after some bluster, the more prudent Nixon prevailed. Usually, he looked for ways to blame someone else if he had to back off. The fall guys in this case were the peaceniks. "The only chance for my ultimatum to succeed was to convince the Communists that I could depend on solid support at home if they decided to call my bluff. However, the chances I would actually have their support were becoming increasingly slim."[59]

The antiwar movement was spreading off the campuses and into communities. It had taken a violent turn, with burnings and bombings, but also become more mainstream. Mothers and fathers were upset about their alienated and lost children. Antiwar organizers were calling for a national day of protest on October 15, a moratorium on work and school to call on Nixon to end the war.

At a press conference at the end of September, Nixon had been asked for his "view" of the coming moratorium. "Under no circumstances will I be affected whatever by it," he responded. Haldeman knew better: "Keeps coming back to the October 15 Moratorium Plan, although he says it doesn't concern him," Haldeman recorded in his diary that night.[60]

On October 15, hundreds of thousands of people gathered in communities all across the country to hold church services, town meetings, and teach-ins. Some were protesting for the first time.[61] From the

White House that night, the staff could see thousands of candles flickering on the Mall. The protests
were mostly peaceful. "A great sigh of relief because
it wasn't nearly as bad as everyone had feared," Haldeman wrote in his diary.[62] But President Nixon was
not relieved. He knew he was losing the country. He
headed to the mountaintop, where he could be alone
to think and plan.

With Bob Finch, John Mitchell, and Spiro Agnew.
Courtesy of the Richard Nixon
Presidential Library and Museum

CHAPTER 14

Silent Majority

On the night of the October 15 Moratorium, Nixon wrote at the top of a yellow pad, "Don't get rattled—don't waver—don't react." Then he went to Camp David to try to figure out the smartest way to seize back the initiative. For "twelve to fourteen hours a day," he recalled, he wrote and rewrote a speech that would, in time, come to be regarded as a conservative manifesto of the culture wars.[1] He did not get much sleep. "Before big speeches, he'd wander around at night," recalled one of his personal aides, Jack Brennan. "He would find an empty cabin and work there. He wanted to be alone." Endlessly scrawling on his yellow pads, Nixon went through a dozen drafts before he called Haldeman and breezily announced, "Well, the baby's been born."[2]

On a Monday night, November 3, at 9:30 P.M. Eastern time, the president addressed an audience of 70 million people. "There were some who urged that I end the war at once," he said. "This would have been the popular and easy course to follow." A

favorite Nixon speech construction was to set up a
morally dodgy straw man and then say, with humble
sincerity (or unctuous piety, depending on one's
view of Nixon), "but that would be wrong. . . ."
Speaking to the nation in a gentle tone, as if more in
sorrow than in anger, Nixon raised a specter that he
knew would rattle most Americans: "The first defeat
in our nation's history would result in a collapse of
confidence in American leadership, not only in Asia
but throughout the world."

He pledged to "win the peace," using the same
gauzy if uplifting phrase he had employed during
his presidential campaign. He said that he had a
"plan for peace," though he did not spell out what it
was, beyond more fighting and talking, coupled
with gradual troop withdrawals. (He made no mention of Duck Hook.)

Then he began his peroration:

And so tonight—to you, the great silent majority
of my fellow Americans—I ask for your support. . . .
    Let us be united for peace. Let us also be united
against defeat. Because let us understand: North
Vietnam cannot defeat or humiliate the United
States. Only Americans can do that.[3]

The Silent Majority. Nixon had come up with
the phrase himself, at 4 A.M. on the last night he
spent at Camp David.[4] "Silent majority" was an old
phrase meaning dead people, noted Nixon word-

smith William Safire—to join the silent majority meant to die and go to a cemetery.⁵ But Nixon's brilliant reinvention of the term was a political masterstroke. It was a natural extension of a theme he had been working on ever since he figured out how the Orthogonians might trump the Franklins. He had long spoken of "quiet Americans" and "forgotten Americans"; now he had found a way to capture the flag back from the protesters—the "loud minority" who, alone, could humiliate the United States.⁶

Nixon wasn't sure how the speech had played. He dined alone afterward in the Lincoln Sitting Room, refusing to watch the TV commentators. His family did, however, and they were "livid," Nixon recalled. Tricia came in and said to her father, "They talked as if they had been listening to a different speech than the one you made."⁷ ABC News had put on Averell Harriman as a scoffing commentator—the same Harriman who had announced, "I will not break bread with this man" at Joe Alsop's house after the 1950 senate campaign. Most of the TV commentators tried to be balanced. They were not so much biased as dim: They missed the political significance of Nixon's appeal to the Silent Majority.

Between 10:15 P.M. and 1:15 A.M., Haldeman recorded, Nixon called him "at least 15–25 times" wanting to know how the speech had played and ordering a counterattack on critics. Haldeman shorthanded Nixon's request: "If [you] only do one thing get 100 vicious dirty calls to **New York Times** and **Washington Post** about their editorials," he wrote, adding with a note of parenthetical exasperation, "even though no idea what they'll be."[8] The chief of staff got busy, generating a massive campaign of letters and telegrams praising Nixon and denouncing his enemies. For days, Nixon kept the telegrams, stacked in piles, in the Oval Office to show to visitors.[9]

The congratulatory telegrams were partly contrived, but Nixon was not wrong when he told Haldeman that his speech was the greatest turnaround job since the Checkers Speech (or, as Nixon preferred, the Fund Speech) in 1952. Polls showed that more than three out of every four Americans approved of the speech, and Nixon's approval rating shot up from 52 to 68 percent.[10] The White House PR team, working with a patriotic salesman named H. Ross Perot, whose computer company had won some hefty government contracts, began printing American flags on bumper stickers and lapel pins, sending the message, not so subtly, that to be against the war was unpatriotic.[11]

Pat Buchanan, Nixon's most hardline speechwriter, had another idea: Unleash Spiro Agnew on the press. Up to this point, the vice president had been regarded by White House staffers, as well as by the president himself, as a nonentity, if not a nuisance. In April, Nixon had told Haldeman that Agnew "must not be involved in decisions. Mustn't insist on talking to P. He's supposed to help the P.— take his line and sell it."[12] Ehrlichman reproduced a nasty little saying in his office diary on November 14: "The Assassin's Dilemma: if they kill Nixon, they get Agnew."[13] But with some help from Buchanan and especially Safire, who had a fondness for biting alliteration, Agnew made an excellent press basher. He had caused a mild stir in October by referring to antiwar activists as "an effete corps of impudent snobs who characterize themselves as intellectuals." Now he ramped up the rhetoric, referring to the "media elite" as "nattering nabobs of negativism."

Nixon loved it. "P was really pleased with VP talk last night (attacking TV network newscasters) and feels he's become a really good property, and we should keep building him and using him," Haldeman recorded.[14] Going over Agnew's remarks with Buchanan, Nixon used a gross expression: "This really flicks the scab off, doesn't it?" the president said.

Nixon was talking about scabs left by Agnew's earlier slashing attack on "impudent intellectuals," but he might as well have been talking about his own emotional scar tissue. Though Nixon tried to control his anger, he could not, or perhaps would not, let old wounds heal. He used the expression repeatedly: He "kept 'flicking off the scab,' in his skin-crawling metaphor," wrote Safire.[15] It was as if he wished to be reminded of the hurt inflicted on him by his tormenters in the press; he rubbed old wounds raw, like a boy, and they festered.

To be so stridently called out by the vice president of the United States was intimidating to communications executives whose businesses were licensed by the federal government. At first, they were cowed.

They worried, not unreasonably, about losing their broadcast licenses.[16] And for the next massive antiwar demonstration, on November 15, the news coverage was different, more skeptical, cooler. The protest was different, too—uglier, more violent. At the Justice Department, protesters chanting "Smash the state!" tore down the American flag and hoisted a Vietcong flag. Standing on the balcony, Attorney General John Mitchell gave them the finger.[17]

At the White House, ringed by city buses to keep the mob away, there was talk of using helicopters to blow out the protesters' candles. Nixon pretended to ignore the whole thing, watching a football game on TV.[18] He knew that he had shifted the public perception, aligned himself with patriots and identified the antiwar movement with the bombers and flagburners. He was winning the PR war.

But he was not winning the war in Vietnam. In his private communication with Kissinger, Nixon was gloomy. Preparing his Silent Majority speech, he had bluntly asked Kissinger, "Is it possible we were wrong from the start in Vietnam?"[19] On November 24, as the euphoria from the speech reaction wore off, he wrote Kissinger: "I get the rather uneasy impression that the military are still thinking in terms of a long war and eventual military solution. I also have the impression that deep down they realize the war can't be won militarily, even over the long haul."[20]

Kissinger didn't disagree, but he was hopeful that force could be matched with secret diplomacy. He had used Nixon's round-the-world trip in August as cover to slip away in Paris to a secret meeting with North Vietnamese negotiator Le Duc Tho. It was all very "cloak and dagger," as Nixon put it, "with Kissinger riding slouched down in the back seats of speeding Citroens, eluding inquisitive reporters."[21] Kissinger, with sly humor that amused his fellow top aides, took to referring to Le Duc Tho as "Ducky." But he also called the North Vietnamese "insolent" and made little progress.[22] Stonewalling Kissinger, Hanoi was cheeky about the American antiwar movement. "May your fall offensive succeed splendidly," Radio Hanoi had announced to the students and protesters before the Moratorium.[23]

Nixon was beginning to feel what LBJ had felt: trapped. He would come to regret not unleashing Duck Hook. Years later, he told Kissinger's biographer Walter Isaacson: "In retrospect, I think we should have done it."[24]

In an interview with the author in 2013, Kissinger echoed Nixon's regret and said, ruefully, about his Duck Hook plan, "I didn't follow up. Was I covering my ass or making a serious policy recommendation?"[25] In truth, there were probably no simple answers, no good way out.

As his first year drew to a close, Nixon girded himself, once again, for the fight. On December 8, Safire sent him a memo warning the president that "attacks on a biased press and sinister eastern establishment solidify some support, but in the long run, unless tempered, run the danger of appearing thin-skinned and whining." Nixon wrote in the margin, "We don't resent. We are not affected."[26] Three weeks later he explained to Ehrlichman why the press disliked him. It "wasn't personal," Nixon told his aide, according to Ehrlichman's notes. The press's "hatred" was "based on fact." As Nixon explained it, "They don't roll me very often." He went on: "Seventy-five percent of these guys hate my guts. They don't like to be beaten: Hiss, Moscow, Caracas, 1968, 11/3"—referring to his Silent Majority speech on November 3—"the biggest beating," Nixon added. As he so often did, Nixon returned to the Hiss case. "You know, in the Hiss battle I was alone," he said. "Ninety-five percent of the columnists and news stories were against me. They all said Whittaker Chambers was lying." Henry Kissinger, quick to the play, chimed in, "Hiss was the epitome of the Eastern Establishment, Mr. President. You and Chambers were outsiders. The wrongness of Hiss really rankled the press." Nixon nodded. "Intellectuals can't stand a fight and they can't stand to lose," he said.[27]

To prepare for his State of the Union in January, Nixon told his staff to clear his schedule for two weeks in mid-January. He holed up in the Executive Office Building by day and the Lincoln Sitting Room by night, setting off the White House fire alarm at 2:30 A.M. when he tried to light some logs.[28] Finally he headed to Camp David, to wander the cabins.

His determination, as expressed in the notes he made to himself, is touching. At the top of one sheet, he listed the time—10:25 at night—and first wrote himself a reminder to seek out nourishment ("Manola [his valet Manolo, misspelled]—Time to eat something!"). Then he recited a litany that is partly a prosaic to-do list for a State of the Union speech, partly a PR plan, and partly an expression of deep personal longing.

> Goals:
>   Family:
>   Dignity—
>   Glamour—(Martha Mitchell re. Kennedy royalty]*
>   Personal leadership:
> Excitement—Joy in Job—Sharing
> Lift spirit of people
> Pithy—memorable phrases
> Brevity
> Moving conclusion
> Anecdote
> Statesmanship
> Honesty—Candor

He penciled a box around a second list:

> Hard work
> Consideration for subordinates
> Concern for people—
>   Letters—

*This is presumably a reference to advice given him by the flamboyant wife of the attorney general to try to emulate the Kennedys.

Calls—
Intelligence
Effect on small groups
<u>Vitality</u>

Four days later, writing an "analysis of 1st year," he allowed a trace of self-pity to creep in:

No credit for

1. Treatment of staff (doesn't embarrass—blow up). RMW [Rose Mary Woods]—Correction of errors— doesn't blame—
2. New Social Events—W.H.
3. Treatment of opponents

a. LBJ—Park [word illegible; Nixon had attended the dedication of the Lady Bird Johnson Redwood Grove in August 1969]
b. H.H.H. to astronaut [Nixon had invited Hubert Humphrey to a party for the Apollo astronauts; Nixon had not been extended a similar courtesy by JFK]

But then he vowed to redouble his efforts to be an upbeat, communicative, sociable, fun-loving All-American president:

Need—(for emphasis)
Work hard—
Treatment of staff

White House Social events—
Bold—gutsy initiatives
Telephone Calls
Music plus football[29]

Nixon was never going to reconcile the man he wished to be with the man he feared he was. Alone, at night with his yellow pad, he could imagine and yearn for a leader who was tough but compassionate, bold but wise, firm but gentle. In company, overwhelmed by social anxiety, he sometimes could not speak at all. He would spin his hands, helpless to articulate his eager, almost boyish idealism while maintaining the pose of **l'homme serieux.**

On January 20 Nixon celebrated his first anniversary in office. He buzzed two of his closest associates, H. R. Haldeman and Rose Woods—"each of whom cordially despised the other," recalled Safire— into the Oval Office. The room was half-dark in the early winter dusk. Standing in his overcoat, Nixon lifted the lid on a silver music box. It tinkled out "Hail to the Chief," getting a little slow toward the end. Shutting the box, the president said only, "Been a year." Then, as Safire recounted the scene, he "walked through the French doors into the night; end of celebration."[30] That night, Nixon was seated next to Liz Moynihan at a cabinet dinner at Blair House. Vivacious, dressed in a slinky halter top on this evening, Mrs. Moynihan was rarely at a loss for words. "I tried to open him up, saying that he must be happy about the editorials, even the **New York Times**," she recalled, citing a wave of friendly press at the end of Year One. "He couldn't answer. I noticed that his hands kept spinning."[31]

Nixon had outmaneuvered the peace movement to seize back the support of Middle America for Vietnam. Now, as he shaped his State of the Union, he wanted to outflank the liberals and raid their base on the home front as well. Reading his copy of Robert Blake's **Disraeli** and chatting with his social history tutor, Pat Moynihan, he was inspired by the notion that "Tory men with liberal policies" had done what liberals could not—win the support of working men to overcome conservative opposition.[32]

When Nixon took office, Democrats had controlled both houses of Congress for all but four years going back to FDR and the New Deal. LBJ's Great Society had ushered in a raft of programs to help the poor and the middle class. Americans might grumble about government, but they had become accustomed to its benefits and wanted more. Although the country had veered slightly right in 1968, partly in reaction to the over-promising of the Great Society, the body politic was actually tilting leftward again in 1970.[33] Social scientists were still in the ascendancy and dominated federal agencies; the conventional wisdom among most opinion makers held that, with enough money and brainpower, government technocrats could cure society's ills.[34]

That was the political reality in 1970, and Nixon was a realist. His contradictory acts and impulses have to be seen in light of the liberal zeitgeist of the era and political necessity (or expediency). Like the liberals he scorned, Nixon was not above buying votes with government benefits. While Nixon wanted to take the high road to govern, politics—getting elected—was a different matter. "He had an idealistic view of government," recalled Jim Schlesinger, whom Nixon appointed to run three different agencies (Atomic Energy Commission, the CIA, and Defense). "But then politics were dog-eat-dog, get-them-before-they-got-you. It was as if there was no connection."[35] Of course, there **was** a connection—Nixon was perfectly well aware that his ability to govern depended on political skills, his ability to persuade lawmakers that it was in their political interest to back his policies. But Schlesinger's bafflement is understandable. Nixon's approach to government is a riddle that needs to be solved with proper attention to Nixon's political genius and his complex psyche.

Nixon liked to rail against "liberal bureaucrats" and suspected, not wrongly in many cases, that they were working against him. He tried from time to time, without much success, to restrain federal spending, which was largely controlled by a free-spending Congress. In the winter of 1970, Schlesinger was assistant director of the Bureau of the Budget and spent "hours and hours" with the president going over spending requests. He vividly recalled the Nixon approach and the inevitable pushback:

I'd bring up an agency and invariably he would say, "Not worth a damn. Cut 'em in half." I'd go back and say this to the budget examiners, and they would go to pieces before your eyes. "Cut in half? Good God, what can we give up?" They'd come back and say, "We really can't cut that." One day, he leaned over and said, "You know, Jim, I don't know the first thing about these agencies. I figure if I tell you, cut them in half, it will strengthen your hand." It was Nixon on stage, playing a role, like his Madman Theory on Vietnam.[36]

Nixon wanted to take power away from Congress and federal agencies and give it "back to the people," or at least to their elected representatives in state and local government. To do this, he first sought to greatly concentrate power in the White House, a move guaranteed to make him more enemies on the Hill and in the Federal Triangle. ("Bringing power to the White House," he later explained to historian Joan Hoff, was necessary to "dishing it out.")[37] In January of 1970, he was still searching for an animating theme and a label. "Need for a name," he jotted on his yellow pad on the night of January 14 as he prepared for his State of the Union address. He listed those coined by his predecessors: "Square Deal, Fair Deal, New Deal, New Frontier, Great Society."[38] The name Nixon came up with—"the New Federalism"—was more confusing than catchy. It sounded to voters unfamiliar with the papers of

James Madison to be a program for **more** federal government, not less.

The 1960s had been a time of great ferment on social policy. Nixon scorned academic "eggheads" and meddlesome bureaucrats, but his intellectual curiosity was piqued by the new "movements" bubbling up in an age of liberal activism. Ed Cox, Tricia's suitor, was an earnest and fairly liberal Harvard Law School student who had worked for consumer advocate Ralph Nader. Cox would spend many hours talking to Nixon, who liked and sought out stimulating young people. To get ahead of the consumer movement (and to outflank the liberals), Nixon appointed a woman, Virginia Knauer, to direct an Office of Consumer Affairs in the White House. Nader dismissed the new office as a "speech making operation," but Knauer proved to be an aggressive consumer advocate.[39]

Nixon's boldest and best idea was welfare reform. In August, Nixon had proposed getting rid of the existing system, which fostered family breakup because it went to mothers who were single, and instead guarantee the poor a minimum income, provided they took jobs or sought job training. Nixon wanted to call the program "workfare" but was convinced to adopt the safer, if blander, "Family Assistance Program" (FAP). From his own Depression-era experience, seeing hungry and homeless people begging for food at his father's grocery, he knew the shame of asking for handouts. His father had left the family badly strapped by refusing to put Nixon's

dying older brother in a free state-run TB sanatorium and instead paying out of pocket to send Hannah and her sick son out into the desert mountains.[40]

Nixon knew that conservatives would oppose a
guaranteed minimum income—really, a negative
income tax—as a "mega-dole."[41] But he hoped to
win enough moderates and liberals to pass Congress.
For once, he lowballed liberal contempt. Defensive
of the welfare state, which provided jobs for middle-
class whites as well as services for poor people, the
liberal establishment labeled the program as "racist."
FAP, said the lobbyists for the National Welfare
Rights Organization, stood for "Fuck America's
Poor."[42] FAP passed the House but ultimately died
in the Senate—"an idea ahead of its time," Nixon
wrote, correctly, in his memoirs.*

It was probably inevitable that Nixon's infatua-
tion with Moynihan would fade. Once, when
Moynihan was lecturing about ending global poverty, the president turned to fellow tough guy Ehrlichman and stage-whispered, "Doesn't it make you
want to puke?" Moynihan was never going to fit in
with the buttoned-up PR types occupying the West
Wing. Padding around in his slippers ("he went to

---

*Nixon the high-road reformer could become Nixon the expedi-
ent pol in a heartbeat. Nixon turned Machiavellian once he saw
that FAP was in jeopardy from the left. By the summer of 1970,
Nixon had given up on his and Moynihan's bold initiative. On
July 13, Haldeman sounded FAP's death knell in his diary: the
president "wants to be sure it's killed by Democrats and that we
make a big play for it, but don't let it pass, can't afford it."[43]

bed at 5 A.M., so 8 A.M. meetings were tough," recalled wife Liz), Moynihan looked like a "giant Lep-
rechaun" in an office full of handsome young bank
trainees, recalled Nixon advance man Charles Stuart.[44] Moynihan, a deft courtier, generally told the
president what he wanted to hear. Will FAP eliminate social workers? Nixon asked. "Wipe them out!"
Moynihan responded enthusiastically.[45] But Moynihan could not resist jousting with (and usually one-
upping) Nixon's more conservative economic adviser
Arthur Burns. Though he played one man against
the other, Nixon soon grew tired of Moynihan's turf
wars with Burns over domestic policy. In the fall of
1969, he kicked Moynihan upstairs with a "Counsellor to the President" title and named the more
reliable if no less liberal Ehrlichman to reorganize
Moynihan's and Burns's duties under an umbrella
Domestic Affairs Council.[46]

When Ehrlichman, who was ambitious as well as
efficient, took over domestic policy, the "thinkers"
on the staff, both from the left and the right—men
like Safire, Len Garment, Pat Buchanan, and Ray
Price—fretted, as one put it, that "the balloon men
have taken over." As tour director of the 1968 campaign, Ehrlichman had been in charge of dropping
the balloons at the end of Nixon rallies.[47]

A few old Nixon hands (the surviving moderates)
still mark the day when Ehrlichman took over as
chief domestic adviser to the president—only a year
into his first term—as the beginning of the end,
when Nixon the deep thinker and reformer morphed

into Nixon the purely political opportunist.[48] This is a misreading of the man, but an understandable one. The Nixon who spent hours with his yellow pads rethinking the nature of government and dreaming of new world orders is hard to reconcile with the Nixon who often cut deals that seem less than principled. Part of the confusion stems from Nixon's emotional makeup. He needed to vent and blurt—cut that damn agency in half!—before settling down and shrewdly estimating what was possible and what was not. Nixon saw himself as a strategic thinker, but he was also a superb tactician with an instinctive sense of the possible. Nixon, as the optimist he wished to be, saw the potential for the Big Play; Nixon, as the pessimist he really was, stood willing and able to take what he could get. Nixon was a great admirer of Woodrow Wilson, who dreamed of making the world safe for democracy, but he was philosophically closer to Burke, the British statesman who valued realism and compromise.

In his search for the "lift of a driving dream," as he put it in his 1970 State of the Union, Nixon's rhetoric could be overwrought. He drove his speechwriters to manufacture eloquence. Ray Price, author of the "lift of a driving dream" line, stayed up three straight nights until, addled by amphetamines, he began to hallucinate.[49] Nixon was more convincing when he followed Price's instinct toward moderation and his own bent toward pragmatism. For all his pride in American exceptionalism, Nixon understood that he was often operating from a position of

strategic weakness. Abroad, America could no longer count on being the sole superpower as the Soviet
Union and China built and improved their nuclear
arsenals and continued to sell a brand of Marxism
that was remarkably appealing to the postcolonial
world. At home, Nixon was the first newly elected
president in over a century to face a Congress in
which the opposing party controlled both the House
and Senate. Compromise was essential. Nixon was
more of an activist than an obstructionist, and he
worked with the Democrats to pass a great deal of
progressive legislation.

The list of what the Nixon administration accomplished domestically makes Nixon look like a
great liberal as well as one of the last of the big spend-
ers. Historian Melvin Small cites what Congress
passed and Nixon signed into law, sometimes after
resisting but usually by compromising: extension of
the Voting Rights Act, postal reorganization, the
Clean Air Act, the Water Pollution Control Act, the
establishment of the Environmental Protection
Agency (EPA), the establishment of an Office of
Consumer Affairs in the White House, expansion of
the national park system, the Occupational Safety
and Health Administration Act (OSHA), the Rail
Passenger Service Act that created Amtrak, the vote
for eighteen-year-olds, the State and Local Fiscal Assistance Act (revenue sharing), the end of Selective
Service (the draft), the beginning of the federal "war"
against cancer, and dramatic increases in spending
on the arts and public broadcasting. He increased

spending on social security and Medicare faster than inflation—making him, by some measures, a bigger spender on social programs than LBJ had been.[50] In 1974, Nixon proposed massive health care reform that Senator Edward Kennedy blocked—and later regretted that he had.[51]

Much of this was the handiwork of John Ehrlichman, who would come to see himself as a kind of a domestic president while Nixon attended to his first love, foreign policy. Ehrlichman was easy to underestimate. He had been an obscure zoning lawyer in Seattle and, when he stuck out his lower lip, "looked buttoned-up to the point of bursting," wrote the un-buttoned-up Moynihan.[52] But he was politically shrewd, and he understood that progressive politics could win votes. His own politics were moderate to liberal, especially on the environment, which he had learned to cherish living in the Pacific Northwest. "Ehrlichman sold him on the environment," recalled John Whitaker, who became Nixon's chief staffer dealing with environmental issues. "He made Nixon see it was politically dangerous if he didn't get on board. He brought in pollsters to say, 'this thing is catching fire!'"[53]

Nixon could see that his most likely opponent in 1972, Senator Edmund Muskie of Maine, was getting ready to ride the Green wave; he was already deeply involved in plans for a first-ever "Earth Day" in April. In Ehrlichman's diary notes for October 23, 1969, he wrote "need a bold stroke" and "pull the rug from under Muskie."[54] In his State of the Union address, Nixon pledged his administration, in general terms, to cleaning up the environment. Nixon's younger brother Ed, a strong environmentalist who, like Ehrlichman, lived in the Pacific Northwest, weighed in. "He listened," Ed Nixon recalled, "but he would say, 'You have to keep the employer healthy and wealthy.'"[55] With Ehrlichman, Nixon was more blunt: "In a flat choice between smoke and jobs, we're for jobs. . . . But just keep me out of trouble on environmental issues." Depending on the audience, he promised to protect big business **and** the environment. He would proclaim that if the Greens took over, "there won't be any private enterprise, no industry left in America." Then he would privately take aside Chris DeMuth, a twenty-three-year-old White House aide, and tell him to develop an environmental policy—but without consulting the secretary of commerce, Maurice Stans. "If Maury Stans is involved, he'll bring in all his business friends and nothing will happen. So stay away from Stans," President Nixon told young DeMuth. "I'll protect you. We'll let him know when we're done."[56]

Nixon's interest in the environment would wax and wane; in a diary entry in August, Haldeman observed that Nixon skipped a helicopter tour of the smog problem of Los Angeles to play golf instead.[57] But he was sensitive to the times and public sentiment, as well as to nature's beauty. Nixon "saw the polls," recalled Whitaker. "His eyes would glaze over when we got into detail. But if you mentioned 'parks,' he would lighten up again. He said he had gone to Yosemite as a kid."[58]

Delivering his first State of the Union speech on January 22, 1970, Nixon sounded like a champion of government as friend of the poor and healer of the weak. As Nixon biographer Richard Reeves pointed out, he borrowed the rhythms of Martin Luther King Jr. Standing at the Speaker's podium as he addressed the House and the Senate, the Joint Chiefs, the cabinet, and the Supreme Court, he began:

> I see an America in which we have abolished hunger, provided the means for every family in the nation to obtain a minimum income, made enormous progress in providing better housing, faster transportation, improved health and superior education. . . .

He went on to promise to spend $10 billion on "clean water" and concluded with a sweeping declaration that he had remembered from a quote from Thomas Jefferson. We act, Nixon said, "not for ourselves alone, but for the whole human race."

The establishment press was delighted by the liberal tilt of Nixon's State of the Union speech. "Nixon, Stressing Quality of Life, Asks in State of Union Message for Battle to Save the Environment," bannered **The New York Times**. Dan Rather of CBS

saw the political sleight of hand and folksily invoked
Tom Sawyer: "What it boils down to is that the
President has caught the Democrats bathing and
he's walked away with their clothes."[59]*

---

*Jokes about clothes, as in the emperor has none, were back in
the news a few days later. On his foreign trips, particularly at the
Élysée Palace in Paris, Nixon had been impressed by the grandly
turned out guards. He noted that the White House guards
looked like traffic cops. The obliging White House staff got to
work, and for a state visit by British Prime Minister Harold Wilson on January 27, the White House police force appeared
dressed as if for a comic opera, in white double-breasted tunics,
trimmed with gold braid; stars on their epaulets; and tall plastic
caps emblazoned with the presidential seal. The press was merci-
less: "Ruritania, D.C.," jeered **The New York Times. The Chicago Daily News** was reminded of the characters in **The Student
Prince.** Mrs. Nixon was horrified. The uniforms were gone in
two weeks; the hats were donated to a high school band and
eventually surfaced at a rock concert.[60]

Commander-in-chief.
Courtesy of the Richard Nixon Presidential
Library and Museum

CHAPTER 15

The Moviegoer

On October 26, 1969, in the case of **Alexander v. Holmes County Board of Education**, the U.S. Supreme Court ruled that public schools could no longer desegregate "with all deliberate speed," the standard set by the court in its famous school desegregation cases in the mid-1950s. Many school boards, especially in the South, had stalled or outright defied the courts. The High Court ruled that desegregation must be "immediate."

In many places, again especially in the South, the reaction was angry. Congressman Otto Passman of Louisiana came to the Oval Office to show President Nixon a photograph of "his little golden-haired granddaughter" who was "bein' bused right past her neighborhood school" clear across town to the formerly all-black high school. Ehrlichman recalled that Nixon talked "for days" about Passman's visit.[1]

Nixon was not above pandering to Southern voters. To attract their votes in 1968, he had promised to choose "strict constructionists" for the Supreme Court. When his nominee Clement Haynsworth, a reputable Southern conservative judge, was voted down by Senate liberals in the fall of 1969, Nixon was furious. He said to Harry Dent, his White House emissary to the South, "Harry, I want you to go out this time and find a good federal judge **further south and further to the right**."[2] Dent, as aides sometimes did, took Nixon too literally. It soon came out that his next nominee, G. Harrold Carswell, had once declared, "I believe that segregation of the races is proper" and that he had endorsed "the principles of white supremacy." When Nixon read of Carswell's comments in his daily news briefing, he wrote in the margin, "My God!"[3]

When Nixon was trying to sound tough, in the manner of one of the boys in a circa-1950 country club locker room, he would sometimes make racist remarks. "Is there something in it for the jigs?" he asked Henry Kissinger about an upcoming presidential address to Congress that February. With Ehrlichman, he opined that blacks were "just down out of the trees."[4] In March, when Congress considered creating a Martin Luther King holiday, Nixon wrote Haldeman in larger-than-usual handwriting, "No! Never! That would be like making Nero Christ!"[5]

But this was largely vile bluster, Nixon's exhaust pipe opened too wide. On the subject of Nixon and race, the words of Nixon's attorney general, John Mitchell, are also instructive. On July 1, 1969, during a meeting with a group of thirty African Americans who had come to protest administration policies on civil rights, Mitchell puffed on his pipe and said, "You would be better advised to watch what we do instead of what we say."[6] What Nixon did on school desegregation during the course of 1970 is an example of Nixon's political judgment, a quality defined by British philosopher and statesman Isaiah Berlin as "a capacity for integrating a vast amalgam of constantly changing, multicolored, evanescent, perpetually overlapping data."[7] It is an example of Nixon's pragmatic politics—also, his occasionally well-concealed desire to do the right thing.

In Alabama, George Wallace began talking of running for president in 1972 on a ticket of massive resistance to the North. A civil war raged in Nixon's own administration. At the Department of Health, Education, and Welfare, liberal Republican appointees and holdover Democratic bureaucrats were publicly threatening to cut off federal funds for Southern school systems that failed to desegregate. The secretary of HEW, Nixon's old friend Bob Finch, seemed to have lost control. Attorney General Mitchell began, à la LBJ, to refer to Finch as "Fink," and Nixon lamented to his aides about "Poor Bob."[8] The director of the civil rights office of the Department of Health, Education, and Welfare, a liberal Republican from California named Leon Panetta, was ignoring signals from the White House to pipe down. In the harsh way of Washington, Panetta found out that he had "resigned" when

Nixon's spokesman Ron Ziegler announced it at a press conference.[9]*

Fresh off his creation of the vice president as scourge of the liberal media, speechwriter Pat Buchanan wanted to unleash Agnew to deliver a scathing denunciation of forced integration. Leonard Garment, the in-house liberal, protested strongly. Nixon ordered the two men to try to write a speech together, but they ended up spending most of the night yelling at each other. Borrowing Nixon's unfortunate metaphor, Buchanan wanted a speech that would "tear the scab off the issue of race in this country."[11]

Nixon would often pit his aides against each other, the better to produce incisive debate, but in this case he could see that he had to step in and settle the argument. Nixon's views on America's racial problems were carefully considered and usually empathetic, notwithstanding his intemperate or provocative utterances. He believed that the best cure to racism was economic. He wanted to help blacks get jobs. To that end, he had quietly pushed to fund small black businesses and to set up a program ("the Philadelphia Plan") that would require some federal contractors to set aside jobs for minorities (thereby

---

*Panetta switched to the Democratic Party and went on to have a successful public career as a member of congress, White House chief of staff under President Clinton, and CIA director and secretary of defense under President Obama. He also wrote a 1971 memoir entitled **Bring Us Together,** which Nixon labeled a "classic of the screw-the-President genre."[10]

infuriating Democratic-dominated, mostly white trade unions).[12]

Nixon understood that blacks needed better educations to get better jobs. On February 20, he summoned his feuding speechwriting staff, plus Haldeman, and spoke thoughtfully about race. "The nation is at an historic moment," he said. Swiveling his chair around to look out the Oval Office window, he said, "You're not going to solve this race problem for a hundred years. Intermarriage and all that, assimilation, it will happen, but not in our time. Desegregation, though, that has to happen now."

He let the words sink in and went on. "That's why we have to hit this minority enterprise thing so hard—sure, they laugh at it—but better jobs, better housing, that's the only way Negroes are going to be able to move to Scarsdale." He pointed to Haldeman, his fellow Californian. "Bob, that's the only way they're going to get into Palisades High and Whittier High."[13]*

Nixon said that he, not Agnew, would announce the administration's position on school desegregation, but not in a speech. Rather, he would issue a public statement. He wanted "no emotional response," he said.[15] On March 24, the White House

---

*Nixon, devoted to his old coach "Chief" Newman, who was part-Indian, was also sensitive to the plight and rights of Native Americans. His administration pushed to give Indians more self-determination in their struggles with the federal bureaucracy and greatly increased funding for programs affecting Native Americans.[14]

released an eight-thousand-word statement that was balanced (desegregation yes, forced busing no), exhaustive, and tedious. "A golden opportunity missed," grumbled Buchanan, who had wanted a TV address to bash liberal judges and northern hypocrisy.[16] But Nixon's approach to actually solving the problem was a model of smart politics and good governance.

Nixon appointed a cabinet committee, nominally headed by Vice President Agnew—a sop to the South—but in fact run by Labor Secretary George Shultz. A carefully considered Princeton grad but also a tough former Marine, Shultz was among the best of the many Ivy Leaguers Nixon claimed not to want but routinely appointed. "A bull dog," Nixon called him, approvingly, after the stern but patient Shultz had maneuvered the building unions to hire more minority employees.[17]

Shultz, in turn, set up the blandly named State Advisory Committees for the seven Southern states still holding out against the Supreme Court decision in the **Holmes** case. The committees were composed of local leaders, black and white, from Klansmen to activists in the NAACP. They would be invited to the White House and engaged in an orchestrated dance. "It was all a set piece," Shultz recalled. The group, starry-eyed, would be led to the Roosevelt Room, just across from the Oval Office. "I let them argue and get it out of their systems," said Shultz. At about the two-hour mark, Shultz would call in Attorney General John Mitchell, who was known as a no-nonsense law-and-order type and "by whites as 'their man,'" as Shultz described him. In a rehearsed minuet, repeated every time for each of the state committees, Shultz would ask the attorney general what he planned to do about the schools in the South. "I am attorney general and I will enforce the law," Mitchell would say, gruffly, puffing on his pipe, and then leave the room.

At lunch, the group would be trooped over to the diplomatic reception rooms at the State Department and shown the desk on which Thomas Jefferson had written parts of the Declaration of Independence, "dedicated to the proposition that all men are created equal." After lunch, back in the Roosevelt Room, Shultz would let the committee members talk and argue some more, and "when the time was right," walk them across the hall to meet President Nixon. The president would calmly say they were all standing in a room where great decisions had been made. The president had made his decision to enforce the law. Now it was time for the state committees to make their decision.

Shultz had been unimpressed when he met with Nixon in a Los Angeles hotel room during the 1968 campaign. "He was defensive around me." But as president, speaking to the awed Southern community leaders, "he was magnificent. A performer," Shultz recalled to the author.[18]

The newly desegregated schools of the South opened peacefully that fall. There was no rioting, no "massive resistance." In 1968, 68 percent of black children in the South attended all-black schools. By 1972, only 8 percent did. There were fierce battles ahead over court-ordered busing, but Nixon had achieved a milestone in race relations. In August 1970, reflecting on what they had accomplished with the committees and what still lay ahead, Nixon was philosophical. "There are no votes in the desegregation of Southern schools," he said, "and the NAACP would say my rhetoric was poor if I gave the Sermon on the Mount. But I'm a firm believer that the law should and must be carried out." Nixon was determined not to rub it in, however. "I don't believe in kicking the South around; we'll do the job swiftly and fairly." He warned Elliot Richardson, the new secretary of HEW, not to let his young attorneys grandstand. In Ehrlichman's meeting notes, the "old," vituperative Nixon popped up, just for a moment: "Tell all the little pipsqueaks. Eager beavers would like to screw us—don't let them do it."[19]

At the time, the press largely missed the real story of how Nixon desegregated the schools. Instead, they focused on Agnew as salesman of Nixon's so-called Southern Strategy to win white votes in the South. Nixon indulged them. Every winter in Washington since 1885, the press had held its white-tie Gridiron Dinner, a boozy evening of songs and skits. Nixon had been going, grudgingly, since 1950. On March 14, 1970, Nixon and Agnew took the stage. The president asked, "Mr. Agnew, I would like to have your candid response to a few questions. First,

what about this 'Southern Strategy' we hear of so
often?" Agnew, speaking in a broad Southern drawl,
clicked his heels, saluted, and answered, "Yes suh,
Mister President, Ah agree with you completely on
yoah Southern Strategy." Nixon sat down at the
piano and told the audience he wanted to play a few
of the favorite songs of past presidents. He began
with FDR's "Home on the Range." After a couple of
notes, Agnew sat down and began banging out the
familiar notes to "Dixie." Nixon responded with
Truman's "Missouri Waltz," and Agnew started up
"Dixie" again. Nixon tried LBJ's "The Eyes of Texas
Are Upon You," and Agnew came right back with
"Dixie." By now, wrote presidential chronicler Richard Reeves, "the crowd was roaring with laughter
and cheers."[20]

"Hold it! Hold it!" Nixon called out. "Now we'll
play my favorite." He swung into "God Bless America," and everyone joined in. In his diary, Haldeman
wrote, "P called me after we got home, was really
pleased with how it had come off, as he should have
been. Feels he'll never be able to top it, and won't
even go next year."[21]

Nixon's hero worship was fed by the movies. John
Wayne was a favorite leading man, though any
powerful, masculine star could win his plaudits.
Generally speaking, Nixon's taste in movies was
wide-ranging, from light comedies to serious drama,
and generally followed no pattern. He would happily sit through almost anything, as long as it wasn't

too prurient.* But in the beginning of April, he watched a series of movies that had, as their overarching theme, the nature of leadership. On April 3, he watched **Hamlet,** Shakespeare's masterpiece on the perils of paralyzing self-awareness. On April 4, he watched **Patton,** with George C. Scott as the ultimate macho leader, defiant of authority, lover of risk and the smell of war. On April 6, he watched **The Caine Mutiny,** the tragedy of the paranoid Captain Queeg, who almost gets his men killed by taking them into a raging typhoon.[23]

Of the three, Nixon liked **Patton** the best. He seemed to make no mention of the other two movies while repeatedly referring to Scott's portrayal of "Old Blood and Guts." "It comes up in every conversation," Secretary of State Rogers told Darryl Zanuck, head of 20th Century Fox, which released the movie.[24] Haldeman wrote in his diary on April 7 that Nixon had told him to see the movie. General Patton, said Nixon, "inspired people, charged them up." Nixon was struck by the image of General Patton standing in front of a giant American flag, talking about how Americans hated losing a war. A few days later, in a conversation with Haldeman, Nixon complained that he was not getting enough credit for his bold leadership style. He said that de Gaulle, Teddy Roosevelt, and Woodrow Wilson "all got

*Nixon was on a crusade against "permissiveness." On February 11, Haldeman wrote in his dairy, "P ordered me to have **Portnoy's Complaint** [Philip Roth's racy novel] removed from White House library and put out story he'd done it."[22]

enormous coverage of the mystique" while he, Nixon, got none.[25]

Nixon set about emulating Patton, a decision that would do much to create a lasting image in pop culture of Nixon as unhinged as he plunged the nation into the Cambodia "incursion" (the White House term to avoid using the word **invasion**). Nixon was not Patton—fortunately, for Patton would have been a terrible chief executive. But nor was he Hamlet, dithering helplessly, or Captain Queeg, so possessed by his demons that his officers felt compelled to mutiny. Nixon was faced with very difficult choices; disloyal and feuding advisers; massive civil unrest; and the extreme loneliness of command. His decisions on Vietnam may not have been the wisest ones—wisdom was, generally speaking, a rare commodity on the subject of the war—but they were hardly delusional. He was trying to keep faith with his vision for the country and to make hard calls with resolution. Nonetheless, it is true that he was increasingly swept up in his own emotionalism, carried away by his fondness for crisis, blind to his own weakness for self-drama.

On March 18, a coup by a right-wing general set off a civil war in Cambodia, and, within two weeks, the communists, backed by Hanoi, were winning. The North Vietnamese sanctuaries in Cambodia had remained a sore point in the Vietnam War; the mysterious and mobile communist headquarters, COSVN (Central Office of South Vietnam) in the

Pentagon's acronym, continued to elude the secret "Menu" bombing campaign launched by Nixon the year before.

Nixon began thinking of a bold move: a combined U.S.–South Vietnamese sweep into Cambodia to clean out the sanctuaries. He was inspired by a tough, wiry ex-submariner, Admiral John McCain (whose son, a naval aviator, was a prisoner of war). On April 19, as CINCPAC, commander of Pacific Forces, Admiral McCain gave the president a lurid briefing, with red arrows pointing into the heart of Vietnam from the sanctuaries, known as Parrot's Beak and the Fishhook. McCain warned that unless the sanctuaries were eliminated, Vietnamization—pulling out U.S. troops and turning the fight over to the South Vietnamese army—was likely to fail.[26]

The next day, Nixon was scheduled to announce on national TV that 150,000 American troops would be coming home from Vietnam in the next year. He gave the speech from the Western White House after seeing McCain in Hawaii, but as Air Force One continued eastward into the night, Nixon was having more hawkish thoughts. He told Haldeman, "Cut the crap on my schedule. I'm taking over here." He meant personally taking over the military response in Cambodia. "Troop withdrawal was a boy's job," he said. "Cambodia is a man's job."[27]

Nixon was fed up with his own military-intelligence establishment. When the CIA missed the coup in Cambodia in March, Nixon snorted impatiently to Secretary of State Rogers, "What do those clowns do out there at Langley?"[28] Now he ordered Haldeman to set up a back channel to issue orders from the White House directly to the military commanders in Vietnam—not through the secretary of defense, the normal chain of command. He knew that Laird would oppose his attempts to escalate. So would Rogers at State.

As usual during a crisis, Nixon was having trouble sleeping. On April 24, he repaired to Camp David with Bebe Rebozo and apparently had a drink or two while watching the movie **The Cincinnati Kid,** which was about a poker sharpie. As a Kissinger aide (who had been listening on the line) later told the story, Nixon got on the phone to Kissinger to discuss sending troops into Cambodia. "Wait a minute," Nixon said suddenly. "Bebe has something to say to you." A new voice came on the phone. "The President wants you to know, Henry, that if this doesn't work out, it's your ass." Kissinger, who could be indiscreet with his aides, told them, "Our peerless leader has flipped out."[29]

Kissinger was summoned to Camp David. While the president paddled around his heated pool, he suggested going even further and implementing Duck Hook. Kissinger wasn't sure if Nixon was just bluffing and testing him, as he sometimes did. "I replied that we had enough on our plate," he recalled in his memoir. In the late afternoon, Kissinger, Nixon, Rebozo, and John Mitchell, whom Nixon liked to have around when things were tough, went on a cruise down the Potomac on the presidential yacht, the **Sequoia**. "The tensions of the grim military planning were transformed into exaltation by the liquid refreshment," wrote Kissinger, "to the point of some patriotic awkwardness when it was decided that everyone should stand at attention while the **Sequoia** passed Mount Vernon—a feat not managed by everyone with equal success." Back at the White House, Nixon invited everyone to see **Patton** with him, again.[30]

Nixon signed the military orders to send U.S. and South Vietnamese troops into Cambodia—a two-pronged attack into the Parrot's Beak and the Fishhook—with his initials "RN," but then, as if to show that he really meant it, wrote out his full name, "Richard Nixon." He was gathering himself. On a notepad, he wrote, "Bebe at the elevator—'This is the big play.' Need for self-discipline in all areas. Polls v. right decision. Dare to do it right—alone."[31] Nixon wanted his address to the nation, scheduled for Thursday night, April 30, to feel historic, so he proposed making it from the Map Room, where FDR had conducted World War II. "I don't think that's a good idea," Haldeman wrote in his diary.

Nixon's secretaries of state and defense were not on board. "Rogers obviously quite upset, emotional," recorded Haldeman. Both Rogers and Laird felt that they had not been properly consulted and worried about high casualties for low gain. Nixon distracted himself by worrying over minutiae. He was upset when the CBS program **60 Minutes** agreed to allot only 20 to 30 minutes—not the full hour—to a Tricia-led tour of the White House. "Really mad, and said so," Haldeman wrote, "chewed me out worse than he ever has as P. Basically, a release of tensions on the big decision, but potentially damaging if he starts flailing in other directions." Haldeman was less understanding the next day when Nixon "called again to discuss problem of locating his new pool table. Decided it won't fit in the solarium, so wants a room in EOB. Absolutely astonishing he could get into trivia on brink of biggest step he's taken so far."[32]

On Thursday, the day of his speech, Nixon went to bed at 1 A.M., got up at 2 A.M., went to bed again at 5:30 A.M., gave up, and sat in his darkened office in the Executive Office Building, listening to Tchaikovsky.[33] He worked and reworked the speech, bringing in Pat Buchanan, whom he used when he wanted to write speeches, as he put it, "with the bark on."[34]

Nixon gave the speech from the Map Room, invoking Woodrow Wilson in World War I, FDR in World War II, and JFK during the Cuban Missile Crisis. A large map, showing the Parrot's Beak, loomed behind him. He told the American people that "this is not an invasion of Cambodia." Rather, South Vietnamese and American troops were going in to knock out communist headquarters and clear out the sanctuaries. Then his tone darkened:

We live in an age of anarchy. We see mindless attacks on all the great institutions which have been created by free civilizations in the last five hundred years. Even here in the United States, great universities are being systematically destroyed. Small nations all the world over find themselves under attack from within and without. . . . If, when the chips are down, the world's most powerful nation, the United States of America, acts like a pitiful, helpless giant, the forces of totalitarianism and anarchy will threaten free nations and free institutions throughout the world.[35]

After the address, Nixon joined his family for a "light supper" in the Solarium. He had summoned Julie and David down from Smith and Amherst, where they were shortly scheduled to graduate, because he feared a violent campus reaction to his speech. He had also told his daughter that it would be too provocative for him to attend her graduation. She had trouble holding back the tears.[36]

Her father was "still keyed up from the speech" when he entered the Solarium, Julie recalled. "Mother, with unmistakable intensity, led the way in reassuring him of rightness of the decision." Nixon repaired to the Lincoln Sitting Room to be alone. Oddly, but touchingly, he was later visited there by the Chief Justice of the United States, Warren Burger, a Nixon appointee, who drove to the White House to offer words of support. "I think anyone who really listened to what you said will appreciate the guts it took to make the decision," Burger told the president.[37] Ehrlichman escorted the Chief Justice to see Nixon. "P looped," he wrote in his diary. (The teetotaling Ehrlichman may have been observing the effect of one drink on the exhausted president.)[38]

The Eastern Establishment press unloaded on him. His old liberal nemesis, **The New Republic,** began a front-page editorial with the sentence, "Richard Nixon is going down in history, all right, but not soon enough." The speech was "insensitive," "phony," "a fraud," and "dangerous." **The New York Times** opined that Nixon was "out of touch with the nation."[39] Quietly, Nixon asked Kissinger to find out how the speech had played with his "Georgetown friends." The national security adviser called the Alsops and got Susan Mary on the phone—she and Joe had just come back from a dinner attended by Senator Edward Kennedy. How was the "atmosphere," Kissinger wanted to know. "It was very bad," answered Mrs. Alsop. "Everyone was in a rage."[40] Some of Nixon's critics were in-house. William Safire, Nixon's moderate speechwriter who had been excluded this time around, later said, "Nixon had done what only Nixon could do—make a courageous decision and wrapped it in a pious and divisive speech."[41]

But Nixon could not hear the jeers or even the cautions, not at first. He went to a Pentagon briefing in the morning and fulminated, "Let's blow the hell out of them," as Kissinger and Laird looked at each other in embarrassment.[42] In the hallway outside the office of the Joint Chiefs of Staff, the president was "mobbed by people cheering and trying to shake my hand," he recalled in his memoirs. " 'God bless you!'

'Right on!' 'We should have done this years ago!' they shouted." By the time Nixon had reached the Pentagon lobby, where he was thanked by a weeping woman with a husband in Vietnam, he was in full flight. "I have seen them," he said, talking about the soldiers in Vietnam. "They're the greatest. You see these bums, you know, blowing up the campuses. Listen, the boys that are on the college campuses today are the luckiest people in the world, going to the greatest universities, and here they are burning up the books, storming around about this issue."[43]

Widely and quickly reported, the line about "these bums" was a mistake. But Nixon did not realize it right away. Instead, he went for another cruise on the Potomac, this time with just his family, Bebe Rebozo, Rose Mary Woods, and one of his military attachés, Marine Colonel Jack Brennan. Woods was a little worried about the president, who was more wound up than she had seen him in twenty years. The presidential yacht went through its usual ritual of playing the national anthem when it passed the George Washington tomb at Mount Vernon. "Really blast it out," Nixon ordered the captain. He stood at rigid attention and then smiled and shot his right thumb in the air.[44]*

---

*Brennan reported back to Woods that Nixon was "lonely" and "exhausted" but "exuberant." Following Nixon's instructions that the captain "blast out" the national anthem, Brennan wrote Woods, "I excused myself and turned away. He then called me back in a manner which he has not done before. In a deliberately gruff voice he said, 'Hey!' I returned and the President, in a

Nixon was sitting alone in his hideaway, EOB 175, on the afternoon of Monday, May 4, when Haldeman came in, "looking agitated," Nixon recalled. He had just read over the wires that National Guardsmen had opened fire on some antiwar protesters at Kent State University in Ohio. Nixon was "stunned." "Are they dead?" he asked. Haldeman answered that he was afraid so. "Is this because of me, because of Cambodia?" Nixon asked.[45]

Nixon opened the newspaper the next day and saw the photograph. A kneeling girl, arms outspread over a dead student, a Vietnam-era pietà. The father of one of the dead girls was quoted as saying, "My child is not a bum."

"Those few days after Kent State were amongst the darkest of my presidency," Nixon recalled. "I felt utterly dejected." He asked Rose Woods to set up an appointment with Dr. Hutschnecker, who flew down to Washington from New York for a meeting that was kept off of the Secret Service log. An ardent dove, Hutschnecker told Nixon that he should rename the Department of Defense the Department of Peace. That was not the conversation Nixon was looking for. He excused himself after a few minutes. "Our old intimacy was not there," Hutschnecker later told Jonathan Aitken.[46]

---

tough-sounding voice, and with very serious facial expression said, 'As a Marine, do you approve of what I said last night?'" Brennan responded, "I only wish I were over there to help carry out what you ordered." Nixon said, "I do too. I think I'll resign and we'll go together."

Demonstrations rocked over a thousand campuses. Almost five hundred of them closed. More than two million students went on strike. At Harvard, student protesters threatened to trash Pat Moynihan's house. His wife hung a giant peace symbol over the porch to assuage the students, then warned her husband. President Nixon sent "some burly men in unmarked cars," she recalled. (They were probably FBI agents.)[47] A "March on Washington" was called for Saturday, May 9. Around the White House, city buses were lined up bumper-to-bumper in protection, like covered wagons in a circle against the Indians. Hundreds of troops from the Third Army bivouacked in the Executive Office Building. Henry Kissinger slept in his West Wing office to avoid demonstrators. Tape was put on the White House windows to keep them from shattering.[48]

Nixon bravely held a press conference on the night of Friday, May 8. He was visibly anxious and sweating. Of the twenty-six questions, twenty-four were about Cambodia and the protests. Nixon gave an indirect but eloquent apology for his "bums" remark. Of college students he said,

They are trying to say that they want peace. They are trying to say that they want to stop the killing. They are trying to say that they want to end the draft. They are trying to say we ought to get out of Vietnam. I agree with everything that they are trying to accomplish.[49]

"Agitated and uneasy," as he described himself, he went to the Lincoln Sitting Room and began making phone calls—forty-seven calls between 9:22 P.M. and 1:55 A.M. Then he slept for a little and started calling again. He called Kissinger eight times. He called Haldeman seven times and Rose Woods four times. He called Billy Graham and Norman Vincent Peale and two newswomen, Helen Thomas of UPI (1:22 A.M. and 3:50 A.M.) and Nancy Dickerson of NBC.[50] He called Undersecretary of State U. Alexis Johnson to complain about fifty junior foreign service officers who had signed a letter opposing the Cambodian invasion. "This is the President," Nixon told the half-asleep career diplomat. "I want all those sons of bitches fired in the morning!"[51]

Looking out the windows as the blackness turned to gray, he could see small groups of people starting to gather on the Ellipse between the White House and the Washington Monument. He put Rachmaninoff's second piano concerto on the record player and, at 4:22 A.M., placed a final call, to his valet, Manolo Sanchez. As Sanchez came in with a cup of coffee, Nixon asked him if he had ever been to the Lincoln Memorial at night. Manolo said that he had not. "Impulsively," Nixon recalled, "I said, 'Let's go look at it now."[52] So began what Haldeman would record in his diary as "the weirdest day so far."[53]

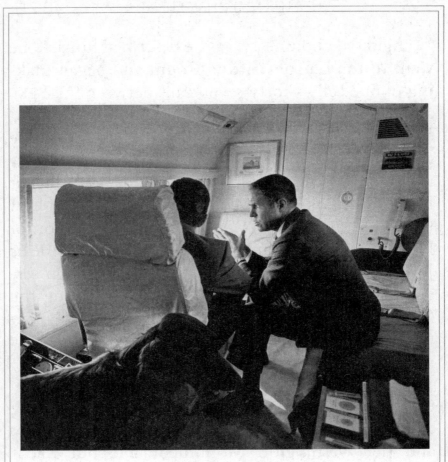

Haldeman.
Courtesy of the Richard Nixon Presidential
Library and Museum

CHAPTER 16

Hippies and Hardhats

"Searchlight is on the lawn. Searchlight has asked for a car."[1] In the Secret Service Command Post, Egil "Bud" Krogh gave a start. Krogh was a young White House staffer working for Ehrlichman on Justice Department matters. He was the "duty officer" on that curious May night, and the last thing he expected was to be jumping in a car shortly before 5 A.M. to chase after the president on the way to the Lincoln Memorial. Running up the Memorial's marble steps, he caught up with Nixon as he stood before the majestic statue of the Great Emancipator. The president had "bags under his eyes," he noted. "He was flushed, drawn, exhausted," Krogh later recalled.[2]

But the president was moved and excited, too. Nixon was making a pilgrimage. His grandmother Milhous had idealized Lincoln; Nixon had read all ten volumes of Lincoln's biography by Lincoln's young secretaries John Nicolay and John Hay.[3] He wanted to feel a bond with a predecessor who had kept the nation together during another, greater civil war. He began reading to Manolo from the inscriptions—the Gettysburg Address and the Second Inaugural—on the temple walls.

By now, "a few small groups of students had begun to congregate in the rotunda of the Memorial," Nixon recalled. He walked over to a group of eight males, dressed in the scruffy uniform of fatigue jackets and jeans, their hair long and unkempt, their sleep-deprived eyes wide as they encountered the 37th president of the United States. Nixon did his best to reach out to the dumbstruck boys. "I know that probably most of you think I'm an SOB," he said, "but I want you to know that I understand just how you feel." He recalled that as a young man, in the late 1930s as war loomed in Europe, he had wanted to believe that British Prime Minister Neville Chamberlain had found a way to stay out of war. He had thought that Winston Churchill, who wanted to fight the Nazis, "was a madman," said Nixon. "In retrospect," he expounded to the students, "I now realize that I was wrong. I think now that Chamberlain was a good man, but that Churchill was a wiser man."

Churchill was not a marble statue or a remote historical figure to Nixon. In 1954, President Eisenhower, eager to educate his young vice president, had summoned Nixon to meet the visiting Churchill at a White House dinner. Two days later Nixon had been Churchill's dinner partner at the British embassy. A fascinated, worshipful Nixon had talked about the defense of the West with the great man;

Nixon's patriotism and idealism had been enlivened and enriched.[4]

Now Nixon was trying to interest half-dazed students in a figure who was little more than a ghost to them, irrelevant to the passions of the day. Churchill was the glorious living past to Nixon; he was a "Dead White Male" to student radicals who hung Che Guevara posters in their dorm rooms.

Nixon might have despaired of his dim-eyed interlocutors, who thought the president was loopy. But he earnestly kept on. "I then tried to move the conversation into areas where I could draw them out," he recalled in an account he wrote the next day. He talked about how young people should not miss opportunities to travel and revealed that he hoped to open up "the great mainland of China." But then, talking about Russia, he veered into arms control and lost his audience again. Still, he tried. He talked about "those elements of the spirit that really matter," as he put it in his diary. "I said candidly and honestly that I didn't have the answer, but I knew that young people today were searching, as I was searching forty years ago, for an answer to this problem. I just wanted to be sure that all of them realized that ending the war, and cleaning up the streets and the air and the water, was not going to solve spiritual hunger, which all of us have and which, of course, has been the great mystery of life from the beginning of time."[5]

By this time, the rising sun over the Capitol was turning the granite memorial pink, and Manolo was signaling that the Secret Service was agitated, or as agitated as men trained to project calm might let on. The agents, "petrified with apprehension," Nixon recalled, were worried that protest rally leaders would try to make a scene. In the world turned upside down of May 1970, the president of the United States was not safe standing at the base of Lincoln's statue.

Nixon walked down the steps, shaking hands with more students, and got in his limousine. A guy with a beard flipped him the bird. Nixon (or so he later told an aide) gave him the finger right back.[6]

The tour was not over. Nixon wanted Manolo to see Congress. Before long, the president's valet was standing at the Speaker's Rostrum while the president, reliving his days in the 46th Congress, clamored, "Speak! Speak!" Manolo said he was proud to be a U.S. citizen, and Nixon and a couple of cleaning ladies applauded. One of them, Mrs. Carrie Moore, asked Nixon to sign her Bible. Nixon held her hand for a moment. "You know," he said, "my mother was a saint." His voice thickened. "You be a saint, too," he said, and Mrs. Moore replied, "I'll try, Mr. President."[7]

Then it was on to the Rib Room of the Mayflower Hotel for breakfast. Nixon skipped his usual—wheat germ—and ordered eggs and hash. "The last time I had this was on a train," he said to his anxious retinue, which by now included Haldeman and the White House physician, Dr. Walter Tkach, Press Secretary Ron Ziegler, and Appoint-

ments Secretary Dwight Chapin, as well as his original minder, Bud Krogh. Nixon was unable to finish
his hearty breakfast. Time to go. They headed for
the limousines. . . .

But Nixon wanted to walk the half-mile back to
the White House. "Stop him, stop him," Haldeman
mouthed to Krogh over the roof of the limo. Krogh
gently grabbed Nixon's arm and said, "Mr. President, you can't walk back. There's no way in." The
ring of buses and troops around the White House
made pedestrian access difficult.

Nixon pulled his arm away. Krogh looked back to
Haldeman, who again mouthed, "Stop him." More
forcibly, Krogh grabbed Nixon's arm, who again
yanked it away and glowered at his by now extremely
uncomfortable thirty-year-old aide. But he got in
the car. Inside the limo, Nixon grumbled, "Whose
idea was those goddamned buses?" Haldeman, who
had a sense of humor, drily answered, "It was Bud's
idea."[8]

In his diary that night, Haldeman wrote, "Very
weird. P completely beat and just rambling on, but
obviously too tired to go to sleep. . . . I am concerned about his condition. The decision, the speech,
the aftermath killings, riots, press, etc.; the press
conference, the student confrontation have all taken
their toll, and he has had very little sleep for a long
time and his judgment, temper, and mood suffer
badly as a result." Haldeman was admiring of Nixon's courage but worried that "the letdown will be
huge."[9]

Colonel Alexander Haig, Kissinger's assistant, was working in his office after midnight when the president—who by now was virtually sleepwalking—appeared in his doorway. "He was slightly disheveled—tie a little askew, coat unbuttoned, hair slightly tousled," Haig recalled. "These signs of disorder were so small that they might have passed unremarked upon in a man less meticulously well-groomed than Nixon. In him they were very noticeable."

Nixon smiled, "also a rare event when he was in private," wrote Haig. Kissinger's aide recalled Nixon telling him, "We've had a tough day, Al. Things are bad out there. But we've got to stick to our guns. We've done the right thing and we have to go on." Haig realized that Nixon had come to his office in the middle of the night to "buck me up," as he put it. The Cambodian operation, code-named "Total Victory" by the South Vietnamese, who code-named every major offensive "Total Victory,"[10] had captured large amounts of North Vietnamese weapons and materiél with few casualties, but the elusive communist COSVN had just moved west, deeper into the jungle. Haig, a highly decorated hawk, had wanted to press on, but Nixon was keeping his promise to pull back once the Parrot's Beak and the Fishhook were cleared. (He had no choice: Congress set a date for withdrawal.) Nixon knew that Haig was disappointed. "It was his way of telling me, to whom he owed no explanation of any kind, that he agreed with the advice I had given him, even though political considerations had caused him to modify his decision," Haig wrote.[11]

The president, worn, emotionally drained, but forging on, was trying to be the good leader he wanted desperately to be. One follower who was mightily impressed was young Bud Krogh. In a report on the strange trip to the Lincoln Memorial, Krogh, writing his boss John Ehrlichman, observed that the students had been "too stunned to respond at all" and that "the students were geared only for the kind of dialogue or rapping which hardly any of us is capable of doing."[12] But Krogh had been deeply inspired by Nixon's compassion and effort to understand the students and his bravery in going out among them. Krogh knew that he would do anything for Nixon.[13]

Nixon was unfairly pilloried for his dawn visit to the Lincoln Memorial. But his emotionalism throughout the Cambodia episode did not well serve him or the country. The better side of Nixon, the president who came to office pledging to "lower our voices" and restore calm to the country, had given way to the excitable, divisive Nixon. It is no wonder that the country felt whipsawed. On April 20, Nixon had announced that he was withdrawing 150,000 troops and declared Vietnamization a success. On April 30, ten days later, he sounded as if the Apocalypse was nigh. The modest military gains garnered by the incursion were far outweighed by the torment at home, as his own defense secretary, Melvin Laird, had warned. Rather than guard against his tendency to lash out, Nixon had given vent to his emotions. Indeed, he had seemed to relish the crisis in a self-dramatizing way, imagining himself, as he saluted George Washington and watched **Patton** at least one too many times, chasing the enemy through the jungle alongside his loyal Marine aide, Colonel Brennan. Nixon was not behaving like the cool-handed leader he so admired. He was too eager to ride his own emotional roller coaster.

The crash came soon enough. The press coverage of the Lincoln Memorial visit was almost jeering. One of the students told reporters that Nixon had spouted condescending irrelevancies about surfing and football, and that became the storyline. Nixon, who had briefly brought up surfing with a California student and football with a Syracuse student, was stung. He behaved peevishly, as he did when wounded. His irritation with a disloyal cabinet secretary deepened. On May 6, Secretary of the Interior Walter Hickel had written a letter urging Nixon to open up lines of communication to young people. The letter leaked before Nixon saw it, and Nixon was furious. Instead of direct confrontation, however, Nixon took the unusually petty step of ordering the White House tennis court—used by Hickel and other cabinet officers, but not by Nixon— "removed immediately."[14] On May 11, two days after his early morning ramble, Nixon wanted to fire Hickel, but instead he was "still demanding the tennis court be removed," Haldeman wearily noted.

The chief of staff, a tennis player himself, stalled until Nixon forgot about it. Hickel was eventually eased out in November.

In his diary entry for that day, Haldeman went on, "E[hrlichman] got pretty direct with P when he was boring in on bad reports from kids about his Lincoln Memorial bit. E told him he was tired and not very effective. This made him mad, and it came up several times later in the day. Real trouble is, he is just totally pooped and is not up to his usual performance."[15]

The hardhats gave him a brief restorative boost. On May 8, the day before his trip to the Lincoln Memorial, a wave of construction workers had charged into an antiwar demonstration in downtown Manhattan. Shouting "All the way U-S-A!" and "Love it or leave it!" the hardhats sang "God Bless America" and beat up some hippies and a stray Wall Street lawyer or two. Some of the construction workers wielded pipes wrapped in American flags. A few hardhats got carried away and ripped the Episcopal Church banner, with its red cross of St. Andrew, off the gate of Trinity Church. They apparently mistook it for a Vietcong flag.[16]

Accused by Mayor John Lindsay of fomenting a "hard hat riot," Peter Brennan, chief of the Building Trades Council of Greater New York, flexed his muscles on May 20 by turning out one hundred thousand construction workers to march on City Hall with banners like "Lindsay for Mayor of Hanoi." (Lindsay had lowered the flags at City Hall after Kent State.) Nixon loved it. "Thank God for the hard hats," he enthused and invited Brennan to the White House on May 26. Brennan gave Nixon a hardhat emblazoned "Commander in Chief." (In 1973 Nixon made Brennan secretary of labor.) Two days later, Nixon, invited by the Reverend Billy Graham, spoke at Youth Day in the University of Tennessee football stadium before eighty thousand people. The Fellowship of Christian Athletes guarded the stage and a paltry protest was hooted down.

Nixon's political antennae were quivering. A Gallup poll showed that 58 percent of Americans held the protesters responsible for the Kent State shootings, while only 11 percent blamed the National Guardsmen. Once again, Nixon eyed the cultural divide between the longhairs and their liberal supporters in the elite press and the rest of America that disapproved of permissiveness and disrespect. Though they were the majority, these voters, in particular blue-collar whites who had traditionally voted Democratic, felt like "forgotten people." Nixon would not forget them. In Orange Country, California, a Republican state senator observed, "Every time they burn another building, Republican registration goes up."[17]

Nixon liked to bolster morale and create bonds with small, jokey, sweet ceremonies. After the 1952 Fund Crisis, he had initiated his staff and some loyal reporters into the "Order of the Hound's Tooth," a play on Eisenhower's admonition that Nixon would have to prove he was "cleaner than a hound's tooth" to stay on the ticket.[18] Now, he had Bebe Rebozo's girlfriend sew up some heart-shaped blue cloth medals, which he duly awarded to Haldeman, Ehrlichman, and Kissinger on Air Force One en route from a break in Key Biscayne in mid-May. He declared the pieces of cloth to be "Blue Heart" medals for all they had endured and suffered and for "those who are true blue." "This will be our secret," he said.[19]

He also looked to cheer up his beleaguered family. They had been badly shaken by the March on Washington after the Kent State shootings. Returning from Camp David on May 9, a few hours after Nixon's early morning adventures, the First Lady, Tricia, Julie, and David had been smuggled into the White House in unmarked cars. They found the Residence tomblike, with the shades drawn, echoing with the eerie, high-pitched whine of distant sound equipment and muffled chanting. Back at Smith and Amherst, Julie and David learned, the protesters had picked up a new chant: "Fuck Julie, Fuck David."[20]

The president decided to hold a mock graduation ceremony for his daughter and her husband in the White House. He impulsively borrowed a set of Notre Dame academic robes from George Shultz, who had just given the commencement speech in South Bend, and dressed up Bebe Rebozo as the official commencement speaker. Rebozo gave a funny speech written by Pat Buchanan. Everyone ate chocolate cake and tried to be jolly. But Julie noticed that her mother was "quieter than usual. . . . She did not seem to be a part of the party."[21]

The First Lady was still having trouble finding a comfortable or meaningful role. The staff came between her and her husband. The president, in his "RN" mode, sometimes delegated to Haldeman or Ehrlichman orders or requests for his wife and daughters. (Tricia reacted with a frosty disdain; Ehrlichman later wrote, "I told her father that I had sized her up as a very tough and troubled cookie.")[22]

The press was rough on the First Lady. She played the role of traditional, dutiful wife at a time when women, or at least the kind of women who worked in the media, were trying on feminism. Her face, guarded and closed and a little sad, kept alive the "Plastic Pat" label and made some reporters wonder if she was depressed.[23]

She may have indeed been depressed during that first year; at least some of the men in the West Wing thought so.[24] But others closer to the Nixons saw how warm she could be, especially with visitors who were frightened or intimidated to be in the White House.[25] Susan Eisenhower, Ike's granddaughter and David's sister, lived on the third floor of the White House in the spring and summer of 1970. She remembered the elevator door opening and finding Mrs. Nixon with her arms open, ready to embrace her and make her feel comfortable. (Susan also found the president to be surprisingly easy company, mostly because he seemed to be genuinely interested in the views of an eighteen-year-old on foreign policy.[26] Nixon's struggle to make small talk worked to make him engage in serious conversation.)

Nixon had trouble showing his affection for Pat in public, and he was often off by himself, but he left her little notes of endearment on her bed. People who spent time around the Nixons had no doubt that he was in love with her. "She **loved** him," said Connie Stuart, the First Lady's chief of staff. Nixon was awkward, distant, and yet solicitous and tender with his wife. Stuart recalls watching them, knee to knee, on Marine One, the president's helicopter. Nixon leaned forward and said, "You look very nice today. Is that a new outfit?" She answered, "Oh Dick, this is an old suit. You've seen it a dozen times." Nixon sat back, chagrined. "He didn't know what to say. But she wasn't angry. She knew he was trying." Their devotion was "real but not demonstrative." When a White House photographer caught the First Couple holding hands, Stuart quickly gave the photo to the press without first checking with the First Lady, who, she knew, would say no to public displays of affection.[27]

Mrs. Nixon bridled at Haldeman's tight rein, Stuart recalled: "We'd get memos saying, 'The President wants,' and she would say, 'Well, maybe he does and maybe he doesn't.'" (Stuart, the wife of one of Haldeman's advance men, Charles Stuart, was initially imposed on the First Lady but grew close to her.)[28] Mrs. Nixon had been her husband's adviser, and Haldeman had shut her out and also her daughters.

Nixon abetted the arrangement. "Pat would complain to the President, who would complain to Haldeman, who would complain to me to tell Mrs. Nixon not to complain," said Stuart.*

The physical setting of the Residence "did not encourage togetherness," said Stuart. "There were a series of rooms off a grand hallway, with no real living room. The Lincoln sitting room was way down the hall from the family living quarters. [The Nixons] often ate off trays in the hallway. They were prisoners of the second floor." The First Lady sometimes escaped with the president to Camp David or Key Biscayne, but "she didn't like Key Biscayne," said Stuart. "It was very modest. There was nothing for her to do. So he would go by himself. It was a Dick and Bebe show."

The war cast a constant shadow. "You can't imagine how it felt," said Lucy Winchester, the White House social secretary. "Protesters would scream things and the press would eat it up." The president was "pre-occupied. We were at war and he took it hard." Pat had one longtime close friend, Helene Drown, who would often visit her. Mrs. Drown was vivacious but perhaps too opinionated around President Nixon. "Mrs. Nixon loved Helene Drown be-

*Haldeman felt caught in the middle. "P called me back up with Bebe about problem of personal household staff, lousy food of wrong kind, etc. Wants me to solve it. Pretty hard when PN [Pat Nixon] won't help and yet won't let someone take over." Haldeman's sympathies were with the "P": "poor guy goes on and on trying to figure out how to have it all go away."[29]

cause she made her laugh," Connie Stuart recalled. "But the President didn't like having Helene around. Helene would tell the president what to do, how to deal with the press or who to have to a White House dinner. Nixon would avoid her. The word was passed through Bob [Haldeman]: No more Helene."

Looking back from the perspective of several decades, Stuart said, "It was a tragedy, the whole damn thing." The stress of war, the officious staff, and their own innate reticence conspired to create distance between two people who loved each other. "There was no screaming or hollering," recalled Stuart, "but there were some cold, stony silences."

Pat was stoical. "Her favorite phrase was 'onward and upward,'" said Stuart. "She got angry but didn't sulk." When Nixon ran for president in 1968, Pat told the **Los Angeles Times,** "We never have fights. We just move away from each other."[30] Actually, the First Lady did tangle with the president from time to time. Nixon was, for his time, unusually far-sighted about hiring women. He had instructed his personnel aide Fred Malek to make an effort to find qualified women (along with minorities, Catholics, and non-Harvard grads).[31] When two Supreme Court seats opened up in September 1971, Pat told reporters, "I think it would be great to get a woman on the Court. And if Congress doesn't approve her, they better see me." She announced that she was working on her husband to make it happen.[32] "Just to play an awful long shot," as he put it to his aides, Nixon did consider a woman, Mildred Lillie, a state court of appeals judge from California. But when the male-dominated American Bar Association balked, he picked two men (Lewis Powell and William Rehnquist) instead. Pat rebuked her husband. "Boy is she mad!" Nixon told Haldeman.[33]

Nixon wanted to please Pat. Frank Gannon, who helped Nixon write his memoirs, compared Nixon to a "high school nerd who could never quite believe he had won the prettiest, coolest girl."[34] Nixon tried, however clumsily, to impress her. Henry Kissinger recalled to the author an evening when the president invited him to dine with the First Couple in the Residence. On the way over, Nixon awkwardly suggested that the national security adviser tell the First Lady a little bit about the president's accomplishments in foreign policy. Nixon absented himself to go to the bathroom, and Kissinger dutifully started in reciting Nixon's achievements. "Oh Henry," Pat sighed, wearily but sweetly. "You don't have to."[35]

Nixon was more worried about John Mitchell's marriage than his own. In May of 1970, Nixon became so concerned about the wild behavior of Martha Mitchell—and its impact on the attorney general—that he considered dismissing his closest adviser.

Waving a cocktail, spouting off in her Southern sorority girl drawl, Martha had become a great favorite of the press. Speaking her own mind in TV interviews and inebriated late-night phone calls to reporters, she even seemed to reveal her husband's true thoughts. "As my husband has said many times, some of the liberals in this country, he'd like to take them and exchange them for Russian Communists," she told the **CBS Morning News.**[36] Mitchell pretended to be amused by his wife's outbursts, but he was having difficulty maintaining what Haldeman called his "usual imperturbable stance."[37] Martha passed out into her soup bowl at one dinner party and threw her shoe at her husband at another.[38] During one of their marital spats, she tossed the attorney general's pants out the window, requiring his FBI detail to retrieve them from the street.[39]

Mitchell seemed to withdraw, like a turtle into his shell, observed Ehrlichman.[40] Never voluble, he was distracted, increasingly silent. Mitchell was stretched thin. He was not only doing the job of attorney general ("Mr. Law and Order"), he was summoned to all important national security meetings. He served on the "40 Committee" that approved covert actions and the equally crucial, if less formal, "Henry Handling Committee" that tried to keep Henry Kissinger from throttling Secretary of State Rogers.

Egged on by Ehrlichman, who saw Mitchell as a rival for power, Nixon began to lose faith in Mitchell, at least as a manager. The ex–Wall Street bond lawyer was not wise to the territorial ways of Washington, and Nixon correctly blamed his attorney general for botching the Haynsworth and Carswell

Supreme Court nominations.[41]* Nixon held Martha
partly responsible. When, after a few drinks, Martha
Mitchell called reporters and suggested that Senator
William Fulbright of Arkansas should be "crucified"
for voting against Carswell, Nixon told Haldeman,
"We have to turn off Martha."[42]

She was starting to place her midnight calls to the
president as well as to reporters. Various aides tried
to fend her off. One of them, White House military
assistant William Gulley, recalled a 4:30 A.M. conversation with Mrs. Mitchell, long breathy silences
punctuated with, "Don't you go back to sleep you
little son-of-a-bitch. Remember that my husband is
the fucking Attorney General of the United States of
America."[43] On April 15, Haldeman's notes show,
Nixon fretted over how to muzzle Martha. "Bebe
take on frontally?" Haldeman jotted on his notepad.
"P. take M[itchell] on directly?"

But for Nixon to directly confront Mitchell was

*Haynsworth, a respected federal judge, had been the first Su-
preme Court nominee to be rejected by the Senate since 1930.
Democrats seized on some minor conflicts of interest in Haynsworth's record in retaliation for the successful Republican effort
to force Justice Abe Fortas (whose conflicts were far worse) to
resign in the summer of 1969. To follow Haynsworth, Mitchell
blundered by choosing Carswell, a true mediocrity. Republicans
as well as Democrats rebelled. "They think he's a boob, a
dummy," Nixon aide Bryce Harlow reported back. "And what
counter is there to that? He is." The senate rejected Carswell by
a vote of 51 to 45 on April 8, 1970.

"unthinkable," notes Mitchell's biographer, James Rosen.[44] Nixon avoided confrontation at all costs, particularly with anyone he regarded as an authority figure. Mitchell was a good deal quieter than Frank Nixon, but he was no less forceful a figure to Richard Nixon. Nixon did not summon Mitchell to the Oval Office; instead, he cast about for an emissary. "Someone has to talk to John," Nixon said to Haldeman. A month later, on May 18, the president blurted to Haldeman, "Mitchell goes—if Martha doesn't."[45]

But Mitchell did not go. Nixon needed him too much. He had counted on Mitchell to be his strong and wise man, his consigliere. Some aides thought that the president would look to Mitchell at meetings to see if he was going on too long. If Mitchell seemed to be puffing strenuously on his pipe, that was the signal for Nixon to cool off or change the subject.[46] Despite Ehrlichman's undercutting, Mitchell remained a constant presence at meetings convened to deal with crises at home and abroad. Nixon was confident enough to play commander-in-chief in the war in Vietnam, but he needed a general he could trust to run the war in the streets, the growing wave of protests, riots, and bombings that threatened upheaval in the cities and on campus.

The tide of unrest was actually cresting in the spring of 1970; soon, troop withdrawals and, in time, the end of the draft would deplete the protester ranks.* But Nixon had inherited an anxious government buffeted by an extremely turbulent time. Ehrlichman recalled that shortly after he came to the White House in January 1969, he had received a visit from an old law school classmate, Warren Christopher, the outgoing deputy attorney general. Christopher handed Ehrlichman a stack of documents and explained that they were martial law proclamations—the president needed only to fill in the date and the name of the city.[48] The leftist rhetoric of the time was pre-revolutionary. Eldridge Cleaver, the minister of communication of the Black Panther Party, whose motto was "Off the Pig," was calling on the masses to kidnap ambassadors, hijack airplanes, and blow up buildings. The Weathermen, a radical fringe of the student protest group Students for a Democratic Society, had become the Weather Underground and ominously disappeared. Between 1969 and the summer of 1970, hundreds of bombings, most of them unsolved, claimed forty-three lives.[49] After a Weather Underground bomb factory blew up in a New York brownstone in March 1970, Pat Moynihan wrote

---

*Nixon, who had a libertarian streak, was persuaded that the draft was "involuntary servitude." He maneuvered, slowly and craftily, through a commission, then a drawn-out legislative battle, to switch to an all-volunteer force. (The draft formally ended on July 1, 1973.) Politically, getting rid of the draft was shrewd in that it disarmed student dissent. By 1986, Nixon—not always philosophically consistent—had reversed himself and once again favored universal conscription.[47]

Haldeman, "It seems to me that we have simply got to assume that in the near future there will be terrorist attacks on the federal government, including members of the Cabinet, the Vice President, and the President himself."[50] So many airliners were hijacked (thirty-three in 1969 alone, most of them by foreigners, not radicals) that the Secret Service told the president that his family members could no longer fly commercial.[51]

Nixon felt sure that foreign agents—Russian? Cuban? North Vietnamese?—were behind the bombings and hijackings. But the U.S. intelligence services were unable to provide any direct proof.[52] Nixon, chronically suspicious of bureaucratic footdragging, correctly believed that turf battles stymied cooperation between the various spy agencies—the FBI, the CIA, the NSA, and military intelligence.

On June 5, Nixon summoned the intelligence agency heads to the Oval Office and "chewed our butts," as one participant recalled.[53] Sitting at the table, along with the likes of the FBI's J. Edgar Hoover and the CIA's Richard Helms, was a gaunt, fierce, twenty-eight-year-old named Tom Charles Huston. A former conservative student activist who had served briefly as an analyst in the Defense Intelligence Agency, Huston was a figure of fascination and some mild mockery among his fellow White House staffers, who referred to him as "Secret Agent X-5." Huston signed some of his memos "Cato the Younger," after an incorruptible Roman statesman, and hung a portrait of John C. Calhoun, the South Carolina Nullifier, on his wall.[54] Nixon was impressed by young Huston, whom he approvingly referred to as a "bomb thrower."[55] The president told Huston to write a report and make recommendations, a task enthusiastically undertaken and completed in three weeks' time. "The Special Report, Interagency Committee on Intelligence (Ad Hoc)," better known as the Huston Plan, would cause a stir when it surfaced three years later during the Senate Watergate hearings. It called for illegal mail-opening and surreptitious "black bag jobs"—break-ins to install taps and bugs on dangerous radicals. The plan was full of lurid rhetoric about the subversive threat, though its tools were not new. Hoover's FBI had for many years conducted black bag jobs and the CIA was already illegally opening mail (Operation Chaos).[56]

Nixon did not trust the CIA or its director, Helms, but he was deeply invested in the FBI's Hoover. "Dick, you will come to depend on Edgar," Lyndon Johnson had told Nixon as he handed over the Oval Office. "He is a pillar of strength in a city of weak men. He's the only one you can put your complete trust in."[57] Nixon almost always turned down invitations to socialize outside of the White House, but in September of his first year in office he had gone to dinner at Hoover's home in a quiet residential neighborhood in northwest Washington. Ehrlichman, who accompanied the president, recalled the "dingy, almost seedy" living room covered ("every square inch") with faded brown photos of Hoover standing with celebrities and presidents. At dinner, Hoover regaled Nixon with tales of FBI black bag jobs and other derring-do. Ehrlichman could see that the crafty Hoover was testing Nixon, seeing how he would react to FBI activities that skirted, if they did not erase, the boundaries of the law. Nixon seemed to lap it all up. After dinner, Hoover took the president down to "the recreation room" for a drink. The walls were covered with girlie pinups, which Hoover made a point of showing off. After one drink, Nixon beat a quick retreat.[58]

Hoover had dutifully supplied Nixon with snippets of political gossip and tapped some phones, but he was no fan of young Tom Huston's "Special Report, Interagency Committee in Intelligence (Ad Hoc)." In early July, the FBI director summoned Huston to his office and, looking down from his elevated desk and referring to Huston as "Mr. Hoffman" and "Mr. Hutchinson," made clear that the FBI was not about to go along with the plan's recommendations.[59] In part, Hoover was wary of sharing with the CIA, the FBI's longtime bureaucratic rival, but he was also showing his political savvy. At age 75, Hoover was ever alert to any threat to the Bureau's legacy, which was to say his own. The 1960s were a time of consciousness raising in the realm of civil liberties. Lawsuits and liberal stirrings in Con-

gress had threatened to expose longtime FBI practices of electronic surveillance. Hoover had already
cut back on black bag jobs. Now, he insisted that the
FBI would conduct illegal surveillance only under
written orders from the president. Hoover knew he
was offering a poison pill; Nixon had an expansive
view of presidential power, but he also wanted to
hide behind a cloak of deniability.[60]

Tom Huston was indignant at Hoover's **lèse-
majesté**. "At some point Hoover has to be told who
is president," Huston spluttered. Hoover "wanted to
ride out of the FBI on a white horse," he grumbled.[61]
Ignoring "Mr. Hoffman," Hoover went to see John
Mitchell to get the answer he wanted. The attorney
general was smart enough to see that Hoover was an
enemy the White House could not afford to make.
Through leaks and the threat of leaks—implicit
blackmail—Hoover had outlasted six presidents.
Mitchell agreed with Hoover that the Huston Plan
"was not something we in the Justice Department
would certainly want to participate in. . . . I called
Mr. Haldeman and the president and objected to
it," Mitchell later testified.

"Once Mitchell got to him [Nixon], that was
pretty much the end of it," recalled the CIA's Richard Helms.[62] But not quite. Nixon was not happy.
He had quietly signed off on the Huston Plan; he
wanted to use the broad powers of the presidency to
win the war at home. Haldeman dutifully looked
for another way to spy on dissidents.

He settled on a newcomer to the White House, the president's brand-new counsel, John Dean. Haldeman explained to Dean that Hoover would no longer deal with Huston, but that Dean should look for a way to get the intelligence agencies on board to step up the fight against the Weather Underground and the Black Panthers.

The thirty-one-year-old Dean, who had practiced law for all of six months and had come to the White House from brief stints as a congressional and Justice Department staffer, was not sure what to do. He was, in a manner of speaking, the president's lawyer, but his job responsibilities were a little vague, except that he would be taking orders from Haldeman and Ehrlichman. Dean was friendly with John Mitchell (who had wisely warned him **against** taking the White House job). So on September 17, Dean went to the office of the attorney general at the Justice Department to see Mitchell. Puffing on his pipe, Mitchell relieved Dean of his anxiety. "He was going to kill the plan, somehow," Dean recorded in a memoir. "John," said the attorney general, speaking slowly, "the President loves all this stuff. But it just isn't necessary." Mitchell and Dean set up an interagency Intelligence Evaluation Committee to at least make a show of sharing intelligence within the government.[63]

It seemed like a bland, toothless compromise, a skillful finesse by Mitchell to save his old friend the president from a rash program of secret break-ins and buggings or a war with Hoover or both. But the plates were shifting under the government. As Hoover gradually took the FBI out of the domestic spying business, the White House would begin to look for ways to fill the void.*

*It remains unclear how much domestic spying continued after the formal rejection of the Huston Plan. Nixon tapes scholar Luke Nichter suggests that aspects of the plan were probably implemented in some form and that the ultra-secret National Security Agency, as well as other agencies, continued to be highly compartmentalized and classified intelligence operations.[64]

CHAPTER 17

Department of Dirty Tricks

John Dean drove a Porsche, liked cocktails and attractive women—he once used the White House switchboard to track down a woman who had refused to give him her phone number—and was quick-witted and eager to please. In his memoir **Blind Ambition**, Dean recalled his job interview with H. R. Haldeman: "I watched as he checked me out and saw a reflection of his own taste in clothes. I was wearing black wing-tip shoes; he was wearing brown wing-tips. He had on a white button-down collar shirt; mine was blue. My suit was as conservative as his. Later I discovered that he and I shopped at the same men's store in Washington."[1]

Nixon liked having sharply dressed, alert young men on his staff. He wanted to surround himself with youth and can-do vigor. He had seen the way President Eisenhower brought along promising young men, including himself, readying them for greater responsibility. Eisenhower had kept watch on his young charges, and if they failed to live up to

With Elvis.
National Archives and Records Administration

his expectations, he had them removed. But Nixon lacked Ike's cold-blooded adroitness as a manager.

Though he periodically threatened to cut federal agencies in half, Nixon did not like to fire anyone. He kept around old hangers-on. One was Murray Chotiner, Nixon's tutor in "rock 'em, sock 'em" politics, who was tainted by an influence peddling scandal in the mid-1950s but still gave Nixon behind-the-scenes political advice.

The brand-new White House counsel ran into Chotiner on his first visit to the White House Mess in July 1970. Still uncertain about his duties, Dean was puzzling over what to do about an "action memorandum" that had landed on his desk. The subject was: "Request that you rebut the recent attack on the Vice President." An attached "confidential memo" explained that a new muckraking magazine called **Scanlan's Monthly** had published a bogus memo linking Spiro Agnew with a secret plan to cancel the 1972 election and repeal the Bill of Rights. Dean had inquired about the "action memo" directive in Haldeman's office and learned that it had come straight from President Nixon. Reading his morning news summary, the president was often inspired to write notes in the margin demanding action.[2] But what action? The word came back from the president: "It was requested that as part of this inquiry you should have the Internal Revenue Service conduct a field investigation on the tax front."

In his memoirs, Dean claimed that he was troubled about opening a tax audit of a publication just because it had published a scurrilous article. So, as he ate lunch at the White House Mess, he asked his new acquaintance Murray Chotiner, an old hand at this sort of thing, what he should do. Bemused, Chotiner responded, "I tell you this, if Richard Nixon thinks it's necessary you'd better think it's necessary. If you don't, he'll find someone who does."[3] Dean was learning from an old hand, but the wrong lesson. Eager to get ahead, Dean did not realize that when the president gave an outrageous order, he often expected it to be ignored.

Nixon kept Chotiner around partly because he wanted someone who knew how to attack his enemies, and Nixon's foes never seemed to go away. In the winter of 1970, Larry O'Brien had become head of the Democratic National Committee. O'Brien had run JFK's campaign in 1960, and Nixon regarded him with the mixture of apprehension and respect he reserved for the Kennedys and their political apparat. On March 4, Haldeman recorded in his diary that the "P" wanted to "move hard on Larry O'Brien now that he is back as DNC chair. P feels this is clear signal that Teddy is in control . . . wants Chotiner to manage Plan O'Brien."[4]

Five days later, Haldeman jotted in his notebook another presidential command: "Chotiner—get O'Brien's tax return audited."[5] Nixon believed that the Internal Revenue Service was a legitimate tool to use to strike at his foes. It was, in his view, simply a matter of payback. Nixon believed that Robert Kennedy, acting as his brother's attorney general and political avenger, had ordered Nixon's tax returns audited three separate times after the 1960 election. The president also told Haldeman that "many" of his friends—he named Bebe Rebozo and Bob Abplanalp—had been the targets of politically inspired tax audits. On February 17, Nixon had ordered Haldeman to "check the income taxes of all our opponents. Harrass them and f[ollow] u[p]— just like they did. Pick [Edmund] Muskie [presumed Democratic front-runner]—check tie-in," Haldeman scribbled as the president talked. "[Clark] Moll[enhoff, a White House operative]—stay on HHH [Humphrey] stuff—but don't use it. Continue on Teddy [Kennedy]—any others."[6]*

Nixon had studied the hardball tactics of his opponents. He focused on Joe Califano, a tart-tongued

---

*The IRS generally resisted being used as a political tool. In 1971, IRS Commissioner John Walters reached out to Nixon's Treasury secretary, George Shultz. Walters had been given a list of names by John Dean (from the "enemies list") to be audited. "What do I tell Dean?" he asked. "Tell him you report to me," responded Shultz. "That was the end of it," Schultz told the author in an interview in 2013.[7] The White House did not stop trying, however, and Shultz's response to Walters was not quite "the end of it." Ehrlichman's files show a transcript of a phone call between Ehrlichman and Shultz on August 29, 1972. Shultz tells Ehrlichman that he has looked into Larry O'Brien's tax records and found nothing wrong. Ehrlichman is still pushing, accusing Shultz of "foot-dragging," and he says to Walters, who is also on the telephone line, "Johnnie, I would just like to feel that the IRS was really with us on this."[8]

former LBJ aide and cabinet secretary who had been publicly deriding the administration. "We need an attitude like Califano—he never misses a day of kicking us," Nixon told Haldeman four days after unleashing the IRS (or trying to) on Muskie, Humphrey, and Kennedy.[9] After leaving the Johnson White House, Joe Califano had gone to work at Williams & Connolly, the liberal establishment law firm of Edward Bennett Williams, best friend of Ben Bradlee of **The Washington Post** and an early candidate for the "enemies list." Nixon wanted young, hard-nosed men of the Califano type to fight back. On September 27, 1970, as he was flying to Europe on Air Force One, Nixon instructed Haldeman to create a "campaign attack group"—he named the "nutcutters," including Colson, Buchanan, Huston, and Chotiner.[10] Haldeman short-handed a list: "Buch[anan], Huston, Moll[enhoff], [Lyn] Nof[ziger], [Jeb] Mag[ruder], Chot[iner], Colson.

Charles "Chuck" Colson was fast becoming Nixon's favorite nut-cutter. "Chuck's got the balls of a brass monkey," Nixon gleefully told his speechwriter, Ray Price.[11] Colson was an ex-Marine, and Nixon liked Marines (Steve Bull, Nixon's personal assistant, was another one). A swamp Yankee* from Boston, Colson was proud to have rejected admis-

---

*"Swamp Yankees" were white Protestants who had been left behind in the "swamp" of Catholic and Jewish immigrants in late-nineteenth-century Boston when the rich WASPs withdrew to their mansions on Beacon Hill.

sion at Harvard, an enormous plus in Nixon's book. (Colson went to Brown instead.) Having closely studied the Kennedy political machine in Massachusetts, Colson was a master of "bloc politics"—he knew how to appeal to ethnic and blue-collar groups. He carefully cultivated labor bosses and the Catholic hierarchy, arranging to have Cardinal John Krol, the archbishop of Philadelphia, invited out on the **Sequoia** with the president. Colson knew how to get things done by, as Nixon approvingly put it, "breaking china." On a Friday night in late 1970, Nixon told Haldeman and Ehrlichman that he wanted an executive order setting up a federal commission to aid parochial schools. Knowing that his two top aides would put this constitutionally dubious order in the do-nothing file, Nixon turned to Colson and said, "Don't pay any attention to Haldeman and Ehrlichman. They're Christian Scientists. They don't understand this." Colson had the executive order on Nixon's desk by Monday morning.

Colson understood right away that he had made enemies of Haldeman and Ehrlichman. "From that day on I was toxic to them," he recalled. But he also knew that he had scored with Nixon, who, like many presidents, was not above pitting his aides against each other. "If he couldn't get them to do what he wanted them to do," Colson said, "he would give it to me to get it done."[12] Haldeman recalled that, at first, he welcomed Colson "because he absorbed a lot of time with Nixon that I would have to sit through—listening to him rant about somebody who's got to be done in, or thrown out of an airplane—and did nothing about. Chuck sat and listened, and wrote it down, and went out and did it." In a reflective, slightly bitter mood after serving a prison sentence for his role in Watergate, Haldeman came to regard Colson as "another of my mistakes."[13] John Mitchell spotted Colson's danger signs right away. "Look out for Chuck Colson," he told Richard Moore, a White House aide, in 1970. "If the president ever gets in real trouble, it will be his fault." Asked by speechwriter Price, "Who is Colson's constituency, anyway?" Mitchell answered, "The president's worst instincts."[14]

Soon Colson was sharing a Scotch or two in the evenings with the president at his Executive Office Building hideaway; Colson's office was conveniently next door. "Those who say that I fed the president's darker instincts are only 50 percent correct," Colson told Jonathan Aitken, "because 50 percent of the time he was feeding my darker instincts." One evening, watching a news report on the Democratic front runner, Senator Edmund Muskie, Nixon remarked, "Wouldn't it be kinda interesting if there was a Committee of Democrats supporting Muskie **and** busing. Couldn't you arrange that Chuck?" In no time "Democrats for Muskie and Busing" was publishing a hundred thousand leaflets, paid for by Chuck Colson. Nixon was delighted by the false propaganda coup, which sowed confusion in the Muskie campaign and alienated the kind of ethnic Democrats who were ripe for the plucking by Nixon.[15]

Some members of the "campaign attack group" were awed and a little intimidated by Colson. Jeb Magruder had been brought into the White House by Haldeman to sharpen the dull PR efforts of Herb Klein, the genial communications director.[16] Klein regaled Magruder with stories of the bogeyman Dick Tuck and Chotiner's shenanigans in earlier campaigns and came to regret it. Magruder was weak and impressionable and got a little too excited about the Department of Dirty Tricks, as some staffers called Colson's office.[17] Handsome and married to a beautiful wife, Magruder was a thoroughly confused young man, spouting sermons from his Williams College chaplain William Sloane Coffin that money isn't everything while he had shinnied up the corporate pole. He was taken aback when Chotiner—"who for twenty years had been stereotyped as a hatchet man"—protested that Colson's tactics went too far. Magruder understood that Chotiner was resentful of Colson, who had supplanted him. But he was uneasy when Chotiner objected to the "attack ads" outlined by Colson, which seemed to go beyond the tactics used by Chotiner and Nixon in the infamous "Pink Lady" campaign of 1950. According to Magruder, Colson instructed his dirty tricksters to lay on the innuendo: "You questioned a man's patriotism, his intelligence, his morality, his manhood, anything you could get away with."[18]

Colson was Nixon's new favorite in part because he knew how to flatter—he rivaled Kissinger in shamelessness—but also because he was upbeat and fun.[19] A fair amount of Colson's boasts, like his quip that he would run over his grandmother for Richard Nixon, was meant in jest.[20] Nixon liked to play practical jokes on his more self-serious aides, like the literal-minded spokesman Ron Ziegler and Kissinger, who veered between self-deprecating charm and self-seriousness.

Kissinger was the only Nixon adviser entitled to walk in the door without getting the permission of Nixon's personal assistant, Steve Bull, but Nixon liked to put him in his place from time to time. Colson was only too happy to help by playing the role of Sorcerer's Apprentice. Once, when Nixon's Executive Office Building door swung open to reveal Kissinger, Nixon, who was in the middle of a conversation with Colson, did not miss a beat. "Well, I think you're right, Chuck, about that," said Nixon, without looking up at Kissinger. "I think it's time we used nuclear weapons. Everything else has failed." Kissinger looked "paralyzed," Colson later recalled.[21]

Heavy-handed joking aside, it's doubtful that Nixon ever seriously considered using nuclear weapons against North Vietnam, but he wasn't exaggerating when he said that "everything else has failed." Kissinger's secret negotiations with the North Vietnamese in Paris were as stymied as ever. Not for the first time, Nixon was harboring the disturbing thought that the war was hopeless, that the North Vietnamese would never accept a peace that was "honorable" or, more precisely as Nixon defined it, one that allowed President Thieu's government to stand in Saigon. On a flight back from Key Biscayne on October 10, he wrote a query to Kissinger, wondering if they had ever understood the war. "Have we misjudged VC from the beginning," he jotted on a yellow pad. Various scenarios—"stop U.S. dissent & they'll talk" and "Give them a jolt & they'll talk"—seemed fruitless.[22]

Kissinger had by now begun to consider that the best the Americans could hope for was a decent interval between the withdrawal of U.S. troops and the collapse of the Thieu government. Nixon, however unhappily, appeared to agree.[23] Inevitably, there were cynical political calculations at work. If the Americans pulled out too quickly, the Saigon government would fall before the 1972 election—and Nixon would get the blame and presumably pay the political price. Better, then, to keep the Saigon government propped up until after Nixon was reelected. Taken to its logical extension, a "decent interval" strategy could be seen as a willingness to prolong a war that could not be won.[24]

Nixon and Kissinger could be deeply cynical practitioners of realpolitik. But Nixon never stopped hoping that the war could be turned around and the politburo in Hanoi brought to their knees, if not to their senses—even as he grudgingly came to respect the obduracy of the enemy. Nixon has been condemned in some quarters as a war criminal, but it is more accurate to blame him for wishful thinking, for a too-optimistic faith in American power. Again and again, he suggested that one more massive blow would bring "peace with honor." Recalling how, on the Herter Committee trip in 1947, he had stood on a hill looking down at devastated Berlin, he was convinced, or had convinced himself, that overwhelming force was moral and justified in the face of evil, which he believed, with all sincerity, communism to be. "He got quite cranked up on this whole subject, and made the point that he will not go out of Vietnam whimpering," Haldeman wrote in his diary in early June of 1971.[25]

Still, Nixon could be crafty and veiled, especially when he was talking to Kissinger. One can read hundreds of pages of transcripts of Nixon and Kissinger conversing without ever knowing for sure the intentions of either. Rivals at pettiness, born manipulators, and geniuses at the darker side of diplomacy, they at once distrusted and needed each other. It did not help the relationship between the president and his national security adviser that Kissinger, on the job and on his frequent social rounds, hinted to newsmen that he was a restraining force on the "madman" president. And Nixon tired of Kissinger's histrionics and paranoia about Bill Rogers at State. "All this really worries the P," Haldeman wrote in his diary on August 17. "P realizes K's basically jealous of any idea not his own."[26] Nixon had assigned Middle East strategy to Rogers instead of Kissinger because he wanted to signal that he was impervious to the pressures of the Israel lobby. The president "had his doubts whether my Jewish faith might warp my judgment," Kissinger wrote in his memoirs.[27] Kissinger, naturally, did his best to undermine Rogers's Middle East peace plans and succeeded; vain but not crafty, Rogers was no match at intramural swordplay.

Despite occasional outbursts of frustration, Nixon by and large tolerated Kissinger's diva act. He understood that Kissinger was just as clever and devious as he was. Scornful of the CIA, he counted on Kissinger to run covert operations. In September of 1970, he and Kissinger were furious that the CIA had failed to stop the election of the leftist leader of Chile, Salvador Allende; "the CIA isn't worth a damn," Nixon railed.[28] (Cynically, CIA Director Richard Helms told his wife Cynthia that he thought Nixon was fronting for his old law client, PepsiCo, whose interests were being threatened by Chilean socialists.)[29] Kissinger and Nixon saw covert action as an integral tool of statecraft. Kissinger was put in charge of a "Track II" operation to subvert the Chilean government that three years later helped cause Allende's overthrow and murder.[30]

Interviewed by David Frost after he left the presidency, Nixon commented on Kissinger's "mood swings" and suggested that he tried to exert a calming influence, never too high or too low, on his mercurial national security adviser. When Kissinger second-guessed a decision, Nixon would say, "Remember Lot's wife, Henry. Never look back."[31] At times, Nixon could be as emotional as Kissinger, but it suited Nixon to see himself as the calm and steady one; it was true that, at the depth of a crisis, Nixon often became serene, almost eerily so. Perhaps it was useful to have others raging around him so that he could play the role he saw for himself, as the cool hand in the crisis—which he often was.

Kissinger never regarded himself as Nixon's friend, but he tried to understand him and came to admire him. He believed that Nixon had been unloved as a child but fought to compensate by achieving greatness. While he made fun of Nixon as "Walter Mitty," he also saw Nixon's sweet side, mawkish when he tried too hard but touching in its sincerity. "He had a kind of desperate courage," Kissinger told the author.[32] In his 1982 memoir **Years of Upheaval,** Kissinger wrote, "No modern president could have been less equipped by nature for political life."[33] Kissinger knew that for Nixon, entering a crowded room or talking to a stranger required an enormous act of will.

In August of 1970, Nixon summoned Kissinger to ride with him and Bebe Rebozo to visit his childhood home in Yorba Linda. The three men and a Secret Service agent climbed into a nondescript brown Lincoln and headed up from San Clemente. When they arrived at the modest bungalow, two other cars filled with press and security pulled up behind them. This was the usual presidential retinue, but suddenly Nixon began yelling at them to leave; he "lost his composure as I had never seen him do before or after," wrote Kissinger. "The orders were delivered at the top of his voice—itself an event so unprecedented that the Secret Service broke every regulation in the book and departed, followed by the press pool."

"When we were alone again Nixon became more relaxed than I have ever seen him," Kissinger recounted. In Whittier, Nixon pointed out the old family gas station, the small college, the nondescript hotel where he had begun his unlikely political career as the underdog Republican candidate. "As he was talking softly and openly for the first time in our acquaintance, it suddenly struck me that the guiding theme of his discourse was how it had all been accidental. There was no moral to the tale except how easily it could have been otherwise," wrote Kissinger. Then Nixon got lost in the canyons of Beverly Hills looking for the fancy house he had built during his brief stint as an L.A. lawyer, and "the relaxed, almost affable Nixon gave way to the agitated, nervous Nixon with whom I was familiar."[34]

Foreign policy was Nixon's first love, but electoral politics finished a close second. Nixon loved playing chief campaign strategist, partly because he knew he was good at it. On the morning of September 9, he held forth for an hour and forty-five minutes with his political advisers, recounting old war stories and laying down a plan of attack for the 1970 midterm elections in November. (Chotiner sat in on the conversation "like the Ghost of Christmas past," recalled Bill Safire, who was there along with Pat Buchanan.) "The P was really in his element," recorded Haldeman.[35] "Have you all read the Scammon-Wattenberg book?" Nixon asked. "The Democrats are all reading it." In **The Real Majority,** Richard Scammon and Ben Wattenberg argued that the election would come down to which party could win the hypothetical forty-seven-year-old Dayton, Ohio, housewife whose husband was a machinist. She was concerned with "the Social Issue," wrote the authors, which, roughly speaking, meant fear of crime and declining morality brought on by hippies and black militants. "Permissiveness is the key theme," said Nixon.* The Democratic Party regulars were scurrying to distance themselves from student radicals and angry blacks by becoming centrists. Don't let them, said Nixon—a Republican candidate should put his Democratic opponent on the defensive by saying, "I don't question his sincerity—he deeply believes in his radical philosophy." This will cause the Democrat to squawk, "Gee, I'm not a radical," said Nixon.[37]

On September 24, Nixon tutored his vice president, his lead paratrooper in the culture wars. Using

---

*Nixon had been having some interesting conversations about permissiveness with Haldeman and Ehrlichman. Ehrlichman's notes from an after-dinner discussion between the three men in "the library in San Clemente" on September 1 are cryptic but suggestive enough:

"Sex and marijuana—Rock festivals
Bikini exposure—sates
Midi
Mini
Porno—dulls mystery"[36]

punchy alliterative scripts written by Buchanan and Safire, Agnew was going around the country denouncing "pusillanimous pussyfooters" and "vicars of vacillation." Nixon wanted him to pick fights with the peaceniks and the Yippies. "If the vice-president were slightly roughed up by these thugs nothing better could happen for our cause. If anybody brushed up against Mrs. Agnew, tell her to fall down," Nixon instructed.[38]

But the Agnew show was getting old, Safire noted, verging into self-parody. The vice president had coined his own term—radic-lib—which "sounded ominously like the 'comsymp' of the John Birchers to some liberal commentators," recalled Safire.[39] The GOP was sinking in the polls. Fearing that the Republicans would lose as many as thirty-five seats in the House—the historic norm for the party in power during the first midterm elections—Nixon decided to take to the hustings himself for the final two weeks of the campaign.[40]

"It's time for the Silent Majority to stand up and be counted!" Nixon told crowds across the country.[41] Nixon seemed to relish his return to the stump, though his social awkwardness never went away. In St. Petersburg, Florida, a policeman was severely injured when his motorcycle flipped over while driving in the presidential motorcade. In his considerate way, Nixon rushed from his limousine to express his sympathies. As was his way, he also didn't know what to say, blurting to the policeman who lay bleeding on the ground, "Do you like your work?"[42]

Nixon's protectors had learned to wear old suits when they traveled into raucous, unruly crowds—his body man, Steve Bull, had once been cut by a protester wielding a razor blade—but the demonstrators were particularly loud and nasty as Nixon approached the San Jose, California, municipal auditorium on October 29.[43] Inside, five thousand uneasy boosters could hear the roar of the angry crowd outside; at one point, protesters tried to bash through the doors.

Haldeman saw an opportunity for Nixon's favorite kind of showmanship. "We wanted some confrontation and there were no hecklers in the hall, so we stalled the departure a little so they could zero in outside, and they sure did," he wrote in his diary that night.[44] Nixon lit a match by climbing on the hood of his limousine and thrusting his arms out in his V-for-victory salute. The crowd reacted explosively. "I couldn't resist," Nixon wrote in his memoirs. "Suddenly rocks and eggs and vegetables were flying everywhere."[45]

The Secret Service hustled the president into his limo, but the staff bus got caught behind a stalled car. Windows shattered. "Just like Caracas!" exclaimed Rose Woods. "She hit the deck in the aisle, shouting at the rest of us to do the same," wrote Safire.[46] That night at the Western White House, the president was too wound up to sleep. In the heat of campaigning, Nixon's penchant for brooding could give way to a kind of joyful giddiness. In his wry, telegraphic style, Haldeman described the evening after the storm in his diary:

After arrival in San Clemente, P went home, then kept calling with ideas about how to push the line. Then called and asked, "How are things at your place?" I said fine and started to talk. He interrupted and said we're having a fire here. Laughed and said house had caught fire from his den fireplace. Told me to come on over. Place full of smoke, hoses, firemen, and water. Not too much damage. P took me in his bedroom (he was padding around the patio in pajamas, slippers, and weird bathrobe when I arrived), said there was no problem. It was full of smoke. I could hardly breathe. He said he loved smoke and would sleep there. I talked him into the guest house. We went over there, had a beer, and talked about the day. Finally to bed about 1:00.

A really weird day, especially the last parts of it. He was very tired, but in great humor. Pulled down his pajamas and showed me horrible bruise on his thigh from motorcade in Rochester.

All through the day he delighted in giving the "V" to peaceniks.[47]

On Election Day, the Republicans lost nine House seats and gained two in the Senate. It was a respectable showing by the incumbent president's party at the midterm, but the press for the most part declared victory for the Democrats. In his election night TV speech, the Democratic champion, Senator Edmund Muskie, had appeared Lincolnesque, speaking in a soft, solemn voice about the "politics of hope" versus the "politics of fear" from his misty cottage in Maine. For his nationally televised address, delivered at a harshly lit rally in Phoenix, Nixon had delivered a strident get-tough speech that made even his allies wince. "He looked like he was running for sheriff," scoffed John Mitchell, normally a law-and-order stalwart.[48]

Bruised again by the press in the wake of the election, Nixon was seized by one of his occasional bouts of self-pity. Traveling to Paris in early November for the funeral of his hero Charles de Gaulle, he wanted to go to a "good restaurant" for lunch but his aides convinced him to keep a low profile. "P then sulked about never gets to do anything fun that he wants to do, always has to do what's right," wrote Haldeman.[49]

But, as ever, he was determined to rally, to be positive. He tried to put on a good show for his family. "My father was the member of the family who most enjoyed the White House," recalled Julie. "As he stepped out of the elevator for dinner, the family could expect to hear a jaunty two-note whistle. He was upbeat and wanted us to be also."[50] On November 15, two days after returning from Paris, Nixon repaired to the Lincoln Sitting Room to write down what, as he put it, "I have learned about myself and the Presidency. From this experience I conclude: The primary contribution a President can make is on Spiritual lift." He listed, as he had the year before, the joyful human qualities he wished to embody and project:

Need for optimistic upbeat psychology.
Need for stimulating people to talk to.
Need for dignity, kindness, drive, youth, brevity,
Spiritual quality[51]

Nixon's dreaminess was duly translated—and deadened—by the too-efficient White House bureaucracy. In early December, a memo went out from Dwight Chapin that staffers were to sit in on meetings to record the president's "warmth." These "anecdotalists"—primarily White House aide Dick Moore and speechwriters Safire, Buchanan, and Price—dutifully set out to find heart-warming human interest stories about the president that could be fed to the press. Naturally, even the most access-hungry reporters resisted such obvious attempts to fluff the president.[52]

The same day that Nixon ordered his staff to contrive feel-good stories, Nixon received some genuinely good news—a small signal from a faraway source that was momentous in its significance. On December 9, at 6 P.M., Kissinger was visited in his office by the Pakistani ambassador bearing an envelope containing a handwritten missive on white, blue-lined paper. It was a personal message from Chou En-Lai, the prime minister of the People's Republic of China, to President Richard Nixon. After some obligatory agitprop about Taiwan, the message stated that a "special envoy of President Nixon's will be most welcome in Peking."

Kissinger later recalled that the participants in a

drawn-out diplomatic process rarely know when
history is being made, but this time he had no doubt.
The national security adviser's initial skepticism that
Nixon could open Red China was fast disappearing.
Nixon's feelers to Beijing, delivered through Pakistan's Yahya Kahn, had teased out a surprising, en-
ticing response. The world order was about to
change, thanks to the farsightedness of a lower-
middle-class boy who had once lain awake listening
to trains in the night. The moment the Pakistani
ambassador left his office, Kissinger hurried down
the hall to the Oval Office to tell Nixon.[53]

The president betrayed no emotion—no excitement, no joy. Watching him react, or rather not
react, Kissinger thought that Nixon had been so
often stung by defeat that he would not let himself
savor victory. He could not reveal his hopes because
they might be snatched away. "He always believed
his enemies would prevail," Kissinger told Richard
Reeves. "He was conditioned for rejection or failure,
confused by success."[54] Or, possibly, he was worried
that Kissinger would leak the news.

Nonetheless, it is odd that Nixon would greet such
a triumph with silence. Nixon could exult wildly over
victories, from ball games to moon shots, at which he
was a mere spectator. Perhaps he needed to show Kissinger his Mr. Cool affect, as a way of reminding him
whose idea the opening to China really was.

Just before Christmas, on December 21, Nixon
was visited by an ambassador from a strange land

close to home. That morning at 8:45, appointments secretary Dwight Chapin, known by his White House buddies as "Slick" for his patent-leather hair and movie-star smile, excitedly reported that Elvis Presley had left a handwritten letter with one of the guards at the Northwest Gate. The rock-and-roll star wanted to see President Nixon. Chapin quickly wrote a memo arguing that "if the President wants to meet some bright young people outside the government, Presley might be the perfect one to start with." In his prim script, Haldeman wrote in the margin, "You must be kidding."[55] But Nixon knew better: Presley was Southern, blue-collar, patriotic. He had not avoided the draft, serving in the army as a private. "Elvis the Pelvis" may have been, by 1970, an over-the-hill pop idol, but here he was, just outside the White House gate, offering himself as an Emissary to Youth. On American Airlines stationery, Presley had written, "The drug culture, The Hippie Elements, the SDS, Black Panthers, etc. do **not** consider me as their enemy or as they call it The Establishment. **I call it America and** I love it." By lunchtime Presley, dressed in tight dark velvet pants, gold medallion, and cape, was shaking hands with Nixon in the Oval Office. (The Secret Service had relieved him of a loaded nickel-plated gun, intended as a gift for the president.)

The conversation between Presley and the president took a few odd turns. At one point, Presley opined, "The Beatles, I think, are kind of anti-American. They came over here. Made a lot of money. And then went back to England. And they said some anti-American stuff when they got back." Nixon looked a little surprised when Presley (who would later die of his drug habit) offered to help with the War on Drugs and asked for a drug enforcement agent's badge. "I've been studying Communist brainwashing for over ten years, and now the drug culture, too," said Presley. The logical leaps were no matter. Nixon seemed glad to meet the King and didn't even flinch when Presley hugged him. The two men fished around in the president's desk drawer where he kept tie clasps and golf balls and other gifts for visitors. Typically, Nixon would hand a guest a tie clip or cuff links with the presidential seal and clumsily joke, "Give this to your wife. Or your girlfriend. We won't tell." Now he loaded the King and two of his friends up with knickknacks and waved farewell with a cheery, "Thank you very much, fellas." Bud Krogh, the young White House aide who had accompanied Presley to the Oval Office, noticed that Nixon seemed unusually relaxed around the faded rock star, who appeared at once forward and shy. The louche, flamboyant Presley, who had once recorded a song called "Poison Ivy League" ("Poison Ivy League, Poison the Ivy League / Gives me an itch, sons of the rich"), and the buttoned-up Nixon understood each other.[56]

CHAPTER 18

Father of the Bride

"I hate exercise," the president told John Ehrlichman on January 9, his fifty-eighth birthday, "but I do it to be better at the job." In addition to his lonely nighttime bowling, Nixon would do "300 or 400 jogs before a press conference to get alert—to get the wind up," Nixon told his aide. He complained that the First Lady was after him for his poor posture. She wanted him to sit in a straight-back chair instead of reclining in his favorite easy chair.

Sitting up a little straighter in his study in San Clemente, the president began to muse on the recreational habits of his predecessors. "LBJ liked his booze," said Nixon. For JFK, entertainment came from "having a few people around with beautiful dolls." Nixon did not begrudge Kennedy his amusements (though he probably did not know that JFK had cavorted with girls in the White House pool). "That was his right," he told Ehrlichman.[1]

That same day, Press Secretary Ron Ziegler, dutifully trying to display "Nixon the Man," allowed reporters and photographers to watch the president

On the beach.
**Courtesy of the Richard Nixon Presidential
Library and Museum**

walk on the beach below the cliffs at the Casa Pacifica. Nixon loved the beach and often walked it, but
on this chilly day he was wearing dress pants and, it
was widely reported, black wing-tip shoes. (In fact,
a close examination of the photo shows Nixon wearing more casual, Hush Puppies–type shoes.) Unflattering comparison with a barefooted JFK, tossing a
football with his khakis rolled up, was irresistible.[2]

JFK remained a haunting presence in the White
House. Among Secret Service personnel, the assassination of the late president was referred to in
hushed tones as "the Tragedy."[3] Pat Nixon had been
roundly criticized in the press for removing a plaque
in her bedroom that read, "In this room lived John
Fitzgerald Kennedy and his wife Jacqueline during
the two years, ten months, and two days he was
President of the United States." The criticism was
unwarranted. The plaque had been on a mantle,
which the Committee for the Preservation of the
White House had removed. Mrs. Nixon played no
role in the decision.[4]

In her way, Pat showed no resentment and, in
early February, graciously invited Jackie, now Mrs.
Aristotle Onassis, and her children, Caroline and
John Jr., back to the White House for a private
showing of the Kennedys' formal White House portraits. John Jr., who was ten years old, spilled a glass
of milk onto the table and into Nixon's lap, and his
mother was quiet about the portraits, which she felt
were unflattering.[5] Nixon was gentle and warm with

her. The president and the former First Lady talked about the vicissitudes of traveling—how hotels routinely painted their "presidential suites" in anticipation of the arrival of the real thing. Nixon and Jackie agreed that it was hard enough to sleep on the road, but the smell of fresh paint made it impossible.

"Of course, I was determined to keep the conversation away from anything that would distress her or make the visit sad. At one point, she looked at me and said, 'I always live in a dream world,'" Nixon recalled in his memoirs. Nixon wrote that "Pat gave explicit orders that the visit be kept secret until it was over so that no reporters or cameramen would intrude on their privacy."[6] Mrs. Nixon's discretion was considerate, but it was not the whole story. In his diary two days after the Kennedy visit, Haldeman wrote that Pat "was disturbed about no TV coverage of the Jackie Onassis dinner the other night, which was a real coup." (Pat wanted to keep cameras away during the visit, but she wanted credit afterward.) Again and again during the winter of 1971, Haldeman recorded Nixon's complaints that his troops were doing a poor job of generating positive coverage of the First Family. On February 5, Haldeman wrote, "On the PR front, he got going again on the fact that we've done so much and gotten so little credit." Haldeman added, "He's also having a problem with Mrs. Nixon," who was upset that her own efforts were so rarely praised in the press.[7]

Nixon faithfully tried to build up the First Lady's

image. He dictated notes to Rose Woods about his wife and asked Bill Safire to polish them up and feed them to a woman's magazine. Nixon's tone was proud but defensive. "They criticize her because she happens to have the virtues that are no longer 'fashionable'—that is, she was an orphan at an early age and worked her way through school; she has great character and determination and is not the type of person who makes a fool of herself in public in order to get attention," Nixon dictated. He was "bothered by the criticism that she doesn't have warmth and that, of course, is easily answered by anybody who knows her at all." Nixon went on to protest too much on his own behalf: "Mrs. Nixon, of course, as most women do, takes much harder the criticism of her husband than her husband himself does. The critics don't bother me, even though I have the most unfriendly press in history, it has never bothered me, but it deeply bothers Pat and my daughters."[8]

Cabinet members were instructed to spread the word about the president's unsung achievements. "The President should become known next year as 'Mr. Peace,'" Haldeman had told Kissinger before Christmas. Kissinger's aide, Al Haig wrote his boss, "Here we go again. I suppose our best bet is to play along, but I must say some of the rhetoric is a little sickening."[9]

Nixon counted on his national security adviser to be loyal, but at the same time the president was wary and worn out by Kissinger, who could be temperamental. In March, Nixon told Haldeman that Kissinger would fall on his sword for the president. "I agree," replied Haldeman. "But he would do it with loud kicking and screaming and make sure the blood spurted all over the place so he would get full credit."[10]

Kissinger's celebrity was growing. At first, Nixon and his top aides were amused by Kissinger's highly publicized flirtations with movie stars. Ehrlichman had a poster of a scantily clad Jill St. John, Kissinger's frequent escort, hung on Air Force One. Bawdy Kissinger jokes abounded at the White House. "Don't do anything I wouldn't do tonight, Henry," Nixon would say, loudly, in front of reporters. (Kissinger's Secret Service code name was "Woodcutter," which Kissinger mangled as "Woodchopper"—actually, "Vudchopper"—and Safire twisted into "Woodpecker." Ehrlichman just called him "Wiener Schnitzel.") But there was also in Nixon "a little envy" of Kissinger's glamour, wrote Kissinger's biographer, Walter Isaacson.[11] At a morning meeting on February 8, Nixon strongly complained to Haldeman about Kissinger's "insistence on flitting around with movie stars. He's making a fool of himself," Nixon protested. "Grown men know better. Henry has to stop this. Do something. Do something." In his diary for that day, Haldeman recorded the basis for a presidential "action memo": "He wants us at the White House dinners to not put him next to the most glamorous girl anymore, but rather put [Kissinger] near some intelligent and interesting woman instead."[12] White House social secretary Lucy Winchester recalled getting the memo that "Henry was not to sit with pretty girls. I ignored it after a week," she said.[13]

Nixon was irked that Kissinger had been spending a lot of time with **New York Times** columnist James Reston. Increasingly, Kissinger was appearing in the newspapers as the architect, not just the executor, of Nixon administration foreign policy. Newspaper articles, uncorrected over time, could harden into history.* Nixon took steps to protect the record.

Although Nixon had ordered President Johnson's taping system dismantled and removed, he reversed himself. In mid-February, at just about the time he banned dinnertime starlets for Kissinger, Nixon ordered a secret taping system installed in the White House. Johnson had used the Army Signal Corps to install his listening devices. Fearing that he would be bugged by the Pentagon high command, Nixon used the Secret Service, which he could control. Microphones were installed in the Oval Office, the Cabinet Room, and the Lincoln Sitting Room (later, in the Executive Office Building hideaway and at Camp David). Partly because Nixon was all thumbs, the tapes were voice-activated.[15]

"Mum's the whole word," Nixon told his aide.

*Nixon kept Kissinger off TV, too. On February 16, 1971—the day Nixon turned on his White House taping system—Haldeman jotted in his notebook: "Will never have K on TV re substance. Can brief here—but not public."[14]

Alex Butterfield, on February 16, the first day the tapes began to turn. "I will not be transcribed." Stumbling slightly over his words, he went on to say, "There may be a day when we have to have this for purposes of, maybe we want to put out something that's positive, maybe we need something just to be sure that we can correct the record."[16] The record Nixon wanted to correct was the one being made by Kissinger, Haldeman later told Walter Isaacson. "Nixon realized rather early in their relationship that he badly needed a complete record of all they discussed," recalled Haldeman. "He knew that Henry's point of view on a particular subject was sometimes subject to change without notice." Kissinger later remarked, "It was a high price to pay for insurance."[17]

"The first months of 1971 were the lowest point of my first term as President," Nixon recalled in his memoirs. "The problems we confronted were so overwhelming and so apparently impervious to anything we could do to change them that it seemed possible I might not even be nominated for reelection in 1972."[18]

Nixon took pride in his good health. He claimed never to get headaches and rarely complained of other aches and pains. He did, however, partake in what he called "preventive medicine" for tension, regular treatments from an osteopathic doctor named Kenneth Riland. About once a month, Riland would fly down from New York to administer massages, although Riland was indignant if anyone compared him to a chiropractor or an ordinary masseur. He called the treatments a "manipulative, muscle-relaxant technique" in which he would obtain "corrections" by deftly realigning bones and knotted muscle. The garrulous Dr. Riland was a show-off, a collector of celebrities whose names he liked to drop—his patients included Jacqueline Onassis and Nelson Rockefeller. But his treatments must have been soothing, because before long he was giving treatments not just to President Nixon but also to Henry Kissinger, Julie Eisenhower, Rose Mary Woods, Murray Chotiner, and a host of others, including Chief Justice Warren Burger and Nixon's own regular doctor, Walter Tkach. Nixon called Riland "the great miracle man."[19]

Riland accompanied Nixon on trips abroad and marveled at his stamina and punishing schedule. "Inhuman—no rest, wash-up time at all—appears Nixon insists on this," Riland wrote in his diary on Nixon's first trip to Europe.[20] But he worried about Nixon's "martyr complex" and found him hard to reach. On February 3, 1971, he wrote in his diary, "The President, as I have said many times before, is really a loner. He doesn't have any real friends, in spite of what they say about Beebe and the rest of them."

On that same day, sitting in his underwear during a visit from Dr. Riland, Nixon authorized an invasion of Laos to try, one more time, to cut off the Ho Chi Minh trail. "To hell with other countries. We're going to do this," Nixon told Kissinger, according to

Riland's diary.[21] Americans would provide air support and helicopters, but the fighting would be done by ARVN, the army of South Vietnam. Operation Lam Son 719 was a major test of "Vietnamization," and, at first, Nixon was optimistic. Or wanted to be. "The South Vietnamese are going to fight," Nixon said to Kissinger on February 18 in one of their first conversations recorded by the new taping system. "They're going to stand and fight. Aren't they?" "Oh yeah," replied Kissinger.

"We can lose an election," Nixon had declared earlier in the conversation, "but we're not going to lose this war, Henry. That's my view. Do you agree with it?"

"I agree, Mr. President."

"I have a feeling about Laos as well."

"That's right," said Kissinger.[22]

A couple of weeks later, Haldeman found the president, sitting in the dark with a fire blazing and his stereo on full blast, still feeling hopeful. "The P clearly has a sort of mystic feeling about the Laotian thing, and says so," Haldeman recorded.[23]

But the South Vietnamese did not stand and fight for long. By late March, they were in full retreat. TV images showed panicked ARVN soldiers forcing their way onto American helicopters or clinging to the helicopters' skids. Nixon was downcast. "If the South Vietnamese could just win one cheap one. . . . Take a stinking hill. . . . Bring back a prisoner or two. Anything," he had said to Kissinger in late February. Now he exploded when he was informed that the South Vietnamese air force had failed to attack North Vietnamese trucks just because they were "moving targets." "Bullshit!" the president exclaimed. "Just, just, just cream the fuckers!"[24]

The Establishment press treated Operation Lam Son as a humiliating defeat. Nixon was in a funk when he spoke to Kissinger in his Executive Office Building hideaway on April 7. "Do you think if America loses, what this goddamn country is going to be like?" Nixon muttered. "I don't understand why the intellectuals, they really just—"

KISSINGER: They don't mind losing. They don't like America, and that's the difference.

NIXON: They don't, huh? That's fine. Isn't that just great? I wish to Christ they had to live someplace else. I wish they did.

KISSINGER: They don't have the patriotism.[25]

Nixon was sinking in the polls.[26] A majority disapproved of his handling of the war. Nixon could always count on Chuck Colson to cheer him up with an outrageous suggestion, and on March 23, the impish Colson suggested to Nixon that the White House pay off pollster Lou Harris. "We can buy him," said Colson, who suggested finding out "how much of a whore Harris is."

Colson was probably having some fun (there is no evidence of bribes, though Harris did start performing polling services for Nixon).[27] But Colson was perfectly serious about trying to smear Senator Edward Kennedy. In December, Colson had managed to procure some photographs of Kennedy dancing the night away with a woman not his wife in Italy, and the self-described hatchet man had connived to get the photos leaked to the **National Enquirer** through friendly congressmen on the Hill.[28]

Haldeman tried, fitfully, to control Colson. "Watch what you tell the president," he warned Colson on March 26. "Be sure your intelligence is right or that you clearly call it a rumor."[29] But Nixon wanted to rub old wounds. He was in one of his periodic Kennedy obsessions. Chatting with Haldeman and Kissinger on the morning of April 15, Nixon started in on a familiar refrain that JFK was "cold, impersonal, he treated his staff like dogs," while "his staff created the impression of warm, sweet, and nice to people." This led to Nixon berating his staff for failing to create a "mythology" about Nixon's own courage. "What is the most important single factor that should come across out of the first two years? Guts! Absolutely. Guts! Do you agree, Henry?" "Totally," Kissinger responded.[30]

Nixon was bothered that a poll showed John and Robert Kennedy far ahead of Nixon in the estimation of young people. He was comforted, at least, that Edward Kennedy did not do so well.[31] The president was determined that the last Kennedy brother not sneak up on him. On the afternoon of May 18, Nixon met with Colson and Haldeman to work out a plan for round-the-clock coverage on

Teddy Kennedy. Nixon was ever hopeful of catching the Massachusetts senator in an indiscretion. Colson had arranged for spies to dog Kennedy wherever he went.

Suddenly, Henry Kissinger burst in the door. "The thing is okay!" exclaimed the national security adviser. Then Kissinger and Nixon began speaking in a strange double-talk as Haldeman motioned for Colson to leave the room.[32]

Kissinger was bringing, at long last, some much-needed good news. The United States and the Soviet Union were close to a historic deal on the control of nuclear weapons. He was speaking in code in front of Colson because the deal was secret. For months, Kissinger had been working his back channel to Soviet Ambassador Anatoly Dobrynin. The two had developed an almost playful relationship as they tried to whittle down the arsenal of doomsday weapons. "I am sitting on [my] back patio thinking about our peaceful coexistence," Kissinger began one phone conversation. "Good for you," responded the Soviet envoy. "I will be in Moscow thinking in the same way."[33]

Colson was not the only one left in the dark about the Kissinger-Dobrynin back channel. In Geneva, the State Department had been conducting formal arms control negotiations with the Soviets. The talks had been an essentially meaningless exercise, diplomatic cover for the real bargaining going on behind the scenes between the president's national security adviser and the Kremlin's man in Washington. Secretary of State Rogers found out about the deal only when Haldeman, dispatched by Nixon, told him later in the afternoon of May 18. Rogers was furious; he said he felt like he had been made a "laughing stock." Rogers called the president, spluttering. Hanging up after trying to calm him down, Nixon heaved a deep sigh, looked out the window, and said, "It would be god damn easy to run this office if you didn't have to deal with people."³⁴*

The following day, May 19, 1971, a warm spring day in Washington, Nixon felt like celebrating the arms control breakthrough. It had been a trying few weeks. Congress was threatening to try to force disengagement from Vietnam. In late April, returning Vietnam veterans, led by an outspoken navy lieutenant named John Kerry, had tossed their medals over a fence in front of the U.S. Capitol (Kerry kept

---

* The State Department experts believed that Kissinger had cut a bad deal. The Soviets had surpassed the Americans in their capacity to launch large missiles, but the Americans were ahead on missile technology that enabled several warheads to fly off a single rocket, or MIRVs (standing for "multiple independently targetable reentry vehicles"). The Strategic Arms Limitation deal worked out by Kissinger and Dobrynin did not ban MIRVs, allowing the Russians to catch up. When Gerald Smith, the head of the arms control agency, began to raise questions, the president scoffed, "That's bullshit, Gerry, and you know it." Smith, a proper old-school gentleman, complained to an aide, "Nobody's ever talked to me that way."³⁵

his).* In early May, antiwar protesters had tried to shut down bridges and block traffic around the nation's capital. Under orders from the Justice Department, the police had rounded up several thousand activists and held them at RFK Stadium. Haldeman's notes show Nixon's PR calculations in releasing them: "Let 'em out. Better to have trashing, etc. Doesn't want evening news of 5 M [five thousand] in a cage."

Colson had been playing to Nixon's dark side. He had advocated hiring some goons to wade into the protesters and tear down their Vietcong flags. "Go ahead and have a fight," Colson urged, according to Haldeman's meeting notes. "Get it thru on TV—dramatize. Also get a fight re tearing down U.S. flag. Be sure cops don't stop our people."[37]

But Colson also made Nixon lighten up. He had sent a crate of oranges to the imprisoned protesters, with a label that read, "Best of luck, Senator Edmund Muskie." Then he tipped off the press. Nixon and Haldeman hooted with laughter when White House counsel John Dean told them of Colson's prank.[38]

---

* Nixon spotted Kerry as a would-be JFK right away. On April 23, he said to Haldeman, "Kerry is pretty well wound up."

HALDEMAN: I think you'll find Kerry running for political office. I mean—

NIXON: Yeah.

HALDEMAN: —the way he's building himself.

NIXON: He's from Massachusetts?[36]

On the evening of May 19, the president asked
Colson to join him, Kissinger, Haldeman, and Ehrlichman for an evening cruise on the **Sequoia**. Colson recalled the way Nixon stopped to salute the flag
on the yacht's stern, and then again when the **Sequoia** paused at Mt. Vernon for the lowering of colors in honor of George Washington (required of
naval vessels). Watching Nixon stand rigidly at attention, Colson observed, "it wasn't a politician's
showmanship."[39] Over a dinner of steaks and fresh
corn in the yacht's mahogany-paneled dining room,
Nixon held forth on his dream of détente through
great power diplomacy. With his giant chessboard
vision of the globe, Nixon had been sidling up to
China in part to throw a scare into Russia. The strategy was working. Moscow was closely watching as
Beijing signaled its new openness to Washington.
Nixon was convinced that the Russians had agreed
to defrost relations with the United States—to sign
a Strategic Arms Limitation Treaty—as a counterweight to an emerging Sino-American rapproche-
ment. "Let me tell you something: without China,
they never would have agreed to the SALT," Nixon
had told Kissinger.[40]

Eyeing Colson, who was ignorant of the secret
diplomacy, Kissinger uncomfortably warned Nixon
not to say too much about his plans for China.
"Relax, relax," Nixon said. He saw a chance to poke
at a soft spot in Kissinger's Germanic countenance.
"If those liberals on your staff, Henry, don't stop giving everything to the **New York Times**, I won't be

going anywhere." Then Nixon jabbed a little harder. "The leaks, the leaks; that's what we've got to stop at any cost. Do you hear me, Henry?"

Kissinger, "who often did not know when he was being kidded," Colson recalled, "launched into an impassioned defense of his own office." The leaks were all coming from "disloyal bureaucrats" at the State Department, he protested. (Across the table, Haldeman "smiled," wrote Colson. "He and I knew, as did Nixon, that Henry himself was often the major source of leaks.")

Nixon by now was off on his favorite subject, his enemies, both on Capitol Hill and elsewhere. "Chuck, your job is to hold off those madmen on the Hill long enough for Henry to finish his work in Paris [his secret talks with the North Vietnamese]. Then we go for the big play, China, Russia."

Nixon began complaining about a freshman senator, Harold Hughes of Iowa, who, in a Law Day speech two weeks earlier, had accused the Nixon administration of "repression, wiretapping, bugging...surveillance...and attempts by government to intimidate the communications media." Colson dismissed "Hughes's accusations as the paranoid prattlings of an ambitious politician," Colson recalled in **Born Again,** his memoir. Then, as Colson told the story: "The President's finger circled the top of his wineglass slowly. 'One day we will get them—we'll get them on the ground where we want them. And then we'll stick our heels in, step on them hard and twist—right, Chuck, right?'"

Nixon's eyes darted to Kissinger. "Henry knows what I mean—just like you do it in negotiations, Henry—get them on the floor and step on them, crush them, show no mercy."

Kissinger smiled and nodded. Colson said, "You're right, sir, we'll get them." Haldeman said nothing. Ehrlichman looked up at the ceiling.[41]

Nixon continued to be an exuberant sports fan. On the White House tapes, he can be heard yelling at his TV while watching football games.* In March, Nixon had waxed on to Haldeman about the spectacle of the Ali-Frazier boxing match, "how the chemistry and drama [had] really lifted public spirits," wrote Haldeman. "The P feels that people need to be caught in a great event and taken out of their humdrum existence." That same day, March 17, Nixon had publicly announced his daughter Tricia's wedding engagement to Edward Cox, the Princeton-

*Nixon claimed never to watch TV, but as a regular consumer of televised baseball and football games, he sometimes dipped into pop culture, if inadvertently. Public tastes and mores were moving away from Nixon's values, which remained firmly rooted in small-town, prewar rural America. On May 13, Safire wrote in his diary this "aside" from Haldeman: "The President turned on the ballgame Tuesday night, and when it was rained out, he watched a show called 'All in the Family.' It really bugged him. He remembers all the dialogue and he acts it out when he tells about it. It had to do with a fag who was portrayed sympathetically. The President feels that the decline of civilizations has always been marked by an acceptance of homosexuality and a general decline of moral values."[42]

and Harvard Law–educated young man who had
been courting her on and off for several years. Noting the positive press about the impending White
House nuptials, Haldeman wrote that it "may be
one of the event-type things that the P's talking
about, if we can take advantage of it properly."[43]

The wedding was scheduled for June 12. Over
four hundred people were invited—but no members of the House or Senate. Nixon had grown tired
of meeting with small groups of congressmen, who
seemed to complain and misinterpret his words. In
January, he had told Haldeman that if he had to
meet with congressmen, they should be assembled
in congregations of fifty or more—"no cozy groups
that just lead to gripes and leaks," Haldeman wrote.[44]

The president also banned **The Washington Post**
from covering the event. Haldeman, as it happened,
had just sat with the **Post**'s owner, Katharine Graham, at a Sunday Night Supper at Joe Alsop's. Mrs.
Graham was a close friend of Kissinger but had never
tried to meet Haldeman. "He made my blood run
cold," she wrote in her memoirs. Attempting his
own local brand of Nixon-goes-to-China diplomacy,
Haldeman had invited the **Post**'s proprietor to call
him if she ever had any problems. She promptly
phoned Haldeman to protest her newspaper's
thwarted access to the wedding. In his memoir, Haldeman recalled that he ignored the president's ban
and allowed the **Post** to attend after all. Mrs. Graham's recollection was that her paper was shut out
but that the **Post** reporter, Judith Martin, wrote the

story from the notes of sympathetic reporters from other papers. (Graham allowed that she would not want Martin to cover the wedding of her own daughter; Martin had already compared Tricia to a vanilla ice cream cone.)[45]

The day of the wedding was cloudy and drizzly. Pat Nixon, supported by Julie and the staff, wanted to play it safe and bring the ceremony indoors. Tricia, who possessed her father's steely will, was determined to be married in the Rose Garden. Nixon, who had avoided the festivities the night before by going for a cruise on the **Sequoia**, had taken refuge in his Executive Office Building hideaway.[46] But he was on Tricia's side. He called the Air Force and learned that there would be a slight break in the weather around 4:30. The seats in the Rose Garden were hastily wiped dry and the ceremony went on. The drops began falling again just as Tricia said, "I do."

Nixon had never danced at the White House. "I won't dance!" he announced during his presidential campaign. "When you're running for sheriff, you dance."[47] But he made an exception for his daughter's wedding. He gave the bride a whirl to "Thank Heaven for Little Girls," then took a spin with Pat, who was a graceful dancer.[48] Nixon's joy and pride were palpable. The PR pay-off was obvious. Americans all over the country were stopping to watch the historic White House wedding, only the fifth of the twentieth century. Nixon's staffers, accustomed to the president's apparent aloofness from his family, were struck by the warmth and emotion of the moment. Longtime aides who flew with the Nixons had observed that Nixon typically sat apart from Pat and the girls and that they affixed their campaign smiles and linked arms only to greet the airport crowd.[49] But now Nixon lovingly embraced his wife and daughters. He let down his guard and allowed his emotions to show.

"P asked me for a rundown on how it all had gone," Haldeman dictated to his diary that night. "I gave him a very enthusiastic report. The P was in great spirits." Haldeman persuaded the president to watch a TV replay of him walking his daughter down the aisle. "Well, at least I'm standing pretty straight," Nixon said. "Obviously, the ladies in the family had been nagging him about standing up straight," Haldeman wrote. "All in all, the whole thing was a sensational day."[50]

In the Rose Garden.
Library of Congress/Wikimedia

CHAPTER 19

"Blow the Safe"

On June 13, the morning after the wedding, Nixon picked up **The New York Times** and saw in the top left-hand corner a photograph of the proud father standing with his radiant daughter in the Rose Garden. "Tricia Nixon Takes Vows" was the headline. Nixon noticed on the front page of the newspaper another headline, "Vietnam Archive: Pentagon Study Traces 3 Decades of Growing U.S. Involvement," but he did not pay much attention.[1] Shortly after noon, Kissinger's assistant Al Haig called to check in, and Nixon asked him about the week's casualties in Vietnam. "Quite low," answered Haig. "Yeah. Should be less than twenty, I would think . . . ," said Nixon. "Nothing else of interest in the world today?"

HAIG: Yes, sir. Very significant. This goddamn **New York Times** exposé of the most highly classified documents of the war.

NIXON: Oh, that! I see. I didn't read the story. But, uh, do you mean that was leaked out of the Pentagon?

HAIG: Sir, the whole study that was done for McNamara, and then carried on after McNamara left by Clifford and the peaceniks over there. This is a devastating security breach of the greatest magnitude of anything I've ever seen.[2]

The secret seven-thousand-page history of United States involvement in the Vietnam War, soon to be known as the Pentagon Papers, did not mention Richard Nixon's name. The study had been commissioned by JFK and LBJ's secretary of defense, Robert McNamara, and completed under his successor, Clark Clifford. "It's a tough attack on Kennedy," Haig told Nixon. "And it's brutal on President Johnson." At first glance, this was hardly bad news for the Nixon team. "The key now for us to keep out of it," Haldeman dictated to his diary that evening, "and let the people that are affected cut each other up."[3]

Al Haig offered the same advice to his boss, Henry Kissinger.[4] But the next morning, Kissinger refused to leave it alone. Compact, bristly, his eyes large behind thick black glasses, the national security adviser bustled into the 8 A.M. meeting, "as angry as I had ever seen him," recalled Chuck Colson. He paced around the Roosevelt Room, threw his papers down, and "pounded his hand on an antique Chippendale table, rattling the pencils and coffee cups," wrote Colson. "There can be no foreign policy in this government. No foreign policy, I tell you!" stormed Kissinger. "Leaks are destroying us."[5]

Kissinger had reason to be anxious about security breaches. He was, at that moment, engaged in the most secret diplomacy with the Soviets and the Chinese. Nixon's dream of "the big play"—an arms control treaty with Russia and opening up China—was close to coming true. An untimely leak could be disastrous.

Even so, Haldeman was suspicious. By now an amateur authority on the Kissingerian psyche, Haldeman detected a whiff of guilty anxiety in the professor's remonstrations. He guessed that Kissinger was worried that the leaker of the Pentagon Papers might be one of his own "boys," the liberal, Harvard-type aides who, from time to time, leaked dissenting opinions to the press or quit in opposition to the administration's war policy.[6]

Nixon was also eyeing Kissinger's rebellious aides as potential culprits. "As to staff leakage, etc., the P is especially concerned about Henry's staff," Haldeman recorded that evening.[7] Based on rumors and guesswork, Nixon speculated that the leaker of the Pentagon Papers was Les Gelb, an ex–Defense Department official who was close to former Kissinger aide Morton Halperin. Nixon had already ordered a wiretap on Halperin for suspected leaking, and Gelb and Halperin both now worked at the Brookings Institution, a think tank Nixon regarded as a government-in-exile for Democrats. Nixon was irked at Kissinger for having even darkened the door at Brookings. "Chrissakes, he went over and talked to Brookings people himself," Nixon fumed. "I warned him about it. I said, 'Henry, don't go over there.' You know, I said, 'Those people—that's the Democratic National Committee.'"

"That's right," said Haldeman.

"They are a bunch of bastards," said Nixon, getting cranked up. "They'll lie, cheat, anything—and then squeal when somebody else does."[8]

When Nixon was in his enemy-bashing mode, he looked for ways to turn the tables. The president's mind began to contemplate ways to take advantage of the Pentagon Papers, to use them as a weapon against the Democrats. Late in the afternoon on June 17, as he sat with Haldeman and Kissinger in his Executive Office Building hideaway, he let his imagination run. Goaded by him, his aides alternately ducked and goaded back.

As he often did in crisis situations, Nixon thought back to the Alger Hiss case. Hiss was a traitor who had leaked government secrets to the Soviets. Nixon told his staff that he had won the Hiss case partly by judiciously leaking information to the press. The way to deal with the leaker of the Pentagon Papers was to do him one better and leak **more** damaging information about Kennedy and Johnson.[9]

Nixon was sure that—somewhere—there were secrets about the Vietnam War that Kennedy and Johnson had wanted to remain hidden forever. He had long suspected, for example, that Kennedy had ordered the assassination of President Ngo Dinh

Diem in a coup in November 1963.* Revving himself up in his Executive Office Building hideaway, Nixon pressed a clearly uncomfortable Kissinger to dig up evidence of Kennedy's role in the fatal coup. (When Kissinger hesitated, Nixon turned to the more reliably can-do Colson. "We're going to put it out," he ordered.)[11]

Haldeman was often a restraint on Nixon's worst urges, but this time he egged on the president by dredging up another murky chapter from the past, the 1968 bombing halt. "You maybe can blackmail Johnson on this stuff." "What?" Nixon asked. "You can blackmail Johnson on this stuff and it might be worth doing."[12] The "stuff" Haldeman was referring to was a supposed report on President Johnson's bombing halt before the 1968 election. Nixon believed that Johnson had tried to time the bombing halt to help Hubert Humphrey at the polls, and after the election Nixon had ordered Haldeman to find out the true facts. At the time, Nixon and Johnson had avoided attacking each other for campaign shenanigans; still, a little intelligence might come in handy down the road. Haldeman had chosen as his investigator Tom Charles Huston, the gung-ho

*The coup was aided by the CIA, but JFK's own role remains murky. The Kennedy administration was split over the wisdom of deposing Diem, who was corrupt and unpopular but a stronger man than his successors. JFK dithered over whether to back the coup, and he was shocked when he learned that Diem had been killed. Still, the evidence deeply implicates the Kennedy administration in the coup.[10]

White House aide who had advocated a program of black-bag jobs against antiwar dissenters. Poking around various government agencies, Huston had heard there was a report on Johnson's bombing halt strategy at the Defense Department.[13] Now, in June of 1971, sitting with a riled-up Nixon in the Oval Office, trying to play to the president's baser instincts, Haldeman was suggesting that the supposed report on the bombing halt could be used to embarrass President Johnson.

There was only one problem. The report was not at the Defense Department. "We can't find it," Haldeman said, a little sheepishly. Huston had told Haldeman that he believed that Les Gelb had taken the report with him from the Pentagon and put it in his files at the Brookings Institution. Unbeknownst to Haldeman, Huston was wrong about this; the over-zealous aide had mixed up the alleged bombing halt study (which probably never existed) with the Pentagon Papers themselves. But Nixon knew nothing of this tangled background; he only knew that Haldeman was dangling an opportunity to get some leverage on Johnson. The mere prospect of potential blackmail sitting in the vaults of the enemy camp seemed to inflame Nixon.[14]

Kissinger, sitting with Haldeman and the president, was wary of getting drawn into one of Nixon's obsessions. The president fumed as the uneasy Kissinger told him, "We have nothing here, Mr. President." Nixon said: "Well, damn it, I asked for that because I need it." Haldeman cut in and said, "Huston swears to God there's a file on it, at Brookings."

Nixon had a sudden inspiration. Hearing Huston's name made him recall Huston's plan to use illegal break-ins against antiwar protesters. "Bob," he said, "Now you remember Huston's plan? Implement it."

Kissinger started to protest.

NIXON: I want it implemented on a thievery basis. Goddamnit, get in and get those files. Blow the safe and get it.

This statement by the president is the first record of him ordering a break-in. It is an astonishing command, especially since simply requesting the material from Brookings might have sufficed. (In fact, that's what Haldeman proposed two weeks later.) Nixon often worked through a problem by venting, by letting off steam with imprecations and threats that were not to be taken literally. His aides generally knew when not to carry out his more outlandish instructions, and Haldeman stalled on this one. But it was not the last time Nixon demanded a burglary at Brookings. He did it three more times over the next several weeks, sometimes in the presence of Kissinger and Defense Secretary Laird. Even given Nixon's penchant for emotional outbursts, his repeated rants about breaking into Brookings, caught on the White House tapes, seem beyond the pale.

June 30, 1971, late afternoon, the Oval Office:

HALDEMAN: Brookings has a lot of [classified] stuff now. Don't you want to send a colonel over and pick it up?

NIXON: The way I want that handled, Bob, is—I want Brookings, I want just to break in, break in, and take it out. Do you understand?

HALDEMAN: Yeah. But you've got to have somebody to do it.

NIXON: That's what I'm talking about. Don't discuss it here. You talk to [E. Howard] Hunt. I want the break in. Hell, they do that. You're to break into the place, rifle the files, and bring them in.

July 1, 1971, mid-morning, the Oval Office:

NIXON: Do you think, for Christ sakes, that **The New York Times** is worried about all legal niceties? Those sons of bitches are killing me. . . . I mean, thank God, I leaked to the press [during the Hiss controversy]. This is what we've got to get. . . . Now you do it. Shake them up. Get them off their goddamn dead asses and say now that isn't what you should be talking about. We're up against an enemy, a conspiracy. They're using any means. **We are going to use any means**. Is that clear?

Did they get the Brookings Institute raided last night? No? Get it done. I want it done. I want the Brookings Institute's safe **cleaned out** and have it cleaned out in a way they make somebody else [unintelligible].[15]

July 2, 1971, mid-morning, the Oval Office:

NIXON: I really meant it when—I want someone to go in and crack that [Brookings] safe. Walk in and get it. I want Brookings cut. They've got to do it. Brookings is the real enemy here. . . . [16]

There is something puzzling about these repeated outbursts. The Pentagon Papers may have seemed like a crisis to Nixon, but it was to some degree a manufactured crisis. Indeed, when the furor started to die down, Nixon instructed his aides to keep it alive.[17] Yet in the weeks after the leak of the Pentagon Papers, Nixon seemed almost out of control, making extreme demands, scoffing at aides who wanted to find lawful solutions, and carrying on about the Hiss case.

Nixon's own explanation in his memoirs of why he wanted to get his hands on the bombing halt file is candid, for Nixon, although he is euphemistic about ordering a break-in:

In the aftershock of the Pentagon Papers leak and all the uncertainty and renewed criticism of the war it produced, my interest in the bombing halt file was rekindled. When I was told that it was still at Brookings, I was furious and frustrated. In the midst of a war and with our secrets being spilled through printing presses all over the world, top secret government reports were out of reach in the hands of a private think tank largely staffed with antiwar Democrats. It seemed absurd. I could not accept that we had lost so much control over the workings of the government we had been elected to run—I saw absolutely no reason for the report to be at Brookings, and I said I wanted it back right now—even if that meant having to get it surreptitiously.[18]

Nixon was often frustrated by bureaucratic intransigence, and it's easy to imagine him conjuring up a conspiracy of liberal elitists to thwart him. Indeed, liberal elitists **were** conspiring against him, and the justification of "national security" was hardly bogus during wartime when the president was engaged in secret diplomacy abroad. Journalists would later scoff at the term **national security** as a cynical excuse to conceal and cover up, but on the White House tapes, Nixon and his aides sound genuinely worried that leaks could, literally speaking, undermine national security. Still, there may be more to the story. Nixon seemed to like playing the tough guy around Kissinger, forcing his Harvard professor adviser to go along with the boys (a role Kissinger was perhaps too willing to play). Ken Hughes, a student of the Nixon tapes at the University of Virginia's Miller Center, has argued that Nixon was moved by fears of his own exposure as well as a desire to get his political enemies. The story has some twists and turns and is based partly on inference, but it bears consideration.

After the 1968 election, Nixon had been told—

falsely—by J. Edgar Hoover that LBJ had bugged Nixon's campaign plane. Nixon had to worry what the Johnson administration, through its own bugging and spying, knew about his own role in trying to sabotage the bombing halt. What if the missing bombing halt report included evidence that Nixon—through his go-between, Madame Chennault—had urged President Thieu to play the spoiler? After the election, Johnson and Nixon had implicitly agreed not to air each other's dirty laundry. Now, in the wake of the Pentagon Papers leak, Nixon had reason to fear that if the report showed that Nixon had also played political games with national security, the Democrats might leak it, in an escalating tit for tat of smears. Nixon never let on why the contents of the mysterious file obsessed him so. But the urgency of Nixon's desire to see the missing report—and the reckless steps he was willing to take to get it—do suggest that he was unusually concerned about what the report might show about him as well as about LBJ.[19]

The real leaker in the Pentagon Papers, Daniel Ellsberg, had surfaced, voluntarily, on CBS News. Nixon was determined to ruin him. When his aides argued, logically enough, that Ellsberg should be prosecuted for stealing government secrets, Nixon was not satisfied. He complained that he was surrounded by lawyers who didn't understand "how the game is played." Ehrlichman and Mitchell, "they're always saying, well, we've got to win the court case through the court." But Nixon scorned the slow-turning wheels of justice. "I mean, just let—convict the son of a bitch **in the press. That's the way it's done**. . . . Nobody ever reads any of this in my biographies. Go back and read the chapter on the Hiss case in **Six Crises** and you'll see how it was done. It wasn't done waiting for the goddamn courts or the attorney general or the FBI. . . . We have got to get going here." And, one more time: "Who's going to break into the Brookings Institute?"*

Nixon began to imagine other potential secret documents that might be unearthed and leaked to the press to shame prior Democratic administrations. He wanted to know who was going to dig through "papers on the Cuban Missile Crisis, on the Bay of Pigs, on World War II and Korea? Who the hell is doing that and pulling out everything that might embarrass members of the establishment. You see? Who's going to do that. . . . I need a man—a commander—an officer in charge here at the White

---

*Nixon's Brookings fixation entered the realm of dark absurdity when Colson plotted with Jack Caulfield, a former New York City cop who did odd jobs for the White House like tailing Teddy Kennedy, to start a fire at the Washington think tank; FBI agents could then enter the building disguised as firemen to "acquire" the documents. According to John Dean, this mad idea was squashed by Ehrlichman. Colson later maintained that he wasn't serious about it. Liddy said that the White House refused to spring for a fire engine. It has never been clear whether the whole scheme was a bad joke or an aborted criminal enterprise.[20]

House that I can call when I wake up, as I did last night, at 2 o'clock in the morning, and I can say, now look here, I want to do this, this, this, and this. Get going. See my point?"

Nixon calmed down for a while and spoke of other matters, then returned to the question of who could play the part of the 2 A.M. action officer. Already overburdened, Haldeman and Ehrlichman did not want the role. Colson didn't either, but, as usual, he had a suggestion for carrying out the president's worst impulses. "There's one guy on the outside," he said, "that has this capacity and ideological bent who might be able to do all of this."

Nixon asked: "Who's that?"

Colson reminded him about a White House consultant named E. Howard Hunt.[21] Colson described a figure out of a James Bond novel. "He's hard as nails. He's a brilliant writer," adding that Hunt had written forty spy novels. "He just got out of the CIA. Fifty. Kind of a tiger."[22]

Colson knew Hunt from the Brown University Club of Washington (they were both grads), but that was about all. He didn't know much about his career in espionage, aside from some tales of derring-do spun by Hunt. Haldeman and Ehrlichman were introduced to Hunt and found him unremarkable, but figured that the ex-CIA man's gray, bland demeanor just made him a good spy. In hindsight, they should have been warned by the way Hunt handled his first assignment. Told to pursue Nixon's theory that JFK had ordered the assassination of President Diem, Hunt met with the CIA operative who had worked on the Diem coup. A tape recorder was set up under a couch in a vacant office, and Hunt invited the CIA man over to share a bottle of Scotch in order to loosen his tongue. After a couple of hours Hunt appeared in Colson's office, reporting in. Bleary eyed, tie askew, Hunt stammered an apology. He sheepishly explained that, by mistake, he had sat on the tape recorder, crushing it. He had taken no notes and was too drunk to remember what the man had said.[23]

Among the several mysteries of the tragedy of Richard Nixon is this one: Why did no one see that Hunt and, even more so, Hunt's partner G. Gordon Liddy were not only comically inept but dangerously so? Within the CIA, Hunt was well known as a bumbler, as the "sort of spy who would trip over his cape and fall on his sword," as he was archly described in a negative efficiency report written by an agency superior.[24] Among his peers, Hunt had a reputation for dreaming up impractical schemes that backfired. He had been marginalized at the agency after his role in the disastrous Bay of Pigs and, eventually, was quietly pushed out. Cynthia Helms, the wife of CIA Director Richard Helms, recalled that Hunt had been recommended to the White House—but only as a "charity case." "Hunt's daughter was blind, and he needed dough," she recalled her husband telling her. She went on: "So Dick talked him up to Haldeman, whom he did not like."* The CIA gave technical support to Hunt—tape recorders, a red wig—until Helms found out and cut it off.[26] "It seemed like such a small thing at the time," Mrs. Helms recalled.[27]

Daniel Ellsberg had been a military analyst working for RAND, the defense think tank, who turned against the war. Nixon thought Ellsberg was a Soviet agent, like Alger Hiss, only worse. Ellsberg was publicly admitting that he was part of a larger conspiracy with the press. "He must be a rat," said Nixon. "I got to say for Hiss, he never ratted on anybody else. Never. He never ratted."[28] The Justice Department internal security division reported, erroneously, that the Soviet embassy had received a set of the Pentagon Papers, and federal agents were checking with MI5, British internal security, to see if Ellsberg was another Kim Philby, the infamous Soviet mole. Nothing materialized.[29]

Kissinger kept Nixon riled up. The release of the Pentagon Papers "shows you're a weakling, Mr. Pres-

---

*Haldeman was gulled by Helms, a very clever bureaucratic infighter who had no qualms about foisting CIA deadwood on the White House. On July 2, the tape recorder in Nixon's EOB Executive Office Building hideaway picked up Haldeman saying, "Get this guy Colson involved [Hunt], the former CIA guy, get him in." Ehrlichman interjected, "You've got to have somebody that knows the business." Haldeman picked up, "Helms describes this guy [Hunt] as ruthless, quiet and careful, low profile. He gets things done."[25]

ident," Kissinger said, according to Haldeman, who once again suspected that Kissinger was covering for himself. A brainy ex-Marine officer, Ellsberg had been a colleague of Kissinger's at Harvard. Kissinger poured on the calumny, telling Nixon that Ellsberg "had weird sexual habits, used drugs, and enjoyed helicopter flights in which he would take potshots at the Vietnamese below."[30] Colson continued to add gas. Nixon said of Ellsberg, "He's our enemy. We need an enemy." To which Colson replied, "Agree completely, and he's a marvelous one. . . . He's a perfect enemy to have."[31]

Ellsberg's fellow conspirators were newspaper reporters. He was a hero to the press. The administration was able to get a court order stopping **The New York Times** from publishing more of the Pentagon Papers and then a gag on **The Washington Post**, which also published a large chunk, but ten other papers began printing parts of the top-secret document. In that season of institution-shaking protest, a constitutional crisis loomed. Could the press defy the executive branch? On June 30, a divided U.S. Supreme Court narrowly sided with the press. It lifted the government ban on publication—the Justice Department had failed to prove that making public the Pentagon Papers harmed national security.

Nixon was furious; Ellsberg was going around speaking on television and at antiwar rallies promoting unlawful dissent, and the American legal system was cowering. Kissinger told Nixon that the country was in a "revolutionary situation." In early July,

Nixon gave a speech to newspaper and TV executives in front of the columned portico of the National Archives. "When I see those columns, I think of what happened to Greece and Rome," the president said. "They became subject to the decadence that destroys civilizations. The United States is reaching that period."[32]

On the morning of July 2, Nixon told Haldeman that he had spoken the night before to J. Edgar Hoover about Ellsberg. "Hoover is not going after this case as strong as I'd like," said Nixon. "There's something dragging him." Hoover had cautioned Nixon not to make a "martyr" out of Ellsberg. Nixon was indignant when he heard that Ellsberg's father-in-law, a toy manufacturer named Louis Marx, was regarded as "F.O.B."—"Friend of Bureau"—and enjoyed Hoover's protection.[33]

The FBI and CIA were useless to Nixon. He railed at Ehrlichman, "If we can't get anyone in this damn government to do something about the problem that may be the most serious one we have, then, by god, we'll do it ourselves. I want you to set up a little group right here in the White House. Have them get off their tails and find out what's going on and figure out how to stop it."[34]

Haldeman's notes refer to "the Jew (Ellsberg)."[35] (Actually, Ellsberg's parents had converted to Christian Science.) Nixon's atavistic rancor over Ellsberg seemed to infect his judgment on other matters. On that same day, July 2, Nixon read a story quoting an anonymous official at the Bureau of Labor Statistics, who explained that a recent dip in the unemployment numbers was a statistical fluke. Colson snooped around and discovered that the official was Assistant Commissioner of Labor Statistics Harold Goldstein. "This drove the P right up the wall tonight, and he started hounding Colson every couple of minutes, demanding that we get Goldstein fired, etc," Haldeman noted.[36]

In the morning, Nixon started in on the Bureau of Labor Statistics:

NIXON: I said [to Colson] is it all Jews? He said, "Yes, every one of them is a Jew."

The president began ventilating to Haldeman about the number of Jews in the federal bureaucracy.

NIXON: All right. I want a look at any sensitive areas around where Jews are involved, Bob. See, the Jews are all through the government, and we have got to get in those areas. We've got to get a man in charge who is not Jewish to control the Jewish . . . do you understand?

HALDEMAN: I sure do.

NIXON: The government is full of Jews.

HALDEMAN: I sure do.

NIXON: Second, most Jews are disloyal.

Fred Malek, the chief of personnel at the White House, was instructed to survey the administration.

But first, a Haldeman aide checked to make sure that Malek wasn't Jewish. (As it turned out, Nixon ended up removing a Protestant as head of the BLS and replacing him with a Jew.)[37]

Nixon's occasional anti-Semitic outbursts were a source of serious discomfort to many of his aides, several of whom were Jewish. In later years, most would insist that Nixon was not really anti-Semitic. Protesting too much, perhaps, one former aide noted that Tricia's first boyfriend, Jeffrey Donfeld, was Jewish, and that he borrowed Nixon's white tie and tails to escort Tricia to the International Debutante Ball. Nixon, it should be remembered, was ardently pro-Israel and counted on Jewish advisers like Kissinger, Safire, Garment, Burns, and economic adviser Herb Stein. He enjoyed and respected—at times, appeared to revere—Israel's earthy, blunt prime minister, Golda Meir. Nixon's defenders say that his offensive rants sprung from his anti-elitist resentment or partisanship; he was irked that Jews continued to vote Democratic despite his strong efforts for Israel. While not subscribing to the hoary canard of an international Jewish cabal, Nixon believed that the East Coast liberal establishment, by the 1960s, included a disproportionate number of Jews at the upper reaches of the federal bureaucracy, the media, and the arts.

The excuses of his followers aside, there is no hiding the ugliness of Nixon's remarks. Nixon's derisive anti-Semitic remarks were not uncharacteristic of many men from his generation or earlier. As a Harvard overseer, FDR supported a Jewish quota. Truman—who in 1948 brushed aside State Department opposition and ordered diplomatic recognition of Israel—casually referred to Jews as "kikes."[38] But Nixon was more imperative.*

While Nixon was bemoaning his inability to control his own government, he was on the verge of changing the balance of nations. On July 7—the day after Nixon gave his gloomy speech about America's decline to the newspaper editors in front of the National Archives—Kissinger feigned a stomachache on a stopover in Pakistan and slipped over the Chinese border. His secret trip to Beijing was codenamed "Marco Polo," after the fourteenth-century Venetian traveler to China, and his mission was to arrange a meeting between Nixon and Mao Tse-Tung and the Chinese leadership.

On July 11, while Nixon was looking out over the Pacific in San Clemente, he received a call from Kissinger's aide, Al Haig. "Any message?" Nixon asked. Haig answered with a pre-designated code word: "Eureka," meaning success.

*Nixon was generally respectful of deep religious faith, even though he belonged to no organized church. "I could be comfortable being a Catholic," he told Chuck Colson. Nixon admired the stability of the church and the depth of Catholic faith. One day in 1970, he asked Pat Moynihan, a Catholic, "You believe in the whole thing?" Moynihan was his usual irreverent self. "Not only that," he replied, cocking his head at Haldeman and Ehrlichman, both Christian Scientists. "I even believe in doctors."[39]

Kissinger had been "literally trembling," Haldeman wrote, when the national security adviser first told Nixon that the Chinese had invited him to Beijing in early June.[40] Nixon and Kissinger had raised a glass of Courvoisier to themselves and their achievement. "Let us drink to generations to come who may have a better chance to live in peace because of what we have done," Nixon had toasted. Now Kissinger presented Nixon with a report on his seventeen hours of intense negotiations with Chou En-lai, the smooth Chinese prime minister who was representing the aging and ailing Chairman Mao. "We have laid the groundwork for you and Mao to turn a page in history," Kissinger's report began.[41]

From Casa Pacifica, Nixon flew by helicopter to an NBC studio in Burbank to tell the world about the China opening. The international reaction was stunned and full of praise. "Le Coup de Nixon" headlined **France-Soir** in Paris. "The politics of surprise leads through the Gates of Astonishment into the Kingdom of Hope," wrote the normally anti-Nixon columnist Max Lerner. Nixon, who could be easy and sweet with his secretaries, turned to Marjorie Acker and asked, "Whaddya think?"[42]

That evening, Nixon rounded up his staff and took them to Perino's, a Wilshire Boulevard restaurant that had once been a celebrity haunt but now catered more often to tourists. Nixon ordered a magnum of Chateau Lafite-Rothschild 1961 (the Secret Service had to talk down the bill for the bottle from $600 to $300).[43] As he was leaving, Nixon stopped at the front of the dining room to introduce Kissinger as "the man who has traveled to Peking." Most of the diners, who had not been glued to their TV sets, had no idea what he was talking about. Kissinger described the scene: "Nixon was not boastful; he acted almost as if he could not quite believe what he had just announced. There was a mutual shyness; Nixon was always ill at ease with strangers, and the other guests were not comfortable in approaching a president. In his hour of achievement Richard Nixon was oddly vulnerable."[44]

Even before Kissinger returned from Beijing, Nixon was fretting that Kissinger would get all the credit. "When Henry gets back, he'll be the mystery man of the age," Nixon told Haldeman.[45] Nixon initially tried to forbid Kissinger from briefing newsmen, but that was a futile gesture, so the president essentially tried to climb on board the bandwagon. On July 19, Nixon sent Kissinger a memo that began, "One effective line you could use with your talks with the press is how RN is uniquely prepared for this meeting [with the Chinese leaders]." Nixon ticked off his attributes, including "3. At his best in crisis. Cool. Unflappable," and "9. A man who is subtle and appears almost gentle. The tougher his position, usually, the lower his voice." That description would not have fit Nixon as he ranted about Ellsberg and "the Jews," but it was true enough at other times, and Kissinger dutifully used Nixon's self-image when he fed Time-Life's Hugh Sidey, whose column in **Life** clearly reflected Nixon's talking points.[46]

More significantly, Nixon's opening to China succeeded in getting the Kremlin's attention. In a conversation with Kissinger on June 29, on the eve of
Kissinger's secret trip to China, Nixon crudely but
accurately predicted the Russian reaction to such a
precipitous thaw in Sino-American relations: "Boy, if
they [the Russians] only knew what the hell was coming up, they'd be in here panting for that summit,
wouldn't they? Huh?" "I'm sure," answered Kissinger.[47] Right on cue, on the Monday after Nixon's
breakthrough to Beijing, Ambassador Dobrynin—
"at his ingratiating best," Kissinger recalled—
appeared at the White House to ask if the Americans
and Soviets could have a summit meeting **before**
Nixon went to China. "To have the two communist
powers competing for good relations with us could
only benefit the cause of peace," Kissinger wrote. "It
was the essence of triangular strategy."[48]

On the short helicopter ride back to San Clemente
after dinner at Perino's, Kissinger, the national security adviser, protested that one of his young aides,
David Young, was being reassigned from his staff.
Young was to head up a new secret unit, ostensibly
set up to plug the sort of leaks that Kissinger had so
vociferously complained about when the Pentagon
Papers first appeared the day after Tricia's wedding.
Speaking over the noise of the helicopter as it thud-
ded above the lights of Los Angeles, Ehrlichman
overruled Kissinger's objections. Haldeman would
later muse that Ehrlichman's inclusion of a Kissinger

man in the secret unit was "a typical stroke of bureaucratic genius. He knew all too well how Henry
would happily ignite a fuse, then stand off swearing
that he knew nothing about it, or had even been
against it."[49]

Young was assigned to a new office, Room 16, on
the ground floor of the Executive Office Building.
The office was equipped with a telephone scrambler
and a safe. When he told his mother of the job running the Special Investigative Unit and plugging
leaks, she replied that his grandfather would have
been proud, because he too had been a plumber.
Young, who had a droll sense of humor, hung a sign
on the door of Room 16 that read, "Mr. Young:
Plumber." Journalists, later hearing of the sign,
began to write about the Plumbers.[50]

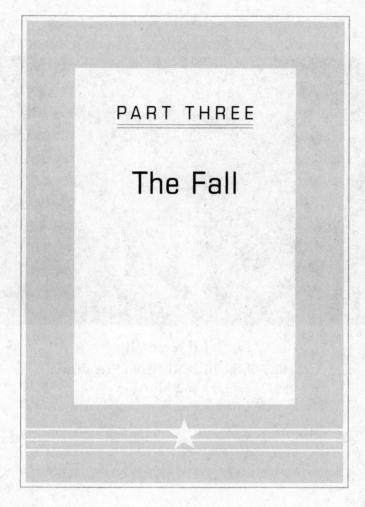

PART THREE

The Fall

Big John Connally.
**Courtesy of the Richard Nixon Presidential
Library and Museum**

CHAPTER 20

Big Plays

It is not illegal, unconstitutional, or unprecedented for a president, stymied by a federal agency, to look for other means to execute the will of the executive. But the high-handed and heedless way the Nixon administration went about staffing and running the Plumbers almost guaranteed illegal and unconstitutional acts, not to mention getting caught.

The chief operatives were E. Howard Hunt—recommended by Colson—and G. Gordon Liddy, a former assistant DA and ex–FBI agent. As a prosecutor, Liddy had once fired a pistol in a courtroom to make a point (using a blank). He loved to tell tall tales about his lethality: to the wife of a young White House staffer sitting next to him, he explained how to kill someone with a pencil to the neck.[1] Liddy's first self-assigned task with the Special Investigative Unit (SIU) was to come up with a more evocative name. He chose ODESSA, short for "Our organization has been directed to eliminate subversion of the secrets of the adminstration." The acronym was more commonly associated

with an organization of fugitive Nazi war crimi-
nals. Tongue in cheek or not, Liddy drew on the
Nazis; he once gave a secret showing of Leni Rief-
enstahl's film of Hitler's Nuremberg Youth Rally at
the National Archives. ("Great advance!" someone
shouted from the back of the darkened room. "So
this is what the second term is going to be like,"
cracked another.) Ehrlichman told Liddy to drop
the acronym but he did not get rid of Liddy.[2]*

Liddy had been recruited by Egil "Bud" Krogh
from the Treasury Department, which was only too
happy to lose the wild-swinging former G-man from
its narcotics enforcement bureau. Krogh missed
subtle hints from Liddy's former employers ("Gordon is a very **aggressive** investigator"), who, in time-
honored bureaucratic fashion, blandly endorsed
Liddy's transfer.

Ehrlichman had tapped Krogh, along with David
Young from Kissinger's staff, to run the SIU. Krogh
was not Ehrlichman's first choice; several aides, including speechwriter Pat Buchanan, had wisely declined the job. An Eagle Scout and a Christian
Scientist like Ehrlichman, Krogh saw his co-
religionist as a kind of father figure. He was nicknamed by his White House pals "Evil Krogh" because
he so plainly was not.[4]

Krogh was a lawyer, not yet thirty, who knew
nothing about plugging leaks or—the SIU's more

---

*"I have absolutely no sympathy for Adolf Hitler and Nazism,"
Liddy told **Playboy** in 1980.[3]

nefarious job—stealing secrets that could be leaked. "Howard Hunt was presented to me as a crackerjack CIA operative who knew his way around. I didn't know he was a clown. I didn't even know he was writing spy novels. They told me he could practice some good spycraft," Krogh recalled to the author many years later. "What did I know?" Krogh did have an inkling that Liddy might be trouble when the mustachio'd, ramrod-erect ex-G-man brandished a large combat knife he carried on "ops." "It is hard to understand why we were so blind to the risks," he recalled, "but I was living in a cocoon of high-pressure expectation."[5]

On Saturday, July 24, at around 10 A.M., Krogh was summoned by Ehrlichman to see President Nixon. A **New York Times** story had revealed some secrets about the American negotiating position in the SALT talks.

Krogh's last visit to the Oval Office had been to introduce Elvis Presley. Whenever he met the president, Krogh felt a "chill and tightening in my gut," he recalled. The Oval Office felt "cold and austere," despite a bright and suitably Californian blue-and-gold color scheme installed by the First Lady. "The president was pacing behind his desk, and his mood was obvious: he was extremely upset and very angry," Krogh wrote in a memoir. "His face was darkly flushed." When he was anxious or agitated, Nixon's dark eyes would dart about, then bore in. Krogh shifted uncomfortably under the presidential gaze.

The president said that he was not going to stand

for it anymore. He slammed his hand into his palm to make his point. "This crap is never ending. I studied these cases long enough, and it's always the son of a bitch that leaks. . . ."

"Ellsberg," Krogh piped up. "Ellsberg!"

"Sure," the president responded.

The leaks were jeopardizing national security. "Now goddamn it, we're not going to allow that. We're not going to allow it." He dismissed Krogh with a wave and a cursory "Good luck."

As they were leaving, Ehrlichman emphasized that the president had invested the work of the SIU with "the highest degree of national security." Krogh later recalled, "I did not dare ask, what does that mean?"[6]

On August 10, Nixon took an evening cruise on the **Sequoia** with Billy Graham. "The P went into considerable detail on his leadership decadence theory at dinner," Haldeman recorded. The problem, said the president, was not the "hippies or youth," but rather "our leadership class"—the ministers ("except for the Billy-Graham type fundamentalists"), the teachers, the business leaders, the politicians—who had "become soft."[7]

Nixon believed that he had found an exception in the former governor of Texas, John Connally. With his wavy silver hair and chiseled chin, Connally exuded self-assurance. "The boss has fallen in love again," joked Bill Safire and his pals in the White House speechwriting shop when Connally began

showing up in the Oval Office in the fall of 1970.
Kissinger scoffed that Nixon was fulfilling his Walter Mitty fantasy through Connally—"Big Jawn," as
the tall Texan was known, was the handsome, ath-
letic Man of the West Nixon could never be.[8] It
would be more generous and accurate to say that
Connally "bucked up" Nixon, to use a favorite Nix-
onism. The former naval officer, who had been decorated for bravery in World War II, had a curious tie
to the Kennedys: Seated in front of President Kennedy in the Dallas motorcade on November 22,
1963, he had been wounded by one of the bullets
that killed JFK. Connally was deft at boosting the
president, urging him to project more confidence,
to be manly, upbeat, optimistic—all things Nixon
wished to be and, in truth, often was, when he was
not brooding. Connally was replacing the weary
John Mitchell as the president's one true peer, the
adviser he could look up to.

Nixon liked to say that every president's cabinet
should include a potential president, but his did not.
(Disliking fractious cabinet meetings, Nixon was
having fewer and fewer of them.) Nixon saw Connally as his heir apparent. By the winter of 1971, the
president was actively wooing Connally and his wife
Nellie, inviting them to a Camp David screening of
his favorite movie, **Around the World in 80 Days**.
("The P," wrote Haldeman, "was hysterical through
it; as each scene was coming up, he'd say, 'You're
going to love this part,' or 'the scenery is just great,
now watch closely.' ")[9] Connally, for his part, praised

Nixon as the only president who understood "the uses of power."

In the spring, Nixon was soon talking about dumping Vice President Agnew and swapping him out for Connally.[10] Nixon and Connally began discussing "five-year plans" and "twenty-five-year plans," until Mitchell quietly persuaded Nixon that Connally, a turncoat Democrat, would arouse too much opposition in Congress.[11] Still, Nixon wanted to find some way to put "Big Jawn" in charge, to rally the flagging troops the way he had inspired the chief executive. Nixon had already found him a prominent place in the cabinet as secretary of the Treasury. On June 28, Nixon summoned his economic advisers and told them that, from now on, Connally would be the administration's spokesman on economic policy. "Nixon was in a harsh mood," John Ehrlichman recalled. "That same day Daniel Ellsberg had admitted his theft and dissemination of the Pentagon Papers, and Kissinger was riding Nixon hard, urging revenge on Ellsberg." In the future, Nixon informed his economic advisers, when Connally "announced that some policy line would be taken, everyone was to hew to that line," wrote Ehrlichman. "Or else," Nixon said brusquely, "you can quit." Nixon abruptly walked out of the meeting.[12]

Connally had little economic training but joked, "I can add." He was a nationalist who had once said, "My view is that the foreigners are out to screw us, and therefore it's our job to screw them first."[13] Connally's ignorance of economic matters matched Nixon's own; although Nixon was a substantive, unusually well-read political leader, his economic expertise was surprisingly shallow.

In early August, Connally faced his first test, a true international crisis. Under the international monetary system adopted after World War II, other countries could convert the dollars they accumulated into gold at a fixed price—$35 an ounce. But because the United States did not own nearly enough gold to pay off all the dollars, the system counted on other nations to treat the dollar as "good as gold." In May, Belgium, Netherlands, and France had traded $400 million for gold. Now Britain, in the throes of its own postwar economic decline, was insisting that its $3 billion in dollar reserves likewise be reimbursed in gold.[14]

Nixon was faced with a dilemma. If America kept the "gold window" open, more countries might overwhelm the Treasury with demands for gold, starting, as it were, a run on the global bank. On the other hand, if the United States "closed the gold window" and let the dollar float against all other national currencies, the dollar would weaken. The effect would likely be inflationary; imports would become much more expensive.

Rarely in doubt if not deeply informed, Connally proposed "a bold stroke," as Nixon called it. The United States would close the gold window, to prevent a run, but at the same time freeze wages and prices, to lasso inflation. Such an approach was sure to stun the American political scene and much of the rest of the world. Wage and price controls were favored by **liberal Democrats,** after all. Nixon had stated publicly that he would never impose such government fetters on economic freedom. Yet, as Connally well knew, Nixon loved to confound the enemy. Stealing the Democrats' clothes was Nixon's old Tom Sawyer trick—he had pulled it on Senator Ed Muskie by pushing for environmental laws. "Nixon imposes wage and price controls" would be a move along the lines of "Nixon goes to China": going for it all, the surprise "big play."[15]

On August 13, all of Nixon's top economic advisers went to Camp David to be given their marching orders.[16] They were not allowed to make phone calls. There was but one dissenter to shutting the gold window: Arthur Burns, the supposedly independent chairman of the Federal Reserve.

Burns and Nixon had an on-again, off-again relationship. At the start of his administration, Nixon had brought the brainy but long-winded Burns into the White House as a top domestic policy adviser, then shunted him aside for the more spritely Moynihan, then kicked both men upstairs when he tired of their battling. At the Federal Reserve, Burns was sure to annoy Nixon some more. Nixon had long been wary of the Fed, which he blamed (among others) for costing him the 1960 election by refusing to ease the money supply and prolonging the "Republican Recession." In the balance between creating jobs and holding down inflation, Nixon wanted to "err on the side of inflation." Burns did not share this view and, from time to time, publicly indicated as much. In his memoirs, Nixon wrote that he respected Burns for not always telling him what he wanted to hear, but in the summer of 1971, in his state of Ellsberg-induced agitation, the president wanted to put the Fed chairman in his place. Nixon cut off Burns's access to the Oval Office. "Just tell Arthur to report to Connally," Nixon instructed Ehrlichman. "The president won't see him."[17]

More callously, Nixon instructed Colson to plant a leak that Burns had lobbied for a nearly 50 percent salary hike for himself while calling for a wage freeze for everyone else. Burns, a devoted public servant, was humiliated by the fabrication, which appeared in **The Wall Street Journal**.[18] Nixon then personally, and shamelessly, knocked down the story as "unfair" and, at a press conference, praised Burns as a valuable public servant. "This he did to pacify rumors that we floated at his instruction, which were designed to stir up Burns a little bit," wrote Haldeman in his diary, explaining Nixon's not-so-subtle gambit to intimidate Burns. "It was a masterful stroke both ways and should have the result of getting Burns back in the fold, but on a basis where he won't bang us around so much from now on."[19]*

*Burns, who had revered Nixon, was shaken and "saddened" by the president's transformation in the weeks after the release of the Pentagon Papers. "I watched his face, as he spoke, with a feeling of dismay," Burns wrote in his diary on July 8, "for his features became twisted and what I saw was uncontrolled cruelty."[20]

At Camp David, Burns tried to make the case against leaving the gold standard, but he was rolled by Connally. Others, like OMB Director George Shultz, who had privately told a friend that wage and price controls would be a "disaster," played "good soldier," as Safire described it, and protested not at all. Mostly free marketers, they knew the risk of such a heavy government hand, but no one raised any serious objection.[21] "Connolly took complete command," Haldeman noted. The code of silence stilled otherwise strong voices. Paul Volcker,* Connally's deputy at Treasury, warned against leaks because "fortunes could be made with this information." Haldeman eased the tension by leaning forward and asking, with mock seriousness, "Exactly how?"

At about 9 P.M., Haldeman found Nixon in Aspen Lodge, sitting in his study with the lights out and a fire burning, even though it was a hot August night outside. "He was in one of his sort of mystic moods," Haldeman wrote. Nixon told Haldeman and another visitor, White House budget aide Caspar Weinberger, that he was sitting where Franklin

---

*Volcker, influenced by Milton Friedman, was the brains behind Connally's plan to go off the gold standard. ("I can play it round or flat," Connally would say. "Just tell me how to play it.")[22] But Volcker wanted higher interest rates to control inflation. Nixon wanted low interest rates to heat the economy and create jobs at election time. In Volcker's view, Nixon bullied Burns at the Fed into easing up on the money supply, feeding the inflationary spiral. Volcker later regretted his support for wage and price controls.[23]

Roosevelt had made all his "big cognitions," as he put it.

At such moments, Nixon was boosted, not weighed down, by his historic duties. When Nixon became wound up on a big subject, like leadership or America's role in the world, he would grow highly animated. He would gesture broadly with his hands and smile widely—not just his student-body-president grin, but a toothy, crinkly beam of pleasure. His arms would wave, slightly out of sync with his words. Or, pondering the immensity of a challenge, he would frown darkly, a grimly purposeful St. George facing the dragon. Occasionally, as he warmed to the task, he would wipe the sweat from his upper lip with a finger or handkerchief. He might catch himself and stiffen his pose to convey wise-man gravitas, but then his enthusiasm would bubble back up. To the end of his life, serious philosophical debates about the future of America were rejuvenating to Nixon. Holding forth on, say, America's duty to save the world from global communism, he could seem as gawky as a teenager at his first dance, peppy as a cheerleader, and disarmingly patriotic. There was no doubt that he was sincere. The cynical Nixon vanished, replaced by the boyish dreamer.

At Camp David on this August night, Nixon was psyching himself up to deliver another "stunner" to the nation. With Haldeman and Weinberger as his rapt audience, Nixon held forth on the future and his role in it. America was leaving an age, begun by FDR, when "we were saying that government should do everything." Now, said Nixon, he had to find a way to inspire people to have a goal greater than self, or neither the people nor the nation would be great.[24]

The president announced his "New Economic Plan" the next night on national television, risking voter wrath by preempting the Sunday night family favorite, **Bonanza**. Wage and price controls were popular and gave the economy a boost—at first. But as the temporary controls were lifted, wages and prices jumped up, and Nixon would feel compelled to impose more, and more highly regulated, limits (by then, Nixon was in the coils of Watergate; Shultz, elevated to Treasury secretary and no longer playing the "good soldier," quietly quit in protest). Pent-up inflation eventually burst loose, reaching double digits by the end of the decade. In his memoirs, Nixon admitted that the "New Economic Policy" (the name was dropped when someone figured out that Lenin had used it) was a short-term boost but a long-term bust. "The piper must always be paid," wrote Nixon.[25]

On August 9, a few days before his secret economic summit at Camp David, Nixon had been sitting in a cabin in Grand Teton National Park in Wyoming, looking out at the lake and still fretting about the Pentagon Papers. "We've got to keep the Pentagon Papers story going," Nixon said, according to Haldeman's notes, "because Larry O'Brien has decided to try to kill it." (O'Brien, the former JFK aide and Democratic Party chairman, was forever cast as Nixon's bugaboo.) Dictating his diary that night, Haldeman went on to say, "The P's afraid that Krogh and our crew are too addicted to the law and are worrying about the legalisms rather than taking on the publicizing of the papers. His point here is not getting **The New York Times**; it's getting the Democrats."[26]

Nixon need not have worried about Krogh's "addiction to the law." Still shaken by his trip to the Oval Office in late July, Krogh was willing to entertain almost any scheme to get Daniel Ellsberg. Krogh and his team asked the CIA for a psychological profile of Ellsberg and were disappointed by the results: The CIA concluded that Ellsberg had been motivated by patriotism. G. Gordon Liddy had a bright idea: a black bag job, breaking into the office of Ellsberg's psychiatrist, Dr. Lewis Fielding, to steal records showing Ellsberg's mental instability. The records could then be leaked to the press through the ever-ready Colson. On July 28, Howard Hunt sent a memo to Colson entitled "Neutralization of Ellsberg" with a "skeletal operations plan" on "how to destroy his image and credibility." On August 11, Krogh sent a lawyerly, lightly veiled memo to Ehrlichman: "We would recommend that a covert operation be undertaken to examine all the medical files still held by Ellsberg's psychoanalyst covering the two-year period in which he was undergoing analysis."

In an "Approve" box provided by Krogh, Ehrlichman wrote his initial, "E," plus the notation, "if done under your assurance that it is not traceable."

Three weeks later, Krogh sent Liddy and Hunt on their way to break into Dr. Fielding's office in Los Angeles. "For God's sake, don't get caught," were his parting instructions. Liddy and Hunt decided that Krogh's code name would be "Wally Fear."[27]

On September 5, Hunt and Liddy returned to Washington and repaired to Room 16 in the Executive Office Building, where they showed Polaroid photos to Krogh of their raid on Dr. Fielding's office. The office was trashed; they had wanted to make it look like a "drug burglary gone awry," the two Plumbers explained. But they apparently hadn't found any files on Ellsberg. Krogh later wrote that he was "stunned and appalled" and that Ehrlichman, too, "seemed shocked and surprised" by the scene of scattered papers and over-turned furniture.[28]

Ehrlichman soon recovered his can-do advance-man cool. During a September 8 meeting, the president's deputy reported on "dirty tricks." Ehrlichman told the president, "We had one little operation that aborted out in Los Angeles, which, I think is better that you don't know about. But we've got some dirty tricks under way that may pay off."[29] Two days later, Ehrlichman was suggesting that his team could "steal" documents on the Pentagon Papers from the National Archives and photograph them.[30] Nixon continued to be impatient with the FBI's investigation of Ellsberg. "I think we may just be doing it too damn legalistically," he said.[31] Meanwhile he was crudely imploring Haldeman to use the IRS to get other enemies ("Now here's the point, Bob, **please** get me the names of the Jews, you know, the big Jewish contributors to the Democrats. . . . All right. Could we please investigate some of the cocksuckers?").[32]

The Plumbers were reorganized, but the Nixonites continued to give Liddy and Hunt employment and even promotions. Two weeks after the botched burglary, eager to satisfy his boss's incessant demands to "do something," Ehrlichman praised the two men to the president. "We have a couple of fellows under Krogh—Liddy and Hunt—who know what they're doing and have been around," he boasted.[33] The two galoots took on new assignments. Liddy's ludicrous plan to put LSD in Ellsberg's soup was called off, but Hunt blundered on trying to find evidence that JFK had ordered Diem's assassination. Unable to find any actual proof, he forged a State Department cable and leaked it to **Life** magazine— which had the good sense not to print it.[34]

The Plumbers did uncover one leak, although it wasn't the one they were looking for. On December 14, investigative columnist Jack Anderson published transcripts of a top-secret White House meeting on a war that had broken out between Pakistan and India. The White House was backing Pakistan—a crucial go-between in Nixon's secret diplomacy with Red China—even though Pakistan had tolerated mass slaughter when its eastern provinces broke away. In the leaked transcripts, Henry Kissinger was exposed making intemperate remarks about the Indians, who were in disfavor at the White House.*

Under harsh questioning, Charles Radford, a young navy yeoman working at the White House, tearfully admitted that he had rifled the files and "burn bags" of Henry Kissinger and his staff. He denied leaking the information to Anderson. He admitted, however, that he had given top-secret documents—including highly sensitive materials like transcripts of Kissinger's conversations on his secret trip to China—to the Chairman of the Joint Chiefs of Staff, Admiral Thomas Moorer.[36]

This revelation was, on its face, shocking. The Joint Chiefs had been caught red-handed spying on the president of the United States. "Jesus Christ!" Nixon exclaimed when Ehrlichman told him. The president banged the table and threatened prosecutions.[37] But then Nixon simmered down and saw a way to use the scandal to his advantage. In his memoirs, Nixon wrote that he was "disturbed" but "not really surprised."[38] Not wanting to cause a major flap over tensions between the White House and Pentagon, Nixon decided to bury the matter. Admiral Moorer was not even chided—-Nixon, in his Machiavellian way, knew that he would gain an extra

*Nixon loathed the Indian prime minister, Indira Gandhi, who spoke to him in a condescending tone redolent of the British Raj. In a taped conversation with Kissinger, Nixon referred to Gandhi as a "bitch" and a "witch."[35] Nixon vastly preferred Pakistan's Yahya Khan, a bluff soldier and his secret go-between to China.

measure of control over the Chairman of the Joint Chiefs by sitting on his flagrant dereliction. As Ehrlichman, always the phrase-maker, put it, Moorer would now come "pre-shrunk." Six months later, Nixon reappointed Moorer Chairman of the Joint Chiefs. The leaky yeoman was exiled to Oregon.

Kissinger, however, staged a foot-stomping tantrum. "He [Nixon] won't fire Moorer!" he shouted at Ehrlichman, railing at a ubiquitous "they" of enemies. "They can spy on him and they can spy on me and betray us and he won't fire them!"[39]

Nixon was becoming increasingly concerned about Kissinger's mood swings. According to Ehrlichman, "Nixon wondered aloud if Henry needed psychiatric care." Nixon seemed "sincere" about it—but he didn't want to confront Kissinger personally. "Talk to him, John," Nixon said.[40] Ehrlichman shied away, too. "No one would bell the cat and tell Henry he needed to see a psychiatrist," Ehrlichman recounted to Kissinger biographer Walter Isaacson. Asked about it many years later, Nixon denied that he had ever said that Kissinger should seek psychiatric help. "Others brought up the idea, Nixon admitted, and it was discussed." But then Nixon launched into his standard dismissal of psychiatrists: "He tended to think that those who saw them came out worse rather than better."[41]

In private conversations with Ehrlichman and others, Nixon could be psychologically shrewd about Kissinger—and about the hubris of other powerful, egotistical men. "People get the feeling that they can do no wrong, and then, well, their defense is always to show, whenever they do make a mistake, they didn't do it. But that, actually, they were right all the time," Nixon said to Haldeman and Ehrlichman on December 23, as they talked about Kissinger's "intellectual arrogance." The president went on, more broadly and insightfully:

NIXON: Whenever you make a mistake, unless you cut your losses and get out, you compound it by trying to prove you're right. That was the trouble with Kennedy and Johnson on Vietnam. Assuming it was a mistake, they compound it by trying to prove that it wasn't.

EHRLICHMAN: Yeah, yeah.

NIXON: So it got deeper, and deeper, and deeper, and deeper, and deeper.[42]

Truer words, perhaps, but Nixon—like so many powerful men—seemed incapable of following his own advice.*

---

*In his diary, Haldeman recorded the same wishful thinking over Vietnam that afflicted the Kennedy and Johnson administrations. In August of 1971, he described how Kissinger lamented U.S. Senate efforts to cut off funding for the war because, Kissinger insisted, "we really won" and "if we just had one more dry season," the North Vietnamese would "break their backs." Haldeman wrote: "This, of course, is the same line he's used for the last two years, over and over, and I guess all Johnson's advisers used with him [Johnson], to keep things escalating. I'm sure

On rare occasions, a flicker of self-awareness would creep into the presidential mind. At Christmastime in 1971, Nixon spoke with John Mitchell about the extraordinary degree of subterfuge among his own advisers. One reason he did not want to fire Admiral Moorer was that Moorer had been the White House back channel to go around Defense Secretary Mel Laird, who himself was spying on the president through the intercepts of the National Security Agency.[44] For a moment, Nixon was able to see what a tangled web he had woven. In a soft, halting voice, the president said to Mitchell, "I created this whole situation, this—this **lesion**. It's just unbelievable. Unbelievable."

But within two weeks he was blithely back to using the Joint Chiefs to circumvent the secretary of defense.[45]

For all his bluster, Kissinger was not blind to his own shortcomings. On December 30, during a long heart-to-heart with Haldeman, Kissinger admitted that he was "egotistical" and "nervous." He knew that Nixon was tiring of his histrionics. But then, as Haldeman noted, "he tossed in the thing of being essential to the China trip." Kissinger's job security—or so he believed—was that only he could

---

they really believed it at the time, but it's amazing how it sounds like a broken record."[43] Nixon could be more fatalistic, telling Haldeman that the war would never be won, just "dribble on," but at other times he wanted to double down with Duck Hook–type bombing campaigns.

handle the immense complexities of arranging the president's trip to Beijing, coming up in February.[46]

Nixon usually tried to be philosophical about his national security adviser's self-promotion, even when it came at the president's expense. In discussing the endless squabbling between Kissinger and Rogers, Nixon could affect a lofty, forbearing tone. "Both think the other is an egomaniac," Bill Safire remarked to Nixon on January 18. "And in a sense they're both right," Nixon replied. "Ego is something we all have, and then you either grow out of it or it takes you over. I've grown out of it," Nixon said to his speechwriter, who may have struggled to keep a straight face. The president continued: "It's really compensation for an inferiority complex. Henry has that, of course, and Bill has it too—because this isn't his field, and he knows Henry knows more than he does."[47]

Kissinger was a deft courtier who usually knew his place. Still, he couldn't resist dangerous liaisons. Stepping out to Georgetown had become risky to Kissinger, but that was part of the thrill. Skipping the First Lady's birthday party in March 1971, Kissinger had instead gone to dinner at Kay Graham's. In a telephone conversation picked up by Kissinger's own taping system—everyone, it seems, had one—Kissinger worried to Mrs. Graham what would happen "if one of the Nixon courtiers points out that I was at your house." The proprietor of **The Washington Post** agreed, "We'd both be beheaded." They laughed, anxiously, giddily.[48]

Nixon's suspicions of Kissinger's perfidy grew. In the convoluted world of White House court politics, Kissinger's reputation as a double agent both threatened his continued employment and protected it. Early in the new year, Haldeman recorded that the president "has really been thinking about the Kissinger thing, and that maybe we've got to bite the bullet now and get him out. The problem is, if we don't, he'll be in the driver's seat during the campaign, and we've got to remember he leaked things to us in '68, maybe we've got to assume he's capable of doing the same to our opponents in '72."[49] In the end, with the China trip looming, Nixon decided to keep his vexing but essential national security adviser. Locked in a Machiavellian embrace, they embarked on a journey to a long-forbidden continent that Nixon likened to "going to the moon."[50]

"I know of no presidential trip that was as carefully planned nor of any president who ever prepared himself so conscientiously," Kissinger wrote of their trip to China.[51] Nixon pored over massive briefing books. (Years later, Haldeman's aide, Larry Higby, recalled, "I had to lug those things around China, but he didn't need them. He had memorized them.")[52] Clumsy with a soup spoon, Nixon practiced for hours using chopsticks. He invited scholars and old China hands to the White House, including the writer André Malraux, who had known Mao and Chou as young revolutionaries in the 1930s. Kissinger regarded Malraux as a has-been and a bit of a faker, but the French philosopher said the right thing to Nixon: If de Gaulle were still alive, he would salute the American president and say, "You are about to attempt one of the most important things of the century."[53]

Worried about Nixon's chronic sleeplessness, Nixon's aides spread out the trip from Washington to Beijing over three days, with layovers in Hawaii and Guam, to let the president adjust to the thirteen-hour time change. Al Haig, who had been sent to Beijing to advance the historic meeting, warned about the 100-proof mao-tai brandy that Nixon would be required by his hosts to drink. Haig cabled, perhaps unnecessarily: UNDER NO REPEAT NO CIRCUMSTANCES SHOULD THE PRESIDENT ACTUALLY DRINK FROM HIS GLASS IN RESPONSE TO BANQUET TOASTS.[54]

On February 17, 1972, Air Force One—renamed **The Spirit of '76** by Nixon—took off from Andrews Air Force Base. As they flew halfway around the world, Kissinger and Nixon picked up their intricate minuet and staged a bit of role reversal. With mild disingenuousness, Nixon acted the part of world-weary, cynical statesman while Kissinger, for his part, reflected a refreshing sense of wonder about trotting the globe that was much closer to Nixon's true feelings. That night, Nixon, who had begun a recorded personal diary three months earlier, dictated, with perhaps more self-consciousness than self-awareness: "As Henry and Bob both pointed out on the plane, there was almost a religious feeling in the messages we were receiving from all over the country, wishing us well. I told Henry that I thought it was all really a question of the American people being hopelessly and almost naïvely for peace, even at any price. He felt that perhaps there was also some ingredient of excitement about the boldness of the move, and visiting a land that was unknown to so many Americans."[55]

The handshake.
**Courtesy of the Richard Nixon Presidential
Library and Museum**

CHAPTER 21

Speak Quietly

Aboard **The Spirit of '76** on the morning of February 21, 1972, the chief of President Nixon's security detail radioed an advance man on the ground at the Beijing Airport: "What about the crowd?"* The answer came back: "There is no crowd."

"Did you say, 'No crowd'?"

"That is an affirmative."[1]

Beijing Airport was dull, sooty with coal smoke, and almost empty. Giant banners denounced Western imperialism.

Nixon peered out the window of the airplane as it came to rest and saw a solitary figure in a gray overcoat standing on the tarmac. When de Gaulle, tall and erect but coatless against the winter chill, had greeted the American president in Paris in February 1969, Nixon had taken off his overcoat, too. Now,

---

*I am using the modern Chinese spelling for Peking, but the old system for familiar names like Mao Tse-tung (now Mao Zedong) and Chou En-lai (now Zhou Enlai).

seeing that Prime Minister Chou En-Lai, thin and frail, was wearing an overcoat, Nixon kept his on.

Five steps from the bottom of the ramp, Nixon extended his hand and kept it out as he walked the several paces toward Chou. Nixon knew that, almost three decades earlier, when John Foster Dulles had met Chou En-lai at a peace conference in Geneva, the American secretary of state had reportedly refused to shake the hand of Red China's foreign minister. The Chinese had added the snub to their centuries-long list of grievances against the West.

In the limousine, a bulky Soviet-made vehicle with curtains, Chou said, with rehearsed formality, "Your handshake came over the vastest ocean in the world—twenty-five years of no communication."[2]

Nixon had been pleased when a Chinese military band struck up "The Star Spangled Banner" at the airport. A chill had run up his spine ("it always has that effect on me," he recalled to Frank Gannon); he noted, gratefully, that the band had not mangled the tune, as foreign military bands usually did.[3] Nixon knew that the TV footage back home would be excellent.[4] Once at his guest house, he could not bring himself to look his host in the eye. "I found it extraordinary that Chou En-lai would be focused on the President, would drill in on him, but the President kind of would look off or look down on the floor," recalled Dwight Chapin, the president's aide, who was closely watching the body language.[5] Aside from his normal social awkwardness, Nixon was distracted. He was anxious to hear if Chairman Mao would meet with him. Nixon knew that the trip would be deemed a failure if he did not see the Chinese ultimate leader face-to-face.

Chou left, and Nixon stripped down to his underwear in order to take a shower. A breathless Kissinger burst in: They had been summoned to Mao's residence. In imperial China, the emperor had always kept visitors on edge, making them wait for an audience. Truly, Communist China was still the Middle Kingdom.[6] Five minutes later, Nixon clambered into another limousine (with the Secret Service in hot pursuit) to drive to Mao's villa, a modest house at the edge of the ancient imperial Forbidden City.

On that cold winter morning, Mao was so weak from bronchitis that he could only walk a few steps, supported by the pretty nurses he kept around. He held Nixon's hand for a minute—"the most moving moment," Nixon recorded in his diary.[7] Mao's overstuffed chair was surrounded by books, many of them lying open. Recalling his briefing on Mao's Little Red Book, the chairman's sayings and required reading for China's nine hundred million people, Nixon opened the conversation in a literary vein. "The Chairman's writings moved a nation and have changed the world," he said. In a guttural, almost gasping voice, Mao replied, "I haven't been able to change it. I've only been able to change a few places in the vicinity of Beijing."

Nixon, relaxing now, began bantering with Mao about calling the Nationalist Chinese "bandits."

Noticing Kissinger standing nearby, Mao showed that he was familiar with the national security adviser's high standing with the Western media. "We two must not monopolize the whole show," Mao said to Nixon. "It won't do if we don't let Dr. Kissinger have a say." He nodded toward Kissinger. "You have been famous about your trips to China."

KISSINGER: It was the president who set the direction and worked out the plan.
MAO: He is a very wise assistant to say it that way.

The chairman and his number two, Chou, had a good chuckle. Nixon began broadly joking about Kissinger and girls, which provoked a laugh from Chou and, after a beat, from Kissinger as well.

Nixon showed off his homework again. "Mr. Chairman," he said, "we know you and the Prime Minister have taken great risks in inviting us here. For us also it was a difficult decision. But having read some of the Chairman's statements, I know he is one who sees when an opportunity comes, that you must seize the hour and seize the day."

Mao seemed more interested in teasing and dropping oblique pearls of wisdom. There was no substantive discussion of tricky issues like Russia and Taiwan. Nixon tried relating in his familiar persona of the poor boy who overcomes the odds:

Mr. Chairman, the Chairman's life is well known to all of us. He came from a very poor family to the top of the most populous nation in the world, a great nation. My background is not so well known. I also came from a very poor family, and to the top of a very great nation. History has brought us together. The question is whether we, with different philosophies, but both with feet on the ground, and having come from the people, can make a breakthrough that will serve not just China and America, but the whole world in the years ahead. And that is why we are here.

Mao looked at Nixon and said, offhandedly, "Your book, **Six Crises,** is not a bad book." Nixon retorted with an aside to Chou and Kissinger: "He reads too much."[8]

Chou was looking at his watch. Mao slowly shuffled his visitors to the door and said that he had not been feeling well. "But you look very good," said Nixon. "Appearances are deceiving," said Mao, with a slight shrug.[9]

Later that night, at the Great Hall of the People, a titanic Soviet-style structure, the Chinese orchestra played a medley of classic American tunes—"Oh! Susannah," "Home on the Range," "Turkey in the Straw." Nixon raised his glass of fiery mao-tai (but did not drink) again and again. His own, carefully rehearsed "extemporaneous" toast was "superb," Haldeman reported in his diary, and the photo opportunity was spectacular. The White House had shipped in tons of TV equipment, and half a world away, millions of Americans watched the evening banquet on the **Today** show. At Yale Law School, a student named Hillary Rodham rented a TV with a rabbit-ears antenna so that she could watch in her room.[10]

Day after day, the improbable images of Nixon in China reeled on—Nixon at the Great Wall, Nixon in the Forbidden City, Nixon in earnest discussion with men in Mao suits. Pat, too, did her part at hospitals, orphanages, and schools. In the sometimes callous way he referred to his wife while discussing her with his chief of staff, Nixon had told Haldeman that the First Lady could come along as a "prop."[11] Watching her mother depart, Julie wrote David, "The difficult part about yesterday [the departure] was seeing how harassed and tired Mother looked. She has really aged! She told me she was sick to her stomach on Saturday and Sunday. It must have been nerves."[12] But the First Lady performed gamely, as she invariably did on foreign tours. (On a visit to a kitchen, she did puzzle her hosts slightly by using a dry Americanism to describe food that looked "good enough to eat.")[13] She had mastered a few Chinese phrases; Bill Safire had recommended that she study Chinese because "it would make Jackie Kennedy's knowledge of French, which went over so big in Europe, look totally insignificant." ("Good, if PN willing to develop some key phrases—or a brief little speech," Nixon had scribbled on the margin of Safire's memo.)[14]

Mao's wife made no effort to charm Nixon. She had become a power during China's Cultural Revolution, ironically named because it had sought to erase millennia of Chinese culture by burning books and forcing scholars to become rural peasants. Vindictive and humorless, she once described herself as "Chairman Mao's dog. When he said, 'Bite,' I bit."[15] At the opera with Nixon, she was abrasive, demanding to know why he had not come to China sooner. Nixon, who was watching the performance, did not respond. The opera, **The Red Detachment of Women,** celebrated a pre-revolutionary woman who had led the people of her town in a revolt against an oppressive landlord. "It was rather a sight to see the P clapping at the end of this kind of thing, which would have been horrifying at home," Haldeman wrote in his diary that night, "but it all seems to fit together, somehow, here."

Nixon and Chou En-lai made an odd couple. The American politician was awkward and stiff, the Chinese diplomat smooth and urbane. But they understood each other; survivors, they had learned from setback and defeat. As they traveled around the country, applauded by vast crowds now permitted to see the spectacle of the visiting American head of state, Nixon and Chou engaged in a deepening dialogue, at once personal and universal. On Saturday, February 26, Nixon dictated to his diary:

Chou En-lai and I had a very interesting conversation on the way to the airport in Peking. He spoke of Mao's poem which he wrote on returning to his hometown after thirty-two years. He returned to the point he has made quite often, that adversity is a great teacher. I related it to adversity generally, and pointed out that an election loss was really more painful than a physical wound in war. The latter wounds the body—the other wounds the spirit. On the other hand, the election loss helps to develop the strength and character which are essential for future battles. I said to Chou that I found that I had learned more from defeats than from victories, and that all I wanted was a life in which I had just one more victory than defeat.

I used also the example of de Gaulle in the wilderness for a period of years as a factor which helped build his character. He came back with a thought that men who travel on a smooth road all their life do not develop strength.

Chou said that I had a poetic turn of mind like Mao, when I had in my last toast said that it was not possible to build a bridge across 16,000 miles and twenty-two years in one week. Much of the Mao poetry, of course, is simply a vivid and colorful example.

He referred again to his admiration for **Six Crises,** and I jokingly said that he shouldn't believe all the bad that the press said of me, and that I would follow the same practice with regard to him.[16]

By day six, Nixon was exhausted and cranky. He complained privately that the press did not understand him, notwithstanding the best media coverage of his life. Still, he had been a masterful diplomat, plotting his game of triangular chess between China and Russia, winning no guarantees of help on North Vietnam but shrewdly playing rivals against each other. The endgame was tense—Kissinger had to find a formulation to paper over the future of Taiwan. The island refuge of the Nationalist Chinese government driven from the mainland by the Communists in 1949 had been a protected ally of the United States—and a potential flashpoint in the Cold War. As vice president, Nixon had sat through anxious meetings of Eisenhower's National Security Council, deliberating whether protecting Taiwan from a Red Chinese invasion was worth World War III. The crises over Taiwan seemed like relics of an earlier age, but the island remained a sore spot between China and America.

"That place is no great use for you," Chou told Kissinger, "but a great wound for us." Nixon had come a long way since the days when he and other Republican senators would toast "Back to the Mainland!" at banquets hosted by the Nationalist Chinese; even so, he had to worry about his right flank at home, which would revolt if he were to be seen abandoning America's old allies. Working all night, Kissinger found an artful finesse—the Americans acknowledged that Taiwan was part of "one China" but left it to the "Chinese themselves" to settle the matter peacefully.[17]

"This was the week that changed the world," Nixon said in a farewell toast. That night he could not sleep. He kept awake the dead-on-his-feet Kissinger as he downed a few farewell mao-tais. "P sort of recapping problems and triumphs of the whole visit," Haldeman recorded. "His admiration for Henry's accomplishments and the whole thing, with Henry sitting on the couch just itching to get out and go to bed, which I tried to bring about several times, but the P made the point that Chou En-lai stays up all night, so will he."

Nixon came home to hosannas of praise from around the world. Conservatives protested their astonishment. Columnist William F. Buckley wrote that as he had watched Nixon toast Mao, "I would not have been surprised if Mr. Nixon had lurched into a toast to Alger Hiss." But any carping in the press was overwhelmed by the stunning visual images, seen by virtually every American. Ronald Reagan, the California governor who had emerged as Nixon's possible successor, complained to Kissinger about Taiwan but joked that the China visit had been a great television "pilot" and ought to be made into a series.[18]

Meeting with his cabinet at the White House, Nixon handed out teacups as souvenirs. "Now you can say you drank from the cup Mao Tse-tung and Chou En-lai drank from," he said. The president was weary but breezy and down-to-earth. He scoffed at "the naïve assumption, particularly among Americans, that problems evaporate when nations get to know one another. That's nonsense. The idea that either of us is going to be affected by mere personal visitors is baloney." But he relished recounting his eyeball-to-eyeball personal diplomacy. Describing Chou, he said, "Another characteristic of his is similar to mine: Whenever he said anything particularly tough, he became much cooler. When it was really down to extremely controversial issues, both of us spoke in a way our interpreter couldn't quite hear. Of course, talking loudly tends to make you much less impressive." Secretary Rogers observed that while they were talking to Chou, a "girl came up and handed him the galleys of the next day's newspaper, and there he was—rearranging the front page." Nixon muttered, "I'd like to rearrange a front page now and then."[19] Everyone had a good laugh. The president was wry, confident, in command.

The mood did not last. He began complaining again about the press coverage, badgering his aides for a PR campaign that would emphasize his personal role (and thus downplay Kissinger's) in the China breakthrough. "Once more we encountered the curious phenomenon that success seemed to unsettle Nixon more than failure," Kissinger wrote. "He seemed obsessed by the fear that he was not receiving adequate credit."[20] Dwight Chapin, too, noted that Nixon "couldn't seem to celebrate. After China it was all, how are we going to exploit this politically? How are we using this? It was almost as if he was surrendering the high he could have had."[21]

Two days after Nixon returned, columnist Jack Anderson reported what appeared to be a scandalous payoff of the Nixon administration. In his

Washington Post column, the muckraker claimed to have a memo proving that the global conglomerate, International Telephone and Telegraph, had given the Republican Party $400,000 for its upcoming convention expenses. The quid pro quo was a favorable resolution in a federal antitrust case that threatened to break up the company. Led by Larry O'Brien, the Democrats jumped on the story as a way to diminish Nixon's China triumph. Senator Edward Kennedy began Judiciary Committee hearings on the scandal, which the establishment press duly hyped. Or so it seemed to Nixon, who was furious. In fact, the president **had** tried to quash the antitrust case—but not in return for a political contribution. As Nixon later explained in his memoirs, he had intervened because Justice Department bureaucrats had defied his order not to break up a company simply because it was big.[22]

The White House was sure that the incriminating payoff memo, supposedly written by an ITT lobbyist named Dita Beard, was a forgery. To prove it, E. Howard Hunt was dispatched to confront Beard in her hospital bed, where she had collapsed in the midst of the scandal. Wearing a red wig and a voice-altering device supplied by the CIA, the Plumber grilled the lobbyist, who protested her innocence in the whole affair (she had been bragging, exaggerating her clout). The case quickly devolved into acrimonious and confusing charges and countercharges until, after a few weeks, the press lost interest.[23]

· · ·

Hunt was still working out of the White House, but his partner, Liddy, had gone on the payroll of the Committee for the Re-Election of the President, CRP, or as it was soon dubbed, "Creep." With the November election approaching, resources were being poured into the effort to ensure the president a second term. Nixon had declared that he was not going to be outspent in 1972 the way he had been by the Kennedy machine in 1960. Influence ped-dlers and seekers were put on notice that ambassa-dorships would go to generous donors.[24]* Chatting with Nixon, Haldeman marveled that the fundrais-ers had "sucked" in so much money that it was going to be hard to spend it all.

Liddy was doing his best. Flying first class around the country and staying in fancy hotels, Liddy was recruiting operatives with blandishments of cash and excitement. On board came some Cuban exiles who called Liddy "El Halcón"—the Falcon, the "birds other birds fear." Liddy scared off one potential secre-tary when he put his hand in a flame to demonstrate his ability to endure pain, but he signed up a pair of blond prostitutes to ensnare wayward Democrats.[26]

On January 27, equipped with charts and graphs,

*Peter Flanigan, a close Nixon adviser who handled the business community, tried to fend off the egregious cases. When C. V. "Sonny" Whitney, a polo-playing philanthropist and a hefty Nixon donor, called demanding to be made ambassador to Spain, Flanigan told him, "Sonny, you're not qualified to be am-bassador to Spain. Barbados, maybe."[25]

Liddy, accompanied by White House Counsel John
Dean and CRP deputy chief Jeb Magruder, had
gone to the Office of the Attorney General at the
Justice Department to brief John Mitchell on a proposed "Operation Gemstone." Liddy wanted campaign intelligence that was "offensive" as well as
"defensive." To secure the Republican Convention
from antiwar protesters, Liddy suggested kidnapping their leaders, drugging them, and spiriting
them away to Mexico. He labeled these disappear-
ances **Nacht und Nebel,** "night and fog," a term
used by Nazi stormtroopers. Liddy explained that
he already had a lease on a houseboat in Miami
Beach, site of the Democratic Convention, to house
the prostitutes (this was "Operation Sapphire").
Liddy ticked off various other ideas for black bag
jobs and bugging operations to hit the headquarters
of Democratic candidates.[27]

Puffing his pipe, the attorney general listened impassively. John Dean later claimed that when he caught
Mitchell's eye, the attorney general winked. According
to Dean, Mitchell drily told Liddy that Operation
Gemstone was "not quite what I had in mind."[28] In
Liddy's world, the line between kidding and crime was
often fuzzy. (Liddy addressed the attorney general as
"General," with a hard "g.") Mitchell later said, "I
should have thrown Liddy out the window."

But at the time, he merely agreed to another meeting. Liddy pared down the million-dollar plan, cutting out the houseboat (but keeping the prostitutes)
and dropping a "chase plane" to pursue Democratic

candidates.[29] A third meeting followed in Florida, where Mitchell was vacationing. It has never been clear what Mitchell approved. He later claimed to have said no at all three meetings, but between the pipe-puffing and the drollery, it was sometimes unclear what he had intended. He was exhausted and distracted—Martha was collapsing, again—and he wanted to go back to his New York law practice after managing the Nixon campaign. The Liddy-Hunt team continued to scheme, along with other Dirty Tricksters in the employ of CRP or the White House. H. R. Haldeman signed off on $300,000 for "intelligence gathering," and no one put a stop to the madness.[30] Liddy's nominal boss at CRP, Jeb Magruder, was afraid of "El Halcón," especially after Liddy said to him, "Jeb, if you don't take your arm off my shoulder, I'm going to tear it off and beat you to death with it." Magruder later wrote that he was instructed to get along with Liddy, who appeared to have the backing of Dean and Colson. "Liddy's a Hitler, but at least he's our Hitler," he was told by Gordon Strachan, the White House aide assigned by Haldeman to keep an eye on Magruder. Liddy claims that he even proposed to assassinate Jack Anderson but was told to "forget it" by Hunt.[31]

What did Richard Nixon know of Operation Gemstone or Liddy's various plots? Probably nothing. Though Haldeman may have kept Nixon apprised of political intelligence operations in general terms, Nixon in the winter and spring of 1972 was absorbed by China, Russia, and Vietnam. While massively winning reelection was always a top priority, presidential politics consumed less time than geopolitics. As the president rose in the polls, his Democratic challengers fell by the wayside until Senator George McGovern, an uncharismatic liberal from South Dakota, was the last man standing. Nixon knew he was going to win; the only question was by how much. It's possible that Nixon had a warning or two of the rot down below. Nixon assistant Henry Cashen recalled standing with Murray Chotiner, the original Nixon nut-cutter, as they looked up at the CRP's plush new headquarters at 1701 Pennsylvania Avenue, across the street from the Executive Office Building, in the fall of 1971. "These guys have nothing to do," said Chotiner. "We're going to win going away. They"—he gestured to the shiny campaign headquarters—"are going to get in trouble." Chotiner told Cashen that he had warned Haldeman of his premonition in writing but had received only an acknowledgment.[32]

Nixon would later be compared to Henry II, who cried out, "Will no one rid me of this troublesome priest?" thus inspiring his attentive knights to murder Thomas Becket, the archbishop of Canterbury. In the Nixon White House, as well as at the CRP, the gathering and spreading of dirt was sanctioned, implicitly and sometimes explicitly, from on high. Chuck Colson, Nixon's self-described hatchet man, explained to Jonathan Aitken, "It was like a culture taking root in a corporation. Haldeman, no doubt with the president's blessing, ran a sort of system by which a nod, a smile, or a word of approval or an invitation to a White House function was bestowed on those who brought in dirt on our opponents. You could always get rewarded if you showed up in the White House with a bit of negative intelligence, so the puppies kept coming in with their bones."[33]

Pressed by Haldeman (or so he later testified), White House counsel John Dean began drawing up a White House "enemies list." Actually, there were several lists—so many that it became confusing. In an almost farcical attempt to avoid overlap or omission, Alex Butterfield wrote Haldeman:

I received a copy of the very sensitive Eyes Only "Opponents List" put together by Messrs. Colson and Bell, I do not see in the media section of that list the names of Kandy Stroud of **Women's Wear Daily** [she had coined the "Plastic Pat" label], Judith Martin or Maxine Cheshire of the **Washington Post**, who, according to my understanding, are on the current "Freeze List." At the same time, I do note the names of others on the "Freeze List"—namely, Senators Nelson, Kennedy, and Muskie, Congressman Robert Kastenmeier and Sander Vanocur of PBS. Am I wrong to assume that the "Freeze List" is something over and above the "Opponent List"? . . . If you will straighten me out on this matter, I will pass the word to Colson, Bell, Rose Mary Woods . . . and others who have a need to know.[34]

The enemies lists (or "opponents lists" or "freeze lists") were fed by Nixon, compiled from the angry notations on the president's copy of the Daily News Summary. Nixon was hardly the first (or last) president to make lists—literal or notional—of his enemies. Eisenhower made a practice of writing down the names of his enemies and tossing them in a drawer.[35] But Nixon was unusually vituperative. In April, he ordered Haldeman and Ziegler to banish **Time** magazine's Sidey and **The New Republic**'s John Osborne (to whom Ehrlichman regularly leaked) for their coverage of the ITT scandal. "Both have spoken in the most vicious derogatory terms of RN in the place where you really find out what people think—the Georgetown cocktail parties," Nixon dictated. "The evidence on this is absolutely conclusive. You do not need to ask me where I got it."[36]

Nixon seemed oblivious to the corrosive power of his own rage. On May 9, Walter Annenberg, the wealthy publisher appointed ambassador to Britain by Nixon, chatted with the president about "our friend Norman Vincent Peale," whose sermons on the "power of positive thinking" Nixon had regularly taken in when he lived in New York. Annenberg recited Peale's teaching that it wise to "practice being dispassionate" because "resentful feelings complicate things, even affect your health." But then, as if he had never heard of Norman Vincent Peale, Annenberg became passionate about avenging his enemies—one in particular.

With the president murmuring in agreement,

Annenberg began talking about how much he resented Katharine Graham. The publisher (**TV
Guide**, **The Philadelphia Inquirer**) said that he was
thinking of commissioning a reporting team to investigate the life of Mrs. Graham's late husband
Philip, who had committed suicide in 1963. Annenberg claimed that during a social encounter in
London, he had told the **Post**'s proprietor that her
"journalistic operation was an absolute disgrace."
Nixon hooted and chortled as Annenberg continued: "This bitch has got it coming." "Right," said
Nixon. John Ehrlichman was taking notes on the
conversation, which was also recorded. His cryptic
jottings reflect the abrupt turn from high-mindedness
to crude japes:

> Norman V. Peale
> Resentful feelings affect health
> Practice being dispassionate
> P—power of positive thinking
> Told K G: paper is a disgrace
> A: someone will do the Phil Graham story in re-
> venge
> Do it in paperback
> She's got it coming
> "Bitch"[37]

Nixon didn't just laugh at vulgar jokes about
The Washington Post's owner. In the fall of 1971,
in the wake of the Pentagon Papers disclosure,
groups organized by Bebe Rebozo and other pro-

Nixon businessmen had begun challenging the FCC licenses of TV stations owned by Graham's publishing company. The effect on the newspaper's staff was predictable. **Washington Post** executive editor Ben Bradlee recalled: "Our stock price nose-dived as the word got out that the **Post** was going to lose its TV station income. It was a scary time, and it had an absolutely critical impact on us internally. From that time on we knew that Nixon hated us and we reciprocated. Without that, the **Post** would never have behaved so confidently in its reporting of Watergate."[38]

When he met with Annenberg on May 9 (he gave the ambassador a set of cuff links), Nixon was unwinding from one of the most momentous decisions of his presidency. The night before, he had told the nation that he was ordering the mining of Haiphong Harbor, where Russian ships delivered supplies to the North Vietnamese. The president was gambling his foreign policy and his presidency.

By the spring of 1972, Nixon had wound down U.S. forces in Vietnam from over half a million when he took office to under seventy thousand. But the secret peace talks with North Vietnam were stalled as usual, and at the end of March, North Vietnam launched a major invasion of the South, using Russian-made T-54 tanks. Nixon ordered a full-on bombing campaign against North Vietnam, but cloud cover obstructed the U.S. Air Force. "The air force isn't worth a shit," Nixon complained, according to Haldeman's notes. "They won't fly."[39]

"Just get that weather cleared up over there," Nixon said to Kissinger. "The bastards have never been bombed [nervously chuckles]. They're going to be bombed this time."[40]

Nixon was feeling isolated and unsupported. He accused the military of ducking action to avoid casualties. He told the Chairman of the Joint Chiefs, Admiral Moorer, that General Creighton Abrams, the U.S. ground commander, was "drinking too much" and was thus ordered to "go on the wagon throughout the balance of this offensive." A month later, he railed about the secretary of defense, "goddamn Laird is playing his usual games, saying we can't find targets and so forth. He is a miserable bastard, really."[41]

He was disappointed with Kissinger, whom he accused of naïveté in his dealings with Hanoi. "The point is, Bob, we've got to realize that on this whole business of negotiating with North Vietnam, Henry has never been right," Nixon told Haldeman on May 2.[42] Kissinger was anxious that if Nixon blockaded North Vietnam, the Russians would scotch the summit meeting scheduled for June in Moscow—the first-ever visit to Moscow by a U.S. president and the culmination of the Nixon-Kissinger triangular diplomacy. Gloomily, Kissinger put the odds of cancellation at 80 percent.[43]

Squeezed on all sides—by the Pentagon, the Kremlin, and Hanoi—Nixon lashed out at Kissinger and then privately regretted it. He wrote in his diary: "I think perhaps I was too insistent and rough on

Henry today, but I am so disgusted with the military's failure to follow through that I simply had to take it out on somebody."[44]

For some time, Nixon had allowed himself to dream that after the election he could join with his favorite, John Connally, to build a new party—"the Independent Conservative Party, or something of that sort," Haldeman recorded—that would bring together Southern Democrats and middle-of-the-road to conservative Republicans. "Get control of the Congress without an election, simply by the re-alignment, and make a truly historic change," wrote Haldeman.[45] Nixon had hoped to build a whole new establishment to replace the liberal elite.

Now he could only think of striking a mighty blow against Hanoi, the political fallout be damned. "For once, we've got to use the maximum power of this country against a shit-ass little country to win the war," he told Kissinger on May 4.[46] But as he contemplated radical military action—a blockade, heavy bombing of Hanoi, maybe even threatening with a nuclear weapon—he realized that the voters would revolt and drive him from office in November.[47] He began thinking of a successor: Rockefeller? Reagan? Chief Justice Burger? "Henry threw up his hands and said none of them would do," Nixon wrote in his diary. "Henry then became very emotional about the point that I shouldn't be thinking this way or talking this way to anybody. . . . He made his pitch that the North Vietnamese should not be allowed to destroy two presidents."[48]

Alone, Nixon turned to his family. Retreating to Camp David on Friday, May 5, he brought Julie with him. He told her that he was planning on mining Haiphong Harbor and striking targets around Hanoi. Warm but independent-minded, Julie told her father of her worries that the public might not back him. If we do not act, Nixon responded, we will cease to be a great power. "She rejoined with the observation that there were many who felt that the United States should not be a great power," Nixon wrote in his diary. "This, of course, is the kind of poison that is fed to so many of the younger generation by their professors."

Tricia's reaction, Nixon wrote, "was immediately positive because she felt we had to do something." That Friday night, wandering and insomniac, Nixon looked for an empty cabin to write his speech. "Very late" that night, he entered Aspen, his main residence, and noticed that Pat's light was still on. "When I went in, she got up and came over, and put her arms around me, and said, 'Don't worry about anything,'" Nixon noted in his diary.

Back in Washington on Monday, "I had my usual light pre-speech dinner of a small bowl of wheat germ for energy around six. . . . I jogged in place for about ten minutes and took a long cold shower."[49]

The speech was short. "There is only one way to stop the killing," he said. "That is to keep the weapons of war out of the hands of the international outlaws of North Vietnam." If the Russians kept delivering tanks and other weapons on ships entering Haiphong Harbor, they would have to take the risk of losing the ships.

On the three TV networks, the commentators unanimously foresaw a superpower confrontation that would doom the summit.[50] But the Russians made only pro forma protests, even after losing one of their freighters to an American mine. The antiwar protests were relatively muted; with the draft ended and the troops coming home, the movement was fading. As American B-52s pounded their targets, the North Vietnamese invasion faltered.

The summit was still on. The Russians had watched America sidle up to China with real apprehension; the Kremlin leaders were eager for détente with the West. Nixon had gambled and won.

In his memoirs, Kissinger poked mild fun at his boss in the throes of deciding whether to risk the summit by striking Hanoi. "Instead of slouching in an easy chair with his feet on a settee as usual, he was pacing up and down, gesticulating with a pipe on which he was occasionally puffing, something I had never previously seen him do," Kissinger wrote. "On one level he was playing MacArthur. On another he was steeling himself for a decision on which his political future would depend."

Kissinger noted that, "play acting aside," the president was "crisp and decisive, his questions thoughtful and to the point." At "moments of real crisis, Nixon would become coldly analytical," Kissinger recalled. There would be endless meetings, more writing on yellow legal pads, sometimes contradictory orders that were actually invitations to argument. But then "nervous agitation would give way to calm decisiveness," Kissinger wrote. Nixon would get to "the essence of the problem and take the courageous course, even if it seemed to risk his immediate political interest."[51]

E. Howard Hunt.
Bettmann/Corbis

CHAPTER 22

Triumph and Tragedy

On Saturday, May 20, 1972, as Air Force One lifted off from Washington en route to the Moscow Summit, Kissinger came into the president's cabin and exclaimed, "This has to be one of the great diplomatic coups of all times! Three weeks ago everyone predicted it would be called off, and today we're on our way!"[1] Though he had been one of the doubters, Kissinger had worked night and day to set up the meeting, right down to the exchange of gifts. Ambassador Dobrynin had suggested that Nixon might like a little hydrofoil speedboat for tooling along the Potomac. Kissinger had inquired, What would please Secretary Brezhnev? "A Cadillac," answered the Kremlin's man.[2]

Nixon had teased Kissinger about his reputation as an international playboy after Kissinger's advance trip to Moscow in late April. Sitting with Rose Woods, who also enjoyed ribbing Kissinger, Nixon suggested that the national security adviser had been hard to reach in Moscow because, as Woods interjected, he was "probably out with some babe." A bit stiffly, Kissinger demurred but added, "I'll tell you one thing, Mr. President, it wasn't through lack of offers."

Nixon perked up. "Is that right?" Woods chimed in, "Oh my word. Aren't you modest, Henry." Kissinger spluttered, "No, no, there it's got nothing to do with modesty. The head of their state security, General [Sergei] Antonov, greeted me at the airport and said he had a whole bunch of girls, all twenty-five years and younger—"[3]

Nixon enjoyed inflating, then deflating Kissinger's ego. He thought he could manipulate Kissinger, though he sometimes inadvertently created a reciprocating engine that served neither man well. William Safire, an astute observer of Nixon and his convoluted relationship with Kissinger, commented that Nixon's lack of self-awareness—his need to see himself as someone other than who he really was—caused the president to be played by the man he thought he was playing. "Nixon, who thought of himself not as he was but as he thought of himself," Safire wrote, "could use Kissinger as a marionette, and then place himself in his own marionette's hands because the President profoundly understood in his assistant the needs he refused to examine himself."[4] Safire, who enjoyed playing with language, was creating a Russian doll of psychological insight. More plainly stated, Nixon saw himself as the cool one calming the emotional Kissinger. But Nixon's insecurities made him susceptible to Kissinger's neediness—which was not so different from Nixon's.

Safire, who as a budding PR man had first seen Nixon in action at the 1959 Kitchen Debate with Khrushchev, was aboard Air Force One as it flew east. The speechwriter noted that "Nixon had been euphoric, filled with wonderment and the sense of history, at the prospect of going to China, but he was withdrawn and filled with a sense of caution in returning to Moscow."[5] In describing the Soviet mind-set, Nixon was fond of quoting Lenin: "Thrust with the bayonet until you hit steel." Nixon was steeling himself for the hard-edged Kremlin leaders.

The public reception in the Russian capital was chilly. The crowds had been restricted to side streets, sealed off from the main roads by buses. The Nixons were given an entire floor in the Grand Palace inside the Kremlin, but to avoid eavesdropping devices, Nixon had to conduct meaningful conversations out-of-doors. As usual he was unable to sleep, and he startled the Secret Service at 4:30 A.M. by slipping out, dressed in a sports jacket, to tour the streets of Moscow in the gray northern light of summer. He spoke to some anxious Soviet guards—the only people on the street at this hour—and felt a rush of emotion looking back at the onion domes of the Kremlin to see the American flag flying over his guest quarters. (The flag was shown again and again on American TV to a public becoming more and more appreciative of their globetrotting president-for-peace.)[6]

To Nixon, Brezhnev came across as a tough American labor leader. Nixon was extremely effective with foreign leaders because he did not offer high-minded lectures about freedom. He spoke instead of interests, never acted superior, and always showed respect.[7] With Brezhnev, he knew that it was important to look past the rough manners and see the crafty intelligence that had allowed the longtime apparatchik to outlast cutthroat rivals. The two men had met thirteen years before at the Kitchen Debate, when Brezhnev was serving as an aide to Khrushchev. Now, over tea in Brezhnev's ornate office, the bushy-eyebrowed, solidly built Soviet leader offered a fixed smile and warily eyed the American president.

After some opening bluster, Brezhnev warmed, slightly. He recalled that Franklin Roosevelt had been a hero to the Soviet people for his alliance with Moscow against Hitler. Nixon carefully noted that he had studied the relationship between Stalin, Roosevelt, and Churchill and found that they had been able to overcome the doubts of their subordinates by establishing personal relationships. That is what Nixon wanted, too, he said. "If we leave all the decisions to the bureaucrats, we will never achieve any progress," Nixon added drily. "They would bury us in paper." At this Brezhnev "laughed heartily and slapped his palm on the table," Nixon recalled in his memoirs. "It seemed like a good beginning."[8]

Brezhnev interrupted talks on the second day to take the American president for a speedboat ride, slapping Nixon's knee in the limousine on the drive to the Volga River and cracking off-color jokes. It was all very jolly; at their own tea, Mrs. Brezhnev began referring to Mrs. Nixon as "sister." But then, just before dinner, Brezhnev and two other Politburo members began stalking about the room denouncing American involvement in Vietnam, which Brezhnev called "barbaric" and "just like the Nazis." The American delegation suspected that the Kremlin leaders were making a transcript to send to Hanoi to reassure their North Vietnamese comrades.[9]

Nixon was unfazed. He sat impassively while the insults flew. At one point he asked the Soviet leader, "Are you threatening here?" Brezhnev calmed down, and at the delayed dinner, the jokes and toasts resumed. The negotiations over the nearly completed arms limitation treaty dragged on another day. Brezhnev doodled little rockets with his red pen and tried to take back some earlier concessions. Nixon listened; later, lying naked on Dr. Riland's massage table, he calmly instructed Kissinger not to bend.[10] Two days later, the Politburo accepted all of the American terms. At about 11 P.M. on Friday, May 26, the Americans and Russians signed the first-ever arms control treaty, freezing nuclear arsenals while work progressed on a more comprehensive deal. "Everyone's spirits were high," recalled Nixon. Brezhnev and Nixon exuberantly drank cognac toasts to each other and to peace.

Pat Nixon asked her husband if she could attend the historic ceremony in the grand, gleaming white St. George's Hall in the Kremlin. Since none of the other wives would be permitted, Nixon suggested that she slip in and stand behind one of the large columns, which she did.[11]

That same evening, some five thousand miles away, in the Continental Room of the Watergate Hotel in Washington, D.C., Hunt and Liddy were hosting a banquet to celebrate an impending burglary. There were snifters of brandy and cigars after dinner, and then they went to work. Hunt and one of the Cubans from the Ellsberg break-in, Virgilio Gonzalez, remained after dinner, hidden in a closet. They intended to break into the Democratic National Committee, only a corridor and elevator ride away. But the alarm on a door was unexpectedly armed, and the duo spent the night trapped in the banquet room. The next night, a different group of burglars, lacking the proper tools to pick the locks, failed as well. On the third try, the burglars got into the Watergate and placed bugs on the phone of DNC chairman Larry O'Brien and another official. One of the bugs didn't work. The Plumbers broke into the DNC's Watergate offices again on the night of June 16, but one of the burglars taped the door's locks horizontally, instead of vertically, allowing the tape to show. A security guard saw the telltale sign and called the police. The burglars were arrested in the early hours of June 17. In their rush to flee the Howard Johnson Motor Lodge, where they were monitoring the operation from across the street, Hunt and Liddy left behind some consecutively numbered hundred-dollar bills, a notebook with

Hunt's name and White House telephone number, and a $6.36 check to Hunt's country club. Thus did amateurish bumbling doom the presidency of Richard Nixon.[12]

On Sunday morning, June 18, Nixon smelled coffee brewing and went into the kitchen at Key Biscayne to get a cup. He glanced at a headline over a small story in the middle of the front page of the **Miami Herald**: "Miamians Held in D.C., Try to Bug Demo Headquarters." He scanned the opening paragraph. Five men, four of them from Miami, had been arrested in the Democratic National Committee Headquarters. One of the five identified himself as a former employee of the CIA. Three were Cuban natives. They had been wearing rubber gloves. "I dismissed it as some sort of prank," Nixon wrote in his memoirs. He spent most of the day taking restful swims and, in his diary that night, vowed to go bowling for a half hour at the end of each day. In the evening he reread the last chapters of Churchill's memoir, **Triumph and Tragedy**.[13]

There is an aura of disengagement, detachment, even mild bemusement in Nixon's recounting of his initial reaction to the Watergate break-in. He regarded spying on opponents as normal and accepted, and from the very beginning of the Watergate scandal complained about a "double standard" in the press that let Democrats get away with dirty tricks but not the Republicans.[14] "They're all doing it," Nixon said to Haldeman on June 20. "That's the standard thing. Why the Christ do we have to hire people to sweep our rooms?" When Haldeman began to answer, "We know they're—" Nixon finished his sentence. "Yeah, they're bugging." He recalled J. Edgar Hoover's (false) report that LBJ had bugged his campaign plane in 1968. "We have been bugged in the past, right?" he asked rhetorically.[15]

His diary entry on June 19 did note some "disturbing news." The ex-CIA employee caught breaking into the Watergate was a security consultant named James McCord. McCord had been hired to do security work by the Committee to Re-Elect the President. But Nixon's reaction to this alarming tidbit seems to have been typically tit-for-tat. He noted that he had learned from "one of [Murray] Chotiner's operatives" that McGovern had tried to bug the Republican National Committee. Nixon's response was to "get somebody on the PR side" to put out the story of the Democrats' alleged bugging attempt to distract, or at least to even the score.

On Tuesday morning, June 20, Nixon read a front-page headline in **The Washington Post**: "White House Consultant Tied to Bugging Figure." The Post had learned that E. Howard Hunt's name had turned up in the address books of two of the burglars caught inside DNC headquarters. The story said that until March, Hunt had worked as a consultant to Chuck Colson. "The mention of Colson's name gave me a start," Nixon later wrote. "I had always valued his hardball instincts. Now I wondered if he might have gone too far."[16]

Nixon's reaction may have been more violent than he let on in his memoirs. According to Colson, Nixon told him that he had "smashed an ashtray down" when he first learned about the break-in that Sunday.[17] In any case, after reading the **Post** story linking Hunt to both the break-in and to Colson, Nixon called Colson over from his Executive Office Building office next door. Colson was all wounded innocence and self-pity. "Pick up that goddamn **Washington Post**. See the guilt by association," Colson grumbled, blaming the **Post** for smearing him. Colson told the president that he didn't see how his man Hunt could be involved—not that Hunt wouldn't stage a black bag job, just that the former spy would have been more skillful about it. "I think he's, he's too smart to do it this way, he's just too damn shrewd," said Colson. "It doesn't sound like a skillful job," Nixon agreed. "If we didn't know better, we'd have thought it was deliberately botched." Nixon was all nonchalance. "I'm not going to worry about it. I've—shit, the hell with it. We'll let it fly, we're not going to react to it." The conversation later turned to Katharine Graham. Colson said he wanted to use the Securities and Exchange Commission to investigate the Washington Post Company because he believed Graham was a "vicious" woman primarily concerned with social niceties and who wanted someone in the White House to "kiss her ass."[18]

Nixon did not entirely trust Colson to tell him the truth, so he checked with Haldeman, who had tried, with mixed success, to keep an eye on the

president's favorite "nut cutter." As was his way,
Nixon did not ask directly but tested a proposition
to get Haldeman's reaction. "Colson protested his
innocence in this," Nixon told Haldeman. "As I've
told you, I've come to the conclusion that Colson's
not that dumb."

Haldeman agreed. He began to explain, warily,
cryptically, that others in the White House had tried
to respond to the president's steady demand for
campaign intelligence by undertaking certain
projects—but nothing so crude and clumsy as the
Watergate break-in. "In fact," said Haldeman, "we
all knew that there were some—"

"—intelligence things," the president interjected.

"Some activities, and we were getting reports, or
some input here and there. But I don't think Chuck
specifically knew that this project was under way or
that these people were involved."[19]

So began a series of opaque conversations between
the president and his chief of staff about who, if
anyone, on the White House staff or at the Committee to Re-Elect the President was responsible for
the break-in. The two men were speaking in a by-
now familiar shorthand that did not need to spell
out precise meanings. Still, judged by the standards
of their normal discourse, Haldeman was guarded
and elliptical. The next morning at 9:30, Nixon
pressed Haldeman again about Colson's involvement. "You're convinced, though, that this is a situation where Colson is not involved, aren't you?"

HALDEMAN: Yes. As far as you can be convinced of anything. As far as I can determine, it is.

NIXON: I'm just concerned about. . . . I just want to be sure what the facts are.

"Well, I think that is a fact," Haldeman responded. But then he began using fudge words. "The problem is that there are all kinds of other involvements, and if they start a fishing thing on this they're going to start picking up tracks. That's what appeals to me about trying to get one jump ahead of them and hopefully cut the whole thing off and sink all of it."[20]

The "they" he was referring to were both the FBI, brought in by the local cops to investigate the break-in, and the Democratic National Committee, which had immediately filed a civil law suit alleging a White House and Republican plot to violate their civil liberties. Haldeman would later write and say that he was thinking of political "containment," not breaking the law.[21] At the time, none of the president's men were using terms like "obstruction of justice" or "suborning perjury" (coaching witnesses to lie) or even "cover up." Although several of Nixon's top men, including Ehrlichman and Mitchell, were lawyers, their command of criminal law was shaky at best. Eager to please his masters, White House counsel John Dean later claimed that he warned of criminal wrongdoing but was brushed off by Ehrlichman.[22] Leaving the inexperienced

Dean to handle the investigation was a fatal blunder; he quickly incriminated himself in a cover-up
in a way that no careful criminal lawyer would ever
countenance. Viewed with perfect hindsight, Dean
looks like a poor choice to defend the office of the
president. But at the time of the break-in and for
many months thereafter, Nixon and his top aides
regarded the White House counsel as a bright young
man commendable for his willingness to step in
and step up. In the experience of all these men,
campaign dirty tricks were a time-honored cliché of
politics, the norm, on both sides. After the election,
campaign shenanigans were expected to be swept
under the rug, as it were, with no more than a wink
and a nod.

Ehrlichman, Haldeman, and Mitchell had met in
Ehrlichman's office early on the morning of June 20
to discuss what to do. Dean, sitting in on the meeting, was struck by their mutual wariness.[23] The
meeting was clearly not meant to get to the bottom
of things. Ehrlichman and Mitchell disliked each
other, and both men had something to hide. Ehrlichman had signed off on the Plumbers' "covert operation" to break into Ellsberg's psychiatrist's office.
He had already told Dean to "deep six" the contents
of Hunt's safe at the White House.[24] Mitchell had
presided over two meetings at which Liddy outlined
the appalling "Gemstone" plans to bug, blackmail,
and kidnap. He may not have given a clear green
light to Liddy, but he did not fire him either.

Everyone—Mitchell, Haldeman, and, for that matter, possibly the president himself—knew that
Magruder had been given a large budget for intelligence gathering. Liddy had done **something** with
the money. Mitchell knew that the president risked
exposure for what he later called "the White House
horrors," the various intrigues of Liddy and Hunt,
as well as wiretapping and campaign donations of
dubious legality.[25]

Haldeman was also at risk—at this stage, probably more of embarrassment than of going to jail. As
the president's all-controlling chief of staff, he was
supposed to be on top of the projects and plans flow-
ing from Nixon's commands. Nixon wanted campaign intelligence and "dirty tricks"; Haldeman was
expected to provide them. How much Haldeman
actually knew remains uncertain, even to this day.
Dean later noted that Haldeman, for all his vaunted
"tickler system" to ensure compliance with presidential orders, was spread thin as well as wide.[26] He
could not know everything. Possibly, he did not
wish to. Haldeman had instructed his aide Gordon
Strachan to act as "liaison" to Jeb Magruder, the
number two at CRP, hand-picked by Haldeman for
the job. Did Strachan report back everything that
Magruder was doing at CRP—including sending
out Liddy and Hunt to break in to the DNC? Right
after the break-in, Strachan cleaned out his files.
Later testimony about who knew what and when
was conflicting but suggests that Strachan, and hence

Haldeman, did not know about the break-in before the fact.[27]*

Nixon's diary shows that he was remarkably unconcerned after his first full day of dealing with Watergate. At 11:30 on the night of June 20, he closed his diary entry with the note, "I feel better today than I have really for months—relaxed yet able to do more work than even we usually do with far more enthusiasm." Watergate at this stage was "an annoying problem," he wrote in his memoir, "but it was still a minor one among many."[30] Dealing with the Russians, the Chinese, the North Vietnamese, and Henry Kissinger was far more consuming.

The next day, June 21, Haldeman came to Nixon with a plan: Liddy would take the rap. "Liddy?" asked Nixon. "Who's he? He's the guy with the detective agency?" Nixon asked, confusing Liddy with

*Remarkably, the Watergate break-in remains something of a mystery. Various conspiracy theories have described every motive and responsibility from a "silent coup" by the military dissatisfied with Nixon, to a CIA plot to undermine the president, to an attempt by CRP to learn more about a call-girl ring. Though there are some interesting clues to support these theories, the best guess of who ordered the break-in and why is more prosaic.[28] Feeling pressure from Haldeman, Colson, and Mitchell to dig up dirt on the Democrats, especially Nixon's bête noire Lawrence O'Brien, Magruder unleashed Liddy and Hunt. (To counter the Democrats' charges of corruption in the ITT case, the burglars seemed to be looking for evidence of sweetheart deals at the Democratic Convention in Miami.) Nixon almost surely did not know of the break-in before the fact.[29]

McCord. "No, Liddy is the general counsel for the Re-Election Finance Committee, and he is the guy who did this," said Haldeman.

"Oooh," the president groaned softly. Though Liddy's job as counsel to the Re-Election Finance Committee was largely a cover, it seemed to remind Nixon that Liddy ultimately reported to John Mitchell, who was the chairman of the Committee for the Re-Election of the President. This apparently prompted Nixon's mind to wander into dangerous territory: Had Mitchell known about the break-in before the arrests?

"Mitchell?" said Haldeman, guardedly. "I'm not sure how much—he obviously knew something. I'm not sure how much. He clearly didn't know any details." Nixon agreed, or wanted to.

Yet Nixon would come back to Mitchell again and again, probing warily, speculating gingerly, changing his mind back and forth. Haldeman and Ehrlichman wanted to hang the break-in on Liddy. "Apparently, he is a little bit nuts," Haldeman told Nixon. "He sort of likes the dramatic. He's said, 'If you want to put me before a firing squad and shoot me, that's fine. I'd like to be like Nathan Hale.'" But Nixon was worried that the investigators' path would lead through Liddy to Mitchell. "If it involved Mitchell, then I would think that you couldn't do it, just because it would destroy him," said Nixon. Haldeman responded, "Well, that's what bothers Ehrlichman. He's not sure it doesn't."

NIXON: Doesn't involve Mitchell?

HALDEMAN: Yes. I put it almost directly to Mitchell this morning, and he didn't answer, so I don't know whether it does or not.

NIXON: Probably did, but don't tell me about it. But you go ahead. If Liddy takes the rap on this, that's fine.[31]

Nixon continued to wonder about Mitchell's involvement. But he never asked Mitchell directly. He told Haldeman that he had called Mitchell the night before—not to find out what had really happened behind the scenes but to buck up an old friend. "I gave Mitchell a call," Nixon told Haldeman. "Cheered him up a little bit. I told him not to worry. He's obviously quite chagrined."[32]

Mitchell was worn out, eager to quit and get back to his New York law practice. At lunch with Nixon at the White House a few days later, his hands shook so much that he had trouble holding his soup spoon.[33] Martha was acting up again. In a drunken rage, she had loudly declared that her husband had ordered the bugging of every Democrat in Washington and threatened to call a reporter. A doctor had to subdue her with a shot in her rear end, Haldeman reported in his diary. Mitchell was afraid his wife was suicidal and would throw herself off a balcony at the Watergate, where, coincidentally, the Mitchells lived.[34]

Nixon could not bear to raise awkward issues with the depressed Mitchell. In his memoirs, the president explained:

I never personally confronted Mitchell with the direct question of whether he had been involved in or had known about the planning of the Watergate break-in. He was one of my closest friends, and he had issued a public denial. I would never challenge what he had said; I felt that if there was something he thought I should know, he would have told me. And I suppose there was something else, too, something I expressed rhetorically months later: "Suppose you call Mitchell . . . and Mitchell says, 'Yes, I did it,'" I said to Haldeman. "Then what do we say?"[35]

In his post-presidential interview with David Frost, Nixon was colorfully emphatic about the high cost of Mitchell's distraction in the months leading up to Watergate:

If it hadn't been for Martha, there'd have been no Watergate. Because John wasn't mindin' that store. He was practically **out of his mind** about Martha in the spring of 1972! He was letting Magruder and all these boys, these **kids**, these **nuts** run this thing! The point of the matter is that if John had been watchin' that store, Watergate would have never happened.[36]

Nixon's explanation to Frost was self-serving. It deflected blame away from where it belonged—at Richard Nixon's doorstep. It was Nixon who created the toxic environment in which his lieutenants felt pressure to spy on the president's perceived enemies. And Nixon was being generous to Mitchell by excusing his malfeasance to weariness and domestic distraction. Nonetheless, Nixon was touching on a central cause of his own downfall. The president could not bring himself to have an honest and direct conversation with his former attorney general, and tragically, Mitchell could not, or did not, see fit to bring his troubles into the Oval Office. Mitchell was one of the few men—perhaps the only man—who could proverbially tell truth to power in the administration of Richard Nixon. Had he not been depressed and increasingly withdrawn, he might have cut off Liddy and Hunt before they began buying burglars' tools, and he might have warned Nixon to not overindulge his hunger for campaign intelligence. Nixon's sympathy for his friend Mitchell— his sensitivity to Mitchell's troubled marriage—was tender. But it is also true that in the summer of 1972, Nixon's deep-seated dislike of personal confrontation served him very poorly.

J. Edgar Hoover had died on May 2. Nixon had tried to fire Hoover six months earlier but characteristically shied away in a face-to-face meeting. With Hoover finally gone, Nixon set about finding his own man to take over as FBI director. "I want one that's our boy," he instructed.[37] He settled—on an "acting" basis—on a Justice Department official and former navy submarine commander named L. Patrick Gray III. Gray was a hard-line Nixon loyalist, but he was regarded by the hidebound FBI as an interloper.[38]

On the morning of June 23, Haldeman reported to Nixon that "we're back to the problem area" on the Watergate investigation. "The FBI is not under control, because Gray doesn't exactly know how to control them, and . . . their investigation is now leading in some productive areas." The Bureau had been able to trace the hundred-dollar bills found on the burglars. The money trail would lead straight to some Nixon campaign donors who did not wish to be identified because some of them were Democrats hedging their bets. The donors were being sucked into the case because Liddy, in his double role as counsel to the Republican Finance Committee, had carelessly used the cash from their donations to finance the burglary. Nixon's advisers came up with the idea of enlisting the CIA to head off the FBI's investigation into the account of one of the burglars, Bernard Barker.

Haldeman made their recommendation to the president: "The only way to solve this is for us to have [CIA Deputy Director Vernon] Walters call Pat Gray and just say, 'Stay the hell out of this . . . we don't want you to go any further on it.'" After some back and forth, Nixon approved. "All right, fine," he said.[39]

The recording of this exchange in the Oval Office was to become known as "the smoking gun tape." When it was finally turned over to prosecutors during the feverish impeachment summer of 1974, it was immediately seized on as proof that the president had obstructed justice by trying to use the CIA to cut off the FBI investigation. Nixon was forced to resign shortly thereafter.

In fact, like so much in Watergate, the "smoking gun" is subject to different interpretations. Some Watergate scholars now argue, as John Dean later wrote in his 2014 book, **The Nixon Defense**, that "the smoking gun was only firing blanks."[40] It is clear from the context surrounding the conversation that Haldeman, supposedly at the instigation of Mitchell and Dean, was trying to head off some awkward questions for some fat cat contributors who wanted to stay in the shadows. There was no crime involved in these donations; they were perfectly legal. (One of the donors was Dwayne Andreas, a close friend and financial backer of Hubert Humphrey; others were Texas oilmen who had supported LBJ.) It is at least possible that Haldeman and the others were not trying to shut down the entire Watergate investigation (with FBI agents in the field it was already too late for that) but trying only to protect the identity of the donors. Nonetheless, as was often the case, Nixon's language became hyperbolic and suggests that whatever others may have intended, Nixon meant to shut down the whole investigation. As he delved into old conspiracies, the president fixed on CIA operative E. Howard Hunt. Talking to Haldeman on the morning of June 23, Nixon seized on one of his pet theories—that the CIA had covered up for some shady activity, including plots to kill Castro, after the failed Bay of Pigs invasion of Cuba during the early days of the Kennedy administration. An implicit threat to expose these secrets might work to pressure CIA Director Richard Helms into going along with the White House request to turn off the FBI as it followed the money trail. The key was Hunt. Nixon grabbed on to the fact that Hunt had been deeply involved with the Bay of Pigs; indeed, some of the Cubans hired by the Plumbers had worked for Hunt on the failed CIA-backed invasion.

"Of course, this is Hunt. That'll uncover a lot of [undecipherable]," said Nixon. Then he employed his familiar crude metaphor: "You open that scab, there's a hell of a lot of things. . . . It would be very detrimental to have this thing go any further. This involves these Cubans, Hunt, and a lot of hanky-panky that we have nothing to do with ourselves."

Nixon might have stopped there, but, wound up by his old animus toward the CIA, he went on to use language suggesting that he wanted the CIA to shut down the entire FBI investigation into Watergate—not just the inquiry into the hundred-dollar bills that could be traced to the anonymous donors. As the secret Oval Office tapes silently turned on the morning of June 23, Nixon coached Haldeman on what to say to Helms and Deputy Director Walters:

When you get these people in, say: "Look, the problem is that this will open the whole Bay of

Pigs thing, and the President feels that"—without going into the details—don't lie to them to the extent to say there is no involvement, but just say this is sort of a comedy of errors, bizarre, without getting into it. "The President's belief is that this is going to open the whole Bay of Pigs thing up again. And because these people are plugging for, for keeps, and that they should call the FBI in and say that we wish for the country, don't go any further into this case," period.

Don't go any further into this case, period. Nixon's aides may have had a narrow intention, to keep the FBI from questioning and embarrassing anonymous campaign donors. But Nixon's restless mind wandered off and focused on Hunt. Nixon seems to have thought they were getting the CIA to warn the FBI off of **anything** involving Hunt—including the break-in itself. By using cryptic euphemisms, Haldeman and Nixon talked past each other. In his 1978 memoir, Nixon wrote that when Haldeman reported back to say that Helms "got the picture," Nixon was relieved because "this was the end of our worries about Watergate"—presumably meaning the entire case, not just the inquiry into the donors. A couple of days after that, Nixon was "surprised" to learn that the FBI was still going after Hunt. "I had thought they were going to keep away from him as a result of Haldeman's meeting with Helms and Walters," Nixon wrote. In other words, his aides may have thought they were simply protecting the donors, but Nixon apparently thought he was shutting down the whole investigation. Such misunderstandings were typical of Nixon's handling of Watergate: He wanted to stay out of it but couldn't resist meddling, in ways that were often ambiguous, confusing, and ultimately incriminating.

At the time, Nixon told Haldeman, "I'm not going to get that involved." Haldeman responded, "No, sir. We don't want you to." But then Nixon added, "Play it tough. That's the way they play it, and that's the way we're going to play it."[41]

After an initial stir, the press—with the notable exception of **The Washington Post** and **Time** magazine—lost interest in what White House spokesman Ron Ziegler dismissed as a "third rate burglary." The public seemed unmoved by "the Watergate caper," as Haldeman somewhat jauntily referred to it. Nixon remained far ahead of George McGovern in the polls.

And yet, cracks in the cover-up began showing almost right away. The CIA went along with the White House request—but not for long. Director Helms, who held no brief for the president, was irritated by the very mention of the Bay of Pigs. His deputy, Vernon Walters, was an old Nixon loyalist who had been installed at the CIA as a quasi-spy by the president (as a military translator, Walters had been with Nixon during the Caracas stoning in

1958). But Walters was also a man of considerable integrity, and he soon told Pat Gray at the FBI that the CIA had no interest in the FBI's investigation. The Bureau was free to follow the money wherever it led.[42]

Nixon was trying to relax in San Clemente on July 6 when Gray telephoned him, sounding anxious. The acting FBI director had called to say that he was "greatly concerned about the Watergate case and that Walters had come in to see him indicating that the CIA had no interest in the matter and that pursuing the investigation would not be an embarrassment to the CIA," Nixon wrote in his diary that night. "He said that he and Walters both felt that some people either at the White House or at the committee were trying to cover up things which would be a mortal blow to me—rather than assisting the investigation."[43]

There was a slight pause, Pat Gray later recalled, then Nixon replied, "Pat, you just continue to conduct your aggressive and thorough investigation."[44]

Nixon, as he never ceased to remind his aides, had been an expert on cover-ups ever since the Alger Hiss case. On July 19, he gave John Ehrlichman a short homily in the dos and don'ts of handling a sensitive investigation. Ehrlichman had come to talk to him about, among other matters, Jeb Magruder, who faced an FBI interview the next day for his role in the break-in. Nixon bluntly asked Ehrlichman to tell him about Magruder's involvement. The conversation is revealing of Nixon's almost schizophrenic approach to Watergate:

NIXON: Did he know?

EHRLICHMAN: Oh, yes. Oh Lord, yes. He's in it with both feet.

NIXON: He can't contrive a story, then. You know, I'd like to see this thing work out, but I've been through these. The worst thing a guy can do, the worst thing—there are two things and each is bad. One is to lie and the other one is to cover up.

EHRLICHMAN: Yes.

NIXON: If you cover up, you're going to get caught.

EHRLICHMAN: Yes.

NIXON: And if you lie you're going to be guilty of perjury. Now, basically, that was the whole story of the Hiss case.

EHRLICHMAN: Yes.

NIXON: It was the story of the five-percenters [officials taking graft in the Truman administration] and the rest. It's a hell of a goddamn thing. I hate to see it, but let me say we'll take care of Magruder immediately afterwards. . . . [45]

Having emphatically laid out the high road, Nixon proceeded to veer off it.[46] Not only did he promise to "take care" of Magruder—thus subtly sending a signal that Magruder would ultimately be rewarded—the president soon became involved, as a kind of too-interested bystander. Nixon could have stayed out of the Magruder case entirely. Or he could have inserted himself to make sure that Magruder told the truth. Instead, he hovered around the case, asking just enough questions to raise suspicions about his own involvement in the cover-up.

There was the awkward question of how Liddy had gotten the money to conduct his antics— where else, logically, but from his boss, Magruder, with the ultimate sign-off of **his** boss, Mitchell? In coaching Magruder's testimony, the goal of Nixon's advisers—endorsed by Nixon—was to keep the criminal responsibility "at the Liddy level," as Nixon put it, and no higher.[47] Magruder did not know all the particulars, but he knew enough to go to jail if caught. He would have to dissemble and say that he knew nothing about the break-in.[48] As he persistently inquired into what Magruder might tell the FBI and the grand jury, Nixon was probably thinking, as he put it, in terms of political "containment," not perjury or obstruction of justice. Still, in his memoirs he acknowledged, albeit circumspectly, that he had been determined to protect Mitchell—even if that meant, implicitly, that Magruder had to hide or fuzz up the truth in his testimony. "Whatever the actual case, I told Haldeman, Magruder simply had to draw the line on anything that might involve Mitchell," wrote Nixon.[49] **Whatever the** actual case.* Nixon worried with Ehrlichman that the "callow" Magruder would break under tough questioning. "There's just too much riding on this thing, you cannot put John Mitchell in this thing," Nixon told his subordinates.[50]

The next day, talking to Haldeman, Nixon said that he had experienced a troubling premonition about Watergate. "I had a strange [dream?] last night. It's going to be a nasty issue for a few days. But I can't believe that—we're whistling in the dark, but I can't believe they can tie the thing [to me]."[51]

---

*Again, it remains unclear how much Mitchell knew—he may have signed off on money for Liddy without knowing exactly what he intended to do with it. In any case, Nixon never asked Mitchell directly. Instead, he sanctioned a cover-up. Nixon was not just protecting Mitchell, of course. If Mitchell was guilty of a crime, and Nixon found out, Nixon knew that he would have to report his friend—or risk committing an impeachable offense.

Landslide, 1972.

**Courtesy of the Richard Nixon Presidential
Library and Museum**

CHAPTER 23

"An Exciting Prospect"

In mid-July, Nixon invited John Connally to San Clemente to watch the last night of the Democratic National Convention on TV. After squabbling with the White House staff, Connally had quit as secretary of the Treasury that spring, but Nixon still saw "Big Jawn" as his successor in 1976, possibly to build a whole new political party around the Silent Majority.[1] After dinner on the night of July 12, Nixon and Connally settled into the Casa Pacifica living room overlooking the darkening ocean and tuned in to the raucous scene at the convention hall in Miami, where the Democratic nominees were scheduled to give their acceptance speeches. Nixon and Connally wanted to see how George McGovern would look on a national stage.

Incredulous, they waited hour after hour while Senator Tom Eagleton of Missouri and then thirty-nine other vice-presidential candidates were nominated, including Mao Tse-tung and Martha Mitchell. To get away from rule by party bosses and "the smoke-filled room," the Democrats had overcorrected. Every hitherto "underrepresented" group was allowed to have its moment. "The scene had the air of a college skit that had gotten carried away with itself and didn't know how to stop," Nixon recalled. Finally, Connally gave up and went to bed. Nixon and Pat held on until, at 2:48 A.M., "prime time in Guam," Senator McGovern at last appeared. Tricia also stayed up to watch. The president's steely daughter tartly remarked of the Democratic presidential nominee, "He's a boring evangelist, and there's nothing more boring than an evangelist who's boring."[2]

On July 25, Haldeman handed the president a wire service bulletin that McGovern and Eagleton had just held a joint press conference to disclose that the Democrats' vice-presidential nominee had been hospitalized three times and had received electro-shock therapy for mental depression. Columnist Jack Anderson piled on with an untrue report that Eagleton had been arrested several times for drunken and reckless driving.

Nixon was thinking of his ordeal in the 1952 Fund Scandal as he watched Eagleton appear on **Face the Nation** a week later, on Sunday, July 30. One of the reporters remarked on how much Eagleton was sweating, to which Eagleton pointed out that the lights were very hot. The reporter observed that no one else on the TV set was sweating and commented that Eagleton was fidgeting with his fingers.

Nixon was appalled and filled with empathy for Eagleton. "I perspire even though I may not be under any tension whatever!" he dictated into his diary that night. Inevitably, within a couple of days, Eagleton was forced off the ticket, replaced by a Kennedy, Sargent Shriver, who was married to JFK and RFK's sister Eunice. The next day, thinking once more of his own and his family's suffering in 1952 and again in 1960 and '62, Nixon pulled out a pen and wrote a letter. It was addressed to Eagleton's young son, Terry, who had visited the Oval Office with his father the year before. "Politics is a very hard game," Nixon wrote the thirteen-year-old boy. After quoting Churchill ("Politics is even more difficult than war because in politics you die many times; in war you die only once"), Nixon wrote, feelingly, "What matters is not that your father fought a terribly difficult battle and lost. What matters is that in fighting the battle he won the admiration of foes and friends alike because of the courage, poise, and just plain guts he showed against overwhelming odds."[3]*

Then Nixon returned to trying to savage his opponents. The next day, August 3, he hounded Haldeman and Ehrlichman to run an IRS audit on Larry O'Brien. O'Brien's firm had taken a $190,000 retainer from secretive financier Howard Hughes;

*When he came home from summer camp, Terry Eagleton wrote back, "Do you know what my Dad said when he read your letter? 'It's going to make it all the tougher to talk against Nixon.' I think both Dad and you are excellent politicians. Even though you and Dad don't always agree, I think the country is lucky to have both of you. My favorite subject in school is history. I now feel I am part of history since you wrote a letter to me."

Nixon was still seething over press reports from a decade earlier that Hughes had given a sweetheart loan to his own brother Don ("that stupid brother," Nixon called him; Nixon had ordered Don wiretapped "for his own protection").[4] Now he wanted to expose that DNC chairman O'Brien—"a grand master in the art of political gamesmanship"—was somehow on the take from Hughes.[5]

"The problem we have here is that all of our people are gun-shy as a result of the Watergate incident and don't want to look into files that involve Democrats," Nixon dictated to his diary that night. In the Oval Office earlier that day, Nixon had angrily denounced foot-dragging. "We have all this power and we aren't using it," he exploded. "Now, what the Christ is the matter?" Haldeman wearily protested, "We don't have the bureaucracy with us and we don't have the press with us. They do." Nixon was not satisfied. The Democrats were down, and he wanted them out. "I mean, it's like Dempsey going for the kill with Firpo," he said, referencing the 1923 heavyweight boxing championship. "I mean you have to . . . keep whacking, whacking, and whacking." Finally, Ehrlichman offered up, "Well, we've got a file a foot thick on [McGovern Finance Chairman] Henry Kimelman, and this is over in the Department of the Interior, where we have fewer problems. I do have some work going on that."

NIXON: Scare the shit out of them. Scare the shit out of them.[6]

. . .

At the end of August, Haldeman came into the Oval Office looking morose. "Bad news," he said glumly. "I really mean it—it's really bad." He handed Nixon the latest Gallup poll. It showed Nixon ahead of McGovern by 34 points, the largest spread between presidential candidates since Gallup started polling in the 1930s. Haldeman was grinning when Nixon looked up.

Nixon wanted to feel happy about everything he had seen and experienced on his royal progress to an historic landslide reelection: Youth for Nixon roaring "Four More Years! For More Years!" at his clockwork convention. The jumpers and squealers in Michigan and San Diego as his motorcade passed by (just like the Kennedys, "although it will, as usual, be difficult to get the press to write about it," he recorded in his diary). The puzzled look of the face of peaceniks when Nixon flashed them the "V" sign ("this really knocks them for a loop, because they think it is their sign," Nixon gloated). Even organized labor was abandoning McGovern, skillfully framed by the Nixon campaign as the candidate for "amnesty [for draft dodgers], abortion, and acid." After a round of golf followed by cigars at the all-male Burning Tree Club, AFL-CIO President George Meany gruffly told Nixon, "Just so you don't get a swelled head about my wife voting for you, I want to tell you why—she don't like McGovern."

So much to celebrate, but he would later recall that he felt oddly dissatisfied: "Against Kennedy or

Muskie or Humphrey I would have had to fight a close-in, one-on-one battle. Against McGovern, however, it was clear that the less I did, the better I would do. This was a totally unaccustomed situation for me, and it was not one in which I felt particularly comfortable or even knew instinctively what was best to do."[7]*

In late August, Leonard Garment, with little to do at the Republican Convention in Miami, lay in the sun on the deck at the Doral Hotel. "One afternoon at the pool," he later recalled,

> I noticed a sizeable group of administration stalwarts huddled together at the outdoor bar. The shifting assemblage included, as I recall, Gordon Strachan, Bob Mardian, Fred LaRue, John Dean, Jeb Magruder, and Dwight Chapin, joined from time to time by Commander-in-Chief Charles Colson, dressed in a polyester sport shirt, faded Bermuda shorts, street shoes, and short black socks. They were whispering worriedly, chain-smoking, chain-drinking, and obviously not having any convention fun. With Nixon sure to win, what were they so worried about?[9]

*Billy Graham advised Nixon to "ignore McGovern. . . . The McGovern people are going to defeat themselves." He told Nixon that he had asked LBJ about "the Watergate bugging business." Johnson, who may have done worse in his time, had just laughed and said, "Hell, that's not going to hurt him a bit."[8]

. . .

A week earlier, on August 17, Magruder and LaRue had gotten together for a more intimate drinking session at a famous Washington saloon. LaRue was the CRP official who handled the payments to the Watergate burglars (for lawyers fees and living expenses; the term "hush money" was not yet used).[10] Magruder had just learned that he would not be indicted. He had successfully misled the grand jury and persuaded the prosecutors that he—and, by extension, his boss John Mitchell—had not known about the Watergate break-in. "That night," Magruder recalled,

> Fred LaRue and I celebrated with dinner at Billy Martin's Carriage House Restaurant in Georgetown. We laughed and joked and unwound, celebrating this apparent victory after two months of intense pressure. But there were times during our celebration when we lapsed into silence, when we found our depression returning, when we grimly asked each other if we could possibly get away with this incredible cover-up. . . . [11]

On September 15, the indictments handed down by a federal grand jury named only Hunt and Liddy and the five men arrested at the Watergate. Nixon shrugged in his diary: "This was the day of the Watergate indictment, and we hope to be able to ride the issue through in a successful way from now on."[12]

Late in the afternoon in the Oval Office, he had met with John Dean to congratulate the White House lawyer on his ability to keep the lid on the investigation. "The way you've handled it, it seems to me, has been very skillful, because you—put your finger in the dike every time leaks have sprung here, sprung there . . . the Grand Jury is dismissed now?" the president asked hopefully. "That is correct," answered Dean. The conversation soon turned to punishing the president's enemies in the second term. "They are asking for it and they are going to get it," said Nixon. "We have not used the power in this first four years, as you know."

DEAN: That's true.

NIXON: We have never used it. We haven't used the Bureau, we haven't used the Justice Department, but things are going to change now. And they're going to change, and they're going to get it right.

DEAN: That's an exciting prospect.

NIXON: It's got to be done. It's the only thing to do.

HALDEMAN: We've got to.[13]

The enemy Nixon most wanted to get was, more than ever, **The Washington Post**. The war between Nixon and the **Post** was escalating, on both sides. Back in June, Kissinger, playing the role of meddlesome double agent, told Nixon that Katharine Graham had said of the president: "I hate him and I'm going to do everything I can to beat him."[14] In his mounting vexation with the **Post**, Nixon had gone from petty punishment—ordering that Mrs. Graham be seated as far away as possible from the guest of honor at a White House dinner—to trying to wreck her business. On September 14, he discussed with Colson ways to cancel the broadcasting licenses of TV stations owned by the Washington Post Company.[15]

While the rest of the press had largely backed off Watergate, the **Post** continued to hammer away with daily page one stories. On September 28, Carl Bernstein of the reporting duo of Woodward and Bernstein awakened John Mitchell to get his comment on a story running the next day: that Mitchell controlled a secret fund of $350,000 to $700,000 to gather information about the Democrats. "Jeeeeesus!" Mitchell gasped. "Katie Graham's gonna get her tit caught in a big fat wringer if that's published." The story was exaggerated, but the **Post** was on a roll, fed by a mysterious source known in the newsroom, and later to history, as "Deep Throat."[16]

Deep Throat was in real life Mark Felt, the deputy director of the FBI.* His motive was not so much to save the Republic from Richard Nixon as it was to secure the top job at the Bureau for Mark Felt. He hoped to accomplish this by leaking so much information that the White House would see that Acting Director L. Patrick Gray was incapable of controlling the Bureau and choose an insider—

---

*Felt's nickname inside the incestuous FBI was "the White Rat" because he had white hair and was known to leak to reporters.[17]

the number two man—instead. Felt's strategy failed. The White House discovered that Felt was the leaker and held off from firing him only because, as Haldeman pointed out, he knew too much.[18]

Meeting Woodward in a garage late at night after a series of prearranged signals, "Deep Throat" told the **Post** reporter much that was true about the FBI's investigation into Watergate, but on a couple of occasions he hinted at more than he knew. On October 12, the **Post** ran with a larger-than-usual headline, "FBI Finds Nixon Aides Sabotaged Democrats." The article revealed a "massive campaign of political spying and sabotage" and claimed that the FBI had uncovered "at least 50 undercover Nixon operatives." The report was hyped, but the **Post** did surface the Nixonites' answer to Dick Tuck: Donald Segretti, a USC pal of Dwight Chapin who conducted "black advance operations." Some of them were silly, like sending pizza, collect, to a Muskie fundraiser, but some were sordid, like distributing a flyer on Muskie stationery accusing his opponents Hubert Humphrey and Henry "Scoop" Jackson of illicit sexual activity.[19] Like other White House dirty tricksters, Segretti was not so much wicked as in over his head. Indeed, Chapin had recommended Segretti partly because he figured that his college chum, a recent USC Law grad, would know how far to go without breaking the law.[20]

In his diary, Nixon dismissed **The Washington Post** article as "the last burp of the Eastern Establishment," but in a later diary entry, he noted something unusual and, to him, disturbing. A **Post** story on October 25 reported that the CRP treasurer Hugh Sloan had told the grand jury that Haldeman controlled a secret fund for political espionage. The story was inaccurate—Sloan had not so testified, and Haldeman's actual involvement was unclear— but it seemed to jolt the normally imperturbable chief of staff. "Haldeman spoke rather darkly of the fact that there was a clique in the White House that were out to get him. I trust he is not getting a persecution complex," Nixon dictated to his diary.[21]

Here was a role reversal. Haldeman had sometimes fed Nixon's insecurities, but he never expressed anxiety himself. Haldeman's job was to guard Nixon from his enemies and his own worst instincts. If Haldeman was distracted by his own concerns, who was to protect Nixon?

Pat Nixon did not want to add to her husband's burdens. She had strong opinions—primarily that Haldeman and the inner circle were keeping her husband isolated and insulated from the cabinet, from most of his own staff, and from his own wife. "If I were in charge of the campaign it wouldn't be running the way it is being run," she wrote her friend Helene Drown. She saw that her husband had seemed oddly depressed on the night of his acceptance speech at the Republican Convention. But "she tried to avoid bringing up what she referred to as the 'unpleasant subjects,'" recalled Julie in her memoir. The president's daughter did not spell out precisely what those "unpleasant subjects" were, but, generally speaking, Pat's aversion to confrontation was at least as great as Nixon's. As ever, she tried to bear tribulation stoically, silently, and with good, if forced, cheer. It stung when McGovern, flailing, compared her husband to Hitler. Both she and Nixon looked "thin and haggard," Julie wrote David. "I think I made a mistake protecting Daddy too much and in giving in too much," Pat later told Julie, "but I knew he was busy, the war was hanging over us."[22]

Years later, Nixon's personal assistant, Steve Bull, struggled to find the right word to describe the atmosphere in the White House in the early fall of 1972. He uttered the word **poisonous** and immediately retracted it as too harsh, too melodramatic. But something was off-key as the Nixon bandwagon tooted its own horn. Perhaps, Bull later speculated, the never-ending war in Vietnam was to blame. The War President could never stand down. "The feelings of being under siege never wore off," he said. "It had a corrosive effect. We never really relaxed. I never heard Nixon say he was happy or sad. He was so formal."[23]

On the evening of October 12, Kissinger bustled into Nixon's hideaway in the Executive Office Building. As usual, the blinds were drawn—"Nixon liked his working offices to convey the atmosphere of a cocoon," Kissinger recalled—and the president was reclining on his easy chair with his feet up on the settee. Coming straight from his plane from Paris, where he had been negotiating with the North Vietnamese, the national security adviser was exultant.[24] "Well, you've got three out of three, Mr. President. It's well on the way." By "three out of three," Kissinger meant the opening to China, détente with the Soviet Union, and now—after so many painful years—a peace agreement with North Vietnam.

"You got an agreement? Are you kidding?" said Nixon.

"No, I'm not kidding," answered Kissinger.

Nixon began to tease Kissinger, looking over to Al Haig, who was not smiling. "I'm going to ask Al, because you're too prejudiced, Henry. You're so prejudiced to the peace camp that I can't trust you. Don't you think so, Al?"[25] Nixon later wrote that Haig appeared "subdued," but "a better word might have been **despondent**," Haig recalled in his memoirs.[26] Kissinger's assistant had just returned from Saigon. He doubted that Thieu would go along with the deal, which the South Vietnamese president was sure to regard as a sellout.

Back in EOB 175, Kissinger, who thought Nixon was "affecting nonchalance" with his japes to Haig, opened his red folder marked "Eyes Only" and began going over the elements of the deal. The key was a new concession by Hanoi: The North Vietnamese no longer required that Thieu be driven out of office and replaced by a coalition government.

Nixon became "cranked up," Haldeman recorded

in his diary, and began interrupting Kissinger to hold forth on why the North Vietnamese were suddenly backing down: the "Linebacker" bombing and mining of Hanoi and Haiphong in May had convinced the Politburo that Nixon would not give up, and the president's trips to Moscow and Beijing had shaken Hanoi's faith in its allies. (The "usual litany," wrote Haldeman.)

Nixon called for a celebration. He ordered a steak dinner prepared and served in his suite, and broke out his best wine for a toast. Haldeman drily recorded, "The P told Manolo to bring the good wine, his '57 Lafite-Rothschild, or whatever it is, to be served to everyone. Usually, it's just served to the P and the rest have some California Beaulieu Vineyard stuff."[27]

A month before the election, the polls continued to predict a landslide. Nixon looked at the numbers and believed that the nation was on the verge of an epochal shift. The Silent Majority was reasserting control, and Richard Nixon was their tribune. The country, he told Haldeman on October 14, was tired of demonstrators and "permissiveness," tired of the elites telling them what to think and how to live; most voters wanted a return to "basic American values." Nixon instructed that his troops were not to speak of the coming "landslide" but rather of "the New American Majority"—the "N.A.M." Nixon's triumphalism was more than politics; the president wanted to lead a restoration of "moral and spiritual values," as he expansively explained to Haldeman. "Our N.A.M. appeals across the board," said Nixon. "The 'movement' has had it," he said, referring to the leftist "movement" that had seized the campuses and transfixed the media elite. "Square America is coming back. We didn't just gather a bunch of haters. The real issue is patriotism, morality, religion." If just taxes and prices were the issue, he added, the voters would be "for McGovern."[28]

So often a political visionary, Nixon was right again—or almost right. The riotous years known as "the '60s," with their revolutions in individual and group rights and social and sexual mores, were finally ending. His prediction about the political landscape prefigured the so-called Reagan Revolution by almost a decade.

But Nixon's vision was also premature, partly for reasons of his own making. The furious revolt against authority that ran through the mid- and late 1960s, that had rocked the establishment and weakened hierarchies in the church and academe, that had turned children against their parents, was not quite spent. Some changes, like women's liberation and an emboldened press, were permanent. There was one final authority figure waiting to fall in this great national melodrama, though he did not know it.

More immediately, the Vietnam nightmare had not ended, not quite yet. Haig's premonition about Thieu was correct. When Kissinger appeared at the Presidential Palace in Saigon on October 23 to try to persuade Thieu to sign on to the peace deal he had worked out in Paris, the South Vietnamese president rebuffed him. The terms of the agreement did not require the North Vietnamese to withdraw its more than 120,000 soldiers already in South Vietnam. Without American support, Thieu knew that he was doomed. He told Kissinger a story about a man catching a thief in his bedroom. The police arrive, but the thief refuses to leave the house. So, after a while, the police chief holsters his gun and says, "He's not such a bad guy. Why don't you learn to live with him? After a while he may get homesick and go back to his own family." Or, Thieu said, "He might rape your wife."[29] Listening impassively to Kissinger spell out the terms of the deal, Thieu recalled, "I wanted to punch him in the mouth." As it was, Thieu had to turn away from Kissinger to hide his tears.

"This is the greatest failure of my diplomatic career," Kissinger huffed as he stood up to leave. "Why," asked Thieu bitterly, "are you rushing to get the Nobel Prize?"[30]

Nixon was not unsympathetic to Thieu. Possibly, Nixon had a sense of the irony: In 1968, he had wanted the Saigon leader to balk at LBJ's offer of peace talks and a bombing halt. The president cabled Kissinger, "We must have Thieu as a willing partner in making any agreement. It cannot be a shotgun marriage."[31] There were other reasons not to rush. Colson had persuaded Nixon that a deal before the election would look politically expedient.

The constituencies so carefully cultivated by Colson—Catholics, labor, blue-collar ethnics—had heartily approved of Nixon's bombing campaign in the spring. They regarded McGovern as an agent of surrender.[32]

The North Vietnamese could read the polls, and they wanted a deal before the November election. They knew Nixon would win, and they feared that he would have a free hand to bomb away. To push things along, on October 26 Hanoi went public with the terms of the proposed deal and on Radio Hanoi accused Nixon of dragging out the talks to cover up his "scheme of maintaining the Saigon puppet regime for the purpose of the continued war of aggression."[33]

Kissinger tried to grab back the microphone by holding a hastily organized press conference. Surprisingly, given Kissinger's by-now global celebrity, his actual voice had rarely been heard by the public. Although Kissinger constantly stroked and fed reporters "on background," he had never faced the press live before the TV cameras. ("The White House public relations people were convinced that my accent might disturb Middle America.") Now Nixon authorized his national security adviser to try to publicly reassure both Hanoi and Saigon that a deal suitable to all sides was still possible. This was a delicate task, and Kissinger may have been anxious about his maiden performance before the cameras, because his choice of words was unfortunate. He declared, "We believe that peace is at hand." Nixon at

first congratulated Kissinger on his TV press conference performance but soon came to realize that his
chief foreign policy adviser had blundered: Even
Kissinger eventually realized that he had gone too
far. The words "peace is at hand"—"so redolent of
Neville Chamberlain and the effete 1930s cult of
appeasement," as Haig put it—were sure to harden
North Vietnam's resolve and further stiffen Thieu's
spine as well.[34]

Nonetheless, Kissinger was a hero in the press.
"Good-bye Viet Nam" proclaimed the cover of
Newsweek. "How Kissinger Did It" ran the headline of the story. Nixon was "so mad his teeth
clenched" when he learned that Kissinger had tipped
off **The New York Times** to the peace deal. "I suppose now everybody's going to say that Kissinger
won the election," he told Colson.[35] Haig, who liked
to blow on the coals, told Haldeman that Kissinger
was motivated by a desire to get credit.[36]

Haldeman was more philosophical. In his diary
for October 26, he recorded that he predicted to
"the P" that the flap over "peace is at hand" would
"turn out to be the best lucky break of the campaign
because it takes the corruption stuff off the front
pages, totally wipes out any other news."[37]

The "corruption stuff" was not going away. **The
Washington Post** was pushing the Segretti story.
Nixon was not pleased to learn from Haldeman that
Segretti had learned dirty tricks (called "rat fucking"
by campus politicians) at USC, where he had been a

fraternity brother of Gordon Strachan as well as a pal of Dwight Chapin.[38] Chapin and Strachan were on the White House staff. Nixon had wanted to keep Watergate out of the White House. Though the press had mostly yawned over Watergate, on October 27 CBS News gave it fourteen minutes—an eternity on a twenty-three-minute evening news program—and planned to do a second installment. The show consisted mostly of repackaged **Washington Post** stories, but it now had Walter Cronkite's imprimatur. Colson called CBS News executives and bullied them into cutting the second segment in half, but some damage was done.[39] "The P had a strong reaction to CBS's special report on the Watergate last night," Haldeman recorded. "Says, 'That finishes them.' He means he's ready to write CBS off."[40] After the election, Colson called CBS News President Frank Stanton and threatened, "We'll break your network," but by then Colson's own days in the White House were numbered.

As Nixon got ready to depart for the last campaign swing of his life, Tricia came into the Lincoln Sitting Room and said, "I want this week to be a real last hurrah." Nixon's final rally took place in Ontario, California, a few miles from his first rally twenty-six years before. He told the overflow crowd that the country, which had seemed so divided when he was elected president in 1968, was "getting together." The nation may have been more exhausted than united, but Nixon had at least succeeded in muting the anger.

The day before the election, he walked on the beach for two miles and noticed that the peace sign that someone had carved into the red sandstone cliff had been "worn down by weather. It was very dim," he wrote in his diary. "It looked like a man with a frown on his face. This may be an indication that those who have held up this sign have had their comeuppance and they are really ready for some heavy depression."

His November 6 diary entry concluded "on a rather subdued and analytical note," he wrote in his memoir. "We are not going to lose," he wrote. He thanked God in a Quakerish way ("I must say that someone must have been walking with us") and took pride in his accomplishments over the previous year. "The Peking trip, the Moscow trip, the May 8 decision [to mine Haiphong Harbor], and then the way we have handled the campaign—must deserve some grudging respect even from our critics. The only sour note of the whole thing, of course, is Watergate and Segretti. This was really stupidity on the part of a number of people."[41]

CHAPTER 24

Peace at Last

For Nixon, the night of November 7, 1972, should have been the greatest in his life. He won reelection to the presidency by one of the greatest landslides in history, 47,169,841 votes to Senator McGovern's 29,172,767. Nixon swept every state but Massachusetts and the District of Columbia. He was the first Republican to win the Catholic vote, and he had done surprisingly well with labor and youth. He had even won 35 percent of Democrats.

The stock market was up, inflation was down, and the world, thanks in no small part to the efforts of President Nixon, seemed to be a more peaceful place.

But Nixon was not at peace. In his memoir, he would later write, "I am at a loss to explain the melancholy that settled over me that victorious night. . . ."[1]

Election Day had started well enough. On a gray, misty morning, Nixon voted in San Clemente, California, near the Western White House. No one on Nixon's staff was surprised when the president

With Bebe Rebozo.
**Courtesy of the Richard Nixon Presidential
Library and Museum**

dropped his ballot on the floor, though press secretary Ron Ziegler called out, "Stop it! Stop it! No
pictures!" to press photographers.[2] That afternoon,
flying east aboard Air Force One, Theodore White,
the veteran campaign chronicler, was "struck" by the
president's "somber, almost emotionless mood," but
he wrote it off to "weariness."[3] Following dinner,
Nixon retired from his family to go to the Lincoln
Sitting Room to listen to **Victory at Sea** on the record player, with the volume turned up. "We in the
family all seemed to be in different rooms in the
second and third floors of the White House during
most of election night," his daughter Julie recalled.
This was normal; Nixon was following his usual
election night practice of secluding himself.[4]

An hour after dinner, a cap on one of the president's front teeth fell off, requiring emergency den-
tal work. It hurt very much, and Nixon knew that if
he smiled too widely the temporary cap might fall
off, so he was a little subdued when he later appeared
before the cameras to declare victory around midnight.[5] Retiring to his hideaway in the Executive
Office Building, he reclined in his easy chair and
began badgering Haldeman for more precise vote
totals. Haldeman was used to this. Still, recalled
Larry Higby, Haldeman's aide, "It was sort of grim
that evening. We couldn't get results and he got frustrated. He kept calling and calling. 'What are we
hearing?' We thought he'd be walking around saying, 'We did it! Great job!' People were saying,
'What's going on?' It was just weird."[6]

Summoned to Nixon's hideaway after 1 A.M., Chuck Colson watched while Nixon composed a telegram accepting McGovern's concession. Usually, Nixon was gracious with his defeated foes; he could empathize. But this time the words would not come. Speechwriters kept trying. "No, I won't say that," Nixon grumbled, flinging the sheet of paper across the little table between Colson and Haldeman.[7] As dawn approached, the president kept on muttering about the poor returns in congressional races.

A few days later, Nixon tried to rationalize what he described in his memoirs as "a curious feeling, perhaps a foreboding, that muted my enjoyment of this triumphal moment. . . ." In his diary he wrote:

> I had determined before the election evening to make it as memorable a one as possible for everyone concerned. The tooth episode probably interfered to a considerable extent. Certainly by the time I had to prepare for the office telecast I was not as upbeat as I should have been.
>
> The rest of the family seemed to think they got enough of a thrill out of it. I think the very fact that the victory was so overwhelming made up for any failure on my part to react more enthusiastically than I did.[8]

On the morning after the historic landslide, the senior staff of the White House was instructed to assemble in the Roosevelt Room. Many shuffled in looking sleepy-eyed and hungover.[9] Kissinger had joined the victory celebration at the Shoreham Hotel the evening before, but in his memoirs he recorded, in his slightly formal manner, that the "festivities seemed . . . to lack the boisterous spontaneity that usually marked such events." Now, as the national security adviser watched Nixon enter the room through the door from the Oval Office at precisely 11 A.M., the president seemed "not at all elated," wrote Kissinger. "Rather he was grim and remote as if the more fateful period of his life still lay ahead."

Nixon's election night melancholia had not worn off. The president seemed "perfunctory" as he thanked his staff, Kissinger observed. Looking worn, sounding vexed, Nixon launched off on one of his riffs from the biography of Disraeli about "exhausted volcanoes," by which he apparently meant his staff and the cabinet.[10]

Herb Klein, Nixon's communications director, was struck by Nixon's dour mood. He knew that the cap on the president's front tooth had fallen off the night before as he was preparing for his TV victory speech. "Momentarily, I thought that was the problem," Klein recalled. But then he realized that Nixon's discomfort reached deeper.[11] Abruptly ending his own remarks, Nixon turned the meeting over to his chief of staff and walked out of the room. With his brush cut, faded tan, and cold eyes, Haldeman glowered at the by-now awakened assemblage. "I stood up and, in chilling tones that actor Robert

Vaughn* might envy, told the numb-struck staff members that each and every one of them must have his resignation on my desk by nightfall. Period," Haldeman recalled saying.[12]

Peter Flanigan, a longtime Nixon loyalist and presidential assistant, was dumbfounded by the abruptness. By custom, White House staffers submitted resignations at the end of the first term. But Nixon's somewhat opaque historical allusions (something about "embers which once shot sparks into the sky"), followed by Haldeman's terse diktat, were worse then demoralizing. "It was demeaning," Flanigan recalled. "Nixon wouldn't have done that at an earlier stage of his career. I didn't think he was a prideful man. I guess he had come to think that he was invincible," Flanigan said, struggling, many years later, to explain to the author how a man so politically shrewd could have become so callous and aloof at precisely the moment he needed goodwill and allies to govern with a Democratic-controlled Congress. Searching for a meaningful saying, Flanigan adapted a famous quotation from Euripides ("Those whom the gods would destroy they first make mad"). "Whom the gods wish to destroy," said Flanigan, "they first make proud."[13] In his memoirs, Nixon would regret calling for the resignations of the entire White House staff and cabinet. "I see this now as a mistake. I did not take into

---

*Robert Vaughn played the master spy Napoleon Solo on **The Man from U.N.C.L.E.**, a popular TV show of the 1960s.

account the chilling effect this action would have on . . . morale."[14]

Nixon flew to Key Biscayne that evening for a brief rest, returned to Washington for only a day, and retreated to Camp David. He stayed there for the rest of the month. Staffers waited to be summoned to the mountaintop to learn their fates (the helicopter ride became known as the "Mount Sinai Shuttle").[15] With Haldeman and Ehrlichman furiously making notes, Nixon began with a memorable rant—"Clean the bastards out!" "He's got to go!"—and then spent days going back and forth rearranging the boxes and names on the organization chart.[16] He was going to remake the government top to bottom, and he was determined to do it by Christmas. "No goddamn **Harvard** men, you understand!" he ordered Haldeman. "Under no condition."[17] The president brandished a Pat Buchanan study of Ivy Leaguers in the Foreign Service to confirm what he expected—that while Ivy Leaguers made up less than 2 percent of college grads, they accounted for more than half the ambassadors. Ehrlichman's notes captured Nixon's scorn—how the Ivy Leaguers "play those frilly games, squash and crew."[18]

Then, having vented, Nixon proceeded to hire and promote Ivy Leaguers: Elliot Richardson of Harvard to replace Mel Laird at Defense and Caspar Weinberger, another Harvard man, to replace Richardson at Health, Education, and Welfare; Schlesinger, another Harvard man, to replace Helms at CIA; George Shultz, of Princeton, not only to run

Treasury but also to oversee all economic matters in Nixon's proposed new "super Cabinet," designed to concentrate power in the White House and ride herd on the bureaucrats. "He'd pound on the desk and say, 'We have too many Ivy Leaguers! No more Ivy Leaguers!' So you'd give him three names and tell him the one you're going to recommend was an Ivy Leaguer, and he'd approve it. You got used to it. It's just the way he was," recalled Fred Malek, his personnel chief (and a Harvard MBA).[19]

For days, Haldeman and Ehrlichman made more and more lists and charts while anxious government servants rode the Mount Sinai Shuttle. Largely ignored in all the to-ing and fro-ing was the United States Congress. Aside from a brief meeting with House Republican Minority Leader Gerald Ford and some tortured conversations with Senator Bob Dole, whom he was easing out as head of the Republican Party, Nixon avoided meetings with congressmen.[20] To George H. W. Bush (another Ivy Leaguer getting a top job, as chairman of the Republican National Committee), Nixon dismissively said, "Our Senate lineup is depressing. Old farts or young farts."[21]

Peace in Vietnam was proving maddeningly elusive. The Paris talks broke down. When Kissinger cabled Nixon with the news, the president wrote in his diary, "The North Vietnamese surprised him by slapping him in the face with a wet fish."[22] The question arose: Who would tell the American people?

Kissinger insisted that the president had to go on national TV. Nixon's aides felt that Kissinger should be the one, via opening remarks at a press conference. "The president should explain success. The staff explains failures," said Ehrlichman, who had been summoned to Camp David to help deal with the latest crisis.

As his aides read Kissinger's cables, Nixon was swimming in his heated pool outside Aspen Lodge. Clouds of steam rose into the December night. Nixon emerged from the pool and donned a giant terry cloth robe. He was limping badly; he had cracked his toe on the side of the pool.* "That damn 'Peace is at hand'!" the president muttered, drying his hair.[24]

Kissinger returned from Paris blaming the North Vietnamese. "Tawdry, filthy shits," he stormed. "They make the Russians look good."[25] Kissinger was on the defensive. He had heard about Nixon's plan to create a "new establishment,"† and he feared that he was too closely identified with the old one.

---

*Dr. Riland, Nixon's osteopathic physician, diagnosed the president's toe as broken. "He refuses to have an x-ray and wants me to keep the whole thing very, very quiet. What a hang-up he has on health! His low back was very much locked up in the attempt to compensate. I got the impression that his fall was a State secret in fact. Sometimes I get the feeling he is not for real."[23]

† At Camp David, Nixon repeatedly spoke of the need "to build up a new establishment." As part of his plan, Nixon talked to Haldeman about finding suitable congressional seats for his brother Ed and his sons-in-law, Ed Cox and David Eisenhower.[26]

"The depths of bitterness against the **Post** here is not to be described," he had told Kay Graham by phone a week after election while arranging to attend a dinner party of the "Georgetown set" that would be held at a private home safely in the Maryland suburbs.[27] Kissinger had further jeopardized his standing at the White House by giving an unguarded interview to an Italian journalist named Oriana Fallaci in which he compared himself to a "lone cowboy" riding into town to dispatch the villains. Sparring, boasting, and flirting with Fallaci, he seemed to take credit for all of Nixon's foreign policy successes. As Walter Isaacson noted, for a man who made fun of Nixon's Walter Mitty tendencies and had never himself climbed on a horse, the picture of Kissinger as Lone Ranger was almost sweetly laughable. ("The president would have cast Henry, I suspect, as Tonto," said Ehrlichman.)[28]

Kissinger pleaded with Haldeman that he had been "just joking" with the Italian journalist. "She shafted me." Nixon was not amused. The president wanted to send a warning shot—to let Kissinger know that he should not try to take credit or to make Nixon the bad guy when he went to write his memoirs. Haldeman wrote in his diary that he was to "let Henry know that the EOB and Oval Office and Lincoln Sitting Room have been recorded for protection—so the P has a complete record of your conversations which, of course, you can carry when you write your book."[29] (Nixon quickly retracted the order.)

Kissinger's Machiavellian aide Al Haig described Kissinger to the president as "completely paranoid." Nixon told Haldeman that he thought Kissinger might be suicidal and instructed him to keep records on his mental state (and to remove all Nixon-Kissinger memos from Kissinger's files, another order Haldeman ignored).[30] In a moment of vexation, Nixon apparently considered easing out Kissinger, according to Haldeman's diary and the recollection of Chuck Colson. Colson claimed that Nixon led him into a hallway at Aspen Lodge to whisper, "In the next Administration, Kissinger is gone. I don't want him around." (Colson later speculated that Nixon was whispering because the room was bugged.)[31]

But Nixon and Kissinger needed each other. Nixon ordered Kissinger to break the news about the stalled peace talks at a press conference. Kissinger acquiesced—but made sure to mention Nixon's name fourteen times.[32] In mid-December, Nixon and Kissinger agreed to resume the bombing of Hanoi, this time with B-52s, massive strategic bombers that were deadly though not always accurate. Once and for all, they were hoping to bring the stubborn North Vietnamese to their knees. The press reaction to the "Christmas bombing" was intensely negative. James Reston of **The New York Times** called it "war by tantrum."[33] Kissinger "talked rather emotionally about the fact that this was a very courageous decision," Nixon wrote in his diary. Then the president was furious to learn, inevitably, that Kissinger was telling his friends in the liberal media that he had opposed the bombing. When Haldeman confronted Kissinger with the time and date he had talked to one reporter (to catch the leaks, Nixon had ordered Kissinger's calls monitored), Kissinger responded, "Yes, but that was only on the telephone."[34]

Nixon, who tried so hard to "buck up" others, endeavored to raise his own morale on the day before Christmas. At 4 A.M., he dictated to his diary:

> I must get away from the thought of considering the office at any time a burden. I actually do not consider it a burden, an agony, etc., as did Eisenhower and also to an extent Johnson. As a matter of fact, I think the term glorious burden is the best description. . . .
>
> From this day forward, I am going to look upon it that way and rise to the challenge with as much excitement, energy, enthusiasm, and wherever possible, real joy that I can muster.
>
> God's help will be required as will the help of loyal people on the staff and the family.
>
> A new group of Nixon loyalists, of course, is an urgent necessity. . . . [35]

The president needed someone he could talk to, someone more politically astute and knowledgeable about the issues than Bebe Rebozo. Nixon felt lonely in Key Biscayne over the holidays. The Nixons were

away from their children for the first time at Christmas (Julie, Tricia, and their husbands were traveling
in Europe), and Nixon was "tense and preoccupied,"
Pat related to Julie. At night after dinner, Pat would
hear him on the phone with Kissinger. She decided
not to probe; the details were too complex, she told
Julie, and she felt wary of second-guessing.

On Christmas morning, Pat suggested to her husband that they open the gifts by the tree. He mum-
bled something about "later," and the packages were
taken back to Washington, still wrapped.[36] That evening, Nixon made a rare admission of his own and his
wife's loneliness. Referring to himself and to Pat in
the third person, he wrote: "It is inevitable that not
only the President but the First Lady become more
and more lonely individuals in a sense who have to
depend on fewer and fewer people who can give them
a lift when they need it."[37] Writing in retrospect,
Nixon noted in his memoirs that "in the last weeks of
December and the beginning of January, the ground
began to shift, however subtly," on Watergate. "On
the White House staff there were the first signs of
finger pointing."[38] Haldeman and Ehrlichman began
to blame Colson, and Colson began to blame Haldeman and Ehrlichman, and everyone blamed Mitchell, who, back in New York, blamed everyone but
said nothing. The accusations were "tentative, without evidence," wrote Nixon. Observing Haldeman
and Ehrlichman, Nixon recorded in his diary on January 6, "I could see that something was eating them
without knowing what."[39]

Nixon did not ask. Back in November, he had declared that he wanted John Dean to write a report, to be made public, showing that "no present member" of the White House staff had been involved in Watergate.[40] He was advised to keep the report narrowly focused, lest it "open the doors, doors, doors, and doors," as Ehrlichman put it.[41] Nixon did quietly push Colson and Chapin out of their jobs in the White House. Though he valued them, especially Colson, they were "lightning rods." Nixon felt guilty about Chapin, who had worked for him as far back as the 1962 governor's race and who, in hiring the prankster Segretti, had been carrying out Nixon's orders to find someone who could do "Dick Tuck–type stuff."[42]

Colson persuaded Nixon to let him stay on at the White House for a few more months and proceeded to drag him, half-wittingly, into the cover-up. E. Howard Hunt was using his pal Colson to extort the White House, threatening to tell all if he did not get more money and a promise of clemency.[43] Colson appealed to Nixon's sympathies—Hunt's wife had died in a plane crash in December, and the former spy, a father of four, was deeply depressed. Nixon agreed, at least tacitly, to consider a pardon for Hunt on humanitarian grounds. In his memoirs, he acknowledged that "it is also true that implicit in Hunt's growing despair was a threat to start talking, although I was never sure exactly about what." Nixon, at this stage, was probably ignorant of Hunt's more outlandish activities, like the break-in at the office of Ellsberg's psychiatrist—just one of the doors Ehrlichman wished to keep closed.[44]

While Nixon struggled to end the Vietnam War and to remake the Republican Party and the U.S. government closer to his image, Watergate kept bubbling back up. On January 8, trial began for the five burglars and Hunt and Liddy. Meanwhile, Congress was stirring with anti-Nixon rebellion. Nixon's plan to reorganize the executive branch into four major departments "blew all the fuses in town," recalled Roy Ash, the director of the Office of Management and Budget.[45] Congressmen regarded federal agencies as their own fiefdoms and were anxious to hang on to them. Nixon, for his part, refused to be a "supplicant" to Congress. "We won the election," he told Haldeman. "We should let them come to us."[46] Nixon had made little effort to elect congressmen in November. "They should support P— not he them," Haldeman had noted on September 20. "Ok to go on endorsement letters but beyond that they should grab P's coattails."[47] During the first term, his long-suffering congressional liaison, Bill Timmons, had arranged a series of half-hour sessions with the president for selected members of Congress—informal, get-to-know-you coffees in the Oval Office. "More than once, afterward, he jammed his finger in my chest and demanded, 'What was that for? What was that for?'" recalled Timmons.[48] Urged to see more senators by Republican Minority Leader Hugh Scott, Nixon sneered, "Our senators are nothing but a bunch of assholes. You never get anything from them. All I can say is fuck the Senate! You bring them down and give them cookies and you can't count on them."[49]

In a Nixon nightmare come true, Senator Edward Kennedy was maneuvering behind the scenes. In the House, the new Democratic majority leader, Thomas P. "Tip" O'Neill, startled his colleagues by telling them that they should begin preparing for impeachment. O'Neill had inherited JFK's congressional district and was closely tied to the Kennedys. Senator Kennedy pushed for Senator Sam Ervin of North Carolina, a segregationist Southerner and strict-constructionist popular with Republicans, to run a special select committee to investigate campaign abuses. Prodded by Majority Leader Mike Mansfield, Kennedy wanted the committee to avoid any taint of partisanship. John Dean soon pegged Ervin as a "puppet" for Kennedy. The down-home, Harvard Law–educated Ervin was his own man, but he was helped mightily by the Kennedy forces. Out of public view, Kennedy's staffers from the Judiciary Committee had been investigating Watergate for six months and now turned over their files to what would become known as the Senate Select Committee on Presidential Campaign Activities of 1972 or, more popularly, the Watergate Committee.[50]

On January 12, Haldeman came up with an ingenious plan, which he attributed to John Dean, to get the Democrats to back off. Haldeman recalled J. Edgar Hoover's claim, frequently cited by Nixon, that LBJ had ordered the FBI to bug Nixon's campaign plane in 1968. The White House should demand that the Senate Select Committee investigate irregularities in the 1968 campaign as well as the one in 1972.

Nixon was not eager to violate the old mutual nonaggression pact with LBJ; in any event, the Haldeman/Dean plan fizzled. There was the inconvenient fact that the FBI never had bugged Nixon's plane. Then there was LBJ's reaction: He "got very hot," according to Haldeman's diary, and threatened to expose Nixon's connection to Mrs. Chennault.[51]

Ten days later, on January 22, LBJ died, "of a broken heart," as Nixon wrote. President Johnson had "longed for the popular approval and affection that continued to elude him." Notwithstanding the late flare-up over Mrs. Chennault, Nixon and Johnson had grown close toward the end, talking on the phone and exchanging visits. "Tell the president I love him," Johnson said before he died. "He was uniquely able to understand some of the things I was experiencing, particularly with Congress and the media over Vietnam," Nixon wrote.[52*]

But it's doubtful that the two presidents really opened up to each other. Outside of extraordinary circumstances, Nixon was not capable of soul-baring

*Nixon admired LBJ's earthiness. Interviewed by Pat Buchanan in 1982, and thinking that the cameras were off, Nixon commented on a Robert Caro biography of LBJ. "Shit, it makes him appear like a goddamn animal," said Nixon. Pause. Smile. "Of course, he was." Pause. "He was a **man**."[53]

conversations. He could discuss the darker side of human nature in the abstract: In October, assessing the electorate, he had remarked, "Hell, the young don't like the old and never have. And the women don't like the men, generally. The men don't like the women. They live together because of reasons that have nothing to do with love."[54] But he very rarely alluded to, much less discussed, any dark feelings of his own. He shied from frank personal conversation, even with friends and family.

Nor did he invite others to open up to him about their own fears and doubts. Nixon's "bucking up" sessions were pep talks and expressions of sympathy; they were not invitations to share.

Nixon could be cagey about not wanting to know too much. He knew that leaders of countries with large national security operations needed "plausible deniability," to be able to deny credibly that they had been involved in some of the baser acts required of global superpowers. But Nixon's aversion to unpleasant truths had a personal, visceral element, rooted in old wounds that never healed.

The Watergate Nixon is generally portrayed as scheming and Machiavellian by the press, and the White House tapes provide no shortage of material to buttress this view. But the overwhelming impression left by listening to the tapes is of a man who is **not** clever, who is all too human—who rambles, gets lost, changes his mind, knows too much and too little all at once.[55] Nixon the brilliant political analyst is nowhere to be seen. His judgment is clouded by human frailty. One moment he sounds cold-blooded and ruthless. The next moment he is naïvely idealistic, prattling on about the lesson of the Hiss case as related in **Six Crises**—the cover-up is worse than the crime!—while plunging into an ever-deeper cover-up. Perhaps he was being cynical and manipulative. Or maybe he was just torn and confused. He was motivated by arrogance and pride, yes, but also by their close cousins, fear and denial.

For whatever reason—probably for all of these reasons—Nixon did not press too closely when his top aides began pointing fingers at each other in the early winter of 1973. Nixon would prod a little, tentatively ask what one man knew about the other—but then retreat when the answers were vague or guarded, as they usually were.[56] Perhaps Nixon was tenderly protecting his old friend, John Mitchell. And—or—perhaps he was protecting himself, knowing, as a lawyer, that he could be held responsible for failing to disclose the crimes of his subordinates. In any case, until it was too late, and not really even then, did Nixon grill his chief subordinates on what they knew and when they knew it. Nor did he bring in a trustworthy outsider who could be counted on to do the job for him. As a result he was often ignorant, misinformed, or confused as Watergate surfaced as a mortal threat.

Of course, until the scandal consumed him late that winter and spring, he had much else on his mind, matters of state that seemed far more consequential. He had to get a peace settlement in Vietnam and to secure the release of the POWs—a cause especially dear to him.[57] Still, Nixon's isolation is striking. He didn't want to hear bad news. He would not seek counsel from the First Lady—Pat later told Julie, with regret, that she had assumed Nixon wanted to be left alone and could handle the complexities of Watergate, as he had managed so many crises before.[58] At some level Nixon did not want to hear more bad news from anyone. It's impossible to know his inner struggles, but he clearly did not want to add to them. He was searching for relief—the sort of escape that careworn leaders sometimes crave when the burdens of state threaten to become overwhelming. Early that January, when LBJ was starting to fail, Nixon offered to send him to Bebe Rebozo's place in Key Biscayne because, as Nixon told LBJ over the phone, "Ole Bebe is a great guy to have around. He cheers people up, you know. He never brings up unpleasant subjects."[59]

Nixon, too, wanted to cheer up people, himself included, and stay away from "unpleasant subjects," such as: Who had ordered the Watergate break-in? If he really knew who was to blame, he might have to fire him—and all those involved, including, he was beginning to suspect, his closest aides. Nixon dreaded the prospect of firing anyone. He had used Haldeman for that. But what if Haldeman, too, was implicated? Fond of quoting British statesmen, Nixon was familiar with William Gladstone's maxim that "The first essential for a Prime Minister is to be a good butcher."[60] Nixon, by his own admission, was not a good butcher.[61]

On January 9, his sixtieth birthday, Nixon was sitting in the Oval Office at noon when Haldeman handed him an "Eyes Only" telegram. Putting on his reading glasses—which he never showed in public—Nixon read, "We celebrated the president's birthday today by making a major breakthrough in the negotiations."[62] Nixon looked up and told Haldeman, "Henry's probably overoptimistic again," but then he dictated his response—that it was the best birthday present he'd had in sixty years.[63]

In the early morning hours of January 11, he took up his yellow pad to write his resolutions, among them "restore respect for the office; New idealism—respect for flag, country; Compassion—understanding."[64] Nixon had taken to sporting a little American flag in his lapel; he had gotten the idea, a burst of defiance, from two movies, **The Man** and **The Candidate,** in which the bad guys—Republicans—wore tiny flags in their lapels. "I told Haldeman I was going to wear the flag, come hell or high water, from now on. . . ." The staff was instructed to do likewise.[65]

At midnight on January 11, Kissinger arrived in Key Biscayne with, at long last, a peace deal. As Nixon walked Kissinger to his car at 2:30 A.M., he noted, "I felt an odd tenderness towards him. . . . We spoke to each other in nearly affectionate terms, like veterans of bitter battles at a last reunion, even though we both sensed somehow that too much had happened between us to make the rest of the journey together."[66]

On January 15, the bombing stopped. Kissinger spoke to Pat Nixon on the phone and later reported to her husband that he had never heard the First Lady sound so elated. Julie checked in, "bubbly and upbeat," Nixon wrote in his diary.[67] But in her own diary, Julie noted, her father's voice "sounded so tired and old when he said, 'Well, we don't know what will happen. We don't know how it will work out.'"[68]

On the evening of January 23, Haldeman summoned the senior staff into the Roosevelt Room. Taking his customary seat in front of the fire, next to the Remington portrait of Theodore Roosevelt and the Rough Riders charging up San Juan Hill, he explained that the president would address the nation at 10 P.M. to declare "peace with honor." A squabble broke out: Hardliner Pat Buchanan wanted a harsh attack on the president's liberal critics, while other staffers did not want to play "the sore winner." Haldeman, who knew that his boss's preference would be to unload on his critics, found a Solomonic compromise: Let proxies do the bashing while keeping Nixon on the high road.

Nixon arrived acting "irritable," Bill Safire recalled. The president made no effort to hide it. "He was not stepping up to a crisis, which required calm and the infectious quality of confidence, he was an-

nouncing a peace and felt he could let the strain of
the past few weeks show in his face and voice." Haldeman sighed to Safire, "The Boss is great in adversity, but he's always had this problem handling
success."[69]

Finished with his broadcast, Nixon returned to
the Solarium in the Residence. Pat came over and
silently put her arms around her husband. After a
while, Nixon retreated to the Lincoln Sitting Room
to sit by the fire and listen to records. He wrote a
short, tender note to the newly widowed Lady Bird
Johnson. "I know what abuse he took—particularly
from members of his own party—in standing firm
for peace with honor. Now that we have such a settlement, we shall do everything we can to make it
last so that other brave men who sacrificed their lives
for this cause have not died in vain."[70]

Over eleven years, some fifty-eight thousand
American soldiers had been killed in Vietnam. The
final deal was about the same one the North Vietnamese had agreed to in October. All the American
POWs would come home, but North Vietnam's in-
vading army would remain inside South Vietnam.
Thieu had finally, grudgingly, bitterly signed the
peace deal when he was given a secret guarantee by
Nixon that the United States would "react strongly
in the event the agreement is violated."[71]

That evening, standing outside the door to the
Roosevelt Room, Kissinger and John Ehrlichman
had a brief chat. "How long do you figure the South
Vietnamese can survive under this agreement?"

asked Ehrlichman. Kissinger, who may have sounded more pessimistic than he meant to, answered, "I think that if they're lucky they can hold out for a year and a half."[72] In the event, South Vietnam held out for twenty-eight months.*

The cease-fire went into effect at midnight on January 27. "I had always expected that I would feel an immense sense of relief and satisfaction when the war was finally ended," Nixon wrote. "But I also felt a surprising sense of sadness, apprehension, and impatience."[73]

Nixon was not expecting trouble from the trial of the Watergate burglars, all of whom pleaded guilty or were convicted. But at a bail hearing on February 2, a federal district court judge, John Sirica, announced that he did not believe the testimony given by the government's witnesses, all of whom had denied any involvement by White House higher-ups. From the bench, Judge Sirica stated his hope that the coming Senate investigation would "get to the bottom" of Watergate.

Nixon was furious. "Here is the judge, and saying this," Nixon protested to Colson the next morning. "His goddamn conduct is shocking, as a **judge**." Colson tried to cool him down by saying that Sirica

---

*Probably, South Vietnam could have held out longer if Congress had not taken away from President Ford the funds necessary to support South Vietnam, but, ultimately, it seems clear that Hanoi was never going to give up until it forcibly united all of Vietnam.

was a Republican law-and-order judge. "I know him pretty well," said Colson, a little too breezily. "He's a hot-headed Italian, and he blew on it."[74]

At the courthouse, Judge Sirica was known as "Maximum John" for his sentences and his practice, of dubious constitutionality, of using the threat of prison time to pressure the accused to talk. In the Watergate case, Sirica was letting the defendants stew for a while before he pronounced sentence.[75]

Bebe Rebozo would later recall an old Cuban expression, "Sooner or later, everyone walks under the lanai." It meant that you should treat people well because when you walk under the veranda they can wave to you—or push a flowerpot onto your head. In 1970, Judge Sirica had presided at the swearing-in of William Casey as head of the Securities and Exchange Commission. After the ceremony, Sirica had said to the president, "I was the head of Italians for Eisenhower-Nixon in 1956 in New York City. I'd like to be on the court of appeals." Nixon had brushed him off.[76]

John Dean.
**Courtesy of the Richard Nixon Presidential
Library and Museum**

CHAPTER 25

Ides of March

As he entered his second term, Nixon's approval rating stood at 68 percent.[1] "I don't think the country is all that stirred up" about Watergate, Nixon told Colson on February 3, 1973. "What do you think?" Colson answered, "No. Oh, God, no, the country is bored with it. . . . The Watergate issue has **never** been a public issue. It's a Washington issue. It's a way to get at us. It's the way Democrats think they can use to embarrass us."[2]

"That's right," said Nixon. "Well. . . ." He wanted to believe that Colson was right. But as the Senate prepared to hold hearings, Nixon sensed that Watergate was "starting to snowball." He also had a nagging feeling that Colson, Haldeman, and Ehrlichman were holding back, perhaps protecting themselves. He decided, as he put it in his memoirs, to give Watergate "my personal attention."[3]

That meant working directly with John Dean, the White House lawyer who had been managing the scandal day to day. On February 27, the president met with Dean, their first session alone together since the indictments of the Watergate burglars had been handed down on September 15. "The talk with John Dean was very worthwhile. He is an enormously capable man," Nixon dictated to his diary that night. The next day he wrote, "I am very impressed by him. He has shown enormous strength, great intelligence, and great subtlety."[4] To Haldeman, Nixon described Dean as "really a gem." Haldeman replied, "He's a real cool cookie, isn't he?"[5] Nixon was impressed that Dean had gone back to read not only **Six Crises** but also his congressional speeches during the Hiss case.

Dean was more deeply caught up in Watergate than Nixon knew. Some Watergate scholars believe that Dean, who is regarded as a brilliant manipulator by his detractors, was aware of the original break-in, an allegation Dean denies.[6] In any case, he had been deeply engaged in the cover-up, arranging for bundles of cash, which were handled with rubber gloves and delivered in brown paper bags to the Watergate defendants—money lawfully and legitimately paid out for legal fees and living expenses but also, it was becomingly increasingly clear, intended to buy silence.[7]

By mid-March, Dean's role had become a little clearer to Nixon. Pat Gray, the earnest Nixon loyalist picked to run the FBI, had been talking loosely at his Senate confirmation hearings. The acting director told the panel that he had shared raw FBI files on Watergate with White House Counsel Dean. Gray offered to do the same with Congress. The

president was appalled by Gray's indiscretion.
"What's the matter with him?" Nixon exclaimed.
"For Christ's sake, I mean, he must be out of his
mind."[8] At his confirmation hearings, Gray continued to thrash about until he was finally forced to
withdraw.[9] Nixon's nominee should be left to "twist,
slowly, slowly in the wind," said the acerbic Ehrlichman, coining a phrase that would enter the national lexicon.[10] In addition to potentially exposing
White House secrets to Congress, Gray's testimony
had dragged Dean—the president's lawyer, but heretofore a nonentity—into the scandal.

Nixon had repeatedly declared that no White
House staffer had been involved in Watergate. Now
it appeared that the White House counsel, tipped
off every step of the way, had been a little too cozy
with FBI investigators.

Compromised or not, Dean was to be Nixon's
guide through the Watergate thicket. The superfi-
cially confident but deeply anxious young lawyer
found the whole process unsettling. Nixon "continually asked questions I had already answered," Dean
recalled. "This disturbed me. He would have bursts
of lucidity and logical thinking, but mostly he was
rambling and forgetful, and as I grew used to talking
to him I nursed the heretical thought that the President didn't seem very smart."

Dean was unfamiliar with Nixon's way of circling
around problems, a process that the tart Ehrlichman
had dubbed as "chewing his cud."[11] (Indeed, appearing disengaged is an old presidential trick, practiced

by, among others, FDR, Eisenhower, and Reagan.) The thirty-four-year-old White House counsel was taken aback at Nixon's clumsiness. Dean would later describe Nixon trying to take notes: First, the president would put on his dark-rimmed glasses ("To my surprise, I thought they made him look much better"). Then he would fish around in his suit's inside pocket for a scrap of paper while reaching into the opposite inside pocket for a pen. When both objects eluded his grasp, he would struggle, with his arms crossed, until he finally secured a fountain pen, and bit off the top. (Nixon's clumsiness might have been natural—or staged to buy time while Nixon thought what he wanted to think. It was sometimes hard to know, even for Nixon aides who had spent far more time with the president than Dean.)

Though Dean dutifully paid homage to **Six Crises** as he tried to ingratiate himself with the president, he was privately "baffled" by Nixon's constant analogies between the Hiss case and Watergate. "I thought the President had everything backward," recalled Dean in his memoir, **Blind Ambition**. "I identified with Hiss, not the investigators, and I winced whenever the President talked about how he finally 'nailed' him."[12]

Slowly unspooling the complicated Watergate plot for Nixon, Dean brought progressively worse news to the president. On March 13, he told Nixon that Gordon Strachan, Haldeman's liaison to Jeb Magruder at CRP, had known in advance about the break-in. Nixon was "stunned," the president recalled in his memoirs. Strachan led straight to Haldeman: "It was well known that Haldeman's staff acted as an extension of Haldeman; it would seem unlikely that Strachan would have known about anything as important as the Watergate break-in plan without having informed Haldeman of it," Nixon wrote. From across his desk in the Oval Office, Nixon asked incredulously, "He knew about Watergate, Strachan did?" Dean answered, "Uh-huh." Nixon sighed, "I'll be damned. Well, that's the problem in Bob's case, isn't it?"[13]

Nixon's surprise may have been slightly feigned. In his gentle poking and prodding at Haldeman and Ehrlichman, he had earlier picked up suggestions that Strachan was somehow involved (the Haldeman aide's role has long remained murky and may have been marginal; criminal charges against Strachan were dropped by the prosecutors).[14] But now Nixon was genuinely worried about the prospect of a congressional investigation and possible prosecution of his closest aides. Dean did not reassure him. "There are going to be a lot of problems if everything starts falling," Dean said as their meeting ended. "So there are dangers, Mr. President. I'd be less than candid if I didn't tell you . . . there are."[15]

Nixon's apprehensions grew when Dean told the president about Ehrlichman's possible exposure in another break-in—the Plumbers' botched raid on the office of Daniel Ellsberg's psychiatrist in September 1971.

"What in the world. . . ." Nixon said. "This is the

first I ever heard of it."[16] Again, Nixon may have been exaggerating his surprise. There are suggestions in earlier tape-recorded conversations that Nixon had already picked up some hint of the Ellsberg break-in.[17] But whatever his prior inklings, Nixon was beginning to get a better idea of what John Mitchell had dubbed "the White House horrors"— the crimes, seemingly unrelated but tied in by the malign presence of Hunt and Liddy—that might be exposed if the Watergate cover-up unraveled.

Day after day, Dean was becoming the bearer of bad tidings. On March 21, 1973, at just after ten o'clock in the morning on an early spring day, cloudy and windy, Dean walked into the Oval Office. "Sit down, sit down," Nixon greeted him cheerfully. "Well, what is the Dean summary of the day about?"

DEAN: Uh, the reason I thought we ought to talk this morning is because in, in, our conversations, uh, uh, I have, I have the impression that you don't know everything I know—

NIXON: That's right.

DEAN: —and it makes it very difficult for you to make judgments that, uh, that only you can make on so many things.

NIXON: That's right . . .

DEAN: I think, I think that, uh, there's no doubt about the seriousness of the problem we're, we've got. We have a cancer—within—close to the Presidency, that's growing. It's growing daily. It's compounding, it grows geometrically now, because it compounds itself. Uh, that'll be clear as I explain, you know, some of the details, uh, of why it is, and basically it's because (1) we're being black-mailed; (2) uh, people are going to start perjuring themselves very quickly that have not had to per-jure themselves to protect other people and the like. And . . . there's no assurance—

NIXON: That it won't bust.

DEAN: That, that won't bust. So let me give you sort of the basic facts. . . . [18]

Dean began reciting the details. "Some of them I had heard before. Some were variations of things I had heard before. And some were new," Nixon wrote in his memoirs. He was disturbed to hear that Colson, in Dean's opinion, had a "damn good idea" of what Hunt and Liddy were up to as they plotted to bug the Dem-ocrats. "Colson!" Nixon recalled thinking to himself. "My earliest fears returned."[19] Dean explained how the hush money had been paid out—initially, and recklessly, through Nixon's personal lawyer, Herb Kalmbach. Haldeman had let him use a $350,000 cash fund from the White House. Haldeman and Ehr-lichman had decided, according to Dean, that there was "no price too high to pay to let this thing blow up in front of the election."

Dean delivered his punch line: "Bob is involved in that; John is involved in that; I'm involved in that; Mitchell is involved in that. And that's an obstruc-tion of justice."

Dean returned to the problem of Hunt, who was

due to be sentenced in two days—and who was demanding $122,000 in hush money. Hunt's threat had been explicit: "I will bring John Ehrlichman down to his knees and put him in jail. I have done enough seamy things for he and Krogh that they'll never survive it." Hunt's deadline, Dean told Nixon, was "close of business yesterday."[20]

Nixon felt that Dean was being "melodramatic." He failed to see that he had arrived at a moment of truth. Here was the chance to finally "prick the boil," to use a Nixon term, to get Watergate behind him, at great cost and amid inevitable tumult, but in a way that would save his presidency. It was too late to spare his top advisers from criminal investigations or to spare himself from serious embarrassment. But had Nixon called in an outside lawyer and run a truly open investigation, his presidency would have endured—weakened, badly shaken, but also purified. Nixon did, for a brief instant, consider the possibility of coming clean. He wanted Dean to write a report, and he asked, "Are you going to put out a complete disclosure? Isn't that the best plan? That'd be my view on it," Nixon said.

Dean began talking about trying to get immunity for witnesses to testify before the grand jury.[21] In these few seconds—as he had before and would again— Nixon missed a chance to do the proverbial right thing, to take the step that would have saved him and preserved his legacy. The president had already pondered ways to buy Hunt's continued silence.

"How much money do you need?" Nixon asked Dean.

DEAN: I would say these people are going to cost, uh, a million dollars over the next, uh, two years.

There was a long silence.

NIXON: We could get that. . . . If you need the money . . . you could get the money. . . . What I mean is, you could, you could get a million dollars. And you could get it in cash. I know where it could be gotten.
DEAN: Uh-huh.
NIXON: I mean, it's not easy, but it could be done. But the question is, who the hell would handle it?

The conversation wandered off with Nixon floating hypotheticals. Clemency for Hunt? "No, it's wrong, that's for sure," said Nixon. But as Haldeman joined the conversation, Nixon clarified, "We could get the money. There is no problem in that. We can't provide the clemency. The money can be provided." Nixon concluded, "You've got to keep the cap on the bottle. . . . Either that or let it all be blown right now."[22]

After the meeting, Nixon greeted Olga Korbut, the Russian Olympic gymnast, and ran a session on efforts to hold down government spending. "But all the time Howard Hunt and his threats and demands for money were weighing on my mind," Nixon recalled. His memoir continued: "As soon as these meetings were over I called Rose Woods and asked her if we had any unused campaign funds. She told me that we did—she would have to see how much. It turned out to be $100,000."[23]

Later that evening, Hunt was paid $75,000 out of a different fund (the $350,000 approved by Haldeman) by one of John Mitchell's former aides, Fred LaRue, who had spoken to Dean that morning. It does not appear that Nixon knew about the payoff, or that he had actually, formally, authorized paying Hunt.[24] But he had signaled—and not in a vacillating way—that he was willing to meet Hunt's demands in order to at least buy time. That morning, he had told Dean, "You've got no choice with Hunt, with the 120 or whatever it is. You've got to damn well get that done."[25]*

Late on the night of March 21, Nixon dictated a long note in his diary "about a day," he wrote in his memoir, "that was later to be seen as a disastrous turning point in my presidency." The entry began, "As far as the day was concerned, it was relatively uneventful except for the talk with Dean. Dean really in effect let it all hang out when he said there was a cancerous growth around the President. . . ." The tone of the note is stunningly detached. The

---

*Nixon was already well aware of the hush money. On March 6, he had discreetly thanked Greek oilman Tom Pappas for helping out John Mitchell with some of the cash needs to keep the Watergate burglars silent. In return, Pappas got to keep his friend Henry Tasca as ambassador to Greece.[26]

president appears more worried about Dean—"he is obviously depressed"—than about himself. In his diary entry, Nixon seems to have regarded Dean as a despondent young man rather than the harbinger of doom that he was. In his memoir, Nixon wrote that he had left his meeting with Dean "more disturbed than shocked; more anxious than alarmed." Only in retrospect, he wrote, did he understand the full import of what Dean was telling him. (Dean told the author he was not depressed but "flabbergasted" at the president's almost eerie nonchalance.)[27]

It is hard to explain this failure of judgment, the most critical mistake Nixon ever made. Favoring hush money over full disclosure was a moral lapse, regardless of whether Nixon had committed a crime, but the reasons for his actions are complex and not easy to sort out. It is generally true, as his defenders have argued, that Nixon was continuing to view his problems as political when they were by now legal— criminally so.[28] But this explanation begs deeper questions. Nixon suffered from a blind spot brought on by mixed motives, some of them decent but ultimately fatal to his presidency. His need to put a positive spin on calamitous events is in some ways admirable, but in this case he was fooled, or he fooled himself. His analytical powers, his early warning system, failed. He saw Dean's "cancer on the presidency" warning as just one more crisis to be bluffed and battled through. And he was further done in by his incapacity to deliver bad news to the people who most needed to hear it.

. . .

The next day, on the afternoon of Thursday, March 22, Nixon brought together Haldeman, Ehrlichman, Mitchell, and Dean in his Executive Office Building hideaway. Mitchell had flown down from his law firm in New York. It was the first—and only—time the president invited the main actors in Watergate to face each other in his presence. The four men had met in Haldeman's office beforehand. There had been "nervous pleasantries and indirect ribbing, but no confrontation," Dean recalled. "It was as if four men were discussing adultery; each knew the others were cheating, each was reluctant to admit it first."[29]

The conversation was no more forthcoming in Nixon's presence. There were jokes about a "modified, limited hang-out" (Ehrlichman the phrasemaker, again). "Anticipated Armageddon never happened," wrote James Rosen, Mitchell's biographer and Watergate historian. "Instead, after strained pleasantries, the session swiftly degenerated into the kind of aimless, purposeless colloquy Nixon favored."[30] Nixon made no attempt to get to the heart of the matter—who was responsible for the Watergate break-in and cover-up and who should bear the blame. After a while, Nixon cleared the room to meet alone with Mitchell.

It was the last time the two old friends would meet during Nixon's presidency. Nixon immediately journeyed into the past, recalling how Ike had forced the resignation of Sherman Adams, his chief of staff, for taking illegal payments. "Now let me make this clear," said Nixon. "I don't want it to happen with Watergate." Eisenhower, in Nixon's view, had made a mistake, one that Nixon would not repeat. He grew impassioned: "I don't give a shit what happens. I want you all to stonewall it, let them plead the Fifth Amendment, cover up or anything else, if it'll save, save the plan," Nixon spluttered. Then he calmed down: "And I would particularly prefer to do it the other way, if it's going to come out that way anyway. And that's my view, that with the number of jackass people that they've got that they can call, they're going to. . . ." Nixon paused and rephrased his thought. "The story that'll get out, through leaks, charges, and so forth, innuendo, will be a hell of a lot worse than the story they're going to get out just by letting it out there."*

Having come out on both sides—for covering up and coming clean—Nixon did not choose either. Rather, he continued to wander into his own past. "Eisenhower—that's all he ever cared about. Christ. 'Be sure he was clean.'" Nixon began to think

---

*The White House's own transcription of the tape was subtly, but significantly different: "I don't give a shit what happens. Go down and sto—, stonewall it; Tell 'em, 'plead the Fifth Amendment, cover-up' or anything else, if it'll save 'em—save it for them. That's the whole point." There is no mention of a "plan." Even with audio enhancement technology, the quality of the recording is poor and difficult to decipher, a significant problem for researchers who sometimes must spend hours listening to a single White House tape. Inevitably, debates over interpretation have been shaded by sympathy and ideology.[31]

back to his own humiliation in 1952, the Fund Crisis and the agony of the Checkers Speech. Nixon would not be a self-protecting prig. "I don't look at it that way," he said to Mitchell, who as usual said very little. "And I just—that's the thing I am really concerned with. We're going to protect our people if we can."[32]

The next morning, Friday, March 23, Judge Sirica informed his crowded courtroom that he had a "surprise." He began to read aloud a letter to him from one of the Watergate burglars, James McCord, the former CIA man and security chief for the Committee to Re-Elect: "There was political pressure applied to the defendants to plead guilty and remain silent. . . ."

Reporters began to run for the phones. "Bingo!" exclaimed **Washington Post** editor Ben Bradlee.[33] Watergate was no longer just a "Washington story." In his memoir, Bradlee recalled, "I was so damned excited I couldn't sit down. I called Mrs. Graham. . . ."[34]

Nixon was in his study in Key Biscayne. "Bombshell," he dictated to his diary. Nixon tried to rationalize the news that the cover-up had broken. "I suppose this is something that had to be expected at some point," he continued. But the news that McCord was talking to the prosecutors, even if what he had to say was mostly hearsay from Liddy, galvanized Nixon's aides. For months, Ehrlichman had been maneuvering against his old rival Mitchell, hoping to get "the Big Enchilada," as Ehrlichman called the former attorney general, to take the fall.[35]

Nixon finally seemed ready to go along, though grudgingly. "From a combination of hypersensitivity and a desire not to know the truth in case it turned out to be unpleasant, I had spent the last ten months putting off a confrontation with John Mitchell," Nixon recalled with rare self-candor. "Now it seemed impossible to avoid." For the sake of everyone else, Mitchell would have to admit guilt for the break-in and cover-up.

But, as ever, Nixon could not stand to deliver the news himself. He sent Ehrlichman, armed with a little speech the president had prepared, to face Mitchell: "I told Ehrlichman to tell Mitchell that this was the toughest decision I had ever made— tougher than Cambodia, May 8 [mining Haiphong Harbor], and December 18 [the Christmas bombing] put together. I said he should tell Mitchell that I simply could not bring myself to talk to him personally about it." He added a vow that Mitchell "would never go to prison."[36]

As it turned out, Mitchell would not admit anything (and indeed, may have been innocent of ordering the actual break-in, though he was more generally culpable).[37] Mitchell did say that Dean had talked Magruder into perjuring himself, Ehrlichman reported to the president. "And what does Dean say about it?" Nixon asked. "Dean says it was Mitchell and Magruder," Ehrlichman answered and gave a wry smile. "It must have been the quietest meeting in history, because everybody's version is that the other two guys talked."[38]

. . .

On March 28, Nixon's osteopath, Dr. Kenneth Riland, arrived at the White House to treat the president and his retinue of patients on the White House staff and found Henry Kissinger in a state of high agitation. Sitting on Riland's "treatment table," Kissinger poured out a gossipy and mean-spirited tale to Riland, which the doctor recorded in his diary:

> He says . . . the President is concentrating entirely on Watergate and he, Henry, is doing the entire foreign policy. He told me confidentially that Bob Haldeman is crying his eyes out and Henry went to him and said, "You better find out who the top man is and stop this thing." Well, quite frankly, Henry thinks it goes right on up to and including the President; and he says the President is too greedy. I can hardly see that, but perhaps he's right; anything can happen.

Nixon, on the other hand, was cool, or pretending to be so, when Riland treated him after Kissinger. Riland had learned to read Nixon, or so he thought. In May 1972, as Nixon was gambling the Moscow Summit by mining Haiphong Harbor, Riland had recorded, "I am beginning to recognize when he's under pressure. He underplays all his actions, whistles, lets me take the initiative regarding conversation. . . ." Now, with his presidency shaken and his aides panicking, "Nixon does not appear worried or excited or upset," Riland wrote in his diary.* But the president was masking his anxiety, which showed up in other, familiar ways. In January, Riland had prescribed a stiff dose of pharmacology to battle Nixon's insomnia. "He is still unable to sleep and continually looking for a new pill," Riland had recorded on January 24. "I again suggest Valium 5 mg. a half hour before bed and a Seconal before retiring." Now, two months later, Riland wrote, "I discussed his sleeping pills, and the valium is working, but he still says he can't sleep, and I'm beginning to understand why."[40]

The bad news kept breaking. On Sunday afternoon, April 15, after the White House worship service, Richard Kleindienst, Mitchell's successor as attorney general, appeared at Nixon's hideaway in the Executive Office Building. Kleindienst was red-eyed from staying up all night and near tears. His voice choked and broke as he told the president some alarming information. John Dean had gone

---

*Nixon always tried to be cool with Riland whenever Kissinger was not. As Kissinger seemed to be collapsing along with the peace deal in early January, Riland described the president's relaxed demeanor while the two men discussed Kissinger's tendency to overreact. Of Nixon, Riland wrote: "His calm and complete detachment is something to see." Nixon asked his doctor about Kissinger, "Why is he so emotional?" Riland, who fancied himself as more worldly than the president, whom he once described as "rather provincial," explained to Nixon, "It's his Jewish heritage, as that racial group, particularly the German Jew, has a great inferiority factor which oddly is not a factor with the Israelites."[39]

over to the other side. He had gotten himself a white-collar crime lawyer—one, it turned out, with close connections to the Kennedys[41]—and had gone to the prosecutors hoping to make a deal. He would tell all in exchange for immunity from prosecution. The White House counsel was accusing Haldeman and Ehrlichman of obstruction of justice.[42] Dean was telling prosecutors that Ehrlichman had told him to "deep six" materials from Hunt's safe after the break-in and informing them of the $350,000 authorized by Haldeman to pay legal fees and hush money. Trying to appear unperturbed, Nixon asked what the evidence was.

Later that afternoon, Kleindienst returned with Henry Petersen, a career government lawyer who ran the Justice Department's criminal division. Petersen was wearing a smudged T-shirt, sneakers, and blue jeans; he had been working on his boat when Kleindienst summoned him on a Sunday afternoon. The Justice Department official acknowledged that the evidence against Haldeman and Ehrlichman was not solid. But he said, "The question isn't whether or not there is a criminal case that can be made against them that will stand up in court, Mr. President. What you have to realize is that these two men have not served you well. They already have, and in the future will, cause you embarrassment, and embarrassment to the presidency."

Nixon resisted. "I can't fire men simply because of the appearance of guilt. I have to have proof of their guilt."

Petersen "straightened," Nixon recalled, and said, "What you have just said, Mr. President, speaks very well of you as a man. It does not speak well of you as a President."[43]

In late March, as Watergate was erupting, Nixon had met with all the White House secretaries on "Secretaries' Day." He spoke for twenty minutes, without notes, about how he would be lost without them. "He was warm, witty, relaxed," observed Douglas Parker, a young White House lawyer.[44] Some eighteen months earlier, Jim Schlesinger had seen the same personable Nixon at a speech at the opening of a power plant in Walla Walla, Washington. "He spoke off the cuff and he was relaxed and delightful," recalled Schlesinger. "I thought, here was the man from Yorba Linda, this must be how he feels with his own people, real Americans." But on the plane, Schlesinger watched uncomfortably as the First Lady tried to "be affectionate with the president, and he just brushed her off," recalled Schlesinger.[45]

That was not so unusual. Schlesinger and other cabinet officers did not see the quiet moments of tenderness that the Nixons hid. At Nixon's second inaugural in January, the solicitor general, Robert Bork, had thought that Pat's face looked like a "death mask." It did not go unnoticed by the press that Pat failed to kiss her husband at the swearing in.[46] But the reporters did not see the First Couple holding hands behind the podium. In his diary that night,

Nixon expressed relief that the First Lady had not embarrassed him with a public display of affection—and he recorded his pride that she had refused a Secret Service order to sit down in the open-top limousine when some spectators along the parade route began throwing garbage.[47]

At Key Biscayne over Easter weekend, "my father was more tense and uncommunicative than I ever remembered him," Julie recalled. "He had withdrawn into his own world and away from the family." Pat, meanwhile, "spent most of her time reading in a lounge chair beneath several palms, a small oasis of escape in our yard." Later, Julie confided to Bill Safire:

He didn't try to cheer Mother up, and that was very rare. In Key Biscayne, around 5 in the afternoon he'd go for a swim, and came back not saying anything, and after dinner he was feeling low. You know how Mother is, always thinking of other people, she wanted him to know that we were with him all the way, but he was just closed off.

I felt he wasn't giving her enough credit for having such confidence in him, so during a movie I sat next to him and said, "Mother's trying so hard to make things right, and you don't realize it. It's hard for her too." He just said, "I guess so," and all through the movie I felt horrible that I had blurted that out, he didn't need any more burdens from us, but then after it was over he turned to me and said, "You're right, it's hard for her too. I'll try." And he did.

Pat "felt helpless," Julie recalled. "She had long ago come to understand that my father did not want his family to be involved in his political decisions. He liked to tackle problems by turning them over and over again in his mind until they became digested and resolved. It was a solitary process, and because both my parents were very private people, their relationship was a delicate, private one that did not allow for much second guessing."[48]

Pat and the girls did try subtle—or not so subtle—forms of suasion. They had conducted a quiet but persistent campaign to undermine Haldeman because they believed that the chief of staff had isolated the president—from his own family, among others. In January, after the staff lodge at Camp David had been rebuilt, Pat and Bebe Rebozo, "knowing that words of criticism would not be as effective with my father as a firsthand view," decided to show the president the new lodge, Julie recalled. The huge living area, with its cathedral ceiling, had been reserved for senior staff by Haldeman. The room was empty. Then the First Lady and Rebozo showed Nixon a small room, "just crowded to overflowing with the doctors, military aides, and helicopter pilots," Julie recorded in her diary.

But Pat had more or less given up speaking directly against Haldeman. She knew that her husband wanted his chief of staff to act as gatekeeper, to guard his time alone to think, to keep away complainers and hangers-on. She left her morose, distant husband alone as he agonized over whether to fire his closest aides.[49]

CHAPTER 26

Praying Not to Wake Up

On Saturday morning, April 28, Nixon walked into the living room at Aspen Lodge looking for Manolo and a cup of coffee. He found his daughter Tricia sitting by the fire. She had been up all night talking to Julie, she said, and the two girls had talked to their mother in the morning. The Nixon women were all agreed: Haldeman and Ehrlichman had to go. "I want you to know that I would never let any personal feeling about either of them to interfere with my judgment," she began, even though she added, "You know that I never felt the way they handled people served you well. . . ." Tears were brimming in her eyes, Nixon recalled, "but unlike Julie, Tricia would seldom allow them to overflow." Tricia told her father she would support him whatever he decided to do. They hugged. Nixon had already decided to fire both men. He had been talking to Leonard Garment and Bill Rogers, two old friends whom Nixon had marginalized as president but whose personal advice he still valued. They had been adamant: Nixon had to sacrifice his closest aides to save himself.[1]

With Brezhnev.
**Courtesy of the Richard Nixon Presidential
Library and Museum**

The next day, Sunday April 29, was a beautiful spring day at Camp David. The sun burned off the morning fog and the woods shone with new growth. Haldeman had been summoned, along with Ehrlichman, to the mountaintop. Haldeman was carrying a book of writings by Mary Baker Eddy, the founder of his faith, the Christian Science Church. Aspen Lodge, where the president stayed, was a couple hundred yards from Laurel, the roomy staff lodge recently remodeled by Haldeman. "I chose a bike to pedal over to meet the president, which is, I suppose, rather an unusual way to ride to political doom," recalled Haldeman.[2]

"When I got to Aspen the P was in terrible shape," Haldeman recorded in his diary. "Shook hands with me, which is the first time he's ever done that." Nixon took Haldeman out on to the back terrace overlooking the blooming valley. The president was having trouble speaking. Finally he said, "This is so beautiful. These lovely tulips down here." Nixon told Haldeman, "I have to enjoy this, because I may not be alive much longer."[3] The president began to talk about his religion. He told Haldeman that every morning since his election, he had gotten to his knees and prayed for guidance. ("I thought he looked somewhat surprised," Nixon recalled.) "When I went to bed last night, I hoped, and almost prayed, that I wouldn't wake up this morning," the president said.[4] Haldeman did his best to comfort the man who was dismissing him.

After about forty minutes, Haldeman emerged

and told Ehrlichman, "Your turn." Ehrlichman asked, "How did it go?" Haldeman answered, "About as we expected."

Ehrlichman entered the living room at Aspen without knocking. Wearing a checked sports coat, Nixon appeared from the bedroom. "His eyes were red-rimmed and he looked small and drawn," Ehrlichman recalled. Ehrlichman himself struggled to remain composed as Nixon told him that he had hoped and prayed that he might die during the night.* "He began crying uncontrollably," Ehrlichman recalled. "It's like cutting off my arms," the president sobbed. "You and Bob. You'll need money; I have some—Bebe has it—and you can have it."

Ehrlichman responded, "That would just make things worse. You can do one thing though, sometime." Ehrlichman recalled that it was "hard for me to talk." (In Nixon's account of the conversation, Ehrlichman's "mouth tightened.") "Just explain all this to my kids, will you?" he told the president. "Tell them why you had to do this." Ehrlichman turned and left, wiping his eyes with a handkerchief.[6]

As darkness fell that night, Nixon turned to his spokesman Ron Ziegler, who was becoming a kind of

---

*Haldeman later wrote that he was "hurt" to learn that Nixon had used "exactly the same words about his 'praying not to wake up.' . . . I had been moved and felt a kinship with him. Now I see that this was just a conversational ploy—a debater's way of slipping into a difficult subject—used on both of us." Possibly, but Nixon was not feigning his agony.[5]

all-purpose sounding board, the role so dutifully played by Haldeman. "It's all over, Ron. Do you know that?" said the president, searching for reassurance and sympathy.[7]

The next night, Monday, April 30, 1973, Nixon went on national television to give his first-ever speech on Watergate. He made it sound as if he had discovered and exposed the cover-up. He announced that he had accepted the resignations of Haldeman and Ehrlichman and had fired John Dean. "The easiest course would be for me to blame those to whom I delegated the responsibility to run the campaign," he said, and gravely shook his head. "But that would be the **cowardly** thing to do." His Checkers-style sanctimony was wearing thin. He hoped, he later wrote in his memoirs, that he had "put Watergate behind me as a nagging national issue. I could not have made a more disastrous miscalculation."

In his memoir, Nixon wrote with unusual directness and candor:

In the April 30 speech I gave the impression that I had known nothing at all about the cover-up until my March 21 meeting with Dean. I indicated that once I had learned about it I had acted with dispatch and dispassion to end it. In fact, I had known some of the details of the cover-up before March 21, and when I did become aware of their implications, instead of exerting presidential leadership aimed at uncovering the cover-up, I embarked in an increasingly desperate search for ways to limit the damage to my friends, my administration, and myself.[8]

On his way to the Oval Office to deliver his speech that night, he passed an FBI agent standing in front of Haldeman's office, which had been sealed off to keep anyone from entering and destroying documents. Suddenly, the president turned around. "What the hell is this?" he demanded, and shoved the shocked FBI man against the wall.[9]

After the speech, Nixon went to the Lincoln Sitting Room and may have had a drink. He waited for calls of ritualistic reassurance from cabinet officials. The calls, save one from Health, Education, and Welfare Secretary Caspar Weinberger, never came, partly because Haldeman was no longer around to arrange them. At 10:16 P.M., Nixon took a call from Haldeman.

"I hope I didn't let you down," the president said, his voice slurring.

HALDEMAN: No, sir. You got your points over, and now you've got it set right and move on. You're right where you ought to be.

NIXON: Well, it's a tough thing, Bob, for you and for John and the rest, but, goddamn it, I'm never going to discuss this son-of-a-bitching Watergate thing again—**never, never, never, never**. Don't you agree?

HALDEMAN: Yes, sir. You've done it now, and you've laid out your position. . . .

Nixon began to complain that no cabinet officers, except for Weinberger, had called. After some more presidential bucking up—"by God, keep the faith"—Nixon ventured to ask his old chief of staff for a favor:

NIXON: I don't know whether you can call and get any reactions and call me back—like the old style. Would you mind?

HALDEMAN: I don't think I can. I don't—

NIXON (hearing himself): No, I agree.

HALDEMAN: I'm kind of in an odd spot to try and do that.

NIXON: Don't call a goddamn soul. To hell with it. . . .

Nixon complained some more about cabinet members who needed to check the polls before calling. Haldeman tried to explain that the switchboard had been instructed not to put calls through. Finally, Nixon signed off with an exceedingly rare declaration:

NIXON: God bless you, boy. God bless you.

HALDEMAN: Okay.

NIXON: I love you, as you know.

HALDEMAN: Okay.

NIXON: Like my brother.[10]

At 10:34 P.M., Elliot Richardson called. Nixon had named Richardson attorney general to replace Kleindienst, who had resigned that day, tainted by his association to Mitchell.[11] Nixon had told Kissinger that he picked Richardson—whom he described to speechwriter Ray Price as "sort of Mr. Integrity, Mr. Clean"—because he would be "trusted by the so-called damned establishment."[12] In his televised speech, Nixon had announced that he was giving his new attorney general "complete authority to make all decisions bearing on the prosecution of the Watergate case and related matters"—including the potential appointment of a special prosecutor. Over the phone that night, a grateful Richardson knew how to flatter:

RICHARDSON: Well, I was very—I thought that was really great.
NIXON: Well, you're very kind to say that.
RICHARDSON: In a real sense, your finest hour.

Then, after some more mutual stroking, Nixon got down to business:

NIXON: Elliot, the one thing they're going to be hitting you on is about the special prosecutor.
RICHARDSON: Yeah.
NIXON: The point is, I'm not sure you should have one.[13]

Richardson replied that he would think about it. The new attorney general proceeded to appoint as Watergate special prosecutor a man Nixon would come to fear and loathe. Archibald Cox, a Harvard

Law professor, was, like Richardson, a true believer
in the rule of law and a high Wasp whose tribal loyalties did not lie with Richard Nixon. Cox proceeded
to recruit a staff heavily laced with Harvard grads
and former aides to Senator Edward Kennedy. Appointed solicitor general by President Kennedy, Cox
himself was so close to the Kennedys that he had
watched the 1960 election returns with JFK. At
Cox's swearing-in ceremony in late May, Senator
Kennedy and members of his family were guests, a
fact duly reported to Nixon, who had been warned
by Kissinger that Cox, a former fellow Harvard professor "has been fanatically anti-Nixon all the years I
have known him." (At first, Nixon professed to be
unconcerned, telling Haig that Cox was an ineffec-
tual Harvard professor who would take five years
and still not get to the bottom of the case.)[14]

Nixon's April 30 speech was unpersuasive, even to
his allies. Bud Krogh told Ehrlichman that the president was on "darn thin ice," and conservative strategist Kevin Phillips wrote in his newsletter that the
"wheels of government" had "ground to a halt." He
predicted that more and more people would ask "is
Richard Nixon going to be involved" in the scandal
and the answer would be "yes." The polls suggested
as much: Nixon's approval rating, which had been
running about two to one positive as late as early
April, showed him in negative territory by early
May. Six Republican senators had said they would
not run for reelection unless the president spoke

out on Watergate, but now that he had, no one was satisfied.

The national press, which had been initially slow to react to Watergate, was now overcompensating. In the White House press room, reporters were openly jeering Ziegler, who found himself trying to explain that some of the president's earlier statements on Watergate had become "inoperative." Night after night the broadcast news led with Watergate; every week, **Time** and **Newsweek** featured the scandal on their covers. A torrent of stories— many of them true, but some hyped, garbled, or wrong—flooded the news. Newspapers and magazines reported erroneously that the Plumbers had wiretapped U.S. senators and the friends of Mary Joe Kopechne, the woman who died in Teddy Kennedy's car at Chappaquiddick.[15] In the new world of "investigative" journalism, "sources say" was sufficient authority. When Dean left the White House, he took with him boxes of documents that he would use to try to barter for immunity from prosecution. His lawyers were soon parceling out the juicier tidbits to reporters.[16] The most sensational revelation was the botched break-in at the office of Daniel Ellsberg's psychiatrist, but there were many other leaks, duly fed by staffers on the Senate Watergate Committee. The headlines soon blared about "enemies lists" and Nixon administration plots to bug and wiretap, including spying on reporters.

Nixon correctly, but futilely, complained to his family and his aides about a double standard. Pat

Nixon began collecting examples from earlier administrations, including a quotation from Franklin Roosevelt's son John, who told a newspaper columnist, "Hell, my father just about invented bugging. He had them spread all over, and thought nothing about it."[17] William Sullivan, a former high-level FBI official close to Nixon, provided the Senate Watergate Committee with a memo detailing widespread political bugging and wiretapping by the FBI under earlier Democratic administrations. But the report was buried by the Democratic staff as unproven, too personal, or irrelevant.[18]

Nixon "felt discouraged, drained, and pressured," he recalled in his memoirs.[19] He was no longer pretending to be jaunty with his family or dictating upbeat passages to his diary—or anything at all, for that matter. His last entry was April 30.

Nixon's one bright light was the return of the 591 prisoners of war from Vietnam. At a ceremony at the State Department in May, he greeted them, one by one. When Everett Alvarez, the first pilot to be shot down and captured, reached him in the line, Nixon grabbed Alvarez's arms and shoulders and began feeling them. "You look good," he said to the naval aviator who had spent over eight years in captivity. Looking down, avoiding Alvarez's eyes, Nixon said in a somber tone, "I tried. I really tried."[20]

The president and First Lady wanted to give these men, some of whom had been in brutal captivity for years, the biggest party in the history of the White

House. On the rainy night of May 24, some twelve hundred guests dined on the South Lawn in a great white tent that was larger than the executive mansion itself. Beforehand, a POW chorus of thirty-five men sang a hymn that one of them had written in prison, and the former prisoners of war and their families were invited to wander through the Nixons' private quarters on the second floor. The men presented Nixon with a plaque inscribed, "Our leader— our comrade, Richard the Lion-Hearted." Among the invited celebrities, John Wayne rose and toasted the POWs by saying, "I'll ride into the sunset with you anytime." Nixon introduced Irving Berlin, the aged songwriter who, in a gravelly voice, led them all in his famous song "God Bless America." The men shouted and cried the last words, "God bless America, my home sweet home."

At 12:30 A.M., with the party still going strong, Nixon kissed Pat good night and went upstairs to the Lincoln Sitting Room. Sitting before the fire, listening to the sounds of laughter and music coming from below, he felt, he recalled, "that this was one of the greatest nights of my life." Then he thought of Watergate and was struck "by an almost physical force." Picking up the phone, he called Julie and Tricia in their rooms and asked them to join him.

"My father seemed drained, as if the emotion of the evening had been too much for him," Julie recalled. With the girls there, Nixon telephoned his friend, the TV producer Paul Keyes, who had organized the evening's performances (Bob Hope and

Sammy Davis Jr.; "no girlie show," as per the First Lady's instruction). With Keyes, the creator of **Laugh-In**, Nixon tried a few jokes, "but it was almost painful for us to see how sad Daddy's face looked despite the laughter in his voice," Tricia recorded in her diary.

Nixon hung up. There was silence. Then the president asked his daughters, "Do you think I should resign?" They burst out with "a wave of exclamations," according to Tricia: "Don't you dare! Don't even think of it!" Tricia, who knew her father, wrote in her diary, "He really wanted us to give him reasons for not resigning."[21]

One reason was to preserve his foreign policy achievements, particularly détente with the Soviet Union. The policy was under attack from the right and the left—by conservatives who accused Nixon of going soft on Communism and by liberals who wanted to pressure the Kremlin to free Soviet Jewry. Nixon was determined to keep détente alive with the personal diplomacy he did best.

On June 16, Brezhnev arrived in Washington for a long-scheduled summit meeting. The Senate Watergate Committee agreed to postpone John Dean's much-anticipated testimony in order not to embarrass Nixon. Baffled by Watergate—what superpower would indulge the luxury of destroying its leader over petty nonsense like bugging the opposition?—the Soviets made clear that they were prepared to ignore it.

Nixon greeted Brezhnev in the Oval Office. The Soviet leader embraced him as an old friend. It occurred to Nixon that "the last time such tactile diplomacy had been used in that room was when Lyndon Johnson wanted to make a point." At Camp David, Nixon gave the Soviet leader a personalized Camp David windbreaker, which Brezhnev wore most of the time he was there, and a customized Lincoln Continental. Brezhnev immediately insisted on a test drive. As the head of Nixon's Secret Service detail turned pale, the Kremlin boss motioned Nixon to get into the front seat beside him. Brezhnev was going 50 miles an hour on a one-lane road approaching a turn marked "Slow, Dangerous Curve" when Nixon finally leaned over and said, "Slow down, slow down." Brezhnev ignored him and, with a squeal of rubber, the four-wheel drifted around the turn. "This is a very fine automobile. It holds the road very well," Brezhnev remarked. "You are an excellent driver," Nixon managed to reply. "I would never have been able to make that turn at the speed at which we were driving."[22]

On the trip from Washington to California on Air Force One, Nixon pointed out the Grand Canyon and mentioned John Wayne. Brezhnev jumped back and pretended to draw a pair of six-shooters. Flying by helicopter from California's El Toro Air Base to San Clemente, Nixon made sure that the Soviet leader saw all the highways, cars, and middle-class homes. At Casa Pacifica, where Brezhnev insisted on staying overnight, he was assigned to Tricia's room, decorated in white wicker furniture with pink-flowered wallpaper. The secretary general had not brought Mrs. Brezhnev but was accompanied by a bosomy masseuse; Nixon noted that she wore Arpège, Mrs. Nixon's perfume. Brezhnev shared a narrow hallway with Pat's bedroom, so, as Julie put it, "Mother was aware of the secretary general's activities throughout this visit."[23] "He was always kind of bragging" about being "a ladies' man," Nixon recalled. "Mrs. Nixon did not particularly appreciate that aspect of him."[24]

On the first night, Brezhnev retired early, complaining of jet lag, then roused Nixon out of his bed at 10:15 P.M. to try to bully him on the Middle East. Crammed into Nixon's tiny study with their translators and top advisers, the two superpower leaders went at it. (Nixon was "as always calm under pressure," recalled Kissinger.)[25] Brezhnev insisted that the United States and Soviets work out a Middle East peace deal right there. Nixon, who was sure that the Russians were fronting for their Egyptian clients and trying to marginalize Israel, said no—a peace deal imposed on the Middle East, he believed, was sure to fail.[26]

With the Russians, Nixon could still stand firm. Congress was a different matter. In the spring of 1973, the North Vietnamese began moving down the Ho Chi Minh Trail to resupply their troops inside South Vietnam. It was a clear violation of the peace accords signed just a few months earlier. Nixon wanted to bomb the North Vietnamese, but he knew that he could not, that a majority of senators would openly revolt. He was too weakened by Watergate to act.[27]

At 5:30 A.M. on July 12, Nixon awakened with a stabbing pain in his chest. The pain was "nearly unbearable," he recalled.[28] Nixon had pretended not to watch John Dean's testimony before the Watergate Committee at the end of June, but he understood television well enough to measure the impact. With his beautiful wife sitting demurely behind him and Senator Howard Baker asking, repeatedly, "What did he know, and when did he know it?" the handsome, bespectacled young lawyer had seemed humble and credible. The former White House counsel delivered, in detail that was at once numbing and sensational, a scathing indictment of his former boss. Most of Dean's revelations had already been leaked, but he managed to hold millions of TV viewers spellbound with a vision of life inside the White House that was dark and conspiratorial, paranoid, and vengeful against its enemies.

In the bright early light of a June morning, Nixon lay coughing and burning in his bed at the White House, unable to arise. At about 9 A.M., Nixon summoned Al Haig, his new chief of staff, to his bedroom. Haig was surprised to find Nixon still in bed; he had never seen the president lying down before. Haig had filled in for Haldeman with take-charge brio. (An aide to Haig once described him as "pathologically ambitious.")[29] The only dissenter to Haig's appointment had been Kissinger, who did not like the idea of reporting to his former assistant and who resented Haig for undercutting him with the president. Kissinger had threatened to resign (again), spurring Rose Woods to tell him, "Henry, for once in your life, act like a man."[30]

Huddled under the bed covers in his pajamas, Nixon began coughing violently. Seeing blood on the president's pillow, Haig urged Nixon to go to the hospital. But Nixon resisted. His fever (102 degrees) rose when he took a call from Senator Sam Ervin at 11 A.M. The chairman of the Watergate Committee wanted Nixon to turn over presidential papers relating to Watergate. In a letter citing "executive privilege"—the well-established doctrine that the executive can't function without some degree of confidentiality—Nixon had refused. Ervin wrote Nixon what he called a "little note" beseeching him to reconsider. The senator's note was promptly leaked to the press, enraging Nixon.

"I read about your letter," Nixon began. "Your committee leaks, you know." The conversation deteriorated. "Your attitude in the hearings was clear," Nixon told Ervin. "There's no question who you're out to get."[31]

"We are not out to get anything, Mr. President, except the truth," replied Ervin.

When Ervin hung up, "his face was flushed," recalled his chief counsel, Sam Dash. "The president is screaming at the top of his lungs, 'You are out to get me; you are out to get me!'" Ervin told his staff.[32]

The next day the entire exchange was in **The New York Times**.

"The joust with Ervin seemed to rejuvenate Nixon," Haig recalled in his memoirs. But he was obviously very sick, and by late afternoon the president was admitted to Bethesda Naval Hospital, where he was diagnosed with pneumonia. Breathing with difficulty, Nixon was unable to sleep.

On the morning of Monday, July 16, Haig received some shocking news: Haldeman's former aide, Alex Butterfield, had testified to the Watergate Committee about the secret taping system in Nixon's offices and residences.* Haig immediately ordered, "Tear it out," and headed to Bethesda to talk to the president. Nixon was "not in a talkative mood," Haig recalled. The president's first reaction was that Butterfield's revelation would make him a laughingstock. Indeed, one headline read, "Nixon Bugs Himself."[34] Haig was worried where the tapes would lead. He recalled telling the president, "Mr. President, I've been in a good many meetings with you, and we both know how the conversation goes. You set up straw men; you play devil's advocate; you say things you don't mean. Others do the same. There is gossip and profanity. Imagine publishing

---

*Butterfield had stood outside the inner circle of loyalists. Haldeman later suggested that the ex–Air Force officer was a CIA plant. "Haldeman is full of shit," former CIA director Richard Helms told Jonathan Aitken, but Watergate conspiracy theorists have continued to dig for a plot by the national security establishment to bring down the president.[33]

every word Lyndon Johnson ever said in the Oval Office. No president could survive it."

Still feverish, Nixon appeared unsure what to do, though he seemed—in Haig's view—to be leaning toward destroying the tapes. He told Haig to go back to the White House and talk to the two lawyers who had been deputized to handle Watergate.[35]

Nixon's lawyers were opposites: Fred Buzhardt was a slow-speaking, cagey South Carolinian and, like Haig, a West Pointer. Leonard Garment, Nixon's old friend and colleague from his New York law days, was known as voluble and excitable—"the Nuclear Non-reactor" was his nickname. Buzhardt agreed with Haig about the risk of letting the world hear the unfiltered Nixon. "You know how he talks in the Oval Office; you would think he was Beelzebub reincarnated," Buzhardt said. He argued that the tapes were Nixon's property and that, at least until a subpoena arrived, he was free to destroy them. Garment responded that Nixon would be impeached if he did such a thing and threatened to resign.[36]

Haig, Buzhardt, and Garment piled into a car and drove out to Bethesda to confer with the president. The debate was typically wandering and inchoate. Spiro Agnew dropped by and ventured his opinion. "Boss," he told the bedridden Nixon, "you've got to have a bonfire." According to Haig, Nixon "gazed at a picture on the wall and feigned temporary deafness."[37] At one point, there was discussion of who would light the match. Bebe Rebozo?

Nixon's dog King Timahoe? Haig later recalled that
Nixon asked him if he would be willing to destroy
the tapes. "I can't do that, I can't put my family in
that position," Haig replied—but suggested that
maybe Manolo could do the deed.[38]

In the morning—Tuesday, July 17—after his
fever broke, Nixon told Haig, "Al, those tapes are
going to defend me. They're going to protect me
from what I'm being charged with." He would come
to rue his decision not to destroy the tapes. Indeed,
he had second thoughts almost right away. In the
early hours of Thursday, July 19, he made a note on
his bedside pad: "Should have destroyed the tapes
after April 30, 1973." In early April, Nixon and
Haldeman had discussed getting rid of all the tapes
save the ones recording his major foreign policy decisions.[39] Distracted and caught up in Watergate,
Nixon and Haldeman had not acted on this instinct.
By July 19, it was too late: The subpoenas from investigators had begun to arrive.

Nixon and Haldeman believed, wrongly, that the
tapes might be exculpatory, that they would contra-
dict Dean's damning testimony. Nixon's recorded
statements are not as incriminating as Dean's testimony promised. But veering back and forth on subjects like hush money—condoning it one moment,
rejecting it the next—Nixon's utterances were, ton-
ally at least, unsavory and demeaning to the office.
Surely Nixon must have known, at some level, how
the tapes would sound if made public. But he believed that his conversations were protected by ex-

ecutive privilege and that he would be shielded by
the courts. He was wrong in this judgment, but not
irrational. Less reasonably, he seems to have clung to
the tapes as a kind of insurance policy against betrayal by others, including his closest aides. At one
point, he said to Haig, "Al, I don't know what Haldeman and Ehrlichman are going to accuse me of."[40]

Nixon could not let go of his deep desire to shape
the historical record. In 1971, Elliot Richardson had
discussed Nixon's favorite biography, Blake's **Disraeli**. Richardson, who could play the courtier, was
quick to grasp the comparison between Nixon and
the great nineteenth-century British statesman.
"The similarities are great, Mr. President," said
Richardson, "but what a pity that Blake could not
quote Disraeli's conversation." For years, Richardson would wonder if he had helped bring on Watergate by thus encouraging Nixon to record **his**
conversations.[41]

There was one Nixon intimate who recognized
right away the risk in hanging on to the tapes. "My
mother saw immediately that unlimited access to
the President's private, candid conversations spelled
disaster," Julie recalled. "She told me later that she
felt the tapes should have been destroyed." But at
the time, "at the hospital she said nothing about the
tapes, relying on an even stronger instinct: her implicit faith in her husband. She would not worry
him by probing, especially when he was ill—and
vulnerable." When Pat picked up her daughter to go
to the hospital, Julie noticed that her mother was

"uncharacteristically wearing sunglasses. She was very quiet in the car, and I remember how she protectively put her hand on top of mine."[42]

Nixon returned to the White House "on a beautiful summer day," he recalled, and tried to buck up the staff, which had turned out to greet him in the Rose Garden. Rumors that he might resign, he told them, were, "in one of my father's favorite words, pure poppycock." The president vowed: "Let others wallow in Watergate, we are going to do our job."

After thirty-seven days and 325 hours of network broadcast time, the Senate Watergate hearings were at last winding down. One of the last witnesses, Pat Buchanan, gave a feisty defense of political spying and pranks and finally got across the point that Democrats, too, indulged in them.[43] But the weight of testimony, in all its tawdry detail, left a strong impression of a White House that had lost its moral bearings. The president's credibility was badly wounded, and Nixon knew it. On the July 23 White House "News Summary" he underlined an item that showed how low his standing had sunk even among the midwestern faithful. The item began, " 'Facts Batter Sense of Trust' is Trib head on first of 4-part series." The "Trib" was the **Chicago Tribune,** historically a pro-Republican organ. The "4-part series" promised to lay out Nixon's lies about Watergate. Nixon jotted a note to Haig and Ziegler, "Al and Z—this is the basic problem." The heartland's trust in Nixon, battered by the facts emerging from the Watergate hearings, was fading.

For his first four and a half years in office, Nixon had underlined his Daily News Summary and festooned the margins with reactions ("Good!") and instructions ("Order the jerk to pipe down!").[44] But by the Watergate summer, Nixon's commentary on the Daily News Summary had dwindled to almost nothing.

Perhaps he thought there was no longer any point. Nixon had tried to manipulate and control a press corps that had grown increasingly skeptical of authority through the gyrations of the late 1960s and the "credibility gap" left by LBJ's deception over the Vietnam War. The facts of Watergate, as they dribbled out, were bad enough, but an inflamed press corps did not stop at the facts. Gossip became headlines. "At some point in the hot, muggy summer of 1973, some of the more influential members of the Washington press corps concluded that I was starting to go off my rocker," Nixon recalled.[45] Nixon fed the rumor mill with his own erratic behavior. On August 20, he flew to New Orleans to address the Veterans of Foreign Wars. The trip was intended to show off Nixon's popularity outside the Beltway, with cheering crowds lining the roads. But an assassination threat forced a change in the motorcade route, and when Haig handed the president a bulletproof vest, Nixon exploded: "Al, get that damn thing away from me!"[46] Moments later, as he entered a special VIP holding room trailed by press secretary Ron Ziegler and the usual gaggle of reporters, Nixon abruptly spun Ziegler around and shoved him, snarling, "I don't want any press with me, and you take care of it!" CBS News played the video twice, in slow motion.[47]

In the **New Republic,** John Osborne, perhaps the most respected Nixon-watcher in the press, wrote that reporters detected "something indefinably but unmistakably odd" about the president's gait. There was a frisson of excitement, Osborne later wrote, at the thought that "he might go bats in front of them at any time."[48] A story spread that Nixon had slapped an airman at a military base. Actually, in a bout of clumsiness, he had hit him in the face while trying to shake his hand.[49]

Nixon could see morale sinking in the White House staff, but he did not know quite how low.[50] An entry by a staffer who was keeping a running diary for Leonard Garment suggests the level of cynicism even among Nixon's lawyers:

Wednesday, August 15

at 9:00 pm that evening President gave speech on TV—more or less the same thing, i.e. "had no prior knowledge of break-in; never took part in or knew about any of the subsequent cover-up activities; neither authorized nor encouraged subordinates to engage in illegal or improper campaign activities . . . that was and is the simple truth." (simple, all right, as in if you are simple enough to

believe this, you'll believe anything!) They (Zei-
gler [sic], possibly Haig and certainly the President himself) seem to think if he keeps saying it
over and over again, it will become the truth or be
accepted as such, but still won't give up the tapes
which presumably would at least give some clari-
fication of what the truth is.[51]

Nixon had defied a subpoena from special prosecutor Archibald Cox to turn over tapes on certain
dates, and the matter was in the courts. Nixon was
not just trying to keep Cox at bay. He refused to let
his own lawyers listen to the tapes. Doug Parker, the
young White House attorney who was working with
Garment on Nixon's defense, recalled going with
Garment to see William Rogers to try to enlist the
secretary of state's support in persuading Nixon to
level with the men hired to defend him. Rogers was
Nixon's old friend, and Nixon himself had turned to
Rogers for advice in April when he was pondering
the fates of Haldeman and Ehrlichman. Garment
and Parker made their pitch: "We told Rogers, 'We
think the President knows more than he's saying,'"
Parker recalled. "'We need to get it out, and you
could be just the person to persuade him.' Rogers
made it very clear to us: He was not going to sign up
for that committee!"[52]*

---

*In August, Nixon decided to remove Rogers as secretary of state
and replace him with Kissinger. Nixon did not want to deliver
the bad news to Rogers, so he told Haig to do it. Rogers reportedly told Haig, "Tell the president to go fuck himself."[53]

Back in the second week of June, Attorney General Richardson had come to Haig with some disturbing news: Federal prosecutors were investigating Vice President Agnew for kickbacks on public construction projects during his time as governor of Maryland. As vice president, he had allegedly continued to take bags of cash at the office. "In my own mind, two words formed: **double impeachment**," recalled Haig. "I called Fred Buzhardt and told him what Richardson had just told me and what I feared. 'Oh, shit,' said Fred."[54]

Nixon had known about the charges against Agnew since April 10, but he had wanted to believe his veep's protestations of innocence. "Damn lies," Agnew had told Nixon. But by the end of September, Richardson was informing Nixon that the government had "an open-and-shut case" against the vice president.[55] Garment's diarist recorded:

Some people in WH think this might take some heat off the President's problems—does it help to have a VP charged with taking "bribes"?? If so, things are really bad.[56]

CHAPTER 27

The Saturday Night Massacre

October 1973 was the most dramatic month of Nixon's presidency. The president was caught in a dizzying swirl of crises, some forced on him, some self-inflicted. He was at once bold, foolish, defiant, and blind to the precariousness of his position. He was brave and decisive at moments, withdrawn and absent at other times. His sense of reality seemed blurred by stresses that were becoming ever more personal.

On October 6, the Nixon administration was caught completely off guard by an Arab attack—Syrians from the north, Egyptians from the south—against Israel. Just the day before, the CIA had reported to the president that war was unlikely. Nixon was unsurprised by the incompetence of the CIA, his old hobbyhorse, but he was "stunned" by the failure of Israeli intelligence.[1] Attacking on the Day of Atonement—the holiest day on the Jewish calendar, when most Israelis were home with their families—the Arab invaders inflicted heavy losses on Israeli forces. For the sake of a peace deal that

Archibald Cox.

would bring a balance of power to the region, the Nixon administration was willing to see Israel bloodied, but only up to a point, and that point was quickly passed.[2]

At 1:30 A.M. on October 9, the Israeli ambassador to Washington, Simcha Dinitz, awakened Secretary of State Kissinger to warn that Israel was losing the war and badly needed supplies.[3] The U.S. response was sluggish, partly because President Nixon was distracted by events closer to home. At 6 P.M. earlier the same night, Vice President Agnew had appeared at the Oval Office to resign. For weeks, the corrupt former governor of Maryland had been forcefully proclaiming his innocence: "Small and fearful men have been frightened into furnishing evidence against me. . . . I will not resign if indicted! **I will not resign if indicted!**" he had recently bellowed at a cheering rally of Republican women in Los Angeles, who were chanting "Spiro is our hero!" Under pressure from Justice Department lawyers, who wanted to send Agnew to prison for bribery, Al Haig had been trying to persuade Agnew to accept a face-saving plea bargain. Agnew had resisted, angrily. (Haig told his wife, "only half in jest," that in case he disappeared they might "want to look inside any recently poured bridge pilings in Maryland"; Agnew later wrote that he in turn feared that Haig would arrange for him to have a convenient "accident.")[4] To avoid a jail sentence, Agnew finally took a deal— three years probation and a $10,000 fine for tax evasion—and stepped down. His visit to the Oval

Office was unannounced, though not unexpected. The scene would play out with ritual insincerity.

Nixon looked "gaunt and sorrowful," Agnew recalled, as he shook Agnew's hand. Agnew asked if the president could help him find some corporation to put him on retainer as a consultant. Nixon told Agnew he'd always be his friend. Agnew's eyes welled up, and Nixon put his arm around Agnew's shoulders. Agnew began to realize that Nixon couldn't wait to get him out of there. They never spoke again.[5]

The president was immediately consumed with trying to find a successor to his defrocked number two. His first choice was John Connally, but a few phone calls to Capitol Hill revealed the hopelessness of that cause. Connally could never be confirmed by the Senate: Many Democrats saw him as a traitor to the party and a potential presidential opponent on the GOP ticket in 1976. High-profile candidates like Ronald Reagan and Nelson Rockefeller would split the Republicans. The safe choice—practically speaking, the only choice—was House Republican Minority Leader Gerald Ford. The genial Ford was popular on the Hill, on both sides of the aisle.

Nixon regarded Ford, his fellow charter member of the Chowder and Marching Club, as decent but not exceptionally bright.[6] With the poor political judgment that increasingly afflicted him, Nixon believed that Ford provided him with a layer of protection against impeachment—the affable but limited congressman from Michigan was a "good insurance policy," the president told Chuck Colson. Congress,

Nixon predicted, would not want to remove the incumbent and bequeath the presidency to a rank amateur who knew so little about foreign policy.[7] At a White House ceremony on Friday evening, October 12, to announce Ford as his choice, Nixon mistook the loud applause from members of Congress in the audience; the president thought they were cheering for him. Nixon was "exuberant" when Kissinger encountered him the next morning at the White House. "As always after a successful public performance, Nixon was exhilarated," Kissinger recalled. "He still reveled in the applause that had greeted his brief, graceful speech the night before. He failed to recognize that it was a tribute above all to Ford."[8]

Secretary of State Kissinger had been up most of the night. At 11:20 on Friday night, Ambassador Dinitz had appeared at his White House office to plead for help. Israel had lost a third of its air force and a fifth of its tanks in intense fighting. Israeli forces were running out of fuel and ammunition while the Egyptians and Syrians were being resupplied by the Soviets. Nixon had ordered the Pentagon to restock the Israelis, but the supply chain was bottlenecked, partly for bureaucratic reasons and possibly because of pro-Arab sentiment at the Pentagon.[9]

As so often in the past, Nixon felt isolated, unable to trust his closest advisers. He was getting foot-dragging excuses from the Pentagon, and he continued to wonder about Kissinger's divided or ambivalent loyalties—to him, to his liberal friends, to the Jewish state.[10] Nixon himself was constantly weighing competing interests—access to cheap Arab oil, the Jewish vote at election time, worries about provoking a conflict with the Soviet Union over primacy in the Middle East. Along with Kissinger, he had a tendency to delude himself with the presumption that America could cold-bloodedly calibrate the fate of other peoples as part of some grand global "geostrategy."[11] And yet, in a critical moment in the history of Israel, Nixon—who could so casually utter ethnic slurs—decisively and forcefully came to the rescue of the people of Israel. When Kissinger told him that the Pentagon had authorized three C-5A transports to fly to Israel—any more would "cause problems" with the Arabs and Soviets— Nixon was exasperated. "We're going to get blamed just as much for three planes as for 300," he told Kissinger.[12] The president called Secretary of Defense James Schlesinger and told him that he was aware of the gravity of his decision and that he would accept the responsibility if the Arabs cut off oil to America. If the Pentagon could not arrange private charter flights, it should use military aircraft. "Do it, **now,**" the president ordered.

Informed by Kissinger that Pentagon officials were arguing over the type of aircraft to be used, Nixon exploded: "Goddamn it, use every one we have. Tell them to send everything that can fly."[13] The next morning, anxious residents in Tel Aviv were awakened to a loud droning in the sky. One after another, giant American air force transports rumbled overhead as they descended to nearby airports and airfields. Cars stopped in the streets and people began to shout "God bless America!" Relieved and grateful, Golda Meir, Israel's hard-bitten prime minister, wept.[14]

On the same day that Israel asked to be saved by the United States, the U.S. Court of Appeals ruled 5 to 2 that President Nixon had to turn over the tapes of nine White House conversations subpoenaed by the Watergate Special Prosecution Force. Nixon had been dreading the court's decision, in part because of the prospect that the judges would shred his constitutional defense of executive privilege and in part because he feared the unleashed zeal of Archibald Cox. "Firing him," Nixon wrote in his memoirs, "seemed the only way to rid the administration of the partisan viper we had planted in our bosom."[15]

For months, the special prosecutor, with his graying crew cut and jaunty bow ties, had been engaged in what Nixon regarded as a witch-hunt.* Cox had used his wide mandate, empowering him to investigate the presidential abuse of powers, to look into Nixon's personal finances as well as those of his friend, Bebe Rebozo. The aggressive young lawyers in Cox's office were examining the hefty expenditure of taxpayer dollars to improve Nixon properties in Key Biscayne and San Clemente, as well as a sizable

---

*"The opposite was true," Richard Ben-Veniste, Cox's senior prosecutor, told the author. "Cox was constantly quizzing us: 'But is it fair?'"

tax break Nixon had claimed when donating his private papers to the National Archives. Nixon prided himself in believing that he was above the sort of venality that had brought down Agnew and so many politicians. "Never let a dollar touch your hand" was Nixon's maxim for avoiding any stain on his personal probity. But, following the precedent set by Lyndon Johnson and his Texas ranch, the Nixon White House spared no expense while making presidential retreats more comfortable and secure. While Pat remained frugal, Nixon had paid little attention as Haldeman had spent freely to please his boss.[16]

With investigators poking around in Nixon's finances and a distraught Bebe Rebozo complaining that he was a target in a money-laundering investigation, Nixon felt like he was reliving the Fund Crisis. Pat was "heartsick," Julie recalled.[17] The president's anger at Cox and his team, known as the "Coxsuckers" around the White House, was beginning to cloud his judgment. "If it costs me the presidency, Cox is going to go," Nixon fumed to Haig.[18]

Nixon's chief of staff, working with Nixon's lawyer, Fred Buzhardt, tried to head off a confrontation with Cox over the tapes. Haig proposed a compromise: The White House would make "summaries" of the subpoenaed recordings, and Senator John Stennis would vouch for their accuracy. Stennis was old and hard of hearing, but he was respected in the Senate. (He was also someone Buzhardt thought he could trust to cover up inconvenient truths; Stennis's nickname as chairman of the Senate Appropriations Committee was "the Undertaker" because he could bury controversial spending items so deep in the federal budget that nobody could dig them up.) Haig thought that he had persuaded Attorney General Richardson to sell the compromise to Cox, but he was mistaken.[19] The president's chief of staff underestimated the deep bonds between the two Yankee lawyers. They valued their loyalty to the rule of law, and to each other, far above any allegiance to Nixon. As Harvard Law School grads, both men had been law clerks to Judge Learned Hand, who was known for his flinty honor. As he defied President Nixon on the night that became known as the "Saturday Night Massacre," Richardson read to Cox from Homer's **Iliad**. The passage (slightly improved by Richardson) had been inscribed, in Greek, in a signed photo given to Richardson by Judge Hand:

> **Now, though numberless fates of death beset us, which no mortal can escape or avoid, let us go forward together, and happily we shall give honor to one another, or another to us.**[20]

Matched against such self-conscious pillars of rectitude, Nixon was bound to look like a small and mean tyrant. Saturday, October 20, 1973, unfolded with Shakespearean—that is to say, convincingly contrived—drama. At a press conference early that afternoon, Cox rejected the "Stennis Compromise" and said that he would go to the Supreme Court to force the president to turn over the tapes.

In **Breach of Faith: The Fall of Richard Nixon,** presidential chronicler Theodore White (Harvard '38) rendered the scene in the ballroom at the National Press Club: "Gangling, gentle and firm, combining the qualities of old Mr. Chips and Joan of Arc, the Special Prosecutor opened at his best—and then proceeded to get better." Sheepishly, perhaps a bit disingenuously, Cox apologized for disturbing reporters on a beautiful fall day. "I am certainly not out to get the President of the United States," said Cox, as the cameras zoomed in. "I am even worried, to put it in colloquial terms, that I am getting too big for my britches." But he felt honor-bound, he explained, "to stick by what I thought was right." Cox went on to state that under the law only the attorney general—not the president—could fire him.

Nixon was prepared to fire Richardson if he declined to fire Cox. "If Elliot feels that he has to go with his Harvard boy, then that's it," Nixon told Haig.[21] Shortly after 4:30 P.M., Richardson was ushered into the Oval Office. The attorney general, refusing to axe Cox, resigned instead. "Let it be on your head," responded Nixon, grimly. He said that he was sorry Richardson had put his own concern above the nation's interest at a time when the Russians were watching for signs of irresolution in the Middle East. Richardson usually spoke in a slurred New England drawl (often mimicked by the departed Agnew, to Nixon's entertainment). But now the ex–attorney general crisply uttered: "I like to feel that what I'm doing **is** in the national interest."[22]

At 8:22 P.M., Ron Ziegler stepped before the cameras to announce that Cox had been fired and that Richardson, as well as his deputy, William Ruckelshaus, had resigned. (Solicitor General Robert Bork, the number three official at Justice, finally fired Cox because, while he disagreed with the decision, Bork believed that Nixon was within his rights and he recognized the need for continuity of government.) The networks broke into their Saturday night programming to show images of FBI agents arriving at the Justice Department to seal off the offices of the special prosecutor. NBC anchorman John Chancellor opened his newscast by saying, "The country tonight is in the midst of what may be the most serious constitutional crisis in its history." A dinner party in New York City at the home of CBS chairman William S. Paley "erupted in a maelstrom of hysteria," recalled Jonathan Aitken, who was a guest, along with an array of prominent Establishment types. "Excitable phrases like 'coup d'etat'; 'What's next? Gas ovens?'; 'Reichstag fire'; 'thump of jackboots'; 'White House madman'; and 'Nixon's insane' filled the air," recalled Aitken. Around midnight, Paley proclaimed, "It's the last straw. He's bound to be impeached now."[23]

Feeling low, fearful that he had failed the president, Haig went to find Nixon, who was alone in the darkened Oval Office. The president, too, seemed dispirited. Haig dutifully briefed Nixon on the spiraling events at home and abroad. Haig noticed that Nixon seemed to be reviving. "Well,

Al," he said, his voice regaining its timber, "it's going to be tough, but we'll handle it. It will work out."

Haig recalled, "I realized that he was reassuring me, letting me know that he still had confidence in me. Deeply touched by his simple kindness in what must have been one of the most difficult hours of his life, I felt a surge of admiration and sympathy for this complex, unpredictable, and indomitable man." But Haig also wondered if Nixon could survive the firestorm.[24]

"I was taken by surprise by the ferocious intensity of the reaction," Nixon recalled. "For the first time I recognized the impact Watergate was having on America. I suddenly realized how deeply its acid had eaten into the nation's grain."[25] Nixon expected a revolt by the likes of Bill Paley's dinner party. But when he saw that, almost overnight, his approval rating had sunk to an unprecedentedly low 17 percent, he again fell into a deep depression.

Nixon's aides could feel the gloom. Charles Wardell, Haig's young assistant who delivered briefing books to the president, could see Nixon becoming morose. Nixon rarely spoke to Wardell, but one day during this low time, as Nixon took a Department of State briefing book he had no intention of reading, the president said to Wardell, "I'm the bridge between two generations and neither likes me. They like the president [meaning the office it-self], but they don't like me."[26]

Brent Scowcroft, Kissinger's deputy, often dealt with the president, especially as Kissinger traveled to Moscow and the Middle East and Scowcroft ran the national security staff. By the third week of October, Kissinger had succeeded in arranging a cease-fire between Israel and the Arabs, but the Russians threatened to create a far greater crisis. At 9:35 P.M. on October 24, Soviet leader Brezhnev signaled that the Soviets were considering sending troops to the region. Intelligence showed that seven Soviet airborne divisions, representing some fifty thousand men, had been put on alert.

It was obvious that the Kremlin was testing American resolve. Scowcroft assembled a White House meeting of the president's top advisers in the Situation Room. They agreed that America needed to put its nuclear forces on alert—a powerful return signal to the Soviets that they needed to back off. The decision was reached with Nixon's concurrence—but without his presence. Haig twice left to consult with Nixon, but Nixon himself stayed away from the meeting.[27]

When stories about Nixon's absence leaked into the press, there was a stir of rumor, fed by Kissinger's aides, that the president was somehow incapacitated. In a phone call to Kissinger earlier that day, the president had said, "I may physically die." Nixon had just learned that the House would begin impeachment proceedings against him. His enemies, Nixon told Kissinger, "want to kill the president. And they may succeed."[28]

Scowcroft later recalled to the author that he was not surprised by the president's absence that night in the Situation Room, as the nation went to DEFCON 3 (two grades higher, DEFCON 1, means imminent war). "He wasn't well," said Scowcroft. "By then he had taken to not showing up at meetings." Nobody at the time said anything about the president's drinking, recalled Scowcroft, but it was becoming more noticeable, in part because of the president's limited capacity for alcohol. In the winter of 1973–74, as Kissinger began his "shuttle diplomacy" to try to reach a more permanent peace in the Middle East, it fell to Scowcroft to brief the president every day on Kissinger's cables. Usually counseling restraint, the messages were often written in Kissinger's opaque diplo-speak. "Nixon would call me mid-afternoon and ask, 'What do you think he meant by that?'" Scowcroft recalled. "At six he'd call after a martini and he'd slur a little and again ask what Kissinger meant. Then at 8:30 after several drinks with his friend Bebe he would tell me to put the troops on alert. If I'd done what he said we would have been at war three times over. But the next morning nobody would say anything." Scowcroft did not find the president's behavior alarming; by watching Kissinger and Haldeman before him, he had learned that Nixon was just "blowing off steam."

By then, Scowcroft said, "I knew enough not to think it was dangerous."[29]*

Nixon gained nothing by firing Cox. He was compelled by popular and political pressure to appoint a new special prosecutor, Leon Jaworski, a prominent Texas lawyer who turned out to be almost as persistent as his predecessor. Nixon still had to hand over the tapes. His woes only deepened when Judge Sirica announced that there was an eighteen-and-a-half-minute gap on one of the tapes, a recording of a conversation between the president and Haldeman on June 20, just as the Watergate scandal was breaking. Rose Woods claimed that she might have accidentally caused the gap, or at least five minutes of it. Posing for photographers, she awkwardly, and implausibly, contorted herself to show how she might

---

*The concern—or lack thereof—about Nixon's drinking shows in a recorded phone call between Scowcroft and Kissinger at 7:55 P.M. on October 11. Scowcroft called Kissinger to say that Edward Heath, the British prime minister, wished to speak to the president. Kissinger asked Scowcroft, "Can we tell them no? When I talked to the president he was loaded." Scowcroft suggested that they describe Nixon as unavailable until the morning, but that the prime minister could speak to Kissinger. "In fact, I would welcome it," Kissinger told Scowcroft to say. Historian Robert Dallek observed, "What seems striking in this exchange is how matter-of-fact Kissinger and Scowcroft were about Nixon's condition, as if it were nothing out of the ordinary." It also shows the eagerness of Kissinger, who sometimes exaggerated Nixon's drinking, to run foreign policy himself.[30]

have pressed the wrong buttons while taking a phone call. "Rose Mary's Boo Boo" was the headline over the photograph on the cover of **Newsweek**.[31] The bad dream had become black comedy.

At the time, Al Haig made a joke about "sinister forces" erasing the tape. Much later, in an oral history for the Nixon Library, he claimed, "I think Rose did it" at the request of Bebe Rebozo. "God, she loved Nixon and she would do anything for him," said Haig.[32] The eighteen-and-a-half-minute gap remains an enduring Watergate mystery. Nixon denied any responsibility, but very few people had access to the tapes, and someone made five to nine erasures. It's unclear what Nixon and Haldeman were talking about on the June 20 tape—Haldeman's notes of the meeting are benign but inconclusive ("PR offensive to top this")—but Nixon plainly did not want to be heard discussing what to do about Watergate with his chief of staff within three days of the break-in. At the time, he was insisting that he had been ignorant of the cover-up until the infamous cancer-on-the-presidency conversation with John Dean of March 21, 1973.[33]

"I know that most people think that my inability to explain the 18½ minute gap is the most unbelievable and insulting part of the whole of Watergate," Nixon wrote in his memoirs. Nixon kept adding to his own caricature. Rattled by the headlines about investigations into his personal finances, he told a press conference on November 18—in the same defiant but brittle tone he had once told reporters,

"You won't have Nixon to kick around anymore"—"I welcome this kind of examination, because people have got to know whether or not their president is a crook. Well, I am not a crook."

Nixon's statement was "not spur-of-the-moment," he recalled. "The attacks on my personal integrity were more disturbing for me and my family than all the other attacks put together." But, he conceded, saying "I am not a crook" was "a mistake." The remark became "an almost constant source of criticism and ridicule."[34]

"HONK FOR IMPEACHMENT" read signs in Lafayette Park across from the White House, and motorists on Pennsylvania Avenue did. The Nixon girls, long accustomed to the vulgar chants of antiwar protesters, tried to ignore the cacophony. But they could see the toll on their father as his press aides fended off questions like: Is the president seeing a psychiatrist? Is he using drugs? Does he still believe in prayer? "The drinking rumors were the most persistent," Julie recalled, "perhaps because it seemed he **was** drinking a little more than ever before, but at dinnertime, when he was trying to unwind."[35] For months, Julie had been on the road making speeches in her father's defense, sometimes as many as six times a week, but it was hard for her, too. After a night of caustic jokes at the annual Radio and Television Correspondents' Dinner, when the Nicaraguan ambassador tried to show some sympathy, she burst into tears and fled the room. When her father suggested she become less involved, she responded, "But Daddy, we have to fight." Tricia, quieter but no less fierce in her resolve, took to staying with her father at night in the Lincoln Sitting Room, saying little if anything, but just trying to show her loyalty and affection.[36]

The holidays brought no respite. On December 23, 1973, at Camp David, Nixon wrote across a page of notes, "Last Christmas here?"[37] At Christmas dinner, Nixon was subdued, Pat quieter than usual. An Arab oil embargo—punishment for Nixon saving Israel—had plunged the nation into an energy crisis. Long lines of automobiles snaked around fuel-starved gas stations. Around the country, thermostats and speed limits were lowered. At the White House, once brightly lit at Nixon's command, there were 80 percent fewer Christmas lights than the year before. For appearances' sake, Nixon decided to park Air Force One and fly commercial to San Clemente over New Year's. Tricia remembered the family's intense discomfort: The other passengers in first class kept their eyes "glued" on the Nixons, even during the movie.[38]

The sun did not shine at Casa Pacifica. The California weather was unusually wet and cold, and electric heaters were moved from the living room to the bedrooms at night. A small earthquake and the highest tides in three hundred years added an eerie feel to the refuge. Nixon sat for hours, staring out at the slate gray ocean; at night, unable to sleep, he played the piano in the darkness.[39] At 1:15 A.M. on

January 1, 1974, the president made a note: "The basic question is: Do I fight all out or do I now begin the long process to prepare for a change, meaning, in effect, resignation?" His note continued:

The **answer—fight**.

At 5 A.M., he made another note:

Above all else: Dignity, command, faith, head high, no fear, build a new spirit, drive, act like a President, act like a winner. Opponents are savage destroyers, haters. Time to use full power of the President to fight overwhelming forces arrayed against us.[40]

"The White House staff Christmas party that year was a wake," recalled Chuck Colson. Steve Bull, Nixon's personal assistant, took Colson aside to say, "No one here is trying to save the President; everyone is knifing him, protecting themselves." Haig was threatening to quit unless Ziegler was demoted; Ziegler refused to attend the party because Haig was scheduled to be there. Neither showed up. "Never have I seen liquor flow more freely or produce fewer smiles," Colson recalled. His former assistant, Dick Howard, compared the White House to Hitler's bunker in its backbiting and hedonism.[41]

Bryce Harlow, brought back to the White House for his political skills in reaching out to congressmen, quit. So did Mel Laird, who had been trying, and failing, to arrange meetings between the president and Laird's many friends on the Hill. "By January [1974], as far as we were concerned, Nixon was almost incommunicado," Harlow recalled. "If he wouldn't let us help, it was time to go."[42] Fred Malek was trying to mentor a promising thirty-three-year-old White House Fellow and army officer named Colin Powell. Powell wanted to go back to uniformed duty as a battalion commander. "You know," said Malek, "you could get them to extend it [the fellowship]. I really want you to stay with us here. We've got a great team." Powell replied, "You don't understand. Nobody's going to be here a year from now."[43]

On January 24, Dr. Riland arrived to treat the president and staff and recorded in his diary, "the entire place is like Campbell's Funeral Home." Rose Mary Woods collapsed in the doctor's arms. She "looks terrible, thin, bloated—obviously drinking too much," wrote Riland. "She is very close to the breaking point. If she were not Catholic, I'm certain she would take her life—she is that desperate." Dr. Tkach showed Riland the president's schedule—to make the point that it was virtually empty.

Riland was having his own problems—he had been indicted for tax evasion (Riland blamed Haldeman for tipping off the IRS)—and Nixon had dropped him for a time. But the president had resumed his treatments that winter, and was gossiping again with his gregarious osteopath, asking about his tax case. He wanted to know if Riland's prosecutor was Jewish, and asked, "They won't send you to jail, will they?" Riland wrote, "Jail has been the furthest thing from my mind but obviously isn't the furthest thing in the President's mind." Still, Riland recorded, the president "looks great except a little tired, a little older and when he's sitting down, he's noticeably stooped, more than before."[44]

In February, Jaworski, the new special prosecutor, attended an off-the-record dinner with the editors of **Time** magazine. "Let's suppose, hypothetically, just hypothetically, that we come across evidence that the president of the United States had committed an impeachable offense. What do you think the president would do?" Jaworski asked the editors. He continued to speculate, "Suppose the president knows we have this tape which is so damaging. . . ." One of the editors, Jason McManus, wrote a note and passed it to one of the writers, Ed Magnuson. The note read: "We've got him."[45]

On March 1, 1974, Haldeman, Ehrlichman, Mitchell, and Colson were indicted on charges of conspiracy and obstruction of justice (they all served prison terms ranging from seven to nineteen months). On March 16, Pat's sixty-second birthday, she appeared on stage at the Grand Ole Opry House in Nashville, where her husband played "My Wild Irish Rose," "God Bless America," and "Happy Birthday" on the piano. As he finished, Pat rose and approached her husband, arms outstretched. But he had already turned toward the master of ceremonies. Helen Smith, Pat's press secretary, "winced," and the press piled on about the president's apparent cold indifference. Pat was bothered more by the press reaction than by her husband, whose awkwardness she well understood.[46]

In the last weeks of 1973, Nixon had conducted a small, private experiment. He had asked Pat Buchanan to type up transcripts of some of the Watergate tapes and show them to Haig. "Even I, who had been present during many such conversations and knew what to expect, was shocked by the flavor of what I read," recalled Haig. Haig asked Bryce Harlow, who had good political instincts, to read the transcripts. Harlow appeared at Haig's office and "sat down in heavy silence. He seemed reluctant to express an opinion," recalled Haig. "I did not press him. Finally he said, 'What do **you** think?'"

Haig replied, "He'll never survive this."

"Amen, brother," said Harlow.

Haig went to see Nixon and, without preamble, said, "Mr. President, there is no way you can release the transcripts Pat and his people have prepared. If you do, what they contain will destroy you."

Nixon "wagged his head, thrust out his jaw, glared at me," Haig recounted. "All right," said the president, angrily. Then, with a wave of the hand as if to make both Haig and the transcripts vanish, he exploded, **"All right!"**[47]

But the demand for the tapes was growing. In January both the special prosecutor and the House Judiciary Committee, now cranking up for full impeachment hearings, demanded more tapes. Nixon was threatened with contempt of Congress if he didn't turn them over.

Once more, the Nixon staff began putting together transcripts, only this time they were carefully edited by Nixon to excise some of the more embarrassing moments, including dozens of instances of what became known as "expletive deleted." Nixon explained to his lawyers that his mother would have disapproved of his salty language and certainly any blasphemy.[48]

A certain amount of wishful thinking was creeping in as the White House prepared to release the tapes. Nixon hoped that his recorded conversations would show that John Dean had misled the Senate Watergate Committee, that the president had **not** been an active participant in the cover-up.[49] Nixon failed to see that, while he might not sound like a crook, he would certainly not appear presidential.

Perhaps, he did understand, at some level, the mortal danger in the tapes, even if he didn't let on. During that bleak winter, Tricia, no fool, wrote in her diary:

Something Daddy said makes me feel absolutely hopeless about the outcome. He has since the [Alex] Butterfield revelation [of the tapes existence] repeatedly stated that the tapes can be taken either way. He has cautioned us that there is nothing damaging on the tapes; he has cautioned us that he might be impeached because of their content. Because he has said the latter, knowing Daddy, the latter is the way he really feels.

"Sometimes," Nixon wrote in his memoir, "People around you understand things better than you understand them yourself."[50]

CHAPTER 28

"I Hope I Haven't Let You Down"

At 9:01 P.M. on April 29, 1974, Nixon appeared on national television from the Oval Office, looking haggard but sounding confident. On his desk was a stack of thirty-eight slender binders, comprising 1,300 pages of transcripts from forty-six White House tapes. "Once and for all," he said, the tapes would show what he knew and what he had done about Watergate. "The President has nothing to hide," he said. He said he trusted in the "basic fairness of the American people."

The "Blue Book," as the collection was dubbed by the White House, went on sale for $12.25. It immediately sold more than three million copies. The reaction was delayed, but violent. Reading the transcripts, Billy Graham said he felt like throwing up.[1] Senator Hugh Scott, the Republican minority leader, denounced the contents as "deplorable, shabby, disgusting, and immoral." Newspapers once supportive of the president turned on him. The **Chicago Tribune** called for his resignation: "He is devious. He is vacillating. He is profane. He is willing to be

Julie with Martha Mitchell.
**Courtesy of the Richard Nixon Presidential
Library and Museum**

led. . . ."² Jokes about "expletives deleted" abounded. "Somebody told me, 'He talks even worse than you do, Bradlee,'" **Washington Post** editor Ben Bradlee recalled.³

A little disingenuously, old Nixon hands like Kissinger and George Shultz expressed surprise: They had **never** heard the president talk like that, they insisted; he must have saved his profanity for his political cronies like Chuck Colson.⁴ The tapes that have been released over the decades tell a story that is less cut-and-dried. It is true that Nixon's tough-guy crudeness was more likely to emerge when he was discussing political "nut-cutting" than global strategy or economic policy, but there was some overlap. Nixon could be vulgar and anti-Semitic with Kissinger as well as Colson. It is also true that Nixon was more blasphemous than obscene and that he probably swore no more, and possibly less, than his two immediate predecessors.

The one place Nixon did not swear was at the family dinner table. The release of the tapes made Nixon's family very uncomfortable. "The Richard Nixon on the tapes was not the Richard Nixon the family saw every day," Julie recalled.⁵ Mrs. Nixon told her chief of staff, Connie Stuart, that she was "shocked" by the tapes; she had never heard her husband use such words.⁶

The furor surprised Nixon, who had once again miscalculated the reaction of the public, a majority of whom now favored impeachment. The tapes did not serve to rebut Dean's testimony, as he had once hoped. Instead, Nixon's meandering, back-and-forth style of speech, his equivocation and uncertainty, as well as his occasional vulgarity, came across as erratic and weak—certainly not what Americans, however unrealistically, imagined or hoped for in a president. Nixon had wanted to be de Gaulle, remote, mysterious, grand. Instead, he lamented, the tapes showed the American people "things they did not want to know."[7]

On May 12, Julie jotted in her calendar book a quotation from Rose Woods. "If there is hell on earth, we are living through it now," Nixon's faithful secretary had told her. "The feeling of helplessness," Julie wrote, "was almost unbearable."[8]

Still, Nixon did not give up. Deeply distracted by Watergate, he nonetheless tried fitfully to govern. On May 13, the president made a national radio address proposing comprehensive national health insurance. His proposal, with its federal mandates, was not significantly different from the one that Barack Obama finally pushed through Congress nearly four decades later.[9] But in May 1974, such a massive piece of social welfare legislation had no chance of passage. Nixon had been surprisingly effective on Capitol Hill, given that the Democrats controlled both chambers, but the game was over. Bill Timmons, his congressional liaison, had long since lost hope of creating bonds between the president and congressmen; now, with the release of the tapes, Nixon lost any chance to use the power of the office. "He was an activist president who wanted to do a lot of things nobody had ever tried, and by a floating coalition of Republicans and Southern Democrats, we got some of it passed," Timmons recalled. "We were able to cut deals, to compromise, and we built a lot of courthouses and bridges [trading pork barrel projects for votes]. But the tapes killed him. He was not the Nixon they knew or they thought they knew."[10]

By the summer of 1974, the U.S. government was essentially running without an effective president. Indeed, it had been running on autopilot for at least a year. "After Haldeman and Ehrlichman left in April 1973, everything I sent to the White House was approved—everything," said Paul O'Neill, the associate director of the Office of Management and Budget who oversaw all domestic policy. As an OMB official from the beginning of Nixon's first term, O'Neill, who would go on to serve as George W. Bush's Treasury secretary, had been impressed by the "Brandeis Briefs" demanded by Nixon from all his advisers—fact-based arguments the president sent back covered with incisive comments. By 1974, "I'm not sure Nixon even read my recommendations," O'Neill recalled. "I guess he was huddled down in a bunker, wishing he were dead."[11]

Foreign leaders had not abandoned Nixon, not quite. Anwar Sadat of Egypt gave the American president something he craved and missed: public adulation. In June 1974, Nixon made a triumphant trip to the Middle East, allowing him to escape, however briefly, the jeering at home.

Israel, Egypt, and Syria had fought to a draw, more or less, in the October War—which amounted to a victory for Sadat. (Nixon had urged the revived and rearmed Israeli army not to destroy Egyptian forces.) An able and up-and-coming leader, Sadat was eager to salve Egypt's bruised pride and to sidle away from Egypt's overbearing Soviet sponsors. Nixon wanted to play the role of "honest broker" between Arabs and Jews and indeed succeeded at laying the foundation for a rare period of relative peace in the Middle East.[12] He also wanted to catch up to Kissinger, who, rightfully, had been lauded for his tireless "shuttle diplomacy." **Newsweek**, the Washington Post Company–owned magazine that had published dozens of gleeful Watergate covers, fronted its June 10 issue with a drawing of Kissinger in a Superman costume.[13]

Arriving in Cairo on June 12, Nixon received "perhaps the most tumultuous welcome any American president has ever received anywhere in the world," Nixon boasted in his memoirs.[14] Nixon had shown the Egyptian people the respect they craved. A lover of crowds and spectacle, Nixon was often heard proclaiming "the greatest day of my life," but he had reason to exult. "When we moved to the highway, it was like hitting a tidal wave," Nixon recounted a decade later. "It was just a sea of humanity surging around us."[15] More than a million people chanted "Nik-son! Nik-son!" as the motorcade inched into the city. (Somewhat uncharitably, Kissinger noted that trucks were picking up people as soon as Nixon passed and moving them farther down the parade route.)[16] Later, on a three-hour train ride in an ornate, open-sided, Victorian-era carriage, Nixon bathed in the adulation of an estimated six to seven million people.

Nixon stood for hours in the nearly hundred-degree heat even though his right leg was swollen to nearly twice its normal size. He was suffering from phlebitis, a potentially fatal swelling of the veins. Nixon was visibly limping, though he later recalled that he felt no pain on either the motorcade or the train ride. He did permit himself a morbid thought when he noticed that a hearse was driving along on the highway that paralleled the track. He wondered for a moment if Haig had leaked the president's potentially mortal condition but later learned that the hearse had been ordered up in case of an assassination.[17]

Sick or not, Nixon took another "Journey for Peace" two weeks later to the Soviet Union. Stopping first at a NATO meeting in Brussels, he was treated "with the solicitude shown to terminally ill patients," wrote Kissinger. Deeply gloomy on the limousine ride from the airport, Nixon told the U.S. Ambassador Donald Rumsfeld that the State Department staffers handling the trip were "a bunch of fairies." Rumsfeld tried to protest that they were actually Defense Department staffers and highly competent, but Kissinger took him aside and whispered, "Rummy, we don't argue with him anymore."[18] On the plane to Moscow, there were dark jokes among the newsmen that Nixon would ask for political asylum.[19] As Nixon and Kissinger joined on their last crusade to get an arms control treaty with the Soviets, each sensed a coolness in the other. Meeting in the presidential limousine outside the Kremlin to avoid electronic eavesdropping, they spoke guardedly. Nixon thought Kissinger was "depressed," and Kissinger thought Nixon was "preoccupied and withdrawn."[20] No more diplomatic surprises or triumphs were in the offing. Brezhnev was signaling that he had overextended himself for détente and now had to worry about the hardliners on the Politburo. On a trip to the general secretary's palatial villa in Yalta, Nixon and Brezhnev tried to recapture some of their chumminess and made gauzy declarations of peace. But the realpolitik side of Nixon did not want to alienate the conservatives in his own party: he would need their votes to avoid conviction in the Senate if, as many now thought likely, he was impeached in the House.[21]

On July 12, Nixon retreated to San Clemente to prepare for his last stand. Tricia and her husband Ed Cox decided to take an evening walk and were upset to see that the three-hole golf course, built by some "Friends of Nixon" on Bob Abplanalp's adjoining property, had been allowed to die. "Wasted, neglected, ugly, dead," Tricia bitterly wrote in her diary.

Nixon was not surprised. He understood the fickleness of politics, which was why he often wrote sympathetic letters to losers.[22]

Nixon was a shrewd vote counter, and he spent hours with Bill Timmons on the potential ayes and nays for impeachment in the House. Most congressmen declared themselves undecided, but Nixon knew from experience that "undecided" usually meant the congressman was getting ready to vote against the White House. Still, he was shaken to hear, on the afternoon of July 23, that the three Southern conservative Democrats on the House Judiciary Committee had turned on him.

Nixon instructed Haig to call the governor of Alabama, George Wallace. Ever since Wallace had won ten million votes in the 1968 presidential election, Nixon had tried to keep the wily demagogue on his good side or, alternatively, to ruin him. A Justice Department corruption case against Wallace's brother Gerald had fizzled, and an attempt to secretly fund Wallace's primary opponent in 1970 also proved fruitless. When a would-be assassin's bullet knocked Wallace out of the 1972 race, "Nixon's agents gave Wallace $750,000 to keep his staff together as a sort of bribe, offered to fly him to the Republican Convention in a C-147 hospital plane, and had Billy Graham and John Connally try to convince him to endorse Nixon," wrote Nixon scholar Melvin Small. Wallace had refused—but he did not endorse McGovern, either.[23]

Now, with critical support among Southern conservatives collapsing, Nixon turned to Wallace for help. When he first came on the line, Wallace pretended that he couldn't hear Nixon very well, then said he hadn't expected the call, then that he hadn't examined the evidence, then that he had prayed for Nixon.[24] Finally, as Haig recollected the conversation, Nixon asked, "George, I'm just calling to ask if you're still with me."

Wallace replied, "No, Mr. President, I'm afraid I'm not."

Nixon beseeched: "George, isn't there some way we can work this out?"

"I don't think so, Mr. President," Wallace replied.

Nixon did not try to argue. He hung up the phone and said in an even voice to Haig, "Well, Al, there goes the presidency."[25]

That night, Nixon sat up late in his study working on a speech about inflation, which had already soared to more than 11 percent after the removal of the ill-conceived wage-and-price controls. What became known as "stagflation" had plunged the economy into the worst recession since the Great Depression. It is likely that the president's approval ratings would have bottomed out even without Watergate; without doubt, voter anger over the economy further drained Nixon's nearly empty reserves of goodwill in Congress. Wallace's rebuff was wounding, but only one of many signs that Nixon's grasp on the presidency was slipping away.[26]

"My mind kept wandering back to the afternoon, and a sense of hopeless loss and despair kept welling up in me," he recalled. He knew that if he resigned, he "could expect an onslaught of lawsuits that would cost millions of dollars and take years to fight in the courts." On the margin of his speech, he wrote, "12:01 A.M. Lowest point in the presidency, and Supreme Court still to come."[27]

He overslept, a rarity, and awakened to learn that the Supreme Court had unanimously ruled that he had to turn sixty-four more tapes over to the special prosecutor. One of them, he knew, was the June 23, 1972, tape, on which he and Haldeman had discussed importuning the CIA to block FBI investigators from following the money trail in the early days of Watergate.

Nixon had listened to the tape in May and knew it was troublesome, though he tried to convince himself it was not fatal. Incredibly, he had not permitted his lawyer, Fred Buzhardt, to listen to the tape, but now he did. Buzhardt came back and told one of his young lawyers, Geoff Shepard, that Nixon was doomed. Shepard put together a transcript and gave it to Buzhardt. "Smoking gun," said Shepard.[28]

Haig was also convinced that the tape was fatal. He later told Bob Woodward of **The Washington Post**, "You only had to read it once." At the time, when Haig confronted Nixon with the transcript of the tape, the president protested that he had ordered the FBI to press on with the investigation when the CIA refused to get involved. Nixon "waved his arm as if clearing off his desk," Haig recalled to Woodward. Haig swore, "Goddamnit," to try to make the gravity of the tape "sink in."[29]

On July 27, the House Judiciary Committee voted 27 to 11 to pass the first article of impeachment, charging Nixon with obstruction of justice. Nixon was swimming at a beach near his house at the time. "I was getting dressed in the beach trailer when the phone rang and Ziegler gave me the news," Nixon recalled.

> That was how I learned that I was the first President in 106 years to be recommended for impeachment, standing in the beach trailer, barefoot, wearing old trousers, a Banlon shirt, and blue windbreaker emblazoned with the Presidential Seal.[30]

A day later, Nixon returned from California to a capital city feverish with rumor and expectation. On the night of July 30, Nixon couldn't sleep. He took out a pad of notepaper from his bedside table and wrote the time—3:50 A.M.—and began listing the pros and cons of resigning. He could see that he was putting the country through an ordeal, that he was crippled politically, but the idea of quitting was horrid to him. From his days sitting on the bench for Coach Newman through the Fund Scandal and the wilderness years in New York, he had built a whole persona around **never quitting**. At San Clemente, he had gazed at a portrait of his mother, remembering what a "saint" she was, but perhaps more clearly the words she had uttered as she lay dying: "Richard, don't **you** give up. Don't let anybody tell you that you are through." As Nixon tried to make rational arguments for and against stepping down, his basic instincts kicked in. Shortly before dawn, Nixon turned the notepaper over and wrote on the back, "End career as a fighter."[31]

His staff had other ideas, however. Jim St. Clair, a trial lawyer hired by Nixon to argue his case before the House, had read the transcript of the June 23 tape and agreed with Buzhardt that Nixon needed to resign. St. Clair and Buzhardt had become anxious about their own exposure, fearful that they would be accused of obstruction of justice if Nixon did not quickly turn over the tape. Nixon turned to Haig for his opinion. "Mr. President," Haig said, "I am afraid that I have to agree with Fred and Jim St. Clair. I just don't see how we can survive this one." The president nodded "almost imperceptibly," Haig recalled.[32] By this point, Haig wanted Nixon to go. He was weary of serving as "Acting President," and he had been jolted by the "smoking gun" tape. "He felt disquieted, sick, misused—like finding out your wife has had an affair," recalled Haig's personal assistant, Charles Wardell.[33]*

Nixon's mood had been swinging between despondency and eerie calm. In an oral history for the

---

*Haig and Kissinger would complain about Nixon to **Washington Post** columnist Joe Alsop, who had long defended Nixon's Vietnam policy but had turned on the president during Watergate. Alsop became an important source for Woodward and Bernstein's **The Final Days**. According to Carl Bernstein's notes of an interview with Alsop, both Kissinger and Haig "were very concerned about RMN's mental stability."[34]

Nixon Library, Haig recalled an astonishing scene as
Nixon entered his final days in office. Haig claimed
that Nixon told him, "In the army, you open the
drawer, and you put a pistol in, and you close the
drawer, and you leave, and the fellow takes care of
himself. I'm beginning to think maybe you better
put that pistol in my drawer." Haig "didn't know
what to say," he recalled. "We weren't joking or kidding. He hadn't had a Scotch. So I told the doctors
to be careful what they gave him."[35]

Nixon's reason began to push back against his instincts. On Thursday, August 1, the president calmly
told Haig that he had decided to resign. "His manner was cool, impersonal, matter-of-fact," recalled
Haig. Nixon said, "Al, it's over. We've done our best.
We haven't got the votes. I can't govern. Impeachment would drag on for six months. For the sake of
the country, this process must end." He told Haig to
signal Gerry Ford to be ready.[36]

But Nixon still had to tell his family. He began
with Julie, who came by his room at the Executive
Office Building on the morning of August 2. Wearing a soft cashmere smoking jacket, sitting in the
comfort of his favorite easy chair, he told Julie "in a
low, steady voice that he had no support left, that he
would have to resign," she recalled.

"My heart racing, I hurried across East Executive
Avenue in the hot, hazy air," Julie recounted. She
was on her way to find her mother. "I felt as if my
heart would break. I could hardly bear to tell her the
fight was over, just as my father could not."

Nixon had not told Pat of his decision. Julie found the First Lady in her bedroom, "which Lady Bird Johnson had decorated, and which Mother, in her practical and saving way, had not changed. As a result, the room was not a reflection of her," Julie wrote, adding a note of self-abnegation to the pitiful scene. The loyal daughter continued:

> Now she stood near the door, as if she had been waiting for something to happen or for someone with news. I told her immediately that Daddy felt he had to resign. A look of alarm spread across her face and she asked, "But why?"
>
> I answered something like, "He has to for his own good or he'll be impeached."
>
> Her mouth began to tremble. We embraced for a moment, our arms around each other very lightly, barely touching, knowing that if we drew any closer we would both break down and not let go. When I stood back I saw that Mother had tears in her eyes. For me, those tears that she shed so briefly were the saddest moment of the last days in the White House.

When Julie left, Pat went upstairs, found boxes, and started packing. She called Clement Conger, who worked with her on White House restoration projects and was helping her order new White House china, a cobalt blue plate with fluted edges. "I won't explain, Clem, but don't go ahead with the porcelain," she said, in a wavering voice. "Call it off."[37]

Tricia arrived from New York in mid-afternoon. At LaGuardia airport, she had been heckled and booed. She found her father in the Lincoln Sitting Room, seated with his feet up on the ottoman. He was fussing with his pipe. Calmly, he explained the June 23 tape to her. She put her arms around him, kissed his forehead, and burst into tears. "You're the most decent person I know," she said.

Tricia, unlike Julie, almost never cried. "But when Daddy said, 'I hope I have not let you down,' the tragedy of his ghastly position shattered me," she wrote in her diary.

One by one—Pat, Tricia, and Julie; their husbands Ed and David; and Bebe Rebozo—assembled in the Lincoln Sitting Room. The small, now-crowded air-conditioned room was cheerfully, if bizarrely, warmed by firelight even though it was a hot, humid August night outside. Manolo handed out transcripts of the June 23 tape and the discussion began. Tricia and Julie adamantly opposed resigning. Their husbands were less sure. Bebe said little, and Pat said almost nothing. "I am not sure she even looked at the transcript," Julie recalled. But the First Lady's opinion, when voiced, was clear and no different from her position all the other times she had seen her husband wobble. He should not give up, she said. He should fight to the finish.

"Was it worth it?" Nixon asked. His family told him what he needed to hear, and then they left him as they had found him, alone.

"My family's courage moved me deeply," Nixon recalled in his memoirs.[38] He had intended to resign that Monday, when the tape transcripts were to be released to the public, but now he decided to wait. He wanted to see the reaction. He was clinging to hope. Later, William Safire would write:

> Nixon's last year in office was spent playing for time, hoping for a break, delaying as long as he could, always living with the knowledge that his guilt could be established, thinking he was watching a bad movie, and saying to himself, "Wait— it'll get better," as it got worse.[39]

The endgame began on Monday, as soon as the transcripts of the tapes were released at a 4 P.M. press briefing. Nixon took his family on a cruise aboard the **Sequoia** so that they wouldn't "have to endure the ordeal of watching the evening news broadcasts," Nixon wrote. "Everyone valiantly tried to make the evening as happy as possible. . . . They talked about everything but what was on everybody's mind."

After dinner, as the yacht turned and headed back up the Potomac, under bridges that were crowded with newsmen and photographers—"we were the subject of a death watch," Julie recalled—Nixon went below and lay down. He put up his swollen leg and tried to close his eyes. A few minutes later Rose appeared to read her shorthand notes of a conversation with Haig, who had been watching the news back at the White House. "Just tell them that this thing is coming about the way we expected," Haig had told her.[40]

Back at the White House, sleep would not come. At 2 A.M., Nixon returned to the Lincoln Sitting Room. No fire had been laid, so he tried to build his own, and he promptly set off the fire alarm. At 3 A.M. he returned to bed. "We had passed through the first firestorm, but it was still raging," he recalled. "I knew that it would be following me for the rest of my life."

A cabinet meeting the next day was "tense and subdued," Nixon recalled. When the president started talking about long-range economic planning, the latest attorney general, William Saxbe, interjected, "Mr. President, don't you think we should be talking about next week, not next year?" Nixon looked around the table. No one said a word, Saxbe recalled.* The president picked up his papers and left the room.[42]

The good-byes, the last-minute pleas and placations and lamentations had begun. Staffers greeted him with an unnaturally cheery, "Good morning, Mr. President!" when he walked by; the Secret Service agents looked on edge. Worried that the president might do something desperate, Defense

*In Kissinger's recollection of the meeting, GOP head George H. W. Bush followed Saxbe by saying that Watergate needed to be ended quickly for the sake of the party's fortunes in November, and Kissinger cut in, "We are not here to give the President excuses. We are here to do the nation's business."[41]

Secretary James Schlesinger passed the word that all commands to the troops from the White House must pass through him; years later, Deputy National Security Adviser Brent Scowcroft scoffed at Schlesinger's melodrama, saying that "Nixon wouldn't even have known how to give the orders."[43]

Nixon called Haldeman, who was making an eleventh-hour plea for a blanket pardon for all Watergate defendants, with amnesty for draft dodgers thrown in for equity's sake. Haldeman sounded just as detached as if he was discussing revenue sharing, Nixon recalled. "As he talked my mind wandered back to the campaign days and the White House days, when his proud and brusque way of dealing with people had aroused fear in some and inspired loyalty in many others." Nixon said good-bye without giving Haldeman an answer, which, Haldeman knew, meant no.[44]

At midday on Tuesday, Nixon told the faithful Rose that he was resigning. He picked up his yellow pad and wrote on the top, "Resignation Speech." In her diary that night, Tricia wrote: "Rose in tears this afternoon told us (Mama, Julie, me) in the solarium that Daddy had irrevocably decided to resign . . . We must not let him down."

On Wednesday afternoon, Senator Barry Goldwater appeared with a solemn delegation of Republican lawmakers. They had come to try to force him to resign—unaware that he had already decided. "I don't have many alternatives, do I?" asked Nixon. The senators said nothing. "Never mind," said

Nixon. "There'll be no tears from me. I haven't cried since Eisenhower died."[45] Kissinger appeared, and Nixon and he wondered what Chairman Mao must be thinking.[46]

Across the globe men and women were watching and wondering at the news emanating from the capital of the world's greatest democratic republic.

During the Saturday Night Massacre, Nixon's envoy to China, David Bruce, had written in his diary, "In Peking, while Washington burned, we fiddled . . . and saw our unhappy domestic political scene as through a glass darkly. We might as well be . . . isolated on another planet." Learning of Nixon's resignation on August 9, Bruce wrote simply, "Hosanna."[47] In New Delhi, when Ambassador to India Patrick Moynihan got word, he wrote in his diary, "Nothing to do, so I got everybody out of bed and told the Marines to double the guard. . . . Three Presidents destroyed. Kennedy by an assassin's hand, Johnson by the hand of his enemies, Nixon by his own hand. I should think my string has run out."[48]

On Wednesday night, the family, joined by Rose, assembled in the White House Solarium. Entering the room, Nixon noticed that his wife sat up straight on the edge of the couch and "held her head at the slightly higher angle that is her only visible sign of tension, even to those who know her," he wrote. She came over and kissed her husband. "We're all very proud of you, Daddy," she said. Nixon loved to stage-manage photos of himself and his family and large groups generally, and he had brought along the White House photographer, Ollie Atkins. "I could see from Mother's expression that she was upset," wrote Julie. "Softly, she explained to Ollie that no one really felt much like posing. But my father interrupted. He had requested the picture, he said, 'for history.'" At first, Julie tried to hide behind her mother so her tears wouldn't show. The group ate dinner in silence.[49]

At 9 P.M., Nixon called Kissinger. The White House operator found the secretary of state dining with Joe Alsop. "Could you come over right away?" Nixon asked. The president was a "basket case," Kissinger later told friends. In his memoir, Kissinger recalled finding the president "slouched in the brown-covered chair, his legs on the settee, a yellow pad in his lap—a last crutch at the moment of despair."

Nixon wanted to know: What would history say of him? Kissinger answered that history would say that he showed courage. "Depends who's writing the history," Nixon answered. For over an hour, they revisited their triumphs and tribulations. At one point, Nixon padded down the hallway to find the bottle of cognac they had cracked when Kissinger reported the breakthrough to China. They raised a glass, two rivals and comrades in dramatic times. Kissinger began to weep. Nixon broke down, too.

Kissinger began to perspire. He wanted to free himself. He got up to leave the Lincoln Sitting

Room, but Nixon steered him to the Lincoln Bedroom next door. The president told Kissinger that every night he followed the practice of his Quaker mother of kneeling and silently praying before bed. Nixon asked Kissinger to pray with him now, "and we knelt," Nixon recalled.

"My own recollection is less clear on whether I actually knelt," Kissinger wrote in his memoirs. He had not prayed in many years, and praying in his religion did not involve kneeling.

Kissinger was drenched with sweat when he returned to his office and found Scowcroft and Lawrence Eagleburger. "Nothing I have ever been through has been so traumatic," he said, and filled them in on the details. Kissinger's private line to Nixon rang. Eagleburger picked up an extension to listen in. Nixon begged Kissinger not to tell anyone about what had occurred or that he had seen the president weep. It would show weakness.

The story was leaked to **The Washington Post** within a few days. In Woodward and Bernstein's book, **The Final Days**, Nixon was portrayed as sobbing and beating the carpet, crying out, "What have I done? What has happened?" In his memoir Kissinger said he did not remember this. Like the image of Nixon talking to portraits, the truth, whatever it was, has long since blurred into myth.[50]

Nixon showed grace at the end. On the morning of Thursday, August 8, his last full day as president, Nixon met with his successor, Gerald Ford. Ford asked Nixon if he had any advice. Nixon responded that the only man who would be "absolutely indispensible" was Henry Kissinger. There was no one else with Kissinger's "wisdom and tenacity." Nixon told Ford about a call he had received from Eisenhower the night before his inaugural in 1969, when Ike said it was the last time he could call him "Dick." Nixon said to Ford, "It's the same with me. From now on Jerry, you are Mr. President." Ford's eyes welled up, as did Nixon's.[51]

At 8 P.M. on the eve of his resignation, there were more tears at a farewell session with longtime supporters in the Cabinet Room. The hallways smelled faintly of burnt paper; some aides were throwing documents into their office fireplaces. Nixon was scheduled to address the nation at 9 o'clock. He was crying so hard that the makeup lady, Lillian Brown, was worried that he wouldn't be able to make it through his speech.[52] Slowly, Nixon was able to master his emotions. When the red light went on at 9:01 P.M., he was calm. "This is the 37th time I have spoken to you from this office," he began. He explained that he no longer had the political support to stay in office. Quitting, he said, "is abhorrent to every instinct in my body." But for the good of the nation, the time had come. "Then," Nixon wrote in his memoirs, "I came to the most difficult sentence I shall ever have to speak":

Therefore, I shall resign the presidency effective at noon tomorrow.

He wanted the healing to begin, he said. "To have served in this office is to have felt a very personal sense of kinship with each and every American. In leaving, I do so with this prayer: May God's grace be with you in the days ahead."

The red light blinked off. Nixon returned to the Family Quarters and found Pat, Tricia, Julie, David, and Ed. "Slowly, instinctively," Nixon recalled, "we embraced in a tender huddle, drawn together by love and faith."

Suddenly, Nixon began to shake violently. Tricia reached over to hold him. "Daddy!" she exclaimed. "The perspiration is coming clear through your coat!" Nixon tried to reassure them, it was just a passing chill.

"A tragicomic scene followed," Nixon recalled. In her diary that night, Tricia recorded it:

On Pennsylvania Avenue voices of a crowd chanting were heard. Mama misinterpreted and thought the group was one of supporters when actually it consisted of the same people who throughout Daddy's presidency had hounded his every effort. Now they were singing, "Jail to the Chief."

Mama tried to propel Daddy toward the window so that he could see the crowd. Ed and I tried desperately to talk loudly so as to drown them out. We hoped Daddy would not hear their sick message. Even so, I am sure this last injustice did not escape him.[53]

CHAPTER 29

"Richard! Wake Up!"

"I woke with a start," Nixon recalled of his last morning in the White House. He had slept for four hours, more than usual. Shortly before 9:30 A.M., he found his family waiting in the hallway of the Family Quarters. Pat was wearing a pale pink and white dress and dark glasses; she had barely slept in the previous two days, which she had spent packing up the family belongings. Only that morning had she begun to weep.

The farewell ceremony with the White House staff was scheduled for 9:30 A.M. Steve Bull, Nixon's personal aide, explained where everyone should stand in the East Room and mentioned that there would be three TV cameras. "At that news, Pat and Tricia became very upset," Nixon recalled. "It was too much, they said, after all the agony television had caused us." Nixon was firm. Television had saved him (the Checkers speech) and hurt him (the first Kennedy debate), but he knew that he had been one of the first politicians to exploit the power of television to reach over the "elites" to the masses.

The last night.
Courtesy of the Richard Nixon Presidential
Library and Museum

Nixon, in this moment, was thinking more about his place in history than about his family, who, he knew, would support him regardless. "That's the way it has to be," he said. "We owe it to our supporters. We owe it to the people."

Nixon was "fighting a floodtide of emotions" as he began to speak. The night before, working on his speech while his son-in-law Ed Cox retrieved his favorite books from their shelves, Nixon had remarked that he was caught up in a "Greek tragedy," one that had to "play out." Nixon had been matter-of-fact, not maudlin, with Cox.[1] But standing before his staff and his followers, he did not hide his feelings. He talked, with an edge of populist resentment, about his father's bad luck. He was sentimental about his mother ("a saint") and then began reading from a tribute Theodore Roosevelt had written to his dead wife, Alice, which ended: "And when my heart's dearest died, the light went out of my life forever." The audience was a little puzzled that Nixon chose to talk about Roosevelt's wife and not his own wife standing behind him. In his memoirs, he explained that he couldn't talk about his own family without breaking down. His point in his farewell remarks was that Roosevelt was only in his twenties when he thought the light had gone out of his life forever, but that he had rallied from despair. Speaking softly, with unpolished eloquence and from the heart, Nixon said of defeat:

It is only a beginning, always. The young must know it; the old must know it. It must always sustain us, because the greatness comes not when things go always good for you, but the greatness comes and you are really tested when you take some knocks, some disappointments, when sadness comes, because only if you have been in the deepest valley can you ever know how magnificent it is to be on the highest mountain. . . .

Always give your best, never get discouraged, never be petty; always remember, others may hate you, but those who hate you don't win unless you hate them, and then you destroy yourself.[2]

A flash of self-knowledge, disguised as advice—and then it passed. Nixon refused to be introspective, at least for long. Too much self-reflection was, he believed, a sign of weakness; he was unable to see that lack of self-awareness **was** his weakness.

As the audience snuffled and sobbed and applauded, Nixon and his family swept out the door, down the stone steps, and on toward the helicopter that would fly the Nixons to exile. Just before he ducked into the aircraft, Nixon turned, flung out his victory salute, and smiled broadly.

Inside the helicopter there was silence.[3] Nixon thought he heard his wife say, "It's so sad, it's so sad."[4] But Nixon was already thinking "not of the past but of the future," he later recounted. "What could I do now? What? It seems presumptuous that I thought it then, but I did. That's the way it was. A little couplet kept coming into my head that I had received from Clare Booth Luce in the spring of 1973 when Watergate had just exploded all over the place. It was the ballad of Sir Andrew Barton:

> I am hurt but I am not slain
> I'll lie me down and bleed awhile
> Then I'll rise and fight again.[5]

Some of the young lawyers in the office of the special prosecutor were pressing Leon Jaworski to indict the former president. A Gallup poll showed that a majority of Americans wanted Nixon to face a criminal trial.[6] At his confirmation hearing for vice president in the fall of 1973, Gerald Ford had said that if he became president he would not issue a pardon because the country "wouldn't stand for it." But now that he was president, Ford knew that a criminal trial for Nixon would drag on for at least two years and tear the country apart. In early September, after less than a month in office, Ford secretly sent his private attorney, Benton Becker, to San Clemente to negotiate a pardon.

By a U.S. Supreme Court ruling, the acceptance of a federal pardon represents an admission of guilt. Nixon did not believe he was guilty of anything more than stupidity. For two days, Nixon's lawyers dickered with Becker over the statement Nixon would sign. "Contrition is bullshit," said Ron Ziegler, the former spokesman who was acting as Nixon's chief of staff in exile. Finally, Becker, under orders from Ford, delivered a now-or-never ultimatum. He threatened to get on a plane and go home.

Ford's lawyer was at last granted an audience with the former president. Nixon was standing in an unadorned office in a temporary building near Casa Pacifica. He was formally dressed in a suit, as always, but his shirt collar seemed too large. He offered Becker a weak handshake and sat down. Becker started to explain to Nixon that a pardon entailed a confession of guilt.

"Where do you live?" asked Nixon. When Becker answered "Washington," Nixon began asking how he thought the Redskins would do in the football season just begun. After twenty minutes of such filibustering, Becker got up to leave. He was in a car about to depart for the airport when he was summoned back to Nixon's office.

The former president seemed contrite. "You've been a gentleman," Nixon said to the young lawyer. "We've had enough bullies." His voice faltered. "I want to give you something. But look around the office. I don't have anything anymore. They took it all away from me."

Becker awkwardly tried to reassure Nixon, but the former president fumbled around in his desk drawer and finally produced some cuff links. "I used to have all kinds of things, ashtrays, you know, paperweights and all that. Lots of them," he said. "I'm sorry this is the best I have now."

Becker returned to Washington with Nixon's signature accepting the pardon and a statement from Nixon very indirectly acknowledging wrongdoing. The young lawyer told Ford that he wasn't a medical doctor, but he wasn't sure Nixon would live much longer.[7]*

On September 8, the day Ford announced the pardon to an explosion of criticism, Nixon said to Pat, "This is the most humiliating day of my life." That night, he felt a stabbing pain in his lower abdomen. His phlebitis had returned, more dangerous than ever. An unusually large blood clot threatened to break off and move to his heart. Nixon stubbornly refused to go to the hospital, saying that if he did, he'd "never get out alive."

In late September, Ken Clawson, who had run the White House communications shop after Herb Klein, visited Casa Pacifica and found Nixon staring out at the ocean, his swollen leg elevated on the ottoman. For the briefest of moments, Nixon let down his guard with Clawson while describing how he had learned how to fight back. He spoke in general

---

*After pardoning Nixon, Ford's popularity dropped twenty-two points in the Gallup poll, the largest single drop in history. Ford's action was politically brave and possibly cost him the 1976 election. There is some evidence that after midnight on August 2, a week before Nixon resigned, Ford ever so subtly signaled Al Haig that he might grant a pardon—or, at least, used ambiguous language that Haig, who was looking for any way to get Nixon to resign, might want to interpret as a signal. In the light of day, reading from note cards, Ford stressed to Haig that nothing he had said the night before should be construed as a deal.[8]

terms but was obviously referring to himself. "What starts the process, really, are the laughs and snubs and slights you get when you are a kid. Sometimes, it's because you're poor or Irish or Jewish or Catholic or ugly or simply that you are skinny. But if you are reasonably intelligent and if your anger is deep enough and strong enough, you learn you can change those attitudes by excellence, by personal gut performance, while those who have everything are sitting on their fat butts."

Clawson asked him about his leg. "They say it's very bad," Nixon answered. "But I've already told them to go to hell. I've told them I wasn't setting foot outside the wall around my property no matter what. They can cut off the damn leg, let it rot, or just wait for the clot to reach the end zone. I don't care."

Clawson was speechless. Nixon looked at him closely. "You see, don't you? You've got to be tough. You can't break, boy, even when there's nothing left. You can't admit, even to yourself, that it is gone. Now some people we both know think that you've got to go stand in the middle of the bull ring and cry, '**mea culpa, mea culpa,**' while the crowd is hissing and booing and spitting on you. But a man doesn't cry." Nixon clenched the pipe stem in his teeth. "I don't cry. You don't cry." Both men became teary-eyed.[9]

The leg worsened, swelling to three times its normal size. On October 30, Nixon was finally convinced that he needed emergency surgery. Weakly sitting up in bed after the operation, his eyelids began to flutter, and he passed out. Attempts to revive him were fruitless. A nurse slapped his face, urgently repeating, "Richard, wake up, Richard!"[10] He was near death from internal bleeding.

Nixon came to, briefly. He later recalled the nurse calling him by a name only his mother had used. Then he drifted away again. Three hours later, after a massive transfusion, he regained consciousness to find his doctor anxiously hovering.[11] He asked to see Pat. Nixon later recalled:

I now knew that I was in pretty desperate shape. Throughout the time we have known each other, Pat and I have seldom revealed our physical disabilities to each other. This time I couldn't help it. I said that I didn't think I was going to make it.

She gripped my hand and said almost fiercely, "Dick, you can't talk that way. You have got to make it. You must not give up." As she spoke, my thoughts went back again to the Fund crisis in 1952. Just before we went on stage for the broadcast, when I was trying to get all of my thoughts together for the most important speech of my life, I told her, "I just don't think I can go through with this one." She grasped me firmly by the hand and said, "Of course you can." The words were the same but now there was a difference. Then I had something larger than myself to fight for. Now it seemed that I had nothing left to fight for except my own life.[12]

Slowly, through the winter and spring of 1975, he recovered. Jack Brennan, the Marine colonel and former military aide who would become Nixon's chief of staff after Ziegler departed, took him to play golf every day. Nixon was not a natural golfer—his swing was painfully herky-jerky—but he compensated with determination. (True White House story: "I scored 128 today," Nixon announces. "Your golf game is getting better," says Kissinger. "I was **bowling,** Henry," Nixon snaps.) Every day Brennan, a scratch golfer with saintly patience, headed out with Nixon to a small public course. "It was a real lousy course, but it was empty—no hecklers," Brennan recalled. "His swing never got better, but he was so disciplined that he could just plunk it down the course."[13]

Pat found her own solace. "Gardening became my Mother's salvation," Julie wrote. "Many days she worked side by side with our gardener for seven hours or more." She removed a rose garden and replaced it with purple, pink, and white flowers. She also read, mostly long historical novels by Taylor Caldwell laced with conspiracies and intrigues. She came to believe that Watergate was "partly an international scheme, or at the very least that double agents were involved," wrote Julie.[14]

On July 7, 1976, Pat suffered a stroke. "In the morning, she had read part of **The Final Days,** which, despite my Father's protests, she had finally borrowed from one of the secretaries in his office," Julie recorded. Woodward and Bernstein's huge bestseller portrayed her as a lonely drunk, but "for Mother, the most unbearable part of the book was the analysis of her marriage as loveless," wrote Julie. Feeling listless and ill, Pat could barely walk when she went to bed. The next morning, she struggled to the kitchen to make coffee for her husband, but could not open the lid on the coffee can. As her husband watched her, he noticed that the right side of her mouth was drooping and that she was slurring her words. He said nothing, quickly downed his juice, and announced that he was going to the office. Instead, he woke up Julie. "I think your mommy had a stroke," he said.

The Nixons' mutual aversion to sharing their suffering had reached a low point that morning. But as Pat recovered in the weeks ahead, her husband was tender, in his own fashion. Julie recalled:

From the very first day he established a ritual for his daily morning visit with Mother: he would come into her room very upbeat, kiss her on the cheek, and then say immediately, "Well, let me feel your grip." Mother, who could barely lift her hand from where it lay inert, a heavy weight by her body, each day gritted her teeth and tried determinedly to grasp his fingers, and each day she grew stronger.[15]

The Nixons were in financial trouble. They owed back taxes and lawyers' fees that would run into the millions of dollars. There was a staff to maintain, and Democrats in Congress kept cutting back the former president's stipend. Nixon was "worried about food on the table, literally," recalled Ken Khachigian, a White House aide who had come west with the Nixons. "We were working with balance sheets. It was sad. He agonized, keeping it from Mrs. Nixon. He was sleepless about it."[16] Ed Cox and Tricia loaned his father-in-law their personal savings.[17]

Rebozo and Abplanalp helped out, buying Key Biscayne from Nixon for about $2 million. Nixon hired the flashiest agent in Los Angeles, Irving "Swifty" Lazar, to negotiate a book contract (over $2 million) for his memoirs. Lazar also sold, for slightly less than $600,000 (plus 20 percent of the profits), a long (twenty-eight-hour) sit-down with David Frost, a TV celebrity interviewer from England known for light but lively and provocative chats.[18]

For twelve days in the spring of 1976, Frost and Nixon met on a set in a rented house near Casa Pacifica. Frost, at first, was outmatched. The former president seemed smarter, better prepared, almost cocky as he batted away the interviewer's questions or launched forth on self-serving soliloquies. "When the president does it, that means it's not illegal," he asserted. (Nixon elaborated that when national security was at stake, "the President's decision in that one instant is one that enables those who carry it out, to carry it out without violating the law. Otherwise, they're in an impossible situation.") Searching, vainly, for self-reflection, Frost asked about Nixon's

parting admonition not to hate your enemies because, as Nixon had put it, "you then destroy yourself." Nixon non-answered by talking about his
respect for the White House barber, Milton Pitts,
and concluded by quoting Coach Newman's homily
that a loser's anger should be directed at himself, not
his opponent. Frost egged on the ex-president to
take a swipe at Kissinger for back-stabbing. Nixon
answered with an air of weary patience, cleverly
comparing Kissinger to Alice Roosevelt Longworth,
who so liked to be wickedly provocative at Georgetown dinner parties. Before they sat down on the
sixth day of the interviewing, Nixon greeted Frost
by casually inquiring, "Well, did you do any forni-
cating this weekend?"[19]

But on the subject of Watergate, Nixon finally
began to sweat. He accused Frost of taking incriminating quotes from the tapes out of context, which
was true enough, but the ex-president came across as
defensive and squirrelly. Frost kept after Nixon for
an apology to the nation, to go beyond the bland
formulation "mistakes were made." Prodded behind
the scenes by some of his own aides to show some
remorse, if only to move on, Nixon finally came as
close to confessing as he could. He did not concede
moral guilt but rather that he had suffered a self-
inflicted wound in a political duel. "I brought myself down. I gave them the sword. And they stuck it
in. And they twisted it with relish. And I guess if I'd
been in their position, I'd have done the same thing."
He was still Machiavelli's fallen prince, not a sinner

redeemed. Even so, he looked and sounded suitably wretched and acknowledged that he had let down the country and that he would carry that burden for the rest of his life.[20]

About 45 million people watched the first Frost-Nixon interview on May 4, 1977. By the end of the four episodes, more than two-thirds thought Nixon had been guilty of obstruction of justice, but by 38 percent to 28 percent, viewers felt more sympathetic toward the exiled president. Frost later wrote that he was "moved—awed" by Nixon's tortured, if modi-fied, limited, mea culpa. After the show, he sug-gested to the fallen statesman that whatever burdens he had been shouldering would be lighter now. "I doubt it," said Nixon. His enemies would never let up; neither would he.[21]

Frost-Nixon offered a brief interruption in the massive undertaking of writing the Nixon life his-tory. For three years, Nixon labored to tell his side of the story. Every morning at about 7 A.M., he would appear in his office dressed in a suit, white shirt, and somber tie. He would dictate—over a million words—and then trim and edit and argue with his researchers and his chief editorial assistant, Frank Gannon.* It was a slow, often grueling process.

---

*Brent Scowcroft was summoned to help Nixon with the for-eign policy parts of the manuscript. Scowcroft told the author that he was permitted to read portions of Nixon's ten-thousand-typescript-page daily journal, which Scowcroft described as a "Walter Mitty" diary, borrowing Kissinger's sobriquet.[22]

The researcher charged with handling Watergate was Diane Sawyer. A former "America's Junior Miss," Sawyer had gone to Wellesley and quoted Shakespeare and George Eliot in casual conversation. Nixon referred to her as "the smart girl."[23] Gannon recalled that Sawyer would emerge shaken after long sessions with the former president, saying that she felt that Nixon himself did not truly understand what had happened and resisted having to write about it. She tried to educate him and then had to cope with his pained reaction, as he alternately dismissed the scandal as trivial, inveighed against the unfairness of double standards, and angrily fought back—before dealing, grudgingly but dutifully, with the uncomfortable facts. Gannon himself had been delegated by Nixon to read the Watergate segments to the family. Tricia, he recalled, looked strained but understanding. Pat's lips were pursed and her veins stuck out from her neck. Julie sobbed quietly.[24]

Gannon was impressed by the depth of loyalty in the Nixon family—and by their almost Victorian reticence and discretion. He recalled: "During the final days of Watergate, it was amazing how little the Nixon family talked about the difficult and embarrassing subjects. At dinner they would talk about mundane things, but then they sent each other notes on pillows or under doors of bedrooms. It was like the Tolstoy house—no one was speaking but everyone was popping little notes."[25]

RN: The Memoirs of Richard Nixon, which became an instant bestseller after its publication in

May 1978, is a thoroughgoing thousand-page argument for the former president's place in history. The autobiography is often tendentious and shaves the facts here and there, but it is also surprisingly personal and revealing, intentionally or not. Reviews ranged from harshly negative to grudgingly respectful. "Informative, explicit, even suspense-ridden," wrote **The New York Times.**[26]

By then, Nixon was beginning to sally forth, testing the climate for yet another New Nixon. In 1976, he visited the safest ground of all: the People's Republic of China, where he was flown to Beijing on a special Chinese airliner and toasted at a banquet in the Great Hall of the People. On July 1, 1978, he sampled another friendly precinct, the Republican blue-collar town of Hyden, Kentucky, where the crowd greeted him with "Nixon Now More than Ever" signs, and he dedicated the Richard M. Nixon Recreational Facility with a tub-thumping patriotic speech. Improbably, afterward he signed a book for the old Democratic prankster, Dick Tuck, who had been sent by **New York** magazine to cover the event. More at home among audiences abroad, he ventured in November 1978 to Britain to debate at the Oxford Union and to dine in a lavish suite at the Dorchester Hotel with former Labour prime minister Harold Wilson. Nixon and Wilson discovered a mutual affinity for Gilbert and Sullivan and sang, while beating time on the table and alternating couplets from memory, all four verses of "When I Was a Lad" from **H.M.S. Pinafore.** Leaving the dinner at

1:30 A.M., Nixon remarked to Jonathan Aitken, "Harold sure knows how to make a party go."[27]

Gradually, he made peace with most of his former aides. He encountered Kissinger at the funeral of Hubert Humphrey in January 1978. "You as mean as ever, Henry?" Nixon teased. "Yes," answered Kissinger, "but I don't have as much opportunity as before."[28] Ehrlichman remained estranged from his old boss, but Nixon reconciled with Haldeman and periodically stayed in touch with Mitchell. On Labor Day weekend of 1979, he gave a birthday party for his old friend, who had recently been released from prison. He had to be prodded a bit by Colonel Brennan—"He's been loyal to you, you be loyal to him"—but he gave a gracious toast: "John Mitchell has friends. And he stands by them."[29]

Nixon missed the arena. He did not want to become a slothful retiree playing too much golf. Both Tricia and Julie had children and lived on the East Coast. Feeling isolated at Casa Pacifica, Pat was frank with Julie: "We're just dying here slowly."[30] In February 1980, the Nixons moved back to New York City. Rejected by the stuffy boards of two cooperative apartments, he bought a brownstone—as it happened, the same one where Judge Learned Hand, patron saint of Elliot Richardson and Archibald Cox, had dwelled for a half-century. Kennedy amanuensis Theodore White lived across the street, Arthur Schlesinger Jr. across the back garden. David Rockefeller was a neighbor.

Nixon had slipped inside the gates of the enemy camp. He relished the coup, creating a foreign policy salon that became a coveted invitation among the prominent journalists and establishment figures who had once scorned him. News anchors, famous authors and pundits, esteemed scholars, publishing tycoons—all felt a little thrill to be greeted at the door by the soft handshake of the 37th president, to hear him reminisce about globe-trotting triumphs and show off his political acumen. "You'd ask yourself, am I really sitting next to Richard Nixon?" recalled a **Time** columnist who was invited twice.[31] Nixon, who still worked the phones and could rattle off the names of precinct leaders in obscure congressional districts, loved making electoral predictions, most of which came true.

His dinner parties, usually "stag affairs" (Mrs. Nixon was always absent) every two weeks or so, had a decidedly Chinese motif. He would lead tours of his residence, showing off silks bestowed on him by Chairman Mao. Manolo and Fina had retired and been replaced by a Chinese couple, and the food was often Chinese, though the wines were vintage French.[32] Nixon liked to invite journalistic up-and-comers, particularly from **Time** magazine, on whose cover Nixon had appeared more than sixty times, more than any other figure in history. Michael Kramer, a young political columnist at **Time**, asked Nixon if he could use the phone in Nixon's study. With a journalist's nosy curiosity, he looked at the papers lying on the ex-president's desk: the ever-prepared Nixon had written out, word for word, his small talk as well as his substantive remarks for the evening.[33]

A regular at these performances was **Time** columnist Hugh Sidey. Generous and genial, Sidey, feeling guilty about having indulged in the Watergate orgy, now pronounced Nixon to be a "strategic genius" in the pages of **Time**. In an oral history, Sidey later recounted his evenings at Nixon's:

> He always has a Chinese dinner in memory of his great moment at the Great Wall. Then after dinner we drank that dreadful Mao Tai. If you've been to China you know it tastes like kerosene. Nixon drinks it, one right after another, and he really does get a little bombed. But let me tell you, he is absolutely amazing. In my judgment, he has a better grasp of world power than any man on the scene, except Kissinger.[34]

The old media establishment softened. In 1984, Don Hewitt of CBS bought ninety minutes of Nixon interviewed on tape by Frank Gannon and aired particularly revealing segments on magazine shows, including the hugely popular **60 Minutes**. In April 1986, Nixon gave one of his no-notes, tour-of-the-horizon speeches to the American Newspaper Publishers Association. The audience was impressed and hooted when he gave his usual one-liner about what he had learned from Watergate: "Just destroy all the tapes." In the audience was Katharine Graham, the owner of **The Washington**

Post. The two old adversaries were photographed sharing a laugh, and Mrs. Graham delivered an order disguised as a suggestion to the editors at **Newsweek**, which she also owned: "Put Nixon on the cover." A six-page spread was laid out plus another three-page interview with the "Sage of Saddle River." (Nixon had moved from New York City to a spacious estate in New Jersey, fifty minutes from downtown, where his four grandchildren could play.)* At the last moment, the editors tried to bump him off the cover for a news story, but Nixon, relishing the chance to play hardball, threatened to cancel the interview. The cover story ran with the memorable headline: "He's Back: The Rehabilitation of Richard Nixon."[36]

Nixon **was** back, at least on the op-ed pages of the major papers and the TV network interview shows, where he was treated more respectfully than he ever had been as a politician or president. There were, of course, a few awkward or uncomfortable moments. In the spring of 1982, Diane Sawyer, now the co-anchor of the **CBS Morning News**, asked him on air if he thought about Watergate when he was "just sitting alone." "Never," Nixon growled. "No. . . . I'm not going to spend my time just looking back and wringing my hands about something I can't do

---

*After the Nixons moved from Sixty-fifth Street, Theodore White—who had been so close to Jack Kennedy that he used the first person plural "we" when writing to JFK about the progress of **The Making of the President, 1960**—wrote Nixon, "I'm sorry you are no longer a neighbor across the street. I felt we had the beginning of a friendship going then."[35]

anything about." Nixon understood that his former aide had to show off her independence; still, he felt betrayed and inwardly hurt, according to Jonathan Aitken, the British member of Parliament who had become close to Nixon.[37]

Such cracks in the facade were rare. Nixon's extraordinary ability to pick himself up and get moving, to **not** brood, even as he harbored old slights, sustained him. He would not be exiled; he would not sulk on Elba overlooking the sea. With his love of the big play, the surprise attack, he simply chose to move in among his afflicters and play their game. The ex-president wasn't just putting up a brave front for television. He did not talk about Watergate with his family, either. "He looked forward, not back," recalled his son-in-law Ed Cox.[38]

And yet, the inner Nixon, the boy who found it hard to be loved or to show his love, was never hidden very far away. From time to time, Leonard Garment, Nixon's law partner during the wilderness years in New York and the White House lawyer who most urgently counseled him not to burn the tapes, called on Nixon at his office in Manhattan at 26 Federal Plaza. "Nixon liked to shmooze with me about politics," Garment recalled.

> He was always hospitable, announcing his views with, well, Nixonian authority. One of these meetings (I think the agenda was the Middle East) went on for two hours. Nixon was terrific, not only full of powerful insights but unusually warm

and funny. When we finished and walked out the door, I made my goodbye very personal— something like "You know, I really miss you." This was a mistake. Nixon literally shuddered. He walked away from me and took a position behind his desk, head down, his face working painfully as I took my embarrassed leave. It was a trip-wire revelation of Nixon's memories of unrequited friendships, of disappointment, abandonment, personal loss, and, of course, death.[39]

Nixon remained the loner in the crowd, seeking in the faces of others some mirror of his worth. He returned a few times to Bohemian Grove, the annual summer camp of the establishment in the California Redwoods. Darrell Trent, a former White House aide, found the former president sitting alone in the amphitheater, listening to the orchestra practice. Nixon told Trent that he had been up that morning at 7 A.M. going between the various camps in the Grove. "Really freaked them out," said Nixon. He was in a playful mood. "Watch this," he said. He got up and went to sit in the orchestra. Before long he was mugging with a saxophone.

One evening, Nixon ran into Brook Byers, a founder of Kleiner Perkins Caufield & Byers, the Silicon Valley venture capital firm. Nixon asked Byers what he had been doing in school back in 1970. "Protesting Cambodia," answered Byers. Nixon looked at him and asked, with a kind of naked sincerity, "Do you hate me?"[40]

CHAPTER 30

Elder Statesman

Nixon was not content to hobnob with opinion-makers and tycoons. He wanted to be on the inside, counseling presidents. His successors were not always eager for his advice, but Nixon was undeterred and, by a steady flow of memos and letters, public and private, he eventually achieved the status of respected elder statesmen at the White House. With the last of his successors, Bill Clinton, he became an unlikely consigliere. The term **wise man** can be a misnomer for Former Greats who come calling on the president. Often, they are operating on out-of-date information, and their biases can harden with age. But, characteristically, Nixon did his homework and made an effort to be realistic about the politics and exigencies faced by his successors.

Having saved Nixon from likely prosecution, Ford wanted to keep his distance. The 38th president was furious when the 37th president visited China in February 1976, three days before the New

At Pat's funeral.
Reuters/Corbis

Hampshire primary. Ford was trying to fend off a primary challenge from Ronald Reagan, who was accusing Ford of going soft on communism. It did not help Ford's cause for TV viewers to see Nixon toasting Chairman Mao. "Nixon is a shit," said Brent Scowcroft, Ford's usually restrained national security adviser.[1]

Jimmy Carter more or less snubbed Nixon, refusing the small courtesy of letting the former president stay at the White House guest quarters, Blair House, when Nixon came east for Hubert Humphrey's funeral in 1978.[2] But Ronald Reagan was receptive to a back-channel relationship with Nixon—as long as it remained secret. "I am yours to command," Nixon wrote Reagan, who had successfully reassembled Nixon's Silent Majority by appealing to disaffected Democrats.[3] Nixon showered Reagan with "Eyes Only" memos on everything from brass-knuckle politics to lofty geostrategy. Reagan listened: He accepted Nixon's recommendation of Al Haig to become secretary of state. A confidential memo on January 14, 1982, from Nixon to William Clark, Reagan's national security adviser, gives a flavor of Nixon's cagey advice:

This brings me to a very delicate suggestion. During the Eisenhower years, [John Foster] Dulles played the role of the hawk and allowed Eisenhower, who was just as tough as Dulles, to be the great conciliator. During my presidency, it was the other way around. Kissinger, due in part to his concern about his relationships with academics and the liberals in the media, played the reasonable dove and I was the intractable hawk. . . .

Nixon suggested that Haig could play the hardliner with the Soviets, leaving Reagan to be the conciliator. The prickly, controlling Haig was soon pushed out at State, but Nixon kept on urging Reagan to set up good-cop/bad-cop dynamics in his administration. "You need at least two or three nut-cutters who will take on the opposition so that you can take the high road," Nixon wrote Reagan in November 1982.[4]

When Reagan proposed abolishing nuclear weapons to Soviet leader Mikhail Gorbachev at the Reykjavik Summit in the fall of 1986, Nixon concluded that Reagan had himself gone soft on communism, if not soft in the head. He surfaced his doubts in public—in a shared op-ed with Kissinger in April 1987 wondering if Reagan had been somehow seduced by Gorbachev. The shot across the bow was felt. Two days later, Reagan invited Nixon to the Residence in the White House—Nixon's first visit since August 1974, when his staff had been burning documents in the fireplaces.[5]

They met in Reagan's study, a room that had served as Nixon's and LBJ's bedroom. Nixon reminisced that he had once sat in that room as Lady Bird crawled into bed with LBJ. Reagan offered cocktails; Nixon declined. "I assume this place isn't taped!" Nixon joked to forced laughter. Would

Nixon support Reagan's attempt to get an arms control treaty with the Soviets on intermediate range
missiles? Nixon declined. He was "no longer Reagan's to command," noted Michael Duffy and Nancy
Gibbs in their book **The Presidents Club**.[6]

Nixon's relationship to Reagan's successor was
problematic. Nixon told his family that he thought
Bush was "the perfect vice president."[7] Bush had his
own doubts about Nixon, which he expressed in a
perceptive letter to his four sons in July 1974, three
weeks before Nixon resigned:

> He is enormously complicated. He is capable of
> great kindness. . . . I am not that close to him as a
> warm personal friend, for he holds people off
> some. But I've been around him enough to see
> some humor and to feel some kindness. . . . He
> has enormous hang-ups. He is unable to get close
> to people. It's almost as if he's afraid to be reamed
> in some way—people who respect him and want
> to be friends get only so close—-and then it is
> clear—no more!

Bush was sensitive enough to know what Nixon
thought of him: "Deep in his heart he feels I'm soft,
not tough enough, not willing to do the 'gut job'
that his political instincts have taught him must be
done."[8] Nonetheless, Nixon tried to tutor Bush, offering his blunt if somewhat banal advice from his
own experience in presidential debates ("above all,
don't get bogged down with the facts") and trying to

stiffen his resolve in foreign policy.[9] In particular, he tried to steer Bush away from backing Gorbachev and instead swinging U.S. support to a rougher but more democratic rival, Boris Yeltsin. Presciently, Nixon understood that Russia was at great risk of reverting to autocracy after the fall of communism. Yeltsin, in Nixon's view, stood the best chance of rooting a democracy. On a trip to Moscow in 1991, in a conversation with three carefully chosen newsmen, Nixon looked at the Soviet Union through his own prism: "Gorbachev is Wall Street and Yeltsin is Main Street; Gorbachev is Georgetown drawing rooms and Yeltsin is the Newark factory gate." Nixon's populist instincts were right: Yeltsin, with the Bush administration's somewhat belated support, supplanted Gorbachev.[10]

Nixon understood Russia in part because he kept traveling there—eight trips as an ex-president. Hugh Sidey asked him how he could deal so handily with an "Evil Empire," in Reagan's famous description. "Because I'm evil," Nixon answered, tongue-in-cheek.[11]

Nixon refused to cash in as an ex-president by sitting on corporate boards and taking directors' or speaking fees. He supported himself by writing nine books, a mélange of memoir and foreign policy advice with titles like **In the Arena** and **Real Peace**. The books were moderately interesting and sold moderately well. In 1990, he hired an attractive young researcher, a political science student named

Monica Crowley, who later published two books of her own reminiscences, **Nixon Off the Record** and **Nixon in Winter**. The Nixons had moved from their estate to a smaller, more manageable townhouse in suburban New Jersey, and Nixon established himself in a book-lined study he called "the Eagle's Nest." One afternoon, Crowley found Nixon, feet up, watching **The Dick Van Dyke Show**, chuckling away at the sitcom. Mortified, he dropped the remote control and said, "Well, you caught me. You know I don't watch the tube, but every once in a while I like to see what's out there."

Gradually, Nixon began to confide in Crowley, even shyly and innocently flirt a bit. When Bush lost to Bill Clinton in 1992, Nixon related the gossip that Barbara Bush was ready to "kill" James Baker, Bush's closest aide. "Politics is not for the faint of heart," Nixon told Crowley. "Even grizzled types like me get bruised." He paused with a smile. "Never admit it, though."[12]

The hardball Nixon never quite went away: He threatened both Bush and Clinton with going public against them if they did not listen to his advice on Russia. Nixon was anxious when Clinton at first ignored his phone calls and memos. He blamed Hillary Clinton, who had worked on Nixon's impeachment for the House Judiciary Committee. At last, after keeping Nixon waiting on the phone for over an hour, Clinton responded to Nixon on Russian policy. Nixon was ecstatic when he told Crowley about the phone call the next morning. "He was very respectful but with no sickening bullshit," Nixon said. "It was the best conversation with a president I've had since I was president. . . . He really let his hair down. This guy does a lot of thinking."[13] Clinton for his part was impressed by Nixon's lucidity and conviction. "The thing that struck me about Nixon was that he really cared about [Russia] and that his mind was working great," Clinton told Duffy and Gibbs.[14] The best natural glad-hander ever to occupy the Oval Office bonded with quite possibly the worst, because both men understood the need for redemption. Nixon recognized Clinton as a fellow policy wonk and undertook to tutor him in foreign policy. Clinton played the avid pupil in phone calls and at a meeting at the White House, where even Hillary was friendly.[15]

Nonetheless, Nixon was wounded when Clinton failed to attend the funeral of Pat Nixon (he sent an emissary, his lawyer friend Vernon Jordan, instead). Pat's death at the age of eighty-one in June 1993 came as an enormous blow to Nixon.[16] The Nixons had grown closer since leaving the White House. Crowley observed that they were solicitous and affectionate with each other, in their courtly way. "He was always attentive," recalled Heidi Retter, their housekeeper. "He wouldn't sit down for dinner until she came downstairs, and he always pulled out her chair. He would try to think of things she liked, small treats and favors."[17] Pat told Crowley, "Dick can be quite romantic, you know. I think that would surprise a lot of people."[18] A sometime smoker, Pat suffered from emphysema and finally succumbed to lung cancer.

On a cloudy, humid day at the newly built Nixon Library in Yorba Linda, Nixon followed his wife's flag-draped casket. As he came into view of the mourners, a gathering of some three hundred people, he broke down. In the audience, Rose Woods exclaimed, "Oh dear." Seated, Nixon began sobbing uncontrollably. His torso slumped and his shoulders heaved up and down as Billy Graham tried to comfort him.

After the service, the guests milled about in the foyer of the lobby, reminiscing. Bryce Harlow recalled that Nixon was a man who, hearing the fall of a raindrop, could predict a downpour three weeks in the future. But, Harlow added, he believed that someone in Nixon's past had hurt him deeply and wondered what might have happened if, as a boy, he had been well loved.

No one expected Nixon to appear after his public breakdown. But suddenly there he was, standing on a riser, no lectern, no microphone, no notes. His black suit seemed to hang on him. Without preamble, he began talking. In a strong baritone, he said that he never would have succeeded "mentally or physically without Pat." He asked himself, what was his favorite campaign? He answered, "1952." He explained that at "whistle stops," the band always played "You Are My Sunshine," and that reminded him of Pat. "She was the sunshine of my life," he said. He recalled how she had recovered from her stroke (he strongly implied that it had been caused by reading Woodward and Bernstein's **The Final Days**) by riding an exercise bike as her brow was covered with perspiration. "She never quit," he said.

Sensing the emotion rising, he spied George McGovern across the room. "Of course George should be here," said Nixon, becoming again the total-recall politician, "because Pat's forebears were from South Dakota!"

It was a bravura performance. Afterward, Nixon shook everyone's hand. Watching from the audience, Ed Cox realized that, without his companion of more than five decades, his father-in-law might not have so long to live himself.[19]

Still, he plowed ahead. He visited Russia for the tenth time as an ex-president in the late winter of 1994. The trip did not go well. Yeltsin canceled a meeting, and Nixon caught the flu. Back in New Jersey, he was correcting the galleys of his latest book, **Beyond Peace,** and he stepped out into the April sunshine for a moment. He was sunning himself when the stroke hit. His housekeeper found him, looking dazed. "I knew right away because the right side of his face was hanging down," Retter recalled. "He was clinging to the door frame. I couldn't get him to let go."[20]

He died four days later, on April 22, 1994, at the age of eighty-one. Clinton offered the family a state funeral, but Nixon had wanted to be buried at the

Nixon Library, built beside his childhood home in Yorba Linda. Clinton had called the family, angling, in a subtle, gracious sort of way, for an invitation to deliver the eulogy. The family invited him to do so, along with Senator Bob Dole, Governor of California Pete Wilson, and Billy Graham. Henry Kissinger called, asking if he could also give a eulogy. At first, the family balked—they were not inclined to give Kissinger "one more opportunity for self-aggrandizement," recalled a family friend. But then they relented, as long as Kissinger promised to be clear about who was the teacher and who was the pupil.

It rained hard the day before the funeral, but thousands stood in line, for as long as eighteen hours, to say good-bye. Four thousand people, including all the living presidents—Ford, Carter, Reagan, Bush, and Clinton—attended the service, under gray skies, before the modest white bungalow that Nixon's father had built. Governor Wilson borrowed a favorite Nixon line from Sophocles: "One must wait until the evening to see how splendid the day has been." Clinton said, "May the day of judging President Nixon on anything less than his entire life and career come to a close." Dole, through tears, said, "I believe the second half of the 20th century will be known as the Age of Nixon. Why was he the most durable public figure of our time? Not because he gave the most eloquent speeches, but because he provided the most effective leadership. Not because he won every battle, but because he always embodied the deepest feeling of the people he led."

Kissinger spoke first. He was the most direct, and he stated the simplest truth about the man they had come to mourn: "He achieved greatly and he suffered greatly, but he never gave up."[21]

Epilogue

RISE AGAIN

Three years after Nixon resigned, his chief speech-writer Ray Price wrote a memoir discussing Nixon's "light side"—"exceptionally considerate, exceptionally caring, sentimental, generous of spirit, kind"—and his "dark side"—"angry, vindictive, ill-tempered, mean-spirited." (Nixon's "calculating, devious, manipulative parts are ones that I consign to neither side," wrote Price; "these are necessary tools of statecraft.")

Price continued:

> The light side and the dark side are both there, and over the years these have been at constant war with one another. I have seen the light side far more in evidence than I have the dark, and everyone I know who has worked closely with him agrees: while both are part of the "real" Nixon, the light side is by far the larger part, more central, the one that he himself identifies with.[1]

The black-hearted Nixon has been a cartoon version ever since Herblock first drew a caricature of

Farewell.

Nixon crawling out of the sewer in the early 1950s.[2] Far from a cynic, say his defenders, Nixon was a romantic. Nixon's family members still argue that, if anything, Nixon was too idealistic, and that he was clumsy at dirty tricks, certainly no match for the Kennedys in that department. The loyalists protest too much. Though Nixon usually wanted to do "the right thing," anyone listening to the White House tapes would wonder about his moral sensibility as he discussed hush money with John Dean. Still, it's true that Watergate got out of hand in part because Nixon was too shy, too trusting to confront his own staff on exactly what happened and who was to blame.[3]

A Manichaean divide between light and dark is useful in religion and literature and possibly political science, but it is a device, a construct. There was only one Nixon. In Nixon the light and dark strains are inextricably intertwined, impossible to disentangle. They fed each other. Nixon's strengths were his weaknesses, and vice versa. The drive that propelled him also crippled him. The underdog's sensitivity that made him farsighted also blinded him. He wanted to show that he was hard because he felt soft. He learned how to be popular because he felt rejected. He was the lonely everyman to the end.

It is said that great men often compartmentalize.[4] They are able to separate their emotions, their inner and outer lives, freeing their drive for greatness from the limiting demands of family life and ordinary human wants and needs. Nixon certainly tried to separate his political or presidential being from his needier self. In his written communications and even verbally ("You won't have Nixon to kick around anymore"), he would refer to a third-person Nixon—an almost disembodied "RN" or just "the President." To his detractors, of course, he was Tricky Dick, the deceiver, the malign faker. Nixon could be heedless about the truth, and he was, like most successful public figures, an actor who presented an idealized version of himself. But he was a very good actor. To a remarkable degree, he succeeded at inventing a true World Leader, able to take his place on the global stage alongside some formidable personages. So personally ill at ease that he could not look his doctor in the eye,[5] he was perfectly confident in the presence of historical figures from de Gaulle to Mao. How, an insightful Nixon observer once asked me, could you say he was insecure when these powerful men regarded him with such respect?[6]

Nixon often played the role of RN with skill and courage. But he failed to realize that separating RN, the cool hand at global poker, from the vulnerability and yearning of Richard, the desperate-to-please child of Frank and Hannah, was impossible. Nixon's effort to rise above or separate from his neediness was admirable in some ways, but it was also self-deceiving and, in the end, self-destructive. If he had been more self-aware—if he had not pretended so much, tried so hard to be someone he was not—he could have watched for and compensated for his

weaknesses, channeled his emotions without suc-
cumbing to their excesses.

The question I kept asking as I wrote this book is
whether Nixon could see the true Nixon. "No,"
Brent Scowcroft told me, "but sometimes I think he
took a peek."[7] That sounds about right. At some
deep, possibly subconscious level, Nixon seems to
have understood that he was locked in a titanic battle between hope and fear, and he struggled, bravely
if not always wisely, against the dark. Nixon keenly
felt the snubs and slights from his youth and even
more so, in later years, the scorn of the East Coast
elite. He was not paranoid; the press and the
"Georgetown set" really were out to get him. He
must have been aware of his insecurities and his tendency to rub old wounds and to lash out. In **Six
Crises,** he acknowledged—almost seemed to
welcome—his messy emotions at times of high
stress. But, rigidly determined not to reveal weakness, even to his intimates, he would not, or could
not, see the harm in projecting a false and brittle
facade, in extolling the tough-guy "nut-cutter."
Deeply thoughtful about the world, he was not insightful about his impact on others. In particular, he
could not see how his festering resentments and
anger would create a mood of reckless arrogance
among some of his subordinates.

To the end, Nixon resisted self-analysis. "I've
never believed that any individual can analyze them-
self [**sic**]," he told Frank Gannon in a recorded interview in 1983. "I know that's the 'hep' thing these

days. It's what you learn in political science classes, and that's what you learn in psychology classes, and—and I know that everybody's supposed to sit about—around in rap sessions and say, 'Well, these are my weaknesses, these are my strengths,' true confessions and all that stuff. But it's always turned me off. I don't think I'm really very good at it."[8]

Far more important, Nixon argued, was "to believe deeply in a great cause." Skeptics might say Nixon's true cause was his own political advancement, and certainly, he could be coldly manipulative as he pushed past his rivals. But, as Price observed, he could also use cunning and ruthlessness as the tools of statesmanship. There can be no doubt that Nixon believed in America, in its power and purpose and essential goodness. He devoted his life to serving his country. Nixon bemoaned the rise of the "Me Generation," the baby boomers preoccupied with self-realization and self-affirmation. It is ironic that Nixon, by discrediting faith in government through the Watergate scandal, contributed mightily to this inward push, away from selflessness and service.

Nixon's story is a lesson in the limits of power—of hubris and of human frailty. Consumed by ambition, he took on enormous burdens and risks and, just as he ascended to the heights, elected by a landslide to rule as the most powerful man in the world, he fell, as dramatically as if he were a tragic hero in an ancient myth or parable. Aeschylus wrote that from suffering comes wisdom; Nixon's tragedy was that he did **not** gain wisdom, at least about himself, from suffering—certainly, not until it was too late to save his presidency.

And yet, there is something affecting about a president who cries out, as his family and friends get up to walk out on a bad movie, "Wait! Wait! It'll get better!" Nixon's optimism and resiliency may have been defensive, bulwarks in his own battle against self-doubt, but they were nonetheless necessary and even admirable. Even in his bleakest hour he knew he was not done. As the helicopter rose above the Washington Monument on his last day in August 1974, Ed Cox, sitting beside him, said, "You'll be back in ten years, sir." Nixon just nodded.[9]

At critical moments, Nixon was not able to confront his own weaknesses, and he was too averse to conflict and too distracted to tame heedless subordinates. But by intelligence and grit, he accomplished great feats for his country and himself, not the least of which was getting elected, sometimes by overwhelming majorities, when he had to brace himself just to make small talk. He may have lacked self-knowledge, but he knew this: that he could be beaten down, counted out, and yet—always and no matter what the obstacles—rise again.

It is one of the mysteries—and glories—of human nature that sinners can become saints. But only in prayers of another world are saints truly cleansed of sin. Often the most convincing moralists are the very ones who feel the temptation to sin most strongly. Some turn out to be hypocrites, but that does not mean their sermons are hollow. Very few, if any, great men or women are pure of heart, but inner torment and even a touch of wickedness can be catalysts to greatness.

Nixon was no saint. But the fears and insecurities that led him into sinfulness also gave him the drive to push past self-doubt, to pretend to be cheerful, to dare to be brave, to see, often though sadly not always, the light in the dark.

Acknowledgments

In 1988, Nixon came to **Newsweek** magazine, where I worked, to talk to a group of editors and writers. After his talk, he came up to me and said, "Your grandfather was a great man." I was taken aback—I had never met Nixon and I was one of thirty or forty people in the room. Not sure of what to say, I spluttered something about how he had been a good grandfather. My father's father, Norman Thomas, had been the leader of the Socialist Party in America for many years from the 1920s to the 1960s. Nixon, in his careful, always-prepared way, must have looked at the attendance list and done some homework.

I spent twenty-four years at **Newsweek,** the magazine then owned by the Washington Post Company, Nixon's nemesis. By many measures, I am a creature of the East Coast media establishment. Old Nixon hands might have been suspicious of me, and I'm sure some were, but they were helpful in my research nonetheless. I told them that I wanted to get past the cartoon version of Nixon, and they trusted me enough to try to explain a highly complicated, deeply flawed, but capable and fascinating figure.

I want to thank, first, Robert Odle, a Washington lawyer and pro bono counsel to the Nixon Foundation, who opened many doors for me. Rob and I didn't always agree about Nixon, but he was always thoughtful in his arguments and gracious with me. I owe a debt to the many former Nixon aides and cabinet members who spoke with me: Marjorie Acker, Robert Bostock, Lucy Winchester Breathitt, Jack Brennan, Steve Bull, Jack Carley, Henry Cashen, Dwight Chapin, John Dean, Chris DeMuth, Fred Fielding, Peter Flanigan, Frank Gannon, William Gavin, David Gergen, Richard Hauser, Larry Higby, Lee Huebner, Ken Khachigian, Henry Kissinger, Egil Krogh, Melvin Laird, John Lehman, Fred Malek, Paul O'Neill, Gregg Petersmeyer, Ray Price, Jonathan Rose, Donald Rumsfeld, Don Santarelli, Brent Scowcroft, George Shultz, Stuart Spencer, Connie Stuart, William Timmons, Ron Walker, Charles Wardell, and John Whitaker.

In particular, I want to thank Doug Hallett, who was an aide to Chuck Colson, and Jack Carley for their insights into Nixon. Frank Gannon, who helped Nixon with his memoirs and spent many hours with the man, was an invaluable resource to me.

Edward Nixon, Nixon's younger brother, was gracious and informative when my wife, Oscie, and I visited him at his home outside of Seattle. For reasons I understand, other members of Nixon's immediate family chose not to speak with me, although I did receive guidance from a source close to the family who wishes to remain anonymous.

Oscie and I had a very pleasant and interesting lunch with Jo Haldeman, Bob Haldeman's widow, who permitted me to read her unpublished memoir. Haldeman's full, unedited diary, available at the Nixon Library, was a crucial source. So, too, were his handwritten notes of his meetings with Nixon, also at the Library. The Nixon-Haldeman memo file is the best source on what Nixon was thinking and agitating about, particularly on personnel and media issues. For his more spontaneous reactions, his marginalia on the president's daily news summary are revealing. Some of Nixon's late-night musings on his yellow pads are available at the Library, as are a large cache of his school papers and much of his correspondence. His ten-thousand-page diary remains closed, though he quotes extensively from it in his memoirs. John Ehrlichman's handwritten notes of his meetings with Nixon, at the Hoover Library at Stanford, are less complete than Haldeman's but are also significant. My thanks to Peter Ehrlichman for talking to me about his father. Thanks, too, to Susan Eisenhower, who lived with the Nixons at the White House in the volatile spring of 1970 and gave me an interesting, empathetic insight.

The White House tapes capture less than two and a half years of his presidency, but they are a mother lode. Since there are three thousand hours available, I needed experienced guides. The one scholar who has listened to all, or almost all, of the tapes is Luke

Nichter at Texas A&M. Luke and his coauthor of **The Nixon Tapes,** Doug Brinkley, were very helpful to me. I also used John Dean's **The Nixon Defense** and Stanley Kutler's **Abuse of Power**—massive and crucial works on the hard-to-decipher tapes. At the University of Virginia's Miller Center, Ken Hughes has made important contributions to deciphering the mysteries of the tapes, and I am grateful to him for sitting down with me to talk through the 1968 October Surprise.

Oscie and I spent several weeks listening to tapes at the Nixon Library, mostly digital versions of the National Archives originals. I often visited Luke Nichter's website nixontapes.org. Any student of the Nixon tapes should start at Nichter's meticulous site.

The transcripts of the tapes quoted in the book were made by me.

I was fortunate to be advised by some Watergate scholars. James Rosen, author of an excellent biography of John Mitchell, is deeply versed on the topic and read my manuscript carefully. So, too, Geoff Shepard, who was a young White House lawyer engaged in Nixon's defense and is still turning up evidence to support his cause. Max Holland, author of **Leak,** a brilliant study of the source known as "Deep Throat"—FBI Deputy Director Mark Felt—gave me generous and shrewd advice. Tim Naftali, the former head of the Nixon Library, shared his strongly held and informed view of Nixon; I used many of the oral histories conducted by him for the Library.

Of Nixon scholars, Melvin Small has to be one of the best; he offered useful feedback on my manuscript (warning me, for example, to be careful with the memoirs of "that old thespian" Nixon). Thomas Schwartz at Vanderbilt was helpful on Vietnam, as was Jeff Kimball at Miami of Ohio. Annelise Anderson at the Hoover Institute explained the origins of the all-volunteer army, and Earl Silbert, the federal prosecutor on Watergate, and Richard Ben-Veniste, the lead lawyer in the Watergate Special Prosecutor's office, helped me think through some of the many enduring puzzles.

Thanks to my friends Robin West and Ted Barreaux for their Nixon reminiscences and to Rick Smith for introducing me to Darrell Trent and Brent Byers for their Nixon memories from Bohemian Grove.

Oscie and I spent about two months at the Nixon Library, where we were well taken care of by archivists Meghan Lee and Pamla Eisenberg and by archives director Gregg Cumming and audio-visual specialist Ryan Pettigrew. Jonathan Movroydis and Sandy Quinn at the Nixon Foundation opened up the Jonathan Aitken papers and gave me access to Nixon's private library, enabling me to see his many underlinings in his favorite books. At the Nixon Library, my friend and longtime researcher Mike Hill was with us for some of that time (working profitably on Henry Kissinger's phone calls and documentation from October 1973) and ventured as well to the Manuscript Division at the Library of Congress in Washington (Safire, Garment, and Haig papers), the Harry Ransom Center at the University of Texas (Woodward and Bernstein papers), and the Virginia Historical Society (David Bruce papers). Thanks to Elizabeth Moynihan for access to Pat Moynihan's papers as well as for her lively recollections. Mike wishes to thank Rick Watson at the Ransom Center; Jeff Flannery, head of the Manuscript Reading Room, and Patrick Kerwin at the LOC; and Nelson Lankford at the VHS. My thanks to Joe Dmohowski at Whittier College for access to a great oral history collection, an unpublished early biography of Nixon, and his deep knowledge of Quaker Whittier. (Thanks, too, to Hubert Perry, Nixon's Whittier College contemporary, for sharing his recollections.) Stephanie George at California State–Fullerton helped me with hundreds more oral histories of Nixon's early days. My appreciation to my friend Peter Drummey for showing me the Henry Cabot Lodge Jr. papers at the Massachusetts Historical Society; to Jon Darman for some Saturday Night Massacre memorabilia from the private papers of his father, Richard Darman; to Amy Fitch at the Rockefeller Archives for help with the diary of Dr. Kenneth Riland (and to Richard Norton Smith for alerting me to it); to Susan Luftshein at the University of Southern California for the Herb Klein papers; to the reference librarians at Harvard University, which houses the papers of Theodore White; to Dan Linke at Princeton University's Mudd Library, which houses the John Foster Dulles and Arthur Krock papers. My friend Paul Miles, former professor of history at Princeton, shared with me valuable oral histories from the David Halberstam papers at Boston University, and Dr. Matthew Beland at Drew University made available the extensive Bela Kornitzer papers.

I learned about the Kornitzer papers, a treasure trove, from Irwin Gellman. Irv is the only scholar who has read the millions of papers at the Nixon Library. In addition to being the best-informed Nixon expert, he is remarkably generous. I spent many hours on the phone with Irv as he patiently walked me through the vast collections of and about Richard Nixon. He helped me avoid dumb mistakes and forced me to try to think through what the record actually shows about Nixon. Irv was finishing the second of what I hope will be many volumes on the life of Nixon.

I am in a long line of Nixon biographers, including Garry Wills, Tom Wicker, Roger Morris, Conrad Black, Jonathan Aitken, Herbert Parmet, Will Swift, Stephen Ambrose, and Richard Reeves. I drew gratefully on their work. I also learned from Rick Perlstein's studies on the rise of conservatism and David Greenberg's brilliant **Nixon's Shadow**. Dan Frick has written smartly about the impact of Nixon on American culture, and Mark Feeney offers a very clever, original take in **Nixon at the Movies**. The best novel about Nixon is **Watergate** by Thomas

Mallon. Chris Matthews's **Kennedy and Nixon** offers a close and feeling look at a relationship that could have been imagined by Shakespeare.

I was fortunate to talk to a variety of journalists who covered Nixon over the years, including Tom Brokaw of NBC and Strobe Talbott and Michael Kramer, formerly from **Time**. Cynthia Helms, widow of CIA director Richard Helms, offered valuable insights on the Georgetown set that so despised (not too strong a word) Richard Nixon.

I rely on the advice and help of old friends in the writing business, including Michael Beschloss, Stephen Smith, Ann McDaniel, and Walter Isaacson (whose biography of Kissinger was invaluable). Diane Brookes was a smart sounding board. My friend Jon Meacham has helped my family and me for many years, again and again. This book was Jon's idea and he brought it to Random House and greatly influenced my thinking. At RH, my immense gratitude to Gina Centrello, who runs the show; Will Murphy, my gifted line and story editor; his able assistant, Mika Kasuga; my excellent publicist, Greg Kubie; and my superb copy editors, Martin Schneider and Steve Messina. Victoria Wong produced the beautiful book and photo design, and Sally Marvin, the director of publicity, and Benjamin Dreyer, the Random House executive managing editor, performed miracles at the close.

My agent, Amanda Urban, is peerless. She knows how I count on her.

My closest friend (and editor), my wife, Oscie,

has helped me every step of the way. My loving mother-in-law, Oscie Freear, took good care of us in California while we were working at the Nixon Library. To my wonderful daughters, Louisa and Mary, who help me understand human nature, I dedicate this book.

Notes

Archives and Collections

BU Boston University
CSF Cal State/Fullerton
DU Drew University
HL Hoover Library
HU Harvard University
JL Johnson Library
LOC Library of Congress
NL Nixon Library
NSF National Security Files
PDD President's Daily Diary
PPP Pre-presidential Papers
PPF President's Personal Files
POF President's Office Files
SMOF Staff Member and
   Office Files

NT Nixon tapes (National
   Archives)*
PPP Public Papers of the
   Presidents
PC Providence College
PU Princeton University
RA Rockefeller Archives
WC Whittier College
USC University of Southern
   California
UT University of Texas
UU University of Utah
VHS Virginia Historical
Society

*Each citation provides the tape number followed by the conversation number, time of day, and date (e.g. Conversation 451-23, 6:16 P.M., February 18, 1971). The time of day indicates the beginning of the tape sequence in which the conversation occurred, as recorded in the National Archives Subject Log.

Introduction: The Fatalistic Optimist

1. Feeney, **Nixon at the Movies,** p. 278.
2. Safire, **Before the Fall,** p. 805.
3. RN notes, September 7, 1969, PPF, NL.
4. Robin West interview. It should be noted that Andrew Wyeth's wife, Betsy, thought Nixon was "ruggedly handsome." Jack Carley interview. Stories about Nixon's maladroitness are legion, particularly among his detractors. According to Arthur Schlesinger Jr., when Nixon saw Jackie Kennedy at Martin Luther King's funeral, he said, "This must bring back many memories, Mrs. Kennedy." Coming out of Notre Dame after the funeral of Charles de Gaulle (whom he greatly admired), Nixon reportedly exclaimed, "This is a great day for France." Schlesinger, **Journals, 1952–2000,** p. 683.
5. Brent Scowcroft interview.
6. Gregg Petersmeyer interview.
7. Eisenhower, **Pat Nixon,** p. 346.
8. See Small, **Presidency of Richard Nixon,** p. 153; Greenberg, **Nixon's Shadow,** p. 304. Nixon could be cynical about voters, calling them "suckers." Conversation 719-4, 9:06 A.M., May 4, 1972, NT. See also RN to H. R. Haldeman, January 25, 1969, SMOF, NL, urging wide dissemination of presidential remarks because Americans are "really suckers for this kind of commentary and follow it like sheep."
9. Conversation 536-16, 10:41 A.M., July 3, 1971, NT.

Part One: The Striver

Chapter 1: Lives of Great Men Remind Us

1. Virgil, **Aeneid** (Patrick Dickinson, trans.), 64; Stassinopoulos, **Gods of Greece,** p. 12.
2. **RN,** p. 14; Nixon/Gannon interviews. See www.libs/uga.edu/media/collections/Nixon/index.html.

3. Kornitzer, **Real Nixon,** p. 56.

4. Brodie, **Richard Nixon,** p. 116; Albert Upton oral history, WC.

5. 1930 **Cardinal and White** (Whittier High School yearbook), WC.

6. Aitken, **Nixon: A Life,** pp. 59–60; Spalding, **Nixon Nobody Knew,** pp. 91–2; Ola Florence Welch interview in Brodie papers, UU.

7. Haldeman, **Ends of Power,** p. 104.

8. Strober and Strober, **Nixon Presidency,** pp. 48–50.

9. White, **Breach of Faith,** p. 252.

10. Nixon/Gannon interview.

11. Schulte, ed., **Young Nixon,** p. 78; Mary Skidmore oral history, CSF; Roger Morris, **Richard Milhous Nixon,** p. 91.

12. Hannah Nixon interview in Kornitzer papers, DU.

13. Olive Marshburn to Bela Kornitzer, July 12, 1959, Kornitzer papers, DU.

14. Edward Nixon interview.

15. Roger Morris, pp. 77, 85, 87; Jackson, "Young Nixon," **Life,** June 6, 1970.

16. Roger Morris, p. 84; **RN,** p. 10.

17. Nixon/Gannon interview.

18. **RN,** p. 7.

19. Roger Morris, p. 95.

20. Nixon/Gannon interview; Joe Dmohowski, "From a Common Ground: The Quaker Heritage of Jessamyn West and Richard Nixon," **California History,** Fall 1994, p. 222; Aitken, p. 60.

21. RN interview, March 25, 1959, Kornitzer papers, DU.

22. Floyd Wildermuth oral history, CSF.

23. Jessamyn West interview in Brodie papers, UU; Jessamyn West oral history, WC.

24. Hadley Marshburn oral history, CSF.

25. Jessamyn West oral history, WC.

26. Ambrose, **Nixon: Ruin and Recovery,** p. 388.

27. Gardner, "Fighting Quaker," p. 28 (unpublished manuscript, WC).
28. Edward Nixon interview; Lucille Parsons oral history, CSF.
29. **RN**, p. 6; Edward Nixon interview.
30. Lawrene Nixon Afinson oral history, WC.
31. Sheldon Beeson oral history, CSF.
32. Julie Eisenhower oral history, WC.
33. Gardner, p. 25.
34. Roger Morris, p. 61.
35. Kevin Starr interview. There is a contradiction between the inward Quakerism of Nixon's mother and the evangelism of his father. See Dmohowski, "From a Common Ground"; Edith Jessup Comfort oral history, WC; Rev. Charles Ball, Eugene Coffin, Paul Smith oral histories, CSF.
36. Hubert Perry interview; Alsop, **Nixon and Rockefeller**, p. 131.
37. Dean Triggs oral history, CSF.
38. Stewart Alsop, p. 131.
39. William Brock oral history, WC; Herman Fink oral history, CSF.
40. **RN**, p. 17.
41. Hubert Perry interview; Wallace Newman oral history, WC.
42. **RN**, pp. 19–20.
43. Paul Smith oral history, CSF.
44. "School Papers," PPP, NL.
45. Nixon/Gannon interview.
46. Jessamyn West interview in Brodie papers, UU.
47. Dmohowski, p. 223.
48. Roger Morris, p. 147.
49. Hubert Perry oral history, CSF.
50. Kornitzer, p. 100; Helen Larson to Bela Kornitzer, March 17, 1959, Kornitzer papers, DU.
51. Gardner, p. 71.
52. **RN**, pp. 18–9; Roger Morris, pp. 150–6; Thomas Bewley oral history, WC.

53. Ola Florence Welch interview in Brodie papers, UU.
54. Aitken, pp. 60–2; Ola Florence Welch interview in Aitken papers, NL.
55. Jackson, "Young Nixon"; Ola Florence Welch to Fawn Brodie, UU; Brodie, p. 123.
56. RN, "What Can I Believe," October 9, 1933, "School papers," PPP, NL.
57. Edward Nixon interview.
58. Aitken, p. 28.

Chapter 2: Pat and Dick

1. Maynard, **Princeton**, p. 72.
2. **RN**, p. 20; Aitken, pp. 66–8; Spalding, p. 99.
3. Aitken, pp. 63–5; Gail Jobe and Ola Florence Welch interviews with Lael Morgan, CSF.
4. Lyman Brownfield interview in Kornitzer papers, DU.
5. Stewart Alsop, p. 235; Lyman Brownfield oral history, Joseph Hiatt oral history, WC.
6. Aitken, p. 76.
7. **RN**, p. 21.
8. Gellman, **Contender**, p. 8.
9. Thomas Bewley oral history, WC.
10. Stewart Alsop, p. 195.
11. Judith Wingert Loubet oral history, CSF.
12. Morris, p. 186.
13. Joe Dmohowski interview.
14. Kevin Starr interview.
15. Robert Blake interview.
16. Eisenhower, pp. 42–3.
17. Eisenhower, p. 55; **RN**, p. 23; Elizabeth Cloes oral history, WC.
18. Ibid. pp. 63, 58–9, 21, 58, 66, 68.
19. Ibid., p. 69; **RN**, p. 25.
20. Eisenhower, p. 77.
21. **RN**, p. 27.

22. Black, **Richard M. Nixon,** pp. 60–1; Hollis Dole oral history, Carl Fleps oral history, WC.
23. Kornitzer, pp. 146–7; James Udell interview in Kornitzer papers, DU.
24. Swift, **Pat and Dick,** p. 56.
25. Eisenhower, p. 83.
26. Ibid., p. 79.
27. Wills, **Nixon Agonistes,** p. 32.
28. Eisenhower, p. 85.
29. Ibid., pp. 84–6; **RN,** pp. 33–4.
30. **RN,** p. 37.
31. Gellman, **Contender,** p. 32; Roy Day oral history, WC.
32. White, **Breach of Faith,** pp. 53–6.
33. Klein, **Making It Perfectly Clear,** p. 266.
34. Lou Cannon oral history, NL.
35. Wills, **Nixon Agonistes,** p. 72.
36. Kornitzer, p. 184.
37. Morris, p. 292; Gellman, **Contender,** p. 37.
38. Halberstam, **Powers That Be,** pp. 118, 256–7.
39. Gellman, **Contender,** p. 33.
40. Brodie, p. 234.
41. Eisenhower, p. 92.
42. Brodie, p. 179; Tom Dixon and Georgia Sherwood interviews in Brodie papers, UU.
43. Aitken, pp. 122–5.
44. Gellman, **Contender,** p. 88.
45. **RN,** p. 39; Gellman, **Contender,** pp. 70–1.
46. Halberstam, p. 259.
47. **RN,** p. 40.

Chapter 3: The Greenest Congressman

1. Eisenhower, p. 95.
2. See Brinkley, **Washington Goes to War.**
3. Gibbs and Duffy, **Presidents Club,** p. 295.
4. **RN,** pp. 42–3.

5. **Time,** August 17, 1953, April 27, 1959; Noble, "Christian Herter," in **The American Secretaries of State and Their Diplomacy,** p. ix.

6. Eisenhower, p. 94.

7. **RN,** p. 48.

8. **Time,** August 17, 1953.

9. Aitken, p. 136.

10. **RN,** pp. 50–1.

11. Black, p. 101.

12. **RN,** p. 51.

13. Eisenhower, pp. 97–8.

14. See John Erman, "A Half Century of Controversy: The Alger Hiss Case," **Studies in Intelligence,** Winter–Spring 2000–2001, pp. 1–14; Haynes, Klehr, and Vassiliev, **Spies,** ch. 1.

15. Roger Morris, p. 347.

16. Black, p. 98.

17. Gellman, **Contender,** pp. 107, 227.

18. **Six Crises,** pp. 3–7.

19. **Washington Post,** August 5, 6, 1948.

20. **Six Crises,** pp. 9–11.

21. Aitken, p. 155; Gellman, **Contender,** pp. 222–3.

22. **Six Crises,** p. 31.

23. Aitken, pp. 165, 154.

24. **Six Crises,** pp. 15, 21.

25. Black, p. 124; Irwin Gellman interview.

26. Halberstam, pp. 259–60.

27. Chambers, **Witness,** pp. 792–3. Best account of Hiss case is Tanenhaus, **Whittaker Chambers,** pp. 203–335.

28. **Six Crises,** pp. 16–7, 23.

29. Eisenhower, p. 100.

30. See, for example, Abrahamsen, **Nixon v. Nixon;** Mazlish, **In Search of Nixon;** and Volkan, Itzkowitz, and Dod, **Richard Nixon.**

31. **Six Crises,** p. 41.

32. Ibid., pp. 48–9.

33. Black, p. 131.
34. **Six Crises,** pp. 54–5.
35. Parmet, **Richard Nixon and His America,** pp. 26–7.
36. **RN,** p. 71.
37. Aitken, p. 176.
38. **Six Crises,** p. 70.
39. Eisenhower, p. 101; Gellman, **Contender,** pp. 267, 272.
40. Frank Gannon interview.
41. Herbert Klein oral history, NL.

Chapter 4: Rock 'Em, Sock 'Em

1. Halberstam, p. 262; **RN,** pp. 72–3.
2. Murray Chotiner to RN, November 30, 1949, Kornitzer papers, DU.
3. Black, p. 150.
4. Gellman, **Contender,** pp. 289–343.
5. Swift, p. 104; Irwin Gellman interview.
6. **RN,** p. 73.
7. Mitchell, **Tricky Dick and the Pink Lady,** pp. 50, 159.
8. Black, p. 160; **RN,** p. 65.
9. Greenberg, p. 37.
10. Merry, **Taking on the World,** p. 236.
11. Brodie, pp. 244, 535.
12. Thomas, **Very Best Men,** p. 27.
13. Herken, **Georgetown Set,** p. 90.
14. Patricia Alsop interview in Brodie papers, UU.
15. Herken, pp. 187–8.
16. Swift, p. 106.
17. **RN,** p. 138.
18. Eisenhower, p. 111.
19. Marjorie Acker interview.
20. Rose Mary Woods to Hannah Nixon, May 25, 1956, Kornitzer papers, DU.
21. Aitken, p. 196.

22. Gellman, manuscript of **The President and the Apprentice,** ch. 19.
23. Aitken, p. 197.
24. Ibid., p. 198.
25. Eisenhower, p. 112.
26. **RN,** p. 80.
27. Frank, **Ike and Dick,** p. 21.
28. **RN,** p. 81.
29. Ibid.
30. Ibid., pp. 83–4.
31. Felsenthal, **Alice Roosevelt Longworth,** pp. 194, 229.
32. Alice Roosevelt Longworth interview in Kornitzer papers, DU.
33. **RN,** pp. 84–5.
34. Ibid., pp. 85–7.
35. Eisenhower, p. 105.
36. Nixon/Gannon interview.
37. **Six Crises,** p. 76.
38. Eisenhower, pp. 115–6.
39. Nixon/Gannon interview.
40. Ibid.
41. Van Natta, **First Off the Tee,** p. 229.
42. Frank, p. 39.

Chapter 5: Checkers

1. **New York Post,** September 18, 1952.
2. **RN,** p. 92.
3. **Six Crises,** pp. 83–7.
4. Mazo, **Richard Nixon,** p. 121; **RN,** pp. 96–7.
5. Eisenhower, p. 120.
6. **RN,** p. 98.
7. Eisenhower, p. 119.
8. West, **Upstairs at the White House,** p. 389.
9. **RN,** pp. 99–100.

10. Ibid., p. 100.
11. Ibid., p. 101.
12. **Six Crises**, p. 105.
13. **RN**, p. 103.
14. Ibid.
15. For the full text of the speech, see www.americanrhetoric .com/speeches/richardnixoncheckers.html.
16. Aitken, p. 217.
17. Wicker, **One of Us**, p. 108.
18. Ibid. p. 98.
19. Perlstein, **Nixonland**, p. 42.
20. Aitken, p. 218.
21. For the most thorough account, see Gellman, manuscript of **The President and the Apprentice**, ch. 2.
22. Wicker, p. 100.
23. **RN**, pp. 105–7.
24. Eisenhower, p. 126.
25. **RN**, pp. 108–17; Aitken, p. 222.
26. Gellman, manuscript of **The President and the Apprentice**, p. 29.
27. **Six Crises**, p. 161; Aitken, p. 343.
28. Gellman, manuscript of **The President and the Apprentice**, p. 11.
29. See Greenstein, **Hidden-Hand Presidency**.
30. Aitken, p. 226.
31. Eisenhower, p. 137; RN to Mrs. Nixon, April 1, 1972, SMOF, NL.
32. **RN**, pp. 119–37.
33. Thomas, **Ike's Bluff**, p. 57.
34. **RN**, pp. 137–50; RN to Henry Kissinger, March 29, 1972, SMOF, NL ("The Bundy's never gave me any credit for this").
35. Reeves, **Life and Times of Joe McCarthy**, p. 578.
36. Gellman, manuscript of **The President and the Apprentice**, ch. 5.
37. Parmet, p. 262.

38. **RN**, pp. 159, 163.
39. Greenberg, p. 58.
40. Eisenhower, pp. 117, 146.
41. Graham, ed., **Katharine Graham's Washington**, p. 232.
42. Arthur Schlesinger Jr. to Evangeline Bruce, October 13, 1955, Bruce papers, VHS.
43. Eisenhower, p. 152.
44. Mazo, p. 139.
45. Kenneth Thompson, ed., **Nixon Presidency**, p. 301.
46. **RN**, p. 163.
47. Eisenhower, p. 151.
48. Mazo, p. 139.

Chapter 6: "El Gringo Tiene Cojones"

1. Ferrell, **Diary of James C. Hagerty**, p. 234.
2. Kornitzer, pp. 323–4; John Carley interview.
3. **Six Crises**, p. 144.
4. **RN**, pp. 204–5; RN oral history, Dulles Papers, PU.
5. Emmett Hughes, **Ordeal of Power**, p. 317.
6. Mazo, p. 157.
7. Eisenhower, p. 157.
8. **RN**, pp. 166–70.
9. Gellman, manuscript of **The President and the Apprentice**, chs. 19 and 20.
10. Leonard Hall interview in David Halberstam papers, BU.
11. Gellman, manuscript of **The President and the Apprentice**, ch. 18.
12. Thomas, **Ike's Bluff**, pp. 353–5; Caro, **Master of the Senate**, pp. 616–7; Dallek, **An Unfinished Life**, pp. 398–9.
13. Eisenhower, p. 157; Aitken, p. 240.
14. **RN**, pp. 170–1.
15. Kissinger, **White House Years**, p. 264; Haldeman, p. 107.
16. Colson, **Born Again**, p. 92.
17. Frank, p. 149.
18. Safire, p. 418.

19. Gellman, manuscript of **The President and the Apprentice,** ch. 12.
20. **RN,** p. 186.
21. Eisenhower, pp. 171–2; Rose Mary Woods to Hannah Nixon, March 21, 1958, Kornitzer papers, DU.
22. Halberstam, p. 335.
23. Brodie, p. 365.
24. Walters, **Silent Missions,** p. 323.
25. **Six Crises,** pp. 193–204; **RN,** pp. 186–9.
26. Eisenhower, p. 174.
27. **RN,** pp. 189–90.
28. Strober and Strober, p. 40.
29. **RN,** pp. 189–91.
30. Ibid. p. 193.
31. Ibid. p. 195.
32. Eisenhower, p. 179.
33. **RN,** p. 198.
34. Nixon/Gannon interview.
35. Aitken, p. 257.
36. Don Hughes interview in Aitken papers, NL.
37. Jim Bassett interview, January 18, 1959, Kornitzer papers, DU.
38. RN interview, March 25, 1959, Kornitzer papers, DU.
39. Irwin Gellman interview.
40. **RN,** p. 207.
41. Safire, p. 1.
42. Gellman, manuscript of **The President and the Apprentice,** ch. 33.
43. Black, p. 386; **Six Crises,** p. 397.

Chapter 7: Jack

1. **RN,** p. 75.
2. Matthews, **Kennedy and Nixon,** p. 93. **New York Times** columnist Maureen Dowd wrote that her brother Michael, a Senate page, delivered mail to both Senators Kennedy and

Nixon. "He recalled that Kennedy never looked up or acknowledged his presence, but Nixon would greet him with a huge smile. 'Hi, Mike,' he'd say. 'How are you doing? How's the family?' " **New York Times,** April 11, 2015.

3. Rex Scouten interview in Aitken papers, NL.

4. Nixon/Gannon interview.

5. Ibid.

6. For the development of the Franklins v. Orthogonians theme, see Matthews, pp. 24–5; Wicker, pp. 8–9; Perlstein, **Nixonland,** pp. 22–3.

7. Hamilton, **Reckless Youth,** p. 213.

8. Aitken, p. 269.

9. Ibid., p. 268.

10. John Lindsay interview in Brodie papers, UU.

11. **RN,** p. 218.

12. Leonard Hall interview in Halberstam papers, BU; Halberstam, p. 335; West, p. 389.

13. Summers, **Arrogance of Power,** p. 204.

14. Haldeman, pp. 111–2.

15. **RN,** pp. 218–9.

16. Herbert Klein oral history, NL.

17. Halberstam, p. 339.

18. Thomas, **Robert Kennedy,** p. 106.

19. Matthews, p. 136.

20. Irwin Gellman interview.

21. Eisenhower, p. 191, Black, p. 409.

22. Aitken, p. 278.

23. Herken, p. 261.

24. Matthews, p. 155.

25. **RN,** pp. 219–20; Aitken, p. 279.

26. Morris, **Eye on the Struggle,** pp. 171, 201–3, 206, 220–3; Gellman, manuscript of **The President and the Apprentice,** chs. 26, 27, 31; Arthur Krock to Wallace Carroll, October 22, 1957, Krock papers, PU.

27. Herbert Klein oral history, NL.

28. **Six Crises,** p. 362.

29. Herbert Klein oral history, NL.

30. Thomas, **Robert Kennedy,** p. 102.

31. Irwin Gellman interview; James Meriwether, "Worth a Lot of Negro Votes: Black Voters, Africa, and the 1960 Presidential Campaign," **The Journal of American History,** December 2008, p. 762.

32. James Bassett interview in Brodie papers, UU; Aitken, p. 282.

33. Wicker, p. 240; William Safire oral history, NL.

34. **Six Crises,** p. 403.

35. Theodore White notebooks, T. White to P. Salinger, November 11, 1960, White papers, HU.

36. White, **Breach of Faith,** p. 69.

37. Herken, pp. 250, 257–8, 263.

38. White, **Making of the President, 1960,** p. 338.

39. Kenneth Thompson, ed., **Nixon Presidency,** pp. 11–2.

40. Klein, pp. 96–7.

41. Leonard Hall interview in Halberstam papers, BU.

42. **RN,** p. 222.

43. Thomas, **Ike's Bluff,** p. 392.

44. Susan Eisenhower, David Eisenhower interviews.

45. Douglas Hallett and Irwin Gellman interviews.

46. Aitken, p. 288.

47. Ehrlichman, **Witness to Power,** p. 10; Dwight Chapin interview.

48. Frank, p. 215.

49. Aitken, p. 289; Herbert Klein oral history, NL.

50. Eisenhower, p. 194.

51. **Six Crises,** p. 386.

52. Eisenhower, p. 197.

53. **Six Crises,** p. 374.

54. Ibid., 392.

55. Peter Flanigan interview; Peter Flanigan oral history, NL.

56. **RN,** p. 225.

57. Julie Eisenhower interview in Aitken papers.

Chapter 8: Over the Wall We Go

1. Leonard Hall interview in Halberstam papers, BU.
2. **Six Crises**, p. 404.
3. Bradlee, **Good Life**, p. 21.
4. Irwin Gellman interview. Gellman calculates that the real margin was closer to forty thousand votes because the votes cast for independent electors in Alabama were counted by the news media for Kennedy.
5. Matthews, p. 185; **Six Crises**, p. 407.
6. **Six Crises**, p. 405.
7. Greenberg, p. 189.
8. Wicker, p. 257.
9. Aitken, p. 293.
10. **RN**, p. 228.
11. Nixon/Gannon interview.
12. Aitken, p. 295.
13. Nixon/Gannon interview.
14. **RN**, pp. 151–2.
15. Stewart Alsop, p. 20.
16. Aitken, p. 16.
17. **RN**, pp. 236–7.
18. Eisenhower, p. 204.
19. **RN**, p. 240.
20. John Carley interview.
21. Thomas, **The Very Best Men**, p. 103.
22. Matthews, p. 215.
23. **RN**, pp. 242–3; Ehrlichman, pp. 148–9.
24. Klein, p. 59; Halberstam, pp. 348–9.
25. Dwight Chapin interview; Klein, p. 55; Matthews, p. 216.
26. **RN**, pp. 245–6.
27. Perlstein, **Nixonland**, p. 46.
28. Eisenhower, pp. 213–6.
29. **Time**, November 16, 1962.
30. Aitken, p. 294; **RN**, pp. 252–5.

31. Eisenhower, p. 216; **RN**, p. 248.
32. Garment, **Crazy Rhythm**, p. 67.
33. Ibid., p. 85.
34. Ibid., p. 70.
35. Ibid., pp. 86–90.
36. **RN**, p. 265.
37. Stuart Spencer interview.
38. Eisenhower, p. 221. See Barry Goldwater: 1964 Republican National Convention, YouTube.com.
39. John Sears interview in Aitken papers, NL.
40. Sears, "Politics Is Great—Except for People," **Los Angeles Times**, April 24, 1994.
41. See Adler, **Wit and Humor of Richard Nixon.**
42. Sears, "Politics Is Great."
43. Garment, p. 115.
44. Witcover, **Resurrection of Richard Nixon**, p. 170.
45. Nixon/Gannon interview.
46. **RN**, p. 278.
47. Eisenhower, p. 230.
48. RN to Jonathan Aitken, May 29, 1991, Aitken papers, NL.
49. Kimball, **Nixon's Vietnam War**, p. 43.
50. Perlstein, **Nixonland**, p. 111.
51. Eisenhower, p. 218.
52. Perlstein, **Nixonland**, pp. 82–3.
53. Buchanan, **Greatest Comeback**, pp. 137, 149.
54. Annelise Anderson interview; Anderson, "Making of the All-Volunteer Force," Hoover Institution, Stanford University (courtesy Annelise Anderson).
55. Hess, **Professor and the President**, pp. 11–2.
56. Amos Eran interview. Eran was an aide to Rabin.
57. **RN**, p. 248.
58. Aitken, p. 337.
59. **RN**, p. 281.
60. Raymond Price oral history, NL.
61. **RN**, p. 285.
62. Courtesy of Christopher Buckley.

63. **RN,** p. 284.
64. RN speech to Bohemian Grove, July 27, 1967, Aitken papers, NL.
65. Douglas Hallet interview; RN to H. R. Haldeman, March 1, 1971, SMOF, NL.

Chapter 9: The New Nixon

1. Ruth Proffitt interview.
2. Eisenhower, p. 220.
3. **RN,** p. 250.
4. Ibid., p. 291.
5. Eisenhower, p. 234; Hutchshnecker, **Will to Live,** pp. 53–4.
6. **RN,** pp. 288–94; Eisenhower, pp. 233–4.
7. James Bassett interview, January 8, 1959, Kornitzer papers, DU.
8. **RN,** p. 265.
9. Ibid., p. 288.
10. Kenneth Khachigian interview.
11. Kissinger, **White House Years,** p. 247.
12. Safire diary, February 21, 1971, Safire papers, LOC.
13. Alexander Haig oral history, NL.
14. Garment, p. 118; Deborah Gore Dean interview.
15. Safire, p. 336.
16. Garment, pp. 119–20.
17. Rosen, **Strong Man,** pp. 17, 36.
18. Dwight Chapin interview; Dwight Chapin oral history, NL.
19. White, **Breach of Faith,** p. 97.
20. Aitken, p. 303; Haldeman, p. 76.
21. Rob Odle interview.
22. Ehrlichman, pp. 3–9, 21–2.
23. Whalen, **Catch the Falling Flag,** p. 137.
24. Kimball, p. 52.
25. Edward Cox speech, Gerald Ford Museum, May 16, 2011, C-SPAN, YouTube.com.
26. Perlstein, **Nixonland,** p. 81.

27. Wills, **Nixon Agonistes,** p. 88.
28. Halberstam, pp. 589–60.
29. White, **Making of the President, 1968,** pp. 166–7.
30. Haldeman, p. 38.
31. Herken, p. 347.
32. Ehrlichman, p. 24.
33. Aitken, p. 353; Wills, **Nixon Agonistes,** p. 216.
34. Stuart, **Never Trust a Local,** p. 27.
35. Safire, p. 60.
36. Dwight Chapin oral history, NL.
37. Witcover, p. 310.
38. Robert Ellsworth oral history, NL.
39. **RN,** pp. 305–7.
40. For background of the speech, see Gavin, **Speechwright,** pp. 6–13.
41. Safire, pp. 67–8; Safire diary, August 8, 1968, Safire papers, LOC.
42. Henry Cashen interview.
43. Edward Cox speech.
44. Robert Ellsworth oral history, NL.
45. McGinniss, **Selling of the President,** p. 123; Wills, **Nixon Agonistes,** p. 265.
46. Perlstein, **Nixonland,** pp. 277–9.
47. Ibid., p. 224; Buchanan, p. 292.
48. Sherman, **Loudest Voice in the Room,** p. 33.
49. Ibid., pp. 30–41.
50. McGinniss, pp. 67, 73, 100.
51. Ibid., p. 111.

Chapter 10: October Surprise

1. Haldeman, p. 100.
2. Strober and Strober, p. 40.
3. Dwight Chapin oral history, NL.
4. Safire, pp. 86–7; Safire diary, September 18, 1968, Safire papers, LOC.

5. Bradlee, p. 212.
6. White, **Making of the President, 1968,** p. 381.
7. Tom Brokaw interview.
8. John Carley interview.
9. Stuart Spencer interview.
10. Dwight Chapin interview; Strober and Strober, p. 27.
11. Jack Dreyfus interview in Aitken papers, NL. Frank Gannon doubted that Nixon was a regular user of Dilantin.
12. Garment, p. 44; Leonard Garment oral history, NL.
13. Dwight Chapin interview.
14. Ibid.
15. Ehrlichman, p. 39.
16. Eisenhower, p. 241.
17. Constance Stuart oral history, NL.
18. Ehrlichman, pp. 30–5; Safire diary, October 28, 1968, Safire papers, LOC.
19. John Carley interview.
20. Ehrlichman, p. 32.
21. Safire, pp. 63–4.
22. Francis Bator interview. Bator was a Harvard professor and Kissinger colleague.
23. **RN,** p. 323; Isaacson, **Kissinger,** pp. 129–32; Hughes, **Chasing Shadows,** pp. 173–5.
24. **RN,** p. 317.
25. Black, p. 540.
26. **RN,** p. 326.
27. Feeney, p. 86, Safire, p. 785.
28. Forslund, **Anna Chennault,** pp. 19–52; Hughes, **Chasing Shadows,** p. 8.
29. Safire, pp. 73, 111–2; Diem, **In the Jaws of History,** p. 237; Chennault, **Education of Anna,** pp. 175–6.
30. Dallek, **Nixon and Kissinger,** pp. 74–7; Kimball, pp. 56–60.
31. LBJ to George Reedy, January 4, 1956; George Christian to Jake Jacobsen, November 4, 1966; Billy Graham notes of conversation with RN, September 8, 1968; JL; Safire diary, October 14 and 20, 1968, Safire papers, LOC.

32. **RN,** p. 327.

33. Hughes, **Chasing Shadows,** p. 29.

34. Strober and Strober, p. 30.

35. Hughes, **Chasing Shadows,** p. 31.

36. Ibid., pp. 5–6, 37; Walter Rostow, Memo for Record, May 14, 1973, "X Envelope," Reference File: Anna Chennault, South Vietnam and U.S. Politics, JL.

37. Director FBI to Bromley Smith, November 4, 1968, "X Envelope," JL.

38. Hughes, **Chasing Shadows,** p. 40.

39. Ibid., p. 50.

40. Director FBI to Bromley Smith, November 3, 1968, "X Envelope," JL.

41. Hodgson, **American Melodrama,** p. 734.

42. Luke Nichter, Thomas Schwartz, James Rosen interviews.

43. RN to Jonathan Aitken, May 29, 1991, Aitken papers, NL.

44. Tom Charles Huston oral history, NL.

Part Two: At the Mountaintop
Chapter 11: "He Loves Being P!"

1. **RN,** p. 332.

2. Safire, p. 116.

3. Henry Cashen interview.

4. Dwight Chapin interview.

5. Garment, p. 141.

6. **RN,** p. 6.

7. White, **Making of the President, 1968.**

8. Eisenhower, p. 246.

9. **RN,** pp. 332–3; Dwight Chapin interview.

10. Garment, p. 76.

11. **RN,** pp. 334–5; Nixon/Gannon interview.

12. Hughes, **Chasing Shadows,** pp. 59–60.

13. Ibid., p. 55.

14. Lyndon Johnson, **Vantage Point,** pp. 522–8, 548–9.
15. Eisenhower, p. 248.
16. Dwight Chapin interview.
17. Rose Mary Woods to RN, July 21, 1960, PPP, NL.
18. Haldeman, p. 118; Ehrlichman, p. 134.
19. Hughes, **Chasing Shadows,** pp. 66–7.
20. Kissinger, **White House Years,** pp. 10–14.
21. Donald Rumsfeld interview.
22. Irwin Gellman interview; RN to Kissinger, July 7, 1958; Kissinger to RN, June 10, July 1, 1959, PPP, NL.
23. **RN,** p. 341.
24. Kissinger, **White House Years,** p. 14.
25. Isaacson, p. 142.
26. Henry Kissinger interview.
27. Isaacson, p. 107.
28. Safire, pp. 133, 39–40.
29. Jo Haldeman interview.
30. Eisenhower, p. 259.
31. Dwight Chapin oral history, NL.
32. Eisenhower, p. 259.
33. **RN,** pp. 360–1.
34. Eisenhower, p. 258.
35. **RN,** p. 361.
36. Haldeman diary, January 20, 1969, NL.
37. Kenneth Thompson, ed., **Nixon Presidency,** p. 160.
38. Kissinger, **White House Years,** p. 4.
39. Price, **With Nixon,** p. 48.
40. Greenberg, p. 75.
41. **RN,** p. 366.
42. Robert Bostock interview.
43. Haldeman diary, January 21, 1969, NL.
44. Reeves, **President Nixon,** p. 30.
45. Wicker, p. 446; **RN,** p. 42.
46. Stuart, p. 49.
47. **RN,** p. 369.

48. Haldeman diary, January 27, 31, 1969, NL.
49. Reeves, **President Nixon**, p. 31; Strober and Strober, p. 74; Haldeman diary, January 31, 1969, NL.
50. Safire, pp. 140, 366.
51. Reeves, **President Nixon**, p. 29.
52. Safire diary, April 4, 1969, Safire papers, LOC.
53. Black, p. 579.
54. Dwight Chapin interview in Aitken papers, NL.
55. Magruder, **American Life**, p. 60.
56. Wicker, p. 400; Safire diary, September 14, 1970, Safire papers, LOC.
57. Wicker, p. 401.
58. Rather, **Palace Guard**, p. 30.
59. Ehrlichman, p. 60; Haldeman, p. 53.
60. Ehrlichman, p. 58.
61. Douglas Hallett interview.
62. Lawrence Higby interview.
63. Haldeman diary, January 25, 1969, NL.
64. President's Daily Diary, NL.
65. Alexander Butterfield oral history, NL.
66. Haldeman notes, March 16, 1969, NL; Haldeman interview by James Rosen courtesy James Rosen.
67. Dwight Chapin interview.
68. Ehrlichman, p. 49.
69. Eisenhower, p. 278.

Chapter 12: Statesman and Madman

1. Small, **Presidency**, p. 53.
2. Safire, p. 99.
3. Ibid., p. 131.
4. Butterfield oral history, NL.
5. Henry Cashen interview.
6. William Safire oral history, NL.
7. Elizabeth Moynihan interview.
8. Feeney, p. 158.

9. Hodgson, **Gentleman from New York,** pp. 25–6.

10. Weisman, ed., **Daniel Patrick Moynihan,** p. 152.

11. Christopher DeMuth oral history, NL.

12. **RN,** p. 342.

13. Eisenhower, p. 254.

14. Weisman, ed., p. 176.

15. Nixon's underlined copy of a biography of Disraeli by André Maurois is at the Nixon Library; Moynihan later recommended the more popular biography by Robert Blake. Patrick Moynihan to RN, November 30, 1970, Moynihan papers, LOC.

16. Reeves, **President Nixon,** p. 33; White, **Making of the President, 1968,** p. 171.

17. RN to Patrick Moynihan, January 15, 1969, Moynihan letters, LOC.

18. Weisman, ed., p. 173; Hess, pp. 92–103, 118.

19. See Hoff, **Nixon Reconsidered;** Wicker, p. 409; Small, pp. 153–4, 309; Greenberg, p. 304, 327.

20. William Timmons interview.

21. Price, p. 45.

22. Reeves, **President Nixon,** p. 32; Price memo, January 23, 1969, POF, NL.

23. Hoff, p. 118; **RN,** p. 353.

24. RN notes, February 6, 1969, PPF, NL.

25. Haldeman diary, May 2, 1969, NL.

26. Sidey, "The Man with the Four-Button Phone," **Life,** January 31, 1969.

27. Halberstam, p. 604.

28. Jim Keogh to Leonard Garment, February 17, 1969, POF, NL. Richard Reeves writes that Nixon responded, "You don't understand, they're trying to destroy us," but those words do not appear on the memo. Reeves, p. 40 (no citation). It is possible he said them or wrote them to someone else.

29. RN to H. R. Haldeman, January 6, 1970, SMOF, NL.

30. Rosen, p. 42.

31. Aitken, p. 377.
32. Strober and Strober, p. 72; see also Mort Allin exit interview, NL.
33. Ambrose, **Nixon: The Triumph of a Politician,** p. 409.
34. Lawrence Higby interview.
35. Ambrose, **Nixon: The Triumph of a Politician,** p. 410. Ambrose cites a June 16, 1969, memo from RN to Haldeman. I was unable to find it in Haldeman's Presidential memos file at the Nixon Library.
36. Strober and Strober, p. 42.
37. Aitken, p. 369.
38. Herken, p. 349.
39. Isaacson, p. 142.
40. Graham, **Personal History,** p. 433.
41. Cynthia Helms interview.
42. Aitken, p. 371.
43. Isaacson, p. 143.
44. Strober and Strober, p. 125.
45. Small, p. 98.
46. Elliot Richardson interview in Aitken papers, NL.
47. Kissinger, **White House Years,** pp. 138–43; Dallek, **Nixon and Kissinger,** pp. 109–12.
48. Moynihan diary, July 21, 1974, Moynihan papers, LOC.
49. Aitken, pp. 380–1; **RN,** p. 371.
50. Safire notes, February 27, 1969, Safire papers, LOC.
51. **RN,** p. 371.
52. Kissinger, **White House Years,** p. 93.
53. Safire, p. 160.
54. Kissinger, **White House Years,** pp. 107–8; Nixon/Gannon interview.
55. **RN,** p. 374.
56. William Safire oral history, NL.
57. Haldeman, p. 120.
58. Ibid., p. 122.
59. Kimball, p. 101.
60. Isaacson, p. 166.

61. **RN**, p. 733.
62. Evans and Novak, **Nixon in the White House,** p. 75.
63. Melvin Laird interview; Small, **Presidency,** p. 65; Kimball, pp. 138–9; Van Atta, **With Honor,** p. 133.

Chapter 13: "Need for Joy"

1. **RN**, p. 380.
2. Kissinger, **White House Years,** p. 243.
3. Kimball, pp. 123–35; Haldeman diary, March 10, 1969, NL.
4. Kissinger, **White House Years,** pp. 246–7.
5. Safire meeting notes, August 18, 1969, Safire papers, LOC.
6. Haig, **Inner Circles,** pp. 205, 195.
7. Kimball, p. 135. On Nixon's Vietnam policy generally, see Kimball, "The Vietnam War" in Small, **Companion to Richard M. Nixon;** for a balanced overview, see Herring, **America's Longest War** and **From Colony to Superpower.** For a strong critique, see Berman, **No Peace, No Honor.**
8. Swift, p. 220, Lucy Winchester Breathitt interview.
9. Jo Haldeman interview.
10. Cynthia Helms interview.
11. Dwight Chapin, Steve Bull, Lawrence Higby, Brent Scowcroft interviews.
12. Magruder, p. 61.
13. Haldeman, p. 110.
14. Haldeman diary, March 28, 1969, NL.
15. Price, pp. 61–2.
16. Black, p. 596.
17. Safire diary, March 31, 1969, Safire papers, LOC.
18. **RN**, pp. 387–8.
19. Isaacson, p. 213.
20. Ibid., p. 225.
21. Haldeman notes, June 16, 1969, NL.
22. Isaacson, p. 229.
23. Haldeman diary, September 4, 1969, NL.

24. Swift, p. 254.

25. Gulley, **Breaking Cover,** pp. 176–90.

26. Safire, p. 801.

27. Haldeman diary, July 18, 1969, NL.

28. Isaacson, p. 209.

29. **RN,** p. 394.

30. Haldeman diary, July 21, 24, 25, 1969, NL.

31. Ibid., July 30, 1969.

32. Reeves, **President Nixon,** p. 88.

33. Henry Cashen interview.

34. **RN,** p. 395.

35. Haldeman, p. 132.

36. Henry Kissinger interview; Van Atta, pp. 272–3.

37. Notes on lunch with William Rogers, March 16, 1973, Safire papers, LOC.

38. Haldeman diary, July 19, 1969, NL.

39. Safire, p. 188; Safire diary, July 20, 1969, LOC.

40. Haldeman notes, July 19, 1969, NL.

41. Klein, p. 110.

42. Safire, p. 192.

43. Haldeman notes, July 21, 1969, NL.

44. Ibid., March 26, 1969, NL.

45. Strober and Strober, p. 263; Alexander Butterfield oral history, NL.

46. Haldeman diary, August 4, 1969, NL.

47. Safire, pp. 194–5. Dwight Chapin does not believe Safire could have observed this scene because he says Nixon and Kennedy met alone.

48. RN notes, September 7, 1969, PPF, NL.

49. Perlstein, **Nixonland,** p. 417.

50. Haig, pp. 229–31.

51. Haldeman diary, October 3, 1969, NL.

52. Dallek, **Nixon and Kissinger,** p. 154; Perlstein, **Nixonland,** p. 420.

53. Isaacson, p. 246.

54. Kimball and Burr, "Nixon White House Considered Nu-

clear Options Against North Vietnam, Declassified Documents Reveal," **National Security Archive Briefing Book No. 195,** July 31, 2006.

55. Thomas, **Ike's Bluff,** pp. 77–81.
56. **RN,** p. 400.
57. Kimball, p. 169.
58. Haldeman diary, October 13, 1969, NL.
59. **RN,** p. 398.
60. Haldeman diary, September 29, 1969, NL.
61. Perlstein, **Nixonland,** p. 424.
62. Haldeman diary, October 16, 1969, NL.

Chapter 14: Silent Majority

1. **RN,** pp. 403, 408.
2. Haldeman diary, November 1, 1969, NL; Jack Bennan interview.
3. **PPP,** p. 425, November 3, 1969.
4. **RN,** p. 409.
5. William Safire oral history, NL.
6. Perlstein, **Nixonland,** p. 435.
7. **RN,** p. 410.
8. Haldeman diary, November 3, 1969, NL.
9. Alexander Butterfield oral history, NL.
10. **RN,** p. 410.
11. Alexander Butterfield oral history, NL. Nixon personally launched a letters-to-the-editor operation. See Alex Butterfield to Dent et al. ("November 3 Game Plan"), October 28, 1969, Klein papers, USC.
12. Haldeman notes, April 25, 1960, NL.
13. Ehrlichman notes, November 14, 1969, Ehrlichman papers, HL.
14. Haldeman diary, November 13, 1969, NL.
15. Safire, p. 472.
16. Haldeman diary, November 15, 1969, NL; Perlstein, **Nixonland,** p. 440.

17. Rosen, p. 94; **RN,** p. 413.
18. Haldeman diary, November 4, 1969, NL.
19. Reeves, **President Nixon,** p. 142. Reeves cites RN to Henry Kissinger, October 27, 1969. I was unable to find this memo in the President's Personal File or his memos to staff.
20. Dallek, **Nixon and Kissinger,** p. 183. Dallek cites RN to Henry Kissinger, November 24, 1969. I was unable to find this memo.
21. **RN,** p. 396.
22. Kimball, p. 187.
23. **RN,** p. 402.
24. Isaacson, p. 163.
25. Henry Kissinger interview.
26. William Safire to RN, December 8, 1969, PPF, NL.
27. Ehrlichman notes, December 29, 1969, Ehrlichman papers, HL; Ehrlichman, p. 246.
28. Haldeman diary, January 17, 1970, NL.
29. RN notes, January 14, 16, 1970, PPF, NL.
30. Safire, pp. 781–2; Safire diary, January 23, 1970, Safire papers, LOC; Haldeman diary, January 20, 1970, NL.
31. Elizabeth Moynihan interview.
32. Wicker, p. 536.
33. Liberalism peaked in 1966, headed down through 1969, but then turned up again in 1970–71. See James Stimson's "Policy Mood Index," www.unc.edu/~cogginse/Policy _Mood.html.
34. Greenberg, p. 315.
35. James Schlesinger interview.
36. Ibid.
37. Hoff, p. 67.
38. RN notes, January 14, 1970, PPF, NL.
39. "Virginia Knauer, Consumer Advocate, Dies at 96," **New York Times,** October 27, 2011. Nixon wanted his own version of Nader's raiders to catch government waste: "I am sure you have seen how much mileage Nader has gotten out of giving his young squirts something to do." RN to H. R. Haldeman, June 16, 1969, SMOF, NL.

40. Wicker, p. 530; See Daniel Moynihan to RN, May 17, 1969, Weisman, ed., p. 188.
41. **RN**, p. 427.
42. Ambrose, **Nixon: The Triumph of a Politician**, p. 315.
43. Haldeman diary, July 13, 1970, NL.
44. Stuart, p. 99.
45. Reeves, p. 100.
46. Ehrlichman, pp. 218–21.
47. Weisman, ed., p. 286.
48. Donald Rumsfeld interview.
49. Schlesinger, **White House Ghosts**, pp. 207–9.
50. Small, **Presidency**, pp. 153, 190. When congressional Democrats proposed to increase social security benefits by 20 percent in 1970, Nixon pushed for an automatic annual cost-of-living adjustment instead—more rational, but ultimately costly. William Timmons interview.
51. Strober and Strober, p. 114.
52. Weisman, ed., p. 285.
53. John Whitaker interview.
54. Ehrlichman notes, October 23, 1969, HL.
55. Edward Nixon interview.
56. Reeves, **President Nixon**, p. 163; Christopher DeMuth interview.
57. Haldeman diary, August 26, 1969, NL.
58. John Whitaker interview.
59. Reeves, p. 163. In a moment of pettiness, Nixon refused to invite the author of the Clean Air Act, Senator Muskie, to the White House signing ceremony.
60. Stuart, p. 109; Ambrose, **Nixon: The Triumph of a Politician**, p. 325; Black, p. 654.

Chapter 15: The Moviegoer

1. Ehrlichman, p. 200.
2. Dent, **Prodigal South Returns to Power**, p. 210.
3. Small, **Presidency**, p. 169.

4. Ibid., pp. 142, 161.
5. Haldeman diary, March 25, 1970, NL; Reeves, p. 159.
6. Rosen, p. 136; **RN**, p. 436.
7. Brooks, "The CEO in Politics," **New York Times,** January 12, 2012.
8. Klein, p. 316; Ehrlichman, p. 200.
9. Haldeman diary, February 9, 1970, NL.
10. Douglas Hallett interview.
11. Garment, p. 207.
12. **RN**, p. 438; Haldeman diary, February 4, 1970, NL; Ehrlichman, p. 204.
13. Safire, p. 303; Haldeman notes, February 20, 1970, NL.
14. Hoff, pp. 28–44; Bobbie Kilberg oral history, NL.
15. Haldeman notes, February 20, 1970, NL.
16. Safire, p. 310.
17. Ehrlichman papers, December 29, 1969, HL.
18. George Shultz interview; George Shultz, "How a Republican Desegregated the South's Schools," **The New York Times,** July 8, 2003.
19. Ehrlichman, p. 204; Ehrlichman notes, August 4, 1970, HL.
20. Reeves, **President Nixon,** p. 170.
21. Haldeman diary, March 14, 1970, NL.
22. Haldeman diary, February 11, 1970, NL.
23. Feeney, p. 341.
24. Feeney, p. 67.
25. Haldeman diary, April 7, 16, 1970, NL.
26. Isaacson, p. 259; Kissinger, **White House Years,** p. 480.
27. Reeves, **President Nixon,** p. 195; Haldeman diary, April 20, 1970, NL.
28. **RN**, p. 447.
29. Isaacson, p. 262.
30. Kissinger, **White House Years,** p. 498.
31. RN notes, April 26, 1970, PPF, NL.
32. Haldeman diary, April 28, 29, 1970, NL.
33. **RN**, p. 453; Kissinger, **White House Years,** p. 503.

34. Safire, p. 233. The expression is sometimes "with the bark off," but linguist Safire quoted Nixon correctly.

35. **PPP,** p. 409, April 30, 1970.

36. **RN,** p. 447.

37. Eisenhower, pp. 285–6.

38. Ehrlichman papers, April 30, 1970, HL.

39. **RN,** p. 453.

40. Herken, p. 351.

41. Safire, p. 239.

42. Isaacson, p. 269.

43. **RN,** pp. 453–4.

44. Jack Brennan interview; Brennan to Rose Mary Woods, May 4, 1970, Brennan papers, PC.

45. Haldeman diary, Haldeman notes, May 4, 1970, NL; **RN,** p. 457.

46. Aitken, p. 404.

47. Elizabeth Moynihan interview.

48. Kissinger, **White House Years,** p. 514; Lawrence Higby interview.

49. **RN,** p. 459.

50. Safire, p. 260; PDD, May 8–9, 1970.

51. Isaacson, p. 270.

52. **RN,** p. 460.

53. Haldeman diary, May 9, 1970, NL.

Chapter 16: Hippies and Hardhats

1. Safire, p. 261.

2. Egil Krogh oral history, NL.

3. Aitken, p. 406.

4. **RN,** p. 158.

5. Ibid., p. 465; RN to H. R. Haldeman, May 13, 1970, SMOF, NL; H. R. Haldeman to William Safire, May 14, 1970; W. S. to H. R. H., March 19, 1970; H. R. H. to W. S., June 8, 1970, Safire papers, LOC.

6. Kenneth Thompson, ed., **Nixon Presidency,** p. 292.
7. Safire, p. 268.
8. Egil Krogh oral history, NL.
9. Haldeman diary, May 9, 1970, NL.
10. Safire, p. 247.
11. Haig, p. 239.
12. Egil Krogh to John Ehrlichman, May 9, 1970, POF, NL.
13. Safire, p. 272, Egil Krogh interview.
14. Haldeman diary, May 7, 1970, NL.
15. Ibid., May 11, 1970, NL.
16. Perlstein, **Nixonland,** pp. 493–5.
17. Ibid., pp. 498–501; **RN,** pp. 466–7.
18. Morris, p. 853.
19. **RN,** p. 466.
20. Eisenhower, p. 290.
21. Ibid., p. 291.
22. Ehrlichman, p. 42; Eisenhower, p. 299.
23. Swift, pp. 236–45.
24. Dwight Chapin interview.
25. Strober and Strober, p. 35.
26. Susan Eisenhower interview.
27. Connie Stuart interview.
28. Haldeman diary, October 7, 1969, NL.
29. Ibid., January 8, February 5, 1970.
30. Swift, p. 177.
31. Fred Malek interview. He hired a Harvard Business School grad, Barbara Franklin, who brought in scores of women. Nixon only balked when Franklin suggested to Nixon that he engage in "rap sessions" with women. Herb Klein to RN, re Rita Hauser's memo, "Emergent Responsible Feminism," July 8, 1971, Klein papers, USC.
32. Swift, p. 277.
33. Haldeman diary, September 25, October 20, 21, 1971, NL; Dean, **The Rehnquist Choice,** p. 51.
34. Frank Gannon, Lucy Winchester Breathitt, Connie Stuart interviews.

35. Henry Kissinger interview.
36. Rosen, p. 118.
37. Haldeman diary, February 21, 1970, NL.
38. Rosen, p. 122.
39. Strober and Strober, p. 296.
40. Rosen, p. 403.
41. Ehrlichman, p. 117; Haldeman diary, November 21, 1969, NL.
42. Haldeman notes, April 11, 1970, NL.
43. Reeves, **President Nixon,** p. 204.
44. Rosen, p. 125.
45. Haldeman notes, April 13, 15, May 18, 1970; Haldeman diary, May 18, 1970, NL.
46. Strober and Strober, p. 294.
47. Rob Odle interview; Anderson, "The Making of the All-Volunteer Armed Forces."
48. Kenneth Thompson, ed., **Nixon Presidency,** p. 138.
49. **RN,** p. 43.
50. Weisman, ed., p. 216.
51. Eisenhower, p. 282.
52. Tom Charles Huston oral history, NL.
53. Small, **Presidency,** p. 56.
54. Lukas, **Nightmare,** p. 31; Safire, p. 379.
55. Haldeman diary, June 16, 1969, NL.
56. **RN,** p. 473; Weiner, **Enemies,** pp. 266–8.
57. **RN,** p. 358.
58. Ehrlichman, pp. 138–41. Nixon sought the invitation; see RN to John Mitchell, September 22, 1969, SMOF, NL (in Haldeman files).
59. Reeves, **President Nixon,** p. 236; Lukas, pp. 30–7; Tom Charles Huston oral history, NL.
60. **RN,** p. 472.
61. Small, **Presidency,** p. 57; Dean, **Blind Ambition,** p. 33.
62. Rosen, pp. 494–5.
63. Dean, **Blind Ambition,** pp. 8, 17, 33–4.
64. Luke Nichter interview.

Chapter 17: Department of Dirty Tricks

1. Dean, **Blind Ambition**, p. 7.
2. Haldeman diary, September 30, 1969, NL.
3. Dean, **Blind Ambition**, pp. 27–9; John Dean oral history, NL.
4. Haldeman diary, March 4, 1970, NL; Nixon used Chotiner to explore the connection between O'Brien and Howard Hughes. Murray Chotiner to Herb Klein, April 24, 1970, Klein papers, USC.
5. Haldeman notes, March 9, 1970, NL.
6. Ibid., February 17, 1970, NL.
7. George Shultz interview.
8. Ehrlichman notes, August 29, 1972, HL; RN to H. R. Haldeman, August 9, 1972, SMOF, NL.
9. Haldeman notes, March 31, 1970, NL.
10. Raymond Price interview.
11. Charles Colson oral history, NL.
12. Strober and Strober, p. 274.
13. Ibid., pp. 278, 280.
14. Haldeman notes, September 27, 1970, NL.
15. Aitken, p. 415.
16. Magruder, p. 81. Nixon let Colson push aside Klein. See H. R. Haldeman to Colson, September 21, 1970; Herbert Klein to Colson, November 5, 1971, Klein papers, USC.
17. Klein, pp. 121, 139.
18. Magruder, pp. 28, 71, 137.
19. Steve Bull interview; Lawrence Higby interview.
20. Douglas Hallett interview.
21. Charles Colson oral history, NL.
22. RN notes, October 10, 1970, PPF, NL.
23. Haldeman diary, December 20, 1970, NL.
24. Kimball, pp. 239–40.
25. Haldeman diary, June 2, 1971, NL; Jeffrey Kimball, "The Case of the 'Decent Interval': Do We Now Have a Smoking Gun?" **SHAFR Newsletter**, September 2001, pp. 35–39;

"Decent Interval or Not? The Paris Agreement and the End of the Vietnam War"; and Larry Berman, "A Final Word on the 'Decent Interval' Strategy," **SHAFR Newsletter,** December 2003.

26. Haldeman diary, August 17, 1970, NL. For further understanding of Nixon's motives, see also Thomas Schwartz, "'Henry . . . Winning an Election Is Terribly Important': Partisan Politics in the History of the U.S. Foreign Relations," **Diplomatic History,** April 2009, pp. 173–90.

27. Kissinger, **White House Years,** p. 559.

28. Haldeman diary, September 25, 1971, NL.

29. Cynthia Helms interview.

30. Weiner, **Legacy of Ashes,** pp. 309–16.

31. Frost, **Frost/Nixon,** pp. 73, 361; Haldeman diary, September 25, 1970.

32. Henry Kissinger interview.

33. Kissinger, **Years of Upheaval,** p. 1181.

34. Ibid., pp. 1185–6.

35. Haldeman diary, September 9, 1970.

36. Ehrlichman notes, September 1, 1970, HL.

37. Safire, pp. 410–1; Haldeman diary, September 26, 1970, NL.

38. William Safire notes, September 9, 1970; Patrick Buchanan to Bryce Harlow and Spiro Agnew, September 9, 1970, Safire papers, LOC.

39. Safire, p. 417; Haldeman diary, October 12, 1970, NL.

40. **RN,** p. 492.

41. Haldeman diary, October 19, 1970, NL.

42. Evans and Novak, pp. 6–7.

43. Steve Bull interview.

44. Haldeman diary, October 29, 1970, NL.

45. **RN,** p. 492.

46. Safire, p. 426.

47. Haldeman diary, October 29, 1970, NL.

48. **RN,** p. 494; Safire, p. 421.

49. Haldeman diary, November 11, 1970, NL.

50. Eisenhower, p. 299.

51. RN notes, November 15, 1970, PPF, NL.
52. Reeves, **President Nixon,** p. 279; Haldeman diary, December 9, 1970, NL.
53. Kissinger, **White House Years,** p. 701.
54. Reeves, **President Nixon,** p. 54.
55. Feeney, p. 235.
56. Egil Krogh interview; Krogh, **Day Elvis Met Nixon;** Feeney, p. 239.

Chapter 18: Father of the Bride

1. Ehrlichman notes, January 9, 1971, NL.
2. Jo Haldeman interview. She noted that her husband and Nixon knew immediately that the photo shoot was a mistake.
3. Krogh, **Day Elvis Met Nixon,** p. 27.
4. Gwendolyn King oral history, NL.
5. Matthews, p. 294.
6. **RN,** pp. 502–3.
7. Haldeman diary, February 5, 1971, NL.
8. Safire, pp. 786–7.
9. Dallek, **Nixon and Kissinger,** p. 246; Dallek cites H. R. Haldeman to Henry Kissinger, November 25, 1970; Alexander Haig to Kissinger, December 12, 1970 in Box 817, NSC Files.
10. Reeves, **President Nixon,** p. 300; Haldeman diary, March 3, 1971, NL.
11. Isaacson, pp. 314, 364.
12. Haldeman diary, February 8, 1971, NL.
13. Lucy Winchester Breathitt interview.
14. Haldeman notes, February 16, 1971, NL.
15. Nichter and Brinkley, **Nixon Tapes,** pp. viii–ix; Steve Bull interview; Luke Nichter interview.
16. Conversation 450-10, 10:28 A.M., February 16, 1971, NT.
17. Isaacson, pp. 494–5; Conversation 891-1, 9:47 A.M., April 9, 1973, NT.

18. **RN,** p. 496.
19. Kenneth Riland diary, "The Nixon Saga, February 16, 1969"; Maxine Cheshire, **New York Daily News,** February 12, 1973, RA.
20. Riland diary, February 22, 1969, RA.
21. Ibid., February 3, 1971; Reeves, p. 301; Kimball, pp. 241–8.
22. Conversation 451-23, 6:16 P.M., February 18, 1971, NT.
23. Haldeman diary, March 26, 1971, NL.
24. Dallek, **Nixon and Kissinger,** pp. 259–60.
25. Conversation 246-17, 3:15 P.M., April 7, 1971, NT.
26. Haldeman diary, March 30, 1971, NL.
27. Dallek, **Nixon and Kissinger,** p. 262.
28. Haldeman diary, December 5, 6, 1970, NL.
29. Haldeman notes, March 26, 1971, NL.
30. Conversation 249-6, 8:59 A.M., April 15, 1971, NT; Haldeman diary, April 16, 1971, NL.
31. Haldeman diary, February 17, 1971, NL.
32. Ibid., May 18, 1971, NL.
33. Dallek, **Nixon and Kissinger,** p. 219.
34. Reeves, p. 326; Haldeman diary, May 19, 1971.
35. Dallek, **Nixon and Kissinger,** p. 218.
36. Conversation 487-1, 9:15 A.M., April 23, 1971, NT.
37. Haldeman notes, April 27, May 3, 1971, NL.
38. Reeves, **President Nixon,** p. 321; Dean, **Blind Ambition,** p. 41.
39. Colson, p. 50.
40. Conversation 487-21, 2:52 P.M., April 23, 1971, NT.
41. Colson, pp. 51–2.
42. Safire diary, May 13, 1971, Safire papers, LOC.
43. Haldeman diary, March 17, 1971, NL.
44. Ibid., January 1, 2, 1971, NL.
45. Haldeman, p. 245; Graham, pp. 443–4.
46. Haldeman diary, June 11, 12, 1971, NL.
47. Safire diary, November 20, 1968, Safire papers, LOC.
48. Eisenhower, pp. 314–5.

49. James Bassett interview in Brodie papers, UU.
50. Haldeman diary, June 12, 1971, NL.

Chapter 19: "Blow the Safe"

1. **RN**, p. 508.
2. Conversation 5-50, 12:18 P.M., June 13, 1971, NT.
3. Haldeman diary, June 13, 1971, NL.
4. Haldeman notes, June 13, 1971, NL.
5. Colson, p. 66; Charles Colson oral history, NL.
6. Haldeman, p. 155.
7. Haldeman diary, June 14, 1971, NL.
8. Conversation 519-1, 8:49 A.M., June 14, 1971, NT.
9. See Conversation 534-2, 8:45 A.M., July 1, 1971, NT.
10. Prados, "The Diem Coup After 50 Years," **National Security Archive Electronic Briefing Book** No. 444, November 1, 2013; Dallek, **Camelot's Court**, pp. 403–19.
11. Conversation 261-16, 6:38 P.M., June 17, 1971, NT; Reeves, p. 334.
12. Conversation 525-1, 5:15 P.M., June 17, 1971, NT.
13. RN to Henry Kissinger, September 22, 1969; Tom Charles Huston to H. R. Haldeman, June 18, 1971, March 13, 1970, SMOF, NL, T. C. Huston oral history, NL.
14. Kenneth Hughes interview; T. C. Huston oral history, NL; Conversation 525-1, 5:15 P.M., June 17, 1971, NT.
15. Conversation 533-1, 5:14 P.M., June 30, 1971; Conversation 534-2, 8:45 A.M., July 1, 1971, NT.
16. Conversation 535-4, 9:15 A.M., July 2, 1971, NT.
17. Haldeman diary. July 6, 1971, NL.
18. **RN**, p. 512.
19. Hughes, **Chasing Shadows**, pp. 3, 164–6; Kenneth Hughes interview.
20. Emery, **Watergate**, p. 48; Dean, **Blind Ambition**, pp. 42–6; Hughes, **Chasing Shadows**, p. 146; Charles Colson oral history, NL.
21. See Hunt, **American Spy**.

22. Conversation 534-5, 10:27 A.M., July 1, 1971, NT.

23. Colson, p. 69.

24. Ted Barreaux interview. Barreaux was senior intelligence adviser to the Chief of Naval Operations. Jim Hougan in **Secret Agenda** argues, with some evidence, that Hunt was not a stumblebum but a clever spy and a CIA plant in the Nixon administration.

25. Conversation 260-21, 5:39 P.M., July 2, 1971, NT.

26. Strober and Strober, p. 277.

27. Cynthia Helms interview.

28. Conversation 535-4, 9:15 A.M., July 2, 1971, NT.

29. Ehrlichman notes, Ehrlichman papers, June 25, 1971, HL.

30. Haldeman, pp. 154–5.

31. Conversation 531-24, 6:50 P.M., June 28, 1971, NL.

32. Weiner, **Enemies,** p. 298.

33. **RN,** p. 513; Conversation 535-4, 9:15 A.M., July 2, 1971, NT.

34. Haldeman, p. 157.

35. Haldeman notes, June 19, 1971, NL.

36. Haldeman diaries, July 3, 1971, NL.

37. Conversation 536-16, 10:41 A.M., July 3, 1971, NT; Fred Malek interview.

38. Rob Odle interview; Medoff, "What FDR Said About Jews in Private," **Los Angeles Times,** April 7, 2013; Kuznick, "We Can Learn a Lot from Truman the Bigot," **Los Angeles Times,** July 18, 2003.

39. Safire, pp. 731–51; Safire diary, December 28, 1972, Safire papers, LOC.

40. Haldeman diary, July 10, 1971, NL.

41. **RN,** pp. 442–4.

42. Marjorie Acker interview.

43. Ehrlichman, p. 266.

44. Kissinger, **White House Years,** p. 760.

45. Haldeman diary, July 10, 1971, NL.

46. Isaacson, p. 351.

47. Conversation 531-31, 6:30 P.M., June 29, 1971, NT.

48. Kissinger, **White House Years,** pp. 766, 835–6.
49. Haldeman, p. 157.
50. Hughes, **Chasing Shadows,** p. 130.

Part Three: The Fall
Chapter 20: Big Plays

1. Rob Odle interview.
2. Emery, p. 57; John Dean interview.
3. Rosen, p. 543.
4. Lukas, p. 73.
5. Egil Krogh interview.
6. Ibid., Krogh, **Integrity,** pp. 45–50.
7. Haldeman diary, August 10, 1971, NL.
8. Safire, p. 643; Kissinger, **White House Years,** p. 951.
9. Haldeman diary, February 27, 1971, NL.
10. Ibid., June 6, 1971, NL.
11. Ibid., August 11, 1971; Ehrlichman, p. 235.
12. Ibid., p. 234.
13. Small, **Presidency,** p. 208; see Matusow, **Nixon's Economy,** pp. 84–7, 117.
14. Silber, **Volker,** p. 80; **RN,** p. 518.
15. Ibid.; Ben Stein interview, Kenneth Thompson, ed., **Nixon Presidency,** p. 176.
16. Nichter and Brinkley, pp. 231–61.
17. **RN,** p. 520; Ehrlichman, p. 324; RN to H. R. Haldeman, March 8, 1971, SMOF, NL.
18. Burns, **Inside the Nixon Administration,** pp. 44–54.
19. Haldeman diary, August 4, 1971, NL.
20. Burns, p. 45.
21. Frank Carlucci oral history, NL; Safire, p. 663.
22. Yergin, **Commanding Heights,** pp. 60–4.
23. Silber, pp. 71–86, 104.
24. Haldeman diary, August 14, 1971, NL.
25. **RN,** p. 521; Safire, pp. 656–86. For excellent analyses, see

Matusow, pp. 84–181, and Nichter, **Richard Nixon and Europe,** chapter 2, "Closing the Gold Window."

26. Haldeman diary, August 9, 1971, NL.
27. Emery, pp. 59–61, 67.
28. Krogh, pp. 74–5. But see Hougan, pp. 47–56 for evidence that Hunt was feeding the CIA with material, including Ellsberg's file.
29. Conversation 274-44, 3:36 P.M., September 8, 1971, NT.
30. Conversation 276-4, 3:03 P.M., September 10, 1971, NT.
31. Conversation 576-6, 10:40 A.M., September 18, 1971, NT.
32. Conversation 571-10, 4:36 P.M., September 13, 1971, NT.
33. Conversation 576-6, 10:40 A.M., September 18, 1971, NT.
34. Emery, pp. 71–2.
35. Nichter and Brinkley, pp. 312–3. The tape (Conversation 615-4), 7:50 A.M., November 5, 1971, has apparently been bleeped out. See Bass, **Blood Telegram.** The Nixon/Kissinger foreign policy driven by national interests and not ideals took extreme form in Pakistan; Bass argues strongly that the United States tolerated a genocide.
36. Haldeman diary, December 21, 1971, NL.
37. Feldstein, **Poisoning the Press,** p. 181; James Rosen, "Nixon and the Chiefs," **The Atlantic,** April 1, 2002.
38. **RN,** p. 532.
39. See Colodny and Gettlin, **Silent Coup,** pp. 1–68.
40. Ehrlichman, pp. 279–80.
41. Isaacson, p. 392.
42. Conversation 641-10, 12:27 P.M., December 23, 1971, NT.
43. Haldeman diary, August 24, 1971, NL.
44. Van Atta, p. 244.
45. Rosen, pp. 172, 180.
46. Haldeman diary, December 30, 1971, NL.
47. William Safire memo of meeting with RN, January 18, 1972, Safire papers, LOC.
48. Herken, p. 375. Telecon, H. K.–Kay Graham, March 15, 1971, NSF (Kissinger phone conversations), NL.
49. Haldeman diary, January 13, 1972, NL.

50. MacMillan, **Nixon and Mao,** p. 17.
51. Kissinger, **White House Years,** p. 1051.
52. Lawrence Higby interview.
53. Kissinger, **White House Years,** pp. 1051–2; **RN,** p. 557.
54. Haig, p. 259.
55. **RN,** p. 559.

Chapter 21: Speak Quietly

1. Kalb, **Kissinger,** p. 266.
2. **RN,** p. 560.
3. Nixon/Gannon interview.
4. Haldeman diary, February 21, 1972, NL.
5. MacMillan, p. 46.
6. Ibid., p. 65.
7. **RN,** p. 560.
8. Burr, ed., **Kissinger Transcripts,** pp. 60–5.
9. **RN,** p. 564.
10. Haldeman diary, February 21, 1972, NL; Frank Gannon interview.
11. Haldeman diary, October 14, 1971, NL.
12. Eisenhower, p. 334.
13. MacMillan, p. 278.
14. William Safire to H. R. Haldeman, November 1, 1971, Safire papers, LOC.
15. MacMillan, p. 281.
16. **RN,** pp. 572–3.
17. Ibid., pp. 566–80; Haldeman diary, February 26, 1972, NL.
18. Ibid., February 27, 1972, NL; James Rosen, "W-Hef-B: Bill Buckley, Playboy, and the Struggle for the Soul of America," Real Clear Politics, July 30, 2008.
19. Notes on Cabinet Meeting, February 29, 1972, Safire papers, LOC.
20. Kissinger, **White House Years,** pp. 1093–4.
21. Dwight Chapin interview.

22. **RN,** pp. 580–1; RN to H. R. Haldeman, March 13, 1972, SMOF, NL.
23. Hunt, **American Spy,** pp. 198–9.
24. Reeves, **President Nixon,** p. 462; Lukas, pp. 112, 138–43; Jonathan Rose interview.
25. Conversation 734-1, 4:02 P.M., June 14, 1972, NT.
26. Emery, pp. 87–8.
27. Rosen, pp. 262–4; Lukas, pp. 172–4.
28. Dean, **Blind Ambition,** pp. 93–5.
29. Emery, pp. 89–92.
30. Ibid., p. 109.
31. Liddy, **Will,** pp. 293–4; Magruder, p. 210. For a good account of Mitchell's role, see Rosen, pp. 262–75.
32. Henry Cashen interview.
33. Aitken, p. 419.
34. Alexander Butterfield to H. R. Haldeman, July 8, 1971, SMOF, NL.
35. Thomas, **Ike's Bluff,** pp. 47–8.
36. RN to H. R. Haldeman and Ron Ziegler, April 14, 1972, SMOF, NL.
37. Ehrlichman notes, May 9, 1972, Ehrlichman papers, HL; Conversation 722-10, 5:01 P.M., May 9, 1972, NT.
38. Aitken, p. 423.
39. Reeves, **President Nixon,** p. 466.
40. Conversation 702-7, 3:45 P.M., April 4, 1972, NT.
41. Conversation 700-5, 10:06 A.M., April 3, 1972; Conversation 718-4, 10:06 A.M., May 3, 1972, NT.
42. Conversation 717-19, 12:08 P.M., May 2, 1972, NT.
43. Conversation 721-11, 12:13 P.M., May 8, 1972, NT.
44. **RN,** p. 589.
45. Haldeman diary, April 22, 1972, NL.
46. Conversation 334-44, 3:04 P.M., May 4, 1972, NL.
47. Conversation 713-1, 3:27 A.M., April 19, 1972, NL.
48. **RN,** p. 591.
49. Ibid., p. 604.

50. Eisenhower, p. 339.
51. Kissinger, **White House Years,** pp. 1179, 1175.

Chapter 22: Triumph and Tragedy

1. **RN,** p. 609.
2. Reeves, **President Nixon,** p. 477; Dobrynin, **In Confidence,** p. 256.
3. Conversation 332-22, 8:53 A.M., April 25, 1972, NT.
4. Safire, p. 567.
5. Ibid. p. 571.
6. **RN,** p. 610; Safire, p. 577.
7. Henry Kissinger to H. R. Haldeman, March 14, 1972, NSF, NL; Aitken, p. 439.
8. **RN,** pp. 609–10.
9. Strober and Strober, p. 167.
10. Safire, pp. 580–4; Kissinger, **White House Years,** p. 1233.
11. **RN,** p. 616.
12. Emery, pp. 119–37; Hougan, pp. 110–204.
13. **RN,** p. 626.
14. Ibid., pp. 629, 637.
15. Conversation 342-16, 11:26 A.M., June 20, 1972, NT.
16. **RN,** pp. 625–9.
17. Charles Colson oral history, NL.
18. Conversation 342-27, 2:20 P.M., June 20, 1972, NT.
19. Conversation 344-6, 4:35 P.M., June 20, 1972, NT.
20. Conversation 739-4, 9:30 A.M., June 21, 1972, NT.
21. Haldeman, pp. 20–40.
22. John Dean interview.
23. Dean, **Blind Ambition,** p. 125.
24. Strober and Strober, p. 357.
25. Emery, p. 180.
26. John Dean oral history, NL.
27. Haldeman, p. 40; Lukas, pp. 226–7; Dean, **Blind Ambition,** p. 9; Emery, pp. 76–7, 93–4, 163, 167, 174, 321;

Haldeman diary, April 14,15, 1973; Dean, **Nixon Defense,** p. 312, footnotes 5–6, pp. 689–90.

28. See Colodny and Gettlin; Hougan; Rosen, pp. 276–96.

29. See Strober and Strober, pp. 318–62; Dean, **Nixon Defense,** pp. 649–51.

30. **RN,** p. 635.

31. Conversation 739-4, 9:30 A.M., June 21, 1972, NL. The tape is very hard to decipher. Another version is: "Hell, he may have said, 'don't tell me about it but you go ahead and do what you want.' But that doesn't cover the rap, you know." Kutler, **Abuse of Power,** pp. 50, 51, 55.

32. Ibid.; Conversation 344-7, 7:52 P.M., June 20, 1972.

33. **RN,** p. 648.

34. Haldeman diary, June 29, 1972, NL.

35. **RN,** p. 636.

36. Rosen, p. 470. See Rosen's argument that Mitchell was framed.

37. Conversation 197-17, 3:05 P.M., July 22, 1972, NT.

38. Holland, **Leak,** pp. 21–2.

39. Conversation 741-2, 9:41 A.M., June 23, 1972, NT.

40. Dean, **Nixon Defense,** p. 56; Geoff Shepard interview.

41. Conversation 741-2, 9:41 A.M., June 23, 1972, NT; **RN,** pp. 640–4.

42. Weiner, **Legacy of Ashes,** pp. 320–1; Helms, **Intriguing Life,** pp. 114, 121; Strober and Strober, p. 351; Cynthia Helms interview.

43. **RN,** p. 650.

44. Emery, p. 207.

45. Conversation 747-14, 12:44 P.M., July 19, 1972, NT.

46. See Black, pp. 824–51.

47. Conversation 747-14, 12:44 P.M., July 19, 1972, NT.

48. Magruder, pp. 228–30, 250–76.

49. **RN,** p. 662.

50. Conversation 747-14, 12:44 P.M., July 19, 1972, NT.

51. Conversation 748-7, 11:52 A.M., July 20, 1972, NT.

Chapter 23: "An Exciting Prospect"

1. Haldeman diary, April 18, 1972, NL; **RN,** p. 674.
2. Ibid., pp. 653–4.
3. Ibid., pp. 663–9.
4. Conversation, 9:12 A.M., August 3, 1972, NT; Edward Nixon interview.
5. **RN,** p. 677.
6. Conversation 760, 9:12 A.M., August 3, 1972, NT; Ehrlichman notes, August 3, 1972, HL.
7. **RN,** pp. 680, 679, 685, 673, 665.
8. Ibid., p. 674.
9. Garment, p. 249.
10. Emery, pp. 200, 220, 230.
11. Magruder, p. 276.
12. **RN,** p. 681.
13. Conversation 779-2, Dean enters at 5:27 P.M., September 15, 1972, NT.
14. **RN,** p. 684.
15. RN to H. R. Haldeman, April 21, 1970, SMOF, NL; Conversation 359-15, 2:50 P.M., September 14, 1972, NT.
16. Rosen, p. 335.
17. Dean, **Nixon Defense,** p. 172.
18. Holland, pp. 99–126.
19. Holland, pp. 89–98; Dean, **Nixon Defense,** p. 167; Lukas, pp. 156–8.
20. Dwight Chapin interview.
21. **RN,** pp. 710–1.
22. Eisenhower, pp. 345–9.
23. Steve Bull interview.
24. Kissinger, **White House Years,** p. 1360.
25. Conversation 366-6, 6:10 P.M., October 12, 1972, NT.
26. Haig, p. 300.
27. Haldeman diary, October 12, 1972, NL.
28. Haldeman notes, October 14, 1972, NL.
29. Reeves, **President Nixon,** p. 536.

30. Isaacson, pp. 453, 456.

31. **RN**, p. 697.

32. Isaacson, p. 441.

33. **RN**, pp. 701–4.

34. Ibid., p. 705; Haig, p. 302; Kissinger, **White House Years,** p. 1400. See "Memoirs v. Tapes: President Reagan & the December Bombings," www.nixonlibrary.gov/exhibits/decbomb/chapter-ii-audio.html.

35. Isaacson, pp. 458–9.

36. Haldeman diary, October 17, 1972, NL.

37. Ibid., October 26, 1972, NL.

38. Conversation 220-12, 9:16 A.M., October 15, 1972, NT.

39. Halberstam, pp. 655–61.

40. Haldeman diary, October 28, 1972, NL.

41. **RN**, pp. 713–4.

Chapter 24: Peace at Last

1. **RN**, p. 717; Reeves, p. 541.

2. Ron Walker interview; Theodore White 1972 campaign notebooks, November 7, 1972, White papers, HU.

3. White, **Breach of Faith,** p. 170.

4. Eisenhower, p. 352; For Nixon's dissatisfied mood, see his 30-page memo analyzing the 1970 election, RN to H. R. Haldeman, November 22, 1970, SMOF, NL.

5. **RN**, p. 715.

6. Lawrence Higby interview.

7. Colson, p. 21.

8. **RN**, p. 717.

9. Haldeman, p. 223.

10. Kissinger, **White House Years,** pp. 1406–7; Minutes of staff meeting, November 8, 1972, Safire papers, LOC.

11. Klein, pp. 377–8.

12. Haldeman, p. 224. Haldeman actually gave them two days, until November 10. Minutes of staff meeting, November 8, 1972, Safire papers, LOC.

13. Peter Flanigan interview.

14. **RN,** p. 769.

15. White, **Breach of Faith,** p. 176.

16. Small, p. 269. See Haldeman notes, September 20, 1972, NL.

17. Haldeman, p. 232.

18. Ehrlichman notes, December 8, 1972, HL.

19. Fred Malek interview.

20. Ehrlichman, pp. 174–81.

21. Ehrlichman notes, November 20, 1972, HL.

22. **RN,** p. 731.

23. Riland diary, December 13, 1973, RA.

24. Ehrlichman, p. 286; Colson, p. 87.

25. **RN,** p. 733.

26. Haldeman diary, December 4, 10, 1972, NL. Cox never considered running for Congress.

27. Herken, p. 377.

28. Isaacson, p. 478; Ehrlichman, p. 285.

29. Ibid., November 18, 1972, NL.

30. Ibid., November 28, December 8, 1972, NL.

31. Charles Colson oral history, NL; Haldeman diary, November 21, 1972, NL.

32. Kissinger, **White House Years,** pp. 1450–1.

33. **RN,** p. 738.

34. Ibid., p. 734; Isaacson, pp. 471–3.

35. **RN,** p. 739.

36. Eisenhower, p. 354.

37. **RN,** p. 740.

38. Ibid., p. 744, 776.

39. Ibid., pp. 744–5, 777.

40. Conversation 815-19, 11:47 A.M., November 24, 1972, NT; Haldeman diary, November 24, 1972, NL.

41. Conversation 819–2, 11:07 A.M., December 11, 1972, NT.

42. **RN,** pp. 773–4; Dwight Chapin oral history, NL.

43. Emery, pp. 226–34.

44. **RN,** p. 776.

45. Strober and Strober, p. 58.

46. Haldeman diary, January 5, 1973, NL.

47. Haldeman notes, September 20, 1972, NL.

48. William Timmons interview.

49. Haldeman diary, March 6, 1973, NL.

50. Matthews, p. 324; Shepard, **Secret Plot,** pp. 31–4.

51. Hughes, p. 156; Gibbs and Duffy, p. 289; Haldeman diary, January 8, 9, 10, 1973, NL.

52. **RN,** pp. 754–6.

53. "Nixon with No Expletives Deleted," CNN, July 31, 2013, youtube.com.

54. Kabaservice, **Rule and Ruin,** p. 288; Conversation 798-15, 11:57 A.M., October 14, 1972, NT.

55. Rosen, pp. 348–50.

56. See Dean, **Nixon Defense,** pp. 186, 189–93.

57. Haldeman diary, March 6, 20, 1973, NL.

58. Eisenhower, p. 354.

59. Gibbs and Duffy, p. 286; RN phone call to LBJ, Conversation 35-67, 4:46 P.M., January, 2, 1973, NT.

60. **RN,** p. 839.

61. Nixon/Gannon interview.

62. **RN,** p. 746.

63. Haldeman diary, January 9, 1973.

64. RN notes, January 11, 1973, PPF, NL.

65. **RN,** p. 763. But see Haldeman notes, September 20, 1972, NL. The custom began, at least occasionally, when his daughters gave him a flag pin after the November 3, 1969, "Silent Majority" speech.

66. Kissinger, **White House Years,** pp. 1469–70.

67. **RN,** p. 748.

68. Eisenhower, p. 356.

69. Safire, pp. 856–73; Safire notes on Cabinet meeting, January 23, 1973, Safire papers, LOC.

70. **RN,** pp. 756–7.

71. Ibid., p. 750. For an excellent summation see "Nixon Legacy Forum: Vietnam and the Paris Peace Accords," December 5, 2014, youtube.com.
72. Ehrlichman, p. 288.
73. **RN**, p. 757.
74. Conversation 840-9, 11:05 A.M., February 3, 1973, NT.
75. Emery, pp. 238–41.
76. Ted Barreaux interview.

Chapter 25: Ides of March

1. **RN**, p. 770.
2. Conversation 840-9; 11:05 A.M., February 3, 1973, NT.
3. **RN**, pp. 778–9.
4. Ibid., pp. 779–80.
5. Conversation 867-16, 1:00 P.M., March 2, 1973, NT.
6. Rosen, p. 338; See Rosen, "John Dean's Watergate Whitewash," **Commentary**, April 2015.
7. Emery, p. 201. See Luke Nichter, "John W. Dean III and the Watergate Cover-up, Revisited," History News Network, April 20, 2009.
8. Dean, **Nixon Defense**, p. 248; Conversation 866-3, 9:18 A.M., March 1, 1973, NT.
9. Gray, **In Nixon's Web**, pp. 150–247.
10. Hearings before the Select Committee on Presidential Campaign Activities of the U.S. Senate, 93rd Congress, 1st Session, Watergate and Related Activities, Phase I Watergate Investigation, July 26, 27, 30, 1973, Book 7, p. 2787.
11. Aitken, p. 383.
12. Dean, **Blind Ambition**, pp. 223–4.
13. **RN**, pp. 781–2; Conversation 878-14, 12:42 P.M., March 13, 1973, NT.
14. Dean, **Nixon Defense**, p. 234.
15. **RN**, p. 783.
16. Ibid., p. 785.
17. Dean, **Nixon Defense**, pp. 222, 268, 293.

18. Conversation 886-8, 10:12 A.M., March 21, 1973, NT.
19. **RN**, pp. 791–4.
20. Conversation 886-8, Dean enters at 10:12 A.M., March 21, 1973, NT.
21. Impeachment of Richard M. Nixon, Report of the Committee of the Judiciary, House of Representatives, August 20, 1974, p. 407.
22. Conversation 886-8, Dean enters at 10:12 A.M., March 21, 1973, NT.
23. **RN**, p. 799; Conversation 886-18, 1:06 P.M., March 21, 1973, NT.
24. Rosen, pp. 353–5.
25. Conversation 886-8, 10:12 A.M., March 21, 1973, NT.
26. Dean, **Nixon Defense,** p. 261; Richard Ben-Veniste interview.
27. **RN**, p. 801; John Dean interview.
28. John Carley interview.
29. Dean, **Blind Ambition,** p. 257.
30. Rosen, pp. 356–8.
31. Geoff Shepard interview; Rosen, pp. 560–1.
32. Watergate Special Prosecutor Files Conversation Transcripts, Conversation 422-33, 1:57 P.M., March 22, 1973, NT.
33. Graham, p. 485.
34. Bradlee, p. 350.
35. Rosen, p. 365.
36. **RN**, pp. 809, 819.
37. Rosen, pp. 273–4.
38. **RN**, p. 820.
39. Ibid., January 3, March 14, 1973.
40. Riland diary, March 28, 1973, May 3, 1972, January 28, 1973, RA.
41. Shepard, pp. 62–5.
42. Haldeman diary, April 15, 1973, NL.
43. **RN**, p. 827.
44. Douglas Parker interview.
45. James Schlesinger interview.

46. Swift, p. 362.

47. **RN**, p. 753.

48. Eisenhower, pp. 366–7.

49. Eisenhower, pp. 363, 366–7.

Chapter 26: Praying Not to Wake Up

1. **RN**, p. 846; Kutler, **Wars of Watergate**, p. 308.

2. Haldeman, p. 373.

3. Haldeman diary, April 29, 1972, NL.

4. **RN**, p. 847.

5. Haldeman, p. 376.

6. Ehrlichman, p. 357, **RN**, p. 847.

7. **RN**, p. 848.

8. Ibid., p. 850.

9. Klein, p. 354.

10. Conversation 45-51, 10:16 P.M., April 30, 1973, NT.

11. Conversation 164-48, 10:42 A.M., April 30, 1973, NT.

12. Conversation 164-28, 10:19 A.M., April 29, 1973, NT.

13. Conversation 45-58; 10:34 P.M., April 30, 1973, NT.

14. **RN**, p. 910; Shepard, pp. 127–46; Richard Ben-Veniste interview.

15. **RN**, pp. 853–4; Kutler, **Wars of Watergate**, pp. 323–4; Halberstam, p. 688; Greenberg, p. 169.

16. Emery, p. 339; Dean, **Blind Ambition**, pp. 358–60, 367–8.

17. Eisenhower, p. 379.

18. Fred D. Thompson, **At That Point in Time**, pp. 126–44.

19. **RN**, p. 874.

20. Everett Alvarez interview.

21. Eisenhower, pp. 371–3; **RN**, pp. 865–9.

22. **RN**, pp. 878–80.

23. Eisenhower, p. 373.

24. Nixon/Gannon interview.

25. Kissinger, **Years of Upheaval**, p. 298.

26. **RN**, p. 885.

27. Ibid., p. 889; Scowcroft oral history, NL.

28. **RN**, p. 898.
29. Charles Wardell interview.
30. Aitken, p. 493.
31. **RN**, pp. 898–9.
32. Strober and Strober, p. 460.
33. Ibid., p. 498; see Colodny and Gettlin; Colodny and Schact-man; Locker, **Nixon's Gamble.** Len Colodny makes a case for the rise of the national security state as a driving force in the fall of Richard Nixon.
34. Aitken, p. 501.
35. Haig, pp. 374–6.
36. Strober and Strober, p. 396; see also Garment, p. 279.
37. Haig, p. 380.
38. Strober and Strober, p. 395; Alexander Haig oral history, NL.
39. **RN**, p. 901; Haldeman diary, April 9,10, 1973; Dean, **Nixon Defense,** p. 366.
40. Aitken, p. 500.
41. Ibid., 501; Kenneth Thompson, ed., **Nixon Presidency,** p. 69.
42. Eisenhower, p. 409.
43. **RN**, pp. 902, 905. Buchanan to RN, July 25, 1973, Haig papers, LOC; Nixon could not understand why the press and Congress seemed to forget that the JFK and LBJ administrations had wiretapped more than his own. RN to Haig, July 7, 1973; Joulwan to Haig, July 10, 1973, Haig papers, LOC.
44. White House News Summary, July 23, 1973, March 16, 1969, POF, NL.
45. **RN**, p. 961.
46. Haig, p. 362.
47. **RN**, p. 962.
48. Greenberg, p, 256.
49. Kenneth Thompson, ed., **Nixon Presidency,** p. 190.
50. **RN**, p. 908.
51. Diary entry, August 15, 1973, Garment papers, LOC.
52. Douglas Parker interview.

53. Isaacson, p. 503.
54. Haig, p. 350; Haig to RN, August 7, 1973, Haig papers, LOC.
55. **RN**, pp. 912–7.
56. Diary entry, August 7, 1973, Garment papers, LOC.

Chapter 27: Saturday Night Massacre

1. **RN**, p. 920.
2. Small, pp. 133–5; William Quandt to Brent Scowcroft, "Arab-Israel Tensions," October 6, 1973; William Quandt to Henry Kissinger, "Middle East Issues," October 9, 1973, NSF, NL.
3. Dallek, **Nixon and Kissinger**, pp. 521–3.
4. Haig, p. 366; Agnew, **Go Quietly . . . or Else**, p. 189.
5. Ibid. pp. 197–8.
6. **RN**, p. 925; Aitken, p. 506; Greene, "Nixon and Ford," in Small, **Companion to Richard M. Nixon.**
7. Ambrose, **Nixon: Ruin and Recovery**, p. 328.
8. Kissinger, **Years of Upheaval**, p. 514.
9. Isaacson, pp. 513–9. See Kissinger–James Schlesinger telcon, October 12, 1973, 11:45 P.M.; Kissinger–Alexander Haig telcon, October 12, 1973, 11:54 P.M., NSF, NL.
10. Nixon/Gannon interview.
11. See, for example, RN–Henry Kissinger telcons, October 8, 1973, 7:08 P.M., October 14, 1973, 9:04 A.M., NSF, NL.
12. Kissinger, **Years of Upheaval**, p. 515.
13. **RN**, p. 927.
14. Isaacson, p. 522.
15. **RN**, p. 929.
16. **RN**, pp. 952–61, 964–7; Aitken, pp. 513–5; Kutler, **Wars of Watergate**, pp. 431–4.
17. Eisenhower, p. 387.
18. Small, **Presidency**, p. 284; Haig, p. 392.
19. Ibid., pp. 392–408; Jonathan Moore oral history, NL; Richard Ben-Veniste interview.
20. Emery, p. 399; Richard Darman diary, January 14, 1998, Richard Darman papers.

21. Haig, p. 396.

22. White, **Breach of Faith**, p. 267; Strober and Strober, p. 434.

23. Aitken, p. 509.

24. Haig, p. 408.

25. **RN**, p. 937.

26. Charles Wardell interview.

27. **RN**, pp. 937–42; Haig, pp. 416–9; Brent Scowcroft interview. See Henry Kissinger to King Faisal, October 14, 1973, NSF, NL.

28. Isaacson, pp. 528–32; Dallek, **Nixon and Kissinger**, pp. 529–31.

29. Brent Scowcroft interview; "I would urge you to keep any Walter Mitty streak under control," Henry Kissinger–Alexander Haig telcon, October 6, 1973, 12:45 P.M., NSF, NL.

30. Dallek, **Nixon and Kissinger**, p. 524. "The crazy bastard really made a mess with the Russians," Kissinger told Haig the day after the alert. Kissinger-Haig telcon, October 26, 1973, 7:55 P.M., NSF, NL.

31. "Rose Mary's Boo Boo," **Newsweek**, December 10, 1973.

32. Alexander Haig oral history, NL.

33. Dean, **Nixon Defense**, pp. 19–21, 656–9, 667; James Robenalt, "Truth in a Lie: Forty Years After the 18½ Minute Gap," May 11, 2014, washingtondecoded.com.

34. **RN**, p. 957. Compare Nixon's November 7, 1962, concession speech with his November 17, 1973, "I am not a crook" press conference at youtube.com. By January 1, 2014, the latter had been viewed almost 600,000 times.

35. Eisenhower, p. 392.

36. **RN**, pp. 963–4.

37. Ibid., p. 968.

38. Eisenhower, p. 396.

39. Ibid., pp. 395–6.

40. **RN**, p. 971.

41. Colson, p. 197. See Joulwan to Haig, December 30, 1973, Haig papers, LOC. Haig was determined to keep total control over the White House staff. When his top aide, Gen.

George Joulwan suggested that Haig adopt a lower profile by no longer having his phone answered, "General Haig's office," Haig checked the box marked "disapprove." Joulwan to Haig, November 29, 1973, Haig papers, LOC.

42. Kenneth Thompson, ed., **Nixon Presidency,** p. 21.
43. Fred Malek oral history, NL. See John K. Andrews to RN, December 13, 1973, SMOF, NL (". . . then Watergate and more Watergate, with no rallying from the boss. This has already cost you a lot of good troops, and the hemorrhaging will only worsen unless some bracing leadership is exerted.").
44. Riland diary, December 18, 1973, January 24, 1974, RA.
45. Halberstam, pp. 693–4.
46. Eisenhower, p. 404; Gwendolyn King oral history, NL; Helen McCain Smith, "Ordeal! Pat's Final Days in the White House," **Good Housekeeping,** July 1976.
47. Haig, p. 447; **RN,** p. 968.
48. Geoff Shepard interview.
49. **RN,** p. 968.
50. Ibid., p. 976.

Chapter 28: "I Hope I Haven't Let You Down"

1. Aikman, **Billy Graham,** p. 217.
2. **RN,** pp. 996–7; Ambrose, **Nixon: Ruin and Recovery,** pp. 336–7.
3. Strober and Strober, p. 44.
4. Henry Kissinger interview; George Shultz interview.
5. Eisenhower, p. 409.
6. Stuart, p. 88.
7. **RN,** p. 996.
8. Eisenhower, p. 407.
9. Hoff, pp. 137–8.
10. William Timmons interview.
11. Paul O'Neill interview. From the records at the Nixon Library, it appears that Nixon virtually stopped writing memos to staff in 1974.

12. Ambrose, **Nixon: Ruin and Recovery,** p. 352.
13. "It's Super K," **Newsweek,** June 10, 1974.
14. **RN,** p. 1010.
15. Nixon/Gannon interview.
16. Kissinger, **Years of Upheaval,** p. 1126.
17. Nixon/Gannon interview.
18. Donald Rumsfeld interview.
19. Ambrose, **Nixon: Ruin and Recovery,** p. 369.
20. **RN,** p. 1027; Kissinger, **Years of Upheaval,** pp. 1163–4.
21. **RN,** p. 1036.
22. Ibid., pp. 1045–6; Nixon/Gannon interview.
23. Small, **Presidency,** pp. 247–52.
24. **RN,** p. 1050.
25. Haig, p. 471.
26. Nixon had pressured Federal Reserve Chairman Arthur Burns to heat up the economy. See RN to Arthur Burns, November 4, 1971, SMOF, NL (in Haldeman files, Box 230). The severe 1973–4 recession contributed greatly to Nixon's downfall.
27. **RN,** p. 1051.
28. Geoff Shepard interview.
29. Alexander Haig interview, September 10, 1974, Woodward and Bernstein papers, UT.
30. **RN,** pp. 1052–3.
31. Ibid., pp. 288, 1046, 1056.
32. Ibid., p. 1057; Haig, pp. 476–7.
33. Charles Wardell comments, draft of **Breach of Faith,** Theodore White papers, HU.
34. Joseph Alsop interview, February 11, 1975, Woodward and Bernstein papers, UT.
35. Alexander Haig oral history, NL.
36. Haig, p. 478; **RN,** p. 1057.
37. Eisenhower, pp. 417–8.
38. Ibid., 418–20; **RN,** 1059–61.
39. Safire, p. 856.
40. **RN,** pp. 1063–4; Eisenhower, p. 421.
41. Kissinger, **Years of Upheaval,** pp. 1203–4.

42. Ambrose, **Nixon: Ruin and Recovery,** p. 418.
43. Brent Scowcroft interview.
44. **RN,** p. 1071.
45. Ibid., p. 1073.
46. Kissinger, **Years of Upheaval,** p. 1206.
47. David Bruce diary, October 25, 1973, August 8, 1974, Bruce papers, VHS.
48. Patrick Moynihan diary, August 9, 1974, Moynihan papers, LOC.
49. **RN,** pp. 1074–5; Eisenhower, p. 424.
50. **RN,** pp. 1976–7; Kissinger, **Years of Upheaval,** pp. 1207–10; Isaacson, pp. 597–601; Aitken, p. 520, Woodward and Bernstein, **Final Days,** p. 423.
51. **RN,** p. 1079.
52. Ambrose, **Nixon: Ruin and Recovery,** p. 434; Christie Brown interview.
53. **RN,** p. 1085.

Chapter 29: "Richard! Wake Up!"

1. **RN,** p. 1072; anonymous source.
2. **RN,** pp. 1086–90.
3. Steve Bull interview.
4. Ibid., p. 1090.
5. Aitken, p. 525.
6. Ambrose, **Nixon: Ruin and Recovery,** p. 453.
7. Werth, **31 Days,** pp. 296–311; "Benton Becker—The Pardon of Richard Nixon—03/10/10," on youtube.com.
8. Thomas, "The 38th President: More than Meets the Eye," **Newsweek,** March 13, 2010; Werth, p. 204; Hartmann, **Palace Politics,** p. 135; Richard Norton Smith interview.
9. Anson, **Exile,** pp. 66–7.
10. Eisenhower, pp. 434–5.
11. Lungren, **Healing Richard Nixon,** pp. 87–8.
12. Ibid., pp. 88–9.
13. Jack Brennan interview; Van Natta, pp. 225–48.

14. Eisenhower, pp. 432, 442.
15. Ibid., pp. 446–50.
16. Ken Khachigian interview.
17. Anonymous source.
18. Aitken, pp. 439–40.
19. Frost, pp. 37, 76–7.
20. Ibid., pp. 122–3; Jack Brennan and Ken Khachigian interviews.
21. Ibid., pp. 136, 125.
22. Brent Scowcroft interview.
23. Anson, p. 180.
24. Frank Gannon interview in Aitken papers, NL.
25. Frank Gannon interview.
26. "RN: The Memoirs of Richard Nixon," **New York Times**, May 6, 1978.
27. Jack Brennan interview, Ambrose, **Nixon: Ruin and Recovery**, p. 489; Anson, p. 194; Aitken, pp. 545–50.
28. Anson, p. 185.
29. Jack Brennan interview; Anson, p. 214.
30. Eisenhower, p. 458.
31. Michael Kramer interview.
32. Greenberg, p. 286.
33. Michael Kramer interview.
34. Kenneth Thompson, ed., **Nixon Presidency**, pp. 307–8.
35. T. H. White to John F. Kennedy, October 11, 1961; T. H. White to RN, October 14, 1983, White papers, HU.
36. Stone, **Nixon's Secrets**, pp. 585–6.
37. Aitken, p. 560; Anson, pp. 263–4.
38. Edward Cox speech.
39. Garment, p. 299.
40. Darrell Trent, Brook Byers interviews.

Chapter 30: Elder Statesman

1. Brent Scowcroft interview.
2. Anson, p. 184.

3. Gibbs and Duffy, p. 357.
4. RN to William Clark, January 14, 1982; RN to Ronald Reagan, November 1, 1982, Aitken papers, NL.
5. Werth, p. 4.
6. Reagan, **My Turn**, p. 258; Gibbs and Duffy, pp. 362–5.
7. Anonymous source.
8. Bush, **All the Best,** p. 179.
9. Jon Meacham interview.
10. Gibbs and Duffy, p. 383.
11. Kenneth Thompson, ed., **Nixon Presidency,** p. 14.
12. Crowley, **Nixon Off the Record,** pp. 74, 141.
13. Ibid., pp. 167–8.
14. Gibbs and Duffy, p. 429.
15. Ibid., pp. 417–8.
16. Crowley, **Nixon in Winter,** pp. 390, 393.
17. Heidi Retter interview.
18. Crowley, **Nixon in Winter,** p. 366.
19. The description of Pat's funeral comes from "The Last Nixon Experience," a private memoir of the Nixons' funerals by Jack Carley.
20. Heidi Retter interview.
21. Eulogies are in Nixon, **Beyond Peace,** pp. 3–16.

Epilogue: Rise Again

1. Price, pp. 29–30.
2. Perlstein, **Nixonland,** p. 45; Block, **Herblock: Special Report.**
3. Anonymous source.
4. Roberts, **Napoleon,** p. xxxi.
5. Riland diary, December 12, 1973, RA.
6. John Carley interview.
7. Brent Scowcroft interview.
8. Nixon/Gannon interview.
9. Edward Cox speech.

Bibliography

Abrahamsen, David. **Nixon v. Nixon: An Emotional Tragedy.** New York: Farrar, Straus and Giroux, 1976.

Adler, Bill. **The Wit and Humor of Richard Nixon.** New York: Popular Library, 1969.

Agnew, Spiro. **Go Quietly . . . or Else.** New York: Morrow, 1980.

Aikman, David. **Billy Graham: His Life and Influence.** New York: Thomas Nelson, 2010.

Aitken, Jonathan. **Nixon: A Life.** Washington, DC: Regnery, 1993.

Alsop, Joseph, with Adam Platt. **"I've Seen the Best of It": Memoirs.** Mount Jackson, VA: Axios Press, 1992.

Alsop, Stewart. **Nixon and Rockefeller: A Double Portrait.** New York: Doubleday, 1958.

Ambrose, Stephen. **Nixon: The Education of a Politician, 1913–1962.** New York: Simon and Schuster, 1987.

———. **Nixon: Ruin and Recovery, 1973–1990.** New York: Simon and Schuster, 1991.

———. **Nixon: The Triumph of a Politician, 1962–1972.** New York: Simon and Schuster, 1989.

Anson, Robert Sam. **Exile: The Unquiet Oblivion of Richard M. Nixon.** New York: Simon and Schuster, 1984.

Bass, Gary. **The Blood Telegram: Nixon, Kissinger, and a Forgotten Genocide.** New York: Knopf, 2013.

Beattie, Ann. **Mrs. Nixon: A Novelist Imagines a Life.** New York: Scribner, 2011.

Bemis, Samuel Flagg, ed. **The American Secretaries of State and Their Diplomacy.** New York: Cooper Square, 1970.

Ben-Veniste, Richard, and George Frampton Jr. **Stonewall: The Legal Case Against the Watergate Conspirators.** New York: Touchstone Books, 1977.

Berman, Larry. **No Peace, No Honor: Nixon, Kissinger, and Betrayal in Vietnam.** New York: Free Press, 2001.

Black, Conrad. **Richard M. Nixon: A Life in Full.** New York: Public Affairs, 2007.

Block, Herbert. **Herblock: Special Report.** New York: W.W. Norton, 1974.

Bradlee, Ben. **A Good Life: Newspapering and Other Adventures.** New York: Simon and Schuster, 1995.

Brinkley, David. **Washington Goes to War.** New York: Ballantine Books, 1996.

Brodie, Fawn. **Richard Nixon: The Shaping of His Character.** New York: W.W. Norton, 1981.

Buchanan, Patrick J. **The Greatest Comeback: How Richard Nixon Rose from Defeat to Create the New Majority.** New York: Crown, 2014.

Burns, Arthur. **Inside the Nixon Administration: The Secret Diary of Arthur Burns, 1969–1974.** Edited by Robert Ferrell. Lawrence: University of Kansas Press, 2010.

Burr, William, ed. **The Kissinger Transcripts: The Top-Secret Talks with Beijing and Moscow.** Washington, DC: National Security Archive, 1999.

Bush, George H. W. **All the Best: My Life in Letters and Other Writings.** New York: Scribner, 2014.

Caro, Robert A. **Master of the Senate: The Years of Lyndon Johnson.** New York: Vintage Books, 2003.

Chennault, Anna. **The Education of Anna.** New York: Times Books, 1980.

Colodny, Len, and Robert Gettlin. **Silent Coup: The Removal of a President.** New York: St. Martin's Press, 1991.

Colodny, Len, and Tom Schactman. **The Forty Years War.** New York: HarperCollins, 2009.

Colson, Charles W. **Born Again.** Grand Rapids, MI: Chosen Books, 1976.

Crouse, Timothy. **The Boys on the Bus.** New York: Ballantine Books, 1973.

Crowley, Monica. **Nixon in Winter.** New York: Random House, 1998.

———. **Nixon Off the Record.** New York: Random House, 1996.

Dallek, Robert. **Camelot's Court: Inside the Kennedy White House.** New York: HarperCollins, 2013.

———. **Nixon and Kissinger: Partners in Power.** New York: HarperCollins, 2007.

Dean, John W. **Blind Ambition.** Updated edition. Palm Springs, CA: Polimedia, 2009.

———. **Lost Honor.** Los Angeles: Stratford Press, 1982.

———. **The Nixon Defense: What He Knew and When He Knew It.** New York: Viking, 2014.

———. **The Rehnquist Choice.** New York: Touchstone Books, 2001.

Dent, Harry. **The Prodigal South Returns to Power.** New York: John Wiley & Sons, 1978.

De Toledano, Ralph. **One Man Alone: Richard Nixon.** New York: Funk & Wagnalls, 1969.

Dickenson, Patrick, trans. **Vergil's Aeneid.** New York: New American Library, 1961.

Diem, Bui. **In the Jaws of History.** Bloomington, IN: Indiana University Press, 1999.

Dobrynin, Anatoly. **In Confidence: Moscow's Ambassador to Six Cold War Presidents.** Seattle: University of Washington Press, 2001.

Homer. **The Aeneid.** Translated by Patrick Dickinson. New York: New American Library, 1961.

Ehrlichman, John. **Witness to Power: The Nixon Years.** New York: Pocket Books, 1982.

Eisenhower, Julie Nixon. **Pat Nixon: The Untold Story.** New York: Simon and Schuster, 1986.

Emery, Fred. **Watergate: The Corruption of American Politics and the Fall of Richard Nixon.** New York: Touchstone Books, 1994.

Evans, Rowland, and Robert Novak. **Nixon in the White House.** New York: Random House, 1971.

Feeney, Mark. **Nixon at the Movies.** Chicago: University of Chicago Press, 2004.

Feldstein, Mark. **Poisoning the Press: Richard Nixon, Jack Anderson, and the Rise of the Washington Scandal Culture.** New York: Farrar, Straus and Giroux, 2010.

Felsenthal, Carol. **Alice Roosevelt Longworth.** New York: Doubleday, 1988.

Ferrell, Robert C., ed. **The Diary of James C. Hagerty: Eisenhower in Mid-course, 1954–1955.** Bloomington, IN: Indiana University Press, 1983.

Forslund, Catherine, **Anna Chennault: Informal Diplomacy and Asian Relations.** Wilmington, DE: Scholarly Resources, 2002.

Frank, Jeffrey. **Ike and Dick: Portrait of a Strange Political Marriage.** New York: Simon and Schuster, 2013.

Frick, Daniel. **Reinventing Nixon: A Cultural History of an American Obsession.** Lawrence: University of Kansas Press, 2008.

Frost, David. **Frost/Nixon: Behind the Scenes of the Nixon Interviews.** New York: HarperCollins, 2007.

Garment, Leonard. **Crazy Rhythm: From Brooklyn and Jazz to Nixon's White House, Watergate, and Beyond.** Cambridge, MA: Da Capo Press, 1997.

Gavin, William F. **Speechwright: An Insider's Take on Political Rhetoric.** East Lansing: Michigan State Press, 2011.

Gellman, Irwin. **The Contender: Richard Nixon, the Congress Years, 1946–1952.** New York: Free Press, 1999.

———. **The President and the Apprentice: Eisenhower and Nixon, 1953–1961.** New Haven: Yale University Press, 2015.

Gibbs, Nancy, and Michael Duffy. **The Presidents Club: In-side the World's Most Exclusive Fraternity.** New York: Simon and Schuster, 2012.

Graham, Katharine. **Personal History.** New York: Knopf, 1997.

————, ed. **Katherine Graham's Washington.** New York: Vintage 2003.

Gray, L. Patrick, III, with Ed Gray and Michael Prichard. **In Nixon's Web: A Year in the Crosshairs of Watergate.** New York: Times Books, 2010.

Greenberg, David. **Nixon's Shadow: The History of an Image.** New York: W.W. Norton, 2003.

Greenstein, Fred I. **The Hidden-Hand Presidency: Eisenhower as Leader.** New York: Basic Books, 1982.

Gulley, Bill, with Mary Ellen Reese. **Breaking Cover.** New York: Warner Books, 1980.

Haig, Alexander M., Jr., with Charles McCarry. **Inner Circles: How America Changed the World.** New York: Warner Books, 1992.

Halberstam, David. **The Powers That Be.** Chicago: University of Illinois Press, 1975.

Haldeman, H. R. **The Haldeman Diaries.** New York: G. P. Putnam's Sons, 1994.

Haldeman, H. R., with Joe DiMona. **The Ends of Power.** New York: Dell, 1978.

Haldeman, Jo. **Watergate Wife: A Memoir by Jo Haldeman.** Unpublished manuscript, 2014.

Hamilton, Nigel. **JFK: Reckless Youth.** New York: Random House, 1993.

Hartmann, Robert. **Palace Politics: An Inside Account of the Ford Years.** New York: McGraw-Hill, 1980.

Haynes, John Earl, Harvey Klehr, and Alexander Vassiliev. **Spies: The Rise and Fall of the KGB in America.** New Haven, CT: Yale University Press, 2011.

Herken, Greg. **The Georgetown Set: Friends and Rivals in Cold War Washington.** New York: Knopf, 2014.

Helms, Cynthia, with Chris Black. **An Intriguing Life: A**

Memoir of War, Washington, and Marriage to an American Spymaster. Lanham, MD: Rowman & Littlefield, 2013.

Herring, George C. **America's Longest War: The United States and Vietnam, 1950–1975.** New York: McGraw-Hill, 2001.

Hess, Stephen. **The Professor and the President: Daniel Patrick Moynihan in the Nixon White House.** Washington, DC: Brookings Institution Press, 2014.

Himmelman, Jeff. **Yours in Truth: A Personal Portrait of Ben Bradlee.** New York: Random House, 2012.

Hodgson, Godfrey. **American Melodrama: The Presidential Campaign of 1968.** New York: Viking, 1969.

———. **The Gentleman from New York: Daniel Patrick Moynihan, a Biography.** Boston: Houghton Mifflin, 2000.

Hoff, Joan, **Nixon Reconsidered.** New York: Basic Books, 1994.

Holland, Max. **Leak: Why Mark Felt Became Deep Throat.** Lawrence: University of Kansas Press, 2012.

Holmes, David L. **The Faiths of the Postwar Presidents: From Truman to Obama.** Athens: University of Georgia Press, 2012.

Hougan, Jim. **Secret Agenda: Watergate, Deep Throat, and the CIA.** New York: Random House, 1984.

Hughes, Emmett John. **The Ordeal of Power.** New York: Macmillan, 1975.

Hughes, Ken. **Chasing Shadows: The Nixon Tapes, the Chennault Affair, and the Origins of Watergate.** Charlottesville: University of Virginia Press, 2014.

Hunt, E. Howard, with Greg Aunapu. **American Spy: My Secret History in the CIA, Watergate, and Beyond.** New York: John Wiley & Sons, 2007.

Hutschnecker, Arnold. **The Will to Live.** New York: Prentice Hall, 1951.

Isaacson, Walter. **Kissinger: A Biography.** New York: Simon and Schuster, 1992.

Johnson, Haynes, and Harry Katz. **Herblock: The Life and Work of the Great Political Cartoonist.** New York: W.W. Norton, 2009.

Johnson, Lyndon. **The Vantage Point: Perspectives of the Presidency, 1963–1969.** New York: Holt, Rhinehart, and Winston, 1971.

Johnson, Paul. **A History of the American People.** New York: HarperCollins, 1998.

Kabaservice, Geoffrey. **Rule and Ruin: The Downfall of Moderation and the Destruction of the Republican Party, From Eisenhower to the Tea Party.** New York: Oxford University Press, 2013.

Kimball, Jeffrey. **Nixon's Vietnam War.** Lawrence: University of Kansas Press, 1998.

———. **The Vietnam War Files.** Lawrence: The University of Kansas Press, 2004.

Kissinger, Henry. **White House Years.** New York: Little, Brown, 1979.

———. **Years of Upheaval.** New York: Little, Brown, 1982.

Klein, Herbert. **Making It Perfectly Clear.** New York: Doubleday, 1980.

Kornitzer, Bela. **The Real Nixon: An Intimate Biography.** New York: Rand McNally, 1960.

Krogh, Egil "Bud." **The Day Elvis Met Nixon.** Bellevue, WA: Pejama Press, 1994.

Krogh, Egil "Bud," with Matthew Krogh. **Integrity: Good People, Bad Choices, and Life Lessons from the White House.** New York: Public Affairs, 2007.

Kutler, Stanley I., ed. **Abuse of Power: The New Nixon Tapes.** New York: Free Press, 1997.

———. **The Wars of Watergate: The Last Crisis of Richard Nixon.** New York: Knopf, 1990.

Lenzner, Terry. **The Investigator: Fifty Years of Uncovering the Truth.** New York: Penguin, 2013.

Liddy, G. Gordon. **Will.** New York: St. Martin's Press, 1980.

Locker, Ray. **Nixon's Gamble: How a President's Own Secret Government Destroyed His Administration.** Guilford, CT: Lyons Press, 2015.

Lungren, John C., with John C. Lungren Jr. **Healing Richard Nixon: A Doctor's Memoir.** Lexington: University Press of Kentucky, 2003.

Lukas, J. Anthony. **Nightmare: The Underside of the Nixon Years.** New York: Viking, 1976.

MacMillan, Margaret. **Nixon and Mao: The Week That Changed the World.** New York: Random House, 2007.

Magruder, Jeb Stuart. **An American Life: One Man's Road to Watergate.** New York: Atheneum, 1974.

Mallon, Thomas. **Watergate: A Novel.** New York: Pantheon Books, 2012.

Manchester, William. **The Glory and the Dream: A Narrative History of America, 1932–1972.** Boston: Little, Brown, 1974.

Marton, Kati. **Hidden Power: Presidential Marriages That Shaped Our History.** New York: Anchor Books, 2001.

Matthews, Christopher. **Kennedy and Nixon: The Rivalry That Shaped Postwar America.** New York: Simon and Schuster, 1996.

Mattson, Kevin. **Just Plain Dick: Richard Nixon's Checkers Speech and the "Rocking, Socking" Election of 1952.** New York: Bloomsbury, 2012.

Matusow, Allen J. **Nixon's Economy: Booms, Busts, Dollars, and Votes.** Lawrence: University of Kansas Press, 1998.

Maynard, W. Barksdale. **Princeton: America's Campus.** University Park: Pennsylvania State Press, 2012.

Mazlish, Bruce. **In Search of Nixon: A Psychohistorical Inquiry.** New York: Basic Books, 1972.

Mazo, Earl. **Richard Nixon: A Political and Personal Portrait.** New York: Harper and Brothers, 1959.

McCord, James W., Jr. **A Piece of Tape: The Watergate Story, Fact and Fiction.** Washington, DC: Washington Media Services, 1974.

McGarr, Kathryn J. **The Whole Damn Deal: Robert Strauss and the Art of Politics.** New York: Public Affairs, 2011.

McGinniss, Joe. **The Selling of the President.** New York: Penguin, 1969.

Merry, Robert W. **Taking on the World: Joseph and Stewart Alsop—Guardians of the American Century.** New York: Viking, 1996.

Michener, James A. **The Bridge at Andau.** New York: Fawcett, 1957.

Mitchell, Greg. **Tricky Dick and the Pink Lady: Richard Nixon vs. Helen Gahagan Douglas—Sexual Politics and the Red Scare, 1950.** New York, Random House, 1998.

Morris, James McGrath. **Eye on the Struggle: Ethel Payne, the First Lady of the Black Press.** New York: HarperCollins, 2015.

Morris, Roger. **Richard Milhous Nixon: The Rise of an American Politician.** New York: Henry Holt, 1990.

Morrow, Lance. **The Best Year of Their Lives: Kennedy, Johnson, and Nixon in 1948.** Cambridge. MA: Basic Books, 2005.

Nichter, Luke A. **Richard Nixon and Europe: The Reshaping of the Postwar Atlantic World.** Cambridge, UK: Cambridge University Press, 2015.

Nichter, Luke, and Douglas Brinkley, ed. **The Nixon Tapes.** New York: Houghton Mifflin Harcourt, 2014.

Nixon, Edward, and Karen Olson. **The Nixons: A Family Portrait.** Bothell, WA: Book Publishers Network, 2009.

Nixon, Richard. **Beyond Peace.** Norwalk, CT: Easton Press, 1994.

———. **In the Arena: A Memoir of Victory, Defeat, and Renewal.** Norwalk, CT: Easton Press, 1990.

———. **Leaders: Profiles and Reminiscences of Men Who Have Shaped the Modern World.** Norwalk, CT: Easton Press, 1982.

———. **1999: Victory Without War.** Norwalk, CT: Easton Press, 1988.

————. **Real Peace: A Strategy for the West: No More Viet-nams.** Norwalk, CT: Easton Press, 1984.

————. **The Real War.** Norwalk, CT: Easton Press, 1980.

————. **RN: The Memoirs of Richard Nixon.** New York: Touchstone, 1978.

————. **Six Crises.** New York: Touchstone, 1962.

————. **Seize the Moment: America's Challenge in a One-Superpower World.** Norwalk, CT: Easton Press, 1992.

Oudes, Bruce, ed. **From: The President: Richard Nixon's Secret Files.** New York: Harper and Row, 1988.

Parmet, Herbert S. **Richard Nixon and His America.** New York: Little, Brown, 1990.

Perlstein, Rick. **The Invisible Bridge: The Fall of Nixon and the Rise of Reagan.** New York: Simon and Schuster, 2014.

————. **Nixonland: The Rise of a President and the Fracturing of America.** New York: Scribner, 2008.

Price, Raymond. **With Nixon.** New York: Viking, 1977.

Rather, Dan, and Gary Paul Gates. **The Palace Guard.** New York: Harper and Row, 1974.

Reagan, Nancy, with William Novak. **My Turn: The Memoirs of Nancy Reagan.** New York: Random House, 1989.

Reeves, Richard. **President Nixon: Alone in the White House.** New York: Touchstone, 2001.

Reeves, Thomas C. **The Life and Times of Joe McCarthy.** New York: Stein and Day, 1982.

Richardson, Elliot. **Reflections of Radical Moderate.** New York: Pantheon, 1996.

Roberts, Andrew. **Napoleon: A Life.** New York: Viking, 2014.

Rosen, James. **The Strong Man: John Mitchell and the Secrets of Watergate.** New York: Doubleday, 2008.

Safire, William. **Before the Fall: An Inside View of the Pre-Watergate White House.** New York: Ballantine, 1975.

Schlesinger, Arthur, Jr. **Journals, 1952–2000.** New York: Penguin, 2007.

Schulte, Renee K. **The Young Nixon: An Oral Inquiry.** Van Nuys, CA: Delta Lithograph Co., 1978.

Sherman, Gabriel. **The Loudest Voice in the Room: How the Brilliant, Bombastic Roger Ailes Built Fox News—and Divided a Country.** New York: Random House, 2014.

Shepard, Geoff. **The Secret Plot to Make Ted Kennedy President: Inside the Real Watergate Conspiracy.** New York: Sentinel, 2008.

Silber, William L. **Volcker: The Triumph of Persistence.** New York: Bloomsbury Press, 2012.

Small, Melvin, ed. **A Companion to Richard M. Nixon.** New York: John Wiley, 2011.

———. **The Presidency of Richard Nixon.** Lawrence: University of Kansas Press, 1999.

Smith, Richard Norton. **On His Own Terms: A Life of Nelson Rockefeller.** New York: Random House, 2014.

Spalding, Henry. **The Nixon Nobody Knows.** Middle Village, NY: Jonathan David, 1972.

Stanford, Phil. **The White House Call Girl: The Real Watergate Story.** Port Townsend, WA: Feral House, 2013.

Stassinopoulos, Arianna. **The Gods of Greece.** New York: Atlantic Monthly Press, 1993.

Stone, Roger, with Mike Colapietro. **Nixon's Secrets: The Rise, Fall, and Untold Truth About the President, Watergate, and the Pardon.** New York: Skyhorse Publishing, 2014.

Strober, Deborah, and Gerald S. Strober. **The Nixon Presidency: An Oral History of the Era.** Dulles, VA: Brassey's, 2003.

Stuart, Charles. **Never Trust a Local: Inside the Nixon White House.** New York: Algora Publishing, 2005.

Summers, Anthony. **The Arrogance of Power: The Secret World of Richard Nixon.** New York: Viking, 2000.

Swift, Will. **Pat and Dick: The Nixons, an Intimate Portrait of a Marriage.** New York: Threshold Editions, 2014.

Tanenhaus, Sam. **Whittaker Chambers: A Biography.** New York: Modern Library, 1998.

Taylor, John H. **Jackson Place: A Novel.** Self-published, 2014.

Thomas, Evan. **Ike's Bluff: President Eisenhower's Secret Battle to Save the World.** New York: Little, Brown, 2012.

———. **Robert Kennedy: His Life.** New York: Simon and Schuster, 2000.

———. **The Very Best Men: Four Who Dared: The Eary Years of the CIA.** New York: Simon and Schuster, 1995.

Thompson, Fred D. **At That Point in Time: The Inside Story of the Senate Watergate Committee.** New York: Quadrangle, 1975.

———. **Robert Kennedy: His Life.** New York: Simon and Schuster, 2000.

Thompson, Kenneth, ed. **The Nixon Presidency: Twenty-two Intimate Perspectives of Richard M. Nixon.** Lanham, MD: University Press of America, 1987.

Van Atta, Dale. **With Honor: Melvin Laird in War, Peace, and Politics.** Madison: University of Wisconsin Press, 2008.

Van Natta, Don. **First Off the Tee: Presidential Hackers, Duffers, and Cheaters, from Taft to Bush.** New York: Public Affairs, 2003.

Volkan, Vamik, Norman Itzkowitz, and Andrew Dod. **Richard Nixon: A Psychobiography.** New York: Columbia University Press, 1997.

Walters, Vernon. **Silent Missions.** New York: Doubleday, 1978.

Weiner, Tim. **Enemies: A History of the FBI.** New York: Random House, 2012.

———. **Legacy of Ashes: the History of the CIA.** New York: Doubleday, 2007.

Weisman, Stephen, ed. **Daniel Patrick Moynihan: A Portrait in Letters of an American Visionary.** New York: Public Affairs, 2010.

Werth, Barry. **31 Days: Gerald Ford, the Nixon Pardon, and a Government in Crisis.** New York: Anchor Books, 2006.

West, J. B. **Upstairs at the White House: My Life with the First Ladies.** New York: Warner Books, 1974.

Whalen, Richard J. **Catch the Falling Flag: A Republican's Challenge to His Party.** Boston: Houghton Mifflin, 1972.

Whitaker, John C. **Striking a Balance: Environment and Natural Resources Policy in the Nixon-Ford Years.** Washington, DC: American Enterprise Institute, 1976.

White, Theodore. **Breach of Faith: The Fall of Richard Nixon.** New York: Atheneum, 1975.

————. **The Making of the President, 1960.** New York: Atheneum, 1961.

————. **The Making of the President, 1968.** New York Atheneum, 1969.

Wicker, Tom. **One of Us: Richard Nixon and the American Dream.** New York: Random House, 1991.

Wills, Garry. **John Wayne's America.** New York: Touchstone Books, 1997.

————. **Nixon Agonistes: The Crisis of the Self-Made Man.** Boston: Houghton Mifflin, 1969.

Witcover, Jules. **The Resurrection of Richard Nixon.** New York: G.P. Putnam's Sons, 1970.

Woodward, Bob, and Carl Bernstein. **The Final Days.** New York: Simon and Schuster, 1976.

Index

Page numbers in **bold** refer to illustrations.

ABOUT THE AUTHOR

EVAN THOMAS is the author of nine books, including **Ike's Bluff**, **Robert Kennedy**, and **The Wise Men** (with Walter Isaacson). He was a reporter, writer, and editor at **Time** and **Newsweek** for thirty-three years, and won a National Magazine Award in 1999. He has taught nonfiction writing at Harvard and Princeton.